Lecture Notes in Computer Science 10482

Formal Methods

Subline of Lectures Notes in Computer Science

More information about this series at http://www.springer.com/series/7408

Deepak D'Souza · K. Narayan Kumar (Eds.)

Automated Technology for Verification and Analysis

15th International Symposium, ATVA 2017 Pune, India, October 3–6, 2017 Proceedings

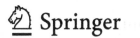

Springer

Editors
Deepak D'Souza
Indian Institute of Science
Bangalore
India

K. Narayan Kumar
Chennai Mathematical Institute
Kelambakkam
India

ISSN 0302-9743 ISSN 1611-3349 (electronic)
Lecture Notes in Computer Science
ISBN 978-3-319-68166-5 ISBN 978-3-319-68167-2 (eBook)
DOI 10.1007/978-3-319-68167-2

Library of Congress Control Number: 2017954903

LNCS Sublibrary: SL2 – Programming and Software Engineering

Printed on acid-free paper

This Springer imprint is published by Springer Nature
The registered company is Springer International Publishing AG
The registered company address is: Gewerbestrasse 11, 6330 Cham, Switzerland

Preface

This volume contains the proceedings of the 15th International Conference on Automated Technology for Verification and Analysis (ATVA 2017), held in Pune, India, during October 3–6, 2017. ATVA is a premier conference in the theoretical and practical aspects of formal verification and has traditionally been hosted in the Asia-Pacific region. This is the second time that the conference has been held in India.

The conference attracted a total of 78 high-quality submissions. Each submission received three reviews during a month-long review period, in which the 31 Program Committee members and 42 external reviewers provided their evaluation of these papers. After a two-week long electronic discussion using the EasyChair system, the Program Committee selected 29 papers (22 regular papers and seven tool papers) for presentation at the conference.

The Program Committee members devoted a significant amount of time in reviewing the papers and in the subsequent discussions. We deeply appreciate their contributions. We also thank the external reviewers for their insightful reviews.

The conference program also included three invited talks, delivered by Carla Ferreira, Gerwin Klein, and Helmut Seidl. We thank them for accepting our invitation and also for providing extended abstracts of their talks for the proceedings.

The conference was hosted by the Tata Consultancy Services at their Sahyadri Park Campus in Pune, India. The meticulous care and enthusiasm of the Organizing Committee from TCS, Pune, contributed immensely to the success of the conference. In particular, we wish to thank R. Venkatesh, the general chair of ATVA 2017, Ulka Shrotri, chair of the Organizing Committee, Kashmira Jhinjina, Kumar Madhukar, and Tukaram Muske.

We express our gratitude to the sponsors of ATVA 2017: The Indian Association for Research in Computing Science (IARCS), Tata Consultancy Services (TCS), Microsoft Research, Mathworks, and Springer.

The proceedings of the conference appears as part of the Springer *Lecture Notes in Computer Science* (LNCS), in the newly introduced Formal Methods subline. We thank Springer for the editorial help in publishing these proceedings.

October 2017

Deepak D'Souza
K. Narayan Kumar

Organization

Program Committee

Mohamed Faouzi Atig	Uppsala University, Sweden
Srivathsan B.	Chennai Mathematical Institute, India
Franck Cassez	Macquarie University, Australia
Rohit Chadha	University of Missouri, USA
Supratik Chakraborty	Indian Institute of Technology, Bombay, India
Deepak D'Souza	Indian Institute of Science, India
Giorgio Delzanno	Università di Genova, Italy
Stephane Demri	CNRS and ENS Paris-Saclay, France
Constantin Enea	University of Paris Diderot, France
Blaise Genest	CNRS and IRISA, Rennes, France
Ashutosh Gupta	Tata Institute of Fundamental Research, India
Teruo Higashino	Osaka University, Japan
Radu Iosif	CNRS and Verimag, University of Grenoble, France
Jie-Hong Jiang	National Taiwan University, Taiwan
Joost-Pieter Katoen	RWTH Aachen University, Germany
Salvatore La Torre	Università degli studi di Salerno, Italy
Nicolas Markey	CNRS and IRISA, Rennes, France
Roland Meyer	TU Braunschweig, Germany
K. Narayan Kumar	Chennai Mathematical Institute, India
Doron Peled	Bar Ilan University, Israel
Pavithra Prabhakar	Kansas State University, USA
Xiaokang Qiu	Purdue University, USA
K.V. Raghavan	Indian Institute of Science, India
R. Venkatesh	Tata Consultancy Services, Pune
S.P. Suresh	Chennai Mathematical Institute, India
Indranil Saha	Indian Institute of Technology, Kanpur, India
Jun Sun	Singapore University of Technology and Design, Singapore
Ashish Tiwari	SRI International, USA
Farn Wang	National Taiwan University, Taiwan
Shaofa Yang	Institute of Software, China
Hsu-Chun Yen	National Taiwan University, Taiwan

Additional Reviewers

André, Étienne
Bazille, Hugo
Bertrand, Nathalie
Brenguier, Romain
Bruintjes, Harold
Chen, Yu-Fang

Chini, Peter
Costa, Gabriele
Darke, Priyanka
Dragoi, Cezara
Emmi, Michael
Ezudheen, P.
Fearnley, John
Garcia Soto, Miriam
Hedrich, Lars
Herbreteau, Frédéric
Jegourel, Cyrille
Junges, Sebastian
Kaminski, Benjamin Lucien
Kapur, Deepak
Kumar, Shrawan
Lahav, Ori
Lal, Ratan
Laurent, Fribourg
Lime, Didier
Longuet, Delphine
Löding, Christof
Madhukar, Kumar
Muskalla, Sebastian
Pandya, Paritosh
Quatmann, Tim
Schewe, Sven
Schweizer, Sebastian
Schwoon, Stefan
Serban, Cristina
Sharma, Subodh
Sighireanu, Mihaela
Suvanpong, Pongsak
Unadkat, Divyesh
Varshney, Pratyush
Wolff, Sebastian
Xu, Xiao
Zheng, Xi

Abstracts of Invited Talks

Consistency Made Easy: Towards Building Correct by Design Cloud Applications

Carla Ferreira

NOVA-LINCS, DI, FCT, Universidade NOVA de Lisboa, Portugal

In the last years, cloud applications have been used to provide increasingly complex services at a global scale. Ensuring quality of service for these applications is challenging, as they need to ensure scalability, availability, and low latency. To achieve these goals the typical approach is to rely on geo-replication, i.e., to maintain copies of the application's shared data across geographically dispersed locations. Ideally, a replicated database should support a strong consistency model, one that behaves as if a single node handles all user requests. But strong consistency requires synchronisation among replicas, thus drastically reducing the application's availability and latency. As a consequence, many applications eschew strong consistency and use weak consistency models instead [4, 8]. Weak models avoid synchronisation altogether: user requests can be executed by the closest replica without synchronising with other replicas so the user gets an immediate reply; any effects are propagated in the background to other replicas. By avoiding synchronisation, replicas may temporarily diverge exposing anomalies to users (e.g. an user might see a reply to a facebook post before seeing the original post). These anomalies are temporary as local effects are eventually propagated to all replicas. An inescapable drawback of weak consistency is that without synchronisation most data integrity invariants cannot be ensured.

To address this tension between availability and safety, large cloud providers (Microsoft Azure and Google's Spanner) have very recently started promoting cloud storage services that support hybrid consistency models [1, 3, 7, 6]. By using hybrid consistency the developer can make fine-grained decisions on the consistency level assigned to each individual operation. The insight is that most operations are asynchronous, and synchronisation is used only when strictly necessary to ensure the application's data integrity invariants. The drawback is that making these choices is very complex and error prone. Requesting stronger consistency in too many operations may hurt performance and availability, while requesting it in too few places may violate correctness.

This talk presents an important milestone in providing verification techniques for cloud applications. With our approach [2], developers no longer have to rely on complex and ad-hoc reasoning to validate an application. The proof rule, defined in [2], is able to check in polynomial time that a particular hybrid consistency model is sufficient to preserve a given integrity invariant. The proof rule is defined over a generic hybrid consistency model expressive enough to instantiate a variety of research and industry consistency models. To illustrate the flexibility of the generic model some encodings of existing consistency models will be shown. In our setting [2], a database computation is defined by a partial order on operations, representing causality, and a conflict relation that further constraints the partial order. The conflict relation specifies which pairs of operations need to be synchronised, as their non-synchronised concurrent execution may lead to an invariant violation. Instead of reasoning about all possible interactions between operations, our proof rule reasons about each operation individually under a set of assumptions on the behaviour of other operations. This allows us to reason in terms of states of a single replica instead of having to consider a set of replicas. We have developed a prototype tool that automates the proof rule proposed in [5]. The evaluation showed the tool can efficiently analyse the correctness of the consistency model of a given application specification. Furthermore, the tool is able to automatically derive a conflict relation (consistency model) that is guaranteed to ensure a given application invariant. In practice, the tool allows developers to build applications assuming a (simple and familiar) sequential execution context. The analysis will then pinpoint what are the problematic operations if the application is executed in a replicated context. In line of this, the developer has two choices. Either devise a consistency model or use the tool to generate one. The use of the tool will be illustrated through some examples.

Acknowledgements. The work presented was partially supported by FCT-MCTES-PT NOVA LINCS project (UID/CEC/04516/2013), EU FP7 SyncFree project (609551), and EU H2020 LightKone project (732505).

References

1. Balegas, V., Preguiça, N., Rodrigues, R., Duarte, S., Ferreira, C., Najafzadeh, M., Shapiro, M.: Putting the consistency back into eventual consistency. In: EuroSys (2015)
2. Gotsman, A., Yang, H., Ferreira, C., Najafzadeh, M., Shapiro, M.: Cause I'm strong enough: reasoning about consistency choices in distributed systems. In: POPL (2016)
3. Li, C., Porto, D., Clement, A., Rodrigues, R., Preguiça, N., Gehrke, J.: Making geo-replicated systems fast if possible, consistent when necessary. In: OSDI (2012)
4. Lloyd,W., Freedman, M.J., Kaminsky, M., Andersen, D.G.: Don't settle for eventual: scalable causal consistency for wide-area storage with COPS. In: SOSP (2011)
5. Marcelino, G., Balegas, V., Ferreira, C.: Bringing hybrid consistency closer to programmers. In: PaPoC (2017)
6. Sovran, Y., Power, R., Aguilera, M.K., Li, J.: Transactional storage for geo-replicated systems. In: SOSP (2011)
7. Terry, D.B., Prabhakaran, V., Kotla, R., Balakrishnan, M., Aguilera, M.K., Abu-Libdeh, H.: Consistency-based service level agreements for cloud storage. In: SOSP (2013)
8. Vogels, W.: Eventually consistent. CACM **52**(1) (2009)

From Trustworthy Kernels to Trustworthy Systems

Gerwin Klein

Data61 and UNSW Sydney, Australia
gerwin.klein@data61.csiro.au

This talk presents an approach for building highly trustworthy systems that derive their assurance from a formally verified OS kernel and a component system that together enforce non-bypassable architectural boundaries within the system through code/proof co-generation. The talk will show how this approach can produce real-word systems, such as autonomous helicopters, that are robust against cyber attacks.

The key ingredients to this approach are: a formally verified microkernel, a component system that provably makes correct use of this verified microkernel, a software component architecture that enforces the desired security property, potentially relying on a small set of trusted (in the best case, formally verified) components, and a high-level formal analysis that the architecture does indeed enforce the security property.

Given these ingredients, we can build systems that are demonstrably highly robust against cyber attack, that can be built by software engineers without deep knowledge of formal methods, and that can be retrofitted with little effort onto suitable existing systems, compared to writing and verifying them from scratch.

The main limitation is that the security properties of interest must be enforceable by architecture with a minimal amount of trusted code. That is not always achievable, and returns are diminishing as the size of trusted code grows. However, when it is achievable, the additional effort that engineers need to invest per system for gaining evidence of high assurance is minimal: the OS kernel proofs are done once and for all and are merely used, the component architecture proofs are automatically generated per system, and the composition of these theorems can in principle be fully automated. If trusted components are involved, their verification may need to be integrated manually, or at least assumed in the high-level security analysis. Compared to formally verifying security properties of real-world systems from scratch, the formal verification effort per system involved in this approach tends towards zero.

The talk will show an example of this approach with the seL4 microkernel [2] as the basis, the CAmkES component system providing the code/proof co-generation for the component architecture [1], and the mission computer of Boeing's Unmanned Little Bird helicopter as the target system. The seL4 kernel comes with a proof of functional correctness from abstract specification down to binary code, as well as proofs of isolation properties. The CAmkES component system generates proofs for correct configuration of seL4 and proofs of correct communication glue code between components. The target system is a full-sized autonomous helicopter with a code base that

Boeing engineers rearchitected during the project for high robustness against cyber attack via the ground link or via maintenance access points. The secured vehicle runs native seL4 components, but also large portions of unverified third-party software, including inside a Linux virtual machine. The vehicle will operate safely even when the third party software is compromised via an unknown attack vector and behaves maliciously.

Acknowledgements. This work is the combined effort of many people, including the Trustworthy Systems team at Data61, and our project partners in the DARPA High-Assurance Cyber-Military Systems (HACMS) program, in particular at Rockwell Collins, Galois Inc, the University of Minnesota, and Boeing.

This material is based on research sponsored by Air Force Research Laboratory and the Defense Advanced Research Projects Agency (DARPA) under agreement number FA8750-12-9-0179. The U.S. Government is authorised to reproduce and distribute reprints for Governmental purposes notwithstanding any copyright notation thereon. The views and conclusions contained herein are those of the authors and should not be interpreted as necessarily representing the official policies or endorsements, either expressed or implied, of Air Force Research Laboratory, the Defense Advanced Research Projects Agency or the U.S. Government.

References

1. Fernandez, M., Andronick, J., Klein, G., Kuz, I.: Automated verification of RPC stub code. In: Bjørner, N., de Boer, F. (eds.) FM 2015. LNCS, vol. 9109, pp. 273–290. Springer, Cham (2015)
2. Klein, G., Elphinstone, K., Heiser, G., Andronick, J., Cock, D., Derrin, P., Elkaduwe, D., Engelhardt, K., Kolanski, R., Norrish, M., Sewell, T., Tuch, H., Winwood, S.: seL4: Formal verification of an OS kernel. In: SOSP, pp. 207–220, Big Sky, MT, USA, October 2009

Proving Absence of Starvation by Means of Abstract Interpretation and Model Checking

Helmut Seidl and Ralf Vogler

Fakultät für Informatik, TU München, Garching, Germany
{seidl,voglerr}@in.tum.de

Abstract. The Avionics Application Software Standard Interface ARINC 653 is meant to increase predictability of safety-critical software systems. It allows to coordinate multiple tasks by means of priorities, semaphores, setting and waiting for events as well as by sending suspend and resume signals. Thus, it is a major challenge to verify that no such tightly coupled task gets ultimately stuck, e.g., by infinitely waiting for an event or a resume signal by another task. We explain how abstract interpretation together with model checking may nicely cooperate to guarantee absence of such concurrency flaws and report on practical experiments.

R. Vogler—This work is supported by the ITEA3 project 14014 ASSUME.

Contents

Hybrid Systems and Control

Invited Talk

Proving Absence of Starvation by Means of Abstract Interpretation and Model Checking

Helmut Seidl(✉) and Ralf Vogler

Fakultät für Informatik, TU München, Garching, Germany
{seidl,voglerr}@in.tum.de

Abstract. The Avionics Application Software Standard Interface ARINC 653 is meant to increase predictability of safety-critical software systems. It allows to coordinate multiple tasks by means of priorities, semaphores, setting and waiting for events as well as by sending suspend and resume signals. Thus, it is a major challenge to verify that no such tightly coupled task gets ultimately stuck, e.g., by infinitely waiting for an event or a resume signal by another task. We explain how abstract interpretation together with model checking may nicely cooperate to guarantee absence of such concurrency flaws and report on practical experiments.

1 Introduction

Safety-critical software as is used in avionic or automotive applications, requires particular care: any kind of malfunction may cause significant financial damage or even have severe consequences to life or well-being of humans. The dream would be to provide for every such system a thorough mathematical proof that the system always does what it is expected to do. Huge progress has been made in for what machine-checkable correctness proofs can be provided. There is a verified implementation of an operating system [19] as well as of compilers [7,18]. Still, these efforts are tremendous and therefore only applied to dedicated, widely usable components. Also, in each of these two cases, the software has been constructed together with the corresponding correctness proof. It is unclear to what extent these techniques could also be applied a posteriori to existing software. Instead, more light-weight methods are sought for, which allow to prove, if not the correctness of a program, so then at least the absence of a certain class of errors. One of the greatest success stories in this area is the development of the static analyzer ASTREE [4–6,25] which has been applied to prove absence of run-time errors in the control software of the A380. Run-time errors could be, e.g., index-out-of-bounds errors when accessing arrays, null pointer dereferences, divisions by 0, or unintended overflows.

Safety-critical software typically is embedded and thus has to meet real-time requirements. Whether or not a task meets hard timing constraints cannot be easily deduced from the high-level source code alone. Also, it cannot be inferred

R. Vogler—This work is supported by the ITEA3 project 14014 ASSUME.

D. D'Souza and K. Narayan Kumar (Eds.): ATVA 2017, LNCS 10482, pp. 3–22, 2017.
DOI: 10.1007/978-3-319-68167-2_1

from a few measurements on example runs, as both the control-flow as well as the hardware status between different runs can be quite different. Another success story in this area therefore is the development of accurate Worst-case execution time analyzers [35]. The effort for developing such tools cannot easily be overestimated as each such analyzer must take into account even tiniest details of the target architecture the application is going to run on.

Moreover, safety-critical embedded software typically consists of multiple tasks which may interact in non-trivial ways. Like timing errors, absence of concurrency errors cannot be proven by inspection of a few example runs of the system. Quite some attention has been attracted by methods which prove absence of data races. In device drivers of the Linux kernel, mutexes are used to protect access to shared data-structures. Then, an analysis of the sets of definitely held mutexes is the method of choice [13,33]. In systems using the operating system Autosar/OSEK, protection is based on dynamic adjustment of priorities [21]. Then, an analysis of defense and offense priorities may be applied [30,33]. More intricate analyses are required if ad-hoc synchronization patterns are used [29].

A much more complicated issue is to prove absence of deadlocks or, more generally, absence of starvation. Early work has, e.g., tried to prove absence of circular wait situations by identifying a partial ordering on mutexes according to which mutexes are acquired [13,36]. Such an approach is insufficient if multiple synchronization primitives, not just mutexes, are used. More recently, a static deadlock detection analysis for JAVA is presented in [26], which, however, neither claims to be sound nor complete. Dedicated methods have also been designed for the *async* construct together with explicit *wait* commands in C$^\sharp$ applications [28]. An interesting analysis based on a translation to Petri net reachability for detecting deadlocks in systems with active objects and futures is proposed in [11]. Other attempts rely on an analysis of what may happen in parallel [14].

A better chance to provide provable guarantees is offered by *software model-checking* as in [8]. There, concurrent C programs are analyzed which communicate via blocking message passing. In order to extract a labeled transition system from the program, predicate abstraction and *counter-example guided abstraction refinement* (CEGAR) is applied. Temporal properties of the resulting models then are checked by a standard LTL model checking algorithm. Deadlock freedom is, as the authors indicate, a prerequisite for the soundness of their method. Still, termination of iterative auxiliary local computation is not considered as an issue. At least naive predicate abstraction is not sufficient to infer termination. As a consequence for our programs of interest, this approach, as is, does not seem appropriate.

Another attempt to apply model-checking to concurrent C programs, in particular for avionics applications, is [12]. The idea is to directly translate C code into PROMELA programs. Such an attempt, however, suffers from the complicated global states encountered in realistic applications and thus is not likely to scale. Other attempts try to improve on that by circumventing PROMELA and directly model-check C code [31].

In contrast, our vision for identifying starvation of tasks is to combine the best of the two worlds *Abstract Interpretation* and *Model-Checking*. In abstract interpretation-based static analysis, we appreciate the efficiency by which sound program invariants — even for large programs with complicated data-structures and complicated control-flow — can be handled. When it comes to the verification of liveness properties of possibly non-terminating concurrent programs, then the algorithms and tools provided for, say, LTL model-checking are well appropriate. Our key idea therefore is to use abstract-interpretation based methods to extract from the given real-time system $\mathcal{S}$ with multiple tasks, a decently small system which still has multiple tasks, but no explicit timings any more so that starvation-freedom of the extracted system implies starvation-freedom of $\mathcal{S}$ — provided that $\mathcal{S}$ is *locally terminating*. Essentially, local termination means that no task of $\mathcal{S}$ performs infinitely many steps, without executing an OS command in between. Local termination is then considered as a separate issue. We explain that *global invariants* [2] can nicely be applied to decompose this problem into proofs of local termination of appropriately defined *sequential* systems for which then the wealth of methods can be applied to solve that particular problem [10,32,37].

We have implemented our approach within the analyzer framework GOBLINT. A particular issue is how to deal with time-dependent behavior of real-time systems. Here, we report on preliminary experiments with our approach for a not-too-large safety-critical real-time application from avionics.

2 Programs

In order to capture the essential features of programs running under an operating system such as ARINC 653 or Autosar/OSEK, we consider a multi-tasking system $\mathcal{S}$ which consists of:

- A finite set of tasks $\mathcal{T}$;
- Finite sets $\mathcal{E}$ and $\mathcal{L}$ of events and mutexes, respectively.

Each task has a unique name $f \in \mathcal{F}$, a priority in $\mathbb{N}$, and is defined by a control-flow graph. Events are considered as boolean flags. Each event is equipped with a queue of tasks waiting for the event to be set to *true*. Initially, each event has value *false* and the corresponding waiting queue is empty. Likewise, a mutex consists of a field containing the task currently owning the mutex (if any) together with a queue of tasks waiting to acquire the mutex. Initially, each mutex is *free*, i.e., not owned by any task, and the corresponding waiting queue is empty.

The edges of each control-flow graph are labeled either with a builtin OS command or with an ordinary statement s. As OS commands, we consider:

- $\mathsf{suspend}(f)$, $\mathsf{resume}(f)$ ($f \in \mathcal{F}$);
- $\mathsf{set\_event}(e)$, $\mathsf{reset\_event}(e)$, and $\mathsf{wait\_event}(e)$ ($e \in \mathcal{E}$), as well as
- $\mathsf{lock}(l)$ and $\mathsf{unlock}(l)$ ($l \in \mathcal{L}$).

We remark that operating systems such as ARINC 653 provide various further commands, e.g., to stop and start other tasks, in addition to other types of resources that can be used for synchronization and communication between tasks. These can be handled in the same style as the subset of commands considered here.

At any moment, each task f is in a particular *task state*. Figure 1 gives an overview of the states we consider here, together with the transitions between them.

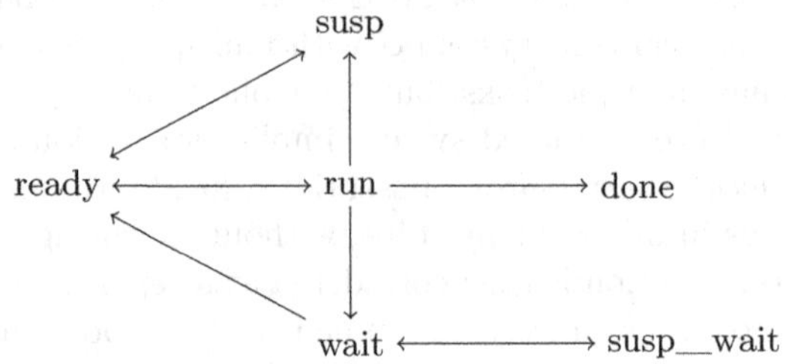

Fig. 1. The task states and the transitions between them.

Initially, all tasks are in state *ready*. From all tasks in state *ready*, the scheduler selects the one of highest priority and sets its state to *run*. This task is then allowed to execute. When the execution of the task terminates by reaching the end point of the task, the state is set to *done*. When a task executes the command yield(), its state is changed from *run* to *ready*. The same happens when a task with higher priority becomes *ready*. A task in state *run* may change its state to *wait* when it tries to acquire a mutex which is already owned, or when executing wait_event(e) for an event e which currently has value *false*. When the task receives the mutex it was waiting for, its state is changed back to *ready*. The same happens when the event it was waiting for, is set to *true*.

A task may also be *suspended*. In this case, its state changes from *run* or *ready* to *susp*. If the task is in state *wait*, the new state is *susp_wait*. A suspended task may be *resumed* by some other task. If the state is *susp*, it is changed to *ready*.

Finally, a task can be in state *susp_wait*, i.e., be both suspended and waiting for some resource. Then it may still complete waiting, i.e., change its state to *susp* alone. This is the case when the task was waiting for an event e which is set to *true*, or receives the mutex it was waiting for. It may also change its state to *wait*, if it was resumed by some other task.

In detail, the semantics of the OS commands are as follows:

yield(). The task state is set from *run* to *ready*.

set_event(e). The value of the event e is set to *true*. Every task f which is in the waiting queue for the event e, receives the state *ready* (if its current state has been *wait*) or *susp* (if its current state has been *susp_wait*). Then the queue of e is set to the empty queue.

reset_event(e). The value of the event e is set back to *false*.

wait_event(e). If the value of the event e is *true*, the current task proceeds. Otherwise, its state is set to *wait*, and the current task is added to the queue of tasks waiting at e.

lock(l). If the mutex l is not owned by any task, l is acquired and the task proceeds. Otherwise, its state is set to *wait*, and the current task is added to the queue of tasks waiting for lock l.

unlock(l). Assume that the mutex l is owned by the current task. If the queue of tasks waiting for l is empty, the mutex l is marked as *free*. Otherwise, the the first task f in the queue is extracted, the mutex is marked as owned by f, and the state of f is set to *ready* (if it has been *wait*) or *susp* (if it has been *susp_wait*).

In each case, when the set of tasks in state *ready* has been changed, the scheduler may subsequently select another ready task for receiving the state *run*.

Program execution proceeds in *atomic steps*. For simplicity, we assume that such a step consists in processing one edge in one of the control-flow graphs. Thus, the execution of a single command, a single assignment, as well as a single guard, is considered atomic. This means that effects of weak memory or multiple cores are ignored.

In the following, we assume that sets of nodes and edges in the control-flow graphs are disjoint. Moreover, we assume each control-flow edge a is labeled by a corresponding action.

Program executions operate on the system's state σ. This state consists of a tuple $\sigma = (q, \eta, \mu, \lambda)$ where

- q represents the global memory state of the system which is accessible to all tasks;
- η maps each event e to a pair (b, w) where b is its boolean value and w is the queue of tasks waiting for e;
- μ maps each mutex l to a pair (f, w) where f is the task currently owning l or indicates that l is *free*, and w is the queue of tasks waiting for l;
- λ maps each task f to its relevant *local* information, namely the pair (v, s, p), where v is the current program point, s is the task state and p is the task-local memory state.

The initial state σ_0 of $\mathcal{S}$ is given by $\sigma_0 = (q_0, \eta_0, \mu_0, \lambda_0)$ for some initial global memory state q_0, $\eta_0 = \{e \mapsto (\mathit{false}, \emptyset) \mid e \in \mathcal{E}\}$, $\mu_0 = \{l \mapsto (\mathit{free}, \emptyset) \mid l \in \mathcal{L}\}$, and $\lambda_0 = \{f \mapsto (v_{f,0}, \mathit{ready}, p_{f,0}) \mid f \in \mathcal{F}\}$ where $v_{f,0}, p_{f,0}$ are the initial program point and the initial local memory state of the task f, respectively.

Starting from the initial state σ_0, a program trace can be represented as a (finite or infinite) sequence Σ of pairs $\langle a_1, \sigma_1\rangle \ldots \langle a_t, \sigma_t\rangle \ldots$ of control-flow edges and system states. The trace Σ is *maximal* if Σ is infinite, or it is finite, but cannot be extended by another pair $\langle a, \sigma\rangle$.

We are particularly interested in *starvation* of tasks. We say that starvation of task f occurs at some step t in a maximal trace Σ if f has not reached state *done*, but at all time points $t' \geq t$, no action of f is executed. In the following, we assume that all control-flow graphs are *well-formed*, meaning that only the end point of the control-flow graph has no outgoing edge; every other node v with an outgoing edge a labeled by a guard with condition b, also has an outgoing edge a' which is labeled with a guard with condition $\neg b$. Then, we can identify two reasons for starvation of f. At each step $t' \geq t$,

- f is either in state *susp* or *ready*, and whenever f is not suspended, then the running task has the same or higher priority than f; or
- the task state of f is either *wait* or *susp_wait*.

In the first case, thread f now and then may become *ready* — but running is prevented by some other task with sufficiently high priority. In the second case, task f fails to become *ready*, because it has started to wait for a resource which is not provided.

The system $\mathcal{S}$ is called *starvation-free* for the initial state σ_0, if on no maximal trace Σ of the system starting in σ_0, starvation of any task occurs.

Proving starvation freedom is a classical verification problem where model-checking has successfully been applied. In practical applications, however, multiple obstacles are encountered. The number of lines of code in realistic applications, grow dramatically. These programs do not just use boolean variables, but compute with integers, floating-point numbers and maintain data-structures. Even if the number of tasks is fixed and small (as is assumed for the applications we consider here), the number of global system states to be explored, grows dramatically.

Thus, this type of starvation problems goes way beyond what can be expected from explicit-state model-checkers, such as SPIN [17]. Also, symbolic model-checkers typically will not be able to deal with programs as large as these and with as complicated a semantics. Tools such as CBMC have successfully been tried on very large programs [20]. As they use *bounded* model-checking only, they are, however, inherently unsound. Moreover, as they explore finite traces only, it is impossible for them to identify whether a task is starving or not.

In the following, we use some C-like syntax where each procedure represents a task with the corresponding name.

Example 1. Consider the following system:

```
int z = 0;

void work() {
  while(true) {
    z++;
    if (z < 65536) set_event(e);
    else break;
  }
}

void ctrl() {
  while(true) {
    reset_event(e);
    resume(work);
    wait_event(e);
    suspend(work);
    ...
  }
}
```

where we assume that e is an event, and the priorities of ctrl and work are given as 10 and 5, respectively. The idea of this program is as follows (cf. Fig. 2). The

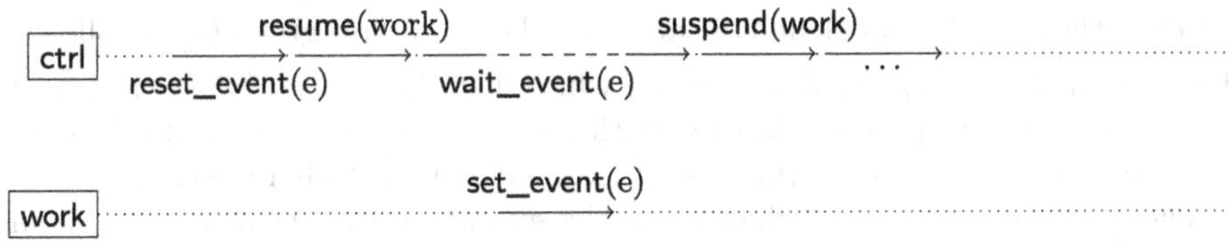

Fig. 2. Execution of example 1

first task to run is the task ctrl. This task first resets the event e. Then the execution of the task work is resumed. As this task has lower priority, its task state is just set to *ready* (if it is not already *ready*). The task ctrl then waits until task work has set the event e, in which case, the task work is suspended. The last command executed by ctrl before execution continues with resetting the event e, is some activity (indicated by ...) to be alternatingly executed with the task work. Note that suspending and resuming the task work is only necessary, if that activity may contain blocking commands where still task work should not be allowed to proceed.

Let us finally explain the behavior of the task work. This task has lowest priority. It runs in close interaction with the task ctrl. When it runs, the task ctrl is waiting for the event e. It increments the global variable z by 1. If the value is less than 65536, it sets event e. Otherwise, it exits the loop and stops. Thus, control is usually handed back to the task ctrl. In the given implementation, it happens, though, that when z reaches 65536, task ctrl remains waiting for event e for ever. Therefore, the system is not starvation-free. □

3 The Abstraction

In order to deal with this situation, we proceed in two stages. In the first stage, we extract a *small* abstract system from the large concrete system. This small system then is (hopefully) small enough to be handled by off-the-shelf model-checkers such as SPIN.

The idea of the abstraction is to strip the control-flow graphs of the tasks of everything which is not related to task interaction and scheduling. The intuition behind this crude abstraction is that application engineers of critical software have a very clear pattern for task interaction in mind. The flow of control in these patterns usually depends on the roles the respective tasks are playing (working, supervising, error-handling, etc.) and rarely on data values.

For every task f, we consider the control-flow graph G_f for f. Let O_f denote the subset of nodes of G_f which consists of the initial node $v_{f,0}$ of G_f together with all end-points of edges labeled with OS commands. To every node v in G_f, we assign the subset $O[v] \subseteq O_f$ of all $v' \in O[v]$, where there is a path from v' to v in G_f without OS commands as labels. These sets $O[v]$ can be computed by some GEN/KILL bit-vector analysis along the lines of a reaching definitions analysis.

Given the sets $O[v]$, we define the abstracted control-flow graph $G^\sharp_f$ as follows. The set of nodes of $G^\sharp_f$ are given by O_f, while there is an edge (v', v_1) in $G^\sharp_f$ iff there is an edge (v, v_1) in G_f labeled with some OS command c, and $v' \in O[v]$ — in which case the label of the abstract edge equals the label of (v, v_1).

The crucial question is in which sense the set of traces of the abstract system reflects the set of traces of the concrete system. Let us call a system *locally non-terminating*, if

N1: There is an infinite trace Σ, some task f and step t so that for all $t' \geq t$, the following holds:

- f is in state *run*, *ready* or *susp* at t';
- f does not perform an OS command, and
- f is in state *run* at some time point $t'' \geq t'$.

According to our scheduling policy, a task not executing any OS command cannot be interrupted. Accordingly, a task is locally non-terminating, iff

N2: there is a step t so that for all $t' \geq t$, f is in state *run* without ever executing an OS command.

A system for which no task is locally non-terminating, is called *locally terminating*. In the system of Example 1, tasks work and ctrl both have non-terminating loops. Still, this system is locally terminating, as each control-flow path traversing the bodies of these loops contains at least one OS command.

For a concrete system state $\sigma = (q, \eta, \mu, \lambda)$, the corresponding abstract state $\alpha(\sigma) = \sigma^\sharp$ is obtained by dropping the global memory state q, and also for each f, the local memory state in $\lambda(f)$. For a concrete trace $\Sigma = \langle a_1, \sigma_1 \rangle \dots \langle a_i, \sigma_i \rangle \dots$ the corresponding abstract trace $\alpha(\Sigma) = \Sigma^\sharp$ is given by $\langle a_{j_1}, \sigma^\sharp_{j_1} \rangle \dots \langle a_{j_n}, \sigma^\sharp_{j_n} \rangle \dots$ where $a_{j_1} \dots a_{j_n} \dots$ is the subsequence of OS commands in Σ and $\sigma^\sharp_{j_n} = \alpha(\sigma_{j_n})$.

Theorem 1. *Assume that the concrete system is locally terminating. Assume that Σ is a trace of the concrete system. Then $\alpha(\Sigma)$ is a trace of the abstracted system. Moreover, starvation of the task f occurs on Σ iff starvation of f occurs on $\alpha(\Sigma)$.*

Proof. Clearly, if starvation of f occurs on $\alpha(\Sigma)$, then also on the trace Σ. Now assume that starvation of f occurs on Σ, but not on $\alpha(\Sigma)$. This means that from some point t on, for all $t' \geq t$, some task f' is running with priority equal or higher than f — without executing an OS command. But this contradicts the assumption that S is locally terminating. □

By Theorem 1, we thus may split the effort of proving starvation freedom of a system into two subtasks: first, to prove that the system is locally terminating. Second, to prove that the abstracted system is starvation-free. The latter system, however, is considerably smaller than the original system. Accordingly, this check can be more easily accomplished by some off-the-shelf model-checker such as SPIN.

To prove that the given system $\mathcal{S}$ is locally terminating, on the other hand, is often reducible to proving termination of sequential tasks alone. Such a reduction can be obtained by means of *global invariants*. A *global invariant* is a superset Q of all global memory states q possibly encountered during any trace of the system when starting in $\sigma_0 = (q_0, \eta_0, \mu_0, \lambda_0)$. Assume that we are given such a global invariant Q. Relative to Q, we consider for each task f the set of all *local traces* starting in the initial local state. The initial local state is obtained from $\lambda_0(f)$ by ignoring the task state. Thus, it is given by $\tau_{f,0} = (v_{f,0}, p_{f,0})$. A local trace then performs only actions of f and for these, only considers the effects on the local state of f. Thus, a local trace of f is a sequence $\langle a_1, \tau_1 \rangle \ldots \langle a_t, \tau_t \rangle \ldots$ where τ_t is the local state of f attained after the tth action of f, and a_t is the tth control-flow edge taken by task f. Let us denote the resulting sequential system by $\mathcal{S}_{Q,f}$. We call it locally non-terminating, if there is an infinite local trace so that from some t on, no OS command is executed. The system is called *locally terminating*, if it is not locally non-terminating. We have:

Theorem 2. *Assume that Q is a global invariant of the system $\mathcal{S}$ with initial state σ_0. If for each task f, the sequential system $\mathcal{S}_{Q,f}$ is locally terminating for the initial local state $\lambda_0(f)$, then so is $\mathcal{S}$ for σ_0.*

Proof. Assume that $\mathcal{S}$ is not locally terminating. Then there is a reachable global state $\sigma = (q, \eta, \mu, \lambda)$ and a task f with $\lambda(f) = (v, run, p)$ and a trace Σ starting in σ where always f is running — without executing an OS command. This trace of $\mathcal{S}$ gives rise to an infinite trace of $\mathcal{S}_{Q,f}$ starting in $\tau = (v, p)$, which does not execute OS commands. Since (v, p) is reachable from $\tau_{f,0}$ in $\mathcal{S}_{Q,f}$, the sequential system $\mathcal{S}_{Q,f}$ cannot be locally terminating. □

In [2], *side-effecting constraint systems* have been proposed to formalize global invariants of multi-tasking systems. In a series of papers, also solvers for such systems have been proposed [1,3,15]. Given such an invariant, off-the-shelf methods for proving termination of loops can be applied [10,27,32,37].

Extensions

So far, we have assumed that priorities are fixed in the beginning. In operating systems such as Autosar/OSEK [30], dynamically adjusted priorities are the central means to guarantee exclusive access to shared data. Also, we simplified our exposition in assuming that OS commands always *succeed.* In POSIX, e.g., acquiring a mutex may also *fail* [34] or just *time-out.* The latter concept will be discussed in detail in the next section. In presence of possibly unsuccessful OS commands, the programmer is required to inspect the return code of a command in order to know what kind of action has been performed. In order to deal with possibly failing commands in the abstract system, a refined slicing procedure must be applied. The abstract system should maintain not only all OS commands, but also all actions that compute with return values of OS commands, e.g., store or retrieve them from local variables as well as guards referring to such values.

4 Time-Dependent Behavior

Operating systems such as ARINC 653 or Autosar/OSEK are designed for the realization of time-critical systems. These systems typically consist of several tasks — some of which are *periodically activated* and must finish within the given period. These tasks may control other tasks with deadlines. Now, each task may set a *time-out* when waiting should be interrupted. Accordingly, we consider the following timed commands. When executed by task f, they mean:

wait_event(e, t). If the event e is not yet set, the state of f is set to *wait*, and f is added to the waiting queue of e. If t time units have elapsed, and f is still in the waiting queue for e, f is removed, the state of f is set accordingly, and the command returns *time-out*. If before t time units have elapsed, the event e has been set, f is removed from the waiting queue of e, the state of f is set accordingly, and and the command terminates by returning *success*.

lock(l, t). If the mutex l is not *free*, the state of f is set to *wait*, and f is added to the waiting queue of l. If t time units have elapsed, and f is still in the waiting queue for l, it is removed, the state of f is set accordingly, and the command returns *time-out*. If before t time units have elapsed, the lock l is handed over to f, the state of f is set accordingly, and the command terminates by returning *success*.

In presence of potential time-outs, the programmer is required to inspect the return code of the commands wait_event() and lock() to detect whether or not the command completed successfully or with time-out.

Moreover, the OS may provide *external timers* which periodically set *timer events* to *true*. These events may be used to periodically trigger tasks. In ARINC 653, e.g., a command periodic_wait() is used by periodic tasks to yield execution until their next release point. The base functionality can be modeled as:

```
reset_event(rel_f);
wait_event(rel_f);
```

if f is a periodic task, and rel_f is the release event of f, which is periodically set by the operating system. In ARINC 653, however, tasks may also have deadlines for their execution times. Their violation may be acted upon using an *error* task. This task is meant to have the highest priority in the system and should only run after a violation occurred. Therefore it should initially be suspended in our setting:

```
void error() {
  suspend(error);
  ...// error handling code
}
```

For each task f — triggered by the release event rel_f and equipped with a deadline t_f — we introduce another event fin_f together with an auxiliary task

watch_f, whose priority is less than the priority of the *error* task, but exceeds the priority of all other user-defined tasks. The task watch_f can be implemented as:

```
void watch_f() {
  while (true) {
    wait_event(rel_f);
    if (wait_event(fin_f, t_f) ≠ success)
      resume(error);
    else reset_event(fin_f);
  }
}
```

For a periodic task f, the event rel_f is the periodic event triggered by the external timer. The event fin_f on the other hand, should now be set during execution of the command periodic_wait():

```
reset_event(rel_f);
set_event(fin_f);
wait_event(rel_f);
```

The task watch_f waits until the event rel_f is set. Subsequently, it starts to wait for the event fin_f — but with time-out t_f. If the event fin_f is not set before t_f time units have elapsed, the *error* task is resumed. Otherwise, i.e., if the event fin_f has been set in time, the fin_f is reset, and the task continues at the beginning of its loop, i.e., waiting for the next event rel_f.

Figure 3 illustrates the execution of some periodic task f which violates its deadline. Since all periodic tasks may run from the beginning, the event rel_f will already be set by the external timer. The task with the highest priority is error, which will therefore run first, and do nothing more than suspend itself. Next, task watch_f will wait for the first release event, which is already set, and then start to wait for task f to yield for the first time. If task f does not manage to call periodic_wait() before t_f time units have passed, watch_f will become ready, thereby preempt f, and resume the error handler.

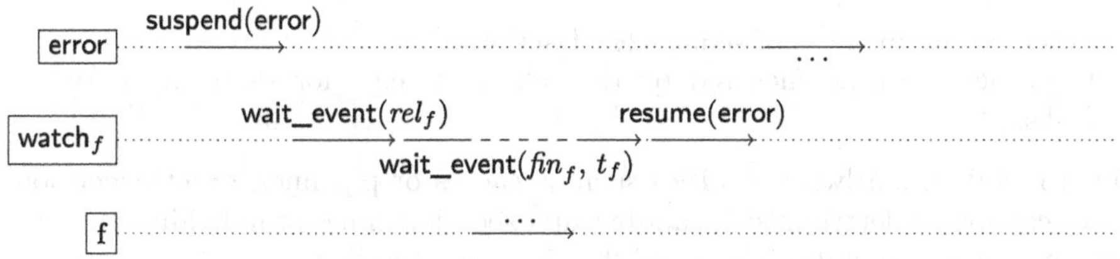

Fig. 3. Execution of a periodic task that violates its deadline.

Figure 4 illustrates the execution of some periodic task f which successfully finishes execution before its deadline by calling periodic_wait(). The error handler is omitted for simplicity.

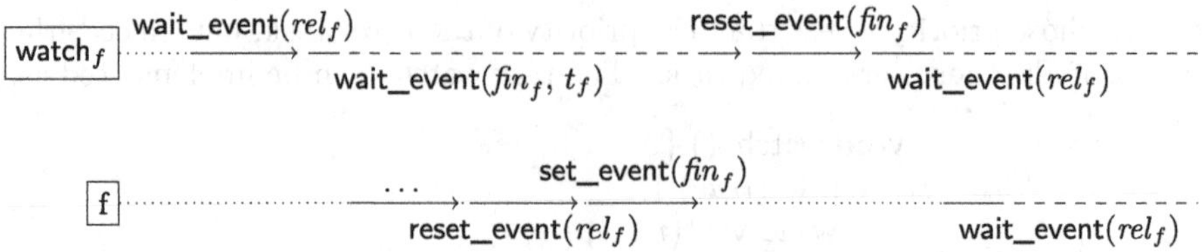

Fig. 4. Execution of periodic_wait before the deadline of a periodic task.

The Example 1 with time-dependent commands may look as follows.

Example 2. Consider the following system:

```
int z = 0;                          void ctrl() {
                                      while(true) {
void work() {                         reset_event(e);
  while(true) {                         resume(work);
    z++;                                if (time-out ≠ wait_event(e, 50))
    if (z < 65536) set_event(e);        suspend(work);
    else break;                         periodic_wait();
  }                                   }
}                                   }
```

Here, we only display the user code, not possibly generated tasks for supervising deadlines and also no *error* code. Again, we assume that we are given an event e, and that the priorities of ctrl and work are 10 and 5, respectively. The idea of this program is that task ctrl only waits for 50 ns before task work is suspended. If within that period, work has set event e, this event is reset. Otherwise, task work is suspended until the next period where ctrl runs. In this case, after sufficiently many iterations of work, event e remains *false*. Thus, from that point on, a time-out of the timed command wait_event will always be observed. Still, no starvation of task ctrl occurs. □

In order to precisely formalize the semantics of such systems, we require

- exact execution times of sequences of actions;
- the exact overhead incurred by the scheduler, e.g., for switching between tasks.

Due to modern hardware facilities such as caches or pipelines, exact execution times cannot be determined by adding up execution times of individual actions (see, e.g., the recent overviews [16,22,35]). For simplicity, let us nonetheless assume that this were so, that execution of each control-flow edge takes exactly one time step, and scheduling incurs 0 overhead. Under these premises, we may assign the time point t to every step at which this step is initiated.

By systematically introducing time-outs, starvation due to infinite waiting for events or mutexes becomes obsolete. Still, starvation may occur, due to missing resume commands or abundance of higher-priority ready tasks.

In order to abstract from the complicated time behavior of the system $\mathcal{S}$, we consider the *time-abstracted* system $\mathcal{S}_0$ where the time-dependent commands are interpreted by means of non-deterministic choice as follows:

wait_event$_0(e, \_)$. This command behaves like wait_event(e, t), only that at any step it may non-deterministically be terminated by the scheduler, in which case the return value is *time-out*. Alternatively, if the event e is set, the task is removed from the waiting queue of e, the state is set accordingly, and the command returns the value *success*.

lock$_0(l, \_)$. Similarly, this command behaves like lock(e, t), only that at any step it may non-deterministically be terminated by the scheduler, in which case the return value is *time-out*. Alternatively, if the mutex l is acquired by the task, the task is removed from the waiting queue of l, the state is set accordingly, and the command returns the value *success*.

For a trace Σ of $\mathcal{S}$ let Σ_0 denote the sequence which is obtained from Σ by dropping the time annotation at every step. The following theorem tells us about the relationship between traces of the system $\mathcal{S}$ with timings and traces of $\mathcal{S}_0$.

A particular abstraction is applied to the command periodic_wait(). As another simplification assume that all periodic tasks have the same period t_0. The abstract command periodic_wait$_0$() sets the current task's state to *wait*. At any point in time later, the state of each task currently executing this command may non-deterministically be set to *ready* (if its state has been *wait*) or *susp* (if its state has been *susp_wait*). Moreover, if no other task is in state *run* or *ready*, and some tasks have not completed a periodic_wait$_0$(), then all of them terminate this command.

As no timing information is available, the event rel_f for a periodic task f is no longer tracked. The same holds for the event fin_f to supervise a potential deadline of f. Accordingly, we abandon the auxiliary task watch$_f$ for f. Instead, the scheduler may execute resume(error) at any time during the execution of f. For a trace Σ of the real-time system $\mathcal{S}$, let Σ_0 denote the corresponding trace of $\mathcal{S}_0$. This trace is obtained by removing the subsequences of commands corresponding to the tasks watch$_f$ (up to the commands resume(error)), and furthermore, by replacing the commands periodic_wait(), wait_event(e, t) and lock(l, t) with periodic_wait$_0$(), wait_event$_0(e, _)$ and lock$_0(l, _)$, respectively.

In general, there could be periodic tasks with several distinct periods where each is equipped with a dedicated deadline. Clearly, exact execution times are no longer available in the time-abstracted system. Still, we can construct an *abstract timer* used by the scheduler of $\mathcal{S}_0$ which at least maintains the *ordering* between significant time points.

Example 3. Assume the given system consists of the periodic tasks f_1, f_2, f_3 where f_1, f_2 have period 100 and deadlines 30 and 40, respectively, while task f_3 has period 50 with deadline 10. Along the full period of 100, the scheduler then should distinguish the time points

$$0, \quad 10, \quad 30, \quad 40, \quad 50, \quad 60, \quad 100$$

before it returns to time point 10.

- At time point 0, the states of all tasks are set to *ready*;
- by time point 10, task f_3 has issued a periodic_wait (or an error occurs);
- by time point 30, task f_2 has issued a periodic_wait (or an error occurs);
- by time point 40, task f_1 has issued a periodic_wait (or an error occurs);
- at time point 50, f_3 continues after the last periodic_wait;
- by time point 60, task f_3 has again issued a periodic_wait (or an error occurs);
- at time point 100, all tasks continue after their last periodic_wait.

Thus, we construct an abstract timer which uses seven states to distinguish between the relevant time points. As no exact time points are known, the abstract timer always stays in the same state, but then non-deterministically may decide to proceed to the next state. According to this construction, the current abstract timer state provides a lower bound to the concrete elapsed time (modulo the maximal period). □

For the time-abstracted system, we have:

Theorem 3. *Assume that $\mathcal{S}$ is a real-time system and $\mathcal{S}_0$ is the corresponding time-abstracted system.*

1. *If Σ is a maximal trace of $\mathcal{S}$ starting in some initial state σ, then Σ_0 is a maximal trace of $\mathcal{S}_0$ starting in σ.*
2. *If $\mathcal{S}_0$ is starvation-free, then so is $\mathcal{S}$.*

The proof of this theorem directly follows from the definition of the time-abstracted system $\mathcal{S}_0$. We remark that $\mathcal{S}_0$ can also be constructed for systems where the execution times of scheduler actions and of sequences of task actions cannot be calculated easily or are unknown. The only property we require is that each step of each user task of the real-time system can be simulated by a corresponding step of $\mathcal{S}_0$. From the time-abstracted system $\mathcal{S}_0$ we proceed as in the last section. This means that we extract a (hopefully small) system $\mathcal{S}_0^\sharp$ which is obtained by removing all actions which are not related to OS commands. Note that now, since some OS commands need no longer necessarily succeed, additionally the return values of OS commands must be tracked. Also, as tasks may spontaneously become *ready* (or *susp*) after a command periodic_wait$_0$(), we must refer to definition **N1** for local termination. In order to establish this property, we again rely on a global invariant Q for $\mathcal{S}_0$. By means of this invariant, we decompose this problem into local termination problems for the sequential systems $\mathcal{S}_{0,Q,f}^\sharp$.

5 Implementation

We have realized this sketched approach. The extraction of the concurrent algorithmic core has been implemented within the abstract interpretation framework Goblint [33]. The latter tool supports the specification of static analyses by means of *side-effecting* constraint systems and thus is well-suited to infer global invariants of systems consisting of multiple concurrent tasks. The analyzer GOBLINT allows to analyze programs context-sensitively, thus distinguishing, e.g., distinct calls of wrapper functions for distinct arguments. This is crucial, e.g., for a precise lockset analysis. GOBLINT also comes with a series of *generic* local fixpoint engines which allow to solve the specified analysis problems in a demand-driven way.

For the purposes of a starvation analysis, GOBLINT is instrumented to extract the set of control-flow edges of the abstract system $\mathcal{S}^\sharp$. The system $\mathcal{S}^\sharp$ is then translated into a PROMELA program which implements the given scheduling policy and provides the semantics for the OS commands. The PROMELA program together with LTL specifications of non-starvation are then fed into the model-checker SPIN [17].

Another instance of GOBLINT is used to analyze the real-time system $\mathcal{S}$ for local termination. The implementation of this second stage is still in a preliminary stage. This analysis first instruments each loop with an explicit loop iteration counter and then tries to prove that each such counter takes values only from some bounded range. For that, a variant of the octagon domain [24] is employed to track bounds as sums and differences of integer variables. This type of analysis is tailored to prove termination for standard *for*-loops. To deal also with more irregular cases, extensive constant propagation together with a dedicated treatment of enums is added.

6 A Case Study

We tried our starvation analyzer on a not-too-large application from the area of avionics. The application is targeted for the ARINC 653 operating system standard and has about 50k lines of (obfuscated) C code. It uses seven tasks, all running at different static priorities. One of them is used for initialization, one for error handling, three are periodic, and two non-periodic. The initialization task creates the other tasks and runs exclusively until it issues a command that starts the scheduler. Among other ARINC primitives, the program makes use of suspend, resume, setting, resetting and timed waiting for a single event as well as a single semaphore. The program does not contain too many of the OS commands, but these may occur deeply nested inside function calls which are dispersed all over the program. In fact, the maximal nesting-depth of function calls is 19. Due to this considerable depth, it pays off, precision-wise, that GOBLINT allows to use the full local states as calling contexts when extracting the system $\mathcal{S}_0^\sharp$, which abstracts first from time and second, from all non-OS related actions. As it is a safety-critical real-time application, the program does not use dynamic memory allocation or recursion, but makes extensive use of arrays and pointers.

Using a 3.7 GHz Intel Core i7 processor, the extraction of the abstract system takes about 3 min. The extraction results in an interprocedural control-flow graph of 4310 edges.

The LTL formula, we want to check for each task f is

$$\mathbf{GF}(\mathsf{run}_f \vee \mathsf{done}_f)$$

where run_f and done_f are the properties that task f is in state *run* and *done*, respectively. From the abstract model together with the LTL formulas, a specification in Promela is generated. On this specification, the SPIN model checker takes 1 min and at most 7.4 GB of memory to finish to verify the formulas. For the given application, it did not find a violation of starvation-freedom.

For our approach to be sound it remains to certify local termination. In order to do so, we tried to prove termination of each loop in the program, given a global invariant for shared data. The results of a manual classification of the different kind of loops is given in Fig. 5.

Terminating	
for-loops	226
do-while	4
contrived loops	61
library functions	7
External reasons	
Time-out	5
Logbook	4
QueuingMessage	2
Unclear termination	9
No termination	4
Total	322

Fig. 5. Manual classification of loops

The program contains 323 loops, of which one had to be unrolled for the analyzer to infer precise information about the created resources. From all loops, our analysis could identify local program variables which control the loop iteration in 282 loops. For 204 of these loops, an octagon analysis is sufficient to prove that the iteration terminates. Additionally in some loops, exit conditions must be tracked as they are stored and inspected later for breaking out of the loop. With some extra effort, we expect termination of all loops from the first three categories in Fig. 5 to be automatically provable.

Upon manual inspection of the remaining loops, we found that the four non-terminating loops are the outermost loops of the three periodic tasks, together with the outermost loop of a non-periodic task that is periodically resumed and suspended. In all these cases, OS commands are encountered on each control-flow path traversing the loop body.

The program code also contains the code for string manipulating system functions such as strlen, strcat, or strcpy, whose termination depends on whether pointers to null terminated strings are provided as arguments or not. There are twenty loops where the criteria for termination are rather contrived.

- In five loops, termination can only be guaranteed due to explicitly programmed time-outs by means of the non-blocking command get_time(), which is not extracted into transitions of the abstract model.
- Termination of six loops depends on the return-codes of non-blocking OS commands like Logbook or QueuingMessage. These commands, however, are extracted to the abstract model.
- Termination of nine loops occurs once a certain value in some data-structure is found.

The latter loops are most difficult, as tailored analyses are required to provide sufficiently strong invariants for these data-structures to deduce that the exit condition ever is met.

The given numbers and observations are specific to the particular given example application. Nonetheless, the experience is encouraging: while most loops can be dealt with automatically, only few loops remain which must be inspected manually to ensure local termination.

7 Conclusion

Proving properties such as definite starvation-freedom in a realistic concurrent real-time system is challenging. We have proposed to use a static analyzer to strip the system of all computation which is irrelevant for the interaction between tasks. We showed that if the resulting abstract system is starvation-free, then so is the original system — given that the original system is locally terminating. This observation allows us to *decompose* the analysis of starvation-freedom into a model-checking problem for a decently small model by means of an off-the-shelf LTL model-checker; and a proof of local termination. In order to attack the latter problem, we relied on *global* invariants. These can again be computed by a static analyzer such as GOBLINT based on abstract interpretation. We finally argued that, relative to a given global invariant, local termination can be reduced to local termination of finitely many sequential systems. To the latter, a variety of known techniques for proving termination of loops can be applied.

Based on an implementation in the static analyzer framework GOBLINT, we indicated that such an approach may indeed be viable. For a realistic safety-critical real-time application based on ARINC 653, we showed that extraction of the abstract model as well as the verification of the appropriate temporal properties is indeed feasible. We also categorized the loops occurring in the application and showed that for most of them, termination proofs are possible by standard means.

Currently, we are extending our approach to other real-time operating systems such as Autosar/OSEK and also to systems running not on a single sequential processor, but on multi-cores.

References

1. Amato, G., Scozzari, F., Seidl, H., Apinis, K., Vojdani, V.: Efficiently intertwining widening and narrowing. Sci. Comput. Program. **120**, 1–24 (2016)
2. Apinis, K., Seidl, H., Vojdani, V.: Side-effecting constraint systems: a swiss army knife for program analysis. In: Jhala, R., Igarashi, A. (eds.) APLAS 2012. LNCS, vol. 7705, pp. 157–172. Springer, Heidelberg (2012). doi:10.1007/978-3-642-35182-2_12
3. Apinis, K., Seidl, H., Vojdani, V.: How to combine widening and narrowing for non-monotonic systems of equations. In: 34th ACM SIGPLAN Conference on Programming Language Design and Implementation (PLDI), pp. 377–386. ACM (2013)
4. Bertrane, J., Cousot, P., Cousot, R., Feret, J., Mauborgne, L., Miné, A., Rival, X.: Static analysis and verification of aerospace software by abstract interpretation. Found. Trends Program. Lang. **2**(2–3), 71–190 (2015)
5. Bertrane, J., Cousot, P., Cousot, R., Jérôme Feret, L.M., Miné, A., Rival, X.: Static analysis and verification of aerospace software by abstract interpretation. In: AIAA Infotech@Aerospace 2010, number AIAA-2010-3385, pp. 1–38. American Institue of Aeronautics and Astronautics, April 2010
6. Bertrane, J., Cousot, P., Cousot, R., Jérôme Feret, L.M., Miné, A., Rival, X.: Static analysis by abstract interpretation of embedded critical software. Softw. Eng. Notes **36**(1), 1–8 (2011)
7. Bourke, T., Brun, L., Dagand, P., Leroy, X., Pouzet, M., Rieg, L.: A formally verified compiler for lustre. In: Cohen and Vechev [9], pp. 586–601
8. Chaki, S., Clarke, E.M., Ouaknine, J., Sharygina, N., Sinha, N.: Concurrent software verification with states, events, and deadlocks. Formal Asp. Comput. **17**(4), 461–483 (2005)
9. Cohen, A., Vechev, M.T. (eds.): Proceedings of the 38th ACM SIGPLAN Conference on Programming Language Design and Implementation, PLDI 2017, Barcelona, Spain, June 18–23, 2017. ACM (2017)
10. Cousot, P., Cousot, R.: An abstract interpretation framework for termination. In: Field, J., Hicks, M. (eds.) Proceedings of the 39th ACM SIGPLAN-SIGACT Symposium on Principles of Programming Languages, POPL 2012, Philadelphia, Pennsylvania, USA, January 22–28, 2012, pp. 245–258. ACM (2012)
11. de Boer, F.S., Bravetti, M., Grabe, I., Lee, M., Steffen, M., Zavattaro, G.: A petri net based analysis of deadlocks for active objects and futures. In: Păsăreanu, C.S., Salaün, G. (eds.) FACS 2012. LNCS, vol. 7684, pp. 110–127. Springer, Heidelberg (2013). doi:10.1007/978-3-642-35861-6_7
12. de la Cámara, P., del Mar Gallardo, M., Merino, P.: Model extraction for ARINC 653 based avionics software. In: Bošnački, D., Edelkamp, S. (eds.) SPIN 2007. LNCS, vol. 4595, pp. 243–262. Springer, Heidelberg (2007). doi:10.1007/978-3-540-73370-6_16
13. Engler, D.R., Ashcraft, K.: Racerx: effective, static detection of race conditions and deadlocks. In: Scott, M.L., Peterson, L.L. (eds.) Proceedings of the 19th ACM Symposium on Operating Systems Principles 2003, SOSP 2003, Bolton Landing, NY, USA, October 19–22, 2003, pp. 237–252. ACM (2003)
14. Flores-Montoya, A.E., Albert, E., Genaim, S.: May-happen-in-parallel based deadlock analysis for concurrent objects. In: Beyer, D., Boreale, M. (eds.) FMOODS/FORTE -2013. LNCS, vol. 7892, pp. 273–288. Springer, Heidelberg (2013). doi:10.1007/978-3-642-38592-6_19

15. Schulze Frielinghaus, S., Seidl, H., Vogler, R.: Enforcing termination of interprocedural analysis. In: Rival, X. (ed.) SAS 2016. LNCS, vol. 9837, pp. 447–468. Springer, Heidelberg (2016). doi:10.1007/978-3-662-53413-7_22
16. Hahn, S., Reineke, J., Wilhelm, R.: Toward compact abstractions for processor pipelines. In: Meyer, R., Platzer, A., Wehrheim, H. (eds.) Correct System Design. LNCS, vol. 9360, pp. 205–220. Springer, Cham (2015). doi:10.1007/978-3-319-23506-6_14
17. Holzmann, G.J.: The model checker SPIN. IEEE Trans. Softw. Eng. **23**(5), 279–295 (1997)
18. Jourdan, J., Laporte, V., Blazy, S., Leroy, X., Pichardie, D.: A formally-verified C static analyzer. In: Rajamani, S.K., Walker, D. (eds.) Proceedings of the 42nd Annual ACM SIGPLAN-SIGACT Symposium on Principles of Programming Languages, POPL 2015, Mumbai, India, January 15–17, 2015, pp. 247–259. ACM (2015)
19. Klein, G., Andronick, J., Elphinstone, K., Murray, T.C., Sewell, T., Kolanski, R., Heiser, G.: Comprehensive formal verification of an OS microkernel. ACM Trans. Comput. Syst. **32**(1), 2:1–2:70 (2014)
20. Kroening, D., Tautschnig, M.: CBMC - C Bounded Model Checker, pp. 389–391. Springer, Heidelberg (2014)
21. Lemieux, J.: Programming in the OSEK/VDX Environment. CMP Media Inc., USA (2001)
22. Lv, M., Guan, N., Reineke, J., Wilhelm, R., Yi, W.: A survey on static cache analysis for real-time systems. LITES **3**(1), 5:1–5:48 (2016)
23. McMillan, K.L., Rival, X. (eds.): VMCAI 2014. LNCS, vol. 8318. Springer, Heidelberg (2014)
24. Miné, A.: The octagon abstract domain. High. Order Symbol. Comput. **19**(1), 31–100 (2006)
25. Miné, A.: Relational thread-modular static value analysis by abstract interpretation. In: McMillan and Rival [23], pp. 39–58
26. Naik, M., Park, C., Sen, K., Gay, D.: Effective static deadlock detection. In: 31st International Conference on Software Engineering, ICSE 2009, May 16–24, 2009, Vancouver, Canada, Proceedings, pp. 386–396. IEEE (2009)
27. Podelski, A., Rybalchenko, A.: Transition invariants and transition predicate abstraction for program termination. In: Abdulla, P.A., Leino, K.R.M. (eds.) TACAS 2011. LNCS, vol. 6605, pp. 3–10. Springer, Heidelberg (2011). doi:10.1007/978-3-642-19835-9_2
28. Santhiar, A., Kanade, A.: Static deadlock detection for asynchronous c# programs. In: Cohen and Vechev [9], pp. 292–305
29. Schwarz, M.D., Seidl, H., Vojdani, V., Apinis, K.: Precise analysis of value-dependent synchronization in priority scheduled programs. In: McMillan and Rival [23], pp. 21–38
30. Schwarz, M.D., Seidl, H., Vojdani, V., Lammich, P., Müller-Olm, M.: Static analysis of interrupt-driven programs synchronized via the priority ceiling protocol. In: Ball, T., Sagiv, M. (eds.) Proceedings of the 38th ACM SIGPLAN-SIGACT Symposium on Principles of Programming Languages, POPL 2011, Austin, TX, USA, January 26–28, 2011, pp. 93–104. ACM (2011)
31. Thompson, S., Brat, G.P., Venet, A.: Software model checking of ARINC-653 flight code with MCP. In: Muñoz, C.A. (ed.) Second NASA Formal Methods Symposium - NFM 2010, Proceedings, Washington D.C., USA, April 13–15, 2010. NASA Conference Proceedings, vol. NASA/CP-2010-216215, pp. 171–181 (2010)

32. Urban, C., Miné, A.: A decision tree abstract domain for proving conditional termination. In: Müller-Olm, M., Seidl, H. (eds.) SAS 2014. LNCS, vol. 8723, pp. 302–318. Springer, Cham (2014). doi:10.1007/978-3-319-10936-7_19
33. Vojdani, V., Apinis, K., Rõtov, V., Seidl, H., Vene, V., Vogler, R.: Static race detection for device drivers: the goblint approach. In: Proceedings of the 31st IEEE/ACM International Conference on Automated Software Engineering, ASE 2016, pp. 391–402. ACM (2016)
34. Walli, S.R.: The posix family of standards. StandardView **3**(1), 11–17 (1995)
35. Wilhelm, R., Altmeyer, S., Burguière, C., Grund, D., Herter, J., Reineke, J., Wachter, B., Wilhelm, S.: Static timing analysis for hard real-time systems. In: Barthe, G., Hermenegildo, M. (eds.) VMCAI 2010. LNCS, vol. 5944, pp. 3–22. Springer, Heidelberg (2010). doi:10.1007/978-3-642-11319-2_3
36. Williams, A., Thies, W., Ernst, M.D.: Static deadlock detection for java libraries. In: Black, A.P. (ed.) ECOOP 2005. LNCS, vol. 3586, pp. 602–629. Springer, Heidelberg (2005). doi:10.1007/11531142_26
37. Zuleger, F., Gulwani, S., Sinn, M., Veith, H.: Bound analysis of imperative programs with the size-change abstraction. In: Yahav, E. (ed.) SAS 2011. LNCS, vol. 6887, pp. 280–297. Springer, Heidelberg (2011). doi:10.1007/978-3-642-23702-7_22

Program Analysis

Precise Null Pointer Analysis Through Global Value Numbering

Ankush Das[1(✉)] and Akash Lal[2]

[1] Carnegie Mellon University, Pittsburgh, PA, USA
ankushd@cs.cmu.edu
[2] Microsoft Research, Bangalore, India
akashl@microsoft.com

Abstract. Precise analysis of pointer information plays an important role in many static analysis tools. The precision, however, must be balanced against the scalability of the analysis. This paper focusses on improving the precision of standard context and flow insensitive alias analysis algorithms at a low scalability cost. In particular, we present a semantics-preserving program transformation that drastically improves the precision of existing analyses when deciding if a pointer can alias NULL. Our program transformation is based on Global Value Numbering, a scheme inspired from compiler optimization literature. It allows even a flow-insensitive analysis to make use of branch conditions such as checking if a pointer is NULL and gain precision. We perform experiments on real-world code and show that the transformation improves precision (in terms of the number of dereferences proved safe) from 86.56% to 98.05%, while incurring a small overhead in the running time.

Keywords: Alias analysis · Global Value Numbering · Static Single Assignment · Null pointer analysis

1 Introduction

Detecting and eliminating null-pointer exceptions is an important step towards developing reliable systems. Static analysis tools that look for null-pointer exceptions typically employ techniques based on *alias analysis* to detect possible aliasing between pointers. Two pointer-valued variables are said to *alias* if they hold the same memory location during runtime. Statically, aliasing can be decided in two ways: (a) *may-alias* [1], where two pointers are said to may-alias if they can point to the same memory location under some possible execution, and (b) *must-alias* [27], where two pointers are said to must-alias if they always point to the same memory location under all possible executions. Because a precise alias analysis is undecidable [24] and even a flow-insensitive pointer analysis is NP-hard [14], much of the research in the area plays on the precision-efficiency trade-off of alias analysis. For example, practical algorithms for may-alias analysis lose precision (but retain soundness) by over-approximating: a verdict that two pointer may-alias does not imply that there is some execution in which

D. D'Souza and K. Narayan Kumar (Eds.): ATVA 2017, LNCS 10482, pp. 25–41, 2017.
DOI: 10.1007/978-3-319-68167-2_2

they actually hold the same value. Whereas, a verdict that two pointers cannot may-alias must imply that there is no execution in which they hold the same value.

We use a sound may-alias analysis in an attempt to prove the safety of a program with respect to null-pointer exceptions. For each pointer dereference, we ask the analysis if the pointer can may-alias NULL just before the dereference. If the answer is that it cannot may-alias NULL, then the pointer cannot hold a NULL value under all possible executions, hence the dereference is safe. The more precise the analysis, the more dereferences it can prove safe. This paper demonstrates a technique that improves the precision of may-alias analysis at a little cost when answering aliasing queries of pointers with the NULL value.

The NULL value is special because programmers tend to be defensive against null-pointer exceptions. If there is doubt that a pointer, say x, can be NULL or not, the programmer uses a check "if ($x \neq$ NULL)" before dereferencing x. Existing alias analysis techniques, especially flow insensitive techniques for may-alias analysis, ignore all branch conditions. As we demonstrate in this paper, exploiting these defensive checks can significantly increase the precision of alias analysis. Our technique is based around a semantics-preserving program transformation and requires only a minor change to the alias analysis algorithm itself.

Program transformations have been used previously to improve the precision for alias analysis. For instance, it is common to use a *Static Single Assignment* (SSA) conversion [5] before running flow-insensitive analyses. The use of SSA automatically adds some level of flow sensitivity to the analysis [12]. SSA, while useful, is still limited in the amount of precision that it adds, and in particular, it does not help with using branch conditions. We present a program transformation based on *Global Value Numbering* (GVN) [16] that adds significantly more precision on top of SSA by leveraging branch conditions.

The transformation works by first inserting an assignment $v := e$ on the *then* branch of a check if ($e \neq$ NULL), where v is a fresh program variable. This gives us the global invariant that v can never hold the NULL value. However, this invariant will be of no use unless the program uses v. Our transformation then searches locally, in the same procedure, for program expressions e' that are *equivalent* to e, that is, at runtime they both hold the same value. The transformation then replaces e' with v. The search for equivalent expressions is done by adapting the GVN algorithm (originally designed for compiler optimizations [10]).

Our transformation can be followed up with a standard alias analysis to infer the points-to set for each variable, with a slight change that the new variables introduced by our transformation (such as v above) cannot be NULL. This change stops spurious propagation of NULL and makes the analysis more precise. We perform extensive experiments on real-world code. The results show that the precision of the alias analysis (measured in terms of the number of pointer dereferences proved safe) goes from 86.56% to 98.05%. This work is used in Microsoft's Static Driver Verifier tool [22] for finding null-pointer bugs in device drivers[1].

[1] https://msdn.microsoft.com/en-us/library/windows/hardware/mt779102(v=vs.85).aspx.

```
var x : int
procedure f(var y : int) returns u : int
{
    var z : int
    L1:
        x := y.f;
        assume (x ≠ Null);
        goto L2;
    L2:
        z.g := y;
        assert (x ≠ Null);
        u := x;
        return;
}
```

```
procedure main()
{
    var a : int;
    var b : int;
    L1:
        a := new();
        b := call f(a);
        goto L2;
    L2:
        return;
}
```

Fig. 1. An example program in our language

The rest of the paper is organized as follows: Sect. 2 provides background on flow-insensitive alias analysis and how SSA can improve its precision. Section 3 illustrates our program transformation via an example and Sect. 4 presents it formally. Section 5 presents experimental results, Sect. 6 describes some of the related work in the area and Sect. 7 concludes.

2 Background

2.1 Programming Language

We introduce a simplistic language to demonstrate the alias analysis and how program transformations can be used to increase its precision. As is standard, we concern ourselves only with statements that manipulate pointers. All other statements are ignored (i.e., abstracted away) by the alias analysis. Our language has assignments with one of the following forms: pointer assignments x := y, dereferencing via field writes x.f := y and reads x := y.f, creating new memory locations x := new(), or assigning NULL as x := NULL. The language also has assume and assert statements:

- assume B checks the Boolean condition B and continues execution only if the condition evaluates to *true*. The assume statement is a convenient way of modeling branching in most existing source languages. For instance, a branch "if (B)" can be modeled using two basic blocks, one beginning with assume B and the other with assume ¬B.
- assert B checks the Boolean condition B and continues execution if it holds. If B does not hold, then it raises an assertion failure and stops program execution.

A program in our language begins with global variable declarations followed by one or more procedures. Each procedure starts with declarations of local

Statement	Constraint
i : x := new()	$aS_i \in pt(x)$
x := NULL	$aS_O \in pt(x)$
x := y	$pt(y) \subseteq pt(x)$
x := y.f	$\dfrac{aS_i \in pt(y)}{pt(aS_i.\mathsf{f}) \subseteq pt(x)}$
x.f := y	$\dfrac{aS_i \in pt(x)}{pt(y) \subseteq pt(aS_i.\mathsf{f})}$

Fig. 2. Program statements and corresponding points-to set constraints

Algorithm 1. Algorithm for computing points-to sets

```
For each program variable x, let pt(x) = ∅
repeat
    opt := pt
    for all program statements st do
        if st is i : x := new() then
            pt(x) := pt(x) ∪ {aS_i}
        if st is x := NULL then
            pt(x) := pt(x) ∪ {aS_O}
        if st is x := y then
            pt(x) := pt(x) ∪ pt(y)
        if st is x := y.f then
            for all aS_i ∈ pt(y) do
                pt(x) := pt(x) ∪ pt(aS_i.f)
        if st is x.f := y then
            for all aS_i ∈ pt(x) do
                pt(aS_i.f) := pt(aS_i.f) ∪ pt(y)
        for all tagged(x) do
            pt(x) := pt(x) − {aS_O}
until opt = pt
```

variables, followed by a sequence of basic blocks. Each basic block starts with a label, followed by a list of statements, and ends with a control transfer, which is either a goto or a return. A goto in our language can take multiple labels. The choice between which label to jump is non-deterministic. Finally, we disallow loops in the control-flow of a procedure; they can instead be encoded using procedures with recursion. This restriction simplifies the presentation of our algorithms. Figure 1 shows an illustrative example in our language.

2.2 Alias Analysis

This section describes Andersen's may-alias analysis [1]. The analysis is context and flow-insensitive, which means that it completely abstracts away the control of the program. But the analysis is field-sensitive, which means that a value can be obtained by reading a field f only if it was previously written to the same field f. Field-insensitive analyses, for example, also abstract away the field name.

The analysis outputs an over-approximation of the set of memory locations each pointer can hold under all possible executions. Since a program can potentially execute indefinitely (because of loops or recursion), the number of memory locations allocated by a program can be unbounded. We consider a finite abstraction of memory locations, commonly called the *allocation-site abstraction* [15]. Each memory location allocated by the same new statement is represented using the same abstract value. This abstract value is also called an allocation site. We

`x := new();`	`x1 := new();`
`assert (x ≠ Null);`	`assert (x1 ≠ Null);`
`y := x.f;`	`y := x1.f;`
`x := Null;`	`x2 := Null;`

Fig. 3. A program snippet before SSA (left) and after SSA (right)

label each new statement with a unique number i and refer to its corresponding allocation site as aS_i. We use the special allocation site aS_0 to denote NULL.

We follow a description of Andersen's analysis in terms of set constraints [26], shown in Fig. 2. The analysis outputs a points-to relation pt where $pt(x)$ represents the points-to set of a variable x, i.e. (an over-approximation of) the set of allocation sites that x may hold under all possible executions. In addition, it also computes $pt(aS_i.\mathsf{f})$, for each allocation site aS_i and field f, representing (an over-approximation of) the set of values written to the f field of an object in $pt(aS_i)$.

The analysis abstracts away program control along with assert and assume statements. It considers a program as a bag of pointer-manipulating statements where each statement can be executed any number of times and in any order. Function calls are processed by adding assignments between formal and actual variables. For instance, in Fig. 1, the call to f from main will result in the assignments y := a and b := u. For each statement, the analysis follows Fig. 2 to generate a set of rules that define constraints on the points-to solution pt. The rules can be read as follows.

- If a program has an allocation x := new() and this statement is labeled with the unique integer i, then the solution must have $aS_i \in pt(x)$.
- If a program has the statement x := NULL, then it must be that $aS_0 \in pt(x)$.
- If the program has an assignment x := y then the solution must have $pt(y) \subseteq pt(x)$, because x may hold any value that y can hold.
- If the program has a statement x := y.f and $aS_i \in pt(y)$, then it follows that $pt(aS_i.\mathsf{f}) \subseteq pt(x)$ because x may hold any value written to the f field of aS_i.
- If the program has a statement x.f := y and $aS_i \in pt(x)$ then it must be that $pt(y) \subseteq pt(aS_i.\mathsf{f})$.

These set constraints can be solved using a simple fix-point iteration, shown in Algorithm 1. (Our tool uses a more efficient implementation [26].) For now, ignore the loop on line 17. Once the solution is computed, we check all assertions in the program. We say that an assertion assert (x ≠ NULL) is *safe* (i.e., the assertion cannot be violated) if $aS_0 \notin pt(x)$. We do not consider other kinds of assertions in the program because our goal is just to show null-exception safety. Andersen's analysis complexity is cubic in the size of the program.

```
assume (x ≠ Null);
y := x;
assert (x ≠ Null);
z := x.f;
```

```
assume (x ≠ Null);
cseTmp# := x;
y := cseTmp#;
assert (cseTmp# ≠ Null);
z := cseTmp#.g;
```

Fig. 4. A program snippet before CSE (left) and after CSE (right)

2.3 Static Single Assignment (SSA)

This section shows how a program transformation can improve the precision of an alias analysis. Consider the program on the left in Fig. 3. A flow-insensitive analysis does not look at the order of statements. Under this abstraction, the analysis cannot prove the safety of the assertion in this snippet of code because it does not know that the assignment of NULL to x only happens after the assertion.

To avoid such loss in precision, most practical implementations of alias analysis use the Single Static Assignment (SSA) form [5]. Roughly, SSA introduces multiple copies of each original variable such that each variable in the new program only has a single assignment. The SSA form of the snippet is shown on the right in Fig. 3. Clearly, this program has the same semantics as the original program. But a flow-insensitive analysis will now be able to show the safety of the assertion in the program because the assignment of NULL is to x2 whereas the assertion is on x1.

3 Overview

This section presents an overview of our technique of using program transformations that add even more precision to the alias analysis compared to the standard SSA. We start by using *Common Subexpression Elimination* [4] and build towards using *Global Value Numbering* [16], which is used in our implementation and experiments.

3.1 Common Subexpression Elimination

We demonstrate how we can leverage assume and assert statements to add precision to the analysis. Consider the program on the left in Fig. 4. Once the program control passes the assume statement, we know that x cannot point to NULL, hence the assertion is safe, irrespective of what preceded this code snippet. Also, note that SSA renaming does not help prove the assertion in this case (it is essentially a no-op for the program). We now make the case for a different program transformation.

As a first step, we introduce a new local variable cseTmp# to the procedure and assign it the value of x right after the assume. These new variables that we introduce to the program will carry the tag "#" to distinguish them from other program variables. For a tagged variable $w^{\#}$, we say that *tagged*($w^{\#}$) is *true*. These tagged variables carry the special invariant that they cannot be NULL; their only assignment will be after an assume statement that prunes away the NULL value. (The same reasoning applies to assert statements too, i.e. once control passes a statement assert(x $\neq$ NULL), x cannot point to NULL.)

After introducing the variable $\mathsf{cseTmp}^{\#}$, we make use of a technique similar to *Common Subexpression Elimination* (CSE) to replace all expressions that are equivalent to $\mathsf{cseTmp}^{\#}$ with the variable itself, resulting in the program on the right in Fig. 4. This snippet is clearly equivalent to the original one. We perform the alias analysis on this snippet as usual, but enforce that $pt(cseTmp^{\#})$ cannot have aS_0 because it cannot be NULL. (See the loop on line 17 of Algorithm 1.) The analysis can now prove that the assertion is safe.

The process of finding equivalent expressions is not trivial. For instance, consider the following program where we have introduced the variable $\mathsf{cseTmp}^{\#}$.

```
assume (x.f ≠ Null);
cseTmp# := x.f;
y.f := z;
z := x.f;
```

In the last assignment, x.f cannot be substituted by $\mathsf{cseTmp}^{\#}$, because there is an assignment to the field f in the previous statement. As there is no aliasing information present at this point, we have to conservatively assume that y and x could be aliases, thus, the assignment y.f := z can potentially change the value of x.f, breaking its equivalence to $\mathsf{cseTmp}^{\#}$.

3.2 Global Value Numbering

We improve upon the previous transformation by using a more precise method of determining expression equalities. The methodology remains the same: we introduce temporary variables that cannot be NULL and use them to replace syntactically equivalent expressions. But this time we adapt the Global Value Numbering (GVN) scheme to detect equivalent expressions. Consider the following program. (For now, ignore the right-hand side of the figure after the "$\Longrightarrow$".)

```
y := x.f.g;           ⟹ t1 ← x, t2 ← t1.f, t3 ← t2.g, y ↪ t3
z := y.h;             ⟹ t3 ← y, t4 ← t3.h, z ↪ t4
assume (z ≠ Null);    ⟹ add t4 to nonNullExprs
a := x.f;             ⟹ t1 ← x, t2 ← t1.f, a ↪ t2
b := a.g.h;           ⟹ t2 ← a, t3 ← t2.g, t4 ← t3.h, b ↪ t4
assert (b ≠ Null);    ⟹ check t4 ∈ nonNullExprs
c.g := d;
```

It is clear that z and b are equivalent at the assertion location, and because z $\neq$ NULL, the assertion is safe. However, none of the previous methods would allow us to prove the safety of the assertion. We adapt the GVN scheme to help us establish the equality between z and b. We introduce the concept of *terms* that will be used as a placeholder for subexpressions. The intuitive idea is that equivalent subexpressions will be represented using the same term.

We start by giving an overview of the transformation for a single basic block, and then generalize it to full procedure later in this section. For a single basic block, we walk through the statements in order and as we encounter a new variable, we assign it a new term and remember this mapping in a dictionary called *hashValue*. We also store the mapping from terms to other terms through operators in a separate dictionary called *hashFunction*. For example, if x is assigned term t_1, and we encounter the assignment y := x.f, we store *hashFunction*[f][t_1] = t_2 and assign the term t_2 to y. We also maintain a separate list *nonNullExprs* of terms that are not null. Finally, for performing the actual substitution, we maintain a dictionary *defaultVar* that maps terms to the temporary variables that we introduced for non-null expressions.

We go through the program snippet starting at the first statement and move down to the last statement. At statement i, we follow the description written in the ith item below. This description is also shown on the right side of the program snippet, after the $\Longrightarrow$ arrow.

1. Assign a new term t_1 to x, and set *hashValue*[x] = t_1. Then, set *hashFunction*[f][t_1] = t_2, and *hashFunction*[g][t_2] = t_3. Finally the assignment to y sets *hashValue*[y] = t_3.
2. We already have *hashValue*[y] = t_3, so assign *hashFunction*[g][t_3] = t_4. The assignment to z sets *hashValue*[z] = t_4.
3. We have *hashValue*[z] = t_4. So, we add t_4 to *nonNullExprs*. We create a new temporary variable gvnTmp$^{\#}$, and construct an extra assignment gvnTmp$^{\#}$:= z, and add it after the assume statement. Because *hashValue*[z] = t_4, we also add *defaultVar*[t_4] = gvnTmp$^{\#}$, which we will use later for substitutions to all expressions that hash to t_4.
4. We already have *hashValue*[x] = t_1 and *hashFunction*[f][t_1] = t_2, so we set *hashValue*[a] = t_2.
5. Since *hashValue*[a] = t_2, *hashFunction*[g][t_2] = t_3 and *hashFunction*[h][t_3] = t_4, the hash value of the expression a.g.h is t_4. We also have *defaultVar*[t_4] = gvnTmp$^{\#}$. At this point, we observe t_4 being in *nonNullExprs* and substitute the RHS a.g.h with gvnTmp$^{\#}$. Finally, we set *hashValue*[b] = t_4.
6. Because *hashValue*[b] = t_4 and *defaultVar*[t_4] = gvnTmp$^{\#}$ and *nonNullExprs* contains t_4, we replace the expression b with gvnTmp$^{\#}$.

The resulting code is shown below.

```
y := x.f.g;
z := y.h;
assume (z ≠ Null);
gvnTmp# := z;
a := x.f;
b := gvnTmp#;
assert (gvnTmp# ≠ Null);
c.g := d;
```

```
L1:
  assume (x ≠ Null);
  gvnTmp1# := x;
  goto L3;
L2:
  assume (x ≠ Null);
  gvnTmp2# := x;
  goto L3;
L3:
  assert (x ≠ Null);
```

```
L1:
  assume (x ≠ Null);
  gvnTmp1# := x;
  goto L3;
L2:
  assume (x ≠ Null);
  gvnTmp2# := x;
  goto L3;
L3:
  gvnTmp3# := x;
  assert (gvnTmp3# ≠ Null);
```

Fig. 5. A program snippet before GVN (left) and after GVN (right)

Clearly, we retain the invariant that #-tagged variables cannot be NULL, and it is now straightforward to prove the safety of the assertion. We also note that the expression substitution is performed in a conservative manner. It is aborted as soon as a subexpression is assigned to. For example, at line 8, we encounter an assignment to the field g, so we remove g from the dictionary *hashFunction*. This has the effect of g acting as a new field, and all terms referenced by this field will now be assigned new terms.

The above transformation, in general, is performed on the entire procedure, not just a basic block to fully exploit its potential. This occurs in two steps. First, loops are lifted and converted to procedures (with recursion), so that the control-flow of each resulting procedure is acyclic. Next, we perform a topological sort of the basic blocks of a procedure and analyze the blocks in this order. This ensures that by the time the algorithm visits a basic block, it has already processed all predecessors of the block.

When analyzing a block, the algorithm considers all its predecessors and takes the intersection of their *nonNullExprs* list and *hashValue* map. This is because an expression is non-null only if it is non-null in all its predecessors and, further, we can use a term for a variable only if it is associated with the same term in all its predecessors. Finally, an important aspect of the algorithm is to perform a sound substitution at the merge point of basic blocks.

Consider the code snippet on the left in Fig. 5. In this example, although x is available as a non-null expression in L3, we cannot substitute x in the assertion by either $\mathsf{gvnTmp}_1^\#$ or $\mathsf{gvnTmp}_2^\#$ because neither preserves program semantics. Instead, we introduce a new variable $\mathsf{gvnTmp}_3^\#$ and add the assignment $\mathsf{gvnTmp}_3^\# := \mathsf{x}$ right before the assertion in L3 and use that for substituting x. This is achieved by the map *var2expr* in the main algorithm. It maps a #-tagged variable to the expression that it substitutes. In the above program, suppose we assign the term t to the non-null expression x. Hence, *nonNullExprs*[L1] and *nonNullExprs*[L2] both contain t. We also have $\mathit{defaultVar}[\mathsf{L1}][t] = \mathsf{gvnTmp}_1^\#$

and $var2expr[\mathsf{gvnTmp}_1^{\#}] = \mathsf{x}$. Since t is available from all predecessors of L3, we know that this term is non-null in L3. The question is finding the expression corresponding to this term t and introducing a new assignment for it. At this point, the map *var2expr* comes into play. We pick a predecessor of L3, say L1. We look for the default variable of t and find $defaultVar[\mathsf{L1}][t] = \mathsf{gvnTmp}_1^{\#}$, we then search for $var2expr[\mathsf{gvnTmp}_1^{\#}] = \mathsf{x}$. At this point, we find that the expression corresponding to term t is x, and we introduce a new assignment $\mathsf{gvnTmp}_3^{\#} := \mathsf{x}$ at the start of L3 and use this for substitution of x in L3. The next section describes the algorithm formally.

4 Algorithm

We present the pseudocode of our program transformation in this section, as Algorithms 2 and 3. The transformation takes a program as input and produces a semantically-equivalent program with new #-tagged variables that can never point to NULL. This involves adding assignments for these new variables, and substituting existing expressions with these variables whenever we determine that the substitution will preserve semantics. A proof of correctness of our transformation can be found in our full version [7].

At a high level, the idea is to use assume and assert statements to identify non-null expressions. We introduce fresh #-tagged variables and assign these non-null expressions to them. Then, in a second pass, we compute a *term* corresponding to each expression. These terms are assigned in a manner that if two expressions have the same term, then they are equivalent to each other. If we encounter an expression e with the same term as one of the non-null expressions e', we substitute e with the #-tagged variable corresponding to e'.

We start by describing the role of each data structure used in Algorithm 2.

- *nonNullExprs* stores the terms corresponding to non-null expressions of a particular block.
- *var2expr* maps a #-tagged variable to the expression it is assigned to in each block. This will be used to perform sound substitution at merge points of basic blocks, as discussed in the last example of Sect. 3.2.
- *defaultVar* maps the term of to an expression to the #-tagged variable that will be used for its substitution. Whenever we compute the term for an expression, if the term is present in *nonNullExprs*, we will use *defaultVar* to find the #-tagged variable that will be used for the substitution.
- *hashValue* maps variables to terms assigned to them in a particular block.
- *hashFunction* stores the mapping from a field and a term to a new term. It is used to store the term for expressions with fields.
- *currBlock* keeps track of the current block (used in helper functions).

We explain the algorithm step by step.

Algorithm 2. Algorithm to perform GVN

```
1: nonNullExprs = {}                                   ▷ block → non-null terms in block
2: var2expr = {}                                       ▷ #-tagged variable → expression
3: defaultVar = {}                                     ▷ block, term → variable for substitution
4: hashValue = {}                                      ▷ block, variable → term
5: hashFunction = {}                                   ▷ operator, terms → term
6: currBlock                                           ▷ current block
7: function DoGVN
8:     for proc in program do
9:         for block in proc.Blocks do
10:            for stmt in block.Stmts do
11:                if stmt is "assert expr ≠ NULL" or "assume expr ≠ NULL" then
12:                    gvnTmp# ← GetNewTaggedVar()
13:                    s ← "gvnTmp# := expr"
14:                    block.Stmts.Add(s)
15:                    var2expr[block][gvnTmp#] ← expr
16:    for proc in program do
17:        sortedBlocks ← TopologicalSort(proc.Blocks)
18:        for block in sortedBlocks do
19:            nonNullExprs[block] ← ∩_{blk∈block.Preds} nonNullExprs[blk]
20:            hashValue[block] ← ∩_{blk∈block.Preds} hashValue[blk]
21:            currBlock ← block
22:            for term in nonNullExprs[block] do
23:                expr ← var2expr[defaultVar[blk][term]]          ▷ for some blk ∈ Preds
24:                gvnTmp# ← GetNewSpecialVar()
25:                var2expr[gvnTmp#] ← expr
26:                s ← "gvnTmp# := expr"
27:                block.Stmts.AddFront(s)
28:        for stmt in block.Stmts do
29:            stmt ← ProcessStmt(stmt)
30:            if stmt is "gvnTmp# := expr" then
31:                term ← ComputeHash(expr)
32:                nonNullExprs[block].Add(term)
33:                defaultVar[block][term] ← gvnTmp#
```

1. Lines 8–15 – In this first pass of the algorithm, we search for program statements of the form "assert expr $\neq$ NULL" or "assume expr $\neq$ NULL". This guarantees that expr cannot be NULL after this program location under all executions. Hence, we introduce a new variable $\mathsf{gvnTmp}^{\#}$ and assign expr to it. This mapping is also added to *var2expr*.
2. Line 17 – Before the second pass, we perform a topological sort on the basic blocks according to the control-flow graph. This is necessary since the information of *nonNullExprs* for the predecessors of a basic block is needed before analyzing it. Note that control-flow graphs of procedures in our language must be acyclic (we convert loops to recursion), thus a topological sorting always succeeds.

Algorithm 3. Helper Functions for DoGVN

```
function PROCESSSTMT(stmt)
    if stmt is "assume expr" or "assert expr" then
        expr ← GetExpr(expr)
        return stmt
    else if stmt is "v := expr" then
        hashValue[currBlock][v] ← ComputeHash(expr)
        expr ← GetExpr(expr)
        return stmt
    else if stmt is "v.f := expr" then
        expr ← GetExpr(expr)
        v ← GetExpr(v)
        hashFunction.Remove(f)
        return stmt
function GETEXPR(expr)
    if expr is v then
        term ← ComputeHash(v)
        if nonNullExprs[currBlock] contains term then
            return defaultVar[currBlock][term]
        return v
    if expr is v.f then
        v ← GetExpr(v)
        return v.f
function COMPUTEHASH(expr)
    if expr is v then
        if hashValue[currBlock] does not contain v then
            hashValue[currBlock][v] ← GetNewTerm()
        return hashValue[currBlock][v]
    else if expr is v.f then
        term ← ComputeHash(v)
        if hashFunction[f] does not contain term then
            hashFunction[f][term] ← GetNewTerm()
        return hashFunction[f][term]
```

3. Lines 18–27 – We compute the set of expressions that are non-null in all predecessors. These expressions will also be non-null in the current block. We also need the term for each variable in the current block, which also comes from the intersection of terms from all predecessors. Finally, for all the non-null expressions, we add an assignment since these expressions may be available from different variables in different predecessors, as discussed in Sect. 3.2.
4. Lines 28–33 – Finally, we process each statement in the current block. This performs the substitution for each expression in the statement (*GetExpr* function in Algorithm 3). *GetExpr* computes the term for the expression (*ComputeHash* function in Algorithm 3), and if the term is contained in *nonNullExprs*, the substitution is performed. Finally, if we encounter a store

statement, "v.f := expr", we remove all mappings w.r.t. f in *hashFunction*. So, for the future statements (and future blocks in the topological order), new terms will be assigned to expressions related to field f.

Following Algorithm 2, we generate a semantically equivalent program, and as we show in our experiments, will have improved precision with regard to alias analysis. The main reason behind this improvement is that these #-tagged variables can never contain aS_0 in their points-to set, hence NULL cannot flow through these variables in the analysis.

5 Experimental Evaluation

We have implemented the algorithms presented in this paper for the Boogie language [19]. Boogie is an intermediate verification language. Several front-ends are available that compile source languages such as C/C++ [17,23] and C# [2] to Boogie, making it a useful target for developing practical tools. (For C/C++, we make the standard assumption that pointer arithmetic does not change the allocation site of the pointer, and thus can be ignored for the alias analysis [29]; due to space constraints we do not describe these details in this paper.)

Our work fits into a broader verification effort. The *Angelic Verification* (AV) project[2] at Microsoft Research aims to design push-button technology for finding software defects. In an earlier effort, AV was targeted to find null-pointer bugs [6]. Programs from the Windows codebase, in C/C++, were compiled down to Boogie with assertions guarding every pointer access to check for null dereferences. These Boogie programs were fed to a verification pipeline that applied heavyweight SMT-solver technology to reason over all possible program behaviors. To optimize the verification time, an alias analysis is run at the Boogie level to remove assertions that can be proved safe by the analysis. As our results will show, this optimization is necessary. The alias analysis is based on Andersen's analysis, as was described in Fig. 2. We follow the algorithm given in Sridharan et al. report [26] with the extra constraint that #-tagged variables cannot alias with NULL, i.e. they cannot contain the allocation site aS_0. We can optionally perform the program transformation of Sect. 4 before running the alias analysis. Our implementation is available open-source[3].

We evaluate the effect of our program transformation on the precision of alias analysis for checking safety of null-pointer assertions. The benchmarks are described in the first three columns of Table 1. We picked 16 different modules from the Windows codebase. The table lists an anonymized name for the module (**Bench**), the lines of code in thousands (**KLOC**) and the number of assertions (one per pointer dereference) in the code (**Asserts**). It is worth noting that the first ten modules are the same as ones used in the study with AV [6], while the rest were added later.

[2] https://www.microsoft.com/en-us/research/project/angelic-verification/.

[3] At https://github.com/boogie-org/corral, project **AddOns\AliasAnalysis**.

Table 1. Results showing the effect of SSA and GVN program transformations on the ability of alias analysis to prove safety of non-null assertions.

Bench	Stats		SSA only		SSA with GVN		
	KLOC	Asserts	Time (s)	Asserts	Time (s)	GVN	Asserts
Mod 1	3.2	1741	9.08	61	11.37	0.88	17
Mod 2	8.4	4035	11.34	233	17.62	1.13	45
Mod 3	6.5	4375	10.26	617	19.43	2.15	52
Mod 4	20.9	7523	24.04	543	33.99	2.43	123
Mod 5	30.9	11184	35.02	1881	59.84	7.11	232
Mod 6	37.8	12128	35.94	2675	70.71	11.13	452
Mod 7	37.2	6840	36.88	1396	53.24	3.44	127
Mod 8	43.8	12209	28.91	2854	62.27	5.38	475
Mod 9	56.6	19030	60.05	5444	106.61	12.40	508
Mod 10	76.5	39955	171.43	2887	839.58	475.08	372
Mod 11	23.5	6966	49.17	875	69.10	10.14	103
Mod 12	14.9	8359	24.57	820	59.13	13.41	210
Mod 13	22.1	11471	38.27	869	87.07	24.03	248
Mod 14	36.2	18026	48.56	2501	149.60	41.93	478
Mod 15	19.4	20555	55.07	586	269.35	134.06	131
Mod 16	54.0	16957	62.86	2821	127.67	30.46	342
Total	**491.9**	**201354**	**701.45**	**27063**	**2036.58**	**775.16**	**3915**

We ran our tool, using either SSA alone or SSA followed by our GVN transformation, followed by the alias analysis. We list the total time taken by the tool (**Time(s)**), including the time to run the transformation, and the number of assertions that were *not* proved safe (**Asserts**). In the case of GVN, we also isolate and list the time taken by the GVN transformation itself (**GVN**). The experiments were run (sequentially, single-threaded) on a server class machine with an Intel(R) Xeon(R) processor (single core) executing at 2.4 GHz with 32 GB RAM.

It is clear from the table that GVN offers significant increase in precision. With only the use of SSA, the analysis was able to prove the safety of 86.56% of assertions, while with the GVN transformation, we can prune away 98.05% of assertions. This is approximately a 7X reduction in the number of assertions that remain. This pruning is surprising because the alias analysis is still context and flow insensitive. Our program transformation crucially exploits the fact that programmers tend to be defensive against null-pointer bugs, allowing the analysis to get away with a very coarse abstraction. In fact, this level of pruning means that investing in more sophisticated alias analyses (e.g., flow sensitive) would have very diminished returns.

The alias analysis itself scales quite well: it finishes on about half a million lines of code in approximately 700 s with just SSA (86.56% pruning) or 2000 s with GVN (98.05% pruning). We note that there is an increase in the running time when using GVN. This happens because the transformation introduces more variables, compared to just SSA. However, this increase in time is more than offset by the improvement presented to the AV toolchain. For example, with the GVN transformation, AV takes 11 h to finish the first 10 modules [6], whereas with the SSA transformation alone it does not finish even in 24 h. Furthermore, AV reports fewer bugs when using just SSA because the extra computational load translates to a loss in program coverage as timeouts are hit more frequently.

6 Related Work

Pointer analysis is a well-researched branch of static analysis. There are several techniques proposed that interplay between context, flow and field sensitivity. Our choice of using context-insensitive, flow-insensitive but field sensitive analysis is to pick a scalable starting point, after which we add precision at low cost. The distinguishing factor in our work is: (1) the ability to leverage information from `assume` and `assert` statements (or branch conditions) and (2) specializing for the purpose of checking non-null assertions (as opposed to general aliasing assertions). We very briefly list, in the rest of this section, some of the previous work in adding precision to alias analysis or making it more scalable.

Context Sensitivity. Sharir and Pnueli [25] introduced the concept of *call-strings* to add context-sensitivity to static analysis techniques. Call strings may grow extremely long and limit efficiency, so Lhoták and Hendren [21] used k-limiting approaches to limit the size of call strings. Whaley and Lam [28] instead use Binary Decision Diagrams (BDDs) to scale a context sensitive analysis.

Flow sensitivity. Hardekopf and Lin [11] present a staged flow-sensitive analysis where a less precise auxiliary pointer analysis computes def-use chains which is used to enable the sparsity of the primary flow-sensitive analysis. The technique is quite scalable on large benchmarks but they abstract away the assume statements. De and D'Souza [8] compute a map from access paths to sets of abstract objects at each program statement. This enables them to perform strong updates at indirect assignments. The technique is shown to be scalable only for small benchmarks, moreover, they also abstract away all assume statements. Finally, Lerch et al. [20] introduce the access-path abstraction, where access paths rooted at the same base variable are represented by this base variable at control flow merge points. The technique is quite expensive even on small benchmarks (less than 25 KLOC) and do not deal with assume statements in any way.

Other techniques. Heintze and Tardieu [13] improved performance by using a demand-driven pointer analysis, computing sufficient information to only determine points-to set of query variables. Fink et al. [9] developed a staged verification system, where faster and naive techniques run as early stages to prune away assertions that are easier to prove, which then reduces the load on more precise but slow techniques that run later. Landi and Ryder [18] use conditional may alias information to over-approximate the points-to sets of each pointer. Context sensitivity is added using k-limiting approach, and a set of aliases is maintained for every statement within a procedure to achieve flow-sensitivity. Choi et al. [3] also follows [18] closely but uses sparse representations for the control flow graphs and use transfer functions instead of alias-generating rules. To the best of our knowledge, none of these techniques are able to leverage assume statements to improve precision.

7 Conclusion

This paper presents a program transformation that improves the efficiency of alias analysis with minor scalability overhead. The transformation is proved to be semantics preserving. Our evaluation demonstrates the merit of our approach on a practical end-to-end scenario of finding null-pointer dereferences in software.

References

1. Andersen, L.O.: Program analysis and specialization for the C programming language. Ph.D. thesis, DIKU, University of Copenhagen, May 1994
2. Barnett, M., Qadeer, S.: BCT: A translator from MSIL to Boogie. In: Seventh Workshop on Bytecode Semantics, Verification, Analysis and Transformation (2012)
3. Choi, J.D., Burke, M., Carini, P.: Efficient flow-sensitive interprocedural computation of pointer-induced aliases and side effects. In: Principles of Programming Languages, pp. 232–245 (1993)
4. Cocke, J.: Global common subexpression elimination. In: Proceedings of a Symposium on Compiler Optimization, pp. 20–24. ACM, New York (1970)
5. Cytron, R., Ferrante, J., Rosen, B.K., Wegman, M.N., Zadeck, F.K.: Efficiently computing static single assignment form and the control dependence graph. ACM Trans. Program. Lang. Syst. **13**(4), 451–490 (1991)
6. Das, A., Lahiri, S.K., Lal, A., Li, Y.: Angelic verification: precise verification modulo unknowns. In: Kroening, D., Păsăreanu, C.S. (eds.) CAV 2015. LNCS, vol. 9206, pp. 324–342. Springer, Cham (2015). doi:10.1007/978-3-319-21690-4_19
7. Das, A., Lal, A.: Precise null pointer analysis through global value numbering. CoRR abs/1702.05807 (2017). http://arxiv.org/abs/1702.05807
8. De, A., D'Souza, D.: Scalable flow-sensitive pointer analysis for java with strong updates. In: Noble, J. (ed.) ECOOP 2012. LNCS, vol. 7313, pp. 665–687. Springer, Heidelberg (2012). doi:10.1007/978-3-642-31057-7_29
9. Fink, S.J., Yahav, E., Dor, N., Ramalingam, G., Geay, E.: Effective typestate verification in the presence of aliasing. ACM Trans. Softw. Eng. Methodol. **17**(2), 9:1–9:34 (2008)
10. Gulwani, S., Necula, G.C.: Global value numbering using random interpretation. In: Principles of Programming Languages, POPL, pp. 342–352 (2004)
11. Hardekopf, B., Lin, C.: Flow-sensitive pointer analysis for millions of lines of code. In: Code Generation and Optimization (CGO), pp. 289–298 (2011)

12. Hasti, R., Horwitz, S.: Using static single assignment form to improve flow-insensitive pointer analysis. In: Programming Language Design and Implementation (PLDI), pp. 97–105 (1998)
13. Heintze, N., Tardieu, O.: Demand-driven pointer analysis. In: Programming Language Design and Implementation (PLDI), pp. 24–34 (2001)
14. Horwitz, S.: Precise flow-insensitive may-alias analysis is NP-Hard. ACM Trans. Program. Lang. Syst. **19**(1), 1–6 (1997)
15. Jones, N.D., Muchnick, S.S.: A flexible approach to interprocedural data flow analysis and programs with recursive data structures. In: Principles of Programming Languages (POPL), pp. 66–74 (1982)
16. Kildall, G.A.: A unified approach to global program optimization. In: Principles of Programming Languages, pp. 194–206 (1973)
17. Lal, A., Qadeer, S.: Powering the static driver verifier using corral. In: Foundations of Software Engineering, pp. 202–212 (2014)
18. Landi, W., Ryder, B.G.: A safe approximate algorithm for interprocedural pointer aliasing. SIGPLAN Not. **39**(4), 473–489 (2004)
19. Leino, K.R.M.: This is boogie 2 (2008). https://github.com/boogie-org/boogie
20. Lerch, J., Spth, J., Bodden, E., Mezini, M.: Access-path abstraction: scaling field-sensitive data-flow analysis with unbounded access paths (t). In: Automated Software Engineering (ASE), pp. 619–629 (2015)
21. Lhoták, O., Hendren, L.: Evaluating the benefits of context-sensitive points-to analysis using a bdd-based implementation. ACM Trans. Softw. Eng. Methodol. (TOSEM) **18**(1), 3 (2008)
22. Microsoft: Static driver verifier. http://msdn.microsoft.com/en-us/library/windows/hardware/ff552808(v=vs.85).aspx
23. Rakamarić, Z., Emmi, M.: SMACK: decoupling source language details from verifier implementations. In: Biere, A., Bloem, R. (eds.) CAV 2014. LNCS, vol. 8559, pp. 106–113. Springer, Cham (2014). doi:10.1007/978-3-319-08867-9_7
24. Ramalingam, G.: The undecidability of aliasing. ACM Trans. Program. Lang. Syst. **16**(5), 1467–1471 (1994)
25. Sharir, M., Pnueli, A.: Two approaches to interprocedural data flow analysis, pp. 189–234. Prentice-Hall, Englewood Cliffs, NJ (1981). Chap. 7
26. Sridharan, M., Chandra, S., Dolby, J., Fink, S.J., Yahav, E.: Alias analysis for object-oriented programs. In: Clarke, D., Noble, J., Wrigstad, T. (eds.) Aliasing in Object-Oriented Programming. Types, Analysis and Verification. LNCS, vol. 7850, pp. 196–232. Springer, Heidelberg (2013). doi:10.1007/978-3-642-36946-9_8
27. Steensgaard, B.: Points-to analysis in almost linear time. In: Principles of Programming Languages (POPL), pp. 32–41. ACM, New York (1996)
28. Whaley, J., Lam, M.S.: An efficient inclusion-based points-to analysis for strictly-typed languages. In: Static Analysis Symposium, pp. 180–195 (2002)
29. Zheng, X., Rugina, R.: Demand-driven alias analysis for c. In: Proceedings of the 35th Annual ACM SIGPLAN-SIGACT Symposium on Principles of Programming Languages, POPL 2008, pp. 197–208. ACM, New York (2008)

May-Happen-in-Parallel Analysis with Returned Futures

Elvira Albert(✉), Samir Genaim, and Pablo Gordillo

Complutense University of Madrid (UCM), Madrid, Spain
elvira@sip.ucm.es

Abstract. May-Happen-in-Parallel (MHP) is a fundamental analysis to reason about concurrent programs. It infers the pairs of program points that may execute in parallel, or interleave their execution. This information is essential to prove, among other things, absence of data races, deadlock freeness, termination, and resource usage. This paper presents an MHP analysis for asynchronous programs that use *futures* as synchronization mechanism. Future variables are available in most concurrent languages (e.g., in the library `concurrent` of Java, in the standard thread library of C++, and in Scala and Python). The novelty of our analysis is that it is able to infer MHP relations that involve future variables that are *returned* by asynchronous tasks. Futures are returned when a task needs to await for another task created in an *inner* scope, e.g., task t needs to await for the termination of task p that is spawned by task q that is spawned during the execution of t (not necessarily by t). Thus, task p is awaited by task t which is in an outer scope. The challenge for the analysis is to (back)propagate the synchronization of tasks through future variables from inner to outer scopes.

1 Introduction

MHP is an analysis of utmost importance to ensure both liveness and safety properties of concurrent programs. The analysis computes *MHP pairs*, which are pairs of program points whose execution might happen, in an (concurrent) interleaved way within one processor, or in parallel across different processors. This information is fundamental to prove absence of data races as well as more complex properties: In [13], MHP pairs are used to discard unfeasible deadlock cycles; namely if a deadlock cycle inferred by the deadlock analyzer includes pairs of program points that are proven not to happen in parallel by our MHP analysis, the cycle is spurious and the program is deadlock free. In [4], the use of MHP pairs allows proving termination and inferring the resource consumption of loops with concurrent interleavings. For instance, consider a loop whose termination cannot be proven because of a potential execution in parallel of the loop with a

This work was funded partially by the Spanish MINECO project TIN2015-69175-C4-2-R, by the CM project S2013/ICE-3006 and by the UCM CT27/16-CT28/16 grant.

D. D'Souza and K. Narayan Kumar (Eds.): ATVA 2017, LNCS 10482, pp. 42–58, 2017.
DOI: 10.1007/978-3-319-68167-2_3

task that modifies the variables that control the loop guard (and thus threatens its termination). If our MHP analysis proves the unfeasibility of such parallelism, then termination of the loop can be guaranteed.

For simplicity, we develop our analysis on a small asynchronous language which uses *future variables* [10,12] for task synchronization. A method call `m` on some parameters $\bar{x}$, written as $\mathsf{f} = \mathsf{m}(\bar{x})$, spawns an asynchronous task, and the future variable `f` allows synchronizing with the termination of such task by means of the instruction **await** f?; which delays the execution until the asynchronous task has finished. In this fragment of code f = m(..) ;...; **await** f?; the execution of the instructions of the asynchronous task `m` may happen in parallel with the instructions between the asynchronous call and the `await`. However, due to the future variable in the `await` instruction, the MHP analysis is able to ensure that they will not run in parallel with the instructions after the `await`. Therefore, future variables play an essential role within an MHP analysis and it is essential for its precision to track them accurately. Future variables are available in most concurrent languages: Java, Scala and Python allow creating pools of threads. The users can submit tasks to the pool, which are executed when a thread of the pool is idle, and may return future variables to synchronize with the tasks termination. C++ includes the components async, future and promise in its standard library, which allow programmers to create tasks (instead of threads) and return future variables in the same way as we do.

In this paper, we present to the best of our knowledge the first MHP analysis that captures MHP relations that involve tasks that are awaited in an outer scope from the scope in which they were created. This happens when future variables are returned by the asynchronous tasks, as it can be performed in all programming languages that have future variables. Our analysis builds on top of an existing MHP analysis [3] that was extended to track information of future variables passed through method parameters in [5], but it is not able to track information propagated through future variables that are returned by tasks. The original MHP analysis [3] involves two phases: (1) a local analysis which consists in analyzing the instructions of the individual tasks to detect the tasks that it spawns and awaits, and (2) a global analysis which propagates the local information compositionally. Accurately handling returned future variables requires non-trivial extensions in both phases:

1. The local phase needs to be modified to backpropagate the additional inter-procedural relations that arise from the returned futures variables. Back-propagation is achieved by modifying the data-flow of the analysis so that it iterates to propagate the new dependencies.
2. The global phase has to be modified by reflecting in the analysis graph the additional information provided by the local phase. A main achievement has been to generate the necessary information at the local phase so that the process of inferring the MHP pairs remains as in the original analysis.

Our analysis has been implemented within the SACO static analyzer [2], which is able to infer the safety and liveness properties mentioned above. The system can be used online at http://costa.ls.fi.upm.es/saco/web/, where the benchmarks used in the paper are available. Our experiments show that our analysis improves the accuracy over the previous analysis with basically no overhead.

2 Language

We present the syntax and semantics of the asynchronous language on which we develop our analysis. A program P is composed by a set of classes. Each class contains a set of fields and a set of methods. A (concurrent) object of a class represents a processor with a queue of tasks which (concurrently) execute the class methods, and access a shared-memory made up by the object fields. One of the tasks will be active (executing) and the others pending to be executed. The notation $\overline{M}$ is used to abbreviate $M_1, ..., M_n$. Each field and method has a type T. The set of types includes class identifiers C and future variable types $fut\langle T\rangle$. A method receives a set of variables as arguments $\overline{x}$, contains local variables $\overline{x}'$, a returned variable, and a sequence of instructions s.

$$
\begin{array}{lll}
CL & ::= & class\ C\ \{\overline{T}\ \overline{f}; \overline{M}\} \\
M & ::= & T\ m(\overline{T}\ \overline{x})\ \{\overline{T}\ \overline{x}'; s\} \\
s & ::= & \epsilon \mid b; s \\
b & ::= & o = \textbf{new}\ C(\overline{x}) \mid \textbf{if}\ (*)\ \textbf{then}\ s_1\ \textbf{else}\ s_2 \mid \textbf{while}\ (*)\ \textbf{do}\ s \mid y = o.m(\overline{x}) \mid \\
 & & \mid \textbf{await}\ y? \mid z = y.\textbf{get} \mid \textbf{return}\ y \mid \textbf{skip}
\end{array}
$$

y and z represent variables of type $fut\langle T\rangle$ and x represents a variable of type T. Arithmetic expressions are omitted for simplicity and are represented by the instruction **skip**. This instruction has no effect on the analysis of the program. The loop and conditional statements are non-deterministic and the symbol $*$ represents *true* or *false*. The instruction $y = o.m(\overline{x})$ corresponds to an asynchronous call. It spawns a new instance of the task m in the object o and binds the task to the future variable y. Instruction **await** $y?$ is used to synchronize with the task $y = o.m(\overline{x})$, and blocks the execution in object o until task m finishes its execution. $z = y$.**get** retrieves the value returned by the method bound to y and associates it with z. W.l.o.g., we make the following assumptions: each **get** instruction is preceded by an **await**, i.e., the task associated to the **get** statement has to be finished to access its returned value; the program has a method call `main` without parameters from which the execution will start; future variables can be used once and they cannot be reused after they are bound to a task; the **get** instruction can be applied once over each future variable; we restrict the values returned by a method to future variables; each method can only have a **return** statement in its body, and it has to be the last instruction of the sequence. We let `ppoints`(m) and `ppoints`(P) be the set of program points of method m and program P respectively, `methods`(P) be the set of method names of program P and `futures`(P) be the set of all future variables defined in program P.

Let us define the operational semantics for the language. A *program state* S is a tuple $S = \langle O, T\rangle$ where O is the set of objects and T is the set of tasks. Only one task can be active in each object. An *object* is a term $obj(o, a, lk)$ where o is

$$(1)\ \frac{l' = l[o \rightarrow bid_1], O' = O \cup \{obj(bid_1, a, \bot)\}, a = init\_atts(C, \overline{x}), bid_1 \text{ is a fresh id}}{\langle O, \{tsk(tid, m, l, bid, \top, o = \textbf{new}\ C(\overline{x}); s) \parallel T\}\rangle \rightsquigarrow \langle O', \{tsk(tid, m, l', bid, \top, s) \parallel T\}\rangle}$$

$$(2)\ \frac{l(o) = bid_1 \neq \textbf{null}, l' = l[y \rightarrow tid_1], l_1 = buildLocals(\overline{x}, m)), tid_1 \text{is a fresh id}}{\begin{array}{c}\langle O, \{tsk(tid, m, l, bid, \top, y{=}o.m_1(\overline{x}); s) \parallel T\}\rangle \rightsquigarrow \\ \langle O, \{tsk(tid, m, l', bid, \top, s), tsk(tid_1, m_1, l_1, bid_1, \bot, body(m_1)) \parallel T\}\rangle\end{array}}$$

$$(3)\ \frac{l_1(y) = tid_2}{\begin{array}{c}\langle O, \{tsk(tid_1, m_1, l_1, bid_1, \top, \textbf{await}\ y?; s_1), tsk(tid_2, m_2, l_2, bid_2, \bot, \epsilon(v)) \parallel T\}\rangle \rightsquigarrow \\ \langle O, \{tsk(tid_1, m_1, l_1, bid_1, \top, s_1), tsk(tid_2, m_2, l_2, bid_2, \bot, \epsilon(v)) \parallel T\}\rangle\end{array}}$$

$$(4)\ \frac{l_1(y) = tid_2, l_1' = l_1[z \rightarrow v]}{\begin{array}{c}\langle O, \{tsk(tid_1, m_1, l_1, bid_1, \top, z{=}y.\textbf{get}; s_1), tsk(tid_2, m_2, l_2, bid_2, \bot, \epsilon(v)) \parallel T\}\rangle \rightsquigarrow \\ \langle O, \{tsk(tid_1, m_1, l_1', bid_1, \top, s_1), tsk(tid_2, m_2, l_2, bid_2, \bot, \epsilon(v)) \parallel T\}\rangle\end{array}}$$

$$(5)\ \frac{obj(bid, a, \top) \in O, O' = O[obj(bid, a, \top)/obj(bid, a, \bot)], v = l(y)}{\langle O, \{tsk(tid, m, l, bid, \top, \textbf{return}\ y) \parallel T\}\rangle \rightsquigarrow \langle O', \{tsk(tid, m, l, bid, \bot, \epsilon(v)) \parallel T\}\rangle}$$

$$(6)\ \frac{\begin{array}{c}(l', s') = eval(instr, O, l) \\ instr \in \{\textbf{skip}, \textbf{if}\ b\ \textbf{then}\ s_1\ \textbf{else}\ s_2, \textbf{while}\ b\ \textbf{do}\ s_3\}\end{array}}{\langle O, \{tsk(tid, m, l, bid, \top, instr; s) \parallel T\}\rangle \rightsquigarrow \langle O, \{tsk(tid, m, l', bid, \top, s') \parallel T\}\rangle}$$

$$(7)\ \frac{obj(bid, a, \bot) \in O, O' = O[obj(bid, a, \bot)/obj(bid, a, \top)], s \neq \epsilon(v)}{\langle O, \{tsk(tid, m, l, bid, \bot, s) \parallel T\}\rangle \rightsquigarrow \langle O', \{tsk(tid, m, l, bid, \top, s) \parallel T\}\rangle}$$

Fig. 1. Summarized semantics

the identifier of the object, a is a mapping from the object fields to their values and $lk \in \{\top, \bot\}$ indicates whether the object contains an active task executing ($\top$) or not ($\bot$). A task is a term $tsk(t, m, l, o, lk, s)$ where t is a unique task identifier, m is the method name that is being executed, l is a mapping from the variables of the task to their values, o is the identifier of the object in which the task is executing, $lk \in \{\top, \bot\}$ indicates if the task has the object's lock or not and s is a sequence of instructions that the task will execute or $s = \epsilon(v)$ if the task has finished and the return value v is available. The execution of a program starts from the initial state $S_0 = \langle obj(0, a, \top), tsk(0, \mathsf{main}, l, 0, \top, body(main))\rangle$ where a is an empty mapping, and l maps future variables to **null**.

The execution starts from S_0 applying *non-deterministically* the semantic rules from Fig. 1. We use the notation $\{t \parallel T\}$ to represent that task t is the one selected non-deterministically for the execution. At each step, a subset of the state S is rewritten according to the rules of Fig. 1 as follows: (1) creates a new object with an empty queue, free lock and initializes its fields (*init_atts*). (2) corresponds to an asynchronous call. It gets the identifier of the object which is going to execute the task, initializes the parameters and variables of the task (*buildLocals*), and creates the new task with a new identifier that is associated with the corresponding future variable. (3) An **await** $y?$ statement waits until the task bound to y finishes its execution. (4) checks if the task bound to the future variable involved in the **get** statement is finished. If so, it retrieves the value associated with the future variable. (5) After executing the **return** statement, the retrieved value is stored in v so that it can be obtained by the future variable bound to this task. Then, the object's lock is released ($O[o/o']$ means that the object o is replaced by o' in O) and the task is finished ($\epsilon(v)$ is added to the sequence of instructions). (6) covers sequential instructions that do not affect synchronization by moving the execution of the corresponding task to the next instruction and possibly changing the state (represented by *eval*). Finally, (7) is used to get the object's lock by an unfinished task and start its execution.

In what follows, given a task $tsk(t, m, l, o, lk, s)$, $pp(s)$ denotes the program point of the first instruction of s. If s is empty, $pp(s)$ returns the exit program point of the corresponding method, denoted $exit(m)$. Given a state $S = \langle O, T \rangle$, we define its set of MHP pairs, i.e., the set of program points that can run in parallel as $\mathcal{E}(S) = \{(pp(s_1), pp(s_2)) \mid tsk(tid_1, m_1, l_1, o_1, lk_1, s_1), tsk(tid_2, m_2, l_2, o_2, lk_2, s_2) \in T, tid_1 \neq tid_2\}$. The set of MHP pairs for a program P is defined as the set of MHP pairs of all reachable states, namely $\mathcal{E}_P = \cup\{\mathcal{E}(S_n) \mid S_0 \leadsto^* S_n\}$.

3 Motivation: Using MHP Pairs in Deadlock Analysis

Let us motivate our work by showing its application in the context of deadlock analysis. Consider the example in Fig. 2 that models a typical client-server application with two delegate entities to handle the requests. The execution starts from the main block by creating four concurrent objects, the client c, the server s, and their delegates dc and ds, respectively. The call start at Line 6 (L6) spawns an asynchronous task on the client object c that sends as arguments references to the other objects. When this task is scheduled for execution on the client, we can observe that it will spawn an asynchronous task on the server (L10) and another one on the delegate-client (L14). The request task on the server in turn posts two asynchronous tasks on the delegate-server (L19) and delegate-client objects (L20). Such delegates communicate directly with each other as we have passed as arguments the references to them.

The most challenging aspect for the analysis of this model is due to the synchronization through returned future variables. For instance at L12 the instruction x.**get** retrieves the future variable returned by request at L21. Thus, we would like to infer that after L13 the task executing result at the object ds has terminated. The inference needs to backpropagate this synchronization information from the inner scope where the task has been created (L19) to the outer scope where it is awaited (L13). This backpropagation is necessary in order to prove that the execution of this application is deadlock free. Otherwise, an MHP-based deadlock analyzer will spot an unfeasible deadlock. Figure 3 shows a fragment of the graph that a deadlock analyzer [13] constructs: the concurrent objects are in circles, the asynchronous tasks in boxes, and labelled arrows contain the program lines at which tasks post new tasks on the destiny objects. In the bold arrows of the graph, we can observe the cycle detected by the analyzer due to the task

```
main() {
  Client c = new Client();
   Server s = new Server();
   DS ds = new DS();
   DC dc = new DC();
   c. start (s,ds,dc);
}
class Client {
 Unit start(Server s, DS ds, DC dc){
     x=s.request(ds,dc);
     await x?;
     z=x.get;
     await z?;
     dc.sendMessage(ds);
  }
}
class Server {
 Fut<Unit> request(DS ds, DC dc){
     y=ds.result(dc);
     p = dc.inform();
     return y;
  }
}
class DS {
 Unit result(DC dc){
     w = dc.myClientId();
     await w?;
 }
 Unit myServerId() {
   skip;
 }
}
class DC {
 Unit sendMessage(DS ds){
     r = ds.myServerId();
     await r?;
 }
 Unit myClientId() {
   skip;
 }
 Unit inform() {
   skip;
 }
}
```

Fig. 2. Example of client-server model

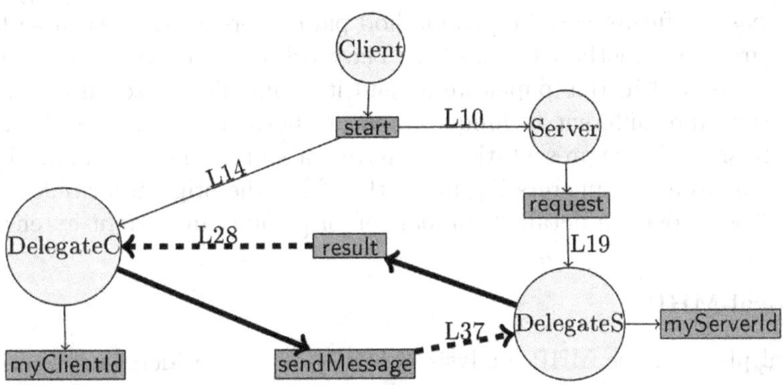

Fig. 3. Partial data-flow graph of example in Fig. 2.

result and sendMessage executing respectively in objects ds and dc. These two tasks wait for the termination of tasks myClientId and myServerId in each other object, thus creating a potential cycle. Our MHP analysis will accurately infer that these two tasks cannot happen simultaneously, and will allow the deadlock analyzer to break this unfeasible deadlock cycle. Figure 4 shows some of the MHP pairs that the analysis in [3] infers, and we mark in bold font those pairs

$L11\|\|L19$	$L11\|\|L20$	$L11\|\|L21$	$L11\|\|L28$	$L11\|\|L29$	$L11\|\|L40$	$L12\|\|L22$
$L12\|\|L28$	$L12\|\|L29$	$L12\|\|L40$	$L14\|\|L22$	**L14||L28**	$L14\|\|L29$	**L14||L40**
$L15\|\|L22$	**L15||L28**	$L15\|\|L29$	**L15||L40**	$L15\|\|L31$	$L21\|\|L29$	$L21\|\|L40$
$L22\|\|L28$	$L22\|\|L44$	$L28\|\|L41$	$L28\|\|L43$	$L28\|\|L44$	$L29\|\|L41$	$L29\|\|L44$
$L29\|\|L41$	$L29\|\|L44$	**L28||L37**	**L28||L38**	$L29\|\|L40$	$L21\|\|L44$	

Fig. 4. Results of MHP analysis.

that our analysis spots as spurious (as will be explained along the paper). For instance, the original analysis infers L15||L28 and L37||L28. However, we detect that at program point L14 the task result is finished so it cannot run in parallel with task sendMessage and hence those pairs are eliminated, this allows us later to discard the potential deadlock described above.

4 MHP Analysis

The MHP analysis of [3] consists of two phases. The first one, the local phase, considers each method separately and infers information (at each program point of the method) about the status of the tasks that are created locally in that method. The second one, the global phase, uses the information inferred by the first phase to construct an MHP graph from which an over-approximation of the MHP pairs set can be extracted. As mentioned already, the limitation of this analysis is that it does not track inter-procedural synchronizations originating from (1) passing future variables as method parameters; or (2) returning future variables from one method to another. The work of [5] extends [3] to handle the first issue, and in this paper we extend it to handle the second one. Both extensions require different techniques, and are both complementary and compatible. To simplify the presentation, we have not started from the analysis with future variables as parameters [5], but rather from the original formulation [3]. In Sect. 6, we provide a detailed comparison of [5] and our current extension.

4.1 Local MHP

The local phase of the MHP analysis (LMHP) of [3] considers each method n separately, and for each program point $\ell \in \texttt{ppoints}(n)$ it infers a LMHP state that describes the status of each task invoked in n before reaching ℓ. Formally, a LMHP state E is a *multiset* of MHP atoms, where an MHP atom is:

1. $y{:}\texttt{T}(m, \texttt{act})$, which represents a task that is an instance of method m and can be executing at any program point. We refer to it as *active* task; and
2. $y{:}\texttt{T}(m, \texttt{fin})$, which represents a task that is an instance of method m and has finished its execution already (i.e., it is at its exit program point). We refer to it as *finished* task.

$$
\begin{array}{ll}
(1) & \tau(y = o.m(\bar{x}), E) = E[y{:}\mathtt{T}(m, X)/\star{:}\mathtt{T}(m, X)] \cup \{y{:}\mathtt{T}(m, \mathtt{act})\} \\
(2) & \tau(\textbf{await}\ y?, E) = E[y{:}\mathtt{T}(m, \mathtt{act})/y{:}\mathtt{T}(m, \mathtt{fin})] \\
(3) & \tau(z = y.\textbf{get}, E) = E' \cup E'' \cup E''' \quad \text{where:}
\end{array}
$$

$$
\boxed{\begin{array}{l}
E' \;\; = \mathtt{eliminate}(\{y\}, E[z{:}\mathtt{T}(m, X)/\star{:}\mathtt{T}(m, X)]) \\
E'' \; = \{z{:}\mathtt{T}(n, X) \mid y{:}\mathtt{T}(f, \mathtt{fin}) \in E,\ \mathtt{T}(n, X) \in \mathit{Ret}(f)\} \\
E''' = \{y{:}\mathtt{T}(f, \overline{\mathtt{fin}}) \mid y{:}\mathtt{T}(f, \mathtt{fin}) \in E\}
\end{array}}
$$

$$
(4) \qquad \tau(b, E) = E \qquad \textit{otherwise}
$$

Fig. 5. Local MHP transfer function τ.

In both cases, the task is associated to future variable y, i.e., in the concrete state that E describes y is bound to the unique identifier of the corresponding task. Intuitively, the MHP atoms of E represent the tasks that were created locally and are executing in parallel. In what follows, we use $y{:}\mathtt{T}(m, X)$ to refer to an MHP atom without specifying if it corresponds to an active or finished task. MHP atoms might also use the symbol $\star$ instead of a future variable to indicate that we do not know to which future variable, if any, the task is bound. Note that if we have two atoms with the same future variable in a LMHP state E, then they are mutually exclusive, i.e., only one of the corresponding tasks might be executing since at the concrete level y can be bound only to one task identifier. This might occur when merging branches of a conditional statement. Note also that MHP states are multisets because we might have several tasks created by invoking the same method. Since LMHP states are multisets, we write $(q, i) \in E$ to indicate that atom q appears $i > 0$ times in E.

The LMHP analysis of [3], that infers the LMHP states described above, is a data-flow analysis based on the transfer function τ in Fig. 5, except for Case (3) which is novel to our extension and whose auxiliary functions will be given and explained later. Recall that the role of the transfer function in a data-flow analysis is to abstractly execute the different instructions, i.e., transforming one LMHP state to another. Let use explain the relevant cases of τ:

- Case (1) handles method calls, it adds a new active task (an instance of m) that is bound to future variable y, and renames all atoms that already use y to use $\star$ since it is overwritten;
- Case (2) handles **await**, it changes the state of any task bound to future variable y to finished; and
- Case (4) corresponds to other instructions that do not create or wait for tasks to finish. In this case the abstract state is not affected.

In addition, the LMHP analysis merges states of conditional branches using union of multisets, and loops are iterated, with a corresponding widening operator that transforms unstable MHP atoms (q, i) to (q, ∞), until a fix-point is reached.

Example 1. Consider a method f with a body **while**$(*)\{$ y = o.m(); $\}$. The first time we apply τ over f, we obtain $\{y{:}\mathtt{T}(m, \mathtt{act})\}$ at the exit program point of the while. At the next iteration, we add a new atom bound to y so we lose the association existing in the current state and add the new atom, obtaining $\{\star{:}\mathtt{T}(m, \mathtt{act}), y{:}\mathtt{T}(m, \mathtt{act})\}$. After applying one more iteration, we lose the relation between y and the task m again obtaining $\{(\star{:}\mathtt{T}(m, \mathtt{act}), 2), y{:}\mathtt{T}(m, \mathtt{act})\}$. When comparing the last two LMHP states, we observe that $\star{:}\mathtt{T}(m, \mathtt{act})$ is unstable, thus we apply widening and obtain $\{(\star{:}\mathtt{T}(m, \mathtt{act}), \infty), y{:}\mathtt{T}(m, \mathtt{act})\}$.

In what follows we present how to extend the transfer function τ and the LMHP states to handle returned futures in Case (3). We first explain it using a simple example, and then describe it formally.

Example 2. Assume we have a method f with an instruction "**return** x", and that at the exit program point of f we have a LMHP state $E_0 = \{x{:}\mathtt{T}(h, \mathtt{act}), w{:}\mathtt{T}(g, \mathtt{act})\}$, which means that at the exit program point of f we have two active instances of methods h and g, bound to future variables x and w respectively. This means that f returns a future variable that is bound to an active instance of h. Now assume that in some other method, at some program point, we have a state $E_1 = \{y{:}\mathtt{T}(f, \mathtt{fin}), r{:}\mathtt{T}(k, \mathtt{act}), u{:}\mathtt{T}(l, \mathtt{act})\}$, which means, among other things, that before reaching the corresponding program point, we have invoked f and waited for it to finish (via future variable y). Let us now execute the instruction $u = y.$**get** in the context of E_1 and generate a new LMHP state E_2. Since y is bound to a task that is an instance of f, E_2 should include an atom representing that u is bound to an active task which is an instance of h (which is returned by f via a future variable). Having this information in E_2 allows us to mark h as finished when executing **await** $u?$ later. We do this as follows:

- any MHP atom from E_1 that does not involve u or y is copied to E_2.
- any MHP atom from E_1 that involves u is copied to E_2 but with u renamed to $\star$ because u is overwritten.
- we transfer the atom $x{:}\mathtt{T}(h, \mathtt{act})$ from E_0 to E_2, by adding $u{:}\mathtt{T}(h, \mathtt{act})$ to E_2 since now the corresponding task is bound to u as well.
- the atom $y{:}\mathtt{T}(f, \mathtt{fin})$ must be copied to E_2 as well, but we first rewrite it to $y{:}\mathtt{T}(f, \overline{\mathtt{fin}})$ (in E_2) to indicate that we have incorporated the information from the exit program point of f already. This is important because after executing the **get**, we will have two instances of h in E_0 and E_2 that refer to the same task, and we want to avoid considering them as two different ones in the global phase that we will describe in the next section.

This results in $E_2 = \{y{:}\mathtt{T}(f, \overline{\mathtt{fin}}), r{:}\mathtt{T}(k, \mathtt{act}), \star{:}\mathtt{T}(l, \mathtt{act}), u{:}\mathtt{T}(h, \mathtt{act})\}$.

To summarize the above example, the local phase of our analysis extends that of [3] in two ways: it introduces a new kind of LMHP atom; and it has to treat the **get** instruction in a special way. In the rest of this section we formalize this extension by providing the auxiliary functions and the data-flow inference. As notation, we let E_ℓ be the LMHP state that corresponds to program point ℓ;

we let E^m_{exit} be the LMHP state that corresponds to the exit program point of method m; and we define

$$Ret(m) = \{\texttt{T}(n, X) \mid \textsf{\textbf{return}}\ y \in body(m),\ y{:}\texttt{T}(n, X) \in E^m_{exit}\},$$

which is the set of tasks in E^m_{exit} that are bound to a future variable that is returned by method m. This set is needed in order to incorporate these tasks when abstractly executing a **get** instruction as we have seen in the example above. We also let $\texttt{eliminate}(Y, E)$ be the LMHP set obtained from E by removing all atoms that involve a future variable $y \in Y$. We first modify the transfer function of [3] to treat the instruction $z = y.\textbf{get}$, similarly to what we have done in the example above. This is done by adding Case (3) to the transfer function of Fig. 5:

- The set E' is obtained from E by renaming future variable z to $\star$, since variable z is overwritten, and then eliminating all atoms associated to future variable y (they will be incorporated in E''' below).
- The set E'' consists of new MHP atoms that correspond to futures that are returned by methods to which y is bound. Note that all are now bound to future variable z.
- In E''' we add all atoms bound to y from E but rewritten to mark them as *already been incorporated.*

Due to the new case added to the transfer function, we need to modify the work-flow of the corresponding data-flow analysis in order to backpropagate the information learned from the returned future variables. This is because the LMHP analysis of one method depends on the LMHP states of other methods (via $Ret(m)$ in Case (3) of τ). This means that a method cannot be analyzed independently from the others as in [3], but rather we have to iterate over their analysis results, in the reverse topological order induced by the corresponding call graph, until their corresponding results stabilize.

Example 3. The left column of the table below shows the LMHP states resulting from applying once the τ function to selected program points, the right column shows the result after one iteration of τ over the results in the left column:

E_{11}: $\{x{:}\texttt{T}(\textsf{request}, \textsf{act})\}$	E_{11}: $\{x{:}\texttt{T}(\textsf{request}, \textsf{act})\}$
E_{12}: $\{x{:}\texttt{T}(\textsf{request}, \texttt{fin})\}$	E_{12}: $\{x{:}\texttt{T}(\textsf{request}, \texttt{fin})\}$
E_{13}: $\tau(z = x.\textbf{get}, E_{12})$	E_{13}: $\{x{:}\texttt{T}(\textsf{request}, \overline{\texttt{fin}}), z{:}\texttt{T}(\textsf{result}, \textsf{act})\}$
E_{14}: $\tau(\textsf{\textbf{await}}\ z?, E_{13})$	E_{14}: $\{x{:}\texttt{T}(\textsf{request}, \overline{\texttt{fin}}), z{:}\texttt{T}(\textsf{result}, \texttt{fin})\}$
E_{15}: $E_{14} \cup \{\star{:}\texttt{T}(\textsf{sendMessage}, \textsf{act})\}$	E_{15}: $\{x{:}\texttt{T}(\textsf{request}, \overline{\texttt{fin}}), z{:}\texttt{T}(\textsf{result}, \texttt{fin}),$ $\star{:}\texttt{T}(\textsf{sendMessage}, \textsf{act})\}$
E_{20}: $\{y{:}\texttt{T}(\textsf{result}, \textsf{act})\}$	E_{20}: $\{y{:}\texttt{T}(\textsf{result}, \textsf{act})\}$
E_{21}: $\{y{:}\texttt{T}(\textsf{result}, \textsf{act}),$ $p{:}\texttt{T}(\textsf{inform}, \textsf{act})\}$	E_{21}: $\{y{:}\texttt{T}(\textsf{result}, \textsf{act}),$ $p{:}\texttt{T}(\textsf{inform}, \textsf{act})\}$
E_{22}: $\{y{:}\texttt{T}(\textsf{result}, \textsf{act}),$ $p{:}\texttt{T}(\textsf{inform}, \textsf{act}))\}$	E_{22}: $\{y{:}\texttt{T}(\textsf{result}, \textsf{act}),$ $p{:}\texttt{T}(\textsf{inform}, \textsf{act}))\}$

Let us explain some of the above LMHP states. In the left column, E_{11} corresponds to the state when reaching program point L11, i.e., before executing the statement **await** x?. It includes x:T(request, act) for the active task invoked at L10. The state E_{12} includes the finished task corresponding to the await instruction of the previous program point. E_{13} cannot be solved, as we need the information from state E_{22} (it is required when calculating E''), which has not been computed yet. Something similar happens with the state E_{14}, which cannot be calculated as the state E_{13} has not been totally computed. Atoms y:T(result , act) and p:T(inform, act) appear in state E_{22} for the active tasks invoked at L19 and L20. The state E_{15} includes $\star$:T(sendMessage, act) for the task invoked at L14, which is not bound to any future variable.

In the right column, after one iteration, we observe that most states are not modified except for E_{13}, E_{14} and E_{15}. As for E_{13}, in the previous step we could not obtain the set E'' when analyzing E_{13} because the function τ had not been applied to request (E_{22} had not been computed). Thus, it considered E_{13}: $E' = \{\}$ as there was no task bound to z; $E'' = \{z$:T(result , act)$\}$ and; $E''' = \{y$:T(request, $\overline{\texttt{fin}}$)$\}$. Having E_{13} calculated, E_{14} is computed modifying the state of result to finished and E_{15} is updated with the new information.

4.2 Global MHP

In this section we describe how to use the LMHP information, inferred by the local phase of Sect. 4.1, in order to construct an MHP graph from which an over-approximation of the set of MHP pairs can be extracted. The construction of the MHP graph is different from the one of [3] in that we need to introduce new kind of nodes to reflect the information carried by the new kind of MHP atom y:T(m, $\overline{\texttt{fin}}$). However, the procedure for computing the MHP pairs from the MHP graph is the same. The *MHP graph* of a given program P is a (weighted) directed graph, denoted by $\mathcal{G}_P$, whose nodes are:

- *method nodes*: each method $m \in$ methods(P) contributes 3 nodes act(m), fin(m) and $\overline{\texttt{fin}}$(m). We use $X(m)$ to refer to a method node without specifying if it corresponds to act(m), fin(m), or $\overline{\texttt{fin}}$(m).
- *program point nodes*: each program point $\ell \in$ ppoints(P) contributes a node ℓ.
- *return nodes*: each program point $\ell \in$ ppoints(P) that is an exit program point, of some method m, contributes a node $\bar{\ell}$.
- *future variable nodes*: each future variable $y \in$ futures(P) and program point $\ell \in$ ppoints(P) contribute a node ℓ_y (which can be ignored if y does not appear in the corresponding LMHP state of ℓ).

Note that nodes $\overline{\texttt{fin}}$(m) and $\bar{\ell}$ are particular to our extension, they do not appear in [3] and will be used, as we will see later, to avoid duplicating tasks that are returned to some calling context.

The edges of $\mathcal{G}_P$ are constructed in two steps. First we construct those that do not depend on the LMHP states, and afterwards those that are induced by

LMHP states. The first kind of edges are constructed as follows, for each method $m \in \texttt{methods}(P)$:

- there are edges from $\texttt{act}(m)$ to all *program point nodes* $\ell \in \texttt{ppoints}(m)$. This kind of edges indicate that an active task can be executing at any program point, including its exit program point;
- there is an edge from $\texttt{fin}(m)$ to the exit *program point node* ℓ of m. This kind of edges indicate that a finished task can be only at the exit program point;
- there is an edge from $\overline{\texttt{fin}}(m)$ to the corresponding *return node* $\bar{\ell}$, i.e., ℓ here is the exit program point of m. This kind of edges are similar to the previous ones, but they will be used to avoid duplicating tasks that were returned to some calling context.

All the above edges have weight 0. Next we construct the edges induced by the LMHP states. For each program point $\ell \in \texttt{ppoints}(P)$, we consider E_ℓ and construct the following edges:

- if $(\star{:}\texttt{T}(m, X), i) \in E_\ell$, we add an edge from node ℓ to node $X(m)$ with weight i. If ℓ is an exit program point we also add an edge from node $\bar{\ell}$ to node $X(m)$ with weight i;
- if $(y{:}\texttt{T}(m, X), i) \in E_\ell$, we add an edge from node ℓ to node ℓ_y with weight 0 and an edge from node ℓ_y to node $X(m)$ with weight i. In addition, if ℓ is an exit program point and y is not a returned future we add an edge from node $\bar{\ell}$ to node ℓ_y with weight 0.

Note that when ℓ is an exit program point, the difference between node ℓ and $\bar{\ell}$ is that the later ignores tasks that were returned via future variables.

Example 4. Figure 6 shows the MHP graph for some program points of interest for our running example. Note that the out-going edges of program point nodes in $\mathcal{G}$ coincide with the LMHP states at these program points depicted in Example 3. At program point $L15$, the LMHP state E_{15} contains the atoms $x{:}\texttt{T}(\text{request}, \overline{\texttt{fin}})$, $z{:}\texttt{T}(\text{result}, \texttt{fin})$ and $\star{:}\texttt{T}(\text{sendMessage}, \texttt{act})$. Each of these atoms corresponds to one of the edges from program point node 15. The first one is represented by the edge that goes from program point node 15 to future variable node 15_x and from 15_x to method node $\overline{\texttt{fin}}(\text{request})$. The second one corresponds to the edge that goes from 15 to 15_z and from there to method node $\texttt{fin}(\text{result})$. The edge which goes from 15 to method node $\texttt{act}(\text{sendMessage})$ originates from the MHP atom $\star{:}\texttt{T}(\text{sendMessage}, \texttt{act})$. This last edge does not go to a future variable node as the task is not bound to any future variable ($\star$). Note that we have two nodes 22 and $\overline{22}$ to represent the exit program point L22, connected to $\texttt{fin}(\text{request})$ and $\overline{\texttt{fin}}(\text{request})$. The edges that go out from 22 correspond to the atoms in E_{22}. As L22 is the exit program point of method request, we have to build an edge. This edge goes from $\overline{22}$ to 22_p and from there to $\texttt{act}(\text{inform})$ and corresponds to the atom in E_{22} whose future variable is not returned by request.

Given $\mathcal{G}_P$, using the same procedure as in [3], we say that two program points ℓ_1, ℓ_2 may run in parallel if one of the following conditions hold:

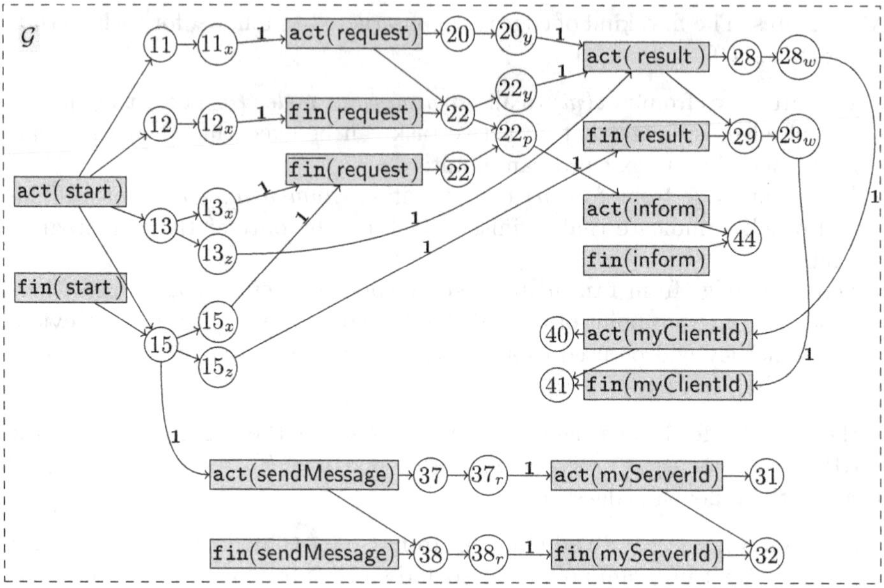

Fig. 6. MHP graph obtained from the analysis of program in Fig. 2.

1. there is a non-empty path from ℓ_1 to ℓ_2 or vice-versa; or
2. there is a program point ℓ_3 and non-empty paths from ℓ_3 to ℓ_1 and from ℓ_3 to ℓ_2 such that the first edge is different, or they share the first edge but it has weight $i > 1$.

The first case is called *direct* MHP pairs and the second one *indirect* MHP pairs.

Example 5. Let us explain some of the MHP pairs shown in Fig. 4 and induced by $\mathcal{G}$. (22,28) and (22,44) are direct MHP pairs as we can find the paths $22 \rightsquigarrow 44$ and $22 \rightsquigarrow 44$ in $\mathcal{G}$. In addition, as the first edge is different, we can conclude that (22,44) is an indirect pair. In contrast to the graph that one would obtain for the original analysis, (15,28) is not an MHP pair (marked in bold in Fig. 4).

Instead, we have the path $15 \rightsquigarrow 29$ which indicates that the task result is finished. Similarly, the analysis does not infer the pair (28,37), allowing us to discard the deadlock cycle described in Sect. 3. We find the path $15 \rightsquigarrow 37$ in $\mathcal{G}$, but the path $15 \rightsquigarrow 28$, needed to infer this spurious pair, is not in $\mathcal{G}$.

Let $\tilde{\mathcal{E}}_P$ be the set of MHP pairs obtained by applying the procedure above.

Theorem 1 (soundness). $\mathcal{E}_P \subseteq \tilde{\mathcal{E}}_P$.

5 Implementation and Experimental Evaluation

The analysis presented in Sect. 4 has been implemented in SACO [2], a *S*tatic *A*nalyzer for *C*oncurrent *O*bjects, which is able to infer deadlock, termination

Examples	Lines	N	PPs^2	OMHPs	MHPs	Lmhp	Gmhp	Mhp	OT	T
ServerClient	69	19	361	176	140	<5	<5	22	64	60
Chat	331	73	5329	1351	1028	<5	<5	606	1686	1014
MailServer	140	28	784	315	284	<5	<5	47	172	166
DistHT	168	27	729	392	367	<5	<5	51	186	183
PeerToPeer	215	42	1764	325	297	8	<5	112	452	238
ETICS	1717	297	88209	30554	30523	175	20	40887	53023	53450
TradingSys^1	1508	216	46656	40562	33038	53	15	13260	32065	31589
TradingSys^2	1508	216	46656	41345	41345	62	26	11765	30308	31057

Fig. 7. Examples and statistics

and resource boundedness [14]. Our analysis has been built on top of the original MHP analysis in SACO and can be tried online at: http://costa.ls.fi.upm.es/saco/web/ by selecting `MHP` from the menu as type of analysis, then enabling the option `Global Futures Synchronization` in the `Settings` section, and clicking on `Apply`. The benchmarks are also available in the folder `ATVA17`. Given a program with a main procedure, the analysis returns a list of MHP pairs and some statistics about the runtime of the local and global phases.

Figure 7 summarizes our experiments. The first benchmark ServerClient corresponds to the complete implementation of our running example. The next four are some traditional programs for distributed and concurrent programming: Chat models a chat application, MailServer models a distributed mail server with several users, DistHT implements and uses a distributed hash table and PeerToPeer which represents a peer-to-peer network. The last two examples, ETICS and TradingSys are industrial case studies, respectively, developed by Engineering® and Fredhopper® that model a system for remotely hosting and managing IT resources and a system to manage sales and other facilities on a large product database. These case studies are very conservative on the use of futures (namely only 3 tasks return a future), however, we have included them to assess the efficiency of our analysis on large programs. For the TradingSys, we have two versions, `TradingSys`^{1} which creates a constant number of tasks (namely 3), and `TradingSys`^{2} which creates an unknown number of tasks within a loop. Experiments have been performed on an Intel Core i7-6500U at 2.5 GHz x 4 and 7.5GB of Memory, running Ubuntu 16.04. For each program P, $\mathcal{G}_P$ is built and the relation $\tilde{\mathcal{E}}_P$ is computed for those points that affect the concurrency of the program (i.e., entry points of methods, awaits, gets and exit points of methods).

Let us first discuss the accuracy of our approach. Columns **Examples** and **Lines** show the name and number of lines of the benchmark. **N** is the number of program point nodes in $\mathcal{G}_P$. **PPs**^{2} is the square of the number of program points, i.e., the total number of pairs that could potentially run in parallel. **OMHPs** and **MHPs** show the number of MHP pairs inferred by the original analysis [3] and by ours. **PPs**^{2}**-MHPs** is thus the number of MHP pairs that are detected not to happen in parallel by the original analysis. Naturally the original analysis already eliminates many pairs that arise from local future variables (not returned). **OMHPs-MHPs** gives us the number of further spurious MHP pairs that our analysis eliminates. We can observe that for all examples (except for `TradingSys`^{2}) we reduce the number of inferred MHP pairs (ranging from a small reduction of 0.2% pairs for `ETICS` to a big reduction of 23.9% for `Chat`). In `TradingSys`^{2} we do not eliminate any pair because the tasks created within the loop use the same future variable to return their results, and the analysis needs to over-approximate and assume that all of them may run in parallel.

As regards the efficiency of the analysis, the next three columns contain the time (in milliseconds) taken by the local MHP (**Lmhp**), the graph construction (**Gmhp**) and the time needed to infer the MHP pairs (**Mhp**). The data presented are the average time obtained across several executions. We can observe that both LMHP and the graph construction are very efficient and they only take 0.175 s in the largest case. The inference of the MHP pairs is more complex and takes more time. This time depends on the number of program point nodes that the graphs contain. For medium programs, the inference technique is also efficient (taking 0.6 s in the largest case), but the time increases notably in bigger examples, reaching 40.8 s in our experiments. However, in most applications we are only interested in a subset of pairs. Besides, the pairs can be computed on demand, spending less time to infer them. The last two columns contain the total time (in milliseconds) taken by the analysis of [3] (**OT**) and our approach (**T**). It can be observed that our analysis is more efficient than the original one for all examples except for the `TradingSys`^{2} and `ETICS`, being the overhead negligible in these cases (less than 2.5%). The reason for the efficiency gain is that when returned futures are tracked, our graph contains less paths that are inspected to infer the MHP pairs. Thus, the process of computing all the feasible paths is faster in these cases, and the global time of the analysis is smaller than [3].

6 Conclusions and Related Work

An MHP analysis learns from the future variables used in synchronization instructions when tasks are terminated, so that the analysis can accurately eliminate unfeasible MHP pairs that would be otherwise inferred. Some existing MHP analyses [1,3,15,16] for asynchronous programs lose all the information when future variables are awaited in a different scope to the one that spawns the tasks bound to the futures. We have presented a static MHP analysis which captures inter-procedural MHP relations in which future variables are propagated *backwards* from one task to another(s). This implies that a task can be awaited in an outer scope from the one in which it was created. Previous work [5] has considered the propagation of future variables *forward*, i.e., when future variables are passed as arguments of the tasks. This implies that a task can be awaited in an inner scope from the one in which it was created. Also, other MHP analyses allow synchronizing the termination of the tasks in an inner scope, passing them as arguments of methods, namely: [11] considers a fork-join semantics and uses a Happens-Before analysis to infer the MHP information; in [6,8], programs are abstracted to a thread model which is then analyzed to infer the MHP pairs; [9]

builds a time based model to infer race conditions in high performance systems; this work is extended in [7], using a model checker to solve the MHP decision problem. The last six analyses are imprecise though when future variables or the tasks identifiers are returned by methods and awaited in an outer scope.

The solutions for the backwards and forward inference (namely as formalized in [5]) are technically different, but fully compatible. Essentially, they only have in common that both the local and global analysis phases need to be changed. For the forward inference, the analysis includes a separated *must-have-finished* (MHF) pre-analysis that allows inferring, for each program point ℓ, which tasks (both the tasks spawned locally and the passed as arguments) have finished their execution when reaching ℓ. In contrast, for the backwards inference, the local phase itself has to be extended to propagate backwards the new relations created when a future variable is returned, which requires changing the analysis flow. In both analyses, the creation of the graph needs to be modified to reflect the new information inferred by the respective local phases, but in each case is different. For the forward inference, the way in which the MHP pairs are inferred besides has to be modified. All in all, both extensions are fully compatible, and together provide a full treatment of future variables in the MHP analysis.

References

1. Agarwal, S., Barik, R., Sarkar, V., Shyamasundar, R.K.: May-happen-in-parallel analysis of x10 programs. In: Yelick, K.A., Mellor-Crummey, J.M. (eds.) Proceedings of PPOPP 2007, pp. 183–193. ACM (2007)
2. Albert, E., Arenas, P., Flores-Montoya, A., Genaim, S., Gómez-Zamalloa, M., Martin-Martin, E., Puebla, G., Román-Díez, G.: SACO: static analyzer for concurrent objects. In: Ábrahám, E., Havelund, K. (eds.) TACAS 2014. LNCS, vol. 8413, pp. 562–567. Springer, Heidelberg (2014). doi:10.1007/978-3-642-54862-8_46
3. Albert, E., Flores-Montoya, A.E., Genaim, S.: Analysis of may-happen-in-parallel in concurrent objects. In: Giese, H., Rosu, G. (eds.) FMOODS/FORTE - 2012. LNCS, vol. 7273, pp. 35–51. Springer, Heidelberg (2012). doi:10.1007/978-3-642-30793-5_3
4. Albert, E., Flores-Montoya, A., Genaim, S., Martin-Martin, E.: Termination and cost analysis of loops with concurrent interleavings. In: Van Hung, D., Ogawa, M. (eds.) ATVA 2013. LNCS, vol. 8172, pp. 349–364. Springer, Cham (2013). doi:10.1007/978-3-319-02444-8_25
5. Albert, E., Genaim, S., Gordillo, P.: May-happen-in-parallel analysis for asynchronous programs with inter-procedural synchronization. In: Blazy, S., Jensen, T. (eds.) SAS 2015. LNCS, vol. 9291, pp. 72–89. Springer, Heidelberg (2015). doi:10.1007/978-3-662-48288-9_5
6. Barik, R.: Efficient computation of may-happen-in-parallel information for concurrent Java programs. In: Ayguadé, E., Baumgartner, G., Ramanujam, J., Sadayappan, P. (eds.) LCPC 2005. LNCS, vol. 4339, pp. 152–169. Springer, Heidelberg (2006). doi:10.1007/978-3-540-69330-7_11
7. Chang, C.W., Dömer, R.: May-happen-in-parallel analysis of ESL models using UPPAAL model checking. In: DATE 2015, pp. 1567–1570. IEEE, March 2015

8. Chen, C., Huo, W., Li, L., Feng, X., Xing, K.: Can we make it faster? Efficient may-happen-in-parallel analysis revisited. In PDCAT 2012, pp. 59–64, December 2012
9. Chen, W., Han, X., Dömer, R.: May-happen-in-parallel analysis based on segment graphs for safe ESL models. In: DATE 2014, pp. 1–6. IEEE, March 2014
10. de Boer, F.S., Clarke, D., Johnsen, E.B.: A complete guide to the future. In: De Nicola, R. (ed.) ESOP 2007. LNCS, vol. 4421, pp. 316–330. Springer, Heidelberg (2007). doi:10.1007/978-3-540-71316-6_22
11. Di, P., Sui, Y., Ye, D., Xue, J.: Region-based may-happen-in-parallel analysis for C programs. In: ICPP 2015, pp. 889–898. IEEE, September 2015
12. Flanagan, C., Felleisen, M.: The semantics of future and its use in program optimization. In: POPL 1995, 22nd ACM SIGPLAN-SIGACT (1995)
13. Flores-Montoya, A.E., Albert, E., Genaim, S.: May-happen-in-parallel based deadlock analysis for concurrent objects. In: Beyer, D., Boreale, M. (eds.) FMOODS/-FORTE -2013. LNCS, vol. 7892, pp. 273–288. Springer, Heidelberg (2013). doi:10.1007/978-3-642-38592-6_19
14. Johnsen, E.B., Hähnle, R., Schäfer, J., Schlatte, R., Steffen, M.: ABS: a core language for abstract behavioral specification. In: Aichernig, B.K., de Boer, F.S., Bonsangue, M.M. (eds.) FMCO 2010. LNCS, vol. 6957, pp. 142–164. Springer, Heidelberg (2011). doi:10.1007/978-3-642-25271-6_8
15. Lee, J.K., Palsberg, J., Majumdar, R., Hong, H.: Efficient may happen in parallel analysis for async-finish parallelism. In: Miné, A., Schmidt, D. (eds.) SAS 2012. LNCS, vol. 7460, pp. 5–23. Springer, Heidelberg (2012). doi:10.1007/978-3-642-33125-1_4
16. Sankar, A., Chakraborty, S., Nandivada, V.K.: Improved MHP analysis. In: CC 2016, pp. 207–217. ACM, September 2016

JTDec: A Tool for Tree Decompositions in Soot

Krishnendu Chatterjee, Amir Kafshdar Goharshady(✉), and Andreas Pavlogiannis

IST Austria (Institute of Science and Technology Austria), Am Campus 1, 3400 Klosterneuburg, Austria
{krishnendu.chatterjee,amir.kafshdar.goharshady, andreas.pavlogiannis}@ist.ac.at

Abstract. The notion of treewidth of graphs has been exploited for faster algorithms for several problems arising in verification and program analysis. Moreover, various notions of balanced tree decompositions have been used for improved algorithms supporting dynamic updates and analysis of concurrent programs. In this work, we present a tool for constructing tree-decompositions of CFGs obtained from Java methods, which is implemented as an extension to the widely used Soot framework. The experimental results show that our implementation on real-world Java benchmarks is very efficient. Our tool also provides the first implementation for balancing tree-decompositions. In summary, we present the first tool support for exploiting treewidth in the static analysis problems on Java programs.

1 Introduction

Treewidth of Graphs. A very widely studied and well-known concept in graph theory for algorithmic analysis is the notion of *treewidth*, which measures the similarity of a graph to a tree [14,16]. Along with its mathematical elegance, the treewidth property has great practical relevance, as many NP-complete problems can be solved in polynomial time on graphs of constant treewidth [3,4].

Constant Treewidth in Verification and Program Analysis. The constant treewidth property has not only been studied in the graph algorithmic community, but has been considered in many problems in verification and program analysis.

Verification. The constant-treewidth property has played an important role in logic and verification; for example, MSO (Monadic Second Order logic) queries can be solved in polynomial time [10] (also in log-space [12]) for constant-treewidth graphs; parity games on graphs with constant treewidth can be solved in polynomial time [15]; and there exist faster algorithms for probabilistic models (such as Markov decision processes) [6]. Recently it was shown for problems in quantitative verification the constant treewidth can be exploited to design much faster algorithms [5], as well as improve space usage [7].

Program Analysis. A very important class of constant-treewidth graphs is the control flow graphs (CFGs) of goto-free programs of many programming languages [17]. It has also been shown that typically all Java programs have small

D. D'Souza and K. Narayan Kumar (Eds.): ATVA 2017, LNCS 10482, pp. 59–66, 2017.
DOI: 10.1007/978-3-319-68167-2_4

treewidth [13]. The small treewidth has been used to develop algorithms for (i) register allocation in polynomial time [2,17], (ii) interprocedural analysis [9], and (iii) intraprocedural analysis of concurrent programs [8].

Relevant Algorithmic Questions. In the context of program analysis, the relevant algorithmic questions are: (a) given an input CFG of constant treewidth, construct a constant-width decomposition; and (b) balance a constant-width tree decomposition Balanced tree decompositions are required to support fast dynamic algorithms (i.e., algorithms that support fast updates given small changes in the input graph) [9] as well as for intraprocedural analysis of concurrent programs [8].

Our Contributions. Although the treewidth property has been exploited for faster algorithms in many problems in verification and program analysis, there exists no tool support for the algorithmic questions we consider. In this work we present JTDec, a tool for constructing tree decompositions of Java programs. We have implemented existing algorithms for the above algorithmic questions, along with several heuristics that exploit the special structure of programs. Our tool is integrated as a plugin in the widely used Soot framework [18]. Our experimental results show that our implementation on real-world Java benchmarks is very efficient. In summary we present the first tool for tree-decomposition and balanced tree-decompositions of CFGs of programs in Java, which can be used by algorithms that exploit the low-treewidth property of graphs.

JTDec is available at http://pub.ist.ac.at/~akafshda/JTDec/ and a full version of this paper at https://repository.ist.ac.at/845/.

2 Definitions

Graphs and Trees. Let $G = (V, E)$ be a finite directed graph (henceforth called simply a graph) where V is a set of n nodes and $E \subseteq V \times V$ is an edge relation. Given a set of nodes $X \subseteq V$, we denote by $G \restriction X = (X, E \cap (X \times X))$ the subgraph of G induced by X. A path $P : u \rightsquigarrow v$ is a sequence of nodes $(x_1, \ldots, x_k)$ such that $x_1 = u$, $x_k = v$, and for all $1 \leq i < k$ we have $(x_i, x_{i+1}) \in E$. The length of P is $|P| = k - 1$. A set of nodes $X \subseteq V$ is called a *connected component* of G, if for every pair of nodes $u, v \in X$, there is either a path $P_1 : u \rightsquigarrow v$ or a path $P_2 : v \rightsquigarrow u$ in $G \restriction X$. Additionally, X is called *strongly-connected* if both P_1 and P_2 exist. A *tree* $T = (V, E)$ is an undirected graph with a root node u_0, such that between every two nodes there is a unique acyclic path. For a node u, we denote by $\mathsf{Lv}(u)$ the *level* of u which is defined as the length of the acyclic path from u_0 to u. A *child* of a node u is a node v such that $\mathsf{Lv}(v) = \mathsf{Lv}(u) + 1$ and $(u, v) \in E$, and then u is the *parent* of v. A tree T is *k-ary* if every node has at most k-children (e.g., a binary tree has at most two children for every node). Finally, the *depth* of T is the maximum level of its nodes, i.e. $\max_u \mathsf{Lv}(u)$, and T is called *balanced* if its depth is logarithmic on its size, i.e. $\max_u \mathsf{Lv}(u) = O(\log n)$.

Tree-Decompositions. A *tree-decomposition* $\mathrm{Tree}(G) = T = (V_T, E_T)$ of a graph G is a tree, where every node B_i in T, which is called a bag, is a subset of nodes of G such that:

C1 $V_T = \{B_0, \ldots, B_b\}$ with $B_i \subseteq V$, and $\bigcup_{B_i \in V_T} B_i = V$ (every node is covered).

C2 For all $(u, v) \in E$ there exists $B_i \in V_T$ such that $u, v \in B_i$ (every edge is covered).

C3 For all i, j, k such that there is a bag B_k that appears in the unique path $B_i \rightsquigarrow B_j$ in T we have $B_i \cap B_j \subseteq B_k$ (every node appears in a contiguous subtree of T).

Conventionally, we call B_0 the root of T, and denote by $\mathsf{Lv}(B_i)$ the level of B_i in T. For a bag B of T, we denote by $T(B)$ the subtree of T rooted at B. A bag B is called the *root bag* of a node u if $u \in B$ and every B' that contains u appears in $T(B)$. We often use B_u to refer to the root bag of u, and define $\mathsf{Lv}(u) = \mathsf{Lv}(B_u)$. A tree decomposition T is called *normal* if for each $B_1, B_2 \in V_T$, such that B_2 is a child of B_1, then $|B_2 \setminus B_1| \leq 1$, i.e. each bag has at most one more node from its parent. The *width* of the tree-decomposition T is the size of the largest bag minus 1. The treewidth t of G is the smallest width among all tree-decompositions of G.

(α, β, γ) Tree-Decompositions. Given a graph G with treewidth t and a fixed $\alpha \in \mathbb{N}$, a tree-decomposition Tree(G) is called *α-approximate* if it has width at most $\alpha \cdot (t+1) - 1$. Given a real constant $\beta < 1$ and an integer constant $\gamma \geq 1$ we say that Tree(G) is (β, γ)-balanced, if for every bag B and every descendant B' of B with $\mathsf{Lv}(B') = \mathsf{Lv}(B) + \gamma$, the size of the subtree $T(B')$ is at most β times as large as the size of the subtree $T(B)$. A (β, γ)-balanced tree-decomposition that is α-approximate is called an (α, β, γ) tree-decomposition.

Algorithmic Questions. We consider the following algorithmic questions:

Q1: Given a constant-treewidth input graph (being the CFG of a method), construct a tree-decomposition of constant width.

Q2: Convert an input tree decomposition to a balanced one.

Q3: Convert a tree decomposition to an (α, β, γ) tree-decomposition, for a single balancing parameter $\lambda \geq 2$, and $\alpha = 2 \cdot \lambda$, $\beta = 2^{-\lambda+1}$ and $\gamma = \lambda$ (see Remark 1 below).

We note that the solution for Q3 subsumes the solution for Q2 (with any constant λ). In the next section we will present details of the algorithms for Q1 and Q3.

Remark 1 (Significance). (1) The basic tree-decomposition has been used for polynomial-time algorithms for register allocation [2,17]. (2) The balanced tree-decompositions have been crucial in algorithms for interprocedural analysis [9] and verification of quantitative properties in graphs [5]. (3) The notion of (α, β, γ) tree-decompositions has been used in algorithmic dataflow analysis of concurrent programs [8]. The ideal value for α and γ is 1, and for β is $\frac{1}{2}$. However, this exact combination is not achieved in any of the known algorithms. In Q3 we consider parameters for which efficient algorithms exist and suffice for the problems considered in [8].

3 Algorithms

We present the algorithms for Q1–Q3. First, we focus on Q1 and then consider Q3 (which subsumes Q2). Our tool JTDec implements all the algorithms of this section.

3.1 Tree-Decomopsitions of CFGs

There exist several general-purpose tree-decomposition algorithms which operate on arbitrary graphs. Here our focus is on tree-decompositions of CFGs. The main part of this section focuses on outlining a tree-decomposition algorithm that operates on input being the source code, as opposed to arbitrary graphs. In particular, the input to the algorithm is a method in Jimple, which is a standard, 3-address representation of Java methods in the Soot framework. As an example, Fig. 1 depicts a Java method and its Jimple representation, and Fig. 2 shows the CFG of a simplified version of the Jimple representation and a balanced tree-decomposition of the CFG.

```
void threeNPlusOne(int n)
    {
  while(n > 1){
   if(n % 2 == 0){
    n /= 2;
   }
   else{
    n = 3 * n + 1;
   }
  }
 }
```

```
1:   n := parameter0: int
2:   nop
3:   if n > 1 goto nop
4:   goto [?= nop]
5:   nop
6:   temp$0 = n % 2
7:   if temp$0 == 0 goto
   nop
8:   goto [?= nop]
9:   nop
10:    temp$1 = n
11:    temp$2 = temp$1/2
12:  n = temp$2
13:  goto [?= nop]
14:  nop
15:  temp$3 = 3 * n
16:  temp$4 = temp$3
17:  temp$5 = temp$4+1
18:  n = temp$5
19:  nop
20:  goto [?= nop]
21:  nop
22:  return
```

Fig. 1. A Java method (left), and its 3-address code representation in Jimple.

```
1 i0 := parameter0: int
2 goto [?= (branch)]
3 $i1 = i0 % 2
4 if $i1 != 0 goto $i2 = 3 * i0
5 i0 = i0 / 2
6 goto [?= (branch)]
7 $i2 = 3 * i0
8 i0 = $i2 + 1
9 if i0>1 goto $i1 = i0 % 2
10 return
```

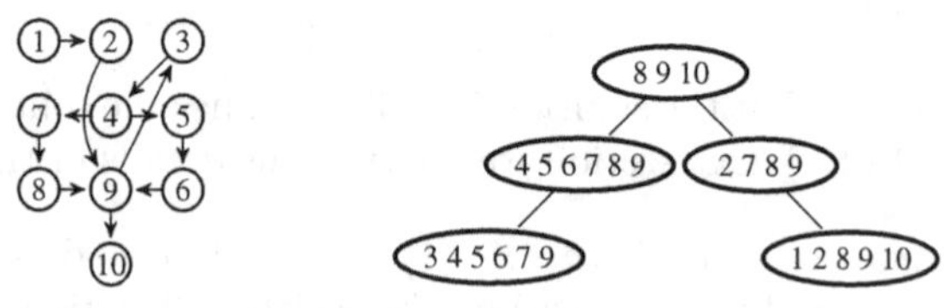

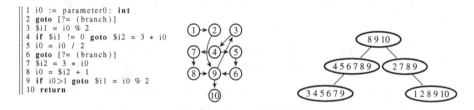

Fig. 2. A simplified Jimple representation of the method in Fig. 1 (left), Its CFG G and an approximate, balanced tree-decomposition Tree(G) (right).

A Dedicated Algorithm for Tree-Decompositions of CFGs. We consider dedicated algorithms that are specific to CFGs, and operate on the source code rather than on the graph itself [17]. In the following we outline the key steps of one such algorithm. We phrase the algorithm on Jimple source code. We start with the notion of complex listings required for the algorithm.

($\leq k$)-Complex Listings. A ($\leq k$)-Complex listing of a graph $G = (V, E)$ is a permutation of the elements of V, such that for each $u \in V$, there exists a set S_u of at most k nodes preceding u in the permutation, and whose deletion from G separates u from all the nodes preceding u in the permutation. In this case S_u is called a *separator* of u. Given a listing and a node u, there is a unique minimal choice for separators of nodes [17]. We always use minimal separators and for brevity drop the word minimal in the sequel. A graph G is called ($\leq k$)-complex if it has a ($\leq k$)-complex listing and is called k-complex if it has a ($\leq k$)-complex listing but no ($\leq k-1$)-complex listings. Given a ($\leq k$)-complex listing L and a pair of distinct nodes u, v, we write $v < u$ to denote that v appears before u in L.

Our main approach for obtaining tree-decompositions from CFGs of Jimple methods is the following theorem and algorithm, which allows us to focus on computing ($\leq k$)-complex listings of the CFG:

Theorem 1. *A graph G has treewidth k if and only if it is k-complex* [11]. *Given any such listing and separators of all the nodes, a tree-decomposition* Tree(G) *of width k can be constructed in linear time* [17].

CFG-Specific Algorithm. Given a listing L, the above algorithm simply creates one bag B_x per node x, and connects the bag B_u to the bag B_v if $v < u$ and v is the latest element of S_u in the listing or to the root if no such v exists. The bag corresponding to u will contain the set $S_u \cup \{u\}$. Hence, computing a tree-decomposition efficiently reduces to two steps:

1. Finding "good" listings, i.e., listings where each separator has small size.
2. Given a listing L, finding efficiently the separator S_u of every node u.

We provide brief and intuitive description of the two steps (following [17]), and refer to the Appendix for the pseudocode.

Heuristic for Good Listings. Our algorithm implements a heuristic of [17] for processing programs in the form of 3-address codes, which is guaranteed to create a listing of small separators for CFGs of goto-free programs, and is expected to perform well for structured programs. Intuitively, given a CFG, a listing with small separators can be obtained using the following two rules for the heuristic:

- The nodes of CFG that correspond to entries and exits of block structures (e.g. if-blocks, while-loops) must appear early in the listing.
- The remaining nodes (e.g. statements within the structures) must appear after the entries and exits of these structures in the listing.

Finding Separators in Listings. Given a listing L, the separators S_u of nodes of L can be created efficiently in $O(n \lg^* n)$ time. This is achieved by a single traversal of L from right to left, and maintaining a *disjoint-set* data-structure, which keeps track of the strongly-connected components of G formed by the set of nodes that have been examined already.

3.2 Constructing (α, β, γ) Tree-Decompositions

Given a CFG G and a binary tree-decomposition Tree(G) of width k, let $\lambda \geq 2$ be the balancing (integer) parameter (c.f. Q3). For $\alpha = 2 \cdot \lambda$, $\beta = 2^{-\lambda+1}$ and $\gamma = \lambda$, the core procedure for constructing an (α, β, γ) tree-decomposition is a recursive one. In each step of the recursion, the algorithm uses one of two rules to split a subtree of Tree(G) to connected components. Informally, (i) Rule 1 controls the height (i.e., parameters (β, γ)), and (ii) Rule 2 controls the width (i.e., parameter α) of the constructed tree-decomposition. The balancing parameter λ specifies how often each rule is used in the recursion, and thus specifies the trade-off between height and width. The algorithm is a simplified and efficiently implementable version of [8, Sect. 3] (see Appendix for the pseduocode). Given a tree-decomposition of $O(n)$ bags, the algorithm runs in $O(n \cdot \log n)$ time and $O(n)$ space.

4 Implementation

We build upon the widely used Soot framework and JTDec is an extension to it. Soot is a framework for language manipulation and optimization that provides tools for different problems in static program analysis. Soot is written in Java and has many different intermediate representation schemes for Java programs. We use the Jimple representation which has a typed 3-address format and is the most widely used of the representations. The main class for representing CFGs is `BriefUnitGraph` in which each node of the CFG corresponds to one Jimple statement, and is represented by the `Unit` class.

Our implementation is placed under the package `JTDec`. We provide an implementation of a class `JTDecTree` which is used to store and manipulate tree decompositions and supports basic tree-decomposition operations, e.g., iterating over the bags of the tree, and adding/removing nodes to bags. Based on this, we have implemented the algorithms of Sect. 3 in another class called `JTDec` in an easy-to-use manner. Specifically, we give the user access to the following functions in `JTDec`:

1. `createTreeDec`: The input is a `SootMethod` method and returns a tree decomposition of the CFG of the method. In the CFG we treat each `Unit` as one node.
2. `normalizeTreeDec`: The input is a tree-decomposition T in form of `JTDecTree` and returns a normalized version of T.
3. `createBalancedTree`: The input is an integer λ and tree-decomposition T in form of `JTDecTree`, and returns a balanced version of T with parameter λ.
4. `process`: The input is a `SootMethod` and (optionally) integer λ, and applies all the above functions in the same order and returns a balanced tree decomposition of the CFG of the method.

Examples of using `JTDec` can be found in the Appendix. The tool and source code are available at http://pub.ist.ac.at/~akafshda/JTDec/.

Table 1. Evaluation results of JTDec. Times are rounded to the nearest millisecond.

Range	#M	Unbalanced			$\lambda = 2$			$\lambda = 3$			$\lambda = 4$			$\lambda = 5$		
		T	W	H	T	W	H	T	W	H	T	W	H	T	W	H
[50, 59]	494	0	3.1	29.7	1	8.5	6.9	1	9.9	5.3	1	10.7	5.1	1	11.0	4.6
[60, 69]	343	1	3.2	33.0	2	8.8	7.1	1	10.6	5.7	2	11.2	5.6	1	11.5	5.0
[70, 79]	232	1	3.4	39.3	2	8.6	7.6	2	10.5	6.4	2	11.1	5.8	1	11.4	5.6
[80, 89]	170	1	3.4	42.8	2	9.0	8.0	2	11.0	6.6	2	11.5	5.9	2	11.9	5.8
[90, 99]	128	1	3.6	45.7	3	9.8	8.4	2	12.1	6.8	2	12.5	5.9	2	13.0	5.8
[100, 149]	394	1	3.6	59.5	4	10.0	8.9	3	12.3	7.2	3	13.1	6.4	3	13.4	6.3
[150, 299]	270	2	4.7	90.6	8	11.3	19.4	8	14.1	8.1	7	14.7	7.2	6	15.2	7.1
[300, 999]	81	5	5.4	203.1	22	17.4	11.8	19	26.6	9.4	17	27.1	8.5	16	27.4	8.0
[1000, 2156]	9	46	2.6	1079.7	98	21.3	15.6	82	20.0	12.2	72.0	26.7	10.9	71	26.7	10.6

5 Evaluation

Experimental results show that JTDec is very efficient. We used JTDec to obtain tree-decompositions for methods from the DaCapo benchmark suit [1], and to obtain balanced tree-decompositions using different values of the balancing parameter λ. The experiments were run on a laptop with Intel Core i5 5200 U Processor (2.7 GHz) and 8 GB of RAM. Table 1 summarizes the results. We divided the benchmark methods based on number of nodes in their CFG to several ranges and for each range we report number of methods in that range (#M), mean execution time of the function `createTreeDec` (T), mean width of the obtained tree-decompositions (W) and their mean height (H). Then for each λ, we report the mean execution time (T) of `createBalancedTree` on the tree-decompositions obtained previously, the mean width of the obtained balanced tree-decompositions (W) and their mean height (H). The table shows the trade-off between the latter two. All times are measured in milliseconds. Soot's analysis typically takes much more time than JTDec.

Acknowledgements. We thank all reviewers for their helpful comments which led to considerable improvements in presentation. The research is partially supported by Vienna Science and Technology Fund (WWTF) ICT15-003, Austrian Science Fund (FWF) NFN Grant No. S11407-N23 (RiSE/SHiNE) and ERC Start grant (279307: Graph Games).

References

1. Blackburn, S.M., Garner, R., Hoffmann, C., Khang, A.M., McKinley, K.S., Bentzur, R., Diwan, A., Feinberg, D., Frampton, D., Guyer, S.Z.: The DaCapo benchmarks: Java benchmarking development and analysis. ACM SIGPLAN Not. **41**(10), 169–190 (2006)
2. Bodlaender, H., Gustedt, J., Telle, J.A.: Linear-time register allocation for a fixed number of registers. In: SODA 1998, pp. 574-583 (1998)
3. Bodlaender, H.L.: A tourist guide through treewidth. Acta Cybern. **11**, 1 (1993)

4. Bodlaender, H.L.: Discovering treewidth. In: Vojtáš, P., Bieliková, M., Charron-Bost, B., Sýkora, O. (eds.) SOFSEM 2005. LNCS, vol. 3381, pp. 1–16. Springer, Heidelberg (2005). doi:10.1007/978-3-540-30577-4_1
5. Chatterjee, K., Ibsen-Jensen, R., Pavlogiannis, A.: Faster algorithms for quantitative verification in constant treewidth graphs. In: Kroening, D., Păsăreanu, C.S. (eds.) CAV 2015. LNCS, vol. 9206, pp. 140–157. Springer, Cham (2015). doi:10.1007/978-3-319-21690-4_9
6. Chatterjee, K., Lacki, J.: Faster Algorithms for markov decision processes with low treewidth. In: Sharygina, N., Veith, H. (eds.) CAV 2013. LNCS, vol. 8044, pp. 543–558. Springer, Heidelberg (2013). doi:10.1007/978-3-642-39799-8_36
7. Chatterjee, K., Ibsen-Jensen, R., Pavlogiannis, A.: Optimal reachability and a space-time tradeoff for distance queries in constant-treewidth graphs. In: LIPIcs-Leibniz International Proceedings in Informatics, vol. 57. Schloss Dagstuhl-Leibniz-Zentrum fuer Informatik (2016)
8. Chatterjee, K., Goharshady, A.K., Ibsen-Jensen, R., Pavlogiannis, A.: Algorithms for algebraic path properties in concurrent systems of constant treewidth components. In: ACM SIGPLAN Notices. vol. 51(1), pp. 733-747. ACM (2016)
9. Chatterjee, K., Ibsen-Jensen, R., Pavlogiannis, A., Goyal, P.: Faster algorithms for algebraic path properties in recursive state machines with constant treewidth. In: POPL. ACM (2015)
10. Courcelle, B.: The monadic second-order logic of graphs. I. Recognizable sets of finite graphs. Inf. Comput. **85**(1), 12–75 (1990)
11. Dendris, N.D., Kirousis, L.M., Thilikos, D.M.: Fugitive-search games on graphs and related parameters. Theoret. Comput. Sci. **172**(1–2), 233–254 (1997)
12. Elberfeld, M., Jakoby, A., Tantau, T.: Logspace versions of the theorems of Bodlaender, Courcelle. In: 2010 51st Annual IEEE Symposium on Foundations of Computer Science (FOCS), pp. 143-152. IEEE (2010)
13. Gustedt, J., Mæhle, O., Telle, J.: The treewidth of Java programs. Algorithm Eng. Exp. pp. 57–59 (2002)
14. Halin, R.: S-functions for graphs. J. Geom. **8**(1–2), 171–186 (1976)
15. Obdržálek, J.: Fast mu-calculus model checking when tree-width is bounded. In: Hunt, W.A., Somenzi, F. (eds.) CAV 2003. LNCS, vol. 2725, pp. 80–92. Springer, Heidelberg (2003). doi:10.1007/978-3-540-45069-6_7
16. Robertson, N., Seymour, P.D.: Graph minors. III. Planar tree-width. J. Comb. Theor. Ser. B **36**(1), 49–64 (1984)
17. Thorup, M.: All structured programs have small tree width and good register allocation. Inf. Comput. **142**(2), 159–181 (1998)
18. Vallée-Rai, R., Co, P., Gagnon, E., Hendren, L., Lam, P., Sundaresan, V.: Soot - a Java bytecode optimization framework. In: Proceedings of the 1999 Conference of the Centre for Advanced Studies on Collaborative Research, p. 13. IBM Press (1999)

Fixing the State Budget: Approximation of Regular Languages with Small DFAs

Graeme Gange[1], Pierre Ganty[2(✉)], and Peter J. Stuckey[1]

[1] Department of Computing and Information Systems, University of Melbourne, Melbourne 3010, Australia
pstuckey@unimelb.edu.au

[2] IMDEA Software Institute, Madrid, Spain

Abstract. Strings are pervasive in programming, and arguably even more pervasive in web programming. A natural abstraction for reasoning about strings are finite-automata. They are a well-understood formalism, and operations on them are decidable and well-known. But in practice these operations either blow up in size or in cost of operations. Hence the attractive automata representations become impractical. In this paper we propose reasoning about strings using small automata, by restricting the number of states available. We show how we can construct small automata which over-approximate the language specified by a larger automata, using discrete optimization techniques, both complete approaches and incomplete approaches based on greedy search. Small automata provide a strong basis for reasoning about strings in programming, since operations on small automata do not blow up in cost.

1 Introduction

Strings are pervasive in programs, and arguably even more pervasive in web programming. They also arise as a natural representation of system configurations for multi-agent systems where agents are linearly ordered [3].

To reason about such systems or programs one has to manipulate possibly infinite sets of strings or languages. To achieve effective reasoning, a natural abstraction for languages is to consider the class of regular languages which were shown to be sufficiently expressive to verify non-trivial properties. Regular languages are well-studied and are supported by multiple description formalism including automata-based representations. The usual operations required for abstract reasoning such as Boolean operations and usual tests such as inclusion

G. Gange—This work was supported by the Australian Research Council through grants DE160100568 and LP140100437.

Pierre Ganty has been supported by the Madrid Regional Government project S2013/ICE-2731, *N-Greens Software - Next-GeneRation Energy-EfficieNt Secure Software*, and the Spanish Ministry of Economy and Competitiveness project No. TIN2015-71819-P, *RISCO - RIgorous analysis of Sophisticated COncurrent and distributed systems.*

D. D'Souza and K. Narayan Kumar (Eds.): ATVA 2017, LNCS 10482, pp. 67–83, 2017.
DOI: 10.1007/978-3-319-68167-2_5

and equivalence can be implemented in polynomial time on deterministic finite-state automata. This contrasts with non-deterministic finite-state automata where inclusion is PSPACE-complete. This has to be taken with a grain of salt since there exist languages whose specification by non-deterministic finite-state automata are logarithmically more succinct than their smallest deterministic automata counterpart [14]. In practice, however, deterministic finite-state automata often blow up in representation size impeding the success automata-based techniques.

In this paper we examine the use of deterministic finite-state automata of bounded size as a way to achieve scalability of automata-based techniques. By bounding the size we combine the benefit of a small representation with the polynomial runtime of the operations and tests on finite-state automata. We consider k-state deterministic finite-state automata as our representation for languages. This restriction avoids the blow up in size, the size of the whole automata is $k|\Sigma|$, and avoids the blow up in cost of operations, each operation is at most $k^2|\Sigma|$.

We start by investigating basic questions and show that, in general, there is no "minimum" k-state DFA that includes a language specified by n-state DFA with $n > k$. Here "minimum" is defined using language inclusion. This result is expected since the intersection of two languages defined by k-state DFAs is in general not representable precisely as a k-state DFA. Therefore we identify criteria besides language inclusion to select between two k-state DFA approximation when language inclusion alone is inconclusive.

To evaluate the effectiveness of those criteria, we formalize the problem of computing a k-state DFA approximating a given a n-state DFA as a search problem. Modeling the problem as a search problem allows to flexibly express the criteria we identified as objective to minimize.

Our first model as a search problem restricts the search space to those k-state DFA resulting from merging state of the n-state DFA in accordance with a k-block partition of the n states. State partitioning is the basis of minimization algorithms for DFAs. Using partitions result in a straightforward encoding of k-state approximation because language inclusion follows immediately from partitioning.

In a second model, we formalize the search problem in full-generality by considering all k-state DFAs. Therefore, in this encoding, we encode the constraint that the language of the k-state DFA includes that of the n-state DFA.

As a consequence of our result on the absence of a least k-state DFA the above search problems have no unique solution. Therefore we rely on the identified criteria to narrow the set of solutions using an objective function.

Modelling the approximation of an automaton as a search problem allows us to find all possible approximations, or find optimal approximations, in practice these problems are challenging to solve. Hence it is worth considering a greedy approach to tackling these problems. We first introduce a greedy approach for finding quotient automata approximations. Then, motivated by the ease in which quotient automata collapse, we introduce a greedy algorithm that preserves more of the structure of the automata while building decreasing size approximations, based on the idea of tracking language dominance of states of the automata.

2 Preliminaries

Strings. We assume a finite alphabet of symbols Σ. A *string* w is either the empty string ε or of the form cw' where c is a symbol in Σ and w' a string. The *length* of a string w, denoted $|w|$, is the number of symbols appearing in the string. We use array notation to lockup the symbols appearing in a string. Suppose $|w| = l$ then $w[i], 1 \leq i \leq l$ is the ith symbol appearing in the string. We assume the reader is familiar with regular expressions.

Finite-State Automata. A finite-state automaton (or simply automaton) is a tulle $R = \langle Q, \Sigma, \delta, q0, F\rangle$ where Σ is an *alphabet*; Q is a finite set of *states* including the *initial state* $q0$ and a set F of *accepting states*; and $\delta \subseteq Q \times \Sigma \times Q$ is a set of *transitions*. The size of an automata R, $size(R)$ is defined as $|Q|$.

A *transition* in automaton R from state q to q', written $q \to q'$, exists if there is $(q, c, q') \in \delta$ for some $c \in \Sigma$. A *computation* for string w of length l in an automaton R is a sequence of transitions $q_0 \to q_1 \to \cdots \to q_l$ where $(q_i, w[i+1], q_{i+1}) \in \delta$. An *accepting computation* for w in R from state q_0 is a computation for w in the automaton R where $q_l \in F$. The *language* of automaton R from state $q \in Q$, $L(q, R)$, is the set of strings w which have an accepting computation from state q. The *language* of automaton R, $L(R) = L(q0, R)$.

A state q is said to be accessible if there is a sequence of transitions from $q0$ to q; co-accessible if there is a sequence of transitions from q to some state $q' \in F$; and useful if q is both accessible and co-accessible. An automaton is *trim* if all its states are useful. An automaton is *deterministic* (DFA) if δ denotes a (partial) function from $Q \times \Sigma$ into Q. In that case, we sometimes use the notation $\delta(q, c)$ where $q \in Q, c \in \Sigma$ to refer to q' where $(q, c, q') \in \delta$, when it exists. An automaton is said to be a *t-DFA* if it is deterministic and trim.

3 Automaton Approximation

In this paper we are interested in defining approximations of DFAs which are as precise as possible given a fixed budget on the number of states.

Definition 1. *Given two automata R and R', we say that R'* approximates *R iff $L(R) \subseteq L(R')$. Given two k-state approximations R_1, R_2 of R we say R_1* dominates *R_2 whenever $L(R_1) \subset L(R_2)$.*

When constructing an approximation of a DFA R we are interested in finding an approximation that is not dominated by any other approximation. Next we exhibit an example showing there might be more than one such approximation.

Example 1. Let A be the 3-state t-DFA $\langle \{0, 1, 2\}, \{a, b\}, \{(0, a, 1), (1, b, 2)\}, 0, \{2\}\rangle$ that accepts exactly $\{ab\}$.

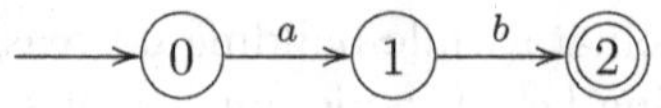

Then for the three 2-state approximations shown in Fig. 1: $L(B_1) = \mathtt{ab}^\star$, $L(B_2) = \mathtt{a}^\star\mathtt{b}$ and $L(B_3) = (\mathtt{ab})^\star$ and none dominates another. □

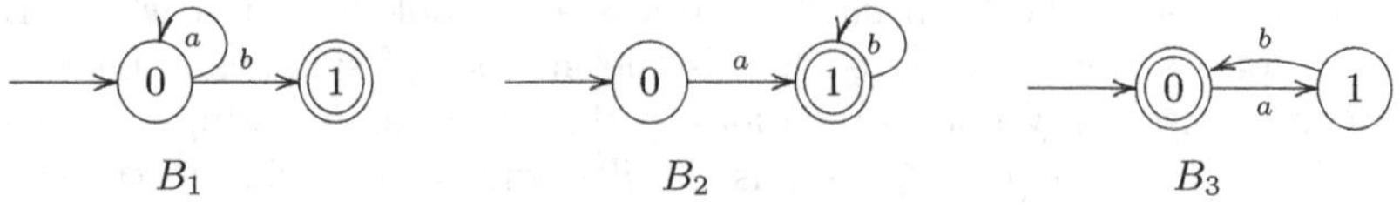

Fig. 1. Three 2 state approximations of the automata A.

While we are mainly interested in over-approximations of DFAs, we can define under-approximations as well using the complement. To compute an under-approximation of n-state DFA $R = (Q, \Sigma, \delta, q0, F)$ such that δ is total, we complement R obtaining $\bar{R} = (Q, \Sigma, \delta, q0, Q - F)$ and compute a k-state over-approximation of $\bar{R}$, $\bar{R}' = (Q', \Sigma, \delta', q0', F')$ and then, assuming δ' is total,[1] complement $\bar{R}'$ to obtain $R' = (Q', \Sigma, \delta', q0', Q' - F')$. R' is a k-state automaton under-approximating R by construction.

4 Approximations Using Equivalence Relations on States

DFA minimization relies on building an equivalence relation of the states of the DFA, or equivalently partitioning the states into equivalence classes. Given an n-state DFA R that minimizes to an equivalent k-state DFA R', we find that R' dominates all other k-state approximations of R since $L(R') = L(R)$. This observation is the starting point of our study of approximations using state partitions.

4.1 Partitions and Quotient Automata

Consider a *partition* $P = \{b_1, \ldots, b_n\}$ of Q into n non-empty, pairwise disjoint subsets covering Q called *blocks* and define the equivalence class of a state q, written $[q]_P$ as the (unique) block b_i such that $q \in b_i$. It is known that the set of partitions of a finite set forms a complete lattice. Thus we find that $(\mathrm{Part}(Q), \preceq, \curlywedge, \curlyvee, \{Q\}, \{\{q\} \mid q \in Q\})$ is a complete lattice where $\mathrm{Part}(Q)$ is the set of partitions of Q; $P_1 \preceq P_2$ iff for all blocks b_1 of P_1 there exist a block b_2 of P_2 such that $b_1 \subseteq b_2$; $P_1 \curlywedge P_2$ is the partition resulting from intersecting all pairs of blocks of P_1 and P_2[2]; $P_1 \curlyvee P_2$ is the partition obtained by merging the blocks of P_1 which have a member in the same block of P_2.

[1] or a $k-1$-state over-approximation, on which we turn δ' into a total function.

[2] Note that the empty set is not a block, hence it is not part of the resulting partition.

Given a t-DFA $R = \langle Q, \Sigma, \delta, q0, F \rangle$ and a partition P of Q, then the *quotient automata* $R_{/P}$ is defined as the automaton $\langle P, \Sigma, \delta_P, [q0]_P, F_P \rangle$ where $F_P = \{p \in P \mid p \cap F \neq \emptyset\}$, and $\delta_P = \{([q]_P, c, [q']_P) \mid (q, c, q') \in \delta\}$. Notice that $R_{/P}$ is not necessarily a t-DFA. The resulting automaton is a t-DFA for a subset of the partitions as we will see later.

A quotient automaton is always an approximation of the automaton it is defined from.

Theorem 1. *Given t-DFA R and partition P of its states, $L(R) \subseteq L(R_{/P})$.* □

Example 2. Consider the t-DFA of Example 1, we have $B_1 = A_{/\{\{0,1\},\{2\}\}}$, $B_2 = A_{/\{\{0\},\{1,2\}\}}$ and $B_3 = A_{/\{\{0,2\},\{1\}\}}$. □

4.2 Determinizing Partitions

Note that the quotient automata of a t-DFA is not necessarily deterministic. A partition P for a t-DFA R is *deterministic* if for all $\{(q, c, q'), (q'', c, q''')\} \subseteq \delta, [q]_P = [q'']_P \Rightarrow [q']_P = [q''']_P$. Hence the resulting quotient automata $R_{/P}$ is also a t-DFA. Given a t-DFA R we define the *language quotients* of R as the automata $R_{/P}$ arising from all deterministic partitions P of R. Lemma 1 shows that the set of deterministic partitions forms a meet semi-lattice.

Lemma 1. *Let P and P' be deterministic partitions for some t-DFA R. Then the partition $P \curlywedge P'$ is deterministic.* □

Lemma 2. *Given a t-DFA R and partition P there is a least deterministic partition $\mathrm{det}_R(P)$ of R such that $P \preceq \mathrm{det}_R(P)$.* □

For any t-DFA R and partition P, we compute the least deterministic partition $det_R(P)$ in $O(|\delta| + |P||\Sigma|)$ time. This algorithm is given in Fig. 2.

Lemma 3. *Procedure determinize-part(P, R) runs in $O(|\delta| + |P||\Sigma|)$ time.* □

Lemma 4. *Let $P' =$ determinize-part(P, R). Then $P' = \mathrm{det}_R(P)$.* □

4.3 Incompleteness of Partition-Based Approaches

It would be convenient if the only k-state DFA approximations we need to consider were quotient automata, since there are many fewer quotient automata of an n-state t-DFA, than there are k-state DFA. Unfortunately, this is not the case.

Example 3. The following 14 state automaton A_1 for (a|b)aaaaaaaaaaaa

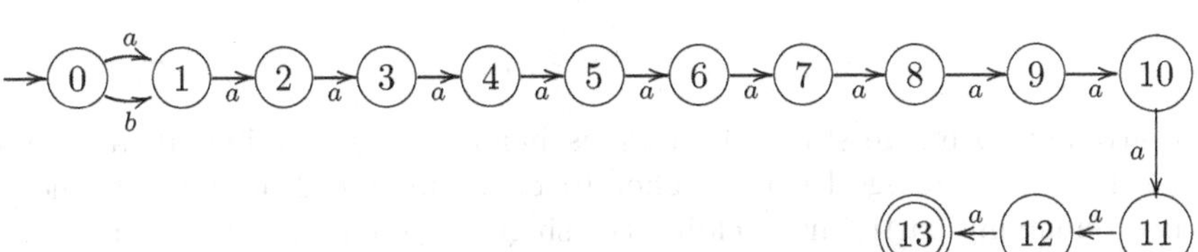

```
determinize-part(P,⟨Q, Σ, δ, q0, F⟩):
  T := ∅
  δ' := ∅
  for(b_i ∈ P)
    for(q ∈ b_i)
      repr[q] := min(b_i)
  for((q, c, q') ∈ δ)
    if((FIND(q), c, q'') ∈ δ')
      T := T ∪ {(q', q'')}
    else δ' := δ' ∪ {(FIND(q), c, q')}
  while(∃(q1, q2) ∈ T)
    T := T − {(q1, q2)}
    UNION(T, δ', q1, q2)
  Rs := {q | q ∈ Q, FIND(q) = q}
  return {{q' | q' ∈ Q, FIND(q') = q} | q ∈ Rs}

FIND(x):
  if(repr[x] ≠ x)
    repr[x] := FIND(repr[x])
  return repr[x]

UNION(T, δ', x, y):
  rx := FIND(x)
  ry := FIND(y)
  if(rx = ry) return
  repr[ry] := rx
  for((ry, c, q) ∈ δ')
    δ' := δ' − {(ry, c, q)}
    if (∃(rx, c, q') ∈ δ')
      T := T ∪ {(q, q')}
```

Fig. 2. Algorithm for computing $\det_R(P)$. It maintains a partition represented by a union-find data structure *repr*.

has this 8 state approximation A_2 such that $L(A_2) = \mathsf{aaa(aaa)}^\star|\mathsf{baaa(aaaa)}^\star$

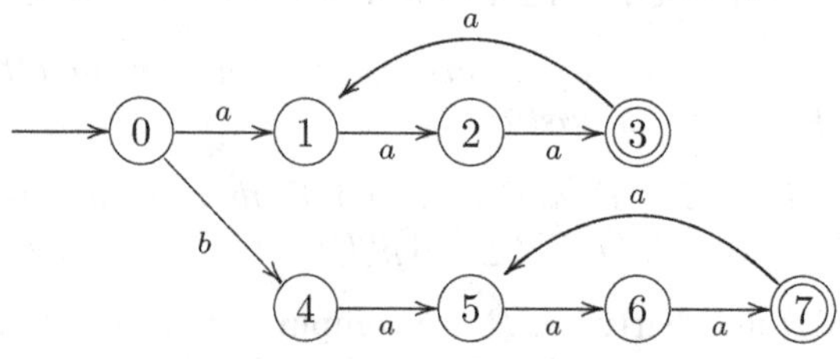

There is no 8-state quotient of A_1 whose language is a subset of $L(A_2)$ since any quotient t-DFA must map state 1 to a single block and hence accepts a language of the form $(\mathsf{a}|\mathsf{b})\ E$ for some regular expression E. □

It is worth noting that when computing quotients of sparse automata, *trimming* is crucial. With a complete DFA, the additional error transitions force us to merge more states than we need to preserve determinism.

Example 4. Recall the automaton from Example 1, now as a complete DFA.

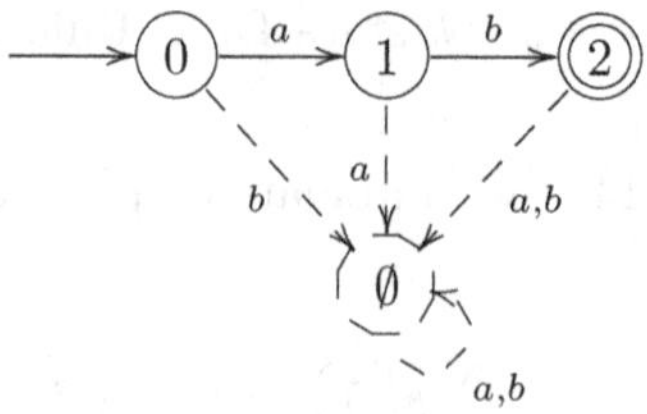

If we attempt to merge states 0 and 2 as before, the transitions $(0, \mathsf{a}, 1)$ and $(2, \mathsf{a}, \emptyset)$ force us to merge 1 with $\emptyset$. Then $(\emptyset, \mathsf{b}, \emptyset)$ and $(1, \mathsf{b}, 2)$ forces us to merge the two remaining partitions, yielding the single-state trivial automaton.

5 Approximations as a Search Problem

We define a discrete satisfaction problem that given an original n-state t-DFA $R = \langle Q, \Sigma, \delta, q0, F\rangle$, finds a k-state DFA $R' = \langle Q', \Sigma, \delta', q0', F'\rangle$ which approximates it. In the next subsection we consider only quotient DFA, before generalizing this to arbitrary DFA in the following subsection.

5.1 Searching Quotient k-state DFAs

Quotient DFAs are an attractive class to consider for approximating arbitrary DFAs since they automatically satisfy the approximation condition, and they can be specified simply in terms of a partition.

Writing this problem as a combinatorial search problem is reasonably straightforward since we are merely deciding a partition. The model is defined by the principal decisions m_q which maps each state $q \in Q$ to a state in Q' where $|Q'| = k$ (which represent the states of the k-state DFA). The constraints are

$$m_q \in Q' \quad (1)$$
$$m_q \quad \text{is surjective} \quad (2)$$
$$q0' = m_{q0} \quad (3)$$
$$F' = \{m_q \mid q \in F\} \quad (4)$$
$$\delta' = \{(m_q, c, m_{q'}) \mid (q, c, q') \in \delta\} \qquad \forall q \in Q, c \in \Sigma \quad (5)$$
$$\delta' \quad \text{is a partial function from } Q' \times \Sigma \text{ to } Q' \quad (6)$$

The size of the system of constraints $O(nk|\Sigma|)$.

Theorem 2 (Correctness). *Let t-DFA R and DFA R' satisfy Eq.* (1)–(6) *then* $L(R) \subseteq L(R')$. □

Theorem 3 (Completeness). *Given t-DFA R and R', if R' is a quotient t-DFA of R then there exist m satisfying Eq.* (1)–(6). □

In practice we improve the model (1)–(6) by adding value symmetry breaking constraints to remove isomorphic k-states automata. We add a symmetry breaking constraint requiring that $\forall q \in Q, u \in \{2, \ldots, k\}$ if $m_q = u$ then there exists $q' < q, m_{q'} = u - 1$. This enforces that we number the partitions P of R in the order of their least element. To be compatible with Eq. (3) we also require that the initial states $q0$ and $q0'$ of both R and R' are the least numbered state.

5.2 Searching All k-state DFAs

Not all k-state DFAs are quotient automata. Furthermore, Example 3 shows there are k-state DFAs approximations which are dominated by no k-state quotient DFA. Hence we are also interested in non-quotient k-state DFA that are approximations.

To model the general approximation problem we reason about the synchronized product of the known n-state t-DFA, and the unknown k-state DFA. The principle decisions are δ' the transition relation for the k-state DFA and F' the set of final states. We ensure that each state reachable in the synchronized product, which represents a final state for the n-state t-DFA, is also a final state for the k-state DFA. The propositional decision variables $r_{q,q'}$ represent that the state (q, q') is reachable in the intersection DFA. The first four constraints ensure that any computation in the n-state t-DFA is reflected in the k-state DFA. The last constraint ensures that each reachable state in the synchronized product which is final for the n-state t-DFA is also final for the k-state DFA.

$$r_{q0,q0'} \tag{7}$$

$$r_{q,q'} \rightarrow \forall (q, c, q_2) \in \delta \, \exists (q', c, q_2') \in \delta' : r_{q_2,q_2'} \tag{8}$$

$$\delta' \quad \text{is a partial function from } Q' \times \Sigma \text{ to } Q' \tag{9}$$

$$r_{q,q'} \rightarrow q' \in F' \qquad \forall q \in F, q' \in Q' \tag{10}$$

The size of this system of constraints in $O(nk|\Sigma|)$.

Theorem 4 (Correctness). *Let t-DFA R and DFA R' satisfy Eq. (7)–(10) then $L(R) \subseteq L(R')$.* □

Theorem 5 (Completeness). *Given t-DFAs R and R' if R' is k-state t-DFA such that $L(R) \subseteq L(R')$ then there is a solution of Eq. (7)–(10).* □

5.3 Complexity

We conjecture that the problem of finding a non-dominated k-state DFA of an n-state t-DFA is NP-hard, even when we restrict to quotient automata.

> NONDOMPART(R,P): given an n-state t-DFA R and deterministic partition P of R decide whether there exists a deterministic partition P' of R where $|P'| \leq |P|$ such that $L(R_{/P'}) \subset L(R_{/P})$.

> NONDOMAPPROX(R,R'): given an n-state t-DFA R and a k-state DFA R' where $L(R) \subseteq L(R')$ decide whether there exists a k-state DFA R'' such that $L(R) \subseteq L(R'') \subset L(R')$.

Conjecture 1. NONDOMPART and NONDOMAPPROX are NP-hard □

Observe that both problems are in NP. For NONDOMPART, guess a partition P' of the n states of R with no more than $|P|$ blocks; check in polynomial time that P' is deterministic; if successful then build the DFAs $R_{/P}$ and $R_{/P'}$; check, in polynomial time, that $L(R_{/P'}) \subseteq L(R_{/P})$ and $L(R_{/P'}) \neq L(R_{/P})$. The argument to show NONDOMAPPROX belongs to NP is similar.

There are some closely related problem which are NP-complete. Gold [8] shows that deciding if there exists a k-state automaton that agrees with a set of examples and counterexamples is NP-complete.

5.4 Objectives

The models above that describe the problem of finding a k-state approximation of an n-state t-DFA, while correctly capturing this question are not that useful in practice. It is always possible to answer with a single-state machine whose initial state is accepting and has self arcs for all symbols in the alphabet.

Ideally what we desire are k-state t-DFA R which are non-dominated. Although this is decidable it seems hard to compute, and we conjecture it is NP-hard. Instead we will consider simpler objectives which are easier to compute. Hence we convert our problem to a discrete optimization problem.

Counting Prefixes. The first thing we consider is counting the number of strings accepted up to some length. We can compute the number of strings accepted $a_{q',l}$ for each state $q' \in Q'$ and each length from $l \in \{0, \ldots, m\}$ as follows

$$a_{q',0} = q' \in F' \tag{11}$$

$$a_{q',l+1} = \sum_{(q',c,q'') \in \delta'} a_{q'',l} \tag{12}$$

The size of this constraint system is $O(k^2|\Sigma|m)$. We can then minimize the expected number of strings of length between 0 and m accepted by the initial state of the k-state DFA $\sum_{l \in 0,\ldots,m} a_{q'_0,l}$.

Using a result of Moore [11] that states that a pair of automata can be differentiated by a string of length less than the sum of their numbers of states we show the following lemma.

Lemma 5. *Suppose* $m \geq 2k - 1$ *then a* k *state DFA* R' *minimizing* $\sum_{l=0,\ldots,m} a_{q'_0,l}$ *is dominated by no* k*-state DFA* R'' *approximating* R. □

Markov-Like Measures. If we assume that the strings of interest have a Poisson distribution in length we can model this as an expected probability p_c for each alphabet symbol x and a probability pe of reaching the end of the string where $pe + \sum_{c \in \Sigma} p_c = 1$. We can define the expected proportion of strings r_q accepted by state q as a system of simultaneous equations

$$r_{q'} = pe \times (q' \in F') + \sum_{(q',c,q'') \in \delta'} p_c r_{q''} \tag{13}$$

The size of this constraint system is $O(k^2|\Sigma|)$. We can then minimize the expected proportion of strings accepted by the automata as $r_{q0'}$.

Other objectives are possible: using a finite corpus of counter-examples, or calculating the expected proportion of strings of some length that are accepted.

6 Greedy Approaches

Independent of whether our conjecture of NP hardness holds, solving the constraint optimization problems defined in the previous section are challenging. Their solving behaviour appears to scale exponentially in k in practice.

Hence we consider incomplete approaches to find k-state approximations to an n-state t-DFA, which may not necessarily return a non-dominated approximation, nor minimize any objective.

The most obvious approach to producing a greedy approximation is by restricting consideration to quotient DFA of the original n-state t-DFA R, and merging partitions in these DFA until we reach a DFA with k or less states.

The greedy algorithm is shown in Fig. 3. At each stage it considers each deterministic automaton $R_{/P_{12}}$ that arises from merging each pair of states in the original automaton R, and calculates a measure (objective value) for the automaton. It greedily selects the best resulting t-DFA. If this has no more than k states the process finishes, otherwise we repeat the merging process.

```
quot(R,k):
  let R = ⟨Q, Σ, δ, q0, F⟩
  P := {{q} | q ∈ Q}
  m := +∞
  for({b1, b2} ⊆ P, b1 ≠ b2)
    P12 := determinize-part(P − {b1, b2} ∪ {b1 ∪ b2}, R)
    M' := R/P12
    if m > measure(M')
      m := measure(M')
      M := M'
  if size(M) ≤ k return M
  return quot(M,k)
```

Fig. 3. Greedy algorithm for building a k-state quotient t-DFA for t-DFA R.

The result crucially depends on the measure used. Note that each of the objective measures defined in Sect. 5.4 is straightforward to calculate for a given fixed automaton $R_{/P_{12}}$.

Example 5. Consider the automaton A from Example 1. We will consider each of the quotient automata B_1, B_2 and B_3 of Fig. 1 arising from partitions $\{\{0,1\},\{2\}\}$, $\{\{0\},\{1,2\}\}$ and $\{\{0,2\},\{1\}\}$ respectively. If we count the number of strings accepted of length up to 3, we find the measures are respectively 3, 3, and 2, and B_3 is preferable. If we use a Markov measure with $pe = 1/3$ and $p_a = p_b = 1/3$ then the measures are respectively $1/6$, $1/6$ and $3/8$ and one of B_1 or B_2 is preferable. □

7 Better State Merging

Quotient automata while easy to understand and construct often collapse quickly by partition determinization into small, and even single-state, automaton. Worse, some interesting classes of automata admit *no* non-trivial deterministic quotient.

Example 6. Consider the following automaton, recognizing the language $(\mathtt{a} \cup \mathtt{b})^\star\mathtt{abaa}(\mathtt{a} \cup \mathtt{b})^\star$:

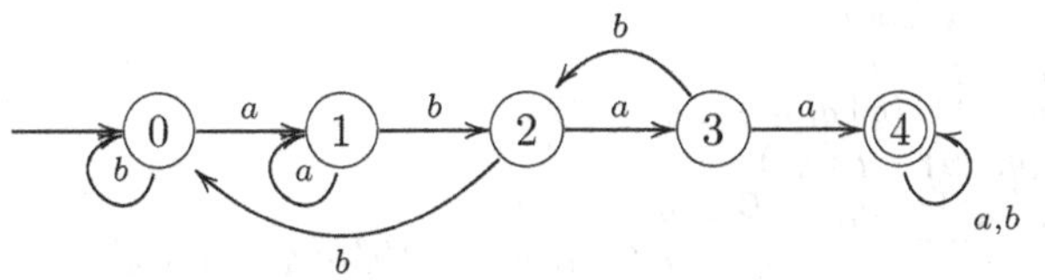

If we attempt to merge states 3 and 4, we find that the outgoing transitions on b conflict, and we are forced to add 2 to the partition. But as 2 transitions to 0 on b, we are again forced to merge 0 with $\{2, 3, 4\}$. But since 0 and $\{2, 3, 4\}$ disagree on a, we are finally forced to add 1 to the partition, obtaining the single-state universal automaton.

The same collapse occurs for any pair of states we choose to merge. However, in some sense it *should* be safe to merge state 3 into state 4, to produce automaton recognizing the shorter substring *aba*. □

This suggests that language quotients describe too restrictive a form of transformation. Instead, consider some partition P such that $[q_1]_P = [q_2]_P$, $\{(q_1, c, q_1'), (q_2, c, q_2')\} \subseteq \delta$, $[q_1']_P \neq [q_2']_P$ and $L(q_1', R) \subseteq L(q_2', R)$. If we replace the transition (q_1, c, q_1') with (q_1, c, q_2'), we resolve the non-determinism of δ_P and obtain an over-approximation of $L(R)$.

In order to use this we have to understand the inclusion relations between the states of the automaton we wish to approximate. To this end, we can use simulation preorders between states. Simulation preorders are computable in time polynomial in the size of the automaton. Moreover, if a simulation preorder $\sqsubseteq$ is such that $q \sqsubseteq q'$ in R then $L(q, R) \subseteq L(q', R)$ holds [6].

We will determinize a t-DFA while shrinking the number of states from n to k by using an approximating version of the NFA to DFA translation. First we map the t-DFA with n-states R to a t-DFA with n-states RR whose state names are $QQ = \{\{q\} \mid q \in Q\}$. During the determinization we will construct new states which always represent sets of the original states Q. This mapping is only used to prevent creating states which already exists. We calculate the inclusion relation D for the t-DFA RR using, for instance, simulation preorders. We then apply the algorithm determinize-tdfa defined in Fig. 4 to R and D choosing two states q_1 and q_2 in QQ to collapse.

The algorithm works by collapsing two states q_1 and q_2 into one. In the case that there is an inclusion relation between them this is easy, we simply eliminate the included state. Otherwise we create a new state q labelled with the union of original states of q_1 and q_2, and replace all occurrences of q_1 and q_2 by q. This

```
determinize-tdfa(R, D, q1, q2):
  let R = ⟨Q, Σ, δ, q0, F⟩
  if (q1, q2) ∈ D
    Q' := Q − {q1}
    F' := F − {q1}
    q0' := (q0 = q1 ? q2 : q0)
    δ' := δ ∪ {(q', c, q2) | (q', c, q1) ∈ δ}
    return ⟨Q', Σ, (δ' ∩ (Q' × Σ × Q')), q0', F'⟩
  elseif (q2, q1) ∈ D
    return determinize-tdfa(R, D, q2, q1):
  q := q1 ∪ q2 % new state
  Q' := Q − {q1, q2} ∪ {q}
  F' := F − {q1, q2} ∪ {q | q1 ∈ F ∨ q2 ∈ F}
  q0' := (q0 ∈ {q1, q2} ? q : q0)
  D' := D ∪ {(q', q) | (q', q1) ∈ D ∨ (q', q2) ∈ D}
  δ' := δ ∪ {(q, c, q'') | (q', c, q'') ∈ δ, q' ∈ {q1, q2}} ∪ {(q', c, q) | (q', c, q'') ∈ δ, q'' ∈ {q1, q2}}
  δ' := δ' ∩ (Q' × Σ × Q')
  R' := ⟨Q', Σ, δ', q0', F'⟩
  while(∃(q', c, q1') ∈ δ', (q', c, q2') ∈ δ', q1' ≠ q2')
    (q12', ⟨Q', Σ, δ', q0', F'⟩, D') := merge-state(q1', q2', R', (D' ∩ (Q' × Q')))
    δ' := δ' − {(q', c, q1'), (q', c, q2')} ∪ {(q', c, q12')}
    R' := ⟨Q', Σ, δ', q0', F'⟩
  return ⟨Q', Σ, (δ' ∩ (Q' × Σ × Q')), q0', F'⟩
```

Fig. 4. Algorithm for computing a $n-1$-state DFA approximation of n-state t-DFA R given inclusion relation D which replaces q_1 and q_2 by their union.

may result in an NFA. We then continue finding non-deterministic transitions going to q_1' and q_2' and merging the states using merge-state which replaces one of these states by a state that over-approximate the union of their languages.

Lemma 6. *The algorithm determinize-tdfa terminates.* □

Lemma 7. *The algorithm determinize-tdfa returns a DFA R' with at most $n-1$ states such that $L(R) \subseteq L(R')$.* □

We can adapt the greedy algorithm quot to use determinize-tdfa to construct the candidate automaton M' in place of determinize-part in an obvious manner. We call this dom.

There is a simpler variation of determinization using dominance. We add a universal accepting state a to the original automata (initially unconnected) and we only consider greedily merging other states q with a. This means that the first `if` condition in determinize-tdfa always holds, so determinization is simple. We call this greedy variant univ (Fig. 4).

merge-state(q_1, q_2, R, D):
  let $R = \langle Q, \Sigma, \delta, q0, F\rangle$
  if $q_1 \cup q_2 \in Q$
    return $(q_1 \cup q_2, R, D)$
  if $(q_1, q_2) \in D$
    return (q_2, R, D)
  elseif $(q_2, q_1) \in D$
    return (q_1, R, D)
  $q := q_1 \cup q_2$
  $r := (\ |\{(q', c, q_1) \mid (q', c, q_1) \in \delta\}| > |\{(q', c, q_2) \mid (q', c, q_2) \in \delta\}|\ ?\ q_2\ :\ q_1)$
  $Q' := Q - \{r\} \cup \{q\}$
  $F' := F - \{r\} \cup \{q \mid q_1 \in F \vee q_2 \in F\}$
  $q0' := (q0 = r\ ?\ q\ :\ q0)$
  $D' := D \cup \{(q', q) \mid (q', q_1) \in D \vee (q', q_2) \in D\} \cup \{(q_1, q), (q_2, q)\}$
  $\delta' := \delta \cup \{(q', c, q) \mid (q', c, r) \in \delta\} \cup \{(q, c, q') \mid (q'', c, q') \in \delta, q'' \in \{q_1, q_2\}\}$
  return $(q, \langle Q', \Sigma, (\delta' \cap (Q' \times \Sigma \times Q')), q0', F'\rangle, (D' \cap (Q' \times Q')))$

Fig. 5. Algorithm for computing an NFA with one of states q_1 and q_2 replaced with their union. It returns the name of the merged state, an NFA and a language inclusion relation for the states of the NFA.

8 Experiments

To evaluate the proposed approximation strategies, we generated a corpus of automata. For an instance `ty-l-m-d.xx`, we generated m random words W with length l over alphabet $\{1, \ldots, d\}$. We then built an automaton of the given type `ty`: exact matching $\{w \in W\}$, prefix $\{w\Sigma^* \mid w \in W\}$, suffix $\{\Sigma^* w \mid w \in W\}$ or substring $\{\Sigma^* w \Sigma^* \mid w \in W\}$. We generated 10 instances for each combination of $l \in \{5, 10, 15, 20\}, m \in \{1, 3, 5, 10\}, d \in \{2, 3, 5, 10\}$, yielding 2560 automata with between 6 and 200 states.

For an automaton having n states, we constructed k-state approximations for $k \in \{n-2, \frac{n}{2}, \frac{n}{4}\}$ using the three greedy merging approaches: quotient determinization (quot), merge-into-universal (univ) and determinization with dominance (dom).

Results for the three greedy approaches are illustrated in Fig. 6. For each initial automaton and target size k, we computed the number of strings of length $\leq 2k - 1$ recognized by the approximation, and reported the average over the 10 instances for each combination of parameters.

It is interesting to note the differences in behaviour of quot and univ. For automata recognizing a single substring, quot cannot produce a non-trivial approximation – after merging any two states, determinization produces the universal automaton. But for these, univ constructs good (frequently minimal) approximations, recognizing a shorter prefix of the target substring. Conversely, quot produces much better approximations for exact string matching automata than univ: univ produces automata matching all prefixes of the target string, whereas quot constructs long loops.

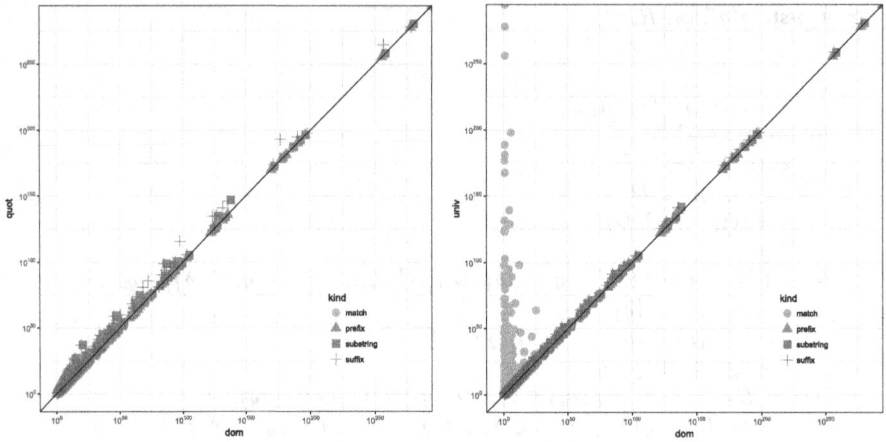

(a) (b)

Fig. 6. For each parameter combination and target size k, the number of strings of length $\leq 2k-1$ recognized by the approximate automaton (averaged over 10 instances).

As hoped, the greater fidelity of dom allows us to achieve tighter approximations than quot or univ. In all but one instance, dom produced an automaton at least as tight, and frequently much tighter, than either quot or univ. A summary of runtimes is given in Fig. 7.

In most cases approximations are constructed quickly. However for large automata, repeatedly evaluating all possible merges (each evaluation simulating the DFA up to $2k - 1$ steps) becomes quite expensive. However, we expect by using previous results as lower bounds, we could avoid many of these evaluations entirely.

	med.	**75%**	**max**
quot	0.02	0.40	382.46
univ	< 0.01	0.04	29.32
dom	0.06	1.46	2819.01

Fig. 7. Runtime quartiles for the greedy approximation methods. The lower two quartiles are <0.01 for all methods.

To test the accuracy of these greedy approximation strategies, we built MiniZinc [13] models for the optimal approximation obtainable in general (Eq. (7)–(10)), and under the quot and univ approximation strategies.[3] We then computed optimal approximations of the smaller test instances using the constraint programming solver CHUFFED [5]. CHUFFED was run with time and memory limits of 10 min and 2 Gb respectively. Figure 8 reports results for those automata where optimal approximations were found for all MiniZinc models.

The observed results match those for the greedy approaches: both quot and univ can represent optimal approximations for matching *single* prefixes, and produce poor approximations for suffix automata; but quot can produce optimal automata for exact matching, but univ produces much tighter (but typically not optimal) automata for substring matching.

[3] We do not include a model for dom, as the natural decision model is semantically equivalent to the general approximation model.

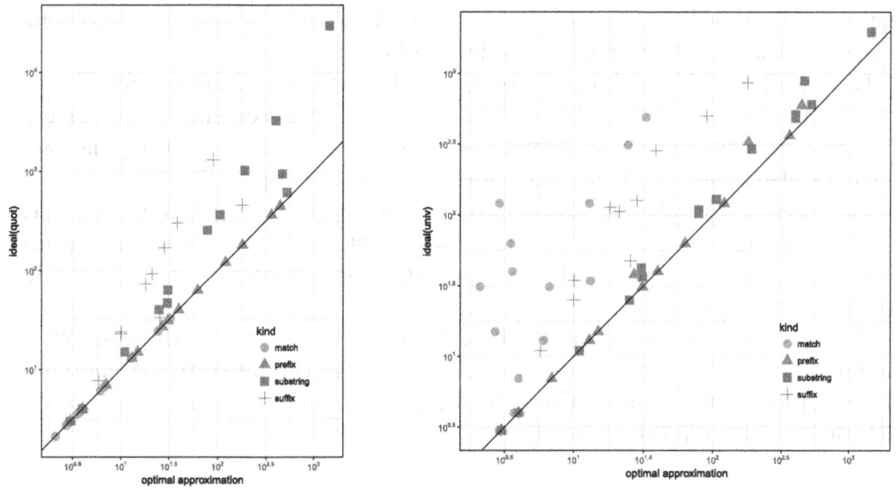

(a) (b)

Fig. 8. Ideal approximations achievable under the (a) quot and (b) univ approximation strategies, compared with the best possible approximation.

9 Conclusion and Related Work

Finding small approximating automata is a challenging problem, but the problem has a number of uses: in static analysis [7], in computer security [10], and elsewhere given the ubiquity of automata. In this paper we have formalized this problem as a search problem, and defined a number of complete and incomplete methods for finding correct approximations.

A related problem is that of computing minimal separating DFAs: Given two DFA defining disjoint languages, compute a DFA with as few states as possible that includes one language and is disjoint from the other. Observe that the minimal separating DFA problem optimizes for size of the resulting DFA while we optimize for its precision with given size k. The minimal separating DFA problem has its origin in the learning of DFA from samples [1,8] where its formulation as a decision problem was shown to be NP-complete. More recently [4,9,12] the problem found applications in formal verification to discover invariants and in the context of assume guarantee reasoning. In that context, the work of Neider [12] is the most relevant to us since he defines a constraint-based approach to the minimal separating DFA problem.

On the other hand, the problem of finding minimal approximations using smaller automaton has been studied in several independent contexts [2,7,10]. D'silva [7] studied the problem in the context of static analysis where abstract states are given by languages of finite-state automaton. To ensure termination of fixpoint computations a widening operator has to be defined. D'silva lays down a principled approach to define widening operators for automata-based representation. Earlier Bouajjani et al. [2] faced identical termination problems in the context of abstract regular model-checking.

Both work put forward an approach based on state equivalences for various notions of equivalences. Equivalent states are then collapsed (merged or identified) yielding a smaller automaton whose language is a superset of original one. The equivalence relation is fixed a priori based on the application domain.

We differ in several aspects: we have a fixed budget on the number of states of the resulting automaton; and using our constraint-based approach we are searching a larger space of candidate automata, not necessarily automata resulting from merging states.

Finally, let us mention the work of Luchaup et al. [10] in the context of computer security where the use of approximations of finite-state automaton is motivated for performance reasons. Again they use an approach merging states with the goal of minimizing the error of classification.

References

1. Angluin, D.: Learning regular sets from queries and counterexamples. Inf. Comput. **75**(2), 87–106 (1987)
2. Bouajjani, A., Habermehl, P., Rogalewicz, A., Vojnar, T.: Abstract regular (tree) model checking. Int. J. Softw. Tools Technol. Transfer **14**(2), 167–191 (2011)
3. Bouajjani, A., Habermehl, P., Vojnar, T.: Abstract regular model checking. In: Alur, R., Peled, D.A. (eds.) CAV 2004. LNCS, vol. 3114, pp. 372–386. Springer, Heidelberg (2004). doi:10.1007/978-3-540-27813-9_29
4. Chen, Y.-F., Farzan, A., Clarke, E.M., Tsay, Y.-K., Wang, B.-Y.: Learning minimal separating DFA's for compositional verification. In: Kowalewski, S., Philippou, A. (eds.) TACAS 2009. LNCS, vol. 5505, pp. 31–45. Springer, Heidelberg (2009). doi:10.1007/978-3-642-00768-2_3
5. Chu, G.: Improving combinatorial optimization. Ph.D. thesis, Department of Computing and Information Systems, University of Melbourne (2011)
6. Dill, D.L., Hu, A.J., Wong-Toi, H.: Checking for language inclusion using simulation preorders. In: Larsen, K.G., Skou, A. (eds.) CAV 1991. LNCS, vol. 575, pp. 255–265. Springer, Heidelberg (1992). doi:10.1007/3-540-55179-4_25
7. D'silva, V.: Widening for automata. Diploma thesis, Institut Für Informatik, Universität Zürich (2006)
8. Gold, E.M.: Complexity of automaton identification from given data. Inf. Control **37**(3), 302–320 (1978)
9. Gupta, A., McMillan, K.L., Fu, Z.: Automated assumption generation for compositional verification. Formal Methods Syst. Des. **32**(3), 285–301 (2008)
10. Luchaup, D., Carli, L.D., Jha, S., Bach, E.: Deep packet inspection with DFA-trees and parametrized language overapproximation. In: 2014 IEEE Conference on Computer Communications, INFOCOM, pp. 531–539. IEEE (2014)
11. Moore, E.F.: Gedanken-experiments on sequential machines. In: Shannon, C., McCarthy, J. (eds.) Automata Studies, pp. 129–153. Princeton University Press, Princeton (1956)
12. Neider, D.: Computing minimal separating DFAs and regular invariants using SAT and SMT solvers. In: Chakraborty, S., Mukund, M. (eds.) ATVA 2012. LNCS, pp. 354–369. Springer, Heidelberg (2012). doi:10.1007/978-3-642-33386-6_28

13. Nethercote, N., Stuckey, P.J., Becket, R., Brand, S., Duck, G.J., Tack, G.: MiniZinc: towards a standard CP modelling language. In: Bessière, C. (ed.) CP 2007. LNCS, vol. 4741, pp. 529–543. Springer, Heidelberg (2007). doi:10.1007/978-3-540-74970-7_38
14. Rabin, M.O., Scott, D.: Finite automata and their decision problem. IBM J. Res. Dev. **3**, 114–125 (1959)

An Equivalence Checking Framework for Array-Intensive Programs

Kunal Banerjee[1,2(✉)], Chittaranjan Mandal[1], and Dipankar Sarkar[1]

[1] Department of Computer Science and Engineering,
Indian Institute of Technology Kharagpur, Kharagpur, India
{kunalb,chitta,ds}@cse.iitkgp.ernet.in
[2] Intel Labs, Bangalore, India

Abstract. Array-intensive programs often undergo extensive loop transformations and arithmetic transformations during code optimization. Accordingly, translation validation of array-intensive programs requires manipulation of intervals of integers (representing domains of array indices) and relations over such intervals to account for loop transformations and simplification of arithmetic expressions to handle arithmetic transformations. Translation validation becomes more challenging in the presence of recurrences because recurrences lead to cycles in the data-dependence graph of a program which make dependence analyses and simplifications (through closed-form representations) of the data transformations difficult. To address the problem of translation validation of array-intensive programs, we have developed an equivalence checking framework, where both the original program and the optimized program are modeled as array data-dependence graphs (ADDGs), that can handle loop and arithmetic transformations along with most of the recurrences.

Keywords: Translation validation · Equivalence checking · Loop transformations · Arithmetic transformations · Recurrence · Array data-dependence graph (ADDG)

1 Introduction

Compiler optimizations targeting better performance in terms of energy, area and/or execution time typically involve extensive applications of loop transformations together with arithmetic transformations for array-intensive programs [3,4,14]. Although effective translation validation techniques exist for programs involving scalar variables [1,7,8], verification of array-intensive programs and accompanying loop transformations requires more complex data-flow analyses. Loop transformations essentially involve partitioning/unifying the index spaces of arrays. Figure 1 shows two programs before and after application of loop fusion and tiling transformations; moreover, the temporary array `T` in Fig. 1(a) has been removed in Fig. 1(b) and the definition of array `Out` has been altered *appropriately*. Specifically, two nested loops in the original program are

D. D'Souza and K. Narayan Kumar (Eds.): ATVA 2017, LNCS 10482, pp. 84–90, 2017.
DOI: 10.1007/978-3-319-68167-2_6

fused into one and then the 8×8 index space of $\langle i, j \rangle$ is covered hierarchically along 4×4 tiles by the outer loop iterators $\langle l1, l2 \rangle$, each tile having 2×2 elements covered by the inner loop iterators $\langle l3, l4 \rangle$; the definition of the array Out in Fig. 1(b) is obtained from that of Fig. 1(a) by substituting for the array T and applying the distributive property of multiplication over addition. Clearly, establishing equivalence/non-equivalence of the two programs shown in Fig. 1 calls for an (elaborate) analysis of the index spaces of the involved arrays and the ability to handle arithmetic transformations.

```
for(i = 0; i <= 7; i++) {
 for(j = 0; j <= 7; j++) {
  T[i+1][j+1] = f(In[i][j]) + 2;
} }
for(i = 0; i <= 7; i++) {
 for(j = 0; j <= 7; j++) {
  Out[i][j] = T[i+1][j+1] * 2;
} }
```

(a) Original program.

```
for(l1 = 0; l1 <= 3; l1++) {
 for(l2 = 0; l2 <= 3; l2++) {
  for(l3 = 0; l3 <= 1; l3++) {
   for(l4 = 0; l4 <= 1; l4++) {
    i = 2*l1 + l3;
    j = 2*l2 + l4;
    Out[i][j] = 2*f(In[i][j]) + 4;
} } } }
```

(b) Transformed program.

Fig. 1. Two programs before and after loop and arithmetic transformations.

An array data-dependence graph (ADDG) based equivalence checking method has been proposed by Shashidhar et al. in [10] which is capable of verifying many loop transformations without requiring any supplementary information from the compiler. Another data dependence graph based method has been proposed by Verdoolaege et al. in [12, 13] that can additionally handle recurrences. However, none of these methods [10, 12, 13] can handle arithmetic transformations, such as distributive transformations, common sub-expression elimination, arithmetic expression simplification, constant (un)folding. The ADDG based method described in [5, 6] has been shown to handle loop and arithmetic transformations. However, since recurrences lead to cycles in the data-dependence graph of a program which make dependence analyses and simplifications (through closed-form representations) of the data transformations difficult, the method of [5, 6], which basically relies on such simplification procedures, fails in the presence of recurrences. The work described in [2] presents a unified equivalence checking framework based on ADDGs to handle loop and arithmetic transformations along with recurrences. Specifically, the slice based ADDG equivalence checking framework [6] which handles loop and arithmetic transformations is extended in [2] so that recurrences are also handled. The tool presented in this paper is basically a product of our earlier works reported in [2, 5, 6].

The rest of the paper is organized as follows. An overview of our tool can be found in Sect. 2. A comprehensive evaluation of our tool and some relevant discussion on the same can be found in Sect. 3. The paper is concluded in Sect. 4.

2 Overview of the Tool

2.1 Overview

Our ADDG based equivalence checker for array-intensive programs has been implemented in C and the tool is available at https://github.com/kunalbanerjee/EquivalenceChecker_ADDG along with the benchmarks, installation and usage guidelines. The tool is an open source free software covered under GNU General Public License as published by the Free Software Foundation.

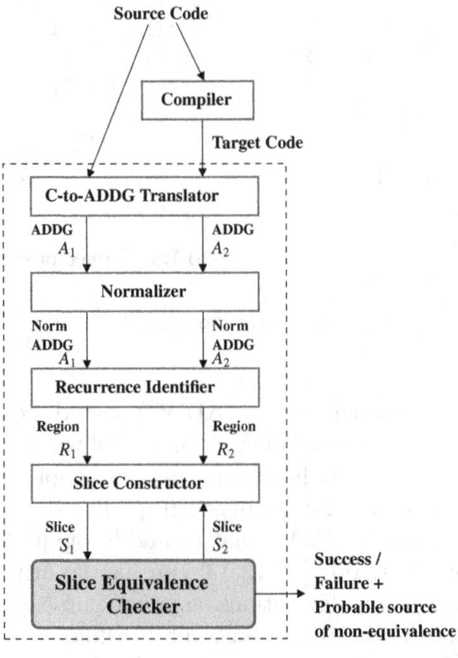

Fig. 2. Framework of the equivalence checker. (Color figure online)

The framework of the equivalence checker is shown in Fig. 2. The modules given in green boxes are integrated within our tool whereas, the box with blue color is external to it. Each of the modules shown in the figure are briefly described below.

1. **Compiler:** This module takes a *source code* as input and produces an optimized version of it known as the *target code*; our objective is to ensure that the target code is bug-free by means of equivalence checking.
2. **C-to-ADDG Translator:** Since our equivalence checker works with ADDGs as inputs, we need this module to translate the source code and the target code into ADDGs. In case the source and/or the target languages of a compiler is something other than C, one will require a different translator; however, it

may be noted that deriving ADDG from any high-level language is easy and straightforward [9].

3. **Normalizer:** Unlike Boolean expressions, no canonical representation exists for expressions involving integers; so, we have developed a normalization technique for integer expressions as given in [1] for comparing such expressions. This module basically converts all operations occurring in the ADDGs A_1 and A_2 into their corresponding normalized forms.
4. **Recurrence identifier:** This module identifies recurrences in an ADDG which, in turn, involves identification of strongly connected components in a directed graph. Some intricacies entailed in recurrence identification has been underlined in [2]. Once the recurrences have been identified, an ADDG is divided into recurrence and non-recurrence regions.
5. **Slice Constructor:** This module constructs slices from each region in an ADDG and tries to pair them with corresponding slices in the other ADDG based on their input/output arrays and data transformations.
6. **Slice Equivalence Checker:** This module takes a slice S_1 from ADDG A_1 and its paired slice S_2 from ADDG A_2 and tries to establish equivalence between the two [2,6]. Since this module constitutes the primary difference from the earlier path based ADDG equivalence checking method [9,10] and the slice based equivalence checking method [2,6], it has been highlighted with gray color.

The output "success" signifies that the two ADDGs are equivalent; in case of a "failure", the probable source of inconsistency (basically, non-equivalent slices in the ADDGs being compared) is outputted. Note that the ADDG based equivalence checking method has been proven to be sound [2] but not complete, i.e., when the checker outputs "success" then the ADDGs (and the programs they represent) are indeed equivalent; however, a "failure" does not necessarily mean that the ADDGs are not equivalent and hence an inspection of the non-equivalent slices outputted may be needed.

2.2 Guidelines

Our tool requires the following softwares to be installed in the system prior to its deployment: *gcc, flex, bison* and *Integer Set Library* [11]; note that all these softwares come for free. Once all the pre-requisite softwares have been installed, one can install our tool using the following command:

```
$ make
```

And run the tool using the following command:

```
$ ./bin/eqChkAddg program1.c program2.c
```

3 Evaluation and Discussion

As mentioned in the Introduction section, loop and arithmetic transformations have been successfully applied to reduce execution time and/or save critical resources in various domains, especially in the areas of multimedia and signal processing. Consequently, codes optimized using the aforementioned transformations may be found in softwares running in safety critical applications or in brand sensitive products on account of which it is extremely important to ascertain that design optimizations do not lead to introduction of errors. So, we tested our tool on several benchmarks from several fields, which primarily included applications from signal processing and multimedia domains [2,6]. Note that the correctness and the complexity issues of the method have been formally treated in [2].

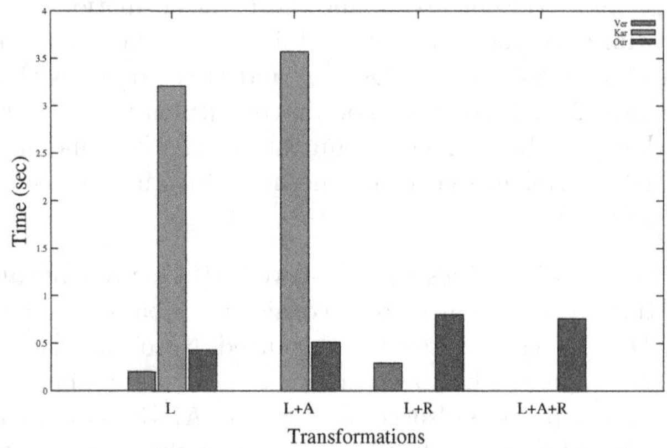

Fig. 3. Average run times for different transformations. (Color figure online)

To validate that our ADDG based equivalence checker [Our] is superior to that of the work reported in [6] [Kar] and to that of another competing method [13] [Ver], we compared our tool with those of [6,13] for several benchmarks undergoing different types of transformations. The average run times taken by the tools of [6,13] and ours have been shown in red, green and blue colors, respectively, in Fig. 3. Note that all the tools succeeded in showing equivalence for benchmarks which involved only loop transformations (denoted by 'L' in Fig. 3); the tool of [13] failed to establish equivalence for benchmarks which contained arithmetic transformations as well (denoted by 'L + A'); the tool of [6] failed for benchmarks which involved loop transformations along with recurrences (denoted by 'L + R') and both the tools of [6,13] failed for benchmarks which involved both arithmetic transformations and recurrences (denoted by 'L + A + R'); our current tool succeeded in showing equivalence in all these cases. Although a comparative analysis with the method of [9] would have also been relevant, we could not furnish it since their tool is not available to us.

To find out the set of loop transformations and arithmetic transformations supported by our tool, the readers are referred to [6]. A pertinent point to note is that although our tool outperforms that of [6] with respect to execution time whenever both the tools are able to establish equivalence, the tool of [13] takes about 2.4 times less execution time on average than that of ours whenever it is successful – this is probably because our tool invokes ISL [11] through system call and communicates with it via reading and writing to files whereas, ISL comes as an integrated package within [13] itself and hence it is faster. The details of these experiments have been reported in [2]. Note that the run times given here have been obtained by executing the test cases on a 2.0 GHz Intel® Core™2 Duo machine.

In another set of experiments, we manually injected data computation errors and/or wrongly wrote the loop iterators to enforce erroneous loop boundary calculations in order to check the efficacy of the equivalence checker in detecting incorrect code transformations. Our equivalence checker reported *failure* in all these cases and correctly identified the subgraphs of the ADDGs where the errors had been injected.

4 Conclusion

Translation validation is a crucial step in software development because it prevents faulty code optimizations from proliferating as software bugs. Accordingly, we have developed an equivalence checking framework which represents both the original and the translated versions of an array-intensive program as ADDGs. The experiments carried out using our tool attest to its robustness by handling various loop and arithmetic transformations even in the presence of recurrences as reported in [2,5,6]. Our tool is an open source free software that can be installed and operated easily. Enhancing the present method to handle co-induction (mutual recurrence) and nested recurrence remain as our future goals.

Acknowledgment. The authors would like to acknowledge Chandan Karfa, currently at IIT Guwahati, for his useful insights during the formulation of this work. The work of K. Banerjee was supported by TCS Research Fellowship. This work was also funded by DST Project No: SB/EMEQ-281/2013.

References

1. Banerjee, K., Karfa, C., Sarkar, D., Mandal, C.: Verification of code motion techniques using value propagation. IEEE Trans. CAD ICS **33**(8), 1180–1193 (2014)
2. Banerjee, K., Mandal, C., Sarkar, D.: Translation validation of loop and arithmetic transformations in the presence of recurrences. In: LCTES, pp. 31–40 (2016)
3. Bouchebaba, Y., Girodias, B., Nicolescu, G., Aboulhamid, E.M., Lavigueur, B., Paulin, P.G.: MPSoC memory optimization using program transformation. ACM Trans. Design Autom. Electron. Syst. **12**(4), 43 (2007)

4. Kadayif, I., Kandemir, M.T., Chen, G., Ozturk, O., Karaköy, M., Sezer, U.: Optimizing array-intensive applications for on-chip multiprocessors. IEEE Trans. Parallel Distrib. Syst. **16**(5), 396–411 (2005)
5. Karfa, C., Banerjee, K., Sarkar, D., Mandal, C.: Equivalence checking of array-intensive programs. In: ISVLSI, pp. 156–161 (2011)
6. Karfa, C., Banerjee, K., Sarkar, D., Mandal, C.: Verification of loop and arithmetic transformations of array-intensive behaviours. IEEE Trans. CAD ICS **32**(11), 1787–1800 (2013)
7. Karfa, C., Sarkar, D., Mandal, C.: Verification of datapath and controller generation phase in high-level synthesis of digital circuits. IEEE Trans. CAD ICS **29**(3), 479–492 (2010)
8. Kundu, S., Lerner, S., Gupta, R.: Translation validation of high-level synthesis. IEEE Trans. CAD ICS **29**(4), 566–579 (2010)
9. Shashidhar, K.C.: Efficient automatic verification of loop and data-flow transformations by functional equivalence checking. Ph.D. thesis, Katholieke Universiteit Leuven (2008)
10. Shashidhar, K.C., Bruynooghe, M., Catthoor, F., Janssens, G.: Functional equivalence checking for verification of algebraic transformations on array-intensive source code. In: DATE, pp. 1310–1315 (2005)
11. Verdoolaege, S.: *isl*: an integer set library for the polyhedral model. In: Fukuda, K., van der Hoeven, J., Joswig, M., Takayama, N. (eds.) ICMS 2010. LNCS, vol. 6327, pp. 299–302. Springer, Heidelberg (2010). doi:10.1007/978-3-642-15582-6_49
12. Verdoolaege, S., Janssens, G., Bruynooghe, M.: Equivalence checking of static affine programs using widening to handle recurrences. In: Bouajjani, A., Maler, O. (eds.) CAV 2009. LNCS, vol. 5643, pp. 599–613. Springer, Heidelberg (2009). doi:10.1007/978-3-642-02658-4_44
13. Verdoolaege, S., Janssens, G., Bruynooghe, M.: Equivalence checking of static affine programs using widening to handle recurrences. ACM Trans. Program. Lang. Syst. **34**(3), 11 (2012)
14. Zory, J., Coelho, F.: Using algebraic transformations to optimize expression evaluation in scientific codes. In: IEEE PACT, pp. 376–384 (1998)

Loop Quasi-Invariant Chunk Detection

Jean-Yves Moyen[1(✉)], Thomas Rubiano[1,2(✉)], and Thomas Seiller[1(✉)]

[1] Department of Computer Science, University of Copenhagen (DIKU), Copenhagen, Denmark
{moyen,rubiano}@lipn.univ-paris13.fr, seiller@lipn.fr
[2] LIPN, Université Paris 13, Paris, France

Abstract. Several techniques for analysis and transformations are used in compilers. Among them, the peeling of loops for hoisting quasi-invariants can be used to optimize generated code, or simply ease developers' lives. In this paper, we introduce a new concept of dependency analysis borrowed from the field of Implicit Computational Complexity (ICC), allowing to work with composed statements called "Chunks" to detect more quasi-invariants. Based on an optimization idea given on a `WHILE` language, we provide a transformation method - reusing ICC concepts and techniques [8,10] - to compilers. This new analysis computes an invariance degree for each statement or chunks of statements by building a new kind of dependency graph, finds the "maximum" or "worst" dependency graph for loops, and recognizes if an entire block is Quasi-Invariant or not. This block could be an inner loop, and in that case the computational complexity of the overall program can be decreased.

In this paper, we introduce the theory around this concept and present a prototype analysis pass implemented on LLVM. We already implemented a proof of concept on a toy C parser (https://github.com/ThomasRuby/LQICM_On_C_Toy_Parser) analysing and transforming the AST representation. In a very near future, we will implement the corresponding transformation within our prototype LLVM pass and provide benchmarks comparisons.

Keywords: Static analysis · Transformations · Optimization · Compilers · Loop invariants · Complexity · Quasi-invariants

1 Introduction

A compiler turns some high-level program into a (semantically) equivalent low-level assembly program. This translation implies many smaller transformations, notably because features such as objects, exceptions, or even loops need to be

J.-Y. Moyen is supported by the European Commision's Marie Skłodowska-Curie Individual Fellowship (H2020-MSCA-IF-2014) 655222 - Walgo; T. Rubiano is supported by the ANR project "Elica" ANR-14-CE25-0005; T. Seiller is supported by the European Commision's Marie Skłodowska-Curie Individual Fellowship (H2020-MSCA-IF-2014) 659920 - ReACT.

D. D'Souza and K. Narayan Kumar (Eds.): ATVA 2017, LNCS 10482, pp. 91–108, 2017.
DOI: 10.1007/978-3-319-68167-2_7

expressed in assembly language. The compiler also performs many optimisations aiming at making the code more efficient. These are often needed to streamline the code generated by the transformations but can also be used to optimise the source code.

A command inside a loop is *loop invariant code* if its execution has no effect after the first iteration of the loop. Typically, an assignment `x:=0` in a loop is invariant (provided `x` is not modified elsewhere). Loop invariants can safely be moved out of loops (*hoisted*) in order to make the program run slightly faster.

While loop invariant code is maybe not so frequent in source code, many transformations along the compilation process can generate some. For example, when compiling the editors `vim` or `emacs`, an average of 10 commands per loop can be hoisted. These are mostly generated by other optimisations.

A command inside a loop is *quasi-invariant* if its execution has no effect after a finite number of iterations of the loop. Typically, if a loop contains the sequence `x:=y; y:=0`, then `y:=0` is invariant. However, `x:=y` is **not** invariant. The first time the loop is executed, `x` will be assigned the old value of `y`, and only from the second time onward will `x` be assigned the value `0`. Hence, this command is *quasi-invariant.* It can still be hoisted out of the loop, but to do so requires to *peel* the loop first, that is execute its body once (by copying it before the loop). The number of times a loop must be executed before a quasi-invariant can be hoisted is called here the *degree* of the invariant.

An obvious way to detect quasi-invariants is to first detect invariants (that is, quasi-invariants of degree 1) and hoist them; and iterate the process to find quasi-invariant of degree 2, and so on. This is, however, not very efficient since it may require a large number of iterations to find some invariance degrees.

We provide here an analysis able to directly detect the invariance degree of any statements in the loop. Moreover, our analysis is able to assign an invariance degree not only to individual statements but also to groups of statements (called *chuncks*). That way it is possible, for example, to detect that a whole inner loop is invariant and hoist it, thus decreasing the asymptotic complexity of the program.

This analysis and transformation has first been implemented as a *Proof of Concept* in a toy C-parser. Next, the analysis has been implemented as a prototype *pass* of the mainstream compiler LLVM and the transformation is under way. The prototype is currently unable to handle several common situations (and leave them untouched) because of choices made for the sake of simplicity. It is, nonetheless, powerful enough to make significant progress compared to the existing loop invariant code motion techniques (it can handle many more cases).

Loop optimization techniques based on quasi-invariance are well-known in the compilers community. The transformation idea is to peel loops a finite number of time and hoist invariants until there are no more quasi-invariants. As far as we know, this technique is called "peeling" and it was introduced by Song *et al.* [16].

Loop peeling and unrolling can also happen for entirely different reasons, mostly to optimise pipelines. In these cases, the decision to unroll is based on loop size and (predicted) number of iterations but not on the presence of quasi-invariants. It may, of course, happen that quasi-invariant removal is performed as a side effect of this unrolling, but only as a side effect and not as the main goal.

The present paper offers a new point of view on invariant and quasi-invariant detection. Adapting ideas from an optimization on a `WHILE` language by Lars Kristiansen [8], we provide a way to compute invariance degrees based on techniques developed in the field of Implicit Computational Complexity.

Implicit Computational Complexity (ICC) studies computational complexity using restrictions of languages and computational principles, providing results that do not depend on specific machine models. Based on static analysis, it helps predict and control resources consumed by programs, and can offer reusable and tunable ideas and techniques for compilers. ICC mainly focuses on syntactic [3,4], type [2,6] and Data Flow [7,9,12,13] restrictions to provide bounds on programs' complexity. The present work was mainly inspired by the way ICC community uses different concepts to perform Data Flow Analysis, e.g. "Size-change Graphs" [12] or "Resource Control Graphs" [13] which track data values' behavior and uses a matrix notation inspired by [1], or "mwp-polynomials" [9] to provide bounds on data size.

For our analysis, we focus on dependencies between variables to detect invariance. Dependency graphs [10] can have different types of arcs representing different kind of dependencies. Here we will use a kind of Dependence Graph Abstraction [5] that can be used to find local and global quasi-invariants. Based on these techniques, we developed an analysis pass and we will implement the corresponding transformation in LLVM.

We propose a tool which is notably able to give enough information to easily peel and hoist an inner loop, thus automatically decreasing the complexity of a program from $O(n^2)$ to $O(n)$.

1.1 State of the Art on Quasi-Invariant Detection in Loop

Modern compilers find loop invariant code by recursively searching for variables whose value only depends on either code that is outside the loop; or other loop invariant code. To our knowledge, no compiler searches for loop quasi-invariant code.

A quasi-invariance detection has been described in [16]. The authors define a *variable dependency graph* (VDG) and detect a loop quasi-invariant variable `x` if, among all paths ending at `x`, no path contain a node included in a circular path. Then they deduce an *invariant length* which corresponds to the length of the longest path ending in `x`. To our knowledge, this analysis has not been implemented in a compiler. Moreover, they only analyse individual commands and do not handle chunks. In the present paper, this *length* is called *invariance degree*.

1.2 Contributions

This paper lies between the fields of Implicit Computational Complexity and Compilation and provides significant advancement to both.

To the authors' knowledge, this is the first application of ICC techniques on a mainstream compiler. One interest is that our tool potentially applies to programs written in any programming language managed by LLVM. Moreover, this work should be considered as a first step of a larger project that will make ICC techniques more accessible to programmers. Thus, we show that 25 years after Bellantoni and Cook breakthrough [3], ICC techniques are ready to move into "the real world".

On a more technical side, our tool aims at improving on currently implemented loop invariant detection and optimization techniques. The main LLVM tool for this purpose, the Loop Invariant Code Motion pass (LICM), does not detect quasi-invariant of degree more than 3 (and not all of those of degree 2). More importantly, LICM will not detect quasi-invariant chunks, such as whole loops. Our tool, on the other hand, detects quasi-invariants of arbitrary degree and is able to deal with chunks. For instance the optimization shown in Fig. 6 is performed neither by LLVM nor by GCC even at their maximum optimization level.

2 Data Flow Graphs

In this section, we sketch the main lines of the theory of *data flow graphs*. While in later sections we will only be studying a specific case of those, the theory is quite general and pinpoints to formal links with various works on static analysis [1,9,12] and semantics [11,14,15].

Here data flow graphs are used to represent (weighted) relations between variables, that is relations that carry some additional information represented by elements of a *semi-ring*. In the next section, for instance, the semi-ring[1] $(\{0, 1, \infty\}, \max, \times)$ will be used to represent various kinds of dependencies between variables. Consequently, all examples will be given with this specific choice of semi-ring.

2.1 Definition of Data Flow Graphs

We will work with a simple imperative `WHILE`-language, with semantics similar to `C`. The grammar is given by:

$$
\begin{array}{lll}
\text{(Variables)} & X & ::= X_1 \mid X_2 \mid X_3 \mid \ldots \mid X_n \\
\text{(Expression)} & exp & ::= X \mid \texttt{op(}exp, \ldots, exp\texttt{)} \\
\text{(Command)} & com & ::= X = exp \mid com;com \mid \texttt{skip} \mid \texttt{while}\ exp\ \texttt{do}\ com\ \texttt{od} \mid \\
 & & \quad \texttt{if}\ exp\ \texttt{then}\ com\ \texttt{else}\ com\ \texttt{fi} \mid \texttt{use(}X_1, \ldots, X_n\texttt{)}
\end{array}
$$

A `WHILE` program is thus a sequence of statements, each statement being either an *assignment*, a *conditional*, a *while* loop, a *function call* or a *skip*. The

[1] The convention here is that $0 \times \infty = 0$.

use command represents any command which does not modify its variables but use them and should not be moved around carelessly (typically, a `printf`). In practice, we currently treat all function calls as *use*, even if the function is pure. *Statements* are abstracted into *commands*. A *command* can be a statement or a sequence of commands. We also call a sequence of commands a *chunk*.

A data-flow graph for a given command C will be a weighted relation on the set V of variables involved in C. Formally, this can be represented as a matrix over a semi-ring, with the implicit choice of a denumeration of the set V. We now fix, until the end of this section, an arbitrary semi-ring $(\mathcal{S}, +, \times)$.

Definition 1. *A* Data Flow Graph *(*DFG*) for a command* C *is a $n \times n$ matrix over the semi-ring $(\mathcal{S}, +, \times)$ where n is the number of variables involved in* C.

We write M(C) *the* DFG *of* C.

For technical reasons, we identify the DFG of a command C with any embedding of M(C) in a larger matrix. I.e. we will abusively call the DFG of C any matrix of the form

$$\begin{pmatrix} \mathrm{M}(\mathtt{C}) & 0 \\ 0 & \mathrm{Id} \end{pmatrix},$$

implicitly viewing the additional rows/columns as variables that do not appear in C.

In all examples, we will be using weighted relations, or weighted bi-partite graphs, to illustrate these matrices. We leave it to the reader to convince herself that these matrices and graphs are in one-to-one correspondence. Moreover, all examples will be based on the semi-ring $(\{0, 1, \infty\}, \max, \times)$, since it is the specific case that will be under study in later sections: it will be used to represent dependencies: 0 will represent *reinitialization*, 1 will represent *propagation*, and ∞ will represent *dependence*. Figure 1 introduces both these notions and the graphical convention used throughout this paper.

Graphically, dependencies are represented by two types of arrows from variables on the left to variables on the right: plain arrows for *direct dependency*, dashed arrows for *propagation*. *Reinitialisation* of a variable z then corresponds to the absence of arrows ending on the right occurrence of z. Figure 1 illustrates these types of dependencies; let us stress here that the DFG would be the same if the assignment $y = y$; were to be removed[2] from C since the value of y is still

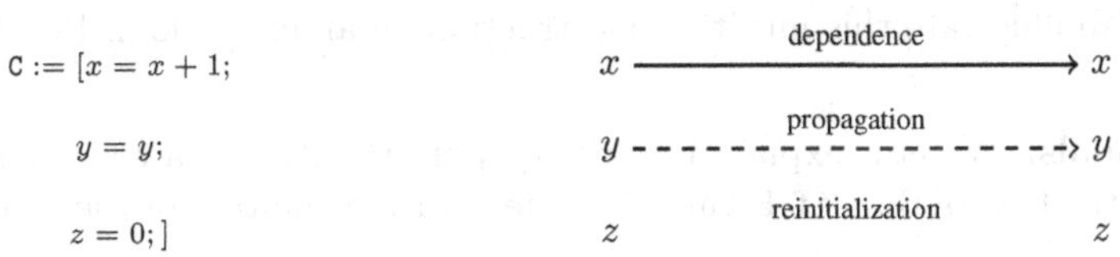

Fig. 1. Types of dependence

[2] Note that $y = y$; does not create a direct dependence.

propagated. Finally $x = x + 1$ can be seen as $x_r = x_l + 1$[3] where x_r depends directly on x_l.

For convenience we define, given a command C, the following two sets of variables.

Definition 2. *Let* C *be a command. We define* In(C) *(resp.* Out(C)*) as the set of variables* used *(resp.* modified*) by* C.

Note that in the case of dependencies, In(C) is exactly the set of variables that are source of a "dependence" arrow, while Out(C) is the set of variables that either are targets of dependence arrows or were reinitialised.

2.2 Constructing DFGs

We now describe how the DFG of a command can be computed by induction on the structure of the command. Base cases (skip, use and assignment) should be defined depending on what the DFG will be used for. The DFG for assignments are obtained by straightforward generalisation of the cases shown in Fig. 1 (see also Sect. 3 for some more explanations). Next, define a variable e – standing for *effect* – not part of the language, and define:

- M(**skip**) as the "empty matrix" with 0 rows and columns[4];
- M(**use**($X_1, \ldots, X_n$)) as the matrix with coefficients from each X_i and e to e equal to ∞, and 0 coefficients otherwise.

Composition and Multipaths. We now turn to the definition of the DFG for a (sequential) *composition* of commands. This abstraction allows us to see a block of statements as one command with its own DFG.

Definition 3. *Let* C *be a sequence of commands* $[C_1; C_2; \ldots; C_n]$. *Then* M(C) *is defined as the matrix product* $M(C_1)M(C_2)\ldots M(C_n)$.

Following the usual product of matrices, the product of two matrices A, B is defined here as the matrix C with coefficients: $C_{i,j} = \sum_{k=1}^{n}(A_{i,k} \times B_{k,j})$.

It is standard that the product of matrices of weights of two graphs F, G represents a graph of length 2 paths. This operation of matrix multiplication corresponds to the computation of *multipaths* [12] in the graph representation of DFGs. We illustrate this intuitive construction on an example in Fig. 2.

Conditionals. We now explain how to compute the DFG of a conditional, i.e. we define the DFG of C := **if** E **then** C_1 **else** C_2; from the DFG of the commands C_1 and C_2.

---

[3] In SSA form.

[4] Up to the identification of the DFG with its embeddings, it is therefore the identity matrix of any size.

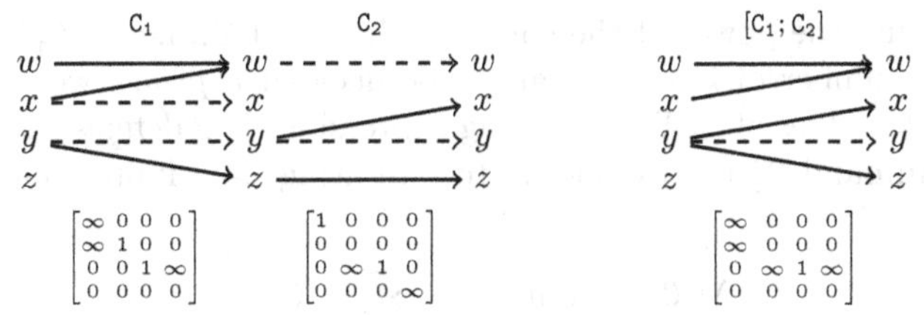

Fig. 2. DFG of composition. Here $\mathtt{C}_1 := [w = w + x; z = y + 2;]$ and $\mathtt{C}_2 := [x = y; z = z * 2;]$

Firstly, we need to take into account that both commands $\mathtt{C}_1$ and $\mathtt{C}_2$ may be executed. In that case, the overall command C should be represented by the sum $\mathrm{M}(\mathtt{C}_1) + \mathrm{M}(\mathtt{C}_2)$.

However, in most cases, it is not enough to consider $\mathrm{M}(\mathtt{C}_1) + \mathrm{M}(\mathtt{C}_2)$, and the DFG of the command C should be obtained by adding a *conditional correction* that may depend on the expressions E and C. This correction will here be written as $\mathcal{C}^{\mathtt{C}}(\mathtt{E})$.

In the case of dependencies, we can notice that all modified variables in $\mathtt{C}_1$ and $\mathtt{C}_2$ should depend on the variables used in E. Denoting E the vector representing variables in[5] Var(E), O the vector representing variables in $\mathrm{Out}(\mathtt{C}_1) \cup \mathrm{Out}(\mathtt{C}_2)$, and $(\cdot)^t$ the matrix transpose, we define $\mathcal{C}^{\mathtt{C}}(\mathtt{E}) = E^t O$. Figure 3 illustrates this on an example.

Definition 4. *Let* $\mathtt{C} = \mathtt{if\ E\ then\ C_1\ else\ C_2;}$. *Then* $\mathrm{M}(\mathtt{C}) = \mathrm{M}(\mathtt{C}_1) + \mathrm{M}(\mathtt{C}_2) + \mathcal{C}^{\mathtt{C}}(\mathtt{E})$.

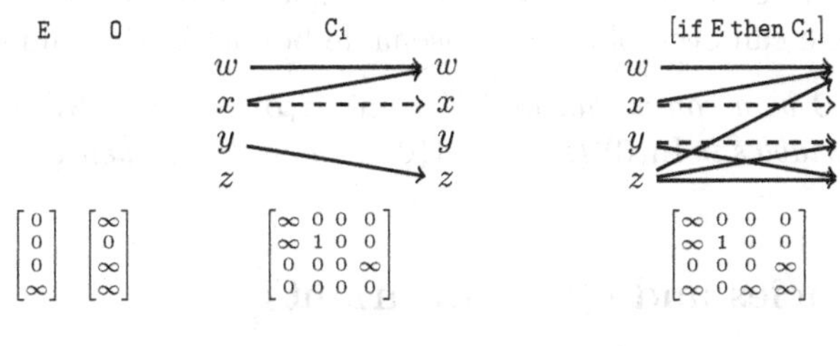

Fig. 3. DFG of conditional. Here $\mathtt{E} := z \geq 0$ and $\mathtt{C}_1 := [w = w + x; z = y + 2; y = 0;]$;

While Loops. Lastly, we define the DFG of a command $\mathtt{C} := \mathtt{while\ E\ do\ C_1;}$ from $\mathrm{M}(\mathtt{C}_1)$. First, we define a matrix $\mathrm{M}(\mathtt{C}_1^*)$ representing iterations of the command $\mathtt{C}_1$. Then, as for conditionals, we introduce a *loop correction* $\mathcal{L}^{\mathtt{C}}(\mathtt{E})$. In the case of dependencies, the loop correction and the conditional correction coincide: $\mathcal{L}^{\mathtt{C}}(\mathtt{E}) = \mathcal{C}^{\mathtt{C}}(\mathtt{E})$.

When considering iterations of $\mathtt{C}_1$, the first occurrence of $\mathtt{C}_1$ will influence the second one and so on. Computing the DFG of $\mathtt{C}_1^n$, the n-th iteration of $\mathtt{C}_1$,

[5] I.e. the vector with a coefficient equal to ∞ for the variables in Var(E), and 0 for all others variables.

is just computing the power of the corresponding matrix, i.e. $\mathrm{M}(\mathtt{C}_1^n) = \mathrm{M}(\mathtt{C}_1)^n$. But since the number of iteration cannot be decided *a priori*, we need to sum over all possible values of n. The following expression then defines the DFG of the (informal) command $\mathtt{C}_1^*$ corresponding to "iterating $\mathtt{C}_1$ a finite (but arbitrary) number of times":

$$\mathrm{M}(\mathtt{C}_1^*) = \mathrm{limit}_{k\to\infty} \sum_{i=1}^{k} \mathrm{M}(\mathtt{C}_1)^i$$

To ease notations, we note $\mathrm{M}(\mathtt{C}_1)^{(k)}$ the partial summations $\sum_{i=1}^{k} \mathrm{M}(\mathtt{C}_1)^i$. Figure 4 illustrate the computation of the DFG of a loop.

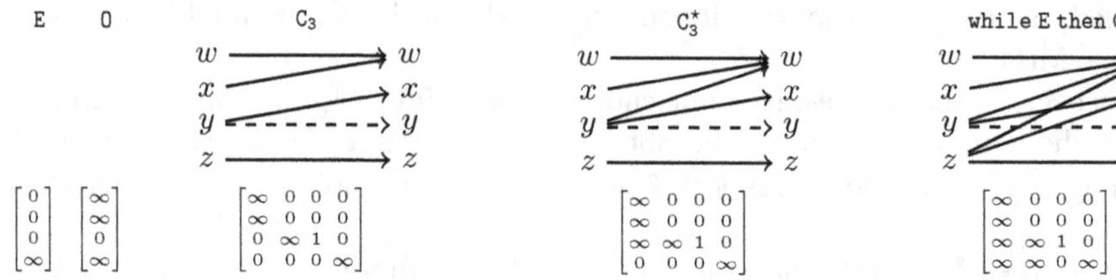

Fig. 4. DFG of while loop. Here $\mathtt{E} := z \leq 100$ and $\mathtt{C}_3 := [w = w + x; x = y; z = z + 1]$;

Definition 5. *Let* $\mathtt{C} = \mathtt{while\ E\ do\ C_1;}$. *Then* $\mathrm{M}(\mathtt{C}) = \mathrm{M}(\mathtt{C}_1^*) + \mathcal{L}^{\mathtt{C}}(\mathtt{E})$.

Note that $\mathrm{M}(\mathtt{C}^*)$ is not always defined (depending on the choice of semi-ring). In the case of the semiring $(\{0, 1, \infty\}, \max, \times)$, the set of all relations is finite and the sequence $(\mathrm{M}(\mathtt{C}_1)^{(k)})_{k\geqslant 0}$ is monotonic, hence this sequence is eventually constant. I.e., there exists a natural number N such that $\mathrm{M}(\mathtt{C}_1)^{(k)} = \mathrm{M}(\mathtt{C}_1)^{(N)}$ for all $k \geqslant N$. One can even obtain a reasonable bound on the value of N.

Lemma 1. *Let* $\mathtt{C}$ *be a command, and* $K = \min(i, o)$, *where* i *(resp.* o*) denotes the number of variables in* $\mathrm{In}(\mathtt{C})$ *(resp.* $\mathrm{Out}(\mathtt{C})$*). Then, the sequence* $(\mathrm{M}(\mathtt{C}^{(k)}))_{k\geqslant K}$ *is constant.*

3 Dependencies and Quasi-Invariants

We now study in more details the DFG representation of programs for the semiring $(\{0, 1, \infty\}, \max, \times)$. Each different weight represents different types of dependencies.

Each weight express how the values of the involved variables *after* the execution of the command depend on their values *before* the execution. There is a *direct* dependence between variables appearing in an expression and the variable on the left-hand side of the assignment. For instance x directly depends on y and z in the statement $x = y + z;$. When variables are unchanged by the command we call it *propagation*; this includes statements such as $x = x;$. Propagation only happens when a variable is not affected by the command, not when it is copied from another variable. If the variable is set to a constant, we call this a *reinitialization*.

3.1 Invariance Degree

We now explain how, based on the computation of DFGs, we are able to define a notion of *dependence degree* for commands within a `while` loop. Based on this notion of degree, we show how the loop can be optimised by *peeling* it in order to extract all quasi-invariant commands, reducing the overall complexity while preserving the semantics.

Before going into details, the reader should be aware that the studied transformation applied on arbitrary `WHILE` programs gives rise to non-trivial renaming issues; in particular when a peeled conditional changes the value of a reused variable (we give an intuition of that in Sect. 4.1). To simplify the exposition while being able to show an interesting example, we here introduce the *φ-function* that, at runtime, can choose the correct value of a variable depending on the path just taken. *φ-functions* are a standard tool of compilation, used when the code is set in *SSA form* (see Subsect. 4.2). Thus, we do not delve into details concerning how they precisely work and assume some sort of "black box" able to select the correct value. Figure 5 shows the dependency graph of a small program.

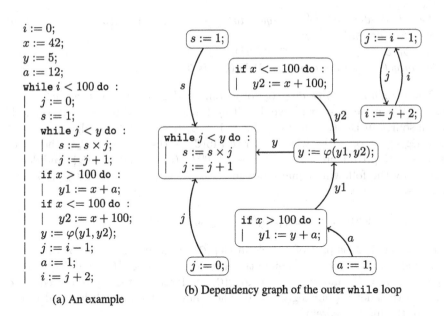

```
i := 0;
x := 42;
y := 5;
a := 12;
while i < 100 do :
|  j := 0;
|  s := 1;
|  while j < y do :
|  |  s := s × j;
|  |  j := j + 1;
|  if x > 100 do :
|  |  y1 := x + a;
|  if x <= 100 do :
|  |  y2 := x + 100;
|  y := φ(y1, y2);
|  j := i − 1;
|  a := 1;
|  i := j + 2;
```

(a) An example

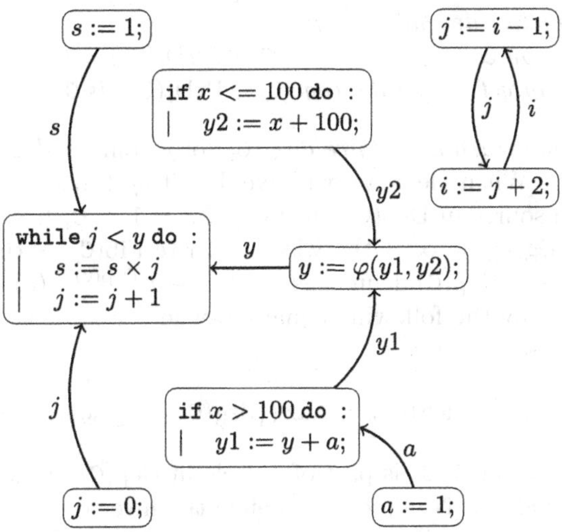

(b) Dependency graph of the outer `while` loop

Fig. 5. Exemple of dependency graph

We now consider a loop $\mathtt{C} := \mathtt{while}\ \mathtt{E}\ \mathtt{do}\ [\mathtt{C_1}; \mathtt{C_2}; \ldots, \mathtt{C_n}]$. We will build a *dependence graph* Dep(C) from the information given by the DFGs.

We will define the subset of *principal dependences* of the command $\mathtt{C_m}$ w.r.t. a given variable i. Intuitively, this principal dependence is the last command preceding $\mathtt{C_m}$ which modified the value of the variable i. However, since `while` and `if` commands may be skipped, we have to consider several main dependences in general. Based on this, we will then build the *dependence graph* which simply consists in writing the principal dependences of each command.

First, we introduce some notations. Given a variable i, we define the set $i^{\prec}$ as $\{\mathtt{C_k} \mid i \in \mathrm{Out}(\mathtt{C_k})\}$, the set of command modifying variable i. Given a command $\mathtt{C_m}$ and a variable $i \in \mathrm{In}(\mathtt{C_m})$, we denote as $\mathrm{PrD}_i(\mathtt{C_m})$ the subset of $i^{\prec}$ – the *use-def chain* over our ordered commands – defined as follows:

- it contains the *smallest* element of $i^{\prec}$ w.r.t. the order $<_m$ defined as

$$\mathtt{C_{m-1}} <_m \mathtt{C_{m-2}} <_m \cdots <_m \mathtt{C_1} <_m \mathtt{C_n} <_m \mathtt{C_{n-1}} <_m \cdots <_m \mathtt{C_m};$$

- if it contains a command $\mathtt{C}_h$ which is either a `while` or `if`, it contains the next element of $i^{\prec}$ w.r.t. the order $<_m$.

Definition 6. *Let* $\mathtt{C} := \mathtt{while\ E\ do}\ [\mathtt{C_1}; \mathtt{C_2}; \ldots, \mathtt{C_n}]$ *be a command. We define the directed graph* $\mathrm{Dep}(\mathtt{C})$ *as follows:*

- *the set of vertices* $V^{\mathrm{Dep}(\mathtt{C})}$ *is equal to* $\{\mathtt{C_1}, \ldots, \mathtt{C_n}\}$ *(the set of commands in the loop);*
- *the set of edges* $E^{\mathrm{Dep}(\mathtt{C})}$ *is equal to* $\biguplus_{m=1}^{n} \biguplus_{i \in \mathrm{In}(\mathtt{C_m})} \mathrm{PrD}_i(\mathtt{C_m})$ *(the set of all principal dependencies);*
- *the source* $s(i)$ *of the edge* $\mathtt{C_k} \in \mathrm{PrD}_i(\mathtt{C_m})$ *is* $\mathtt{C_k}$*;*
- *the target* $t(i)$ *of the edge* $\mathtt{C_k} \in \mathrm{PrD}_i(\mathtt{C_m})$ *is* $\mathtt{C_m}$*.*

The *invariance degree* $\deg_{\mathtt{C}}(\mathtt{C_m})$ of a command $\mathtt{C_m}$ w.r.t. $\mathtt{C}$ is then defined as follows. When clear, we will avoid writing the subscript $\mathtt{C}$ to ease notations. If $\mathtt{C_m}$ is a source in $\mathrm{Dep}(\mathtt{C})$, then $\deg(\mathtt{C_m}) = 1$. If $\mathtt{C_m}$ has a reflective edge in $\mathrm{Dep}(\mathtt{C})$, then $\deg(\mathtt{C_m}) = \infty$. Otherwise, we write $\mathrm{Fib}(\mathtt{C_m})$ – the *fiber* over $\mathtt{C_m}$ – the set of vertices in $\mathrm{Dep}(\mathtt{C})$ defined as $\{\mathtt{C_k} \mid \exists e \in E^{\mathrm{Dep}(\mathtt{C})}, s(e) = \mathtt{C_k}, t(e) = \mathtt{C_m}\}$, and define $\deg(\mathtt{C_m})$ by the following equation, where $\chi_{>m}(i) = 1$ if $i > m$ and $\chi_{>m}(i) = 0$ otherwise:

$$\deg(\mathtt{C_m}) = \max\left(\{\deg(\mathtt{C_i}) + \chi_{>m}(i) \mid \mathtt{C_i} \in \mathrm{Fib}(\mathtt{C_m})\}\right)$$

In particular, if $\mathtt{C_m}$ is part of a cycle in $\mathrm{Dep}(\mathtt{C})$, its degree is equal to ∞.

For all $i \in \mathbf{N} \cup \{\infty\}$, we define the inverse image $\deg^{-1}(\mathtt{i})$, i.e. $\deg^{-1}(\mathtt{i}) = \{\mathtt{C_k} \mid \deg(\mathtt{C})_k = i\}$, and we note $\mathrm{maxdeg}(\mathtt{C})$ the largest integer (i.e. not equal to ∞) such that $\deg^{-1}(\mathrm{maxdeg}(\mathtt{C})) \neq \emptyset$. The following lemma will be used in the proof of the main theorem.

Lemma 2. *Consider the set* $\deg^{-1}(\mathtt{i})$ *for an integer* $i > 0$ *and the relation induced from the dependency graph, i.e.* $\mathtt{C_i} \to \mathtt{C_j}$ *if and only if there is a sequence of edges from* $\mathtt{C_i}$ *to* $\mathtt{C_j}$ *in* $\mathrm{Dep}(\mathtt{C})$*. Then* $(\deg^{-1}(\mathtt{i}), \to)$ *is a partial order.*

Proof. It is clear that $\to$ is transitive and reflexive. We only need to show that it is antisymmetric. I.e. that there are no two commands $\mathtt{C_i}, \mathtt{C_j}$ such that $\mathtt{C_i} \to \mathtt{C_j}$ and $\mathtt{C_j} \to \mathtt{C_i}$. We suppose that two such commands can be found and show it leads to a contradiction. Indeed, if such a situation arises, it means that the dependency graph contains a cycle $\mathtt{P_1}, \dots, \mathtt{P_k}$ with $\mathtt{P_1} = \mathtt{P_k} = \mathtt{C_i}$. By definition of the degree, one has $\deg(\mathtt{P_{i+1}}) \geqslant \deg(\mathtt{P_i})$. More to the point, one has $\deg(\mathtt{P_{i+1}}) > \deg(\mathtt{P_i})$ as long as $\mathtt{P_i} = \mathtt{C_k}$ and $\mathtt{P_{i+1}} = \mathtt{C_h}$ with $k > h$. Now, it is clear that one of the inequalities $\deg(\mathtt{P_{i+1}}) \geqslant \deg(\mathtt{P_i})$ has to be strict, as no sequence $\mathtt{C_{i_1}}, \mathtt{C_{i_2}}, \dots, \mathtt{C_{i_k}}$ with $i_1 < i_2 < \dots < i_k$ can form a cycle. This implies that $\deg(\mathtt{C_i}) > \deg(\mathtt{C_i})$; a contradiction.

Based on the invariance degree, we will be able to *peel* loops. For this purpose, we define the following notation. Given a sequence of commands $[\mathtt{C_1}; \mathtt{C_2}; \dots; \mathtt{C_n}]$, we write $[\check{\mathtt{C_1}}; \check{\mathtt{C_2}}; \dots; \check{\mathtt{C_n}}]^{(i)}$ the subsequence in which all commands of degree strictly less than i are removed. We then define $\mathtt{if}^i = \mathtt{if\ E\ then}\ [\check{\mathtt{C_1}}; \check{\mathtt{C_2}}; \dots; \check{\mathtt{C_n}}]^{(i)}$, and $\mathtt{while}^i = \mathtt{while\ E\ then}\ [\check{\mathtt{C_1}}; \check{\mathtt{C_2}}; \dots; \check{\mathtt{C_n}}]^{(i)}$. We can now state the main theorem of the paper, denoting by $[\![\mathtt{C}]\!]$ the semantics of the command C.

Theorem 1. *Let* $\mathtt{C} := \mathtt{while\ E\ do}\ [\mathtt{C_1}; \mathtt{C_2}; \dots, \mathtt{C_n}]$ *be a command. Then*

$$[\![\mathtt{C}]\!] \equiv [\![\mathtt{if}^1; \mathtt{if}^2; \dots; \mathtt{if}^{\mathrm{maxdeg}(\mathtt{C})}; \mathtt{while}^{\infty}]\!]$$

The proof of this theorem is based on an induction, using the following lemma.

Lemma 3. *Let* $\mathtt{C} := \mathtt{while\ E\ do}\ [\mathtt{C_1}; \mathtt{C_2}; \dots, \mathtt{C_n}]$, *and* $\mathtt{D} := \mathtt{if}^1; \mathtt{while}^2$. *Then* $[\![\mathtt{C}]\!] \equiv [\![\mathtt{D}]\!]$ *and for each command* $\mathtt{C_m}$ *appearing in* $\mathtt{while}^2$, $\deg_{\mathtt{C}}(\mathtt{C_m}) = \deg_{\mathtt{D}}(\mathtt{C_m}) + 1$.

Proof. We start by proving the claim that for each command $\mathtt{C_m}$ appearing in $\mathtt{while}^2$, $\deg_{\mathtt{C}}(\mathtt{C_m}) = \deg_{\mathtt{D}}(\mathtt{C_m}) + 1$. This is a consequence of the fact that the dependency graph Dep(D) is obtained from Dep(C) by removing all vertices $\mathtt{C_m}$ for commands $\mathtt{C_m}$ of degree 1, together with their outgoing edges. Note that this defines a well-formed graph since by definition of the degree, a command of degree 1 may only depend on commands which are themselves of degree 1 (i.e. edges of target $\mathtt{C_m}$ are removed as well). Now, it is clear from the definition of the dependence degree that $\deg_{\mathtt{C}}(\mathtt{C_m}) = \infty$ implies $\deg_{\mathtt{D}}(\mathtt{C_m}) = \infty$, and that if $\deg_{\mathtt{C}}(\mathtt{C_m})) = d$ the command $\mathtt{C_m}$ only depended commands of degree at most d. From Lemma 2 we can prove by induction that $\deg_{\mathtt{D}}(\mathtt{C_m}) = d - 1$.

Then, one should realise that commands of degree 1 are in fact invariants of the loop C. It is then clear that $[\![\mathtt{C}]\!] \equiv [\![\mathtt{D}]\!]$.

4 In Practice

In the previous section, we have seen that the transformation is possible from and to a WHILE-language. This section will progressively show that we can do it in real languages by introducing our implementations. First it will present our *proof of concept*[6] which does both analysis and propose a transformation from C to C. After we will explain how we implemented a prototype analysis in a mainstream compiler.

[6] https://github.com/ThomasRuby/LQICM_On_C_Toy_Parser.

4.1 Proof of Concept (PoC)

To easily and quickly integrate our transformation, we decided to use "pycparser"[7], a `C` parser written in `Python`. The principal interest was to simply get and manipulate an Abstract Syntax Tree. Using a "WhileVisitor" we list all nested `while`-loops, then, with a bottom-up strategy (the inner loop first), this tool analyses and transforms the code if an invariant or quasi-invariant is detected. The analysis is divided in two parts: the DFG construction and the invariance degree computation.

Analysis. The first part aims to list relations between statements. In this implementation we decided to define a relation object by one list of pairs (for the direct dependencies) and two sets (for the propagations and reinitializations) of variables. A relation is computed for each command using a top-down strategy following the dominance tree. The relations are composed when the corresponding command is a sequence of commands. As described previously, we compute the correction and the maximum relations possible for a `while` or `if` statement. With those relations, we compute an invariance degree for each statement in the loop regarding to the relations listed (Algorithm 1).

Peeling Loops from `C` to `C`. On a non-SSA form (see Subsect. 4.2), variables are often reused to store temporary values. The problem is that if we hoist a part of loop which changes the value of one of those variables it is possible to change the semantic. Furthermore, it is harder if those variables are modified in a conditional chunk, in this case a φ*-function* is needed. This issue is illustrated in Fig. 6 if we replace `y1`, `y2` by `y` and φ*-function* is removed.

Implementation Details. For this PoC we decided to not consider renaming issue, or the φ-functions used in the example. Indeed, these are already standard in compilers, our ultimate goal, and there is no need to rewrite a full "put into SSA form" algorithm. The PoC is nonetheless able to peel `C` programs in SSA form with no invariant conditional statements (see the examples in the repository).

This implementation is almost 400 lines of `Python`. It is able to compute relations of each commands or sequence of commands. This tool focuses on a restricted `C` syntax and considers all functions as non-pure. Functions with side effects can be seen as an anchor in the sequence of statements, commands can not be moved around. But we can restrain the conditions for peeling. We can allow to hoist pure functions as in [16]. All other side effects can be broken by this transformation, and thus should not be moved.

[7] https://github.com/eliben/pycparser.

4.2 Prototype Pass in LLVM

Compilers, and especially LLVM on which we are working, use an *Intermediate Representation* (IR) to handle programs. This is a typed assembly-like language that is used during all the stages of the compilation. Programs (in various different languages) are first translated into the IR, then several optimizations are performed (implemented in so-called *passes*), and finally the resulting IR is translated again in actual assembly language depending on the machine it will run on. Using a common IR allows to do the same optimizations on several different source languages and for several different target architectures.

One important feature of the LLVM IR is the *Single Static Assignment* form (SSA). A program is in SSA form if each variable is assigned at most once. In other words, setting a program in SSA form requires a massive α-conversion of all the variables to ensure uniqueness of names. The advantages are obvious since this removes any name-aliasing problem and ease analysis and transformation.

The main drawback of SSA comes when several different paths in the Control Flow reach the same point (typically, after a conditional). Then, the values used after this point may come from any branch and this cannot be statically decided. For example, if the original program is `if (y) then x:=0 else x:=1;C`, it is relatively easy to turn it into a pseudo-SSA form by α-converting the `x`: `if (y) then` $\mathtt{x}_0 :=$ `0 else` $\mathtt{x}_1 :=$ `1; C` but we do not know in `C` which of $\mathtt{x}_0$ or $\mathtt{x}_1$ should be used.

SSA solves this problem by using *φ-functions*. That is, the correct SSA form will be `if (y) then` $\mathtt{x}_0$`:=0 else` $\mathtt{x}_1$`:=1;` `X:=`$\varphi(\mathtt{x}_0, \mathtt{x}_1)$; `C`.

While the SSA itself eases the analysis, we do have to take into account the φ functions and handle them correctly.

Existing. LLVM does have a Loop Invariant Code Motion (LICM) pass which hoists invariants out of loops. Used with unrolling and instruction combination optimizations it can sometimes "peel" quasi-invariants. However, as far as we know, it does not compute invariance degrees and does not detect quasi-invariant chunks. Hence, if peeling occurs, it is as a side effect of another transformation (mostly, pipeline optimisation) and not to hoist quasi-invariants.

Preliminaries. First, we want to visit all loops using a bottom-up strategy (the inner loop first). Then, as for the LICM, our pass is derived from the basic `LoopPass` (loops are detected by the LLVM's `LoopInfo` pass). Which means that each time a loop is encountered, our analysis is performed.

At this point, the purpose is to gather the relations of all instructions in the loop to compose them and provide the final relation for the entire loop.

Then a `Relation` is generated for each command using a top-down strategy following the dominance tree. The *SSA* form helps us to gather dependence information on instructions. By visiting operands of each assignment, it's easy to build our map of `Relation`. With all the current loop's relations gathered, we compute the compositions, condition corrections and the maximums relations possible as described in Sect. 2.2. Obviously this method can be enhanced by an analysis on bounds around conditional and number of iterations for a loop. Finally, with those composed relations we compute an invariance degree for each statement in the loop following Algorithm 1.

```
Data: Dependency Graph and Dominance Graph
Result: List of invariance degree for each command
Initialize degrees of use to ∞ and others to 0;
for each command C_m do
    if the current degree deg(C_m) ≠ 0 then
        return deg(C_m);
    else
        Initialize the current degree deg(C_m) to ∞;
        if there is no dependence for the current chunk then
            deg(C_m) = 1;
        else
            for each dependent command ordered (Subsect. 3.1) compute the degree
            deg(C_d) do
                if deg(C_d) = ∞ or C_d = C_m then
                    return ∞;
                end
                if deg(C_m) ≤ deg(C_d) and d > m then
                    deg(C_m) = deg(C_d) + 1;
                else
                    deg(C_m) = deg(C_d);
                end
            end
        end
        return deg(C_m)
    end
end
```

Algorithm 1. Invariance degree computation.

This algorithm is dynamic. It stores progressively each degree needed to compute the current one and reuse them. Note that, for the initialization part, we are using LLVM methods (`canSinkOrHoist`, `isGuaranteedToExecute` etc...) to figure out if an instruction is movable or not. These methods provide the anchors instructions for the current loop.

Peeling Loop Idea. The transformation will consist in creating as many basic blocks before the loop as needed to remove all quasi-invariants. For each block created, we include every commands with a higher or equal invariance degree. For instance, the first `preheader` block will contain every commands with an invariance degree higher or equal to 1; the second one, higher or equal to 2 etc... to maxdeg. The final loop will contain every commands with an invariance degree equal to ∞.

Of course, hoisting quasi-invariant of high degrees is not necessarily a good idea since it requires peeling the loop many times and thus greatly increase the size of the code. The final decision to hoist or not will depend on the quasi-invariance degree, the size of the loop, ...

Implementation Details. The only chunks considered in the current implementation are the one consisting of `while` (any loops in LCSSA form) or `if-then-else` (any forks which have a common post dominator existing in the loop) statements.

This implementation (including a preliminary version of peeling) is almost 3000 lines of `C++`. It is able to compute relations of each commands or sequence of commands. However, it has, for the moment, some restrictions on the form of the loop analyzed. First, loops with several exit blocks are ignored and left intact (typically a loop including a `break`); furthermore, this tool considers all functions as non-pure as for the Proof of Concept. Even with these restrictions, the pass is able to optimise code that was previously left untouched, thus illustrating the power of the method.

5 Conclusion and Future Work

5.1 Results

Developers expect that compilers provide certain more or less "obvious" optimizations. When peeling is possible, that often means: either the code was generated; or the developers prefer this form (for readability reasons) and expect that it will be optimized by the compiler; or the developers haven't seen the possible optimization (mainly because of the obfuscation level of a given code).

```
(initialisations not shown)

    while (i<n) {
        j=0;                    // 1
        s=1;                    // 1
        while (j<y) {           // 3
            s=s*j;
            j=j+1;
        }
        if (x>100) {            // 2
            y1=x+a;
        }
        if (x<=100) {           // 1
            y2=x+100;
        }
        y=φ(y1,y2);             // 2
        a=1;                    // 1
        j=i-1;                  // ∞
        i=j+2;                  // ∞
    }
    return i;
}
```

peeling →

```
    if (i<n) {
        j=0;
        j1=j;
        s=1;
        s1=s;
        while (j<y) {...}
        if (x>100) {...}
        if (x<=100) {...}
        y21=y2;
        y=φ(y1,y2);
        a=1;
        j=i-1;
        i=j+2;
    }
    if (i<n) {
        j=j1;
        s=s1;
        while (j<y) {...}
        if (x>100) {...}
        y12=y1;
        y2=y21;
        y=φ(y1,y2);
        j=i-1;
        i=j+2;
    }
    if (i<n) {
        j=j1;
        s=s1;
        while (j<y) {...}
        y1=y12;
        y2=y21;
        y=φ(y1,y2);
        j=i-1;
        i=j+2;
    }
    while (i<n) {
        j=i-1;
        i=j+2;
    }
    return i;
}
```

Fig. 6. Hoisting inner loop

Our generic pass is able to provide a reusable abstract dependency graph and the quasi-invariance degrees for further loop optimization or analysis.

In this example (Fig. 6), we compute the same factorial several times. We can detect it statically, so the compiler has to optimize it at least in `-O3`. Our tests showed that is done neither in LLVM nor in GCC (we also tried `-fpeel_loops` with profiling). The generated assembly shows the factorial computation in the inner loop.

Moreover, the computation time of this kind of algorithm compiled with `clang` in `-O3` still computes n times the inner loop so the computation time is quadratic, while hoisting it results in linear time. For the example shown in Fig. 6 (LLVM-IR in Fig. 7a), our pass will compute the correct degrees.

To each instruction printed corresponds an invariance degree. The assignment instructions are listed by loops, the inner loop (starting with `while.cond5`) and the outer loop (starting with `while.cond`). The inner loop has its own invariance degree equal to 4 (line `10`). Remark that we do consider the `phi` initialization instructions of an inner loop. Here `%fact.0` and `%i.1` are reinitialized in the inner loop condition block. So `phi` instructions are analyzed in two different cases: to compute the relation of the current loop or to give the initialization of a variable sent to an inner loop. Our analysis only takes the relevant operand regarding to the current case and do not consider others.

Statistics have been generated by our pass on the editor `vim` to evaluate the magnitude of new possible optimizations (Fig. 7b). Note that the result changes

```
...
while.cond:
  %j.0 = phi i32 [ 0, %entry ], [ %add20, %while.end ]
  %y.0 = phi i32 [ 5, %entry ], [ %y.2, %while.end ]
  %i.0 = phi i32 [ undef, %entry ], [ %j.0, %while.end ]
  %a.0 = phi i32 [ 5, %entry ], [ 0, %while.end ]
  %cmp = icmp slt i32 %j.0, %rem
  br i1 %cmp, label %while.cond5, label %while.end21

while.cond5:
  %fact.0 = phi i32 [ %mul, %while.body8 ], [ 1, %while.cond ]
  %i.1 = phi i32 [ %add, %while.body8 ], [ 1, %while.cond ]
  %cmp6 = icmp sle i32 %i.1, %y.0
  br i1 %cmp6, label %while.body8, label %while.end

while.body8:
  %mul = mul nsw i32 %fact.0, %i.1
  %add = add nsw i32 %i.1, 1
  br label %while.cond5

while.end:
  %cmp10 = icmp sgt i32 %rem3, 100
  %add12 = add nsw i32 %rem3, %a.0
  %add12.y.0 = select i1 %cmp10, i32 %add12, i32 %y.0
  %cmp14 = icmp sle i32 %rem3, 100
  %add17 = add nsw i32 %rem3, 100
  %y.2 = select i1 %cmp14, i32 %add17, i32 %add12.y.0
  %add20 = add nsw i32 %j.0, 1
  br label %while.cond

while.end21:
  ret i32 %i.0
...
```

(a) LLVM Intermediate Representation

```
(LQICM Analysis called before each LICM occurence)
Compiler: clang release_40 -Oz
Time (with - without)
8m8,020s - 7m48,244s
--- vim v8.00442 ---
13407   Number of loop
5009    Loops well analyzed by LQICM
5984    LQICM Quasi-Invariants detected
8126    LICM Invariants Hoisted
656     LQICM Quasi-Invariants blocks detected
7632    LQICM Aborted: several exit blocks
351     LQICM Aborted: Header not exiting
256     LQICM Aborted: Inner loop not analyzed
159     LQICM Aborted: Successor not found
```

(b) Statistics on vim.

Fig. 7. LLVM IR and LQICM's statistics

a lot regarding to when our pass is called. Here, to compare, it is placed before all `LICM` iterations. We can observe that, despite the number of aborted analysis due to the lack of flexibility of our young pass, over less than half of the loops analyzes `LICM`, we find 5984 quasi-invariants instructions, 73% of the total invariants currently hoisted by `LICM`.

The code of this pass is available online[8]. To provide some real benchmarks on large programs we need to finish the transformation. We are currently working on it.

5.2 Further Works

The pass is currently a prototype. The transformation is still in preliminary form and even the analysis is making some approximations (*e.g.* considering all functions as non-pure) that hamper its efficiency. We will obviously work further on the pass to finish the transformation and increase the number of cases we can handle.

On a more theoretical side, the current analysis is strongly inspired by other ICC analysis such as *Size Change Termination* [12] (from which the Data Flow Graphs and Multipaths are taken) or the *mwp*-analysis (from which the loop correction idea is taken) [9]. As shown in Subsect. 2.1, it is easy to adapt the method to similar analysis, and most of the existing code can be reused. Thus, we plan on implementing a *mwp*-inspired complexity analysis in LLVM, which should be able to guarantee the polynomiality of large parts of the code.

Such certificates built at compile-time can be used in a *Proof Carrying Code* paradigm. If the compiler is trusted (for example, untrusted developers upload source-code onto an applications store and the compilation is made by the trusted store), then the certificate ensures that certain properties (in this case, complexity) are valid.

References

1. Abel, A., Altenkirch, T.: A predicative analysis of structural recursion. J. Funct. Program. **12**(1), 1–41 (2002)
2. Baillot, P., Terui, K.: Light types for polynomial time computation in lambda calculus. Inf. Comput. **201**(1), 41–62 (2009)
3. Bellantoni, S., Cook, S.: A new recursion-theoretic characterization of the polytime functions. Comput. Complex. **2**, 97–110 (1992)
4. Cobham, A.: The intrinsic computational difficulty of functions. In: Bar-Hillel, Y. (ed.) CLMPS (1962)
5. Cocke, J.: Global common subexpression elimination. SIGPLAN Not. **5**(7), 20–24 (1970)
6. Girard, J.-Y.: Linear logic. Theor. Comput. Sci. **50**, 1–110 (1987)
7. Hofmann, M.: Linear types and non-size increasing polynomial time computation. In: LICS, pp. 464–473 (1999)
8. Kristiansen, L.: Notes on code motion. Private communication

[8] https://github.com/ThomasRuby/lqicm_pass.

9. Kristiansen, L., Jones, N.D.: The flow of data and the complexity of algorithms. Trans. Comput. Log. **10**(3), 28 (2009)
10. Kuck, D.J., Kuhn, R.H., Padua, D.A., Leasure, B., Wolfe, M.: Dependence graphs and compiler optimizations. In: POPL (1981)
11. Laird, J., McCusker, G., Manzonetto, G., Pagani, M.: Weighted relational models of typed lambda-calculi. In: IEEE/ACM LICS (2013)
12. Lee, C.S., Jones, N.D., Ben-Amram, A.M.: The size-change principle for program termination. In: POPL (2001)
13. Moyen, J.-Y.: Resource control graphs. ACM Trans. Comput. Log. **10**, 29 (2009)
14. Seiller, T.: Interaction graphs: additives. Ann. Pure Appl. Log. **167**, 95–154 (2016)
15. Seiller, T.: Interaction graphs: full linear logic. In: IEEE/ACM LICS (2016)
16. Song, L., Futamura, Y., Glück, R., Hu, Z.: A loop optimization technique based on quasi-invariance (2000)

SamaTulyata: An Efficient Path Based Equivalence Checking Tool

Soumyadip Bandyopadhyay[1(✉)], Santonu Sarkar[1], Dipankar Sarkar[2], and Chittaranjan Mandal[2]

[1] BITS Pilani K K Birla Goa Campus, Goa, India
{soumyadipb,santonus}@goa.bits-pilani.ac.in
[2] Indian Institute of Technology Kharagpur, Kharagpur, India
{ds,chitta}@cse.iitkgp.ac.in

Abstract. An application program can go through significant optimizing and parallelizing transformations, both automated and human guided, before being mapped to an architecture. Formal verification of these transformations is crucial to ensure that they preserve the original behavioural specification. PRES+ model (Petri net based Representation of Embedded Systems) encompassing data processing is used to model parallel behaviours more vividly. This paper presents a translation validation tool for verifying optimizing and parallelizing code transformations by checking equivalence between two PRES+ models, one representing the source code and the other representing its optimized and (or) parallelized version.

Keywords: Eclipse plugin · PRES+ model · FSMD model · Equivalence checking · Cut-point

1 Introduction

Applications written for parallel and embedded systems often go through a series of semantic preserving transformations so that the resulting program can optimally utilize the underlying computing infrastructure. Over the years, the researchers and practitioners have developed tools and methodologies to perform code transformations manually or semi-automatically. For instance, Intel® compiler[1] performs a series of transformations on the applications to improve the performance by utilizing the multi-core and vector registers. There are compilers like PLuTo [1], Par4All [2], Cetus [3] which perform source to source transformation to parallelize a sequential code. There are compilers like ROSE [4] which performs source to source transformation to improve fault-tolerance of a code. In practice, developers often perform a hand-crafted transformation of a code

S. Bandyopadhyay is now working at HPI, Potsdam, Germany, email: soumyadip.bandyopadhyay@hpi.de

[1] https://software.intel.com/en-us/intel-compilers.

D. D'Souza and K. Narayan Kumar (Eds.): ATVA 2017, LNCS 10482, pp. 109–116, 2017.
DOI: 10.1007/978-3-319-68167-2_8

followed by extensive testing. In all these cases, it is absolutely essential to verify that the transformed program preserves the semantics of the original code. Several translation validation methods are reported in [5–10]. In this paper, we propose an Eclipse plugin based verification tool named SamaTulyata, that can verify the semantic equivalence of two programs using Petri-net based model. The plugin is integrated with the Eclipse-CDT environment. The equivalence checking algorithm along with the theoretical treatment is given in [11–14]. The paper has been organized as follows. In Sect. 2 we describe the architecture of the tool. Next, in Sect. 3 we report the experimental results performed for this tool. Finally we conclude the paper.

2 Tool Architecture

The equivalence checker tool has been implemented as an Eclipse plugin, shown in Fig. 1. The lifecycle of the plugin is as follows:

Inactive state: The plugin gets loaded while Eclipse development environment is initialized but it remains inactive at the beginning.

Active state: Since the equivalence checker works on two C programs, the plugin becomes active when two C programs are selected as shown in Fig. 1 under the Eclipse-CDT environment. When the plugin receives the equivalence check event from the user, it converts the source programs into two Petri net based control flow graphs, and then performs equivalence check on the CFGs. The result of the equivalence check is displayed as shown in Fig. 1.

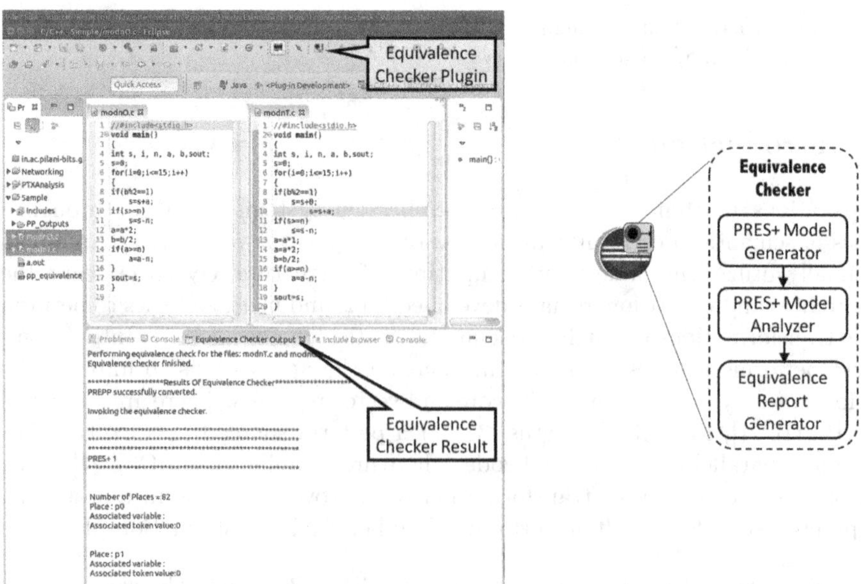

Fig. 1. Architecture of the equivalence checker

2.1 Functional Modules

The tool has been implemented in Java and C, where the plugin functionality and the lifecycle have been implemented in Java and the core equivalence checking algorithm has been implemented in C. The core system comprises of three modules as shown in Fig. 1. The First one, **PRES+ Model generator** accepts a control flow graph and generates a PRES+ model of the program. The second module, **PRES+ Model analyzer**, accepts two PRES+ models and performs the equivalence check. The detailed report of the equivalence check process is generated by **Equivalence Report Generator** module. Currently, the tool displays the results in a textual form. In the future version, we intend to make the results more interactive where the tool will not only show the final result but highlight the source code lines in the Eclipse, to explain why the equivalence checking process has failed. Through the following example, we illustrate the equivalence checking method. Note that here we have considered only integer type variables.

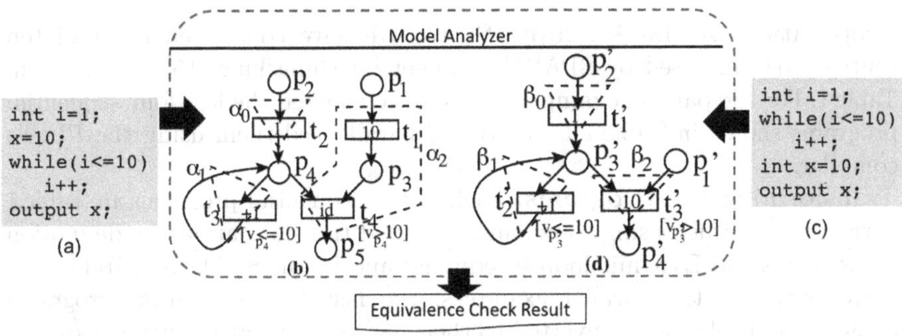

Fig. 2. Illustrative example for the equivalence checking method.

Example 1. Figure 2(c) is the program obtained from the program of Fig. 2(a) by moving the instruction $x = 10$ preceding the loop using code motion across the loop. Figure 2(b) depicts the PRES+ model N_0 corresponding to the Fig. 2(a) and (d) represents the PRES+ model N_1 corresponding to Fig. 2(b) which are constructed by the **PRES+ Model Generator** module. Then the two constructed models are fed into the **Model Analyzer** module which essentially checks the equivalence between two PRES+ models. The working principle of equivalence checking procedure is given below.

The set of variables (for both N_0, N_1) is $V = \{i, x\}$. In Fig. 2(a), the cut-points are p_1, p_2, p_4 and p_5; using path construction module, the set of paths for N_0 is $\{\alpha_0, \alpha_1, \alpha_2\}$. Similarly, in Fig. 2(b), the cut-points are p'_1, p'_2, p'_3, p'_4 and the set of paths is $\{\beta_0, \beta_1, \beta_2\}$. The equivalence checking method consists in establishing that for all path of N_0, there exists a path in N_1 such that two paths are computationally equivalent [11,14] and vise-versa. Now, for α_0, the path

β_0 is chosen as the candidate for examining equivalence with α_0 because their respective pre-places are related by the relation f_{in} and they are computationally equivalent. Hence, it infers that $\alpha_0 \simeq \beta_0$. Similarly, α_1 and α_2 are found to have equivalence with β_1 and β_2, respectively. At last, the method identifies that the non-equivalent path sets of N_0 and N_1 is empty and accordingly declares that the two models N_0 and N_1 are equivalent. ■

3 Experimental Results

The core system has been tested on both sequential and parallel examples on a 2.0 GHz Intel(R) Core(TM)2 Duo CPU machine (using only a single core). We have carried out the experiments on a set of sequential examples and a set of parallel examples. For both the cases, we have performed the following steps systematically.

3.1 Methodology

1. **Preparation of the Example Suite:** We have considered a set of ten source programs used by SPARK compiler benchmarking [15], as shown in Table 1. For the parallel examples, we have considered the last four sequential programs shown in Table 1 from [1] and parallelized them using the PLuTo compiler.
2. **Transforming the Programs:** Each of the sequential programs in Table 1 is then transformed using some human guided transformations (code motion across loops and Dynamic loop scheduling) and by the SPARK compiler [15].
   However, for the parallel examples, the last four sequential programs depicted in Table 1 are converted to their parallel equivalents using a prominent thread level parallelizing compiler PLuTo [1].
3. **Tool Verification:** We feed the original and the transformed version of each example as inputs to our tool and evaluate its performance when the transformed program is semantically equivalent to the original program and when the transformation is erroneous.

Performance: For each example, we observe number of paths, path construction time for both original and transformed programs and the equivalence checking time. We compare the timing with two other reported methods in [13,16]. The entire module is now available online for verification[2].

Faulty Translation: In order to experimentally evaluate the performance of the tool in the presence of faulty translation of code, we inject some errors in the source code of the transformed program and observe the time it takes to detect these errors during equivalence checking process. We have introduced the following types of (both instruction level and thread level) erroneous code transformations:

[2] https://github.com/santonus/equivchecker.

Type 1: non-uniform boosting up code motions from one branch of an if-then-else block to the block preceding it which introduces false-data dependencies; this has been injected in the GCD and MODN examples.
Type 2: non-uniform duplicating down code motions from the basic block preceding an if-then-else block to one branch of the if-then-else block which removes data dependency in the other branch;
Type 3: mix of some correct code motions and incorrect code motions.
Type 4: data-locality transformations which introduce false data-locality in the body of the loop.

Table 1. Equivalence checking results for several sequential and parallel examples

Example	Paths		Need extension	Need extension	FSMDEQX in (μs)	DCPEQX in (μs)		SamaTulyata in (μs)	
	Orig	Transf	(FSMDEQX)	(DCPEQX)	Total	PathConstr	Total	PathConstr	Total
MODN	30	30	YES	YES	16001	22208	37789	19835	30761
SUMOFDIGITS	9	9	YES	YES	8000	12175	25477	11389	23451
PERFECT	53	23	YES	YES	8372	44375	53674	29918	37274
GCD	43	43	YES	NO	12563	28960	41432	28034	38238
TLC	70	70	YES	YES	16121	282876	288671	252251	272129
DCT	18	18	NO	NO	1902	35637	42354	25134	28123
LCM	45	45	YES	NO	16174	30960	43245	29143	39235
LRU	56	56	YES	NO	20001	834323	855785	768790	826716
PRIMEFAC	35	20	YES	YES	6352	21846	27414	17734	24356
MINANDMAX-S	40	38	×	NO	×	24774	40763	21309	37033
BCM	1	1	×	NO	×	912	4659	802	3561
LUP	18	18	×	NO	×	20209	33633	18341	31012
DEKKER	12	12	×	NO	×	8912	16821	6891	10234
PETERSON	10	10	×	YES	×	10526	17652	9521	10387

3.2 Performance Analysis

In Table 1, we discuss the observations regarding the performance of Sama Tulyata vis-a-vis those of the FSMD based equivalence checker (FSMDEQX) [17] and the dynamic cut-point induced PRES+ equivalence checker (DCPEQX) on programs and their equivalent transformed versions.

FSMD Based Approach: As observed from Table 1, FSMDEQX is significantly faster than SamaTulyata for all the examples. The main reason is that an FSMD based equivalence checker unlike PRES+ model based ones (DCPEQX and SamaTulyata), can construct paths by identifying the cut-points only, which are essentially the control flow bifurcation points. In contrast, for PRES+ models, the path construction process involves not only identification of the back edges but also keeping track of the sequence of maximally parallelizable transitions. Nevertheless, PRES+ models are more powerful to capture the data independence, and hence parallelism [11,14], which an FSMD based model is not capable of. Consequently, FSMDEQX is not capable of checking equivalence of several parallel examples as indicated using × in Table 1.

Dynamic Cut-Point Based Approach: Let us now focus on the columns pertaining to DCPEQX and SamaTulyata. It may be observed that SamaTulyata outperforms DCPEQX in terms of total time. Both the approaches use path construction method and they are capable of analyzing sequential as well as parallel examples. The main reason for better performance in SamaTulyata lies in path construction during equivalence checking. Since SamaTulyata creates paths based on static cut points, it cuts the loop (if present in the PRES+ model of a program) in at least one cut point [11,14]. However, DCPEQX generates more cut-points for the same PRES+ model of a program as it seeks to capture the computation syntactically [12,13]. In the process, it has to employ costly path extension during equivalence checking. Due to this reason, SamaTulyata considers less number of paths during equivalence checking, and hence executes faster.

3.3 Performance in Presence of Fault

The last three columns of Table 2 depict the non-equivalence detection times for the three equivalence checkers to identify the set of non-equivalent paths in each cases. The non-equivalence time for SamaTulyata is better than DCPEQX and FSMDEQX. The reason is that for reporting non-equivalent paths, both DCPEQX and FSMDEQX methods call the costly path extension routine; however, in SamaTulyata there is no need for costly path extension.

Table 2. Non-equivalence checking times for faulty translations

Errors	Example	FSMDEQX	DCPEQX	SamaTulyata
		Time (μs)	Time (μs)	Time (μs)
Type 1	MODN	15456	17255	13471
	GCD	10435	12523	10142
Type 2	TLC	14592	16434	13780
Type 3	LRU	19278	23143	16143
	LCM	11412	12834	10619
Type 4	MINANDMAX-P	×	24347	15463
	PETERSON	×	10913	6534

4 Conclusion

In this paper we describe a tool named SamaTulyata that implements an efficient path based equivalence checking. The underlying technique does not use the costly path extension mechanism. In comparison, the current tool has been found to be somewhat better than DCPEQX tool; however, both take more time than FSMDEQX methods primarily because the path construction time for PRES+

model is significantly higher than the corresponding time for FSMD model. The tool has been implemented as an Eclipse plugin, which is active under the CDT environment and can help the programmer to perform the equivalence checking during program development. Some of the limitations of the present work are its inability to handle loop-shifting, software pipelining and other loop transformations for array handling programs which are going to be our focus for the future work.

Acknowledgment. Santonu Sarkar has been partially supported by Science and Engineering Research Board, Govt. of India project (SB/S3/EECE/0170/2014) for this research work.

References

1. Bondhugula, U., Hartono, A., Ramanujam, J., Sadayappan, P.: Pluto: a practical and fully automatic polyhedral program optimization system. In: PLDI (2008)
2. Par4All. http://www.par4all.org/
3. Bae, H., Mustafa, D., Lee, J.W., Aurangzeb, A., Lin, H., Dave, C., Eigenmann, R., Midkiff, S.P.: The cetus source-to-source compiler infrastructure: overview and evaluation. IJPP **41**(6), 753–767 (2013)
4. Lidman, J., Quinlan, D.J., Liao, C., McKee, S.A.: Rose: FTTransform-a source-to-source translation framework for exascale fault-tolerance research. In: DSN Workshop, pp. 1–6 (2012)
5. Necula, G.C.: Translation validation for an optimizing compiler. In: PLDI, pp. 83–94 (2000)
6. Pnueli, A., Siegel, M., Singerman, E.: Translation validation. In: Steffen, B. (ed.) TACAS 1998. LNCS, vol. 1384, pp. 151–166. Springer, Heidelberg (1998). doi:10.1007/BFb0054170
7. Rinard, M., Diniz, P.: Credible compilation. Technical report MIT-LCS-TR-776, MIT (1999)
8. Vafeiadis, V., Balabonski, T., Chakraborty, S., Morisset, R., Nardelli, F.: Common compiler optimisations are invalid in the C11 memory model and what we can do about it. In: POPL, pp. 209–220 (2015)
9. Kundu, S., Lerner, S., Gupta, R.: Validating high-level synthesis. In: Gupta, A., Malik, S. (eds.) CAV 2008. LNCS, vol. 5123, pp. 459–472. Springer, Heidelberg (2008). doi:10.1007/978-3-540-70545-1_44
10. Feng, X., Hu, A.J.: Cutpoints for formal equivalence verification of embedded software. In: Proceedings of the 5th ACM International Conference on Embedded Software, EMSOFT 2005, pp. 307–316 (2005)
11. Bandyopadhyay, S., Sarkar, D., Mandal, C.: An efficient equivalence checking method for petri net based models of programs. In: ICSE, pp. 827–828 (2015)
12. Bandyopadhyay, S., Sarkar, D., Mandal, C.A., Banerjee, K., Duddu, K.R.: A path construction algorithm for translation validation using PRES+ models. PPL **26**(2), 1–25 (2016)
13. Bandyopadhyay, S., Sarkar, D., Banerjee, K., Mandal, C.: A path-based equivalence checking method for petri net based models of programs. In: ICSOFT, pp. 319–329 (2015)
14. Bandyopadhyay, S., Sarkar, D., Mandal, C.: An efficient path based equivalence checking for petri net based models of programs. In: ISEC, pp. 70–79 (2016)

15. Gupta, S., Dutt, N., Gupta, R., Nicolau, A.: SPARK: a high-level synthesis framework for applying parallelizing compiler transformations. In: Proceedings of International Conference on VLSI Design, pp. 461–466 (2003)
16. Banerjee, K., Karfa, C., Sarkar, D., Mandal, C.: Verification of code motion techniques using value propagation. IEEE TCAD **33**(8), 1180–1193 (2014)
17. Karfa, C., Mandal, C.A., Sarkar, D.: Formal verification of code motion techniques using data-flow-driven equivalence checking. TODAES **17**(3), 30 (2012)

Model Checking and Temporal Logics

Tests and Refutation

Mohammad Torabi Dashti(✉) and David Basin(✉)

Department of Computer Science, ETH Zurich, Zürich, Switzerland
{mohammad.torabi,basin}@inf.ethz.ch

Abstract. The purpose of testing a system with respect to a requirement is to refute the hypothesis that the system satisfies the requirement. We build a theory of tests and refutation based on the elementary notions of satisfaction and refinement. We use this theory to characterize the requirements that can be refuted through black-box testing and, dually, verified through such tests. We consider refutation in finite time and obtain the well-known finite falsifiability of hyper-safety temporal requirements as a special case. We extend our theory with computational constraints and separate refutation from enforcement in the context of temporal hyper-properties. Overall, our theory provides a basis to analyze the scope and reach of black-box tests and to bridge results from areas including testing, verification, and enforcement.

1 Introduction

Testing is a widely adopted quality-assurance activity and there is a general agreement as to its purpose and importance. However, a solid understanding of testing's strength and limitations is lacking, despite the manifest importance of this topic. For instance, it is commonly agreed upon that the purpose of testing a system with respect to a requirement is to refute the hypothesis that the system satisfies the requirement [6,15]. Yet, existing testing theory is inadequate for answering basic questions such as: which class of requirements are refutable, given a class of tests? Or, which class of tests, if any, can refute a class of requirements? The need for research advances here is imperative as current analytic frameworks for testing are incapable of even articulating, let alone answering, these fundamental questions in a satisfactory manner. We show how this can be done for black-box testing, the most basic system analysis technique, by presenting a theory of tests and refutation that fully characterizes the class of refutable requirements and provides a foundation for bridging results in testing with other related disciplines.

We start with an abstract model of systems and requirements (Sect. 2) and introduce two types of requirements: obligations and prohibitions (Sect. 3). A requirement is an obligation if it obliges the systems to exhibit certain (desired) behaviors, and it is a prohibition if it prohibits the systems from exhibiting (undesired) behaviors. We show that these two requirement types admit a straightforward order-theoretic characterization. Namely, given a refinement (or abstraction) partial-order on a set of systems, the satisfaction of an obligation

D. D'Souza and K. Narayan Kumar (Eds.): ATVA 2017, LNCS 10482, pp. 119–138, 2017.
DOI: 10.1007/978-3-319-68167-2_9

is abstraction-closed, and for a prohibition it is refinement-closed. We then turn to black-box tests (Sect. 4).

A system is a black-box if we can observe its input and output, but cannot observe *how* the latter is produced from the former. Therefore, a tester can analyze such a system only by interacting with it through its interface. In black-box testing, sometimes called "testing by sampling" [6], testing a system amounts to inspecting a sample of its behaviors. The sample obtained through tests can be seen as a refinement of the system under test, a notion we make precise in the following sections. All a tester learns by sampling is that a system exhibits certain behaviors. From this, the tester cannot infer that the system does not exhibit other behaviors as well. Such a conclusion could only be justified through the sample's exhaustiveness, which black-box testing alone cannot establish. A requirement is therefore refutable through tests if, for any system that violates the requirement, the hypothesis that the system satisfies the requirement can be refuted by inspecting a refinement of the system. It follows that a requirement whose violation is contingent upon demonstrating the absence of behaviors cannot be refuted through black-box testing. Based on this, we prove that any refutable requirement is a prohibition, and all non-trivial obligations are irrefutable (Sect. 5). We then define the notion of verification dual to refutation, and show that any verifiable requirement is an obligation and that non-trivial prohibitions cannot be verified through tests (Sect. 6).

Contributions. We present a theory for reasoning about the strength and the limitations of black-box testing. Our theory has minimal formal machinery, which gives rise to direct, elementary proofs (Appendix A). We use the theory to prove new results and to obtain known results as special cases.

We fully characterize the requirements that can be refuted and those that can be verified through black-box tests. This characterization augments, and in some cases rectifies, the folkloric understanding that exists in the community. For example, we highlight the fundamental role that determinacy assumptions play in making sense of day-to-day black-box tests.

Our theory is abstract. Extending it to account for refutation in finite time and refutation under computational constraints is therefore immediate. We present different applications of our theory of finite refutability (Sect. 7). We demonstrate that the well-known finite falsifiability of hyper-safety temporal requirements [4] can be derived as a special case in our theory. Moreover, we explicate the relationship between finite refutability and system self-composition [3,4], a central technique in information flow analysis. Finally, we use our characterization to separate refutability from enforceability: we show that any enforceable temporal requirement is refutable, but refutable requirements need not be enforceable; we give a precise definition of the notion of enforceable requirements in the following sections. The separation hinges upon analyzing the computational constraints of refutation (and enforcement) via a notion of algorithmically refutable requirements (Sect. 8).

Related Work. Below, we review the most closely related work.

Our definition of refutability is inspired by Popper's notion of *testable* theories [19]. Theories of black-box testing proposed in the software engineering literature are largely concerned with the notions of test selection and test adequacy; see, e.g., [9,10,24,27]. Refutable requirements have not been investigated in prior works. In contrast, *enforceable* temporal requirements have been extensively studied. Intuitively, a requirement is enforceable if there exists a reference monitor that can tell when a system violates the requirement only by observing the system's behaviors [11,16]. Due to its technical nature, we relegate comparing refutability and enforceability to Sect. 7.

Obligations and prohibitions, as requirement types, implicitly appear in various domains of software engineering. For example, Damm and Harel introduce *existential* charts for specifying the obligatory behaviors of a system, and *universal* charts for specifying all the behaviors the system exhibits [5]. An existential chart intuitively corresponds to an obligation, and a universal chart corresponds to a *semi-monotone* requirement in our theory, which is the conjunction of an obligation and a prohibition. The notions of necessity and possibility also have a central role in modal logic. For example, Larsen and Thomsen's modal transition systems specify obligations and prohibitions through, respectively, *must* and *may* transitions [13]. Similarly, Tretmans' IOCO testing theory [24] is based on specifications that define both a lower bound and an upper bound on a system's behaviors, which roughly speaking correspond to, respectively, obligations and prohibitions (see Sect. 6). The existing works define prohibitions and obligations in concrete modeling formalisms. In contrast, we present abstract definitions which can be instantiated by the existing ones.

We briefly discuss the limitations of our theory in Sect. 9.

2 Systems and Requirements

We start with a simple abstract model of systems and requirements. A **system** is an entity that is capable of exhibiting externally observable behaviors. Operating systems, digital circuits and vending machines are all examples of systems. We keep the notion of a behavior unspecified for now. Let $\mathcal{S}$ denote the nonempty set of all systems under consideration. For example, $\mathcal{S}$ may stand for the set of all Java programs. We assume that $(\mathcal{S}, \preceq)$ is a partially-ordered set (poset), where $\preceq$ denotes a refinement relation: $S_1 \preceq S_2$ states that system S_1 refines system S_2, or that system S_2 abstracts system S_1. That is, $S_1 \preceq S_2$ means that S_1 exhibits fewer behaviors than S_2. There exists a large body of research on refinement and abstraction; see for instance [1,14,25]. Examples of refinement relations include trace containment and various algebraic simulation relations. In the interest of generality, we do not bind $\preceq$ to any particular relation. We write $\lceil S \rceil$ and $\lfloor S \rfloor$ respectively for the set of systems that abstract a system S and those that refine it: $\lceil S \rceil = \{S' \in \mathcal{S} \mid S \preceq S'\}$ and $\lfloor S \rfloor = \{S' \in \mathcal{S} \mid S' \preceq S\}$. We assume that the poset $(\mathcal{S}, \preceq)$ is bounded: it has a greatest element $\top$ and a least element $\bot$. The "chaos" system $\top$ (sometimes called the "weakest" system [12]), abstracts every system, and the "empty" system $\bot$ refines every system in $\mathcal{S}$. In short, our abstract model of systems is a four-tuple $(\mathcal{S}, \preceq, \bot, \top)$.

We extensionally define a **requirement** as a set of systems. A system **satisfies** a requirement R if it belongs to R. For now, we need not expound on the satisfaction relation between systems and requirements; we will give examples later. We write χ_R for a requirement R's characteristic function, which maps $\mathcal{S}$ to $\{0,1\}$. A requirement R is **trivial** if all or none of the systems in $\mathcal{S}$ satisfy it, i.e. χ_R is a constant function. Let $\mathcal{R}$ denote the set of all requirements. It is immediate that $(\mathcal{R}, \subseteq)$, where $\subseteq$ is the standard set inclusion relation, is a complete lattice. We define the **conjunction** of two requirements R_1 and R_2, denoted $R_1 \wedge R_2$, as their meet. For a set R of systems, we write $\lceil R \rceil = \bigcup_{S \in R} \lceil S \rceil$ and $\lfloor R \rfloor = \bigcup_{S \in R} \lfloor S \rfloor$. A set R is an **upper set** if $R = \lceil R \rceil$, and a **lower set** if $R = \lfloor R \rfloor$. These terms originate from order theory.

3 Obligations and Prohibitions

A requirement is an obligation if it obliges the systems to exhibit certain (desired) behaviors, often corresponding to intended functionalities and features. For example, a requirement for a database system obliges it to provide the user with an option to commit transactions. Intuitively, this requirement cannot be violated by adding behaviors to the system, for example by providing the user the option to review transactions. The satisfaction of an obligation R is therefore abstraction-closed: $\forall S, S' \in \mathcal{S}.\ S \in R \ \wedge\ S \preceq S' \ \rightarrow\ S' \in R$. That is, an obligation is an upper set.

A requirement is a prohibition if it prohibits the systems from exhibiting certain (undesired) behaviors. For instance, consider the requirement that prohibits a database system from committing malformed transactions. Intuitively, this requirement cannot be violated by removing behaviors from the system, for example removing the option for committing transactions altogether. That is, the satisfaction of a prohibition R is refinement-closed: $\forall S, S' \in \mathcal{S}.\ S \in R \wedge S' \preceq S \ \rightarrow\ S' \in R$. In other words, a prohibition is a lower set of systems.

Definition 1. A requirement R is an **obligation** if $R = \lceil R \rceil$ and R is a **prohibition** if $R = \lfloor R \rfloor$.

The following example illustrates obligations and prohibitions.

Example 2. Consider the system model $(2^{\mathbb{N}\times\mathbb{N}}, \subseteq, \emptyset, \mathbb{N} \times \mathbb{N})$, where a system is extensionally defined as a subset of $\mathbb{N} \times \mathbb{N}$, with $\mathbb{N}$ being the set of natural numbers, and the refinement relation is the standard subset relation. For an input $i \in \mathbb{N}$, a system S can produce an output o, non-deterministically chosen from the set $\{n \in \mathbb{N} \mid (i,n) \in S\}$, and it does not produce any outputs when $\{n \in \mathbb{N} \mid (i,n) \in S\}$ is empty. We call this the **extensional input-output** system model eio.

The requirement P stipulating that systems are deterministic is a prohibition: if S is deterministic, meaning $\forall i \in \mathbb{N}.\ |\{n \in \mathbb{N} \mid (i,n) \in S\}| \leq 1$, then so is any refinement, i.e. subset, of S. In particular, the empty system satisfies the definition of determinacy.

The requirement O stipulating that systems define total relations is an obligation: if S is total, meaning $\forall i \in \mathbb{N}.\ |\{n \in \mathbb{N} \mid (i,n) \in S\}| > 0$, then so is any abstraction, i.e. superset, of S. The requirement R, stating that systems extensionally define total functions is clearly neither a prohibition nor an obligation: from $\forall i \in \mathbb{N}.\ |\{n \in \mathbb{N} \mid (i,n) \in S\}| = 1$ we cannot conclude that an arbitrary subset or superset of S defines a total function. Note that $R = P \wedge O$. ▲

A requirement R is an obligation iff χ_R is monotonically increasing in $\preceq$, that is, $S \preceq S' \rightarrow \chi_R(S) \leq \chi_R(S')$. Similarly, R is a prohibition iff χ_R is monotonically decreasing, that is, $S \preceq S' \rightarrow \chi_R(S') \leq \chi_R(S)$. Therefore, any requirement that is both an obligation and a prohibition must have a constant characteristic function. The following lemma is now immediate.

Lemma 3. If a requirement R is both an obligation and a prohibition, then R is trivial.

This lemma implies that a prohibition cannot in general be replaced with an obligation and vice versa. For example, the prohibition *smoking is forbidden* has no equivalent obligation and the obligation *sacrifice a ram* has no equivalent prohibition. The lemma does not however imply that obligations and prohibitions exhaust the set of requirements. Namely, a **non-monotone** requirement, i.e. one whose characteristic function is neither monotonically increasing nor monotonically decreasing, is neither an obligation nor a prohibition. For instance, the requirement $R = P \wedge O$, defined in Example 2, is not monotone. Therefore, R is neither an obligation nor a prohibition.

Note that prohibitions implicitly define which behaviors are permissible. Namely, the set of permissible behaviors complements the set of prohibited ones, cf. deontic logic [26]. To avoid inconsistency, all obligatory behaviors must be permissible, but not all permissible behaviors need be obligatory. Consequently, the set of permissible behaviors for a system, delimited by the prohibitions, does not necessarily coincide with its set of obligatory behaviors.

4 Black-Box Tests

We start by defining the notion of a test setup. This notion enables us to distinguish system behaviors from what a black-box tester observes. Let $(\mathcal{S}, \preceq, \bot, \top)$ be a system model. By sampling the behaviors of a system $S \in \mathcal{S}$, a tester makes an **observation**. For now, we do not further specify observations. We give examples shortly. A **test setup** is a pair (T, α), where T is an (uninterpreted) domain of observations and α is an **order-preserving** function from $\mathcal{S}$ to 2^T, i.e., $S \preceq S' \rightarrow \alpha(S) \subseteq \alpha(S')$. Intuitively, the set $\alpha(S)$ consists of all the observations that can be made by testing a system S in this test setup. Since α is order-preserving, if t belongs to $\alpha(S)$ for some system S, then $t \in \alpha(S')$ for any system S' that abstracts S. This reflects the nature of black-box testing where analyzing a system S "by sampling" amounts to inspecting a sample of S's behaviors [6]. Therefore, if an observation can be made on S by inspecting the behaviors S exhibits, then the same observation can also be made on any system S' that abstracts S, simply because S' exhibits all of S's behaviors.

We define the function $\hat{\alpha} : T \to 2^{\mathcal{S}}$ to map an observation to the set of systems that can yield that observation. Formally, $\hat{\alpha}(t) = \{S \in \mathcal{S} \mid t \in \alpha(S)\}$, for any $t \in T$. In black-box testing, a tester knows nothing about the behaviors of the system under test beyond what is observed by interacting with it. Therefore, all the tester can conclude from an observation t is that the system under test can be *any* system that could yield t. That is, solely based on an observation t, the tester cannot distinguish between the system under test and any other member of the set $\hat{\alpha}(t)$. We call this condition the **indistinguishability condition**. Clearly black-box tests combined with, say, white-box system inspection [17], are not constrained by this condition.

The above condition delimits the knowledge a tester can obtain through black-box testing. Suppose that Ted (the tester) performs a black-box analysis of a system S. Ted cannot distinguish S from, say, $\top$, simply because $\top$ abstracts every system. This epistemic limitation is not alleviated by **exhaustive** tests: regardless of whether or not Ted samples and analyzes all the behaviors of S during testing, $\top \in \lceil S \rceil$ is still true. That is, black-box testing can neither demonstrate the absence of behaviors nor the exhaustiveness of an observation; otherwise, Ted could tell that the system under test is not $\top$, which exhibits all behaviors, thereby distinguishing S from $\top$. But, as just discussed, this falls beyond the scope of black-box testing. The following example illustrates these points.

Example 4. Consider the eio system model and the test setup $\mathbf{T}_r = (\mathcal{S}, \lfloor \cdot \rfloor)$, where a tester may observe an arbitrary refinement of the system under test. Note that $\lfloor \cdot \rfloor$ is order-preserving and hence $\mathbf{T}_r$ is a test setup. Suppose Ted observes that the system under test S outputs 0 for input 0, and 1 for input 1. That is, Ted makes the observation $t = \{(0,0),(1,1)\}$. Ted can neither conclude that S does not output 1 for input 0, e.g. due to internal nondeterminism, nor that S extensionally defines the identity function. This is because $\top$, which abstracts t and hence belongs to $\hat{\alpha}(t)$, satisfies these requirements, and Ted cannot differentiate S from $\top$ by observing t alone. ▲

Note that the conclusions drawn above hold true regardless of whether or not observations can be carried out in a finite amount of time. We return to this point in Sect. 7.

5 Refutable Requirements

The purpose of testing a system with respect to a requirement is to refute the hypothesis that the system satisfies the requirement [6,15,19]. Below, we characterize the class of requirements that can be refuted using black-box tests, after presenting an illustrative special case.

Any system model $\mathsf{M} = (\mathcal{S}, \preceq, \bot, \top)$ induces a **reflexive** test setup $\mathbf{T}_r^{\mathsf{M}} = (\mathcal{S}, \lfloor \cdot \rfloor)$, where each observation on a system $S \in \mathcal{S}$ is a system in $\mathcal{S}$ that refines S.

When M is clear from the context, we simply write $\mathbf{T}_r$ for M's reflexive test setup, as we did in Example 4. In the reflexive setup, testing a system S against a requirement R amounts to inspecting a refinement S_w of S to refute the hypothesis that $S \in R$. By merely observing S_w, with $S_w \in \lfloor S \rfloor$, the tester cannot distinguish S from any other system that abstracts S_w, due to the indistinguishability condition. Therefore, the tester can infer $S \notin R$ after observing S_w iff every element of $\lceil S_w \rceil$ violates R. Hence R is refutable in a reflexive test setup if, for any S that violates R, there is at least one **witness** system $S_w \in \lfloor S \rfloor$ such that any system that abstracts S_w violates R. That is, R is refutable in $\mathbf{T}_r$ if $\forall S \in \mathcal{S}.\ S \notin R \rightarrow \exists S_w \in \lfloor S \rfloor.\ \lceil S_w \rceil \cap R = \emptyset$.

Example 5. Consider a program whose input and output domains are the set of lists of natural numbers. A requirement R restricts the program's outputs to ascending lists. Suppose that a system S violates R. Then there must exist an input i for which S produces an output list o that is not ascending. Let us refer to the system that exhibits just this forbidden behavior as $S_w = \{(i, o)\}$. Clearly S_w refines S, and any system that abstracts S_w violates R by exhibiting the forbidden behavior. Therefore, R is refutable in the test setup $\mathbf{T}_r$. ▲

We now generalize the above and define refutability in an arbitrary test setup $\mathbf{T}$.

Definition 6. Let $\mathbf{T} = (T, \alpha)$ be a test setup for a system model $(\mathcal{S}, \preceq, \bot, \top)$. A requirement R is **T-refutable** if $\forall S \in \mathcal{S}.\ S \notin R \rightarrow \exists t \in \alpha(S).\ \hat{\alpha}(t) \cap R = \emptyset$.

Let R be a (T, α)-refutable requirement. Then, for any system S, $S \notin R \rightarrow \lceil S \rceil \cap R = \emptyset$, simply because α is order-preserving. The contrapositive implies that if $S_1 \in R$ and $S_2 \preceq S_1$, then $S_2 \in R$. That is, R is a prohibition. The following theorem is now immediate.

Theorem 7. *Let* $\mathbf{T}$ *be a test setup. Any* $\mathbf{T}$*-refutable requirement is a prohibition.*

Example 8. Consider the model where each system extensionally defines a binary tree where each node is colored either red or black, and $\preceq$ is the subtree relation. The requirement R stipulates that the two children of any red node must have the same color. Observing a tree t in which a red node has a red child and a black child implies that any tree that abstracts t violates R. Therefore, R is refutable in $\mathbf{T}_r$ and, due to Theorem 7, it is a prohibition. ▲

Given a system model, we say a test setup $\mathbf{T}_i$ is **more permissive** that a test setup $\mathbf{T}_j$ if any $\mathbf{T}_j$-refutable requirement is $\mathbf{T}_i$-refutable. The following lemma along with Theorem 7 imply that, in any system model M, the reflexive test setup $\mathbf{T}_r^{\mathsf{M}} = (\mathcal{S}, \lfloor \cdot \rfloor)$ is the **most permissive** test setup.

Lemma 9. In any system model M, any prohibition is $\mathbf{T}_r^{\mathsf{M}}$-refutable.

The proof is straightforward: if R is a prohibition and $S \notin R$, then $S' \notin R$ for any S' that abstracts S. Therefore, S itself can serve as the witness system demonstrating R's violation in $\mathbf{T}_r$. To further illustrate, observe that any test setup $\mathbf{T} = (T, \alpha)$ induces a set of obligations: $\mathcal{O}(\mathbf{T}) = \{\hat{\alpha}(t) \mid t \in T\}$. Testing a system S in $\mathbf{T}$ amounts to the conclusion that S satisfies an obligation that includes S, namely the obligation $\hat{\alpha}(t)$, where $t \in \alpha(S)$ is the observation obtained through testing. Therefore, the smaller $\hat{\alpha}(t)$ is, the more we learn about S by observing t; recall the indistinguishability condition. For any system S, the smallest obligation in $\mathcal{R}$ that includes S is $\lceil S \rceil$, which belongs to $\mathcal{O}(\mathbf{T}_r) = \{\lceil S \rceil \mid S \in \mathcal{S}\}$. This intuitively explains why M's reflexive setup $\mathbf{T}_r^{\mathsf{M}}$ is the most permissive test setup in any system model M. In Sect. 7, we show that $\mathbf{T}_r$ is "too permissive" in some settings, going beyond what is in practice refutable in a finite amount of time.

That $\mathbf{T}_r$ is the most permissive test setup implies that a requirement that is irrefutable in $\mathbf{T}_r$ is irrefutable for any test setup. Obligations are prominent examples of such irrefutable requirements, as stated in the following lemma, whose proof is immediate by Lemma 3 and Theorem 7.

Lemma 10. Nontrivial obligations are irrefutable in any test setup.

Example 11. Consider the setting of Example 4 and assume that the system S should satisfy the obligation O stating: systems must exhibit the behavior $(1, 0)$. Suppose Ted observes $t = \{(1, 1)\}$. Based on this, he cannot refute the hypothesis $S \in O$, simply because $\top$ abstracts t and satisfies the obligation. Note that interpreting O as the requirement P stating that *the system may output nothing but 0 for input 1* results in a refutable requirement. But O and P are not equivalent: O is an obligation and P is a prohibition; recall Lemma 3. Clearly if Ted knows that S is deterministic, then observing t would demonstrate O's violation. Determinacy itself cannot however be concluded through black-box tests alone, simply because determinacy is a prohibition (see Example 2) and prohibitions cannot be verified through black-box tests as we prove below in Lemma 15. ▲

As the last example suggests, determinacy assumptions can play a significant role in testing. For example, passing a test that checks a program's output when the input is the empty list is in practice taken as a "proof" that the program behaves correctly on empty lists. This reasoning hinges upon the assumption that the program is deterministic.

We now turn to the irrefutability of non-monotone requirements. Suppose that a requirement R is not monotone. Although R is irrefutable by Theorem 7, it is possible that for *some* systems the violation of R can be demonstrated through tests, as explained in the following. We say a non-monotone requirement is **semi-monotone** if it is the conjunction of two monotone requirements. It is easy to prove that a requirement R is semi-monotone iff $R = \lfloor R \rfloor \wedge \lceil R \rceil$ (see Theorem 26 in Appendix A). Clearly any system S that violates the prohibition $\lfloor R \rfloor$ violates the semi-monotone R as well. Since $S \notin \lfloor R \rfloor$ can be demonstrated through tests, so can $S \notin R$. For instance, the non-monotone requirement $R = P \wedge O$, defined in Example 2, is semi-monotone. For the system $S = \{(0, n) \mid n \in \mathbb{N}\}$, any test that demonstrates $S \notin P$ also demonstrates that S violates R.

For a requirement R that is not semi-monotone, it is possible that testing can demonstrate R's violation for *none* of the systems under consideration, as the following example illustrates.

Example 12. Consider the eio model and the requirement R stating that for each $(i, o) \in S$ there exists some $(i', o) \in S$, with $i \neq i'$. This requirement, which can be seen as a simplified form of a k-anonymity requirement [23], intuitively states that by solely inspecting a system's outputs, an observer cannot determine whether or not the input is some particular $i \in \mathbb{N}$. Note that R is not monotone. Moreover, R's violation (for any system) cannot be demonstrated through tests in any test setup (T, α): every observation $t \in T$ obtained by testing any system belongs to $\alpha(\top)$, and $\top \in R$. It is easy to check that $\lceil R \rceil \wedge \lfloor R \rfloor = \mathcal{S}$ and hence R is not semi-monotone. ▲

6 Verifiable Requirements

We define testing with the purpose of verifying the satisfaction of a requirement as dual to testing for refutation.

Definition 13. Let $\mathbf{T} = (T, \alpha)$ be a test setup for a system model $(\mathcal{S}, \preceq, \bot, \top)$. A requirement R is **T-verifiable** if $\forall S \in \mathcal{S}.\ S \in R \rightarrow \exists t \in \alpha(S).\ \hat{\alpha}(t) \subseteq R$.

In particular, a requirement R is $\mathbf{T}_r^{\mathsf{M}}$-verifiable in the system model $\mathsf{M} = (\mathcal{S}, \preceq, \bot, \top)$ if $\forall S \in \mathcal{S}.\ S \in R \rightarrow \exists S_w \in \lfloor S \rfloor.\ \lceil S_w \rceil \subseteq R$. That is, if there exists a witness system S_w that refines S and any system that abstracts S_w satisfies R, then by observing S_w we have conclusively demonstrated $S \in R$. The following theorem is dual to Theorem 7. Its proof is immediate.

Theorem 14. *Let* $\mathbf{T}$ *be a test setup. Any* $\mathbf{T}$*-verifiable requirement is an obligation.*

An observation $t \in \alpha(S)$ shows that the system S satisfies the obligation $O = \hat{\alpha}(t)$. It also proves that $S \in R$ for any requirement $R \supseteq O$. Therefore, as O becomes smaller, more obligations are proved by the observation. This also explains why $\mathbf{T}_r$ is the most permissive test setup for verification: any $\mathbf{T}$-verifiable requirement is $\mathbf{T}_r$-verifiable. Consequently, a requirement that is not $\mathbf{T}_r$-verifiable is non-verifiable in any test setup. Prohibitions are prominent examples of such non-verifiable requirements. The following lemma's proof is straightforward.

Lemma 15. Nontrivial prohibitions are non-verifiable in any test setup.

The lemma expresses the essence of Dijkstra's often-quoted statement that "program testing can be used to show the presence of bugs, but never to show their absence" [6]. Contrary to the folklore, this does not mean that no requirement is verifiable through black-box tests. For instance, the requirement that obliges a magic 8-ball to output *ask again later* is clearly verifiable through black-box tests: observing this output once demonstrates the obligation's satisfaction. The following example illustrates this point. We return to this example in Sect. 7 where we investigate temporal requirements.

Example 16. Consider the setting where a system S is identified with the set $b(S)$ of its behaviors, and $S_1 \preceq S_2$ denotes $b(S_1) \subseteq b(S_2)$. Suppose that a system behavior is a sequence of events and e is an event. Assume that a system S satisfies the requirement R_e stating that systems exhibit at least one behavior where e eventually appears. Note that R_e is an obligation since its satisfaction is abstraction-closed. Now, observing a refinement S_w of S where S_w exhibits one behavior π in which e eventually appears demonstrates $S \in R_e$: any abstraction of S_w exhibits π as well, hence satisfying R_e. We conclude that the obligation R_e is verifiable through tests in $\mathbf{T}_r$. ▲

We can now sharpen Dijkstra's dictum to: **(D)** *Program testing can be used to show the presence of behaviors, but never to show their absence.* If a software *bug* is a prohibited behavior, then **(D)** coincides with Dijkstra's statement, simply stipulating that prohibitions are refutable, but not verifiable. However, if a bug is the absence of an obliged behavior, then **(D)** translates to: program testing can be used to show the absence of bugs, but never to show their presence. This statement, which is dual to Dijkstra's, simply stipulates that obligations are verifiable, but not refutable.

We conclude this section with an intuitive interpretation of refutability and verifiability. The examples thus far given in the paper suggest that a system S satisfies an obligation O if the set of desired behaviors that O obliges is included in the set of behaviors of S. Any violation of O is therefore due to the behaviors that S "lacks". Consequently, O can be seen as a "lower-bound" for the set of S's behaviors. Similarly, S satisfies a prohibition P iff the set of behaviors of S is contained in the set of behaviors P permits. Any violation of P is therefore due to "excessive" behaviors of S. In this sense, P constitutes an "upper-bound" for the set of S's behaviors; see Fig. 1.

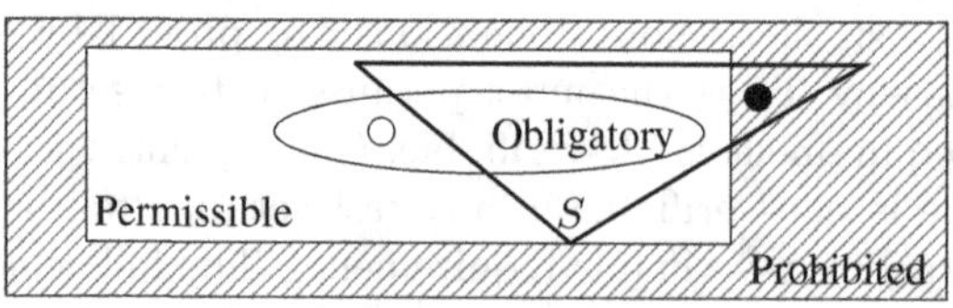

Fig. 1. The hatched area stands for the set of prohibited behaviors. The white box is the set of permissible ones which includes the set of obligatory behaviors, represented by the oval. The triangle represents a system S's behaviors. The white circle represents a violation of the obligation denoted by the oval, and the black circle represents a violation of the prohibition depicted by the hatched area.

7 Refutation in Finite Time

A requirement that is deemed refutable in our theory might not be refutable in practice. For example, a requirement whose refutation hinges upon measuring the exact momentum and position of a quantum object is impossible to refute due to the laws of physics. This limitation, not unexpectedly, does not follow from our logical theory of tests and refutation. Below, we extend our theory to account for a practically relevant limitation of system testing: we consider refutation through black-box tests that proceed in a finite amount of time.

In a system model $(\mathcal{S}, \preceq, \bot, \top)$, to show that a requirement R's satisfaction is refutable through tests in a finite amount of time, we prove that R is $\mathbf{T}$-refutable in a setup $\mathbf{T} = (T, \alpha)$ where (1) every observation in $\bigcup_{S \in \mathcal{S}} \alpha(S)$ consists of finitely many elements and (2) each such element is observable in finite time. In this case, we say R is **finitely refutable** in $\mathbf{T}$. The notion of **finite verifiability** is defined dually.

Condition (2) above refers to the world: determining whether a given element can be observed in finite time falls outside our theory's scope, and this condition's satisfaction must be substantiated by other means. Thus our theory cannot establish a requirement's finite (ir)refutability unless assumptions are made about what can be observed in finite time in the world. The following example illustrates this point.

Example 17. Consider the eio system model and the family $\mathbf{T}_k = ((\mathbb{N} \times \mathbb{N})^k, \alpha_k)$ of test setups, where $k \geq 1$ and α_k maps any system S to S^k, inductively defined as $S^1 = S$ and $S^{k+1} = S \times S^k$. Testing a system S in the setup $\mathbf{T}_k$ amounts to observing k input-output pairs belonging to S. Assume that natural numbers are observable in finite time. Then, observing every element of $(\mathbb{N} \times \mathbb{N})^k$, where $k \geq 1$ belongs to $\mathbb{N}$, takes finite time. The requirement R_{nz} stating that *systems never output zero* is, under this assumption, finitely refutable in $\mathbf{T}_1$. Now consider the requirement R_{fz}, stating that *systems may output zero for at most finitely many inputs.* It is easy to check that R_{fz}, although refutable in the reflexive test setup $\mathbf{T}_r$, is not $\mathbf{T}_k$-refutable for any $k \geq 1$.

It now seems reasonable to conclude that R_{fz} is not finitely refutable: no finite set of behaviors can refute R_{fz}. This conclusion does not however follow from our theory. To illustrate, consider an alternative test setup $\mathbf{T} = (\{*, \omega\}, \alpha)$, where $\alpha(S) = \{*\}$ if S outputs zero for finitely many inputs, and $\alpha(S) = \{*, \omega\}$ otherwise. Since α is order-preserving, $\mathbf{T}$ is formally a test setup. The requirement R_{fz} is finitely refutable in $\mathbf{T}$, under the assumption that the elements of $\{*, \omega\}$ are observable in finite time, which is the essence of Condition (2) above. Whether this is a tenable assumption cannot be settled inside our theory. Although $\mathbf{T}$ hardly appears realizable, such observations are possible in certain cases, for example by measuring the electromagnetic radiation emitted from a black-box system, cf. [22]. ▲

Condition (1) above is satisfied if finitely many behaviors of the system under test are sampled for each observation, and only a finite portion of those behaviors are inspected even when the behaviors themselves are not finite objects. We illustrate this point with an example.

Example 18. Consider the system model $(2^{\mathbb{R} \times \mathbb{R}}, \subseteq, \emptyset, \mathbb{R} \times \mathbb{R})$, where $\mathbb{R}$ is the set of real numbers. This system model is similar to the eio model except its input-output pairs belong to $\mathbb{R}$. Define $pre(r)$ as the set of finite truncations of the decimal expansion of a real number r. For instance, $pre(\sqrt{2}) = \{1, 1.4, 1.41, 1.414, 1.4142, \cdots\}$. Note that a real number can have more than one decimal expansions, for example, 1 and $0.999\cdots$, but accounting for this point is unnecessary for our discussion here. We define the test setup $\mathbf{T} = (\mathbb{F} \times \mathbb{F}, \alpha)$, where $\mathbb{F}$ is the set of rational numbers that have a finite decimal expansion and α maps any system S to the set $\bigcup_{(i,o)\in S} pre(i) \times pre(o)$. An observation of a system S in this setup is a pair (f_1, f_2), where f_1 is a truncation of an input i and f_2 is a truncation of an output o, where $(i, o) \in S$. That is, we may observe only finite portions of the decimal expansions of the inputs and outputs. Assume that $\mathbb{F}$'s elements are observable in finite time. That is, any $\mathbf{T}$-refutable requirement is finitely refutable.

Now consider the requirement $R_<$, stating that system outputs are strictly smaller than $\sqrt{2}$. Clearly $R_<$ is a prohibition, hence $\mathbf{T}_r$-refutable. Below, we show that $R_<$ is not $\mathbf{T}$-refutable. Define the system $S = \{(1, 1.4142\cdots)\}$, which outputs $\sqrt{2}$, decimally expanded, for the input 1. Even though S violates $R_<$, no truncation of S's output's decimal expansion conclusively demonstrates this, because the set of permissible outputs according to $R_<$, namely $\{o \in \mathbb{R} \mid o < \sqrt{2}\}$, is not a closed set in $\mathbb{R}$'s standard topology. That is, there is a number, namely $\sqrt{2}$, that is arbitrarily close to this set, but is not a member of the set. No finite truncation of this numbers decimal expansion can therefore conclusively determine whether it is a member, or not. We therefore conclude that $R_<$ is not $\mathbf{T}$-refutable. An analogous argument shows that the requirement $R_\leq$ stating that system outputs must be less than or equal to $\sqrt{2}$ is $\mathbf{T}$-refutable, and hence finitely refutable, because the set of permissible outputs it induces, namely $(-\infty, \sqrt{2}]$, is topologically closed. ▲

The example suggests that there is a fundamental connection between refutability and topological closure when system behaviors are infinite sequences. This connection has been investigated by Alpern and Schneider in the context of temporal properties [2], which we turn to next.

To investigate temporal requirements, we model systems that induce infinitely long sequences of events, such as operating systems, and their requirements following [4]. Let Σ be an alphabet (e.g. of events or states), where every element of Σ can be observed in finite time. We write Σ^* and Σ^ω for, respectively, the sets of finite and countably infinite sequences of Σ's elements. A behavior is an element of Σ^ω and a system is a set of behaviors. The complete lattice $(2^{\Sigma^\omega}, \subseteq, \emptyset, \Sigma^\omega)$ instantiates our system model, defined in Sect. 2. For a behavior $\pi \in \Sigma^\omega$, we write $pre(\pi)$ for the set of all finite prefixes of π, and we denote the concatenation of an element of Σ^* with one of Σ^ω by their juxtaposition. As usual, a requirement is a set of systems.

We define the test setup $\mathbf{T}_*$ as (T_*, α_*), where T_* is the set of all finite subsets of Σ^*, and $\alpha_*(S)$ is the set of all finite subsets of $\bigcup_{\pi\in S} pre(\pi)$ for a system S. Intuitively, any element of $\alpha_*(S)$ is a possible observation of S where finite prefixes of finitely many behaviors of S are observed. For any $\mathbf{T}_*$-refutable requirement R and any $S \notin R$, there exists a finite (witness) set t_w of finite prefixes of S's behaviors such that any system S' that could have yielded the observation t_w, i.e. $t_w \in \alpha_*(S')$, violates R. Clearly, every $\mathbf{T}_*$-refutable requirement is finitely refutable. Next, we relate $\mathbf{T}_*$-refutability and $\mathbf{T}_*$-verifiability to the notions of *properties* and *hyper-properties.*

A **property** is a set of (permitted) behaviors [2,18], i.e. a subset of Σ^ω. We have (extensionally) defined a system as a set of behaviors. A property can therefore be seen as a system. By overloading the notion of satisfaction, we say a system S *satisfies* a property ϕ if $S \subseteq \phi$. Any property ϕ thereby defines a refinement-closed requirement $R_\phi = \lfloor \phi \rfloor$. A property ϕ is **safety** if $\forall \pi \notin \phi. \exists \sigma \in pre(\pi). \forall \pi' \in \Sigma^\omega.\ \sigma\pi' \notin \phi$ and **liveness** if $\forall \sigma \in \Sigma^*. \exists \pi \in \Sigma^\omega.\ \sigma\pi \in \phi$. That is, safety and liveness properties are closed and dense sets, respectively [2]. The following example illustrates properties.

Example 19. A linear-time temporal logic (LTL) formula ϕ defines a set $b(\phi)$ of behaviors or executions; see, e.g., [18]. A system S satisfies the requirement expressed by ϕ if the set of system behaviors is contained in $b(\phi)$. Clearly if S satisfies the requirement and $S' \subseteq S$, for some system S', then S' satisfies it as well. Here the satisfaction relation is refinement-closed, with $S_1 \preceq S_2$ if $S_1 \subseteq S_2$. Hence, for every ϕ, regardless of whether $b(\phi)$ is a safety property, a liveness property, or an intersection of the two [2], the requirement expressed by ϕ is a prohibition. Note that the obligation R_e of Example 16 is not expressible in LTL, where the satisfaction relation is refinement-closed as just discussed, because then R_e would have to be trivial by Lemma 3. However, R_e is expressed as $\mathsf{EF}\ e$ in the computation tree logic CTL. This argument amounts to a simple proof for the well-known result that LTL is *not* more expressive than CTL [7]. ▲

Theorem 20. *A temporal property ϕ is $\mathbf{T}_*$-refutable iff ϕ is safety. Moreover, all temporal properties are $\mathbf{T}_r$-refutable and any $\mathbf{T}_*$-verifiable property is trivial.*

The theorem, whose proof hinges upon Lemma 3 and Theorem 7, implies that nontrivial liveness properties, although $\mathbf{T}_r$-refutable, are not $\mathbf{T}_*$-refutable; cf. [8]. We now turn to hyper-properties.

A **hyper-property** is a set of properties [4], i.e. a requirement in our model. A system S satisfies a hyper-property $\mathbb{H}$, if $S \in \mathbb{H}$. A hyper-property $\mathbb{H}$ is **hyper-safety** if for any $S \notin \mathbb{H}$, there exists an observation $t \in \alpha(S)$ such that $\forall S' \in \hat{\alpha}(t).\ S' \notin \mathbb{H}$; see [4]. It is easy to check that a temporal requirement R is hyper-safety iff R is $\mathbf{T}_*$-refutable. Now it is immediate by Theorem 7 that any hyper-safety requirement is a prohibition. Therefore, finitely verifiable hyper-safety requirements must be trivial. These results show how existing, specialized concepts and their refutability follow as special cases of the notions we defined. For instance, Example 16's requirement R_e, which is clearly finitely verifiable in $\mathbf{T}_*$, cannot be hyper-safety due to the above results and it is therefore not finitely refutable in $\mathbf{T}_*$.

We conclude this section with another application of our theory and consider refutation through system self-composition. Suppose we want to refute the hypothesis H stating that a plane figure S is a circle by observing a number of points lying on the figure. Since any three (non-collinear) points define a circle, in general we must observe at least four points lying on the figure to refute H. Alternatively, we may consider the fictitious entity defined by the relation r^4, where the relation r is obtained from S: $(x, y) \in r$ iff the point (x, y) lies on S. Then, observing a single element of the set r^4, which consists of four-tuples of the coordinates of the figure's points, can refute H. This line of reasoning is central to the **self composition** technique [3]: to refute a *k-property*, which is a temporal property that cannot be refuted by observing less than k system behaviors [4], one can make a single observation on the fictitious entity that contains k copies of the system under test. Returning now to the family of test setups $\mathbf{T}_k$, with $k \geq 1$, defined in Example 17, we remark that a requirement that is $\mathbf{T}_{k+1}$-refutable, but not $\mathbf{T}_k$-refutable, can be refuted by observing a single behavior of the entity that is found by self-composing the system under test no less than $k + 1$ times. We proceed with an example.

Example 21. The prohibition P, stating that systems are deterministic, given in Example 2, is not $\mathbf{T}_1$-refutable: observing any single behavior of a non-deterministic eio system S is insufficient to refute the hypothesis $S \in P$. However, observing a single element of S^2 can demonstrate P's violation. Therefore, P is $\mathbf{T}_2$-refutable: determinacy can be refuted by self-composing the system under test. ▲

Intuitively, the less stringently a requirement is specified, the larger is the number of times the system under test must be self-composed to facilitate the requirement's refutability. We illustrate this point with a simple example. Consider the eio system model and the prohibition R defined as: S satisfies R iff $\forall (i, o) \in S.\ o = f(i)$, where f is a function from $\mathbb{N}$ to $\mathbb{N}$. Suppose that f is not available, but it is known that f is monotonically increasing: $i_1 \leq i_2$ implies $f(i_1) \leq f(i_2)$. We write R' for the corresponding (less stringent) requirement: $S \in R'$ iff $\forall (i_1, o_1), (i_2, o_2) \in S$, $i_1 \leq i_2$ implies $o_1 \leq o_2$. The requirement R is $\mathbf{T}_1$-refutable, whereas R', which is a superset of R, is not: R''s test oracle cannot make a decision solely based on a single input-output pair; a **test oracle** for a requirement R is a (partial) decision function that given a set of system behaviors tells whether the system violates R. Note however that R' is $\mathbf{T}_2$-refutable. Since $\mathbf{T}_{k+1}$ is strictly more permissive than $\mathbf{T}_k$, we conclude that the less stringently specified R is (in the above sense), the more a system must be sampled, or self-composed, to facilitate a test oracle for R; cf. [21]. That is, a partially specified requirement is harder to refute, because it leaves more leeway.

8 Algorithmic Refutability

We now characterize the requirements whose violation can be demonstrated through algorithmic means. We start with an auxiliary definition. Any requirement R induces a set Ω_R of **irremediable observations** $\{t \in T \mid \hat{\alpha}(t) \cap R = \emptyset\}$ in a test setup $\mathbf{T} = (T, \alpha)$. It follows that a system S violates a $\mathbf{T}$-refutable R iff $\alpha(S) \cap \Omega_R \neq \emptyset$. Intuitively, a requirement is algorithmically refutable only if it induces a recursively enumerable set of irremediable observations. Recall that, given a countable set U, a set $E \subseteq U$ is **recursively enumerable** if there is a (semi-)algorithm $\mathcal{A}_E$ that terminates and outputs *true* for any input $u \in U$ that is a member of E. If $u \notin E$, then $\mathcal{A}_E$ does not terminate.

Definition 22. A requirement R is **algorithmically refutable** in the test setup $\mathbf{T} = (T, \alpha)$ if R is finitely refutable in $\mathbf{T}$, and Ω_R is a recursively enumerable subset of the countable set T.

If a system S violates an algorithmically refutable requirement R in $\mathbf{T}$, then there is at least one observation $t \in \alpha(S)$ that can be carried out in finite time, where $\mathcal{A}_{\Omega_R}$ terminates on t and outputs *true*. Here, *true* means $t \in \Omega_R$, demonstrating $S \notin R$. Observing such a t through testing, therefore, conclusively refutes the hypothesis $S \in R$. The following example illustrates Definition 22.

Example 23. Consider the prohibition P for eio systems stating that a system may never output 0 for an odd input. Clearly, P is $\mathbf{T}_1$-refutable, and whether an observation $\{(i, o)\}$ is irremediable is decidable since the set $\Omega_P = \{\{(2i{+}1, 0)\} \in T_1 \mid i \in \mathbb{N}\}$ is recursive. If natural numbers are finitely observable, then P is algorithmically refutable in $\mathbf{T}_1$: any S that violates P has a finitely observable behavior, e.g. $t = \{(3, 0)\}$, and whether, or not, $t \in \Omega_P$ can be decided by a Turing machine. ▲

Let R be an algorithmically refutable requirement in $\mathbf{T} = (T, \alpha)$, and S be a system. The decision problem that asks whether S violates R is semi-decidable, if $\alpha(S)$ is a recursively enumerable subset of T. We illustrate this point using the following **test algorithm**, which relies on *dovetailing*. For a formal treatment of dovetailing, which is a poor man's parallelization technique, see, e.g., [20].

Algorithm 24. Fix an arbitrary total order on T's elements. Dovetail $\mathcal{A}_{\alpha(S)}$'s computations on the elements of T. In parallel, dovetail $\mathcal{A}_{\Omega_R}$'s computations on those observations for which $\mathcal{A}_{\alpha(S)}$ terminates. Output *true* and terminate, when any computation of $\mathcal{A}_{\Omega_R}$ terminates.

If $S \notin R$, then there exists at least one observation t_w in the set $\alpha(S) \cap \Omega_R$. The test algorithm is bound to terminate on t_w and output *true*, thus demonstrating $S \notin R$ in finite time. However, if $S \in R$, then the test (semi-)algorithm does not terminate. Ideally, standard test selection methods [15] place likely witnesses of R's violation early in the ordering assumed on T. Note that the above test algorithm achieves the (impractical) ideal of testing: it not only has "a high probability of detecting an as yet undiscovered error" [15], the algorithm is in fact guaranteed to reveal flaws in any system that violates an algorithmically refutable requirement. We proceed with an example.

Example 25. Fix an ordering on the set of all Turing machines: $M_0, M_1, \cdots$. In the eio model the requirement R is defined as: $S \in R$ if for any $(i, o) \in S$ the machine M_i diverges on o. It is easy to check that R is $\mathbf{T}_1$-refutable and the set Ω_R is recursively enumerable. Suppose that $\alpha_1(S)$ is recursively enumerable for a system S. That is, $\mathcal{A}_{\alpha(S)}$ is guaranteed to terminate on any $(i, o) \in S$ in the universe $\mathbb{N} \times \mathbb{N}$. If $S \notin R$, then there is a "witness" $(i_w, o_w) \in S$ where M_{i_w} terminates on o_w. Therefore, dovetailing M_i's computations on o for all (i, o) on which $\mathcal{A}_{\alpha(S)}$ terminates is bound to witness a terminating computation, thus demonstrating $S \notin R$ in finite time. ▲

Next, we apply the notion of algorithmic refutability to the temporal requirements introduced in Sect. 7 and the corresponding test setup $\mathbf{T}_*$. It is easy to check that a safety property ϕ is algorithmically refutable iff ϕ's set of *irremediable sequences* $\nabla_\phi = \{\sigma \in \Sigma^* \mid \forall \pi \in \Sigma^\omega.\ \sigma\pi \notin \phi\}$ is recursively enumerable. This condition separates refutability from **enforceability**, as explained below. To enforce the safety property ϕ on a system S, a reference monitor observes some $t \in \alpha(S)$. If t demonstrates that S violates ϕ, then the monitor *stops* S. Otherwise, the monitor *permits* S to continue its execution. For enforcement, the set ∇_ϕ must therefore be recursive [11]. It then follows that any enforceable temporal property is algorithmically refutable. An algorithmically refutable property need not however be enforceable: any property ϕ, where ∇_ϕ is recursively enumerable but not recursive, is algorithmically refutable, but not enforceable.

To further illustrate the relationship between refutability and enforceability, we define **weak enforceability** for a hyper-safety requirement R as follows. By monitoring the executions of a system S, a monitor observes some $t \in \alpha_*(S)$. If t does *not* conclusively demonstrate $S \notin R$, then the monitor permits S to continue. However, if t does conclusively demonstrate R's violation, then the monitor may either stop S, or diverge and thereby stall S. Recall that a system S violates a hyper-safety requirement R iff $\alpha_*(S) \cap \Omega_R \neq \emptyset$. To weakly enforce R, the set Ω_R must therefore be co-recursively enumerable, i.e. $T_* \setminus \Omega_R$ must be recursively enumerable. This observation, which concurs with [16, Theorem 4.2], illustrates that weak enforceability and algorithmic refutability are complementary in the sense that the former requires Ω_R to be co-recursively enumerable and the latter requires Ω_R to be recursively enumerable. This duality between refutability and enforceability becomes evident only after explicating the computational constraints of testing and enforcement.

9 Concluding Remarks

We have formally characterized the classes of refutable and verifiable requirements for black-box tests. Naturally black-box testing can be combined with other analysis techniques, like white-box system inspection; see, e.g., [17]. The indistinguishability condition of Sect. 4, stating that the system under test can be any abstraction of an observation obtained through tests, would then no longer be applicable. For instance, if the system under test is known to be deterministic, then clearly more requirements become refutable as discussed in Sect. 5. In other words, augmenting black-box analysis with knowledge that itself cannot be verified through black-box tests (e.g., coming from white-box analysis) would expand the analysis's capabilities, leading to more powerful refutation methods. Developing such an extension of our theory and exploring its applications remain as future work.

We remark that our theory of tests and refutation is not readily applicable to probabilistic constraints. For example, a gambling regulation requiring that slot machines have a 75% payout cannot be refuted through black-box test. Nevertheless, tests refuting such probabilistic constraints with a controllable margin of error can be devised. Developing a corresponding theory of tests and refutation also remains as future work.

Acknowledgments. We thank E. Fang, M. Guarnieri, G. Petric Maretic, S. Radomirovic, C. Sprenger, and E. Zalinescu for their comments on the paper.

A Proofs

We first present the proofs of the lemmas and theorems that are given in the paper. Afterwards, we formally state and prove the claim that a requirement is semi-monotone iff it is the intersection of its upper set and its lower set, which is mentioned in Sect. 5.

Proof (Lemma 3's Proof). If no system satisfies R, then R is trivial. Suppose that some system S satisfies R. Then, every system in $\lfloor\lceil S\rceil\rfloor$ satisfies R, because R is an obligation and a prohibition. As $\lfloor\lceil S\rceil\rfloor = \mathcal{S}$, for any $S \in \mathcal{S}$, we conclude that every system satisfies R. That is, R is trivial. □

Proof (Theorem 7's Proof). Suppose R is $\mathbf{T}$-refutable, with $\mathbf{T} = (T, \alpha)$. We prove that R is a prohibition. If R is empty, then R is a trivial prohibition. Assume that R is nonempty and let $S \in R$. Now, suppose $S' \preceq S$. All we need to prove is that $S' \in R$. We present a proof by contradiction.

Assume that $S' \notin R$. Then $\exists t \in T.\ \hat{\alpha}(t) \cap R = \emptyset$ simply because R is $\mathbf{T}$-refutable. Since α is order-preserving and $S' \preceq S$, we have $t \in \alpha(S)$. Therefore, $S \in \hat{\alpha}(t)$. This entails $S \notin R$, which contradicts the assumption $S \in R$. We conclude that $S' \in R$. Therefore, R is a prohibition.

Proof (Lemma 9's Proof). Fix a system model $\mathsf{M} = (\mathcal{S}, \preceq, \bot, \top)$, and assume that R is prohibition. We show that R is $\mathbf{T}_r^{\mathsf{M}}$-refutable, where $\mathbf{T}_r^{\mathsf{M}} = (\mathcal{S}, \lfloor\cdot\rfloor)$. Assume that some system S violates R. Since R is a prohibition, any system that abstracts S violates R. Moreover, $S \in \lfloor S\rfloor$. We conclude that $\exists S_w \in \lfloor S\rfloor.\ \lceil S_w\rceil \cap R = \emptyset$, namely $S_w = S$. Therefore, R is $\mathbf{T}_r^{\mathsf{M}}$-refutable.

Proof (Lemma 10's Proof). Suppose R is a nontrivial obligation. We prove by contradiction that R is not refutable in any test setup.

Assume that R is $\mathbf{T}$-refutable in some test setup $\mathbf{T}$. By Theorem 7, R is a prohibition. Then, R must be trivial by Lemma 3, because R is both a prohibition and an obligation. That R is a trivial contradicts the assumption that R is a nontrivial obligation. We conclude that R is not refutable in any test setup.

Proof (Theorem 14's Proof). Suppose R is $\mathbf{T}$-verifiable, with $\mathbf{T} = (T, \alpha)$. We prove that R is an obligation. If R is empty, then R is a trivial obligation. Assume that R is nonempty and let $S \in R$. Now, suppose $S \preceq S'$. All we need to prove is that $S' \in R$. Since R is $\mathbf{T}$-verifiable, from $S \in R$ we conclude $\exists t \in \alpha(S).\ \hat{\alpha}(S) \subseteq R$. As α is order-preserving and $S \preceq S'$, we have $t \in \alpha(S')$. That is, $S' \in \hat{\alpha}(S)$. We conclude that $S' \in R$. Therefore, R is an obligation.

Proof (Lemma 15's Proof). Suppose R is a nontrivial prohibition. We prove by contradiction that R is not verifiable in any test setup.

Assume that R is $\mathbf{T}$-verifiable in some test setup $\mathbf{T}$. By Theorem 14, R is an obligation. Then, R must be trivial by Lemma 3, because R is both a prohibition and an obligation. That R is a trivial contradicts the assumption that R is a nontrivial prohibition. We conclude that R is not verifiable in any test setup.

Proof (Theorem 20's Proof). We split the proof into several parts.

(1) Suppose that a property ϕ is $\mathbf{T}_*$-refutable. We show that ϕ is safety. Assume that $\pi \notin \phi$, for some $\pi \in \Sigma^\omega$. Then, the system $S_\pi = \{\pi\}$ violates ϕ. Now, by ϕ's $\mathbf{T}_*$-refutability, there exists a finite set t of ϕ's finite prefixes that demonstrates $S_\pi \notin R_\phi$, where $R_\phi = \lfloor \phi \rfloor$. Let σ be the longest element in t; note that since $\{\pi\}$ is a singleton, there always exists a single longest element in t. Then, for any $\pi' \in \Sigma^\omega$, the system $S_{\pi'} = \{\sigma\pi'\}$ violates ϕ, simply because t belongs to $\alpha(S_{\pi'})$. We conclude that $\sigma\pi' \notin \phi$, for all $\pi' \in \Sigma^\omega$. That is, ϕ is a safety temporal property.
(2) Suppose that ϕ is safety. We show that ϕ is $\mathbf{T}_*$-refutable. Assume that a system S violates ϕ. That is, $\exists \pi \in S.\ \pi \notin \phi$. Since ϕ is safety, a finite prefix of π, say σ, satisfies the following condition: $\forall \pi' \in \Sigma^\omega.\ \sigma\pi' \notin \phi$. Now, define the observation $t \in T_*$ as $\{\sigma\}$. Note that $t \in \alpha(S)$, and moreover $\hat{\alpha}(t) \cap R_\phi = \emptyset$ due to the above condition. This shows that ϕ is $\mathbf{T}_*$-refutable.
(3) Any temporal property ϕ is $\mathbf{T}_r$-refutable because R_ϕ's satisfaction is abstraction-closed, for any ϕ. Then, by Lemmas 3 and 15, any $\mathbf{T}_r$-verifiable or $\mathbf{T}_*$-verifiable property must be trivial.

Theorem 26. *A requirement R is semi-monotone iff $R = \lfloor R \rfloor \wedge \lceil R \rceil$.*

Proof. We split the proof into two parts, reflecting the theorem's two statements.

(1) Assume that R is semi-monotone. We show that $R = \lfloor R \rfloor \wedge \lceil R \rceil$. Clearly $R \subseteq \lceil R \rceil \wedge \lfloor R \rfloor$, for any requirement R. All we need to prove is that $\lceil R \rceil \wedge \lfloor R \rfloor \subseteq R$. If $\lceil R \rceil \wedge \lfloor R \rfloor = \emptyset$, then the claim trivially holds. Suppose $S \in \lceil R \rceil \wedge \lfloor R \rfloor$ for some system S. From $S \in \lceil R \rceil$, we conclude $\exists S_- \in R.\ S_- \preceq S$. Similarly, from $S \in \lfloor R \rfloor$, we conclude $\exists S_+ \in R.\ S \preceq S_+$. In short, we have $S_- \preceq S \preceq S_+$, $S_- \in R$, and $S_+ \in R$. Then, Lemma 27 below implies that $S \in R$, simply because R is semi-monotone. Therefore, if R is semi-monotone, then $R = \lceil R \rceil \wedge \lfloor R \rfloor$.
(2) Assume that $R = \lfloor R \rfloor \wedge \lceil R \rceil$. We prove that R is semi-monotone. Note that for any requirement Q, the requirement $\lfloor Q \rfloor$ is a prohibition, hence monotone. Moreover, $\lceil Q \rceil$ is an obligation, hence monotone. Therefore, $\lfloor Q \rfloor \wedge \lceil Q \rceil$ is semi-monotone, that is the intersection of two monotone requirements, for any requirement Q. In particular, R is semi-monotone because $R = \lfloor R \rfloor \wedge \lceil R \rceil$.

Lemma 27. If R is a semi-monotone requirement, then for any three systems S_-, S, and S_+ the following condition holds.

$$S_- \preceq S \preceq S_+ \;\wedge\; S_- \in R \;\wedge\; S_+ \in R \;\rightarrow\; S \in R$$

Proof. Either (1) R is monotone, that is R is the conjunction of two prohibitions or the conjunction of two obligations, or (2) R is the conjunction of a prohibition P and an obligation O. The lemma's claim is immediate for case (1). Let us consider case (2). Suppose $S_- \preceq S \preceq S_+ \;\wedge\; S_- \in R \;\wedge\; S_+ \in R$. Note that $S_- \in R$ implies that $S_- \in O$. Then, $S_- \preceq S$ implies that $S \in O$. Similarly, $S_+ \in R$ implies that $S_+ \in P$. Then, $S \preceq S_+$ implies that $S \in P$. These two statements show that $S \in P \wedge O$. That is, $S \in R$.

References

1. Abadi, M., Lamport, L.: The existence of refinement mappings. In: LICS, pp. 165–175. IEEE (1988)
2. Alpern, B., Schneider, F.: Defining liveness. Inf. Process. Lett. **21**(4), 181–185 (1985)
3. Barthe, G., D'Argenio, P.R., Rezk, T.: Secure information flow by self-composition. In: CSFW 2004, pp. 100–114. IEEE Computer Society (2004)
4. Clarkson, M.R., Schneider, F.B.: Hyperproperties. J. Comput. Secur. **18**(6), 1157–1210 (2010)
5. Damm, W., Harel, D.: LSCs: breathing life into message sequence charts. Formal Methods Syst. Des. **19**(1), 45–80 (2001)
6. Dijkstra, E.W.: Notes on structured programming. Technical report T.H. Report 70-WSK-03, Technological University Eindhoven, April 1970
7. Emerson, E.A., Halpern, J.: "Sometimes" and "Not Never" revisited: on branching versus linear time temporal logic. J. ACM **33**(1), 151–178 (1986)
8. Falcone, Y., Fernandez, J.-C., Jéron, T., Marchand, H., Mounier, L.: More testable properties. STTT **14**(4), 407–437 (2012)
9. Gaudel, M.-C.: Testing can be formal, too. In: Mosses, P.D., Nielsen, M., Schwartzbach, M.I. (eds.) CAAP 1995. LNCS, vol. 915, pp. 82–96. Springer, Heidelberg (1995). doi:10.1007/3-540-59293-8_188
10. Goodenough, J., Gerhart, S.: Toward a theory of test data selection. IEEE Trans. Softw. Eng. **1**(2), 156–173 (1975)
11. Hamlen, K.W., Morrisett, G., Schneider, F.B.: Computability classes for enforcement mechanisms. ACM Trans. Program. Lang. Syst. **28**(1), 175–205 (2006)
12. Hoare, C.A.R., Jifeng, H.: Unifying Theories of Programming. Prentice Hall, Englewood Cliffs (1998)
13. Larsen, K., Thomsen, B.: A modal process logic. In: LICS, pp. 203–210. IEEE (1988)
14. Morgan, C.: Programming from Specifications. Prentice Hall (1998)
15. Myers, G., Sandler, C., Badgett, T.: The Art of Software Testing. Wiley, Hoboken (2011)
16. Ngo, M., Massacci, F., Milushev, D., Piessens, F.: Runtime enforcement of security policies on black box reactive programs. In: POPL 2015, pp. 43–54. ACM (2015)
17. Nielson, F., Nielson, H.R., Hankin, C.: Principles of Program Analysis. Springer, Heidelberg (2005)

18. Pnueli, A.: The temporal logic of programs. In: FOCS 1977, pp. 46–57. IEEE (1977)
19. Popper, K.: Conjectures and Refutations: The Growth of Scientific Knowledge. Routledge, London (1963)
20. Rogers Jr., H.: Theory of Recursive Functions and Effective Computability. MIT Press, Cambridge (1987)
21. Segura, S., Fraser, G., Sanchez, A.B., Ruiz-Cortes, A.: A survey on metamorphic testing. IEEE Trans. Software Eng. **42**(9), 805–824 (2016)
22. Standaert, F.-X., Malkin, T.G., Yung, M.: A unified framework for the analysis of side-channel key recovery attacks. In: Joux, A. (ed.) EUROCRYPT 2009. LNCS, vol. 5479, pp. 443–461. Springer, Heidelberg (2009). doi:10.1007/978-3-642-01001-9_26
23. Sweeney, L.: K-anonymity: a model for protecting privacy. Int. J. Uncertain. Fuzziness Knowl.-Based Syst. **10**(5), 557–570 (2002)
24. Tretmans, J.: Model based testing with labelled transition systems. In: Hierons, R.M., Bowen, J.P., Harman, M. (eds.) Formal Methods and Testing. LNCS, vol. 4949, pp. 1–38. Springer, Heidelberg (2008). doi:10.1007/978-3-540-78917-8_1
25. Glabbeek, R.J.: The linear time - branching time spectrum. In: Baeten, J.C.M., Klop, J.W. (eds.) CONCUR 1990. LNCS, vol. 458, pp. 278–297. Springer, Heidelberg (1990). doi:10.1007/BFb0039066
26. von Wright, G.H.: Deontic logic. Mind **60**(237), 1–15 (1951)
27. Weyuker, E.J.: Axiomatizing software test data adequacy. IEEE Trans. Softw. Eng. **12**(12), 1128–1138 (1986)

The Density of Linear-Time Properties

Bernd Finkbeiner and Hazem Torfah(✉)

Saarland University, Saarbrücken, Germany
torfah@react.uni-saarland.de

Abstract. Finding models for linear-time properties is a central problem in verification and planning. We study the distribution of linear-time models by investigating the density of linear-time properties over the space of ultimately periodic words. The density of a property over a bound n is the ratio of the number of lasso-shaped words of length n, that satisfy the property, to the total number of lasso-shaped words of length n. We investigate the problem of computing the density for both linear-time properties in general and for the important special case of ω-regular properties. For general linear-time properties, the density is not necessarily convergent and can oscillates indefinitely for certain properties. However, we show that the oscillation is bounded by the growth of the sets of bad- and good-prefix of the property. For ω-regular properties, we show that the density is always convergent and provide a general algorithm for computing the density of ω-regular properties as well as more specialized algorithms for certain sub-classes and their combinations.

1 Introduction

Given a linear-time property, specified for example as a formula of a temporal logic, how hard is it to guess a model of the property? Temporal models play a fundamental role in verification and planning, for example in the satisfiability problem of temporal logic [19], in model checking [2], and in temporal planning [16]. With this paper, we initiate the first systematic study of the *density* of the linear-time temporal models.

The first choice to be made at the outset of such an investigation is how to represent temporal models. We base our study on ultimately periodic words, i.e., infinite words of the form $u \cdot v^\omega$, where u and v are finite words. This is motivated by the fact that ultimately periodic words are the natural and commonly used representation in all applications, where the underlying state space is finite (cf. [5]). With this choice of representation, our central question thus is the following: Suppose you are given an infinite word $u \cdot v^\omega$, where u and v are two finite words, that have been chosen randomly from all sequences over a given alphabet. How likely is it that $u \cdot v^\omega$ is a model of a given linear-time property?

We consider the *cardinality* and the *density function* in terms of the bound n. The cardinality of a property φ for a given bound n is the number of lassos of

This work was partly supported by the ERC Grant 683300 (OSARES) and by the Deutsche Telekom Foundation.

D. D'Souza and K. Narayan Kumar (Eds.): ATVA 2017, LNCS 10482, pp. 139–155, 2017.
DOI: 10.1007/978-3-319-68167-2_10

length n, that are models for the property φ, denoted by $\#_\varphi(n) = |\{(u,v) \in \Sigma^* \times \Sigma^+ \mid |u \cdot v| = n,\ u \cdot v^\omega \in \varphi\}|$. The density function of a property φ determines the rate of the cardinality of φ over the whole solution space for the specific bound n, and is denoted by $\nabla_\varphi(n) = \#_\varphi(n)/|\{(u,v) \in \Sigma^* \times \Sigma^+ \mid |u \cdot v| = n\}| = \#_\varphi(n)/(n \cdot |\Sigma|^n)$. To answer the question posed above, we study the asymptotic behavior of the density function, i.e., the limit $\lim_{n\to\infty} \nabla_\varphi(n)$, which we denote by ∇_φ^∞ and refer to as the *density* of the property φ.

Consider the following linear-time properties over the alphabet $\Sigma = 2^{\{a,b\}}$. The density function of the property given by the LTL formula $\varphi_1 = a \wedge \bigcirc b \wedge \bigcirc\bigcirc b$ is constant and equal to $\frac{1}{8}$ for bounds larger than two, because there is no restrictions on the labeling once the constraint of a labeling a followed by two b's has been satisfied. The density of the property $\varphi_2 = a\mathcal{U}b$ is equal to $\frac{2}{3}$ as the increase in the number of models is twice as large as the increase in the number of non-models for increasing bounds. Properties like $\varphi_3 = \square(a \wedge \bigcirc b)$ have densities equal to 0, because the cardinality of the set of bad-prefixes increases exponentially with increasing bounds, in comparison to a linear increase in the number of its models.

Two key questions of interest are whether or not the density exists for a linear-time property and, if the answer to the first question is yes, to compute its value. It is not obvious that the density exists for linear-time properties. In the case of ω-regular properties, we show that the density indeed always exists. This stands in contrast to regular properties of finite words, where this is not always true. Consider, for example, the regular property $(aa)^*$. Models for the property exist only for even bounds, and the density function oscillates between 0 and 1 for the alphabet $\{a\}$. The ω-regular property $(aa)^\omega$ for the same alphabet, however, has ultimately periodic models for all bounds and its density function converges to 0. The density for linear-time properties in general, nevertheless, does not necessarily exist. We show that for certain not ω-regular properties, the density function oscillates indefinitely without converging.

In case the density function cannot be computed, we show that it can still be approximated by examining the growth of the sets of good- and bad-prefixes of the property. The density of good-prefixes of a property defines a lower bound on the density. The density of bad-prefixes defines an upper bound on the density. Whether a density exists for property φ depends on the densities of four classes of lassos, that partition the whole space of lassos with respect to φ. These classes represent lassos (u,v), where $u \cdot v$ is a bad-prefix for φ, a good-prefix for φ, or models or non-models of φ where $u \cdot v$ is neither a good- nor a bad-prefix. We present few ways to check the existence of the density of a linear-time property with respect to the densities of each of these classes. To illustrate the affect of these classes consider the property $\bigcirc\bigcirc\bigcirc a$. It is clear that the rate of both the classes of models with no good-prefix and non-models with no bad-prefix converge to 0. This means, the upper and the lower bound of the density, determined by the classes of bad-prefix non-models and good-prefix models, meet in the limit and the density function converges to $\frac{1}{2}$.

For the special case of ω-regular properties, the limit of the density function can be computed algorithmically. This can be done by constructing an unambiguous ω-automaton, that defines the property and computing the probability of reaching an accepting strongly connected component in the automaton. Building on top of the algorithmic ideas, we also investigate the qualitative density checking problems, i.e., we determine if the density of a property is equal to 0 or 1, and provide a complete complexity analysis, determining the lower and upper bounds of these problems. Table 1 gives a summary on the complexity results shown and proven in the paper. A gap between the lower (PSPACE) and upper bound (EXPTIME) remains open for the problem of determining whether the density is smaller than 1 for a given LTL formula.

Table 1. Results for the computational complexity of computing the density of ω-regular languages.

	LTL	Non-deterministic Büchi	Deterministic parity
$\nabla_{\varphi}^{\infty}$	EXPTIME	EXPTIME	P
$\nabla_{\varphi}^{\infty} > 0$	PSPACE-compl	P-compl.	NL-compl.
$\nabla_{\varphi}^{\infty} < 1$	EXPTIME	PSPACE-compl.	NL-compl.

For some sub-classes of ω-regular properties, we can even avoid the costly construction of the automaton. We investigate a series of sub-classes and show how to compute the density for these classes and any of their combinations. In the case of LTL, we match syntactic classes to the introduced sub-classes and show that the density of a boolean combination of these syntactic classes can be reduced to the computation of the density of a much smaller formula.

Related Work. In the setting of finite, rather than infinite, words, the study of density has a long history [3,4,10,12,21]. For each language $\varphi \subseteq \Sigma^*$ of finite words over some alphabet Σ, the *density function* is defined as the quotient $\nabla_{\varphi}(n) = \#_{\varphi}(n)/|\Sigma^n|$, where $|S|$ denotes the cardinality of a set S and $\#_{\varphi}(n) = |\varphi \cap \Sigma^n|$, i.e., the number of words of length n in φ. In 1958, Chomsky and Miller [4] showed that for each regular language φ, there exists an initial length n_0 such that for all $n \geq n_0$, $\#_{\varphi}(n)$ can be described by a linear recurrence. For example, for the language ψ of the regular expression $(ab + baa)^*$, we have that $\#_{\psi}(n) = \#_{\psi}(n-2) + \#_{\psi}(n-3)$. The recursive description of $\#_{\varphi}(n)$ allows for a detailed analysis of the shapes of $\#_{\varphi}(n)$ and $\nabla_{\varphi}(n)$ (cf. [12]). The result was later extended to the nonambiguous context-free languages [12]. Much attention has focussed on *sparse* languages, i.e., languages, where $\#_{\varphi}(n)$ can be bounded from above by a polynomial [6,10,21]. Sparse languages can be used to restrict NP-complete problems so that they can be solved polynomially [6]. An interesting application of the density is to determine how well a non-regular language is approximated by a finite automaton [7]; this is important in streaming algorithms, where the incoming string must be classified quickly, and it suffices if the classification is correct most of the time.

In previous work [9], we have presented automata-based algorithms for computing $\#_\varphi(n)$ for safety specifications expressed in LTL. These algorithms compute $\#_\varphi(n)$ for a specific property φ and a specific value of n, but cannot be used to derive the convergences value of $\nabla_\varphi(n)$ for an entire class of properties. Faran and Kupferman have recently investigated the probability that a prefix of a word not in φ is a bad prefix of φ [8]. This probability is used to quantitatively determine the "safety level" of φ. The analysis again is done with respect to the finite words not the infinite words. A key difference to our work is that the safety level does not give the probability of a model and does not distinguish between properties of the same class but with different density values. Also related is Asarin *et al.*'s investigation of the asymptotic behavior in temporal logic [1]. The authors use the notion of entropy to show the relation between formulas in parametric linear-time temporal logic and formulas in standard LTL as some bounds tend to infinity.

2 Preliminaries

Linear-Time Properties and Models. A *linear-time property* φ over an alphabet Σ is a set of infinite words $\varphi \subseteq \Sigma^\omega$. Elements of φ are called *models* of φ. The complement set $\overline{\varphi} = \Sigma^\omega \setminus \varphi$ is called the set of *non-models* of φ.

A *lasso* over an alphabet Σ of length n is a pair (u, v) of finite words $u \in \Sigma^*$ and $v \in \Sigma^+$ with $|u \cdot v| = n$, that induces the ultimately periodic word $u \cdot v^\omega$. We call $u \cdot v$ the base of the lasso or ultimately periodic word. An *n-model* for the property φ over Σ is a lasso $(u, v) \in \Sigma^* \times \Sigma^+$ of length n such that the induced ultimately periodic word $u \cdot v^\omega \in \varphi$. We call n the bound of the n-model. The language $L_n(\varphi)$ for a bound n is set of n-models of φ. Note that a model of φ might be induced by more than one n-model, e.g., a^ω is induced by (a, a) and (ϵ, aa). The complement language $\overline{L_n(\varphi)}$ is the set of n-non-models of φ. We call the linear-time property over Σ, whose models build up the set of all lassos over Σ the *universal property* and denote it by $\top$. The *cardinality* of a property φ for a bound n, denoted by $\#_\varphi(n)$, is the size of $L_n(\varphi)$.

Safety and Liveness. For an infinite word $\sigma = \alpha_1\alpha_2\cdots \in \Sigma^\omega$ we denote every prefix $\alpha_1 \ldots \alpha_i$ by $\sigma[\ldots i]$. A finite word $w = \alpha_1 \ldots \alpha_i \in \Sigma^*$ is called a bad-prefix for a property φ, if every infinite word $\sigma \in \Sigma^\omega$ with $\sigma[\ldots i] = w$ is not a model of φ. We call a bad-prefix w *minimal*, if no prefix of w is a bad-prefix for φ. We denote the set of bad-prefixes of a property φ by *Bad*(φ). A finite word $w = \alpha_1 \ldots \alpha_i \in \Sigma^*$ is called a good-prefix for a property φ, if every infinite word $\sigma \in \Sigma^\omega$ with $\sigma[\ldots i] = w$ is a model of φ. We call a good-prefix w minimal, if w has no prefix, that is also a good-prefix for φ. We denote the set of good-prefixes of a property φ by *Good*(φ).

A property φ is a *safety* property if every non-model of φ has a bad-prefix for φ. A property φ is a *liveness* property if every finite word w can be extended by an infinite word σ such that $w \cdot \sigma$ is a model of φ. A property φ is a *co-safety* property if every model of φ has a good-prefix for φ. Co-safety properties can be either safety or liveness properties. The only property that is both liveness and safety at the same time is the *universal* property $\top$.

Linear-Time Temporal Logic. We use Linear-time Temporal Logic (LTL) [18], with the usual temporal operators Next $\bigcirc$, Until $\mathcal{U}$, and the derived operators Release $\mathcal{R}$, which is the dual operator of $\mathcal{U}$, Eventually $\diamond$ and Globally $\square$. LTL formulas are defined over a set of atomic propositions AP. We denote the satisfaction of an LTL formula φ by an infinite sequence $\sigma \in (2^{AP})^\omega$ of valuations of the atomic propositions by $\sigma \models \varphi$ and call σ a model of φ. For an LTL formula φ we define $L(\varphi)$ by the set $\{\sigma \in (2^{AP})^\omega \mid \sigma \models \varphi\}$. A lasso (u, v) of length n is an n-model of an LTL formula φ if $u \cdot v^\omega \in L(\varphi)$. If $u \cdot v^\omega$ is not a model of φ, the lasso is called an n-non-model of φ.

Parity Automata. A parity automaton over an alphabet Σ is a tuple $\mathcal{A} = (Q, Q_0, \delta, c)$, where Q is a set of states, Q_0 is a set of initial states, $\delta : Q \times \Sigma \to 2^Q$ is a transition relation, and $c : Q \to \mathbb{N}$ is a coloring function. A run of $\mathcal{A}$ on an infinite word $w = \alpha_1\alpha_2 \cdots \in \Sigma^\omega$ is an infinite sequence $r = q_0q_1 \cdots \in Q^\omega$ of states, where $q_0 \in Q_0$ and for each $i \geq 0$, $q_{i+1} = \delta(q_i, \alpha_{i+1})$. We define $\mathbf{Inf}(r) = \{q \in Q \mid \forall i \exists j > i.\ q_j = q\}$. A run r is called accepting if $\max\{c(q) \mid q \in \mathbf{Inf}(r)\}$ is even. A word w is accepted by $\mathcal{A}$ if there is an accepting run of $\mathcal{A}$ on w.

The automaton is called deterministic if the set Q_0 is a singleton and for each $(q, \alpha) \in Q \times \Sigma$ we have $|\delta(q, \alpha)| \leq 1$. The automaton is called unambiguous if for each accepted word w there is exactly one accepting run of the automaton on w. A parity automaton is called a *Büchi* automaton if the image of c is contained in $\{1, 2\}$. An automaton is *complete* if each state has an outgoing transition for each letter $\alpha \in \Sigma$. In the paper we always consider complete automata.

A strongly connected component (SCC) in $\mathcal{A}$ is a strongly connected component of the graph induced by the automaton. A strongly connected component is called *terminal* if none of the states in the SCC has a transition, that leaves the SCC. An SCC is called *accepting* if the highest color of the states of the SCC is even.

3 The Density of Linear-Time Properties

For a given linear-time property φ, the density function of φ gives the distribution of models of φ for increasing bounds n.

Definition 1 (Density). *The density function of a linear-time property φ over an alphabet Σ and a bound n is the ratio between the cardinality of φ for n and the number of lassos of length n over Σ:*

$$\nabla_\varphi(n) = \frac{\#_\varphi(n)}{n \cdot |\Sigma|^n}$$

The asymptotic density of φ *(short density) is the value* $\lim_{n\to\infty} \nabla_\varphi(n)$ *(in case it exists), which we denote by* ∇_φ^∞.

In previous work we presented an algorithm for computing the cardinality of safety LTL formulas for a given bound. The algorithm is doubly-exponential in the length of the formula yet linear in the bound [9]. An algorithm based on a translation to a propositional formula is exponentially less expensive in the formula than our algorithm, but exponentially more expensive in the bound. With respect to counting complexity classes, the complexity of computing the density of a property φ depends on the complexity of the membership test allowed by the representation of φ. Counting the number of models for a bound n and a property given as an LTL formula has been shown to be in #P [23]. Using these results we summarize the counting complexities of computing the density of ω-regular properties in the following theorem[1].

Theorem 1. *For an* ω*-regular property* φ *given by an LTL formula, a nondeterministic Büchi automaton, or a deterministic parity automaton, and for a given bound* n*, the problem of computing* $\nabla_\varphi(n)$ *is in #P.*

Proof. To show that the problem is in #P, we show that there is nondeterministic polynomial-time Turing machine $\mathcal{M}$, such that, the number of accepting runs of the machine on a given bound n and a property φ, is equal to the number of n-models of φ. We define $\mathcal{M}$ as follows. The machine $\mathcal{M}$ guesses a prefix u and a period v of an ultimately periodic word $u \cdot v^\omega$ with $|u \cdot v| = n$, and checks whether $u \cdot v^\omega$ satisfies φ, which can be done polynomial time when φ is an LTL formula [13], and in logarithmic space when φ is given by a nondeterministic Büchi or a deterministic parity automaton [14]. For each n-model (u, v) of φ there is exactly one accepting run of $\mathcal{M}$. Thus, counting the n-models of φ can be done by counting the accepting runs of $\mathcal{M}$ on the input (n, φ). □

Before getting to the computational complexity of computing the density of a given linear-time property, we illustrate what factors play a role in shaping the density function of a property. Consider the density of the universal property $\top$, which is constant and equal to 1, as its cardinality is defined by $\#_\varphi(n) = n \cdot |\Sigma|^n$. For each bound n, we can transform every n-model of $\top$ to a $(n+1)$-model by extending the base of the n-models with one letter from Σ and adding one of the now $n+1$ possible loops to the new base. The number of bases for n-models for the property $\top$ is $\frac{\#_\top(n)}{n}$. Thus, the number of $(n+1)$-models for $\top$ is equal to $|\Sigma| \cdot \frac{n+1}{n} \cdot \#_\top(n)$. According to the definition of the density function, this means that the monotonicity of the density function of a property in some bound n depends on whether the increase in the number of models in n is larger or smaller than the growth factor $|\Sigma| \cdot \frac{n+1}{n}$.

We define the *growth function* of a property φ by $\varsigma_\varphi(n) = \frac{\#_\varphi(n+1)}{\#_\varphi(n)}$. We call the function $\varsigma_\top(n) = |\Sigma| \cdot \frac{n+1}{n}$ the *universal growth function*. The following

[1] For more on counting complexities and the counting problem for linear-time temporal logic we refer the reader to [9,23,24].

proposition clarifies the relation between the monotonicity of the density function of a linear-time property φ and the universal growth function. Furthermore, the proposition shows the relation between the growth function of φ and the growth function of its complement $\overline{\varphi}$.

Proposition 1. *Given a property φ over Σ the following holds:*

1. $\forall n.\ \nabla_\varphi(n) = \nabla_\varphi(n+1)$ *if and only if* $\varsigma_\varphi(n) = \varsigma_\top(n)$
2. $\forall n.\ \nabla_\varphi(n+1) > \nabla_\varphi(n)$ *if and only if* $\varsigma_\varphi(n) > \varsigma_\top(n)$
3. $\forall n.\ \varsigma_\varphi(n) = \varsigma_\top(n)$ *if and only if* $\varsigma_{\overline{\varphi}}(n) = \varsigma_\top(n)$
4. $\forall n.\ \varsigma_\varphi(n) > \varsigma_\top(n)$ *if and only if* $\varsigma_{\overline{\varphi}}(n) < \varsigma_\top(n)$

For any linear-time property φ, the function $\#_\varphi(n)$ is monotonically increasing. This is due to the fact that any n-model of the property φ can be mapped to a $(n+1)$-model of φ, namely the one that results from unrolling the loop of the n-model by one position. From the last proposition we read thus that the monotonicity of the density function of φ at some bound n depends on the number of new $(n+1)$-models, i.e., those that cannot be rolled back to n-models. A density function, where the increase in models at some bound is higher (lower) than the increase in all lassos (models of the universal property $\top$) is increasing (decreasing) at that bound. This in turn means that the growth factor of the number of non-models is lower (higher) at the same bound. An oscillating function is one, where the increase in the number of models is interchangeably higher and lower than the increase in the total number of lassos.

Whether the density of a property exists, converges, is monotone or oscillating, depends on the densities of the following classes of lassos, that form with respect to a given property a partition of the space of lassos. For a property φ, we split the set of lassos into four classes:

- **Base non-models:** These are non-models (u, v), where $u \cdot v \in \mathit{Bad}(\varphi)$.
- **Base models:** These are models (u, v), where $u \cdot v \in \mathit{Good}(\varphi)$.
- **Loop non-models:** These are non-models (u, v), where $u \cdot v \notin \mathit{Bad}(\varphi)$.
- **Loop models:** These are models (u, v) where $u \cdot v \notin \mathit{Good}(\varphi)$.

In Fig. 1, we show how each of these classes grow over increasing bounds. For any property φ and for all bounds n, the classes of base non-models and base models increase by a factor larger or equal to $\varsigma_\top(n)$, because any extension of a bad-prefix remains a bad-prefix and every extension of a good-prefix also remains a good-prefix. Following Proposition 1, this means that for any bound n, the rates of base n-models and base n-non-models to the set of all n-lassos are monotonically increasing and thus converging. The rate of base models defines for each n a lower bound for the density function $\nabla_\varphi(n)$. Its convergence value defines in turn a lower bound on the limit inferior of the density function. The rate of base non-models defines an upper bound on the density function and its convergence value is an upper bound on the limit superior of the density function. The increase in the number of lassos of the classes of loop models and loop non-models depends highly on the property. An extension of the bases may

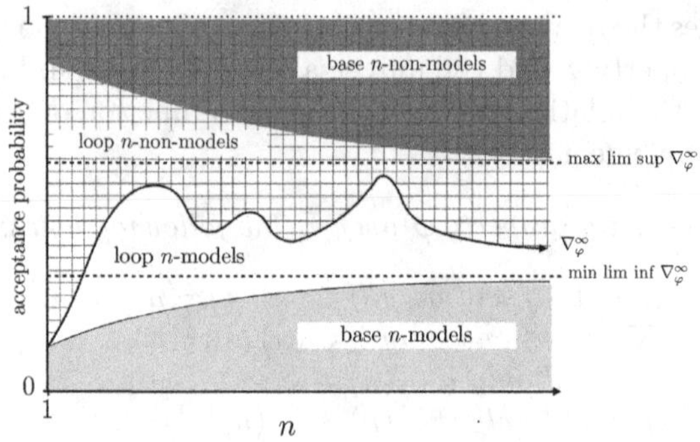

Fig. 1. The change in the density of the different classes of lassos for a linear property φ over increasing bounds n. Notice that both the rates of base n-non-models (lined gray area) and base n-models (plain gray area) is monotonically increasing forming an upper and lower bound on the density.

result in a new bad-prefix a new good-prefix, or a base on top of which new loop models or non-models can be obtained. This means that the rate of these two classes to the set of all lassos might oscillate indefinitely without converging as we show for some properties in the next section. This in turn means that the convergences behavior of the density function of φ is determined by the convergence of the rate of loop models of φ.

3.1 Asymptotic Density

In this section we investigate which linear-time properties have a converging density function. In the case of finite regular properties the density does not always exist. This follows from the fact that some regular properties allow no models for certain bounds as we have seen in the introduction. In contrast, in the case of ω-regular properties we will show that the density always exists. For general linear-time properties however we will see that this does not necessarily hold when considering ω-non-regular properties as shown in detail in Theorem 2.

We classify a property φ according to the convergence of its density function to either: *0-convergent* when $\nabla^\infty_\varphi = 0$, *1-convergent* when $\nabla^\infty_\varphi = 1$, *$\epsilon$-convergent* when $\nabla^\infty_\varphi = \epsilon$ for $0 < \epsilon < 1$, and *$\bot$-convergent* when the density function is non-convergent.

The change in the size of the different classes of lassos presented in the last section plays a key role in the convergence behavior of a property. From the last section we know that the rates of base models and base non-models are always convergent. This means the convergence behavior depends on the rates of loop models and loop non-models. For example, the property $\bigcirc p$, has no loop models nor loop non-models for bounds larger that 2, and the rates of these classes converge to 0. All lassos of length greater or equal to 2 belong to one of the sets of base models or base non-models, depending on whether the second position of the lasso is labeled with p or not, and thus, the density of $\bigcirc p$ is determined by the rates of base models and base non-models. The number of base models of $\bigcirc p$ is equal to $2^{AP-1} \cdot (2^{AP})^{n-1} \cdot n$ for $n > 1$, which results in a density of $\frac{1}{2}$.

The rates of base models and base non-models also determine the density of the safety property $q\mathcal{R}p$ over $AP = \{p, q\}$, which convergences to a value of $\frac{1}{3}$. The property has no loop non-models and n loop models for each bound n, namely those where all positions are labeled with p and not labeled with q. Thus, the rates of loop models and loop non-models converge to 0. In the case of base-models we can count $\sum_{i=1}^{n}(2^{AP})^{n-i} \cdot n$ many base n-models, because for each $1 \leq i \leq n$, there are $(2^{AP})^{n-i} \cdot n$ many base n-models which are labeled with p and q at position $i-1$ and with only p for all positions smaller than i, and arbitrarily for all positions greater than i. Applying Definition 1, the density function of $q\mathcal{R}p$ can be computed as $\sum_{i=1}^{n}(4)^{-i}$, which converges towards $\frac{1}{3}$ when n tends to infinity.

An example, where the density depends fully on the rate of loop models is $\Diamond\Box p$. The property has neither base models nor base non-models. A lasso is a loop model for $\Diamond\Box p$ if all positions in the loop are labeled with p. For a bound n, there are $\sum_{i=1}^{n}(2^{AP})^{i-1}$ many loop n-models (i is the position of the loop). This results in a density function equal to $\sum_{i=1}^{n}\frac{(2^{AP})^{i-1}}{(2^{AP})^{n} \cdot n}$ which converges to 0 when n grows to infinity[2].

If none of the sets of bad- nor good-prefixes is empty, and the rate of loop models is convergent then the density is ϵ-convergent, because none of the rates of base models nor base non-models to all lassos is equal to zero.

Lemma 1. *The density function of a property φ is convergent, if and only if the rate of loop models is convergent.*

Proof. The density function can be defined as the sum of the two rates of base models and loop models. Because the rate of base models is always convergent, it follows that the density function is convergent if and only if the rate of loop models is convergent. □

With the same argumentation the rate of loop non-models plays the same role as the one for loop models.

Lemma 2. *For a given property φ, the rate of loop models is convergent if and only if the rate of loop non-models is convergent.*

Proof. From Lemma 1 we know that when the rate of loop models is convergent then the density of φ is also convergent. This means that the rate of non-models is convergent, and as the rate of base non-models is always convergent, then so is the rate of loop non-models.

With analogous reasoning we can show that the convergence of the rate of loop non-models implies the convergence of the rate of loop models. □

[2] The formula $\Diamond\Box p$ is an example of a 0-convergent liveness formula.

We show now an example of certain types of not ω-regular properties, that have a non-convergent rate of loop models, and thus a non-convergent density function.

Theorem 2. *There is a linear-time property with a non-convergent density function.*

Proof. We divide each of the lasso classes further into cyclic lassos, i.e., lassos, where the loop is at the first position of the lasso, and non-cyclic lassos, which cover the rest of lassos in a class. The property we present is a liveness property, where the classes of base models and base non-models are empty. We show that the rate of loop models is non-convergent and we show that the reason is that the rate of cyclic loop models is non-convergent.

We define a property φ over the set of atomic propositions $AP = \{a\}$ as follows: Let $c_1, c_2 \dots$ and $d_1, d_2 \dots$ be natural numbers such that $c_1 \leq d_1 < c_2 \leq d_2 < \dots$. A lasso is a model of φ if eventually the letter $\{a\}$ is encountered at some position and there is a constant δ in one of the intervals $[c_i, d_i)$ for some number $i \in \mathbb{N}$ such that from then on, $\{a\}$ appears periodically every δ positions.

The number of non-cyclic loop n-models of φ is equal to $|2^{AP}| \cdot \#_\varphi(n-1)$, because we can extend each $(n-1)$-model φ to an n-model by attaching any letter from 2^{AP} to the first position of the $(n-1)$-model. This means that the growth factor of the models of φ is determined by the respective growth in the size of the sets of cyclic models for each bound.

Notice that the rate of cyclic models depends strongly on the bound n. If $c_j \leq n < d_j$ for some j, then we have $|2^{AP}|^n - 1$ many cyclic models of length n, as we only need to have at least one position labeled with $\{a\}$ and the rate of models in this case is increasing. If $d_j \leq n < c_{j+1}$, then there are at most $|2^{AP}|^{n - \lfloor \frac{n}{h} \rfloor} \cdot h$, where h is the largest allowed period in n. In this case, the rate of models is decreasing. This means that in all bounds n that belong to some interval $[c_i, d_i)$ the density is increasing, and all bounds in intervals $[d_j, c_{j+1})$ the density of φ is decreasing. We can choose the numbers $c_1, c_2, \dots$ and $d_1, d_2 \dots$ in a way that the density increases in c_{i+1} to a value larger than the one in c_i, and decreases in d_{i+1} to a value smaller than in d_i. In this way, the density function is oscillating and non-convergent. □

3.2 Density of ω-Regular Properties

In this section we show how to compute the density of ω-regular properties given by non-deterministic Büchi and deterministic parity automata. In the next section we show how these results can be adopted to compute the density of properties given as LTL formulas.

We start by showing the relationship between the density of a property φ and the densities of the terminal SCCs of an automaton representing φ.

Lemma 3. *The density of an ω-regular property φ given as a parity automaton $\mathcal{A}$ is greater than 0 if and only if $\mathcal{A}$ has a reachable terminal accepting strongly connected component.*

Proof. We prove the lemma along the steps of [20]. Let $\mathcal{A}$ be defined over the alphabet 2^{AP} for a set of atomic proposition AP. Let S be an accepting terminal SCC in $\mathcal{A}$ with n states (remember that $\mathcal{A}$ is complete, thus S allows transitions for all letters in 2^{AP} in each state). The probability of choosing a transition with label $\alpha \in 2^{AP}$ is equal to $\epsilon = \frac{1}{|2^{AP}|}$ from any state in S. Let s be a state in S. The probability of not reaching s from any other state in S in n steps is at most $1 - \epsilon^n < 1$. This means for an infinite trace in S, the probability of not seeing s again from every position of the trace is equal to 0. Thus, the probability of choosing an infinite run σ in S such that $s \notin \mathbf{Inf}(\sigma)$ is also equal to 0. This is in particular true for the state $s_{\max}$ with the maximum color in S. This implies that an infinite run σ in S with $\mathbf{Inf}(\sigma)$ equal to the set of states of S, has probability 1. Because $s_{\max}$ is even, it follows that the probability of a lasso with an accepting run in S converges to 1, when the length of the lasso tends to infinity.

If $\mathcal{A}$ has a reachable terminal accepting SCC S, then it is reached by at least one finite prefix with positive probability. The density of φ is then at least equal to the probability of choosing this prefix. If $\mathcal{A}$ does not have a terminal accepting SCC, then the rate of models of φ converges to 0, because the probability of staying infinitely in an accepting cycle in the automaton is 0. □

Using the previous lemma we show the complexity of the following qualitative problems for the density.

Theorem 3. *Let φ be an ω-regular property given by a deterministic parity automaton. The problem of checking whether $\nabla^{\infty}_{\varphi} > 0$ is* NL*-complete.*

Proof. As shown in Lemma 3, to check if the density of the property given by an automaton $\mathcal{A}$ is greater than 0, it suffices to check whether there is an accepting terminal strongly connected component in $\mathcal{A}$. We choose a state q of $\mathcal{A}$ reachable from the initial state and apply the following procedure. Iterating over all states q' of the automaton, we check if q' is reachable from q. If yes, we check if q is reachable again from q'. If this is not the case, then q is not a state in a terminal SCC in $\mathcal{A}$, and we choose a new state in $\mathcal{A}$ different than q and repeat the whole procedure for the new state. Otherwise, if for each q' reachable from q, there is a path leading back to q, then we have found a terminal SCC that contains q. During the iteration we also save the highest color seen. If this color is even then q is a state in a terminal accepting SCC in $\mathcal{A}$. If no terminal accepting SCC is found after iterating over all states of $\mathcal{A}$, then the density is 0.

Checking whether a state is reachable from another can be done in nondeterministic logarithmic space (the reachability problem in automata is in NL). Checking whether a state is not reachable from another can also be done in nondeterministic logarithmic space (the non-reachability problem in automata is in co-NL and NL=co-NL). In each iteration we only need to memorize the binary encoding of the state q and the current state q' and the current highest color seen so far, which require in total an encoding of no more than logarithmically many bits in the size of the automaton.

A matching lower bound is can be proven by a reduction from a nondeterministic logarithmic-space Turing machines. □

Theorem 4. *Let φ be an ω-regular property given by a nondeterministic Büchi automaton $\mathcal{A}$. The problem of checking whether $\nabla_{\varphi}^{\infty} > 0$ is P-complete.*

Proof. We check whether $\mathcal{A}$ has a terminal accepting SCC S. Finding such an SCC can be done in polynomial time. A matching lower bound is achieved by a log-space reduction from the *circuit value* problem. □

We turn now to the problem of checking if $\nabla_{\varphi}^{\infty} < 1$.

Theorem 5. *Let φ be an ω-regular property given by a deterministic parity automaton $\mathcal{A}$. The problem of checking whether $\nabla_{\varphi}^{\infty} < 1$ is* NL*-complete.*

Proof. Following the idea of Theorem 3 we can check if $\mathcal{A}$ has a terminal **non-accepting** SCC in nondeterministic logarithmic space. Because the automaton is deterministic, any lasso that has a run in this SCC is a non-model of φ. If $\mathcal{A}$ contains such an SCC, then the rate of non-models is greater than 0 (at least as equal as the probability of reaching the non-accepting SCC), and thus the density is less than 1. If no such SCC is found, then the density is equal to 1.

A matching lower bound can be shown via a reduction from a nondeterministic logarithmic-space Turing machine.

Theorem 6. *Let φ be an ω-regular property given by a nondeterministic Büchi automaton $\mathcal{A}$. The problem of checking whether $\nabla_{\varphi}^{\infty} < 1$ is* PSPACE*-complete.*

Proof. Using Safra's construction [17], every nondeterministic parity automaton $\mathcal{A}$ can be transformed into a deterministic parity automaton $\mathcal{D}$ of size exponential in the size of $\mathcal{A}$. Each state of $\mathcal{D}$ is a Safra-tree over the states of $\mathcal{A}$. The size of a Safra-tree is equal to the size of $\mathcal{A}$ and we can distinguish exponentially many Safra-trees. In Theorem 5 we presented a non-deterministic logarithmic-space algorithm over deterministic parity automata for checking whether there is an non-accepting terminal SCC. Instead of constructing the whole automaton $\mathcal{D}$ and checking the existence of such an SCC, we will do it on the fly as follows. We can guess a run of the automaton $\mathcal{D}$ by stepwise guessing Safra-trees and checking if two succeeding trees are consistent with transition relation of $\mathcal{D}$. At some position we also guess that a current state q of the run is one in a terminal SCC. As in the procedure of Theorem 3 we check whether all successor states q' allow a path from which q can be reached again. For that we only need logarithmic space in the size of $\mathcal{D}$, thus, polynomial space in the size of $\mathcal{A}$. If a maximum color seen during the traversal of a path is even, then we have found an accepting terminal SCC that contains the state q.

A matching lower bound can be achieved following the steps of [15] by reducing a polynomial space-bound Turing machine $\mathcal{M}$ and a word w to a nondeterministic parity automaton A such that, $\mathcal{M}$ accept w if and only if the density of A is smaller 1.

Using the so far presented results we show now how to compute the density.

Theorem 7. *Computing the density ∇_φ^∞ for an ω-regular property φ can be done in polynomial time if φ is given by an unambiguous parity automaton $\mathcal{A}$.*

Proof. To compute the density of φ we need to compute the density of each terminal accepting strongly connected component in the automaton $\mathcal{A}$. Because $\mathcal{A}$ is unambiguous, it is guaranteed that no model ends in two terminal accepting SCCs of $\mathcal{A}$ and thus the density is the sum of densities of all terminal accepting SCCs. The density of an SCC is given by the probability of reaching the SCC. Computing the probability of an SCC can be seen as a convergence problem of a Markov chain, where the automaton $\mathcal{A}$ can be thought of as a Markov chain, where the label of a transition is replaced by its probability, i.e., a probability equal to $\frac{1}{|2^{AP}|}$. Both finding the terminal accepting strongly connected components and computing their probabilities can be done in polynomial time [3]. □

4 Density of LTL Properties

In this section we reexamine the problems investigated in the last section for properties given as LTL formulas. For any LTL property φ we can compute the density by constructing an unambiguous ω-automaton for φ and using the algorithm given in Theorem 7. However, the construction of the automaton is costly (exponential [2]) and can be avoided for many sub-classes of LTL.

The results for LTL are summarized below, and follow from Theorems 7, 6, and 3, and from the fact that any LTL formula can be turned into an exponential unambiguous parity automaton [2].

Theorem 8. *1. Computing the density ∇_φ^∞ for an ω-regular property φ given as an LTL formula can be done in exponential time.*
2. Checking whether $\nabla_\varphi^\infty > 0$ for an LTL formula φ is PSPACE*-complete.*
3. Checking whether $\nabla_\varphi^\infty < 1$ for an LTL formula φ is in EXPTIME.

In the following we present a series of syntactic LTL classes for which the density can be immediately given. Using these sub-classes we show later that the computation of the density for LTL formulas can be reduced to the computation of the density of a much smaller LTL formula. We distinguish following syntactic LTL classes:

- **Bounded-Safety:** A *bounded-safety* property φ describes a set of infinite words, each with a prefix in a finite set $\Gamma \subseteq \Sigma^k$ for some k. A formula in the LTL fragment with only the temporal operator $\bigcirc$ is a bounded-safety formula.
- **Invariants:** An *invariant* property φ describes an unreachability property over a bounded-safety property ψ and is given by the LTL fragment $\square\psi$.
- **Guarantee:** A *guarantee* property φ is a reachability property defined over some bounded-safety property ψ and is given by the LTL fragment $\diamond\psi$.

- **Persistence:** A *persistence* property φ is a co-Büchi condition defined over a bounded-safety property ψ and is given by the LTL fragment $\Diamond\Box\psi$.
- **Response:** A *response* property φ is a Büchi condition defined over a bounded-safety property and is given by the LTL fragment $\Box\Diamond\psi$.

Theorem 9. *1. Every bounded-safety property φ not equivalent to false or to true is ϵ-convergent.*
2. Every invariant property or persistence property φ is 0-convergent.
3. Every guarantee property or response property φ is 1-convergent.

4.1 Composition of LTL Properties

When given an LTL formula φ composed of formulas from the syntactic classes presented above we can compute the density of φ using the rules given in Table 2. The intersection of properties φ_1 and φ_2 that are convergent to 1 results in a new property that also has an density $\nabla^{\infty}_{\varphi_1 \cap \varphi_2} = 1$. When φ_1 and φ_2 converge to 0 then $\nabla^{\infty}_{\varphi_1 \cap \varphi_2} = 0$. The same also holds when considering the union of the properties φ_1 and φ_2. In the case of ϵ-convergent properties φ_1 and φ_2 the density of the intersection of the properties depends intersected properties. If both φ_1 and φ_2 were bounded-safety properties this value depends on the size of the intersection of characterization sets of φ_1 and φ_2. It can range from 0, when the characterization sets are disjoint, to ϵ when the properties are equivalent. When building the union of two ϵ-convergent properties the density can range from ϵ to 1. If both properties were again bounded safety properties then the density is equal to ϵ when φ_1 and φ_2 are equivalent and to 1 when their characterization sets are disjoint. Given an LTL formula φ composed of the syntactic classes we apply the rules presented in Table 2 and the results from Theorem 9, until no rule is applicable anymore. The remaining formula is a bounded safety formula for which we apply the algorithm given in Theorem 7.

Table 2. Density for conjunctive (lower triangle) and disjunctive (upper triangle) compositions:

$\nabla^{\infty}_{\varphi_1 \cap \varphi_2}$	1	ϵ	0	$\nabla^{\infty}_{\varphi_1 \cup \varphi_2}$
1	1	1	1	1
ϵ	ϵ	$1/\epsilon$ $0/\epsilon$	ϵ	ϵ
0	0	0	0	0

For example, consider the LTL formula over the set of atomic propositions $AP = \{a, b\}$:

$$\varphi = (a \vee \bigcirc b) \wedge (\bigcirc\bigcirc\bigcirc(b \wedge a) \vee \Diamond a) \vee (\Box b \wedge \Diamond(a \wedge \bigcirc b))$$

We start by evaluating the subformulas

$$\nabla^{\infty}_{\Box b \wedge \Diamond(a \wedge \bigcirc b)} = \nabla^{\infty}_{\Box b} = 0 \quad \text{and} \quad \nabla^{\infty}_{\bigcirc\bigcirc\bigcirc(b \wedge a) \vee \Diamond a} = 1$$

Thus the density is equal to the one of the formula $(a \vee \bigcirc b)$, which is a bounded-safety property for which we can use the algorithm in Theorem 7 and compute the density

$$\nabla^{\infty}_{a \vee \bigcirc b} = 0.5 + 0.5 * 0.5 = 0.75$$

5 Discussion

With this paper, we have initiated an investigation of the density of models of linear-time properties. Our work extends the classic results for finite words to ultimately periodic infinite words. In comparison to finite words, the new class of models significantly complicates the analysis; the proof techniques introduced in this paper, in particular the analysis of classes of loop and base models and non-models, have allowed us, however, to obtain a classification of the major property classes according to the convergence of the density. Computing the density for omega-regular properties can be done algorithmically, yet is very expensive. In contrast to expensive LTL algorithms presented above, the qualitative analysis can be obtained for free, for the syntactic fragments for the different property types introduced in the paper (and their combinations).

The obvious next step is to exploit the results algorithmically. It may be possible to steer randomized algorithms such as Monte Carlo model checking [11] towards areas of the solution space where we are most likely to find a model. In planning, the choice between exploration and backtracking in a temporal planner could be biased towards exploration in situations with increasing probability, and towards backtracking in situations with decreasing probability. It may also be possible to develop approximative algorithms that replace a complicated linear-time property with a simpler, but ultimately equivalent property, such as a parity condition with a smaller number of colors. In similar techniques for properties of finite words, the density of the difference language is used to verify that the error introduced by the approximation is small [7].

A big challenge is to extend the results further to tree models and, thus, to determine the density of branching-time properties. A first step into this direction is made by model counting algorithms for tree models [9]. Since tree models can be seen as implementations in the sense of reactive synthesis [22], this line of work might also lead to a better understanding of the complexity of the synthesis problem, and perhaps to new randomized synthesis algorithms.

References

1. Asarin, E., Blockelet, M., Degorre, A., Dima, C., Mu, C.: Asymptotic behaviour in temporal logic. In: LICS 2014. ACM, New York (2014)
2. Baier, C., Katoen, J.-P.: Principles of Model Checking. Representation and Mind Series. The MIT Press, Cambridge (2008)

3. Bodirsky, M., Gärtner, T., von Oertzen, T., Schwinghammer, J.: Efficiently computing the density of regular languages. In: Farach-Colton, M. (ed.) LATIN 2004. LNCS, vol. 2976, pp. 262–270. Springer, Heidelberg (2004). doi:10.1007/978-3-540-24698-5_30
4. Chomsky, N., Miller, G.A.: Finite state languages. Inf. Control **1**(2), 91–112 (1958)
5. Clarke, E., Biere, A., Raimi, R., Zhu, Y.: Bounded model checking using satisfiability solving. Form. Methods Syst. Des. **19**(1), 7–34 (2001)
6. Demaine, E.D., López-Ortiz, A., Munro, J.I.: On universally easy classes for NP-complete problems. Theoret. Comput. Sci. **304**, 471–476 (2003)
7. Eisman, G., Ravikumar, B.: Approximate recognition of non-regular languages by finite automata. In: Proceedings of the 28th Australasian Conference on Computer Science, ACSC 2005, Darlinghurst, Australia, vol. 38 (2005)
8. Faran, R., Kupferman, O.: Spanning the spectrum from safety to liveness. In: Finkbeiner, B., Pu, G., Zhang, L. (eds.) ATVA 2015. LNCS, vol. 9364, pp. 183–200. Springer, Cham (2015). doi:10.1007/978-3-319-24953-7_13
9. Finkbeiner, B., Torfah, H.: Counting models of linear-time temporal logic. In: Dediu, A.-H., Martín-Vide, C., Sierra-Rodríguez, J.-L., Truthe, B. (eds.) LATA 2014. LNCS, vol. 8370, pp. 360–371. Springer, Cham (2014). doi:10.1007/978-3-319-04921-2_29
10. Flajolet, P.: Analytic models and ambiguity of context-free languages. Theoret. Comput. Sci. **49**(23), 283–309 (1987)
11. Grosu, R., Smolka, S.A.: Monte Carlo model checking. In: Halbwachs, N., Zuck, L.D. (eds.) TACAS 2005. LNCS, vol. 3440, pp. 271–286. Springer, Heidelberg (2005). doi:10.1007/978-3-540-31980-1_18
12. Hartwig, M.: On the density of regular and context-free languages. In: Thai, M.T., Sahni, S. (eds.) COCOON 2010. LNCS, vol. 6196, pp. 318–327. Springer, Heidelberg (2010). doi:10.1007/978-3-642-14031-0_35
13. Kuhtz, L., Finkbeiner, B.: **LTL** path checking is efficiently parallelizable. In: Albers, S., Marchetti-Spaccamela, A., Matias, Y., Nikoletseas, S., Thomas, W. (eds.) ICALP 2009. LNCS, vol. 5556, pp. 235–246. Springer, Heidelberg (2009). doi:10.1007/978-3-642-02930-1_20
14. Markey, N., Schnoebelen, P.: Model checking a path. In: Amadio, R., Lugiez, D. (eds.) CONCUR 2003. LNCS, vol. 2761, pp. 251–265. Springer, Heidelberg (2003). doi:10.1007/978-3-540-45187-7_17
15. Meyer, A.R., Stockmeyer, L.J.: The equivalence problem for regular expressions with squaring requires exponential space. In: 13th Annual Symposium on Switching and Automata Theory, SWAT 1972. IEEE, Washington, DC (1972)
16. Patrizi, F., Lipovetzky, N., De Giacomo, G., Geffner, H.: Computing infinite plans for LTL goals using a classical planner. In: Proceedings of the 22nd International Joint Conference on Artificial Intelligence, IJCAI 2011, Barcelona, Catalonia, Spain, 16–22 July 2011. IJCAI/AAAI (2011)
17. Piterman, N.: From nondeterministic büchi and streett automata to deterministic parity automata. In: 21st Annual IEEE Symposium on Logic in Computer Science (LICS 2006), pp. 255–264 (2006)
18. Pnueli, A.: The temporal logic of programs. In: 18th Annual Symposium on Foundations of Computer Science, pp. 46–57. IEEE Computer Society (1977)
19. Rozier, K.Y., Vardi, M.Y.: LTL satisfiability checking. In: Bošnački, D., Edelkamp, S. (eds.) SPIN 2007. LNCS, vol. 4595, pp. 149–167. Springer, Heidelberg (2007). doi:10.1007/978-3-540-73370-6_11

20. Schewe, S.: Synthesis for probabilistic environments. In: Graf, S., Zhang, W. (eds.) ATVA 2006. LNCS, vol. 4218, pp. 245–259. Springer, Heidelberg (2006). doi:10.1007/11901914_20
21. Szilard, A., Yu, S., Zhang, K., Shallit, J.: Characterizing regular languages with polynomial densities. In: Havel, I.M., Koubek, V. (eds.) MFCS 1992. LNCS, vol. 629, pp. 494–503. Springer, Heidelberg (1992). doi:10.1007/3-540-55808-X_48
22. Thomas, W.: Facets of synthesis: revisiting church's problem. In: de Alfaro, L. (ed.) FoSSaCS 2009. LNCS, vol. 5504, pp. 1–14. Springer, Heidelberg (2009). doi:10.1007/978-3-642-00596-1_1
23. Torfah, H., Zimmermann, M.: The complexity of counting models of linear-time temporal logic. Acta Inform. pp. 1–22 (2016)
24. Valiant, L.G.: The complexity of computing the permanent. Theor. Comput. Sci. **8**, 189–201 (1979)

HyLeak: Hybrid Analysis Tool for Information Leakage

Fabrizio Biondi[1], Yusuke Kawamoto[2(✉)], Axel Legay[3], and Louis-Marie Traonouez[3]

[1] CentraleSupélec Rennes, Rennes, France
[2] AIST, Tsukuba, Japan
yusuke.kawamoto.aist@gmail.com
[3] Inria Rennes, Rennes, France

Abstract. We present HyLeak, a tool for reasoning about the quantity of information leakage in programs. The tool takes as input the source code of a program and analyzes it to estimate the amount of leaked information measured by mutual information. The leakage estimation is mainly based on a hybrid method that combines precise program analysis with statistical analysis using stochastic program simulation. This way, the tool combines the best of both symbolic and randomized techniques to provide more accurate estimates with cheaper analysis, in comparison with the previous tools using one of the analysis methods alone. HyLeak is publicly available and is able to evaluate the information leakage of randomized programs, even when the secret domain is large. We demonstrate with examples that HyLeaks has the best performance among the tools that are able to analyze randomized programs with similarly high precision of estimates.

1 Introduction

Automated Security Evaluation. With the increasing complexity of networked systems, it is getting harder and harder for security engineers to analyze a system and give a reasonable guarantee that the system does not jeopardize the security and privacy of the users. A significant effort in research has been devoted towards techniques able to (semi-)automatically identify leakage of confidential information in software and hardware systems, allowing for more formal assurances of security and privacy.

This work was supported by JSPS KAKENHI Grant Number JP17K12667, by JSPS and Inria under the Japan-France AYAME Program, by the MSR-Inria Joint Research Center, by the Sensation European grant, and by région Bretagne.

D. D'Souza and K. Narayan Kumar (Eds.): ATVA 2017, LNCS 10482, pp. 156–163, 2017.
DOI: 10.1007/978-3-319-68167-2_11

Among automated techniques to quantify the information leakage of a system, we distinguish the two approaches: *precise program analysis* providing a precise result (e.g. [2,4,5]) and *statistical analysis* providing an approximate estimation (e.g. [6–8]). The main difference between them is that precise analysis needs to explore the complete behavior of the system to obtain the exact leakage values, while statistical analysis has to cover only a statistically significant sample of the system's behavior to produce their estimation, and thus tends to scale better. However, when statistical analysis fails to cover many rare events in the system, it does not produce an accurate estimation.

Recently, some researchers have been trying to bridge the gap between precise and statistical techniques by introducing *hybrid methods* combining them [10,12]. This paper presents the HyLeak tool, the first publicly available leakage computation tool leveraging both precise and statistical analyses. The implementation is based on the hybrid method for estimating mutual information [10] while it also employs many optimization techniques to enhance the estimation performance. As we explain in Sect. 4 the tool has the best performance in computing leakage among the tools that are able to analyze randomized programs with similarly high precision of estimates.

The HyLeak Hybrid Analysis Strategy. The HyLeak tool takes as input a program written in a simple imperative language (a slight extension of the input language used in the QUAIL tool [4]) and computes its Shannon leakage, i.e., the mutual information between the variables defined as *secrets* and those as *observable outputs* in the given source code.

More specifically, HyLeak divides a program code into (terminal) components and decides for each of them whether to analyze it using precise or statistical analysis, by applying heuristics that evaluate the analysis cost of each component. Then, following the theoretical results in [10], HyLeak composes the analysis results of all components into an approximate joint probability distribution of the secret and observable variables in the program. Finally, the tool estimates the Shannon leakage and its confidence interval.

One of HyLeak's technical novelties lies in the implementation of the code decomposition. The procedure is based on the fact that the cost of analyzing a code fragment with precise analysis is proportional to the amount of traces in the fragment (since precise analysis has to analyze all traces), while the cost of statistical analysis is proportional to the number of possible observable variables (since statistical analysis has to run simulations for each value of the observable variables). Then the amount of traces and observable variable values at each point in the program execution is statically estimated via a heuristic approach. The tool locates in which part of the execution, if any, stochastic simulation becomes more efficient than precise analysis, and records this by inserting a `simulate` statement in the code.

The stochastic simulation usually has to run the code for each value of the secret; however, if in the code fragment the observable variables do not depend on the secret, it is sufficient to simulate the fragment with a single secret value and to apply the results to all the other values of the secret. This technique is called *abstraction-then-sampling* in [10], and can significantly reduce the number of simulations necessary to produce a good estimation, particularly for programs with a large secret domain. If the tool finds it can apply abstraction-then-sampling on the code fragment, it inserts a `simulate-abs` statement instead. In the analysis of the program, when the tool reaches a `simulate` or a `simulate-abs` statement in the code, it switches precise program analysis to stochastic simulation or abstraction-then sampling, respectively.

```
const MAX:=14;
secret int32 sec := [251,750];
observable int32 obs:= 0;
public int32 time := 0;
public int32 loc := 0;
public int32 seed := 0;
public int32 ran := 0;
if (sec <= 425) then
  assign loc:=400;
elif (sec <= 475) then
  assign loc:=450;
elif (sec <= 525) then
  assign loc:=500;
elif (sec <= 575) then
  assign loc:=550;
else
  assign loc:=600;
fi
while (time < MAX) do
  random ran := random(1,6);
  if (ran <= 3) then
    assign loc:=loc+10;
  else
    assign loc:=loc-10;
  fi
  assign time:=time+1;
od
assign obs:=loc;
return;
```

Fig. 1. Random walk.

Motivating Example. Consider the following random walk problem (modeled in Fig. 1).

The secret is the initial location of an agent, encoded by a single natural number representing an approximate distance from a given point, e.g. in meters. Then the agent takes a fixed number of steps. At each step the distance of the agent increases or decreases by 10 m with the same probability. After this fixed number of random walk, the final location of the agent is revealed, and the attacker uses it to guess the initial location of the agent.

This problem is too complicated to analyze by precise analysis, because the analysis needs to explore every possible combination of random paths, amounting to an exponential number in the walking steps. It is also intractable to analyze with a fully statistical approach, since there are hundreds of possible secret values and the program has to be simulated many times for each of them to sufficiently observe the agent's behavior.

As shown in Sect. 4, HyLeak's hybrid approach computes the leakage significantly faster than the fully precise analysis and more accurately than the fully statistical analysis.

2 HyLeak Implementation

We describe how HyLeak estimates the Shannon leakage of an input program. The tool determines which component of the program to analyze with precise analysis and which with randomized analysis, and inserts appropriate annotations in the code. The components are analyzed with the chosen technique and the results are composed into a joint probability distribution of the secret and observable variables. Finally, the Shannon leakage and its confidence interval are computed. The tool implementation consists of the following 4 steps. Steps 1 and 2 are implemented with different ANTLR parsers [14]. The implementation of Step 3 inherits a large amount of code from the QUAIL tool. This means that QUAIL's optimizations, i.e., parallel analysis of execution traces and compact Markovian state representation, are inherited. However QUAIL's restrictions are inherited as well in HyLeak, meaning that the prior distribution on the secret is assumed to be uniform and no private variable can appear in assignments.

Step 1: Preprocessing

Step 1a. Lexing, Parsing and Syntax Checking. The tool starts by lexical analysis, macro substitution and syntax analysis. In macro substitution the constants defined in the input program are replaced with their declared values, and simple operations are resolved immediately. The tool checks whether the input program correctly satisfies the language syntax. In case of syntax errors, an error message describing the problem is produced.

Step 1b. Loop Unrolling and Array Expansion. `for` loops ranging over fixed intervals are unrolled to optimize the computation of variable ranges and thus program decomposition in Step 2. Similarly, arrays are replaced with multiple variables indexed by their position number in the array. Note that these techniques are used only to optimize program decomposition and not required to compute the leakage in programs with arbitrary loops.

Step 2: Program Decomposition and Internal Code Generation

If a `simulate` or `simulate-abs` statement is present in the code, this step is skipped. Otherwise, for each variable and each code line, an estimation of the number of possible values of the variable at the specific code line is computed. This is used to evaluate at each point in the input program whether it would be more expensive to use precise or statistical analysis, as explained in Sect. 5 of [10]. The tool adds `simulate` and/or `simulate-abs` statements in the code to signal which parts of the input program should be analyzed with standard statistical sampling and with abstraction-then-sampling. At the end, the input program is translated into a simplified internal language. Conditional statements and loops (`if`, `for`, and `while`) are rewritten into `if-goto` statements.

Step 3: Program Analysis

In this step the tool analyzes the executions of the program using the two approaches.

Step 3a. Precise Analysis. The tool performs a depth-first symbolic execution of all possible execution traces of the input program, until it finds a `return`, `simulate`, or `simulate-abs` statement. When reaching a `return` statement the tool recognizes the execution trace as terminated and stores its secret and output values. In the cases of `simulate` and `simulate-abs` statements it halts the execution of the trace, saves the resulting program state, and schedules it for stochastic simulation or for abstraction-then-sampling simulation, respectively, starting from the saved program state.

Step 3b. Randomized Analysis. The tool performs all the standard stochastic simulations and abstraction-then-sampling simulations, using the saved program states from Step 3a as starting point of each component to analyze stochastically. The sample size for each simulation is automatically decided by using heuristics to have better accuracy with less sample size. The results of each analysis is stored as an appropriate joint probability sub-distribution between secret and observable values.

Step 4: Leakage Estimation

In this step the tool aggregates all the data collected by the program analysis (performed in Steps 3) and estimates the Shannon leakage of the input program, together with evaluation of the estimation. More specifically, it constructs an (approximate) joint posterior distribution of the secret and observable values of the input program from all the collected data produced by Step 3, as explained in Sect. 3.1 of [10]. Then the tool estimates the Shannon leakage value from the joint distribution, including bias correction (See more details in Sect. 4 of [10]). Finally, a 95% confidence interval for the estimated leakage value is computed to roughly evaluate the quality of the analysis.

3 On Using HyLeak

HyLeak is freely available from https://project.inria.fr/hyleak, in both source code and artifact form. Multiple examples and the scripts to generate the results are also provided.

We show how to use HyLeak to analyze the random walk example presented in Sect. 1. The program code is shown in Fig. 1 on the left; assume it is contained in the file `random_walk_abs-sim.hyleak`. We invoke the tool with the command:

```
./hyleak random_walk_abs-sim.hyleak
```

The tool generates various `.pp` text files with analysis information and the control flow graph of the program (Fig. 2). Finally, it outputs the prior and posterior Shannon entropy estimates, the estimated leakage of the program before and after bias correction, and its confidence interval. HyLeak can also print the channel matrix and additional information; the full list of arguments is printed by `./hyleak -h`.

4 Comparison with Other Tools

The HyLeak tool processes a simple imperative language that is an extension of the language used in the QUAIL tool version 2.0 [3]. The QUAIL tool implements only a precise calculation of leakage that examines all executions of programs. Hence the performance of QUAIL does not scale, especially when the program performs complicated computations that yield a large number of execution traces. On the other hand, HyLeak fully supports the statistical approach and the hybrid approach. Hence HyLeak can analyze large problems that QUAIL cannot handle. Note that an approach combining static and randomized analyses was first proposed by Köpf and Rybalchenko [12] differently.

The stochastic simulation techniques implemented in HyLeak have also been developed in the tools LeakiEst [7] (with its extension [11]) and LeakWatch [8,9]. Below we compare HyLeak's analysis technique against the full simulation technique implemented in these tools.

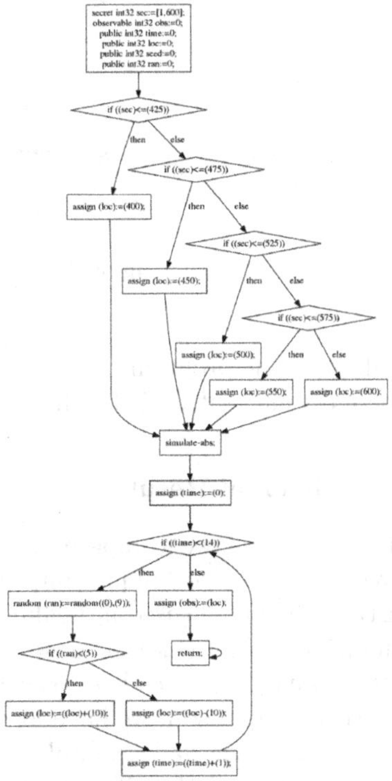

Fig. 2. Control flow graph for the input code of Fig. 1.

The tool Moped-QLeak [5] computes the precise information leakage of a program by transforming it into an algebraic decision diagram (ADD). As noted in [3], this technique is efficient when the program under analysis is simple enough to be converted into an ADD, and fails otherwise even when other tools including HyLeak can handle it.

Many information leakage tools restricted to deterministic input programs have been released, including TEMU [13], squifc [15], jpf-qif [16], QILURA [17], nsqflow [18], and SHARPPI [19]. Some of these tools have been proven to scale to programs of thousands of lines written in common languages like C and Java. Such tools rely on the fact that the Shannon leakage of a deterministic program is bounded from above by the logarithm of the number of possible outputs of the program. The number of possible outputs is usually computed using model counting on a SMT-constraint-based representation of the possible outputs, obtained by analyzing the program. Contrary to these tools, HyLeak can analyze randomized programs[1] and provides a quite precise estimation of the

[1] Some of these tools, like jpf-qif and nsqflow, present case studies on randomized protocols. However, the randomness of the programs is assumed to have the most leaking behavior. E.g., in the Dining Cryptographers this means assuming all coins produce head with probability 1.

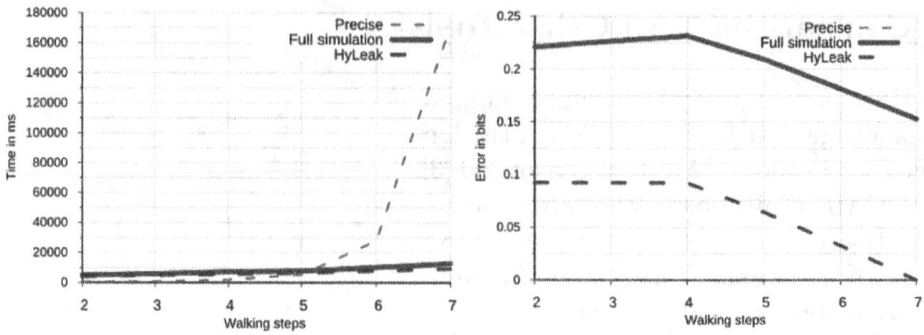

Fig. 3. Random walk experimental results

leakage of the program, not just an upper bound. As far as we know, HyLeak is the most efficient tool that has this greater scope and higher precision.

Experimental Results

In this section we compare the performance of the tool HyLeak against the precise analysis technique (implemented in version 2.0 of QUAIL) and the statistical technique (used in LeakiEst and LeakWatch). In the experiments we use an option of HyLeak that deactivates stochastic simulations and performs fully precise analysis, which has basically an identical behavior to the QUAIL tool. As another comparison, we have forced fully randomized analysis like LeakWatch.

The random walk example in Fig. 1 has a conditional branching inside the `while` loop, and thus it has an exponential number of execution traces in the walking time `time`. Hence precise analysis takes an exponential time while both HyLeak and fully randomized analysis take much less time thanks to random sampling of traces (Fig. 3 on the left). Since HyLeak uses an abstraction-then-sampling technique, it has smaller errors than fully randomized analysis with an identical sample size (Fig. 3 on the right).

See the full version [1] for other examples and the results of their experiments.

References

1. Biondi, F., Kawamoto, Y., Legay, A., Traonouez, L.-M.: HyLeak: hybrid analysis tool for information leakage (2017). https://hal.inria.fr/hal-01546817
2. Biondi, F., Legay, A., Malacaria, P., Wąsowski, A.: Quantifying information leakage of randomized protocols. In: Giacobazzi, R., Berdine, J., Mastroeni, I. (eds.) VMCAI 2013. LNCS, vol. 7737, pp. 68–87. Springer, Heidelberg (2013). doi:10.1007/978-3-642-35873-9_7
3. Biondi, F., Legay, A., Quilbeuf, J.: Comparative analysis of leakage tools on scalable case studies. In: Fischer, B., Geldenhuys, J. (eds.) SPIN 2015. LNCS, vol. 9232, pp. 263–281. Springer, Cham (2015). doi:10.1007/978-3-319-23404-5_17

4. Biondi, F., Legay, A., Traonouez, L.-M., Wąsowski, A.: QUAIL: a quantitative security analyzer for imperative code. In: Sharygina, N., Veith, H. (eds.) CAV 2013. LNCS, vol. 8044, pp. 702–707. Springer, Heidelberg (2013). doi:10.1007/978-3-642-39799-8_49
5. Chadha, R., Mathur, U., Schwoon, S.: Computing information flow using symbolic model-checking. In: Proceedings of FSTTCS 2014, pp. 505–516 (2014)
6. Chatzikokolakis, K., Chothia, T., Guha, A.: Statistical measurement of information leakage. In: Esparza, J., Majumdar, R. (eds.) TACAS 2010. LNCS, vol. 6015, pp. 390–404. Springer, Heidelberg (2010). doi:10.1007/978-3-642-12002-2_33
7. Chothia, T., Kawamoto, Y., Novakovic, C.: A tool for estimating information leakage. In: Sharygina, N., Veith, H. (eds.) CAV 2013. LNCS, vol. 8044, pp. 690–695. Springer, Heidelberg (2013). doi:10.1007/978-3-642-39799-8_47
8. Chothia, T., Kawamoto, Y., Novakovic, C.: LeakWatch: estimating information leakage from java programs. In: Kutyłowski, M., Vaidya, J. (eds.) ESORICS 2014. LNCS, vol. 8713, pp. 219–236. Springer, Cham (2014). doi:10.1007/978-3-319-11212-1_13
9. Chothia, T., Kawamoto, Y., Novakovic, C., Parker, D.: Probabilistic point-to-point information leakage. In: Proceedings of CSF 2013, pp. 193–205 (2013)
10. Kawamoto, Y., Biondi, F., Legay, A.: Hybrid statistical estimation of mutual information for quantifying information flow. In: Fitzgerald, J., Heitmeyer, C., Gnesi, S., Philippou, A. (eds.) FM 2016. LNCS, vol. 9995, pp. 406–425. Springer, Cham (2016). doi:10.1007/978-3-319-48989-6_25
11. Kawamoto, Y., Chatzikokolakis, K., Palamidessi, C.: Compositionality results for quantitative information flow. In: Norman, G., Sanders, W. (eds.) QEST 2014. LNCS, vol. 8657, pp. 368–383. Springer, Cham (2014). doi:10.1007/978-3-319-10696-0_28
12. Köpf, B., Rybalchenko, A.: Approximation and randomization for quantitative information-flow analysis. In: Proceedings of CSF 2010, pp. 3–14 (2010)
13. Newsome, J., McCamant, S., Song, D.: Measuring channel capacity to distinguish undue influence. In: Chong, S., Naumann, D.A. (eds.) PLAS. ACM (2009)
14. Parr, T.: The Definitive ANTLR Reference: Building Domain Specific Languages. Pragmatic Bookshelf, Raleigh (2007)
15. Phan, Q., Malacaria, P.: Abstract model counting: a novel approach for quantification of information leaks. In: Proceedings of ASIA CCS 2014, pp. 283–292 (2014)
16. Phan, Q., Malacaria, P., Tkachuk, O., Pasareanu, C.S.: Symbolic quantitative information flow. ACM SIGSOFT Softw. Eng. Notes **37**(6), 1–5 (2012)
17. Phan, Q.-S., Malacaria, P., Păsăreanu, C.S., D'Amorim, M.: Quantifying information leaks using reliability analysis. In: Proceedings of SPIN 2014, pp. 105–108. ACM (2014)
18. Val, C.G., Enescu, M.A., Bayless, S., Aiello, W., Hu, A.J.: Precisely measuring quantitative information flow: 10k lines of code and beyond. In: EuroS&P 2016, pp. 31–46 (2016)
19. Weigl, A.: Efficient SAT-based pre-image enumeration for quantitative information flow in programs. In: Proceedings of QASA 2016, pp. 51–58 (2016)

Compositional Safety Refutation Techniques

Kumar Madhukar[1,3](✉), Peter Schrammel[2], and Mandayam Srivas[3]

[1] TCS Research, Pune, India
kumar.madhukar@tcs.com
[2] School of Engineering and Informatics, University of Sussex, Brighton, UK
[3] Chennai Mathematical Institute, Chennai, India

Abstract. One of the most successful techniques for refuting safety properties is to find counterexamples by bounded model checking. However, for large programs, bounded model checking instances often exceed the limits of resources available. Generating such counterexamples in a modular way could speed up refutation, but it is challenging because of the inherently non-compositional nature of these counterexamples. We start from the monolithic safety verification problem and present a step-by-step derivation of the compositional safety refutation problem. We give three algorithms that solve this problem, discuss their properties with respect to efficiency and completeness, and evaluate them experimentally.

1 Introduction

Divide-and-conquer approaches are considered to be the blue print solution to scale algorithms to large problems. Compositionality of proofs is the enabler of a map-reduce approach to verification. Compositional verification approaches based on contracts and summaries have been shown to tremendously increase scalability and productivity in real-world formal verification [2,12,19,27].

But what about refutation? Unlike verification, refutation algorithms are usually based on finding a violating execution trace, which seems to be inherently non-compositional. Consequently, the study of the compositional refutation problem is an under-explored area of research. Yet, solutions to this problem have significant impact on other research problems. As a motivation, we give here two algorithmic approaches in verification and testing that will be enabled by efficient compositional refutation algorithms:

- Property-guided abstraction refinement algorithms like CEGAR [6] need to decide whether counterexamples that are found in the abstraction are spurious or true counterexamples. The lack of compositional refutation techniques forces these algorithms to operate in a monolithic manner and is therefore an obstacle to scaling them to large programs.
- Automated test generation techniques based on Bounded Model Checking are successfully used in various industries to generate unit tests (e.g. [25]). However, they do not sufficiently scale to accomplish the task of generating

D. D'Souza and K. Narayan Kumar (Eds.): ATVA 2017, LNCS 10482, pp. 164–183, 2017.
DOI: 10.1007/978-3-319-68167-2_12

integration tests. Compositional refutation techniques achieve exactly this goal: they efficiently produce refutations (from which test vectors can be derived) on unit (module) level and enable their composition in order to obtain system level refutations, i.e. integration tests.

This paper is a first step in this direction and lays the base for a more systematic study of the problem domain.

Contributions. We summarise the contributions of the paper as follows:

- In order to place the problem in a wider context, we give an informal overview on how completeness relates to problem decomposition in safety refutation and verification (Sect. 3).
- We formalise the safety refutation problem in *horizontal decompositions*, e.g. procedure-modular decompositions, and characterise the compositional completeness guarantees of various algorithmic approaches (Sect. 4).
- We describe three refutation approaches with different degrees of completeness (Sect. 5) and give experimental results on C benchmarks, comparing their completeness and efficiency (Sect. 6).

2 Preliminaries

Program Model and Notation. We assume that programs are given in terms of acyclic[1] call graphs, where individual procedures f are given in terms of *deterministic*, symbolic input/output transition systems. F is the set of all procedures in the program. Since the handling of loops is orthogonal to the compositional aspect, we consider only loop-free procedures (respectively bounded unwindings of loops) in this paper. Thus, we simply denote the input/output relation of a procedure f as $T_f(\boldsymbol{x}^{in}, \boldsymbol{x}^{out})$. Inputs $\boldsymbol{x}^{in}$ are procedure parameters, global variables, and memory objects that are read by f. Outputs $\boldsymbol{x}^{out}$ are return values, and potential side effects such as global variables and memory objects written by f. Boolean guard variables (g) are used to model the control flow. Non-deterministic choices are encoded by additional input variables.

The relations T_f are given *as first-order logic formulae* over bitvectors and arrays, resulting from the logical encoding of the program semantics. Figure 1 gives an example of the encoding of a program into such formulae using the loop-free notation. The inputs $\boldsymbol{x}^{in}$ of *foo* are (y, g_6) and the outputs $\boldsymbol{x}^{out}$ consist of (r, g_7) where r is the return value. In addition to the inputs and outputs we need boolean guard variables g^{in}, g^{out} (here g_6, g_7) that are true if the entry and, respectively, exit of the procedure can be reached. They are handled like input/output parameters and have their actual counterparts in the guard variables in the caller (here, e.g. g_1, g_2 for the call foo_0 in *main*). Note that we consider exit in a procedure is not reachable, i.e., $\neg g^{out}$, if either the program is non-terminating or an assertion in a procedure is violated. Hence, the exit guard

[1] We consider non-recursive programs with multiple procedures (cf. model in [5]).

```
void main(int x) {
  if(x < 0) {
    x = foo(x);
    x = foo(x);
    bar(x);
  }
}

int foo(int y) {
  return y+1;
}
void bar(int z) {
  assert(z > 10);
}
```

$$
\begin{aligned}
T_{main}((x_0, g_0), (g_5)) &\equiv g_1{=}(g_0 \wedge (x_0{<}0)) \wedge \\
&\quad foo_0((x_0, g_1), (x_1, g_2)) \wedge \\
&\quad foo_1((x_1, g_2), (x_2, g_3)) \wedge \\
&\quad bar((x_2, g_3), (g_4)) \wedge \\
&\quad g_5{=}(g_0 \wedge \neg(x_0{<}0) \vee g_4) \\
Props_{main} &\equiv true \\
T_{foo}((y, g_6), (r, g_7)) &\equiv (r{=}y{+}1) \wedge (g_6{=}g_7) \\
Props_{foo} &\equiv true \\
T_{bar}((z, g_8), (g_9)) &\equiv g_9{=}(g_8 \wedge (z{>}10)) \\
Props_{bar} &\equiv g_8 \Rightarrow (z{>}10)
\end{aligned}
$$

Fig. 1. Example program and its encoding

condition in the definition of a transition function includes assertion checks as in T_{bar}. We use a single static assignment (SSA) encoding, which gives a fresh name to each update of a variable if it is modified multiple times, such as for example in *main*.

Each call to a procedure h at call site i in a procedure f is modeled by a *placeholder predicate* $h_i(\boldsymbol{x}_i^{p\_in}, \boldsymbol{x}_i^{p\_out})$ occurring in the formula T_f for f. The placeholder predicate ranges over intermediate variables representing its actual input and output parameters $\boldsymbol{x}_i^{p\_in}$ and $\boldsymbol{x}_i^{p\_out}$, respectively. Placeholder predicates evaluate to *true* in the beginning, which corresponds to havocking the program variables in procedure calls. As the analysis progresses, they get strengthened by summaries. We later explain how we use the guard variables in performing this propagation. In procedure *main* in Fig. 1, the placeholder for the first procedure call to *foo* is $foo_0((x_0, g_1), (x_1, g_2))$ with the actual input and output parameters x_0, x_1, respectively, and the corresponding guard variables that encode whether the entry and exit of foo_0 are reachable. Let $Props_f$ denote the property (assertion) in procedure f (e.g. the assertion in *bar* in Fig. 1). Note that we view these formulae as predicates, e.g. $T(\boldsymbol{x}, \boldsymbol{x}')$, with given parameters $\boldsymbol{x}, \boldsymbol{x}'$, and mean the $T[\boldsymbol{a}/\boldsymbol{x}, \boldsymbol{b}/\boldsymbol{x}']$ when we write $T(\boldsymbol{a}, \boldsymbol{b})$. Moreover, we write $\boldsymbol{x}$ and x with the understanding that the former is a vector, whereas the latter is a scalar.

CS_f is the set of call sites in procedure f, and the set of all call sites CS is $\bigcup_{f \in F} CS_f$. $fn(i)$ is the procedure called at call site i. We write X_f for the variables in T_f, and $\hat{X}$ for the entirety of variables in $T_{fn(i)}(\boldsymbol{x}_i^{in}, \boldsymbol{x}_i^{out})$ for all $i \in CS$.

Summaries, and Calling Contexts. Inter-procedural compositional proofs of a sequential program usually use a set of auxiliary predicates to define abstractions of loops and procedures. These abstractions are usually formally defined by means of a set of predicates – *invariants*, a *summary* and a *calling context* ($CallCtx_i$) for every procedure invocation h_i at call site i in a call-graph of the program. These predicates have the following roles: Invariants abstract the behaviour of loops inside functions. Summaries abstract the behaviour of called procedures; they are used to strengthen the placeholder predicates.

Calling contexts abstract the caller's behaviour w.r.t. the procedure being called. When analysing the callee, the calling contexts are used to constrain its inputs and outputs. The set of sub-traces corresponding to a function at a call site is characterised by a conjunction of the calling context and summary predicates associated with the function at that call site. We provide formal definitions for summaries and calling contexts below (invariants are not needed in this paper).

Definition 1. *For a procedure given by T_f we define:*

- *A* summary *is a predicate Sum_f such that:*

$$\forall X_f : T_f(\boldsymbol{x}^{in}, \boldsymbol{x}^{out}) \Longrightarrow Sum_f(\boldsymbol{x}^{in}, \boldsymbol{x}^{out})$$

- *The* calling context *for a procedure call h at call site i in the given procedure is a predicate $CallCtx_i$ such that*

$$\forall X_f : T_f(\boldsymbol{x}^{in}, \boldsymbol{x}^{out}) \Longrightarrow CallCtx_i(\boldsymbol{x}_i^{p\text{-}in}, \boldsymbol{x}_i^{p\text{-}out})$$

For instance, a summary for procedure *foo* in Fig. 1, is $Sum_{foo}((y, g_6), (r, g_7)) = (y<MAX \Rightarrow r>y)$.[2] A (forward) calling context for the first call to procedure *foo* in *main* is $CallCtx_{foo_0}((x_0, g_1), (x_1, g_2)) = (g_1 \Rightarrow x_0<0)$.

We observe that the guard variables are also used in defining summaries and calling contexts. They have the same meaning as in transition functions. The reason we have defined *CallCtx* over both input and output parameters is so we can propagate it in forward or backward directions.

3 Compositional Verification and Refutation Overview

A decomposition of a verification problem intuitively splits the original problem into a set of sub-problems that cover the original problem. The decomposition operator for the problem has a corresponding composition operator for composing the results obtained from the sub-problems in order to obtain a solution of the original problem.

In terms of program executions, a decomposition can be viewed as a way a proof of verification splits the behaviour, i.e. the set of all execution traces of a program, in constructing the proof. Consider a safe version of the code in Fig. 1 where the assertion in *bar* is changed to $z \leq 10$. A safety proof for the program can be constructed hierarchically by using the following summaries for *foo* and *bar*: $Sum_{foo}((y, g_6), (r, g_7)) = (r{=}y+1 \wedge g_6{=}g_7)$ and $Sum_{bar}((z, g_8), (g_9)) = (g_9 \Rightarrow z \leq 10)$. Then, the proof for *main* can be constructed using the recursive Algorithm 1. The proof for the leaves (*foo* and *bar*) involves showing their transition functions imply their respective summary. Proof composition for a non-leaf procedure will use the caller summaries to similarly construct a proof (a summary) for the caller. In our example, the program is indeed proved safe as the algorithm constructs a Sum_{main}, which, in this case, can be a suitable

[2] *MAX* denotes the maximum possible value in the type of y.

Algorithm 1. Composition operator for summaries

```
procedure COMPOSE(f)
    for all i ∈ CS_f do                        ▷ CS_f are the call sites in procedure f
        Sum_fn(i) ← COMPOSE(fn(i))             ▷ fn(i) is the procedure called at call site i
    Sum_f ← proof(f)                           ▷ uses Sum_fn(i), i ∈ CS_f and proof composer operator
    return Sum_f                               ▷ Sum_f can be cached
```

abstraction of the transition function for *main*, that is not *false*, while checking that the constructed summaries verify all the embedded properties.

For sequential programs, decompositions can be *vertical* or *horizontal.* A vertical decomposition usually focuses on entire execution traces and splits the behaviour of the program into subsets of end-to-end traces, e.g. program slicing [16]. A *horizontal* decomposition is usually based on a syntactic decomposition of the program e.g. into procedures. This paper focuses on solving the refutation problem with horizontal decompositions.

The challenge in automating horizontal compositional verification lies in synthesising a set of precise summary predicates for the procedures in the call graph. Note that in the program in Fig. 1, it was essential to constrain the input z to *bar* to be ($z \leq 1$) to get a proof. This effort is made harder if the code has loops, which require *invariants* and use of abstractions. The calling contexts and summaries can be mutually dependent even for non-recursive programs. In general, one requires iterative fix-point computation on the call-graph structure, possibly using abstraction and refinement. A pre-requisite for performing abstraction refinement is the ability to refute safety and check for spurious counterexamples also in a modular and efficient fashion, which is the goal of this paper.

A Practical View of the Modular Refutation Problem. Consider the example in Fig. 1 in Sect. 2. This program is unsafe because when *bar* is called the actual argument to it that takes the place of z can at most be only 1. The question is if we can arrive at this refutation modularly. Analysing procedure *bar* in isolation indeed gives a counterexample, which could be possibly spurious.

Instantiated on the example in Fig. 1, a refutation involves checking $\neg\forall z, g_8 : g_8 \Rightarrow (z > 10)$. A counterexample could be $g_8 \wedge z = 5$, for example. The question is now how to decide whether this counterexample is spurious or not, and to find a valid counterexample if one exists. For instance, $z = 5$ turns out to be spurious if we consider the whole program because it clashes with $x_0 < 0$ in *main*. However, $z = -8$ would be a valid counterexample.

The set of *local* counterexamples found in a procedure f might contain many counterexamples that are spurious for the whole program, i.e. they are infeasible from the entry point of the program. A definite answer to this question cannot be given by looking at the local problems alone, but only by analysing the global one. This is the reason why refutation in horizontal decompositions is hard — unlike refutation in vertical decompositions where a refutation of the local problem implies the refutation of the global one.

Intuitively, the negation of the *assertion* has to be hoisted up along the error path to the entry point of the program. If the obtained weakest precondition for the violation of the assertion is not *false*, then the counterexample is feasible. Propagating up the *counterexample* itself is not sufficient to decide spuriousness as illustrated above.

4 Formalising Horizontal Compositional Refutation

In this section we formalise the problem of safety refutation for sequential programs. To simplify the presentation we focus on *loop-free* programs. The formalisation for programs with loops is structurally similar, but in addition, requires the handling of invariants, which is orthogonal to the compositional aspect.

We give three different formalisations – the first corresponds to a monolithic approach, and the remaining two correspond to compositional approaches.

4.1 Monolithic Safety Refutation Problem

For non-recursive programs, since one can always inline every procedure call at its call site, we can replace every call by recursively inlining its body. Then, to *refute* safety we have to show unsatisfiability of the following formula:

$$\forall \hat{X} : \bigwedge_{j \in CS} g^{in}_{f_{entry}} \wedge T_{fn(j)}(\boldsymbol{x}^{in}_j, \boldsymbol{x}^{out}_j) \wedge \mathit{InlineSums}_{fn(j)} \Rightarrow \mathit{Props}_{fn(j)}(\boldsymbol{x}_j) \quad (1)$$

where

- $\mathit{InlineSums}_f$ is $\bigwedge_{i \in CS_f} \mathit{InlineSum}_{fn(i)}(\boldsymbol{x}^{p\text{-}in}_i, \boldsymbol{x}^{p\text{-}out}_i)$,
- $\mathit{InlineSum}_f(\boldsymbol{x}^{in}_f, \boldsymbol{x}^{out}_f)$ is $T_f(\boldsymbol{x}^{in}_f, \boldsymbol{x}^{out}_f) \wedge \mathit{InlineSums}_f$,
- $\hat{X}$ is the entirety of variables in (1),
- and the conjunction with $g^{in}_{f_{entry}}$ states that the entry procedure is reachable.[3]

Alternatively, we can write:

$$\begin{array}{l} \exists \overbrace{\mathit{Sum}_f, \ldots}^{\text{for all } f \in F} : \bigwedge_{f \in F} \forall X_f : \\ \quad (g^{in}_{f_{entry}} \wedge T_f(\boldsymbol{x}^{in}_f, \boldsymbol{x}^{out}_f) \wedge \mathit{Sums}_f \Longrightarrow \mathit{Props}_f(\boldsymbol{x}_f)) \\ \wedge \left(T_f(\boldsymbol{x}^{in}_f, \boldsymbol{x}^{out}_f) \wedge \mathit{Sums}_f \Longleftrightarrow \mathit{Sum}_f(\boldsymbol{x}^{in}_f, \boldsymbol{x}^{out}_f)\right) \end{array} \quad (2)$$

where Sums_f is $\bigwedge_{i \in CS_f} \mathit{Sum}_{fn(i)}(\boldsymbol{x}^{p\text{-}in}_i, \boldsymbol{x}^{p\text{-}out}_i)$.

This formulation uses a predicate Sum_f to exactly express the behaviours of each procedure f. (1) and (2) are equisatisfiable, i.e., 1 is satisfiable iff 2 is satisfiable. The existential quantifier in (2) can be uniquely eliminated by recursively replacing the Sum_f predicates by left-hand side of the equivalence in the last line in (2), obtaining (1). Note that solving (1) is NP-complete, whereas

[3] This amounts to using $T_{f_{entry}}[\mathit{true}/g^{in}_{f_{entry}}]$ as the transition relation of f_{entry}.

solving (2) is PSPACE-complete. However, (1) may be exponentially larger (in the number of variables) than (2).

Both versions are *monolithic* because they consider the entire program as a whole. In particular, (2) finds summaries *globally*, i.e. for the whole program.

Also note that, proving unsatisfiability of (2) shows the inexistence of a verification proof, but it does not directly allow us to derive a counterexample in terms of an execution trace because of the universal quantification of the variables. Moreover, showing unsatisfiability of (2) is difficult because it involves proving the inexistence of summary predicates. For this reason, many practical techniques, such as SAT-based Bounded Model Checking use (1) (considering bounded unwindings for programs with loops in order to make them loop-free). Note that negating (1) results in an existentially quantified problem, whose satisfiability witnesses a refutation in the form of values for the variables $\hat{X}$.

However, solving (1) monolithically is often intractable. Therefore, we want to decompose the problem into smaller subformulae that are faster to solve. (2) is amenable to decomposition, but it does not allow us to approximate the summaries with the help of abstractions (because of $\Leftrightarrow$ in last line). Therefore we give a third formulation of the monolithic problem that additionally uses *calling contexts*. The calling context for the entry procedure is $g^{in}_{f_{entry}}$.

$$
\begin{aligned}
&\exists \overbrace{Sum_f, CallCtx_f, \ldots}^{\text{for all } f \in F} : \bigwedge_{f \in F} \forall X_f : \\
&\big(CallCtx_f(\boldsymbol{x}^{in}_f, \boldsymbol{x}^{out}_f) \wedge \\
&\ T_f(\boldsymbol{x}^{in}_f, \boldsymbol{x}^{out}_f) \wedge Sums_f \Longrightarrow Props_f(\boldsymbol{x}_f) \wedge \\
&\qquad\qquad\qquad\qquad\qquad\quad Sum_f(\boldsymbol{x}^{in}_f, \boldsymbol{x}^{out}_f) \wedge \\
&\qquad\qquad\qquad\qquad\qquad\quad \bigwedge_{j \in CS_f} CallCtx_{fn(j)}(\boldsymbol{x}^{p\_in}_j, \boldsymbol{x}^{p\_out}_j)\big)
\end{aligned}
\tag{3}
$$

Equation (3) is also equisatisfiable with (2), although (3) admits more solutions to Sum_f including those that are over-approximations adequate to prove the properties. To see this, if (2) is satisfiable, the precise solution of (2) for Sum_f can be used to satisfy (3) by plugging it in for both $CallCtx_f$ and Sum_f in (3). If (2) is unsatisfiable, then so is (3) because one or all behaviour included in Sum_f solution of (2) violates one of the properties. Then, every solution to (3) would violate the properties as they are over-approximations of the precise summaries.

4.2 Modular Safety Refutation Problem

Let us now have a look at the *horizontal* decomposition following the procedural structure of the program. The goal is to compute the summaries Sum_f for each f while considering only f and the summaries for the procedures called in f. We can attempt at achieving this by flipping the existential quantifier ($\exists Sum_f$) and the top-level conjunction ($\bigwedge_{f \in F}$ in (3)). However, this does not result in an equisatisfiable formula because existential quantification does not distribute over conjunctions. Therefore, we need an alternative formulation to solve the existential query per procedure. One approach is to search for a minimal solution for summaries and calling contexts occurring within each calling site of procedure f for a given context for f that satisfies all the embedded properties in f as shown in 4. I.e. for each $f \in F$ we have:

$$\begin{array}{l} \min \mathit{Sum}_f, \overbrace{\mathit{CallCtx}_j, \ldots}^{\text{for all } j \in CS_f} : \forall X_f : \\ \big(\mathit{CallCtx}_f(\boldsymbol{x}_f^{in}, \boldsymbol{x}_f^{out}) \wedge \\ T_f(\boldsymbol{x}_f^{in}, \boldsymbol{x}_f^{out}) \wedge \mathit{Sums}_f \Longrightarrow \mathit{Props}_f(\boldsymbol{x}_f) \wedge \\ \qquad \mathit{Sum}_f(\boldsymbol{x}_f^{in}, \boldsymbol{x}_f^{out}) \wedge \\ \qquad \bigwedge_{j \in CS_f} \mathit{CallCtx}_j(\boldsymbol{x}_j^{p\text{-}in}, \boldsymbol{x}_j^{p\text{-}out})\big) \end{array} \tag{4}$$

$\min P : F(P)$ is defined w.r.t. implication order for a formula F involving predicates P, i.e. as $\exists P : F(P) \wedge \forall P' : (P' \Rightarrow P) \Rightarrow \neg F(P')$. Note that $\min P$ is not unique in a partial order. (4) gives a solution for Sum_f and the calling contexts for all embedded calling sites relative to a $\mathit{CallCtx}_f$, assuming there is a minimal solution for all embedded procedures. But, we have not broken the dependency between calling contexts and summaries. Solving this problem requires computing a fixed point in the composition operator (presented below) and computing minimal solutions for the summary and calling context predicates. That is, what has been an existential second-order satisfaction problem in (3), has now become a second-order minimisation ($\exists\forall$) problem. The reason for this is that the mere existence of a solution for Sum_f and $\mathit{CallCtx}_{fn(j)}$ does not prove that the overall verification problem holds. Therefore, we pessimistically have to assume that we require the *exact* calling contexts and summaries in order to *decide* the problem during proof composition.

The proposed proof composition operator (*compose*) with calling contexts is shown in Algorithm 2 and is more complex than Algorithm 1. The idea is to use the call graph of the program to compute the minimal calling context for each call site of procedure call of f piecewise in a top-down fashion use that calling context to compute a piecewise minimal summary for f for that call site (note the conjunction on Line 12 of Algorithm 2) consistent with all the properties in f. The piecewise summaries and contexts are combined disjunctively as they are built, which takes care of the dependency between summary and calling contexts. In the algorithm, each time *compose* is called recursively for f, it is called with a new piece of entry calling context for f and (4) is solved with summaries computed up to that point for the procedures in the body of f. Solving the equation smay result in new contexts for each call site (if any) inside f and a new piece of summary for f all of which are accumulated.

For a program with entry f_{entry}, a proof can be constructed by calling $compose(f_{entry}, g^{in}_{f_{entry}})$. The calling context $g^{in}_{f_{entry}}$ means that the entry procedure is reachable. The calling context of all embedded functions are initialised to *false* as that is the least element and also makes everything following the first call site unreachable. The summary for each f is initialised to $\neg g_f^{out}$, meaning that its exit is not reachable and hence execution cannot continue beyond any call to f. This initial value for summary has the effect of blocking analysis of all functions following f in the code until a piecewise summary is computed for f.

Algorithm 2. Composition operator with calling contexts

1: **global** $Sum_f \leftarrow \neg g_f^{out}$ for all $f \in F$
2: $CallCtx_f \leftarrow false$ for all $f \in F$
3: **procedure** $compose(f,\ CallCtx_f^*)$
4: **while** $true$ **do** ▷ Repeat until fixed point reached
5: Solve (4) for f with $CallCtx_f^*$ as $CallCtx_f$ ▷ $\begin{cases}\text{obtain } Sum_f \text{ and } CallCtx_j \\ \text{for all } j \in CS_f\end{cases}$
6: **for all** $j \in CS_f$ **do** ▷ join calling contexts for $fn(j)$
7: $CallCtx_{fn(j)} \leftarrow CallCtx_{fn(j)} \vee CallCtx_j(\boldsymbol{x}_{fn(j)}^{in}, \boldsymbol{x}_{fn(j)}^{out})$
8: **if** $CallCtx_{fn(j)}$ for all $j \in CS_f$ has not changed **then**
9: **return** Sum_f
10: **for all** $j \in CS_f$ for which $CallCtx_{fn(j)}$ has changed **do**
11: $Sum_j \leftarrow compose(fn(j), CallCtx_j(\boldsymbol{x}_{fn(j)}^{in}, \boldsymbol{x}_{fn(j)}^{out}))$
12: $Sum_{fn(j)} \leftarrow Sum_{fn(j)} \vee (CallCtx_j(\boldsymbol{x}_{fn(j)}^{in}, \boldsymbol{x}_{fn(j)}^{out}) \wedge Sum_j)$
13: ▷ join summaries for $fn(j)$

Observe that, as opposed to monolithic (3) where the fixed point computation for resolving the mutually dependent summary and calling context predicates (cf. [23]) is done within the solver for solving the monolithic formula, the fixed point in the modular version must be computed during the composition of the individual results. I.e. we have to saturate the Sum_f and $CallCtx_f$ predicates.

Theorem 1. *We obtain* $Sum_{f_{entry}} = false$ *using Algorithm 2 iff (3) is unsatisfiable. I.e. horizontal decomposition is sound and complete.*

Proof (sketch): We prove this by induction on the depth (k) of the top-level function in the call graph of the program.

For the base case ($k = 0$), there is only one procedure call - the call to the entry procedure, f_{entry}. Since the calling context of f_{entry} is $g_{f_{entry}}^{in}$, and there are no other procedure calls, it is evident that computing $Sum_{f_{entry}}$ from Algorithm 2 effectively reduces to finding it by solving (4) (line 5 of Algorithm 2), with *Sums* and $CallCtx_j$ not present. This makes Eqs. (4) and (3) identical and hence the theorem follows trivially.

Proceeding with the induction step for $k+1$ assuming the theorem holds for all functions in the call graph with depth $\leq k$. That is, we assume as hypothesis the summary computed by *compose* satisfies theorem for all function calls in the body of f for all contexts. Suppose (3) is unsatisfiable. We will argue that Algorithm 2 must return *false*.

If (3) is unsatisfiable then there must be at least one function (either the top-level function or something deeper in the call graph) that is unsatisfiable. Suppose it is one of the called functions, say h, that is unsatisfiable. Then, by our induction hypothesis, the algorithm will return *false* for Sum_h. The moment one of the embedded summaries becomes *false* our algorithm immediately saturates because Algorithm 2 is trivially satisfiable with minimal solution of *false* for

Sum_f. If (3) is unsatisfiable because the top-level function f is unsatisfiable, then it must be because $Props_f$ is inconsistent with T_f. In this case, Algorithm 2 can only return *false*.

4.3 Modular Safety Refutation with Witnesses

(4) suffers from the same problem as (3) that we cannot extract counterexamples in terms of an execution trace in case of a refutation because the formulae are unsatisfiable for refutations. Therefore we give next a formulation and a corresponding composition operator that produces refutation witnesses. The idea here is to compute piecewise contexts and summaries backwards starting from exit points of each procedure, much like a weakest-precondition computation works. Additionally, we start with negation of properties and compute maximal summary and contexts that possibly lead the program to an error state. In other words, a summary computed for f represent maximal symbolic witness to all the states reachable to safety violation. Such a summary can be obtained as maximal solutions to the equation shown in 5.

$$\begin{array}{l}\max Sum_f, \overbrace{CallCtx_j, \ldots}^{\text{for all } j \in CS_f} : \forall X_f : \\ \quad Sum_f(\boldsymbol{x}_f^{in}, \boldsymbol{x}_f^{out}) \wedge \\ \quad \bigwedge_{j \in CS_f} CallCtx_j(\boldsymbol{x}_j^{p\_in}, \boldsymbol{x}_j^{p\_out}) \Longrightarrow (CallCtx_f(\boldsymbol{x}_f^{in}, \boldsymbol{x}_f^{out}) \vee \neg Props_f) \wedge \\ \qquad\qquad\qquad\qquad\qquad\qquad\qquad\qquad T_f(\boldsymbol{x}_f^{in}, \boldsymbol{x}_f^{out}) \wedge Sums_f\end{array} \tag{5}$$

where $\max P.F(P)$ is defined as usual: $\exists P.F(P) \wedge \forall P'.(P \Rightarrow P') \Rightarrow \neg F(P')$.

(5) describes maximal solutions for the summary and calling contexts that are *contained* in the behaviour of the procedure. That is the reason the predicates for the summary and the calling contexts (for the called functions) appear on the left-hand side of the implication and the transition relation is on the right-hand side, i.e. reversed in comparison with (4). The disjuncts in the first part of the consequent of (5) are the sources of safety violations: these are safety violations in the caller (which are propagated by $CallCtx_f$), and safety violations in f itself ($\neg Props_f$). Safety violations in callees are propagated through the summaries. Both these are constrained to be consistent with the transition relation of f (with current summaries plugged in for the called functions), which ensures spurious errors are not propagated upwards.

We use the composition operator as in Algorithm 2, but with the following modifications to the initialization. We call this composition operator *compose'* or Algorithm 2' from now on.

- Initially, $Sum_f \leftarrow \neg g_f^{in}$ for all $f \in F$, meaning that the entry of f is not backwards-reachable.
- In Line 5, we solve (5).

The calling contexts for all embedded functions are initialized to *false* as before except for the top-level function f_{entry}. A refutation is constructed by computing $compose'(f_{entry}, \neg g^{out}_{f_{entry}})$. The calling context $\neg g^{out}_{f_{entry}}$ of f_{entry} means that we cannot reach the regular exit of the entry procedure if there is a property violation. If there are no property violations at this level (or no properties), then this choice for top-level context would still work as the second conjunct in Eq. 5, which denotes the transition relation, would ensure the precise contexts propagated to the first embedded call site from exit point. The choice of initial summary of $\neg g^{in}_f$ for all embedded functions will ensure that the summaries are generated in order of dependency of function calls backward from the exit point.

Theorem 2. *We obtain $Sum_{f_{entry}}$ using Algorithm 2' such that $\exists \boldsymbol{x}^{in}, \boldsymbol{x}^{out}$: $g^{in}_{f_{entry}} \wedge Sum_{f_{entry}}(\boldsymbol{x}^{in}, \boldsymbol{x}^{out})$ iff (3) is unsatisfiable.*

Note that the conjunction with $g^{in}_{f_{entry}}$ projects the summary on the inputs, which must be satisfiable to have a refutation.

Proof (sketch): In contrast to Algorithm 2 with (4), Algorithm 2' uses (5) that computes the maximal solutions for the summary and calling contexts contained in the program behaviour. The summaries and calling contexts are computed such that their projection on the input variables of a procedure is the weakest precondition w.r.t. the properties (*Props*), whose complement is the refutation. Thus at the entry function, f_{entry}, we get $Sum_{f_{entry}}(\boldsymbol{x}^{in}, \boldsymbol{x}^{out})$ as weakest precondition for the negation of the property such that $g^{in}_{f_{entry}} \wedge Sum_{f_{entry}}(\boldsymbol{x}^{in}, \boldsymbol{x}^{out})$ is satisfiable iff (3) is unsatisfiable.

4.4 Worked Example

Let us consider the example in Fig. 1, but with the conditional in line 2 being $x < 10$. We start with $Sum_{main}((x_0, g_0), (g_5)) = \neg g_0$, $Sum_{foo}((y, g_6), (r, g_7)) = \neg g_6$, $Sum_{bar}((z, g_8), (g_9)) = \neg g_8$, and $CallCtx^*_{main}((x_0, g_0), (g_5)) = \neg g_5$, $CallCtx_{foo}((y, g_6), (r, g_7)) = false$, $CallCtx_{bar}((z, g_8), (g_9)) = false$.

The composition operator is called for *main*. We solve (5):

$$
\begin{aligned}
&\max Sum_{main}, CallCtx_{foo_0}, CallCtx_{foo_1}, CallCtx_{bar} : \forall X_{main} : \\
&\quad Sum_{main}((x_0, g_0), (g_5)) \wedge \\
&\quad CallCtx_{foo_0}((x_0, g_1), (x_1, g_2)) \wedge \\
&\quad CallCtx_{foo_1}((x_1, g_2), (x_2, g_3)) \wedge \\
&\quad CallCtx_{bar}((x_2, g_3), (g_4)) \Longrightarrow (\neg g_5 \vee \neg true) \wedge \\
&\qquad\qquad g_1 = (g_0 \wedge (x_0 < 10)) \wedge \\
&\qquad\qquad g_5 = ((g_0 \wedge \neg(x_0 < 10)) \vee g_4) \wedge \\
&\qquad\qquad \neg g_1 \wedge \neg g_2 \wedge \neg g_3
\end{aligned}
$$

We obtain the following solutions for the predicates: $CallCtx_{bar} = \neg g_4$, $CallCtx_{foo_1} = \neg g_3$, $CallCtx_{foo_0} = \neg g_2$, $Sum_{main} = \neg g_0 \wedge \neg g_5$.

Then we recur into *bar* with (5) instantiated as:

$$
\begin{aligned}
&\max Sum_{bar} : \forall z, g_8, g_9 : \\
&\quad Sum_{bar}((z, g_8), (g_9)) \Longrightarrow (\neg g_9 \vee \neg(g_8 \Rightarrow z > 10)) \wedge \\
&\qquad\qquad (g_9 = (g_8 \wedge z > 10))
\end{aligned}
$$

Hence, we get for Sum_{bar}: $(g_8 \Rightarrow \neg(z > 10)) \wedge \neg g_9$.

In Line 6 of Algorithm 2', (5) for *main* is then:

$$\begin{aligned}
&\max Sum_{main}, CallCtx_{foo_0}, CallCtx_{foo_1}, CallCtx_{bar} : \forall X_{main} : \\
&\quad Sum_{main}((x_0, g_0), (g_5)) \wedge \\
&\quad CallCtx_{foo_0}((x_0, g_1), (x_1, g_2)) \wedge \\
&\quad CallCtx_{foo_1}((x_1, g_2), (x_2, g_3)) \wedge \\
&\quad CallCtx_{bar}((x_2, g_3), (g_4)) \Longrightarrow (\neg g_5 \vee \neg true) \wedge \\
&\qquad\qquad g_1 = (g_0 \wedge (x_0 < 10)) \wedge \\
&\qquad\qquad g_5 = ((g_0 \wedge \neg(x_0 < 10)) \vee g_4) \wedge \\
&\qquad\qquad \neg g_1 \wedge \neg g_2 \wedge \\
&\qquad\qquad (g_3 \Rightarrow \neg(x_2 > 10)) \wedge \neg g_4
\end{aligned}$$

which results in $CallCtx_{bar} = \neg g_4$, $CallCtx_{foo_1} = g_3 \Rightarrow \neg(x_2 > 10)$, $CallCtx_{foo_0} = \neg g_2$, $Sum_{main} = \neg g_5$. Hence, $CallCtx_{foo}$ is updated to $g_7 \Rightarrow \neg(r > 10)$.

In the next iteration of *compose*(*main*) we recur into foo_1 and solve:

$$\begin{aligned}
&\max Sum_{foo} : \forall y, g_6, r, g_7 : \\
&\quad Sum_{foo}((y, g_6), (r, g_7)) \Longrightarrow ((g_7 \Rightarrow \neg(r > 10)) \vee \neg true) \wedge \\
&\qquad\qquad (g_6 = g_7) \wedge (r = y + 1)
\end{aligned}$$

Thus, Sum_{foo} is updated to $(g_6 \Rightarrow \neg(r > 10) \wedge g_7) \wedge (r = y + 1)$.

Then in Line 6 in *compose*(*main*), we solve

$$\begin{aligned}
&\max Sum_{main}, CallCtx_{foo_0}, CallCtx_{foo_1}, CallCtx_{bar} : \forall X_{main} : \\
&\quad Sum_{main}((x_0, g_0), (g_5)) \wedge \\
&\quad CallCtx_{foo_0}((x_1, g_2)) \wedge \\
&\quad CallCtx_{foo_1}((x_2, g_3)) \wedge \\
&\quad CallCtx_{bar}((g_4)) \Longrightarrow (\neg g_5 \vee \neg true) \wedge \\
&\qquad\qquad g_1 = (g_0 \wedge (x_0 < 10)) \wedge \\
&\qquad\qquad g_5 = ((g_0 \wedge \neg(x_0 < 10)) \vee g_4) \wedge \\
&\qquad\qquad (g_1 \Rightarrow \neg(x_1 > 10) \wedge g_2) \wedge (x_1 = x_0 + 1) \wedge \\
&\qquad\qquad (g_2 \Rightarrow \neg(x_2 > 10) \wedge g_3) \wedge (x_2 = x_1 + 1) \wedge \\
&\qquad\qquad (g_3 \Rightarrow \neg(x_2 > 10)) \wedge \neg g_4
\end{aligned}$$

which gives us $Sum_{main} = (g_0 \Rightarrow \neg(x_0 > 8)) \wedge \neg g_5$. The calling contexts $CallCtx_{bar} = \neg g_4$, $CallCtx_{foo_0} = g_2 \Rightarrow \neg(x_1 > 10)$, and $CallCtx_{foo_1} = g_3 \Rightarrow \neg(x_2 > 10)$ do not result in an update of the calling contexts for *foo* and *bar* (Line 8 in Algorithm 2). $g_0 \wedge Sum_{main}$ is satisfiable, hence, $x \leq 8$ is a (maximal) refutation witness.

5 Examples of Refutation Algorithms

Algorithm 2' is not only applicable to straight-line programs with multiple procedure invocations, it can still be used for programs with loops by introducing invariants into the formula for the modular subproblem (5). However, in general it is hard to solve the problems without using approximations by bounding the number of unwindings and/or using abstractions for computing the predicates involved.

In the previous section, we have described the elements necessary for compositional, horizontal refutation proofs. In this section, we will give three examples of algorithms that instantiate this framework (Algorithm 2'), which we have implemented to compare them experimentally in Sect. 6. We assume that loops have been unwound a finite number of times before application of these techniques. The difference in the following three techniques lies in the abstractions that are used to solve for Sum_f and $CallCtx_f$ in (5). We consider techniques that use constraint solving to find counterexamples.

5.1 Concrete Backward Interpretation

This technique is the one sketched in the example at the beginning of Sect. 3. Formally, we use the domain of predicates that track a single constant value for each variable, defined as follows: Let $P(\boldsymbol{x}) = \{false\} \cup \{\boldsymbol{x} = \boldsymbol{d} \mid d_i \in Dom(x_i)\}$ with the domain $Dom(x_i)$ of variable x_i, then we admit the following predicates for summaries and calling contexts: $Sum_f \in \{g_f^{in} \Rightarrow p \mid p \in P(\boldsymbol{x}_f^{in})\}$ and $CallCtx_f \in \{g_f^{out} \Rightarrow p \mid p \in P(\boldsymbol{x}_f^{out})\}$. We explain now in an example how Algorithm 2' proceeds using this domain.

Example. Let us consider the example in Fig. 1 in Sect. 2. We start with $compose'(main, \neg g_5)$. We obtain the calling contexts $\neg g_2, \neg g_3, \neg g_4$ for foo_0, foo_1, bar, respectively. We recur into $compose'(bar, \neg g_9)$. We have to solve (5) where $\sum_{bar}$ is instantiated with the above domain:

$$\begin{array}{l} \exists d : \forall z, g_8, g_9 : \\ \quad (g_8 \Rightarrow z{=}d) \Longrightarrow (\neg g_9 \vee \neg(g_8 \Rightarrow (z > 10)))\wedge \\ \qquad\qquad\qquad\qquad (g_9 = (g_8 \wedge z > 10)) \end{array} \tag{6}$$

The partial order of our domain has only two levels *false* and the values for $\boldsymbol{d}$. Hence, we can implement max by $\exists \boldsymbol{d}$; if there is no $\boldsymbol{d}$ then $p = false$. A constraint solver may return, for example, $d = -4$; Sum_{bar} is hence $g_8 \Rightarrow (z = -4)$. This is an under-approximative summary of *bar* w.r.t. property violation.

In the next iteration of $compose'(main, \neg g_5)$ we solve:

$$\begin{array}{ll} \exists d_0, \ldots, d_3 : \forall x_0, g_0, \ldots, g_5 : & \\ \quad (g_0 \Rightarrow x_0{=}d_0)\wedge & \\ \quad (g_2 \Rightarrow x_1{=}d_1)\wedge & \\ \quad (g_3 \Rightarrow x_2{=}d_2)\wedge & \\ \quad (g_4 \Rightarrow d_3) \Longrightarrow & (\neg g_5 \vee \neg true)\wedge \\ & g_1 = (g_0 \wedge (x_0 < 10))\wedge \\ & g_5 = ((g_0 \wedge \neg(x_0 < 10)) \vee g_4)\wedge \\ & \neg g_1 \wedge \neg g_2\wedge \\ & (g_3 \Rightarrow (x_2 = -4)) \wedge \neg g_5 \end{array} \tag{7}$$

and obtain $CallCtx_{foo_1} = (g_3 \Rightarrow (x_2 = -4))$. $compose'(foo, g_7 \Rightarrow (r = -4))$ returns $g_6 \Rightarrow (y = -5)$ for Sum_{foo_1}. Note that the boolean variable d_3 stands for the reachability of the exit of *bar*. Since *bar* has no return value, this is how its exit is encoded. Proceeding similarly we get $compose'(foo, g_7 \Rightarrow (r = -5)) = (g_6 \Rightarrow (y = -6))$; and finally $Sum_{main} = (g_0 \Rightarrow x_0 = -6)$. Hence, we have found a true global counterexample.

5.2 Abstract Backward Interpretation

Abstract backward interpretation computes sufficient preconditions to safety violations, i.e. negations of necessary preconditions to safety. The size of the summaries can vary from very concise to larger than the procedure, depending on the abstraction.

There are a couple of techniques to implement such abstract interpretations that are distinguished by the way abstract preconditions are inferred, e.g. (classical) abstract domain transformers (e.g. [20]), template-based synthesis (e.g. [15]) or interpolation (e.g. [1]).

We are going to use the template-based synthesis technique used in [3] to solve (5). We know how to compute over-approximative abstractions with that technique. Hence, we use an over-approximation to compute an under-approximation (similar to computing $\max f$ by $-\min(-f)$). This means we compute predicates $Sum_f^{\tilde{u}}$ and $CallCtx_j^{\tilde{u}}$ whose negations are Sum_f and $CallCtx_j$, respectively. This is done by solving the following formula in place of (5) in Algorithm 2'.

$$\begin{array}{l}\min Sum_f^{\tilde{u}}, \overbrace{CallCtx_j^{\tilde{u}}, \ldots}^{\text{for all } j \in CS_f} : \forall X_f : \\ (CallCtx_f^{\tilde{u}}(\boldsymbol{x}_f^{in}, \boldsymbol{x}_f^{out}) \wedge Sums_f^{\tilde{u}} \wedge \\ \quad T_f(\boldsymbol{x}_f^{in}, \boldsymbol{x}_f^{out}) \wedge Props_f(\boldsymbol{x}_f) \Longrightarrow Sum_f^{\tilde{u}}(\boldsymbol{x}_f^{in}, \boldsymbol{x}_f^{out}) \wedge \\ \qquad\qquad\qquad\qquad\qquad\qquad \bigwedge_{j \in CS_f} CallCtx_j^{\tilde{u}}(\boldsymbol{x}_j^{p\_in}, \boldsymbol{x}_j^{p\_out}))\end{array} \tag{8}$$

This formula is derived from (5) by negating $(CallCtx_f \vee \neg Props)$ on the right-hand side of (5), which yields $(CallCtx_f^{\tilde{u}} \wedge Props)$, reversing the implication, and minimising to obtain an over-approximation for $Sum^{\tilde{u}}$ and $CallCtx^{\tilde{u}}$. Similar approaches are used in [5,10]. Since convex domains are too imprecise for this purpose, we use a disjunctive domain [22]. For our experiments we used intervals as a base domain. Formally, let $P(\boldsymbol{x}) = \{\bigvee_k \boldsymbol{d}'_k \leq \boldsymbol{x} \leq \boldsymbol{d}_k \mid d_i, d'_i \in Dom(x_i), k \geq 0\}$, then $Sum_f \in \{g_f^{in} \Rightarrow p \mid p \in P(\boldsymbol{x}_f^{in})\}$ and $CallCtx_f \in \{g_f^{out} \Rightarrow p \mid p \in P(\boldsymbol{x}_f^{out})\}$. Our implementation also ensures that arithmetic overflows create new disjuncts in order to avoid precision loss. The second source of additional disjuncts that we take into account are Lines 7 and 12 in Algorithm 2'.

Example. For the example in Fig. 1, we compute $compose'(main, \neg g_5)$. We solve (8) with $CallCtx_{main}^{\tilde{u}} = g_5$ and get $CallCtx_{bar}^{\tilde{u}} = g_4$, i.e. $CallCtx_{bar} = \neg g_4$.

We recur into $compose'(bar, \neg g_9)$, i.e. $CallCtx^{\tilde{u}}_{bar} = g_9$ We have to solve (8) instantiated with our domain.

$$\begin{aligned}&\exists d, d' : \forall z, g_8, g_9 :\\ &(g_9 \wedge true \wedge\\ &(g_9 = (g_8 \wedge z > 10)) \wedge (g_8 \Rightarrow (z > 10)) \Longrightarrow (g_8 \Rightarrow (d \leq z \leq d')))\end{aligned} \tag{9}$$

Note that $Sums^{\tilde{u}}_f$ is true because the initial under-approximations are false—the superscript $\tilde{u}$ flags predicates that carry negations of under-approximations. We get $Sum^{\tilde{u}}_{bar} = (g_8 \Rightarrow (11 \leq z \leq MAX))$, i.e. $Sum_{bar} = (g_8 \wedge (MIN \leq z \leq 10))$. MAX and MIN denote the maximum, resp. minimum, possible value for the type of z.

We proceed similarly. Finally, $compose'(main, \neg g_5)$ computes $Sum^{\tilde{u}}_{main} = (g_0 \Rightarrow (9 \leq x_0 \leq MAX))$, i.e. $Sum_{main} = (g_0 \wedge (MIN \leq x_0 \leq 8))$.

Note that (8) expresses an over-approximation of *good* states; the complement is therefore guaranteed not to contain any good states, but only *bad* and *unreachable* states, and hence no strict under-approximation of bad states. However, this does not matter since we project $Sum_{f_{entry}}$ on the initial condition (see Theorem 2) to obtain a true under-approximation of inputs that violate a property.

Abstract backward interpretation is not limited to bounded unwindings of the transition relation, but can also be used for programs with loops (cf. [5,11]) by calling invariants into play in (8).

5.3 Symbolic Backward Interpretation

This technique computes the exact weakest precondition for the bounded problem. The technique is complete for loop-free programs. However, the size of the obtained summaries is in the same order as the procedure size in the worst case.

The domain used are sets of variables, so-called *dependency sets*. These sets of variables, X^{in}_f, X^{out}_f, $X^{p\text{-}in}_j$, $X^{p\text{-}out}_j$, describe which variables should be kept as relevant part of the summary. We then use them to compute an exact summary as the following predicate $Sum_f(\boldsymbol{x}^{in}, \boldsymbol{x}^{out})$:

$$\begin{aligned}&\exists X_f \setminus (X^{in}_f \cup X^{out}_f \cup \overbrace{X^{p\text{-}in}_j \cup X^{p\text{-}out}_j}^{\text{for all } j \in CS_f} \cup \ldots) :\\ &(CallCtx_f(\boldsymbol{x}^{in}, \boldsymbol{x}^{out}) \vee \neg Props_f) \wedge T_f(\boldsymbol{x}^{in}, \boldsymbol{x}^{out}) \wedge Sums_f\end{aligned} \tag{10}$$

We implement the existential quantification in (10) by Gaussian elimination to eliminate as many of the intermediate or irrelevant variables as possible. After elimination the summary contains only variables that have a dependency on the property $Props_f$, on $\boldsymbol{x}^{out}$, or on the placeholder predicates, which are going to be replaced by summaries during the composition. The elimination can have positive and negative effects on the formula size depending on non-determinism and control flow paths in the procedure.

The composition operator is the same horizontal composition operator as in the two previous techniques. Context-sensitivity is exploited exactly in the same way as in the previous two techniques. The calling context at call site j is the set of output variables $X_j^{p\text{-}out}$ that a procedure call backward-transitively depends on the given property. The resulting calling context dependency set X_f^{out} is then used for eliminating intermediate variables in (10) in addition to the dependency sets obtained from $Sums_f$, and $Props_f$. The set of input variables X_f^{in} that have not been eliminated is the dependency set $X_f^{p\text{-}in}$ of the summary Sum_f.

Any satisfiable assignment to $\boldsymbol{x}_{f_{entry}}^{in}$ in the formula obtained by Gaussian elimination of the summary predicates in the entry function is a feasible global refutation.

Example. For example, in Fig. 1 the symbolic backward interpreter starts from the exit of *main* with $X_{main}^{out} = \emptyset$ to start with. As it arrives in *bar*, it retains the negation of the assertion $\neg(g_8 \Rightarrow (z > 10))$ and updates the dependency set to $X_{bar}^{in} = \{z, g_8\}$. On simplification, this gives the summary for *bar* as $g_8 \wedge \neg(z > 10)$.

Then the technique proceeds to the caller of *bar*, replacing the variables in the dependency set by the parameter passed, i.e. $X_{foo_1}^{p\text{-}out} = \{x_2, g_3\}$. Then it recurs into the call to *foo*. The statement $r = y + 1$ gives the summary of *foo* as $r = y + 1$ and the dependency set $\{y, g_6\}$. The next call to *foo* has already been analysed with the same dependency set, hence there is no need to recur.

Proceeding in the main function, we finally get the summary for *main* as $(g_1 = g_0 \wedge (x_0 < 0)) \wedge foo_0((x_0, g_1), (x_1, g_2)) \wedge foo_1((x_1, g_2), (x_2, g_3)) \wedge bar((x_2, g_3), (g_4))$. Substituting the placeholder predicates by their respective summaries (variables are renamed) allows us to evaluate the summary for *main*. Since it is satisfiable, we have found a global refutation.

6 Experiments

We performed a number of experiments to evaluate compositional refutation techniques in comparison with monolithic approaches.

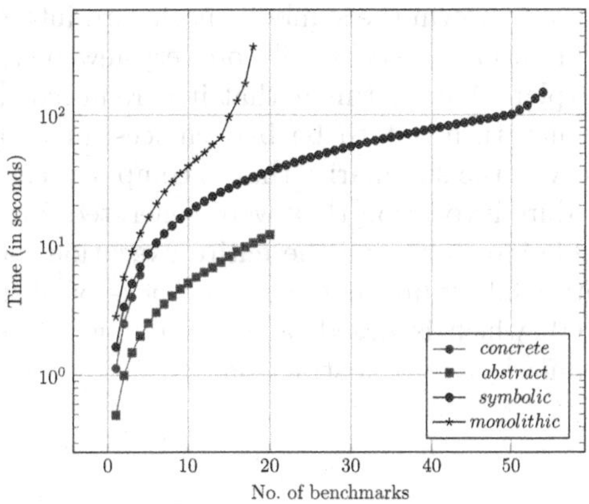

Fig. 2. Comparison on product-lines benchmarks

Implementation. We have implemented these safety refutation techniques as an extension to 2LS [3,24]. 2LS is a verification tool built on the CPROVER framework [9], using MiniSAT 2.2.1 as the backend solver (although other SAT and SMT solvers with incremental solving support can also be used). We limit resources to 900 s CPU time and 13 GB memory per benchmark. To aid reproducibility, we provide[4] the implementation sources along with the compilation instructions, the benchmarks, and scripts that can be used to run the tool on the benchmarks. As explained in Sect. 5, the three techniques are instances of a context-sensitive inter-procedural analysis that traverses the callgraph backwards and propagates summaries and calling contexts. For the concrete interpretation, values for non-deterministic choices are picked by the SAT solver. For the abstract interpretation we use disjunctions of intervals.

Benchmarks. We selected the unsafe examples (265 benchmarks) from the *product-lines* collection of the SV-COMP 2017 benchmarks set for our experiments. These benchmarks have a reasonably complex procedural structure (83 procedures per benchmark on average), which makes it suitable to test the effectiveness of our techniques. We set an unwinding depth of 5 for all the benchmarks, across all the techniques. The chosen depth might have been, in some cases, higher than what would be necessary to find a refutation. However, the aim of our experiments was to compare the scalability of the techniques in general, and not to find out the least amount of time needed to solve a given benchmark.

Results. Figure 2 shows the results plotting for each technique the cumulative time (y-axis) it takes to solve the given number of benchmarks (x-axis). The longer the line for a technique extends to the right the more benchmarks were solved within the resource limits. These results show some interesting tendencies. We observe that the symbolic backward interpretation performs best. It is complete, but could potentially degrade into a monolithic analysis if summaries cannot be sufficiently simplified and reused. But on this benchmark set it works quite well on a certain number of benchmarks. The abstract backward interpretation is very fast on a couple of benchmarks, but then remains inconclusive. This is supposedly due to the imprecision introduced by the weak abstract domain that we use. Yet, this is encouraging that by a clever choice of abstractions one could outperform the symbolic backward interpretation. The concrete backward interpretation succeeds only on very few benchmarks and is surprisingly slow. An explanation for this is that it is required to make non-deterministic choices that may turn out to be bad choices and make a counterexample infeasible. Moreover, the summaries that it computes usually do not generalise beyond the procedure invocation they were generated for. Hence, this technique is likely to degrade into following the entire execution path, spoiling the benefits of modularity while exhibiting the drawbacks of abstraction. The monolithic analysis (BMC), which is based on full inlining is slowest but solves almost as many benchmarks as the abstract one.

[4] https://github.com/kumarmadhukar/2ls/tree/atva17.

7 Conclusion

We investigated compositional refutation techniques in horizontal, e.g. procedure-modular, decompositions of sequential programs. We showed how to derive a compositional refutation framework step by step from the monolithic problem. We also compared the completeness properties of concrete, abstract and symbolic modular refutation approaches. Our experiments show that compositional refutation techniques have an advantage over monolithic approaches, however, not all tested approaches perform equally well because of their varying completeness. Using a portfolio of fast incomplete techniques and slower complete ones may ensure that modular techniques are always at least as fast as monolithic ones in practice.

Open Questions. Modular analyses should be independent of a program's syntactic structure because real-world programs are not written in a nice and balanced way that would enable efficient modular analysis. It would be worthwhile to explore semantic decompositions into modules in order to make these techniques scale on real-world programs. W.r.t. the inter-procedural backward analysis, it remains to be investigated how to handle recursion.

Moreover, it would be interesting to look into compositional refutation in termination analysis. Also there, spuriousness of local refutations can occur due to lack of context information: To find a counterexample to termination one needs to find a stem from the entry point. Compositionality in this context has been explored in the Ultimate tool [17]. We would also consider performance comparisons with testing, i.e. dynamic refutation techniques (random, directed, concolic, etc.) to be beneficial to advance research in static refutation techniques.

Related Work. Compositional automated verification approaches have been considered in the tools Whale [1] and FunFrog [26], for example. Horn clause encodings were used in [18]. These tools eventually use interpolation to compute abstractions. Under-approximating precondition inference techniques have been proposed for polyhedra [20] and with the help of bit blasting and loop iteration estimation [4]. All these techniques can be used in our setting, however, their completeness properties remain to be evaluated. Completeness considerations [21] have been conducted for compositional LTL model checking [7,8] of (parallel) compositions of (infinite-) state transition systems. Since the decomposition of sequential programs can be encoded into a composition of parallel programs (with appropriate synchronisation), their completeness results are expected to hold in our setting. Compositionality has also been explored in the context of dynamic test generation to achieve scalability by memoizing symbolic execution sub-paths as test summaries [13]. This has given rise to an incremental approach for statically validating symbolic test summaries against code changes [14]. In our framework memoization is naturally handled by the composition operator.

References

1. Albarghouthi, A., Gurfinkel, A., Chechik, M.: WHALE: an interpolation-based algorithm for inter-procedural verification. In: Kuncak, V., Rybalchenko, A. (eds.) VMCAI 2012. LNCS, vol. 7148, pp. 39–55. Springer, Heidelberg (2012). doi:10.1007/978-3-642-27940-9_4
2. Alur, R., de Alfaro, L., Henzinger, T.A., Mang, F.Y.C.: Automating modular verification. In: Baeten, J.C.M., Mauw, S. (eds.) CONCUR 1999. LNCS, vol. 1664, pp. 82–97. Springer, Heidelberg (1999). doi:10.1007/3-540-48320-9_8
3. Brain, M., Joshi, S., Kroening, D., Schrammel, P.: Safety verification and refutation by k-invariants and k-induction. In: Blazy, S., Jensen, T. (eds.) SAS 2015. LNCS, vol. 9291, pp. 145–161. Springer, Heidelberg (2015). doi:10.1007/978-3-662-48288-9_9
4. Brauer, J., Simon, A.: Inferring definite counterexamples through under-approximation. In: Goodloe, A.E., Person, S. (eds.) NFM 2012. LNCS, vol. 7226, pp. 54–69. Springer, Heidelberg (2012). doi:10.1007/978-3-642-28891-3_7
5. Chen, H., David, C., Kroening, D., Schrammel, P., Wachter, B.: Synthesising interprocedural bit-precise termination proofs. In: Automated Software Engineering, pp. 53–64. ACM (2015)
6. Clarke, E., Grumberg, O., Jha, S., Lu, Y., Veith, H.: Counterexample-guided abstraction refinement. In: Emerson, E.A., Sistla, A.P. (eds.) CAV 2000. LNCS, vol. 1855, pp. 154–169. Springer, Heidelberg (2000). doi:10.1007/10722167_15
7. Clarke, E.M., Grumberg, O., Long, D.E.: Model checking and abstraction. Trans. Programm. Lang. Syst. **16**(5), 1512–1542 (1994)
8. Clarke, E.M., Long, D.E., McMillan, K.L.: Compositional model checking. In: Logic in Computer Science, pp. 353–362. IEEE Computer Society (1989)
9. Clarke, E., Kroening, D., Lerda, F.: A tool for checking ANSI-C programs. In: Jensen, K., Podelski, A. (eds.) TACAS 2004. LNCS, vol. 2988, pp. 168–176. Springer, Heidelberg (2004). doi:10.1007/978-3-540-24730-2_15
10. Cook, B., Gulwani, S., Lev-Ami, T., Rybalchenko, A., Sagiv, M.: Proving conditional termination. In: Gupta, A., Malik, S. (eds.) CAV 2008. LNCS, vol. 5123, pp. 328–340. Springer, Heidelberg (2008). doi:10.1007/978-3-540-70545-1_32
11. David, C., Kesseli, P., Kroening, D., Lewis, M.: Danger invariants. In: Fitzgerald, J., Heitmeyer, C., Gnesi, S., Philippou, A. (eds.) FM 2016. LNCS, vol. 9995, pp. 182–198. Springer, Cham (2016). doi:10.1007/978-3-319-48989-6_12
12. Flanagan, C., Leino, K.R.M., Lillibridge, M., Nelson, G., Saxe, J.B., Stata, R.: Extended static checking for java. In: Programming Language Design and Implementation, pp. 234–245. ACM (2002)
13. Godefroid, P.: Compositional dynamic test generation. In: Proceedings of the 34th Annual ACM SIGPLAN-SIGACT Symposium on Principles of Programming Languages, POPL 2007, pp. 47–54. ACM, New York (2007)
14. Godefroid, P., Lahiri, S.K., Rubio-González, C.: Statically validating must summaries for incremental compositional dynamic test generation. In: Yahav, E. (ed.) SAS 2011. LNCS, vol. 6887, pp. 112–128. Springer, Heidelberg (2011). doi:10.1007/978-3-642-23702-7_12
15. Gulwani, S., Srivastava, S., Venkatesan, R.: Program analysis as constraint solving. In: Programming Language Design and Implementation, pp. 281–292. ACM (2008)
16. Harman, M., Hierons, R.M.: An overview of program slicing. Softw. Focus **2**(3), 85–92 (2001)

17. Heizmann, M., Hoenicke, J., Podelski, A.: Termination analysis by learning terminating programs. Comput.-Aided Verification **8559**, 797–813 (2014)
18. Komuravelli, A., Bjørner, N., Gurfinkel, A., McMillan, K.L.: Compositional verification of procedural programs using horn clauses over integers and arrays. In: Formal Methods in Computer-Aided Design, pp. 89–96 (2015)
19. Leino, K.R.M.: Dafny: an automatic program verifier for functional correctness. In: Clarke, E.M., Voronkov, A. (eds.) LPAR 2010. LNCS, vol. 6355, pp. 348–370. Springer, Heidelberg (2010). doi:10.1007/978-3-642-17511-4_20
20. Miné, A.: Inferring sufficient conditions with backward polyhedral under-approximations. Electr. Notes Theor. Comput. Sci. **287**, 89–100 (2012)
21. Namjoshi, K.S., Trefler, R.J.: On the completeness of compositional reasoning methods. ACM Trans. Comput. Log. **11**(3), 16:1–16:22 (2010). doi:10.1145/1740582.1740584
22. Sankaranarayanan, S., Ivančić, F., Shlyakhter, I., Gupta, A.: Static analysis in disjunctive numerical domains. In: Yi, K. (ed.) SAS 2006. LNCS, vol. 4134, pp. 3–17. Springer, Heidelberg (2006). doi:10.1007/11823230_2
23. Schrammel, P.: Challenges in decomposing encodings of verification problems. In: Horn Clauses for Verification and Synthesis, EPTCS (2016). p. to appear
24. Schrammel, P., Kroening, D.: 2LS for program analysis. In: Chechik, M., Raskin, J.-F. (eds.) TACAS 2016. LNCS, vol. 9636, pp. 905–907. Springer, Heidelberg (2016). doi:10.1007/978-3-662-49674-9_56
25. Schrammel, P., Kroening, D., Brain, M., Martins, R., Teige, T., Bienmüller, T.: Successful use of incremental BMC in the automotive industry. In: Núñez, M., Güdemann, M. (eds.) FMICS 2015. LNCS, vol. 9128, pp. 62–77. Springer, Cham (2015). doi:10.1007/978-3-319-19458-5_5
26. Sery, O., Fedyukovich, G., Sharygina, N.: Interpolation-based function summaries in bounded model checking. In: Eder, K., Lourenço, J., Shehory, O. (eds.) HVC 2011. LNCS, vol. 7261, pp. 160–175. Springer, Heidelberg (2012). doi:10.1007/978-3-642-34188-5_15
27. SPARK: (2014). http://www.spark-2014.org/

Gradient-Based Variable Ordering of Decision Diagrams for Systems with Structural Units

Elvio Gilberto Amparore(✉), Marco Beccuti, and Susanna Donatelli

Dipartimento di Informatica, Università di Torino, Turin, Italy
{amparore,beccuti,susi}@di.unito.it

Abstract. This paper presents Gradient-Π, a novel heuristics for finding the variable ordering of Decision Diagrams encoding the state space of Petri net systems. Gradient-Π combines the structural informations of the Petri net (either the set of minimal P-semiflows or, when available, the structure of the net in terms of "Nested Units") with a gradient-based greedy strategy inspired by methods for matrix bandwidth reduction. The value of the proposed heuristics is assessed on a public benchmark of Petri net models, showing that Gradient-Π can successfully exploit the structural information to produce good variable orderings.

Keywords: Decision diagrams · Variable ordering · Petri nets

1 Introduction

The use of binary decision diagrams [8] and their variants is at the base of the so-called symbolic model-checking techniques. These techniques have given an incredible boost to state-based verification of systems over the last 30 years and have given rise to a number of successful tools for automatic verification of systems, in particular for discrete event dynamic systems (DEDS) [9]: systems in which the state is composed by a set of variables, taking values on a set of finite and discrete values, and events that change the state of the system.

It is well-known that the size of the decision diagram representation of a state space heavily depends on the chosen order of the variables that represent the state of the system, and that the problem of finding such an ordering is NP-complete. Many heuristics for finding "good" variable orderings have been proposed in the past (see for example the surveys in [23,26]) and they are often crucial for the performances of model-checking tools and of decision diagram libraries [19].

Variable ordering can be *static* or *dynamic*, or, more precisely, can be used statically or dynamically. In the first case an ordering is computed before state space generation and it is kept fixed through the whole generation procedure, while in the second case a new order can be computed and applied at run-time if the decision diagram size grows too large. In this paper we concentrate on static ordering and we aim at understanding *if and how the structure of the system can be exploited for devising a good variable ordering.*

D. D'Souza and K. Narayan Kumar (Eds.): ATVA 2017, LNCS 10482, pp. 184–200, 2017.
DOI: 10.1007/978-3-319-68167-2_13

To answer this question we need to place our research in a specific context, as it is difficult to draw conclusions on the efficacy of a heuristics without referring to a specific state-space generation technique and to an appropriate benchmark of systems on which to exercise our findings. As system specification language we consider Petri Nets, that have proven useful in modelling a large variety of DEDS, from hardware [24] to business process models [1]. The evaluation of the proposed heuristics is based on a benchmark extracted from the public model set of the Model-Checking Contest (MCC2016) [14], which includes 664 model instances. We use symbolic model-checking based on *Multi-terminal Dcision Diagrams* (MDDs) as implemented in the GreatSPN tool [4,5] based on the MDD library Meddly [7]. We assume that MDD levels encode Petri net places, i.e. we do not consider merging multiple places into a single level like in [11]. The state space generation algorithms employs *saturation* [10].

Another reason for choosing Petri nets is the large amount of literature on structural analysis techniques [12], that is to say techniques that allow to check properties of the state space (like invariant properties of the variables, finiteness of the state space and liveness of events) without building the state space itself.

Structural informations are at the base of many of the heuristics designed for the analysis of (Petri net models of) circuits, which exploit the locality of the inter-dependent variables, or the input-output dependencies, as the widely used heuristics based on fan-in [20]. However, only a subset of these heuristics can be used effectively on general Petri net models, which usually have cyclic behaviour and no clear input/output dependencies. Popular static variable ordering heuristics applied to Petri nets include, among others: The Noack and Tovchigrechko [16] methods; The Force and the Mince heuristics [3]; Bandwidth-reduction techniques like the Sloan method [27].

In a previous paper [6] we evaluated 14 different heuristics on 386 model instances (belonging to 62 parametric models) taken from the MCC2016 model set. In that paper we also tested a heuristics called *P-chain* based on P-semiflows (which are subsets of places with constant weighted sum of tokens in all reachable states) to improve variable ordering heuristics. *P-chain* showed rather poor performances, suggesting that the concatenation of P-semiflows which is at the base of the technique is not enough. In this paper we propose Gradient-Π, a new heuristics that modifies the bandwidth-reduction method of Sloan to order places on a subset-basis, using either P-semiflows or Nested Units [15] to provide such subsets. An extensive benchmark enlights that Gradient-Π has better performance than the Sloan method and better than other structural-based methods like P-chain, as well as various other state-of-the-art variable ordering methods.

Note that Gradient-Π assumes that in the MDD we assign one place per level. Other techniques have instead used P-semiflows for identifying places to be grouped in a single level [11] or for state compression for binary decision diagrams [25]. These technique can be seen as orthogonal to the proposed one.

The paper is organized as follows: Sect. 2 introduces the notation used in the paper; Sect. 3 describes the Gradient-Π heuristics; Estimation of the heuristics parameters is done in Sect. 3.1; The effectiveness of the new method is assessed in Sect. 4. Finally, Sect. 5 concludes the paper.

2 Background

This section first reviews the definition of Petri nets [2] and the related notions of P-semiflows and Nested Units. The section then presents a description of the two variable ordering algorithms (the Sloan method [27] and the P-chain method [6]) which influenced the definition of the proposed static variable ordering heuristics.

The Petri net (PN) is a graphical mathematical formalism that has been widely used to model and study real systems in different fields (e.g. communication systems, biological systems, power systems, work-flow management, ...). A Petri net is a bipartite directed graph with nodes partitioned into *places* or *transitions*. An example of PN is depicted in Fig. 4. Places, graphically represented as circles, correspond to the state variables of the system, while transitions, graphically represented as boxes, correspond to the events that determine the state changes. The arcs connecting places to transitions (and vice versa) express the relations between states and event occurrences. Each arc is labeled with a non null natural number representing its "weight". The state of a PN is usually called a *marking* $\mathbf{m}$, a multiset on the set P of places.

Definition 1 (Petri Net). *A PN system is a tuple* $\mathcal{N} = (P, T, \mathbf{I}^-, \mathbf{I}^+, \mathbf{m}_0)$, *where: P is a finite and non empty set of* places*; T is a finite and non empty set of* transitions *with* $P \cap T = \emptyset$; $\mathbf{I}^-, \mathbf{I}^+ : T \times P \rightarrow \mathbb{N}$ *are the* input *and* output *matrices, that define the arcs of the net and that specify their weight; and* $\mathbf{m}_0 : P \rightarrow \mathbb{N}$ *is a multiset on P representing the* initial marking *of the net.*

A *marking* $\mathbf{m}$ (or state) of a PN is a multiset on P. A transition t is *enabled* in marking $\mathbf{m}$ iff $\mathbf{I}^-(t,p) \leq \mathbf{m}(p)$, $\forall p \in P$, where $\mathbf{m}(p)$ is the number of tokens in place p in marking $\mathbf{m}$. Enabled transitions may *fire*, and the firing of transition t in marking $\mathbf{m}$ yields a marking $\mathbf{m}' = \mathbf{m} + \mathbf{I}^+(t) - \mathbf{I}^-(t)$. Marking $\mathbf{m}'$ is said to be reachable from $\mathbf{m}$ because of the firing of t and is denoted by $\mathbf{m}[t\rangle\mathbf{m}'$.

The markings which are reachable from a given initial marking $\mathbf{m}_0$ form the *Reachability Set* (RS($\mathbf{m}_0$)). The *incidence matrix* is the matrix $\mathbf{C} = \mathbf{I}^+ - \mathbf{I}^-$, so that $\mathbf{C}_{t,p} = \mathbf{I}^+(t,p) - \mathbf{I}^-(t,p)$ describes the effect of the firing of transition t on the number of tokens in place p. Any left annuller of matrix $\mathbf{C}$, a vector $x \in \mathcal{Z}^{|P|}$ solution of the matrix equation $x\mathbf{C} = 0$ is called a *P-semiflow*.

The set of P-semiflows are at the base of the first notion of "structure" used in this paper. Indeed if x is a P-semiflow and $\mathbf{m}$ any state reachable from the initial state $\mathbf{m}_0$, we can write that $x \cdot \mathbf{m} = K$, where K is a constant value that can be computed from the initial state, $K = x \cdot \mathbf{m}_0$. This suggests that all the places that are in the same P-semiflow (that is to say the set π_x of all places p with a non-null value of $x(p)$) have a form of "circular" dependency and it is advisable to put them close together in the decision diagram [11]. The intuition is that each P-semiflow usually represents a local sub-component of a more complex model. The set π_x consists of connected places that can be used to identify a PN subnet, the Petri Net structure that will be at the basis of the algorithm proposed in the next section. All the P-semiflows of a PN can be expressed as linear combinations of the set Π_{MPS} of *minimal P-semiflows*

Algorithm 1. Pseudocode of the Sloan algorithm.

Function `Sloan`:
  Select a vertex u of the graph.
  Select v as the most-distant vertex to u with a graph visit.
  Assign to each vertex v' a gradient $grad(v') = dist(v, v')$.
  Initialize visit frontier $Q = \{v\}$
  repeat until Q is empty:
    Remove from the frontier Q the vertex v' that minimizes $P(v')$.
    Add v' to the variable ordering l.
    Add the unexplored adjacent vertices of v' to Q.

(MPS). Since the number of MPS can be exponential in the number of places, their computation is in EXPSPACE. However, on many practical cases, the set of MPS is much smaller and can be computed in almost linear time [12]. In the experimental section we shall detail on which models the computation is feasible.

The second notion of "structure" used in this paper is that of *nested unit* (NU) which is at the base of Nested-Unit Petri Nets (NUPN) [15]. NUPN are ordinary Petri nets (all arcs have weight one) with an additional structure of "nested units". Units constitute a partition of the set P of places and are characterized by having at most one place of the unit marked in any reachable state. NUPN have been developed as the target formalism for the translation from process algebra to Petri nets. Let Π_{NU} be the set of nested units of a NUPN.

Note that while the structure based on MPS can be computed on (almost) any net, the structure of NU applies only to NUPN, and is part of the model definition. This topic will be discussed with more detail in the experimental section. Both NU and MPS express an important property of mutual dependency of the involved variables in PN system. In a NU, at most one place can have a token in any marking. In a MPS, a weighted sum of tokens is constant in any marking. Therefore, we expect that a variable ordering that groups together MDD variables corresponding to places in the same NU/MPS should reduce the MDD size, due to the inter-dependence between the variables [11,25].

The Sloan Algorithm for Static Variable Ordering

The Sloan algorithm [27] is an algorithm to reorder the entries of a sparse symmetric matrix $\mathbf{A}$ around its diagonal. It computes a permutation of the rows/columns of $\mathbf{A}$ such that most of the non-zero entries are maintained as close as possible to the diagonal. Recently, the work in [21] has shown that Sloan is a promising algorithm for variable ordering of Petri net models. The idea is to express variable-variable interactions in $\mathbf{A}$. Compacting $\mathbf{A}$ around the diagonal results in an improved transition locality in the MDD. Since the Sloan method requires $\mathbf{A}$ to be *symmetric*, some form of symmetrization is needed. In our context, we define $\mathbf{A}_{i,j}$ to be non-zero iff there is a transition that connects place i with place j, regardless of the direction of the arcs.

The pseudocode of Sloan is given in Algorithm 1. The method can be divided into two phases. In the first phase it searches a pseudo-diameter of the $\mathbf{A}$ matrix graph, i.e. two vertices v, u that have an (almost) maximal distance. Usually, a

Algorithm 2. Pseudocode of the P-semiflows chaining algorithm.

Function P-chain(Π_{MPS}):
  $l = \varnothing$ is the ordered list of places.
  $S = \varnothing$ is the set of currently discovered common places.
  Select a MPS $\pi_i \in \Pi_{\text{MPS}}$ s.t. $\max_{\{i,j\} \in |\Pi_{\text{MPS}}|} \pi_i \cap \pi_j$ with $i \neq j$
  $\Pi_{\text{MPS}} = \Pi_{\text{MPS}} \setminus \{\pi_i\}$
  $\pi_{curr} = \pi_i$
  Append $V(\pi_{curr})$ to l
  repeat until Π_{MPS} is empty:
    Select a MPS $\pi_j \in \Pi_{\text{MPS}}$ s.t. $\max_{j \in |\Pi_{\text{MPS}}|} \pi_{curr} \cap \pi_j$
    Remove $(l \cap V(\pi_j)) \setminus S$ to l
    Append $V(\pi_{curr} \cap \pi_j) \setminus S$ to l
    Append $V(\pi_j) \setminus (S \cap V(\pi_{curr}))$ to l
    Add $V(\pi_{curr} \cap \pi_j)$ to S
    $\pi_{curr} = \pi_j$
    $\Pi_{\text{MPS}} = \Pi_{\text{MPS}} \setminus \{\pi_j\}$
  return l

heuristic approach based on the construction of the *root level structure* of the graph is employed. The method then performs a visit, starting from v, exploring in sequence all vertices in the visit frontier Q that maximize a priority function $P(v')$. The function $P(v')$ guides the variable selection in the greedy strategy. It is defined as $P(v') = -W_1 \cdot incr(v') + W_2 \cdot dist(v, v')$ where v, v' are vertices in graph $\mathbf{A}$, $incr(v')$ is the number of unexplored vertices adjacent to v', $dist(v, v')$ is the distance of the shortest path between v and v', and W_1 and W_2 are two integer weights. The weights control how Sloan prioritizes the visit of the local cluster (W_1) and how much the selection should follow the gradient (W_2).

The P-chain Algorithm for Static Variable Ordering
The *P-semiflows chaining algorithm*(P-chain) is based on the idea of keeping together the places belonging to the same P-semiflow for the MDD variable ordering. The idea behind this algorithm is to maintain the places shared by two P-semiflows as close as possible in the final DD variable ordering, since their markings cannot vary arbitrarily. The pseudo-code is reported in Algorithm 2.

The algorithm takes as input the Π_{MPS} set and returns as output a variable ordering l. Initially, the MPS π_i sharing the highest number of places with any unit is removed from Π_{MPS} and saved in π_{curr}. All its places are added to l.

Then the main loop runs until Π_{MPS} becomes empty. The loop comprises the following operations. The MPS π_j sharing the highest number of places with π_{curr} is selected. All the places of π_j in l, which are not currently S (the list of currently discovered common places) are removed. The common places between π_i and π_j not present in S are appended to l, followed by the places present only in π_j. After these steps, S is updated with the common places in π_i and π_j, and π_j is removed from Π_{MPS}. Finally π_{curr} becomes π_j, completing the iteration.

Evaluation Methodology

When testing multiple methods on a set of models, we need one or more score functions to determine the efficacy of the methods. We mainly consider the peak node size of the constructed MDD as a basis for the score functions, since it is the upper bound of the MDD computation both in terms of memory and time. Let $\mathcal{A}$ be a set of considered methods, let $\mathcal{I}$ be the set of model instances, and let i be a model instance solved by algorithms $\mathcal{A} = \{a_1, \ldots, a_m\}$ with peak nodes $P_i = \{p_{a_1}(i), \ldots, p_{a_m}(i)\}$. We consider three score functions for each instance i:

- $\mathit{Solved}_a(i)$: 1 if the RS generation using the variable ordering provided by algorithm a finishes in the time/memory constraints, 0 otherwise;
- $\mathit{Optimal}_a(i)$: 1 if algorithm a found the variable ordering among the tested method which leads to the smallest MDD peak size, 0 otherwise;
- *Normalized Score* (NS): is a value between 0 and 1 which weights the "quality" of the variable ordering, and it is defined as:

$$\mathrm{NS}_a(i) = 1 - \frac{\min\{p \in P_i\}}{p_a(i)} \tag{1}$$

The optimal algorithm for an instance i receives a NS score of 0. If an algorithm does not terminate in the given time/space limits, we arbitrarily assign a score of 1 to that algorithm.

3 The Gradient-*Π* Algorithm

This section presents the Gradient-*Π* heuristics, the main contribution of the paper. It is an hybrid algorithm that combines the features of both the Sloan method (which is *gradient-based*) and the P-Chain method (which is based on the idea of ordering the *structural units*). As observed in [6] Sloan performs rather well, especially in terms of the number of "solved" models (models on which the state space is generated within the given time and space constraints), but it is not always the best one. Methods like Tovchigrechko, that takes into consideration some aspect of the net graph (like number of input and output arcs of a place) often exhibit better performances. That analysis also showed that a heuristics like Force, that usually reaches intermediate performances, when modified to include information on the NU (method called Force-NU in [6]) can go beyond the performance of the best performers (like Tovchigrechko and Sloan) on the set of NUPN models.

The idea behind the Gradient-*Π* heuristics is indeed to combine the generality of Sloan, that results in a large number of solved models, with the exploitation of structural informations that could result in better performances. The exploitation of structural info is similar to the idea behind the P-chain algorithm. According to the benchmark results reported in [6], P-chain does not perform well, and our hypothesis is that its poor performances have two motivations: (1) there is no clever choice of the order in which the MPSs are considered and (2) there is no indication on how to order the variables of the same MPS

Algorithm 3. Pseudocode of the Gradient-Π heuristics.

Function Gradient-$\Pi(v_0, \Pi)$:
  // Phase 1: establish a gradient based on v_{first} and v_{last}.
  Start a graph visit from v_0. Let v_{last} the variable that maximizes $dist(v_0, v_{\text{last}})$.
  Start a visit from v_{last}. Let v_{first} be the variable that maximizes $dist(v_{\text{last}}, v_{\text{first}})$.
  for each variable $v \in V$:
    Compute $grad(v)$.
  $S \leftarrow \varnothing$
  $l \leftarrow []$
  // Phase 2: Linearize the elements of Π along the gradient.
  while exists at least one $\pi \in \Pi$ with $\pi \setminus S \neq \varnothing$:
    for each element $\pi \in \Pi$ with $\pi \setminus S \neq \varnothing$:
      Compute $score(\pi)$.
    Let $\pi_{\max}$ be the element with maximum $score(\pi)$ value.
    // Phase 3: Linearize the variables in the selected element π_{max}.
    Append variables in $(\pi_{\max} \setminus S)$ to l in ascending gradient order.
    $S \leftarrow S \cup \pi_{\max}$.
  Append all variables in $(V \setminus S)$ to l in ascending gradient order.
  return l.

(which corresponds to linearize the places inside the MPS which is basically a cyclic structure). In Gradient-Π the choices associated to the two points above are resolved using a gradient-based approach mutuated from Sloan algorithm

The method takes as input an initial vertex and a structure Π of places. We consider two different applications of this method: Gradient-P uses the set of minimal P-semiflows Π_{MPS} as input, and Gradient-NU uses the set of Nested Units Π_{NU} as input. A pseudo-code is given in Algorithm 3.

The algorithm is subdivided into three main phases. In the first phase, the algorithm identifies a *pseudo-diameter* of the system graph, whose vertices v_{first} and v_{last} are the opposite ends. Identification is done using two graph visits. Alternatively, a *root level structure* [18] can be used for this task. The identified diameter is a *pseudo-diameter*, since there is no guarantee that $(v_{\text{first}}, v_{\text{last}})$ forms the maximum diameter of the graph. However, this method usually finds a reasonable approximate of the pseudo-diameter, and it is very fast. Once the pseudo-diameter is established, a scalar *gradient* is assigned to each vertex v. The definition of $grad(v)$ is the subject of study in the next section.

The second phase of the algorithm takes one element of Π at a time, according to the gradient order. To do so, it assigns a *score* value to each element, with the goal of taking the one with the maximum score. The algorithm tracks the set of variables S that have already been inserted in the variable ordering l. Again we shall discuss the considered score function in the next section. Once the element with the maximum score $\pi_{\max}$ has been identified, the algorithm performs the third phase, which consists in a greedy local optimization of the variable ordering. Variables in $(\pi_{\max} \setminus S)$ are ranked according to the $grad(v)$ value, and appended to l. The method continues selecting elements $\pi \in \Pi$ until all variables have been inserted in l. For completeness of the method, if some variable is not covered by any element of Π, it is appended at the end of l. The implemented method also considers the case where the graph is not fully connected. In that case, the algorithm is run separately for each connected component.

3.1 Parameter Estimation of the Score and Gradient Functions

The Gradient-Π method depends on a set of different parameters and functions. We defined a set of experiments to estimate empirically these parameters. The targeted questions are the following:

Q1. What is the best strategy for the selection of the initial vertex v_0?
Q2. What $score(\pi)$ function should be used?
Q3. What $grad(v)$ function should be used?

To answer these questions, we run a prototype implementation of the Gradient-Π method on a benchmark composed of 51 PN model instances, made by a section of the smallest instances of the MCC2016 benchmark, used for the Gradient-Π assessment in Sect. 4. We consider Π_{MPS} as the input set Π.

Q1. We consider three different criterias for the selection of v_0: (1) Take v_0 as the first place P_0 in the net; (2) Take v_0 as a random place in the net; and (3) Take v_0 as the place with the maximum number of input/output arcs.

We run Gradient-Π on the test set, collecting the peak MDD size for each run. Figure 1 shows the comparative results obtained by the three criterias.

Each plot in Fig. 1 shows the MDD peak values of the compared runs, on a log-log scale. Each dot represent a model run, where the x and y coordinates are the MDD peaks obtained in two of the three tested configurations. The data shows that the method is not very sensible to the selection of v_0, with the third configuration only marginally better than the other two. However, since the third configuration is also the typical strategy for the initial vertex selection of Sloan, we adopt it for our implementation of Gradient-Π.

Q2. The score function for an element $\pi \in \Pi$ should balance these quantities:

1. An element π that has many variables already in S should be preferred;
2. The score should be proportional to the gradient;
3. The element cardinality $|\pi|$ can be used as a weight parameter.

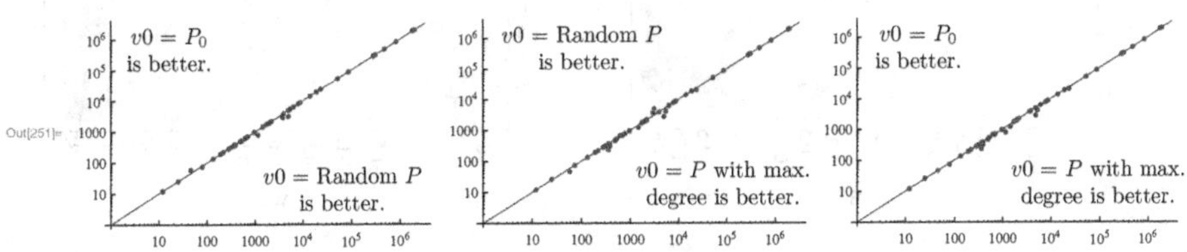

Fig. 1. MDD peaks obtained for different choices of v_0.

To encode these three desiderata into a single score function, we defined (empirically) two parametric score functions:

$$score_{\text{mult}}(\pi) = \overbrace{\left(W_1 \cdot \sum_{v \in \pi \cap S} grad(v) - \sum_{v \in \pi \setminus S} grad(v)\right)}^{d} \cdot |\pi \setminus S|^{E \cdot sign(d)} \quad (2)$$

$$score_{\text{add}}(\pi) = W_1 \cdot \sum_{v \in \pi \cap S} grad(v) - \sum_{v \in \pi \setminus S} grad(v) + W_2 \cdot |\pi \setminus S| \quad (3)$$

These functions are inspired by both the weight function of Sloan and the weight function of the Noack method [16]. In the function $score_{\text{mult}}(\pi)$ the weight of the element size is a multiplicative factor, while for the function $score_{\text{add}}(\pi)$ it is an additive factor. The power in Eq. (2) consideres the sign of d to ensure that when E is positive the score increases for increasing values of $|\pi \setminus S|$ regardless of the sign of d. Vice versa, it should decrease when E is negative. Both functions are controlled by a set of parameters (W_1 and E for the first, W_1 and W_2 for the second). We run a set of experiments on the parameter space of $W_1 \times E$ and $W_1 \times W_2$, in order to determine the best values for both.

Figure 2 shows the normalized scores of Eq. (1) of the runs on the 51 model instances considered. The left plot shows the NS results when the $score_{\text{mult}}(\pi)$ is used, for varying (W_1, E). Similarly, the right plot shows the NS results when using the $score_{\text{add}}(\pi)$, for varying (W_1, W_2). Lighter blocks have a smaller NS, which means that the algorithm running on that pair of parameter's values computes better variable orderings. The resulting plots are remarkably smooth. Interestingly, the left one has a local minimum in $W_1 = 1, E = 0$, while the right one has a local minimum in $W_1 = 1, W_2 = 0$. This analysis suggests that the element size does not bring any advantage to the score function, neither in multiplicative nor in additive form. Therefore, the final score function that we adopt is:

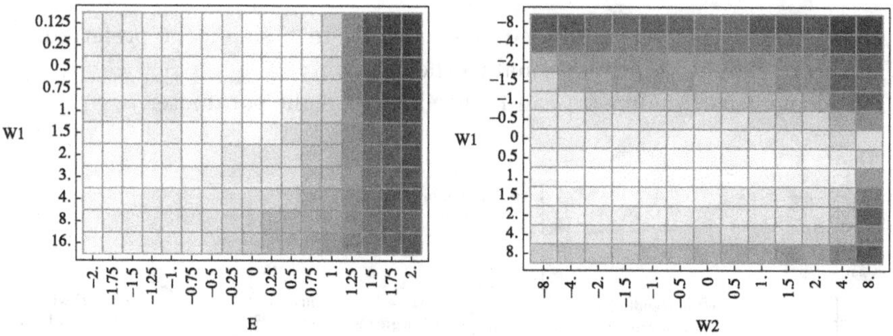

Fig. 2. Normalized scores on the parameter space of $W_1 \times E$ and $W_1 \times W_2$.

$$score(\pi) = \sum_{v \in \pi \cap S} grad(v) - \sum_{v \in \pi \setminus S} grad(v) \quad (4)$$

Q3. Since the Gradient-Π method works using a pseudo-diameter, a critical element is the gradient function $grad(v)$. Let $b = \max_{v \in V} dist(v_{\text{last}}, v)$. We consider two gradient functions: (1) An *integer* function: $grad(v) = dist(v_{\text{first}}, v)$, based solely on v_{first}; (2) A *fractional* function: $grad(v) = dist(v_{\text{first}}, v) + \frac{1}{b}(b + 1 - dist(v_{\text{last}}, v))$. The first function is the same used in the Sloan method. The second function also considers the distance to v_{last} as a fractional part. We investigate if this addition brings benefits to the method.

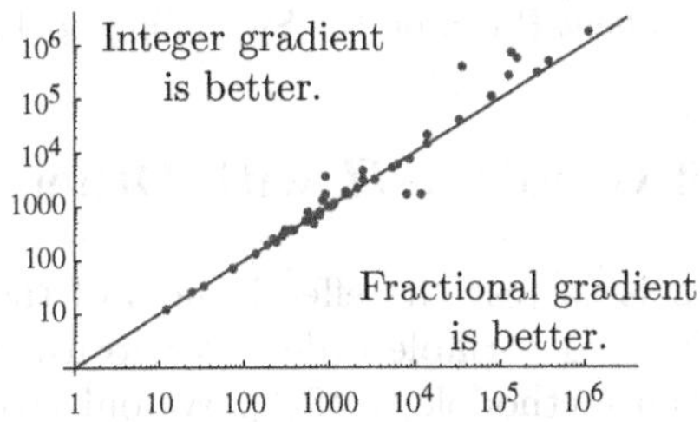

Fig. 3. Effect of the two tested gradient functions.

Figure 3 shows the comparison of the two gradient functions. The plot compares the MDD peaks obtained running the same test using the two different functions. The results show that the integer function is slightly better than the fractional one in some cases, but the advantage cannot be determined clearly.

Example 1 (Gradient-Π example on a Petri net using P-semiflows)
We now illustrate the Gradient-Π algorithm on a small Petri net, taken from the MCC2016 model set. The model is called "SwimmingPool" and describes a sort of protocol to use a pool[1]. We use the set of P-semiflows Π_{MPS} for the input elements Π. Figure 4 shows in the upper-left frame the Petri net model. Numbers written in the places are the ordering computed by the Gradient-P algorithm. Numbers written aside of each place are the computed integer gradient. The three replicas of the model on the right show the three MPS π_1, π_2 and π_3.

The algorithm computes three iterations of the second phase loop. In the first iteration, π_1 is selected, since it has the highest score. Since no variable has been selected yet, all variables in π_1 are taken, in gradient order. In the second iteration, π_2 is selected, which has already two variables in S. Finally, π_3 is selected. Intuitively, the P-semiflows of this model represents closed loops where a constant token quantity circulates. The algorithm attaches these "loops" one after the other, following the gradient order.

[1] Model details can be found in http://mcc.lip6.fr/pdf/SwimmingPool-form.pdf.

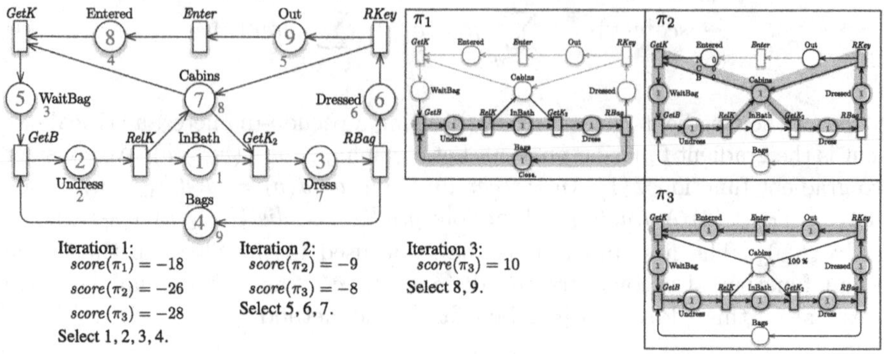

Fig. 4. Gradient-P run on the Swimming pool model.

4 Comparison of Gradient-Π with Other Heuristics

The goal of this section is to test the effectiveness of the proposed heuristics against other commonly used variable ordering algorithms for Petri net models. We use the evaluation methodology of [6]. We only consider static variable ordering methods. The set $\mathcal{A}$ of considered methods is:

- **Force-{PTS, NES, WES}:** variants of the Force heuristics [3] where 200 orderings are generated, and the one with the smallest score is selected. The considered score functions are: *point-transition span* (PTS), *normalized event span* (NES) and *weighted event span* (WES), respectively [26].
- **Force-{P, NU}:** variant of Force where structural elements are also centers of gravity, along with the events. Elements can be either Π_{MPS} or Π_{NU}.
- **Cuthill-Mckee** heuristics, defined in [13].
- **King** heuristics, defined in [17].
- **Sloan/Sloan16** heuristics, defined in [27] and recalled in Sect. 2. We consider two variations of this method: Sloan uses $\frac{W_1}{W_2} = \frac{1}{2}$, while Sloan16 uses $\frac{W_1}{W_2} = \frac{1}{16}$ (the parameters used in [21] and in [6], respectively).
- **P-Chain** heuristics: defined in [6] and recalled in Sect. 2
- **Noack** heuristics, defined in [22], is a greedy heuristics for Petri net models that tries to minimize the locality of the events in the ordering.
- **Tovchigrechko** heuristics, defined in [16], is a variation of the Noack heuristics with a different selection criteria.
- **Markov Cluster** uses the Markov cluster algorithm [28] to identify variable clusters and group them together.

Example 2 (Tested algorithms on the running example model). Figure 5 shows the variable orderings obtained with the tested methods on the SwimmingPool model. The model has a very clear structure of partially overlapped P-semiflows, as shown in Fig. 4, and we expect Gradient-P to perform well as it is designed to exploit this type of structure.

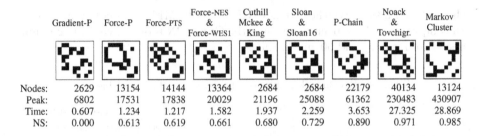

	Gradient-P	Force-P	Force-PTS	Force-NES & Force-WES1	Cuthill Mckee & King	Sloan & Sloan16	P-Chain	Noack & Tovchigr.	Markov Cluster

Nodes:	2629	13154	14144	13364	2684	2684	22179	40134	13124
Peak:	6802	17531	17838	20029	21196	25088	61362	230483	430907
Time:	0.607	1.234	1.217	1.582	1.937	2.259	3.653	27.325	28.869
NS:	0.000	0.613	0.619	0.661	0.680	0.729	0.890	0.971	0.985

Fig. 5. Comparison of Gradient-P with the other tested methods.

Each block shows the algorithm name, the symmetric adjacency matrix of the ordered model, and the performances of the state space generation using that ordering. Algorithms are ordered according to peak nodes (smallest to highest). Some algorithms obtained the same ordering, and have been grouped together in a single column. The matrix has a black square in (i, j) if there exists an event that links the variable at level i with the variable at level j. In this visualization we do not consider the event directionality, and we make the matrix symmetric. The rows below each matrix report the number of MDD nodes, the peak nodes, the time needed to construct the MDD, and the normalized score assigned to that variable order. In this example, Gradient-P performs better and thus receives an NS score of 0. All the other algorithms receive a score that is proportional to how much their peak node size departs from the minimum peak node size found for that instance. Note that Gradient-P has a peak size which is almost one third of the second best ordering algorithm (Force-P, which is also an algorithm that exploits the net structure), one fourth of Sloan (which is a generic algorithm that does not exploit P-semiflows). Note that algorithms that have been specifically performed for Petri nets, like Tovchigrechko and Noack perform rather poorly on this example, with peak sizes more than 30 times bigger than Gradient-P.

4.1 Empirical Assessment on the Benchmark

The model of the previous section is just an example of a structure on which Gradient-P performs very well. In this section we test Gradient-P and Gradient-NU on a broader set of models, to evaluate their average performance. The evaluation is based on a benchmark with two subsets of models, taken from the 664 instances of the Model Checking Contest (MCC) 2016 [14] model set:

- The set $\mathcal{I}_{\text{MPS}}$ where P-semiflows are computable in less than 30 s. The set is made by 408 model instances, belonging to 45 models. In 294 of these instances at least one algorithm finishes in the time/memory limits.
- The set $\mathcal{I}_{\text{NU}}$ of NUPN instances, with well identified nested units that correspond to process algebra terms. The set is made by 80 model instances belonging to 12 different models. For 67 of these instances, at least one algorithm finishes in the time/memory limits.

The excluded instances either are not NUPN, or the MPS set is not computable. All computations have been done using the GreatSPN tool [5], with a maximum of 4 GB of memory and 60 min of time.

Table 1. Benchmark results on the $\mathcal{I}_{\text{MPS}}$ and $\mathcal{I}_{\text{NU}}$ model sets.

	Models (45)			Instances (294)				Models (12)			Instances (67)		
Method	solv.	opt	NS	solv.	opt	NS	Method	solv.	opt	NS	solv.	opt	NS
Gradient-P	**28.61**	**12.42**	**12.73**	240	**76**	**137.22**	Gradient-NU	**9.82**	**7.03**	**2.64**	50	**34**	**23.72**
Sloan16	**28.61**	4.60	21.46	**244**	53	181.29	Sloan16	9.47	0.45	8.10	**55**	9	45.40
Sloan	28.51	4.84	22.07	242	43	188.83	Sloan	9.37	1.31	8.56	53	7	49.07
Tovchigr.	28.29	5.62	18.80	240	52	169.27	Tovchigr.	8.82	0.60	8.51	44	12	47.71
P-Chain	26.81	2.61	24.88	229	21	223.33	Noack	7.83	0.15	8.34	42	3	50.66
Noack	26.31	4.34	19.21	228	36	176.99	Force-NES	6.30	0	10.22	35	0	61.85
Force-NES	22.69	2.90	23.98	192	23	209.52	Force-PTS	5.74	0	10.43	27	0	64.24
Force-P	22.40	4.67	20.75	199	30	188.09	Force-NU	5.71	1.30	8.78	38	5	54.59
Force-PTS	22.33	2.53	24.32	189	19	213.19	Force-WES	5.41	0	10.11	34	0	61.72
Force-WES	22.04	3.40	23.27	190	23	206.30	MarkovCl.	4.91	0	9.19	24	0	60.94
Cuthill-M.	21.32	2.74	24.63	214	52	180.11	Cuthill-M.	2.53	0	10.58	21	0	65.59
King	20.80	1.77	24.99	206	21	199.89	King	2.49	0	10.59	21	0	65.71
MarkovCl.	18.61	1.30	27.29	174	15	235.13							

Table 1(left) reports the results for the $\mathcal{I}_{\text{MPS}}$ set. Since in the MCC model set the number of instances-per-model vary largely (some have just one, others have up to forty instance), the table reports the results on a per-model and per-instance basis. For each algorithm $a \in \mathcal{A}$, the table indicates the number of models for which a terminates (solv.), the number of models where the a found the best variable ordering (opt) and the total NS score for that algorithm. The last three columns replicate the same data for the model instances.

The computation of the NS score for the per-instance analysis of algorithm a just sums the value of $\text{NS}_a(i)$ of Eq. (1) over all instances i. In the per-model analysis the sum is over the $\text{NS}_a(m)$ values for each model m, where the NS score of a model m is computed as $\text{NS}_a(m) = \sum_{i \in m} \frac{1}{|m|} \text{NS}_a(i)$, to balance models that have many instances. Analogous rescaling is done for the number of solved and optimally solved models (which results in fractional numbers).

From the data it emerges that Gradient-P and the variation of Sloan that we propose (Sloan16) are the best performers. In particular if we observe the per-model results, Gradient-P has a significant margin in finding the optimal ordering (thus reducing the MDD peak size) on both Sloan16 and Sloan (and even on their sum) and a much better NS score both with respect to Sloan/Sloan16 and with respect to the second one on the NS column (Tovchigrechko). Surprisingly, neither P-chain nor Force-P methods, which are both P-semiflow based algorithm, reaches similar performances to that of Gradient-P. From these positive results we conjecture that the combination of a Sloan-like gradient order with the structural information of P-semiflows produces variable orderings that are better that those generated by algorithms that use just one of the two elements (gradient or P-semiflows).

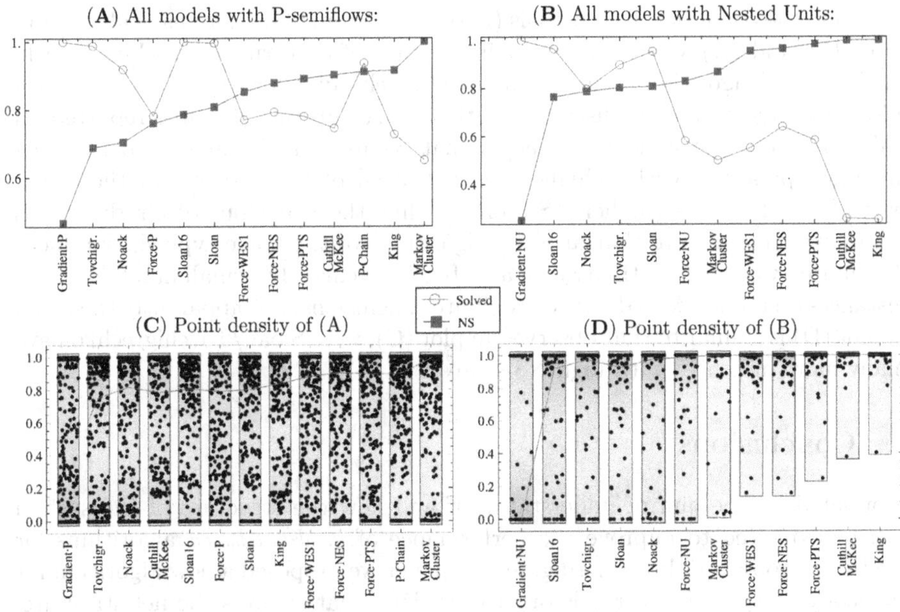

Fig. 6. Performance obtained using Gradient-Π on the benchmark.

In the per-instance analysis, Gradient-P has the best NS score, actually significantly better than the second one in the column (which is, again, Tovchigrechko), a number of solved instances that is only 1.7% less than the best performer on solved instances (Sloan16) and the best number of optimal solved instances. This last results is nevertheless not particularly relevant, since the splitting of Sloan on two variations (Sloan and Sloan16) may have lead to an underestimation of the value with respect to a benchmark in which only one of the two is present.

Table 1(right) reports the results for the $\mathcal{I}_{\text{NU}}$ set. The results are similar to that of the previous case but even more striking for what concerns the number of optimally solved models/instances: Sloan, Gradient-NU and Tovchigrechko methods occupy the top positions in terms of solved models/instances, but Gradient-NU finds the optimal variable ordering among the tested methods more often than the others, with a significantly lower NS score. The number of solved instances is now worse than the best one by 10%, but, as explained before, the results per instance are less stable, since it is enough to have a single model with many instances, on which an algorithm does not perform well, to badly influence the results.

From the data analysis it seems that Gradient-P and Gradient-NU finds better variable ordering compared to state-of-the-art methods like Sloan and Tovchigrechko. To confirm this observation, we look at the point density of the NS scores of each instance. Figure 6 reports on the top row the plots of the NS score and the count of solved models (normalized from 0 to 1), for each algorithm. Plots (C) and (D) shows the NS point density of each run in the benchmark. In the bar of algorithm a there is a single black point for each $\mathrm{NS}_a(m)$, which allows to understand the distribution that makes up the NS value reported on Tables 1. From the plot (C) emerges that Sloan and Tovchigrechko methods are more polarised with a higher concentration of lower scores in the upper part of the diagrams (higher NS scores), while the behaviour of Gradient-P is more distributed. Note that also the algorithms of the Force type show a more distributed values of NS than Sloan and Tovchigrechko. The small number of $\mathcal{I}_{\mathrm{NU}}$ instances do not allow to draw very definite conclusions, but apparently the trend of plot (D) is similar to that observed in plot (C), were Sloan/Tovchigrechko have many more instances with high NS scores.

5 Conclusions

Motivated by the aim of understating if and how the structure of the system can be exploited to improve the performance of *gradient-based* algorithms for devising a good variable ordering, in this paper we proposed a new algorithm for statically computing a variable ordering of DDs that exploits the net structure. The algorithm combines the features of the Sloan method, with the ideas of the P-Chain method. It finds the variable ordering by sorting a set of structural units of the system along a Sloan-like gradient. The structural units should be available or computable, which may limit the applicability of the method on a subset of models. In practice, these units are computable on most models in a reasonable time. For the set of tested models with structural information (294 instances), the efficacy of the proposed algorithm emerges, producing better results over the set of considered state-of-the-art variable ordering methods (13 were tested). Our tests show that the combination of a gradient-based order with the structural units is effective in reducing the MDD peak size. Parameter estimation techniques were used to tune the internals of the proposed heuristics. This allowed the identification of the range of the internal score function coefficients that have been used for the 294 instances test.

We would like to extend the method to formalisms other than Petri nets (like process algebra models or workflows models), to see if the observed performance is consistent. In addition, other kinds of structural informations could be exploited, as for instance the min-cut partitioning.

References

1. Van der Aalst, W.M.: The application of Petri nets to workflow management. J. Circ. Syst. Comput. **8**(1), 21–66 (1998)
2. Ajmone-Marsan, M., Balbo, G., Conte, G., Donatelli, S., Franceschinis, G.: Modelling with Generalized Stochastic Petri Nets. Wiley, Hoboken (1995)
3. Aloul, F.A., Markov, I.L., Sakallah, K.A.: FORCE: a fast and easy-to-implement variable-ordering heuristic. In: Proceedings of GLSVLSI, pp. 116–119. ACM, New York (2003)

4. Amparore, E.G., Balbo, G., Beccuti, M., Donatelli, S., Franceschinis, G.: 30 years of GreatSPN. In: Fiondella, L., Puliafito, A. (eds.) Principles of Performance and Reliability Modeling and Evaluation: Essays in Honor of Kishor Trivedi. SSRE, pp. 227–254. Springer, Cham (2016). doi:10.1007/978-3-319-30599-8_9
5. Amparore, E.G., Beccuti, M., Donatelli, S.: (Stochastic) model checking in GreatSPN. In: Ciardo, G., Kindler, E. (eds.) PETRI NETS 2014. LNCS, vol. 8489, pp. 354–363. Springer, Cham (2014). doi:10.1007/978-3-319-07734-5_19
6. Amparore, E.G., Donatelli, S., Beccuti, M., Garbi, G., Miner, A.: Decision diagrams for Petri nets: which variable ordering? In: Petri Net Performance Engineering conference (PNSE), pp. 31–50. CEUR-WS (2017)
7. Babar, J., Miner, A.: Meddly: multi-terminal and edge-valued decision diagram library. In: International Conference on Quantitative Evaluation of Systems, Los Alamitos, CA, USA, pp. 195–196. IEEE Computer Society (2010)
8. Bryant, R.E.: Graph-based algorithms for boolean function manipulation. IEEE Trans. Comput. **35**, 677–691 (1986)
9. Cassandras, C.G., Lafortune, S.: Introduction to Discrete Event Systems. Springer, Secaucus (2006)
10. Ciardo, G., Lüttgen, G., Siminiceanu, R.: Saturation: an efficient iteration strategy for symbolic state-space generation. In: Margaria, T., Yi, W. (eds.) TACAS 2001. LNCS, vol. 2031, pp. 328–342. Springer, Heidelberg (2001). doi:10.1007/3-540-45319-9_23
11. Ciardo, G., Lüttgen, G., Yu, A.J.: Improving static variable orders via invariants. In: Kleijn, J., Yakovlev, A. (eds.) ICATPN 2007. LNCS, vol. 4546, pp. 83–103. Springer, Heidelberg (2007). doi:10.1007/978-3-540-73094-1_8
12. Colom, J.M., Silva, M.: Convex geometry and semiflows in P/T nets. A comparative study of algorithms for computation of minimal p-semiflows. In: Rozenberg, G. (ed.) ICATPN 1989. LNCS, vol. 483, pp. 79–112. Springer, Heidelberg (1991). doi:10.1007/3-540-53863-1_22
13. Cuthill, E., McKee, J.: Reducing the bandwidth of sparse symmetric matrices. In: Proceedings of the 1969 24th National Conference, pp. 157–172. ACM, New York (1969)
14. Kordon, F., et al.: Complete Results for the 2016th Edition of the Model Checking Contest. http://mcc.lip.6.fr/2016/results.php
15. Garavel, H.: Nested-unit Petri nets: a structural means to increase efficiency and scalability of verification on elementary nets. In: Devillers, R., Valmari, A. (eds.) PETRI NETS 2015. LNCS, vol. 9115, pp. 179–199. Springer, Cham (2015). doi:10.1007/978-3-319-19488-2_9
16. Heiner, M., Rohr, C., Schwarick, M., Tovchigrechko, A.A.: MARCIE's secrets of efficient model checking. In: Koutny, M., Desel, J., Kleijn, J. (eds.) Transactions on Petri Nets and Other Models of Concurrency XI. LNCS, vol. 9930, pp. 286–296. Springer, Heidelberg (2016). doi:10.1007/978-3-662-53401-4_14
17. King, I.P.: An automatic reordering scheme for simultaneous equations derived from network systems. J. Numer. Methods Eng. **2**(4), 523–533 (1970)
18. Kumfert, G., Pothen, A.: Two improved algorithms for envelope and wavefront reduction. BIT Numer. Math. **37**(3), 559–590 (1997)
19. Lu, Y., Jain, J., Clarke, E., Fujita, M.: Efficient variable ordering using a BDD based sampling. In: Proceedings of the 37th Annual Design Automation Conference, DAC 2000, pp. 687–692. ACM, New York (2000)

20. Malik, S., Wang, A.R., Brayton, R.K., Sangiovanni-Vincentelli, A.: Logic verification using binary decision diagrams in a logic synthesis environment. In: IEEE International Conference on Computer-Aided Design (ICCAD), pp. 6–9, November 1988
21. Meijer, J., van de Pol, J.: Bandwidth and wavefront reduction for static variable ordering in symbolic reachability analysis. In: Rayadurgam, S., Tkachuk, O. (eds.) NFM 2016. LNCS, vol. 9690, pp. 255–271. Springer, Cham (2016). doi:10.1007/978-3-319-40648-0_20
22. Noack, A.: A ZBDD package for efficient model checking of Petri nets (in German). Ph.D. thesis, BTU Cottbus, Department of CS (1999)
23. Rice, M., Kulhari, S.: A survey of static variable ordering heuristics for efficient BDD/MDD construction. Technical report, University of California (2008)
24. Roig, O., Cortadella, J., Pastor, E.: Verification of asynchronous circuits by BDD-based model checking of Petri nets. In: De Michelis, G., Diaz, M. (eds.) ICATPN 1995. LNCS, vol. 935, pp. 374–391. Springer, Heidelberg (1995). doi:10.1007/3-540-60029-9_50
25. Schmidt, K.: Using Petri net invariants in state space construction. In: Garavel, H., Hatcliff, J. (eds.) TACAS 2003. LNCS, vol. 2619, pp. 473–488. Springer, Heidelberg (2003). doi:10.1007/3-540-36577-X_35
26. Siminiceanu, R.I., Ciardo, G.: New metrics for static variable ordering in decision diagrams. In: Hermanns, H., Palsberg, J. (eds.) TACAS 2006. LNCS, vol. 3920, pp. 90–104. Springer, Heidelberg (2006). doi:10.1007/11691372_6
27. Sloan, S.W.: An algorithm for profile and wavefront reduction of sparse matrices. Int. J. Numer. Meth. Eng. **23**(2), 239–251 (1986)
28. Van Dongen, S.: A cluster algorithm for graphs. Inform. Syst. **10**, 1–40 (2000)

Model Checking of C and C++ with DIVINE 4

Zuzana Baranová, Jiří Barnat, Katarína Kejstová, Tadeáš Kučera, Henrich Lauko, Jan Mrázek, Petr Ročkai, and Vladimír Štill(✉)

Faculty of Informatics, Masaryk University, Brno, Czech Republic
divine@fi.muni.cz

Abstract. The fourth version of the DIVINE model checker provides a modular platform for verification of real-world programs. It is built around an efficient interpreter of LLVM code which, together with a small, verification-oriented operating system and a set of runtime libraries, enables verification of code written in C and C++.

1 Introduction

Building correct software is undoubtedly an important goal for software developers and we firmly believe that formal verification methods can help in this endeavour. In particular, explicit-state model checking promises to put forth a deterministic testing procedure for non-deterministic problems (such as parallel programs or tests which use fault injection). Moreover, it is quite easy to integrate into common test-based workflows. The latest version of DIVINE aims to make good on these promises by providing an efficient and versatile tool for analysis of real-world C and C++ programs.

2 DIVINE 4 Architecture

The most prominent feature of DIVINE 4 is that the runtime environment for the verified program (i.e. support for threads, memory allocation, standard libraries) is not part of the verifier itself: instead, it is split into several components, separated by well-defined interfaces (see Fig. 1). The three most important components are: the DIVINE Virtual Machine (DiVM), which is an interpreter of LLVM code and provides basic functionality such as non-determinism and memory management; the DIVINE Operating System (DiOS), which takes care of thread management and scheduling; and finally libraries, which implement standard C, C++ and POSIX APIs. The libraries use syscalls to communicate with DiOS and hypercalls to communicate with DiVM.

The verification core below DiVM is responsible for verification of safety and liveness properties and uses DiVM to generate the state space of the (non-deterministic) program.

This work has been partially supported by the Czech Science Foundation grant No. 15-08772S and by Red Hat, Inc.

D. D'Souza and K. Narayan Kumar (Eds.): ATVA 2017, LNCS 10482, pp. 201–207, 2017.
DOI: 10.1007/978-3-319-68167-2_14

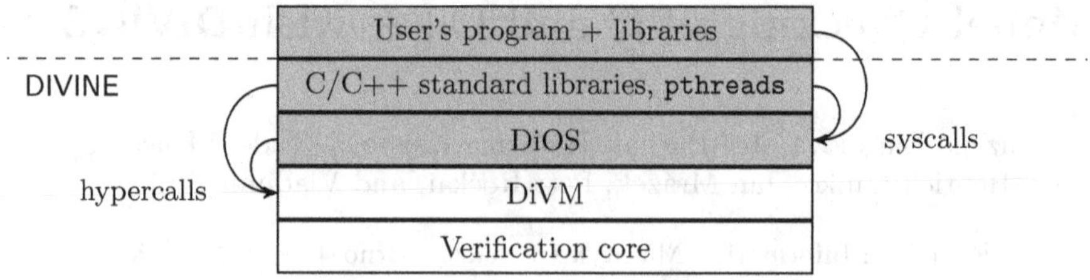

Fig. 1. Overview of the architecture of DIVINE 4. The shaded part consists of LLVM code which is interpreted by DiVM.

2.1 DIVINE Virtual Machine (DiVM)

The basic idea of DiVM is to provide the bare minimum required for efficient model checking of LLVM-based programs. To this end, it executes instructions, manages memory, implements non-deterministic choice, and (with the help of program instrumentation) keeps track of visible actions performed by the program. To the verification core, DiVM provides support for saving and loading snapshots of the program state and for generating successors of a given program state.

When the user program is executed in DiVM, it will be typically supported by a runtime environment (which itself executes on top of DiVM). This environment is expected to supply a *scheduler*, a procedure invoked by DiVM to explore the successors of a given program state. The scheduler's primary responsibility is thread management. It can, for example, implement asynchronous thread interleaving by managing multiple stacks and non-deterministically choosing which to execute. This design allows DiVM to be small, minimising the space for errors in this crucial part of the verifier. Moreover, it allows for greater flexibility, since it is usually much easier to program for DiVM then to change DiVM itself.

DiVM uses a graph to represent the memory of a program: nodes correspond to memory objects (e.g. results of allocation, global variables) and edges to pointers between these objects. Each program state corresponds to one such graph. When exploring the state space, those graphs are stored, hashed and compared directly (i.e. they are not converted to byte vectors). This graph representation allows DiVM to handle programs with dynamic heap allocation efficiently.

Out of the box, memory access in DiVM is subject to sequentially consistent semantics. Nevertheless, analysis under relaxed memory semantics can be added to DIVINE by the means of program transformations on the level of LLVM, as outlined in [7].

More details about DiVM, including an experimental evaluation, can be found in [6].

2.2 DIVINE Operating System (DiOS)

DiOS supplies both a scheduler, which is invoked by DiVM, and a POSIX-like environment for the libraries and the user program. To this end, DiOS exposes a syscall interface to `libc`, in a manner similar to common operating systems. Currently, DiOS implements asynchronous parallelism with threads and supports syscalls which cover an important subset of the POSIX file system interface (provided by the integrated virtual file system). Additional syscalls make thread management and DiOS configuration possible.

2.3 State Space Reductions

To be able to verify nontrivial C or C++ programs, DIVINE 4 employs heap symmetry reduction and τ reduction [5]. The latter reduction targets parallel programs and is based on the observation that not all actions performed by a given thread are visible to other threads. These local, invisible actions can be grouped and executed atomically. In DIVINE, actions are considered visible if they access shared memory. As DiVM has no notion of threads, the *shared status* of a memory object is partially maintained by DiOS. However, DiVM transparently handles the propagation of shared status to objects reachable from other shared objects.

It is desirable that threads are only switched at well-defined points in the instruction stream: in particular, this makes counterexamples easier to process. For this reason, DIVINE instruments the program with interrupt points prior to verification. DiVM will then only invoke the scheduler at these explicit interrupt points, and only if the program executed a shared memory access since the previous interrupt. To ensure soundness, these interrupt points are inserted such that there cannot be two accesses to shared memory without an interrupt point between them.

To further reduce the size of the state space of parallel programs, DIVINE performs heap symmetry reduction. That is, heaps that differ only in concrete values of memory addresses are considered identical for the purpose of verification. On top of that, DIVINE 4 also employs static reductions which modify the LLVM IR. However, it only uses simple transformations which are safe for parallel programs and which cause minimal overhead in DiVM.

2.4 C and C++ Language Support

For practical verification of C and C++ code, it is vital that the verifier has strong support for all language features and for the standard libraries of these languages, allowing the user to verify unmodified code. DIVINE achieves this by integrating ported implementations of existing C and C++ standard libraries. Additionally, an implementation of the POSIX threading API was developed specifically for DIVINE. These libraries together provide full support for C99 and C++14 and their respective standard libraries.

As DiVM executes LLVM instructions and not C or C++ directly, the program needs to be translated to LLVM IR and linked with the aforementioned libraries. This is done by an integrated compiler, based on the clang C/C++ frontend library. How a program is processed by DIVINE is illustrated in Fig. 2.

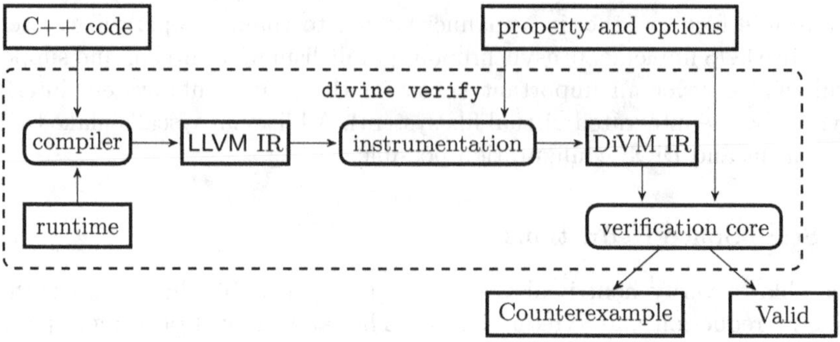

Fig. 2. Verification workflow of the `divine verify` command when it is given a C++ file as an input. Boxes with rounded corners represent stages of input processing.

The inputs to the build are a C or a C++ program and, optionally, a specification of the property to be verified. The program is first compiled and linked with runtime libraries, producing an LLVM IR module. This module is then instrumented to facilitate τ reduction (see Sect. 2.3) and annotated with metadata required for exception support [8]. The instrumented IR is then passed to the verification algorithm, which uses DiVM to evaluate it. Finally, the verification core (if provided with sufficient resources) either finds an error and produces a counterexample, or concludes that the program is correct.

2.5 Property Specification

DIVINE 4 supports a range of safety properties: detection of assertion violations, arithmetic errors, memory errors (e.g. access to freed or otherwise invalid memory), use of uninitialised values in branching, and `pthreads` locking errors.

The libraries shipped with DIVINE can simulate memory allocation failures and spurious wake-ups on `pthreads` conditional variables. The allocation failure simulation can be disabled on DIVINE's command line.

Monitors and Liveness. More complex properties can be specified in the form of *monitors*, which are executed synchronously by DiOS every time a visible action (as determined by τ reduction) occurs. This allows such monitors to observe globally visible state changes in the program, and therefore to check global assertions or liveness properties (using a Büchi accepting condition). Moreover, it is also possible to disallow some runs of the program, i.e. the monitor can specify that the current run of the program should be abandoned and ignored.

In order to check LTL properties in DIVINE, the LTL formula has to be translated to a Büchi automaton encoded as a monitor in C++. This translation can be done automatically by an external tool, `dipot`,[1] which internally uses SPOT [1] to process the LTL formula.

[1] Available from https://github.com/xlauko/dipot.

2.6 Interactive Program Simulator

Model checkers traditionally provide the user with a counterexample: a trace from the initial state to the error state. However, with real-world programs, the presentation of this trace is critical: the user needs to be able to understand the complex data structures which are part of the state, and how they evolve along the error trace. To help with this task, DIVINE now contains an interactive simulator that can be used to perform the steps of the program which led to the error and to inspect values of program variables at any point in the execution [4].

2.7 Major Changes Compared To DIVINE 3

Compared to DIVINE 3, the new version comes with several improvements. From architectural point of view, the most important changes are the introduction of DiVM and DiOS and the graph-based representation of program memory [6]. From user perspective, the most important changes include better support for C++ and its libraries, an improved compilation process which makes it easier to compile C and C++ programs into LLVM IR, an interactive simulator of counterexamples, and support for simulation of POSIX-compatible file system operations.

3 Usage and Evaluation

DIVINE is freely available online[2], including source code, a user manual, and examples which demonstrate the most important features of DIVINE. In addition to the source code, it is also possible to download a pre-built binary for 64bit Linux (which also works on Windows Subsystem for Linux), or a virtual machine image with DIVINE installed (available in 2 formats, OVA for VirtualBox, and VDI for QEMU and other hypervisors). If you choose to build DIVINE from source code, please refer to the user manual[3] for details.

3.1 Using DIVINE

Consider the code from Fig. 3 and assume it is saved in a file named `test.cpp`. Assuming that DIVINE is installed[4], the code can be verified by simply executing `divine verify test.cpp`. DIVINE will report an invalid write right after the end of the `x` array. You can observe that the output of `printf` is present in the `error trace` part of DIVINE's output. Moreover, toward the end, the output includes stack traces of all running threads. In this case, there are two threads, the main thread of the program and a kernel thread, in which the fault handler is being executed.

---

2 https://divine.fi.muni.cz/2017/divine4/.
3 https://divine.fi.muni.cz/manual.html.
4 The binary has to be in a directory which is listed in the `PATH` environment variable.

```
#include <cstdio>
#include <cassert>
void foo( int *array ) {
    for ( int i = 0; i <= 4; ++i ) {
        printf( "writing at %d\n", i );
        array[i] = 42;
    }
}

int main() {
    int x[4];
    foo( x );
    assert( x[3] == 42 );
}
```

Fig. 3. Example C++ code which creates an array `x` of size 4 (on the stack) and then, in function `foo`, writes into this array. `foo` does, however, attempt to write one element past the array, which would normally overwrite the next entry on the stack but not cause an immediate program failure. In DIVINE, this error is detected and reported.

If we wanted to inspect the error state in more detail, we could use DIVINE's simulator. First, we need a way to identify the error state: the counterexample contains a line which reads `choices made: 0^182`; the sequence of numbers after the colon is a sequence of non-deterministic choices made by DIVINE. We can now run `divine sim test.cpp` and execute `trace 0^182` (replacing the sequence of choices with the ones actually produced by `divine`). This makes the simulator stop after the last non-deterministic choice before the error. The error location can be inspected by executing `stepa`, which tells DIVINE to perform a single atomic step (unless an error occurs, in which case it stops as soon as the error is reported). It is now possible to examine the frame of the error handler, although it is more useful to move to the frame which caused the error by executing the `up` command. At this point, local variables can be inspected by using `show`.

Please consult the user manual for more detailed information on using DIVINE. Additionally, `divine help` and the `help` command in the simulator provide short descriptions of all available commands and switches.

3.2 Evaluation

We have evaluated DIVINE 4 on a set of more than 900 benchmarks from various sources, including parallel and sequential tests of parts of C and C++ standard libraries, the `pthread` library, part of the SV-COMP `pthread` benchmark set, and programs from various programming courses. We have compared DIVINE 4 to DIVINE 3 (an older version of DIVINE, also an explicit-state model checker) and ESBMC 4.1 [3] (an SMT-based symbolic model checker).

From our benchmark set, DIVINE 3 was able to process 457 benchmarks in 7 h, while DIVINE 4 processed the same 457 benchmarks in 1 h and 5 min. ESBMC was only able to process 60 benchmarks, mostly due to limitations of its C++ support and worse performance on threaded benchmarks. ESBMC took 2 h 43 min, while DIVINE 4 only took 10 minutes on the same subset. In all cases, there was a timeout of 2 h and benchmarks which timed out were not included in the results. More details are available online.[5]

[5] https://divine.fi.muni.cz/2017/divine4/.

Overall, DIVINE 4 showed substantial improvement over DIVINE 3, both in terms of speed as well as C++ support. Compared to ESBMC, DIVINE 4 has again the advantage of better C++ support (partially due to usage of clang compiler whereas ESBMC has custom C++ frontend) and additionally better performance on programs with threads.

4 Conclusion and Future Work

In this paper, we have introduced DIVINE 4, a versatile explicit-state model checker for C and C++ programs, which can handle real-world code using an efficient LLVM interpreter which has strong support for state space reductions. The analysed programs can make use of the full C99 and C++14 standards, including the standard libraries.

In the future, we would like to take advantage of the new program representation and versatility of DiVM to extend DIVINE with support for programs with significant data non-determinism, taking advantage of abstract and/or symbolic data representation, building on ideas introduced in SymDIVINE [2]. We would also like to add support for verification of concurrent programs under relaxed memory models, based on [7].

References

1. Duret-Lutz, A., Lewkowicz, A., Fauchille, A., Michaud, T., Renault, É., Xu, L.: Spot 2.0—a framework for LTL and ω-automata manipulation. In: Artho, C., Legay, A., Peled, D. (eds.) ATVA 2016. LNCS, vol. 9938, pp. 122–129. Springer, Cham (2016). doi:10.1007/978-3-319-46520-3_8
2. Mrázek, J., Bauch, P., Lauko, H., Barnat, J.: SymDIVINE: tool for control-explicit data-symbolic state space exploration. In: Bošnački, D., Wijs, A. (eds.) SPIN 2016. LNCS, vol. 9641, pp. 208–213. Springer, Cham (2016). doi:10.1007/978-3-319-32582-8_14
3. Ramalho, M., Freitas, M., Sousa, F., Marques, H., Cordeiro, L., Fischer, B.: SMT-based bounded model checking of C++ programs. In: Engineering of Computer Based Systems (ECBS), pp. 147–156. IEEE Computer Society (2013)
4. Ročkai, P., Barnat, J.: A Simulator for LLVM Bitcode. Preliminary version, arXiv:1704.05551 (2017)
5. Ročkai, P., Barnat, J., Brim, L.: Improved state space reductions for LTL model checking of C & C++ programs. In: Brat, G., Rungta, N., Venet, A. (eds.) NFM 2013, vol. 7871, pp. 1–15. Springer, Heidelberg (2013). doi:10.1007/978-3-642-38088-4_1
6. Ročkai, P., Štill, V., Černá, I., Barnat, J.: DiVM: Model Checking with LLVM and Graph Memory. Preliminary version, arXiv:1703.05341 (2017)
7. Štill, V., Ročkai, P., Barnat, J.: Weak memory models as LLVM-to-LLVM transformations. In: Kofroň, J., Vojnar, T. (eds.) MEMICS 2015. LNCS, vol. 9548, pp. 144–155. Springer, Cham (2016). doi:10.1007/978-3-319-29817-7_13
8. Štill, V., Ročkai, P., Barnat, J.: Using off-the-shelf exception support components in C++ verification. In: IEEE International Conference on Software Quality, Reliability and Security (QRS 2017) (2017). doi:10.1109/QRS.2017.15

Dealing with Priorities and Locks for Concurrent Programs

Marcio Diaz[1(✉)] and Tayssir Touili[2(✉)]

[1] LIPN, University Paris Diderot, Paris, France
diaz@lipn.univ-paris13.fr
[2] CNRS, LIPN, University Paris 13, Paris, France
tayssir.touili@lipn.univ-paris13.fr

Abstract. In this paper, we consider the backward reachability problem of multi-threaded programs where the threads have priorities, can be synchronized using locks and are scheduled by a priority based round-robin scheduler. For that, we extend the well known Dynamic Pushdown Network model with priorities and locks (called PL-DPN). We represent potentially infinite sets of configurations of PL-DPNs using finite state automata and show that the backward reachability sets of PL-DPNs are regular and can be effectively computed if we restrict the usage of priorities inside lock usages. Also, we show that allowing an unrestricted usage of nested locks and priorities leads to undecidability. We evaluate the performance of our algorithm on benchmarks drawn from real time systems, device drivers and hypervisor obtaining encouraging results and discovering new bugs.

1 Introduction

Writing multi-threaded programs is notoriously difficult, as concurrency related bugs are hard to find and reproduce. This difficulty is increased if we consider that several software systems consist of different components that react to the environment and use resources like CPU or memory according to a real time need. For instance, in systems that control automobiles we can have a component in charge of the music sub-system and another component in charge of the braking sub-system. Obviously, the braking sub-system should have a higher priority access to the resources needed, since a delay in the action of the brakes can cost lives.

The programming model used in the vast majority of these real time systems, used from automobiles to spacecrafts, defines a set of threads that perform computation monitoring or respond to events. Each thread is typically assigned a priority and are scheduled by a priority round-robin preemptive scheduler: if a thread with a higher static priority becomes ready to run, the currently running thread will be preempted and returned to the wait list for its priority level. The round-robin scheduling policy allows each thread to run only for a fixed amount

This work was partially funded by the FUI project FREENIVI.

D. D'Souza and K. Narayan Kumar (Eds.): ATVA 2017, LNCS 10482, pp. 208–224, 2017.
DOI: 10.1007/978-3-319-68167-2_15

of time before it must yield its processing slot to another thread of the same priority.

Combining threads with priorities and different synchronization primitives like locks can easily lead to a large number of undesirable behaviors. Consider for example the pseudocode of Fig. 1. It consists on five threads that synchronize their access to shared variables using a spin-lock. The program consists of two global variables x and y, and one spin-lock l (lines 1, 2 and 3). The program starts with thread *main* (line 5), of priority one, creating two threads A and B (lines 7 and 8), each of them also of priority one. Thread A increments variable x (line 14), holding the spin-lock, and then it creates thread C (line 16), of higher priority of two. Thread B, holding the spin-lock, reads variable x into variable *tmp* (line 22) and checks if they are equal (line 23). Note that threads A and B can be executed concurrently, but the assert succeeds, since all accesses to variable x are protected by the spin-lock. Thread C is similar to thread A, but this time incrementing variable y and creating again thread A. This creates a loop that executes thread A and C in an interleaved way. A similar behavior is produced by threads B and D.

Now, we may think that the error in this program is the lack of protection to the global variable y on thread D. But the assertion (line 39) will always succeed, since threads C and D will never be executed concurrently. Indeed, either C or D will be created first and will block the creation of the other thread until it finishes. However, the program still has a bug. The problem occurs when thread B owns the spin-lock (lines 22 or 23) and it is interrupted by thread C trying to acquire it (line 30). In this case we have a deadlock, since the only thread that can make progress is thread C (having highest priority) but it cannot acquire the spin-lock.

The program of Fig. 1 shows that there is a real need for formal methods to find automatic verification techniques for *multi-threaded programs with locks and*

```
1  int x = 0;
2  int y = 0;
3  spin_lock l;
4
5  void main() {
6    // Priority 1.
7    thread_create(A,1);
8    thread_create(B,1);
9  }
10
11 void A() {
12   // Priority 1.
13   spinlock_lock(l);
14   x++;
15   spinlock_unlock(l);
16   thread_create(C, 2);
17 }
18
19 void B() {
20   // Priority 1.
21   spinlock_lock(l);
22   int tmp = x;
23   assert(tmp == x);
24   spinlock_unlock(l);
25   thread_create(D, 2);
26 }
27
28 void C() {
29   // Priority 2.
30   spinlock_lock(l);
31   y++;
32   spinlock_unlock(l);
33   thread_create(A, 1);
34 }
35
36 void D() {
37   // Priority 2.
38   int tmp = y;
39   assert(tmp == y);
40   thread_create(B, 1);
41 }
```

Fig. 1. Pseudocode of a multi-threaded program with priorities and spin-locks.

priorities. Indeed, deadlock freedom and absence of conflicts, like data races, are among the most crucial properties that need to be checked for multi-threaded programs.

Dynamic pushdown networks (DPNs) were introduced in [1] as a suitable formalism to model multi-threaded programs. DPNs generalize pushdown systems by a rule that have the additional side effect of creating a new pushdown system that is then executed in parallel. The key concept for analyzing DPNs is computation of predecessor sets. Configurations of a DPN are represented as words over control and stack symbols, and for a regular set of configurations, the set of predecessor configurations is regular and can be computed effectively [1]. Predecessor computations can be used for various interesting analyses, like kill/gen analysis on bit-vectors and context-bounded model checking.

In [2] the DPN model was extended with well-nested locks, generalizing the technique of Kahlon and Gupta [3]. The authors give an algorithm for predecessor computation in a DPN model capable of acquiring and releasing locks. But in this model threads have the same priority and therefore they can preempt each other without restrictions. In [4] we extended the DPN model with priorities in the control states. The model, called P-DPN, is able to model the interaction between threads with different priorities. In a P-DPN, a thread can only be preempted by threads of equal or higher priority (threads of the same priority can interleave). However, P-DPNs do not give any other mechanism to synchronize threads, in particular, they are unable to synchronize using locks.

Previous research [5,6] on verification of multi-threaded programs with priorities using pushdown systems has focused on threads scheduled under a FIFO policy, on which each thread can only be interrupted by another thread of highest priority (threads of the same priority cannot interleave).

Here we consider multi-threaded programs with priorities and locks scheduled under a priority based round-robin scheduler. For this, we extend the DPN model allowing threads to synchronize by using priorities and locks. In this way we obtain a new model, called PL-DPN, more expressive than the models of [2,4]. The contributions of this paper are:

- A suitable definition of the PL-DPN model. There are many ways to combine priorities and locks giving rise to different degrees of expressiveness and complexity of the algorithms. We believe to have found a good balance that allows us to modelcheck real programs with locks and priorities.
- An algorithm for the computation of predecessor sets of configurations. We constructed a finite abstraction that allows us to reduce the *pre** images computation for PL-DPNs to the computation of *pre** images for DPNs, and then use the algorithm of [1]. Our finite abstraction is quite elaborate and we explain it in detail.
- An evaluation of the performance of our algorithm for real programs. We used several benchmark programs extracted from real time systems and device drivers. Our tool was able to find new data races in a hypervisor software, that follows our scheduling policy, consisting of 460,000 lines of code.

- An undecidability result. If we remove a small restriction in our model, allowing threads to change their priority while they hold a lock, our reachability problem becomes undecidable. The undecidability is proved by showing a way to simulate pairwise rendezvous using nested locks and priorities.

2 Model Definition

A PL-DPN can be seen as a collection of threads running in parallel, each of them being able to:

1. Perform pushdown operations. This can be used to model calls and returns from (possible recursive) functions.
2. Change its priority *if it is not holding any lock.* Removing this constraint leads to undecidability (see Sect. 9).
3. Acquire a lock that is not in its set of acquired locks.
4. Release a lock in its set of acquired locks.
5. Create a new thread with any priority.

Definition 1. *A* Dynamic Pushdown Network with Priorities and Locks *(PL-DPN) is a tuple $M = (P, \Gamma, \Delta, \eta_p, \eta_l)$, where P is a finite set of control states, Γ is a finite stack alphabet with $P \cap \Gamma = \emptyset$, $\eta_p : P \to \mathcal{I}$ is a function from control states to a finite set of natural numbers $\mathcal{I}$ representing priorities, $\eta_l : P \to \mathcal{L}$ is a function from control states to a set of locks from the finite set $\mathcal{L}$, and Δ is a finite set of rules of the following forms:*

1. $p\gamma \xhookrightarrow{\tau} qw$, *with* $\eta_p(q) = \eta_p(p)$ *and* $\eta_l(q) = \eta_l(p)$;
2. $p\gamma \xhookrightarrow{n} qw$, *with* $\eta_p(q) = n$ *and* $\eta_l(q) = \eta_l(p) = \emptyset$;
3. $p\gamma \xhookrightarrow{acq\ l} qw$, *with* $\eta_p(q) = \eta_p(p)$, $\eta_l(q) = \eta_l(p) \cup \{l\}$ *and* $l \notin \eta_l(p)$;
4. $p\gamma \xhookrightarrow{rel\ l} qw$, *with* $\eta_p(q) = \eta_p(p)$, $\eta_l(q) = \eta_l(p) \setminus \{l\}$ *and* $l \in \eta_l(p)$;
5. $p\gamma \xhookrightarrow{\tau} q_1w_1 \rhd q_2w_2$, *with* $\eta_p(q_1) = \eta_p(p)$, $\eta_l(q_1) = \eta_l(p)$ *and* $\eta_l(q_2) = \emptyset$.

where $p, q_1, q_2 \in P, \gamma \in \Gamma$, $w, w_1, w_2 \in \Gamma^*, l \in \mathcal{L}, n \in \mathcal{I}$. A Dynamic Pushdown Network (DPN), can be seen as a PL-DPN $(P, \Gamma, \Delta, \eta_p^0, \eta_l^\emptyset)$, where for all $p \in P$, $\eta_p^0(p) = 0$ and $\eta_l^\emptyset(p) = \emptyset$. Given a PL-DPN $M = (P, \Gamma, \Delta, \eta_p, \eta_l)$, its DPN M' is defined as $(P, \Gamma, \Delta, \eta_p^0, \eta_l^\emptyset)$, abbreviated (P, Γ, Δ).

A *global configuration* of a PL-DPN M is a word over the alphabet $P \cup \Gamma$, starting with a symbol in P, representing the state of the PL-DPN. A global configuration can be seen as a sequence of (sub)-words in $P\Gamma^*$ each of them corresponding to the configuration of one of the threads running in parallel on the system, also called *local configuration.* Let $Conf_M$ be the set of all global configurations of a PL-DPN M.

The function η_p assigns a priority to each control state. Intuitively, this means that a thread can be in configurations with different priorities. PL-DPNs must execute first the thread in the configuration with highest priority. We overload the function η_p to global configurations as follows: for all $c = p_1w_1 \dots p_nw_n \in Conf_M$, $\eta_p(p_1w_1 \dots p_nw_n) := max(\eta_p(p_1), \dots, \eta_p(pn))$.

The function η_l assigns a set of locks to each control state. This set of locks represents the locks held (acquired but not yet released) by the thread at such configuration. Transitions in a PL-DPN should follow the *locking rules*: (1) a transition attempting to acquire a lock can only be executed if the lock is free; (2) a transition attempting to release a lock, can only be executed if the lock is in possession of the corresponding thread. We overload the function η_l to global configurations as follows: for all $c = p_1w_1 \dots p_nw_n \in Conf_M$, $\eta_l(p_1w_1 \dots p_nw_n) := \eta_l(p_1) \cup \dots \cup \eta_l(pn)$.

Following previous works we assume that locks are used in a well-nested fashion, i.e. a process has to release locks in the opposite order of acquisition, an assumption that is often satisfied in practice. Note that for non-well-nested locks even simple reachability problems are undecidable [3].

3 Semantics of the Model

Definition 2. *The transition relation $\longrightarrow_M$ is defined as the smallest relation in $Conf_M \times Conf_M$ such that $\forall c_1, c_2 \in Conf_M$:*

1. $c_1\ p\gamma r\ c_2 \longrightarrow_M c_1\ qwr\ c_2$,
   if $\eta_p(p) = \eta_p(c_1\ p\gamma r\ c_2)$ *and* $p\gamma \xhookrightarrow{lab} qw \in \Delta$, *s.t.* $lab \in \{\tau, rel\ l\} \cup \mathcal{I}$;
2. $c_1\ p\gamma r\ c_2 \longrightarrow_M c_1\ qwr\ c_2$,
   if $\eta_p(p) = \eta_p(c_1\ p\gamma r\ c_2)$, $l \notin \eta_l(c_1\ p\gamma r\ c_2)$ *and* $p\gamma \xhookrightarrow{acq\ l} qw \in \Delta$;
3. $c_1\ p\gamma r\ c_2 \longrightarrow_M c_1\ q_2w_2\ q_1w_1r\ c_2$,
   if $\eta_p(p) = \eta_p(c_1\ p\gamma r\ c_2)$ *and* $p\gamma \xhookrightarrow{\tau} q_1w_1 \rhd q_2w_2 \in \Delta$;

where $p, q, q_1, q_2 \in P, \gamma \in \Gamma, w, w_1, w_2, r \in \Gamma^*, l \in \mathcal{L}$. We denote the transitive-reflexive closure of $\longrightarrow_M$ as $\longrightarrow_M^*$.

The semantics above says that:

1. A thread in a local configuration with control state p and top of stack γ can move to a local configuration with control state q, replacing the top of its stack γ by w, if there is a τ, n or release rule $p\gamma \xhookrightarrow{lab} qw \in \Delta$ and its priority ($\eta_p(p)$) is equal to the highest priority among all the threads ($\eta_p(c_1\ p\gamma r\ c_2)$);
2. A thread in a local configuration with control state p and top of stack γ can move to a local configuration with control state q, replacing the top of its stack γ by w, if there is an *acquire* rule $p\gamma \xhookrightarrow{acq\ l} qw \in \Delta$, the lock that the rule attempts to take is free ($l \notin \eta_l(c_1\ p\gamma r\ c_2)$), and its priority ($\eta_p(p)$) is equal to the highest priority among all the threads ($\eta_p(c_1\ p\gamma r\ c_2)$);
3. A thread in a local configuration with control state p and top of stack γ can move to a local configuration with control state q_1, replacing the top of its stack γ by w_1 and create another thread in control state q_2 with stack w_2, if there is a rule $p\gamma \xhookrightarrow{\tau} q_1w_1 \rhd q_2w_2 \in \Delta$ and its priority ($\eta_p(p)$) is equal to the highest priority among all the threads ($\eta_p(c_1\ p\gamma r\ c_2)$).

Note that the semantics of locks corresponds to the one of spin-locks, found in the main libraries for threads (like Pthreads). Spin-locks are similar to mutexes, but they might have lower overhead for very short-term blocking. When the calling thread requests a spin-lock that is already held by another thread, the calling thread spins in a loop to test if the lock has become available. As we saw in the program of Fig. 1, this means that if a thread with lower priority, holding a lock l, is interrupted by a thread with higher priority, attempting to acquire the same lock, then the program becomes blocked (assuming there is only one CPU).

Given a configuration c, the set of immediate predecessors of c in a PL-DPN M is defined as $pre_M(c) = \{c' \in Conf_M : c' \longrightarrow_M c\}$. This notation can be generalized straightforwardly to sets of configurations. Let pre^*_M denote the reflexive-transitive closure of pre_M. For the rest of this paper, we assume that we have fixed a PL-DPN $M = (P, \Gamma, \Delta, \eta_p, \eta_l)$ and let $M' = (P, \Gamma, \Delta)$ be its corresponding DPN as defined in Definition 1.

4 Modeling Programs with PL-DPNs

It was explained in [1] how to use DPNs to model multi-threaded programs without locks and priorities. PL-DPN extends the DPN model by attaching a priority and a set of locks to each control state and restricting the execution of each thread according to the priority and spin-locks semantics.

In order to model our example of Fig. 1, we give to all the control states of a thread the same priority. Also, when modeling the termination of a thread, we must make sure that the priority of its final control state does not prevent other threads from making a transition. To ensure this, we model the end of a thread execution with a transition to a control state with priority zero.

Thus, the PL-DPN of the program of Fig. 1 consists on:

- The set of control states $P = \{p_0, p_{0,l}, p_1, p_{1,l}, p_2, p_{2,l}\}$. The sub-index indicates the priority and the spin-locks of the control state. For instance p_0 is a control state with priority zero and does not hold any spin-lock, while $p_{1,l}$ is a control state with priority one and holds spin-lock l.
- The stack corresponds to program points on each thread: $\Gamma = \{m_0, \ldots, m_3, a_0, \ldots, a_4, b_0, \ldots, b_5, c_0, \ldots, c_4, d_0, \ldots, d_3\}$.
- We show some of the rules of Δ in Fig. 2. For instance, there are three rules corresponding to thread main: the first two rules modeling the creation of threads A and B; and the last rule modeling the end of its execution. Thread A, is modeled by five transition rules, each one representing (in this order): the acquisition of lock l, the write of variable x, the release of lock l, the creation of thread C, and the end of its execution. The rules for the others threads are created in a similar way.
- As said previously, the sub-index of the control states indicates their priority and locks. Thus we have that $\eta_p(p_0) = 0, \eta_p(p_1) = \eta_p(p_{1,l}) = 1$ and $\eta_p(p_2) = \eta_p(p_{2,l}) = 2$. Also, $\eta_l(p_0) = \eta_l(p_1) = \eta_l(p_2) = \emptyset$ and $\eta_l(p_{0,l}) = \eta_l(p_{1,l}) = \eta_l(p_{2,l}) = \{l\}$.

Thread main:

$$p_1\, m_0 \overset{\tau}{\hookrightarrow} p_1\, m_1 \rhd p_1\, a_0$$
$$p_1\, m_1 \overset{\tau}{\hookrightarrow} p_1\, m_2 \rhd p_1\, b_0$$
$$p_1\, m_2 \overset{0}{\hookrightarrow} p_0$$

Thread A:

$$p_1\, a_0 \xhookrightarrow{acq\ l} p_{1,l}\, a_1$$
$$p_{1,l}\, a_1 \overset{\tau}{\hookrightarrow} p_{1,l}\, a_2$$
$$p_{1,l}\, a_2 \xhookrightarrow{rel\ l} p_1\, a_3$$
$$p_1\, a_3 \overset{\tau}{\hookrightarrow} p_1\, a_4 \rhd p_2\, c_0$$
$$p_1\, a_4 \overset{0}{\hookrightarrow} p_0$$

Thread B:

$$p_1\, b_0 \xhookrightarrow{acq\ l} p_{1,l}\, b_1$$
$$p_{1,l}\, b_1 \overset{\tau}{\hookrightarrow} p_{1,l}\, b_2$$
$$p_{1,l}\, b_2 \overset{\tau}{\hookrightarrow} p_{1,l}\, b_3$$
$$p_{1,l}\, b_3 \xhookrightarrow{rel\ l} p_1\, b_4$$
$$p_1\, b_4 \overset{\tau}{\hookrightarrow} p_1\, b_5 \rhd p_2\, d_0$$
$$p_1\, b_5 \overset{0}{\hookrightarrow} p_0$$

Thread C:

$$p_2\, c_0 \xhookrightarrow{acq\ l} p_{2,l}\, c_1$$
$$p_{2,l}\, c_1 \overset{\tau}{\hookrightarrow} p_{2,l}\, c_2$$
$$p_{2,l}\, c_2 \xhookrightarrow{rel\ l} p_2\, c_3$$
$$p_2\, c_3 \overset{\tau}{\hookrightarrow} p_2\, c_4 \rhd p_1\, a_0$$
$$p_2\, c_5 \overset{0}{\hookrightarrow} p_0$$

Thread D:

$$p_2\, d_0 \overset{\tau}{\hookrightarrow} p_2\, d_1$$
$$p_2\, d_1 \overset{\tau}{\hookrightarrow} p_2\, d_2$$
$$p_2\, d_2 \overset{\tau}{\hookrightarrow} p_2\, d_3 \rhd p_1\, b_0$$
$$p_2\, d_3 \overset{0}{\hookrightarrow} p_0$$

Fig. 2. Transition rules corresponding to the PL-DPN of the program of Fig. 1.

5 Execution Hedges

Executions of DPNs can be viewed as trees, on which we specify the order of transitions inside each thread and the father-child relation between threads, but we do not specify the order of transitions between different threads running concurrently.

In Fig. 3 we can observe a graphical representation of a possible execution tree from the PL-DPN of Fig. 2. At the top of the tree we can observe the thread *main* creating thread A. The left subtree corresponds to the execution of thread A, in which it acquires and releases the spin-lock l and creates thread C. The right subtree corresponds to the remaining execution of thread *main*, where it creates thread B, and the execution of thread B, on which it acquires and releases the spin-lock l and then creates thread D.

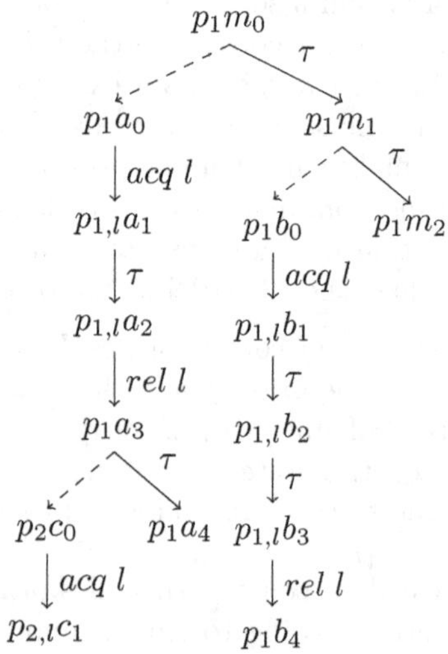

Fig. 3. Graphical representation of an execution tree. The tree $c(lab, t_1, t_2)$ is represented by the edges $c \xrightarrow{lab} t_1$ and $c \dashrightarrow t_2$.

Formally, let X be a variable, we define the set $T[X]$ of *terms* over $P \cup \Gamma \cup \{X\}$, inductively, as follows: $X \subseteq T[X]$, $P\Gamma^* \subseteq T[X]$, if $t \in T[X]$, $c \in P\Gamma^*$ then $c(lab, t) \in T[X]$ with $lab \in \{\tau\} \cup \mathcal{I} \cup \{acq\ l \mid l \in \mathcal{L}\} \cup \{rel\ l \mid l \in \mathcal{L}\}$, if $t_1, t_2 \in T[X]$, $c \in P\Gamma^*$ then $c(\tau, t_1, t_2) \in T[X]$. Terms in $T[]$ are called *trees*, and will be denoted also by T. A *context* C is a term in which X occurs exactly once. Let t be a tree, then $C[t]$ is the tree obtained by substituting in C the occurrence of the variable X with the tree t. We define an *execution hedge* as a finite sequence of trees in T, and denote the set of execution hedges as T^*.

Given a hedge $h \in T^*$, we define the *root configuration* of h, $root(h)$, as the configuration formed by concatenation of the roots of each tree in h from left to right. Given a hedge $h \in T^*$, we define the *yield configuration* of h, $yield(h)$, as the configuration formed by concatenating the leaves of h from left to right.

Since we are interested in execution hedges that can be mapped to at least one valid execution path under PL-DPN semantics, we define now a *scheduler* relation that schedules the transitions of an execution hedge following the priority and spin-locks semantics. The scheduler will consume the execution hedge by choosing, between the roots of the (non-leaf) trees, an edge that respects the PL-DPN semantics. Removing an edge from a root local configuration means that the scheduler executes the transition corresponding to this edge.

Definition 3. *The scheduler* $\rightsquigarrow \subseteq T^* \times T^*$ *is the least relation satisfying the following constraints:*

$$\begin{aligned}
h_1\ c(lab,t)\ h_2 &\rightsquigarrow h_1\ t\ h_2, && \text{if } \eta_p(c) = \eta_p(root(h_1\ c(lab,t)\ h_2)) \\
h_1\ c(acq\ l,t)\ h_2 &\rightsquigarrow h_1\ t\ h_2, && \text{if } \eta_p(c) = \eta_p(root(h_1\ c(acq\ l,t)\ h_2)) \\
& && \wedge\, l \notin \eta_l(root(h_1\ c(acq\ l,t)\ h_2)) \\
h_1 c(\tau,t_1,t_2) h_2 &\rightsquigarrow h_1 t_1 t_2 h_2, && \text{if } \eta_p(c) = \eta_p(root(h_1\ c(\tau,t_1,t_2)\ h_2))
\end{aligned}$$

where $h_1, h_2 \in T^*, t, t_1, t_2 \in T, c \in P\Gamma^*, l \in \mathcal{L}, lab \in \{\tau\} \cup \mathcal{I} \cup \{rel\ l \mid l \in \mathcal{L}\}$. *Its transitive reflexive closure is denoted by* $\rightsquigarrow^*$.

We say that a hedge h is *schedulable* if the scheduler can schedule all its transitions, i.e. the sequence of $\rightsquigarrow$ transitions end up with the yield configuration of h.

Definition 4. *An execution hedge h is* schedulable *if and only if* $h \rightsquigarrow^* yield(h)$.

Then, it is easy to see that a schedulable execution hedge has a valid execution path in M, i.e. under PL-DPN semantics. This leads to the following theorem.

Theorem 1. *Let* $c, c' \in Conf_M$*, then* $c \longrightarrow_M^* c'$ *iff there is a schedulable execution hedge* $h \in T^*$ *with* $c = root(h), c' = yield(h)$.

In the next section we give a finite abstraction to detect if an execution hedge is schedulable without the need to schedule the transitions of the execution hedge in all possible ways.

6 Abstracting Execution Hedges

The main idea of our algorithm is to apply the saturation process of [1] to compute predecessors under DPN semantics, and then filter out the configurations

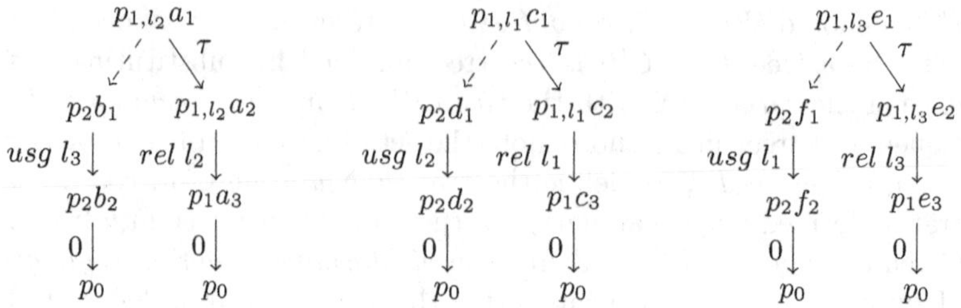

Fig. 4. Execution hedge with three initial threads of priority one, each one of them spawns another thread with higher priority of two.

that cannot be reached under PL-DPN semantics, i.e. considering priorities and locks. To be able to filter out these unreachable configurations we define in this section a finite abstraction of the execution hedges. This abstraction will allow us to decide effectively whether an execution hedge satisfies or not the priority and lock semantics.

In [2], the authors give a finite abstraction of execution hedges called *acquisition structure* and use it to decide whether an execution hedge respects or not the semantics of locks. In [4], we used a similar method and give a finite abstraction called *priority structure* to decide if an execution hedge respects or not the semantics of priorities. However, until now, there was no finite abstraction that can be used to decide if an execution hedge respects *both* semantics: the one of spin-locks and priorities.

6.1 Unsoundness of Previous Abstractions

Given an execution hedge, we call *usage* of l ($usg\ l$) each acquisition of a lock l with a matching release. Acquisitions (releases) of locks without matching releases (acquisitions) are called *final acquisitions* (*initial releases*).

We cannot use priority and acquisition structures in conjunction in order to give an abstraction to decide schedulability of execution hedges with different priorities and lock actions. This method may fail and label a hedge without schedule as schedulable. Indeed, priorities may force the execution of some lock actions before others, introducing lock dependencies not contemplated by acquisition structures.

Consider the execution hedge of Fig. 4, it consists of three initial threads with priority one. Each thread is holding a lock from $\{l_1, l_2, l_3\}$. After releasing the corresponding lock and finishing its execution, each thread spawns another thread of priority two. Each spawned thread uses another lock, and then finishes its execution. Thus, the first tree creates the dependency $usg\ l_3 \rightarrow rel\ l_2$, where the arrow means that the usage of lock l_3 should be executed before the initial release of lock l_2, since the branch of the spawned thread has a higher priority of two. The same happens with the other two trees: the second tree adds the dependency $usg\ l_2 \rightarrow rel\ l_1$ and the third tree adds the dependency $usg\ l_1 \rightarrow$

rel l_3, both for the same reasons as before. Therefore, we have the following dependency path:

$$usg\ l_3 \rightarrow rel\ l_2 \rightarrow usg\ l_2 \rightarrow rel\ l_1 \rightarrow usg\ l_1 \rightarrow rel\ l_3$$

and since we cannot use lock l_3 before releasing it, the whole execution hedge cannot be scheduled. However, this execution hedge is schedulable under only the priority semantics or only the lock semantics, not both. This means that we cannot combine, in an easy way, priority and acquisition structures to decide schedulability under priority and spin-lock semantics.

6.2 Definition of Priority-Lock Structure

In this section we give a finite abstraction that is priority and spin-lock sensitive. The abstraction, called *priority-lock structure* (*pl-structure*), is defined as either a tuple $[\![\mathbf{x}, \mathbf{y}, \mathbf{g_r}, \mathbf{g_a}, \mathbf{la}]\!]$ or the symbol $\perp$. We use $\perp$ to denote the pl-structure of an execution hedge that cannot be scheduled. On the other hand, the pl-structure of an execution hedge that can be scheduled will be a tuple with five elements satisfying some properties. The tuple is composed of the following elements:

- **Lowest transition priority (x):** the lowest priority between the priorities of all configurations that make a transition in the execution hedge. Intuitively, given two execution hedges with different lowest transition priority, it is easy to see that the execution hedge with highest x finish its execution first.
- **Highest final priority (y)**, the highest priority between the priorities of all leaf configurations of the execution hedge. Intuitively, after executing a hedge with highest final priority y we know that the remaining transitions in the execution hedge should have at least a priority of y to be able to execute.
- **The release graph ($\mathbf{g_r}$)**, with edges *usg* $l_1 \rightarrow$ *rel* l_2, representing usages that should be executed before initial releases. These dependencies can be created due to the order of the lock actions inside an execution tree or due to priorities like in Fig. 4.
- **The acquisition graph ($\mathbf{g_a}$)**, with edges *acq* $l_1 \rightarrow$ *usg* l_2, representing final acquisitions that should be executed before usages. As in the previous item, these dependencies can be created due to the ordering of the lock actions inside the execution tree or due to priorities.
- **Lock actions (la)**, set with information of each lock action that occurs in the hedge. This information will be useful to decide if a lock action needs to be executed before another one, dependency that will be added to g_r or g_a. The elements of this set are tuples composed of the following elements:
    - *Name of the lock* on which the action is executed, takes values of $\mathcal{L}$.
    - *Type of the lock action*, take values from $\{acq, rel, usg\}$.
    - *Lowest before priority (lbp)*: lowest priority between the priorities of all ancestor configurations of the action, including the priority of the configuration that makes the transition itself. Intuitively, given two lock actions with different *lbp* values, the action with highest *lbp* value will be executed first because the path from the root to that lock action has highest priority.

- *Lowest after priority (lap)*: lowest priority on which the hedge can be after the execution of this action. Intuitively, given two lock actions a_1 and a_2, if the first one has a lowest before priority lower than the lowest after priority of the second one, i.e. $lbp_1 < lap_2$, then the first action should be executed first. Otherwise it gets blocked by the priorities after the second lock action.

The set of all pl-structures is denoted by PLS. It is easy to see that PLS is finite, with size exponential in the number of locks.

The first two elements of the pl-structure tuple correspond to the priority structure of [4] while the remaining elements correspond to the acquisition structure of [2]. The novelty consist of the attachment of priorities to the elements of lock actions and all the computation necessary to update them.

6.3 Computing Priority-Lock Structures

The computation of the pl-structure of an execution hedge h is carried out inductively over its structure in a bottom-up way, from its leaves to its roots.

The main function of the algorithm is denoted by $\Phi : T^* \rightarrow \mathsf{PLS}$:

- If $h = pw$ then $\Phi(h) = [\![\infty, \eta_p(p), \emptyset, \emptyset, \emptyset]\!]$. Since the hedge does not have transitions, its lowest transition priority is initialized to ∞. Its highest final priority is set to $\eta_p(p)$, the priority of the control state of its unique leaf configuration. The hedge does not have any transition or lock actions, so the remaining elements of the tuple are empty sets.
- If $h = c(lab, t)$ then $\Phi(h) = update(\eta_p(c), lab, \Phi(t))$. The function *update*, explained in detail later, it is in charge of updating the minimum priorities and keeping track of the lock actions found.
- If $h = c(\tau, t_1, t_2)$, we proceed in a way similar to the previous case, $\Phi(h) = update(\eta_p(c), \tau, \Phi(t_1) \oplus \Phi(t_2))$, except that before updating we need to combine the pl-structures of the subtrees. For combining the pl-structures we introduce the operator $\oplus$, explained in detail later, that takes as input two pl-structures and returns a new pl-structure, the *composition* of them.
- If $h = t_1 \dots t_n$ then $\Phi(h) = \Phi(t_1) \oplus \dots \oplus \Phi(t_n)$. If the hedge is a sequence of trees then its pl-structure is the composition of the pl-structures of the trees. This is computed using the operator $\oplus$ by taking pairs of trees, since $\oplus$ will be defined to be associative and commutative.

The function **update** : $\mathcal{P} \times Lab \times \mathsf{PLS} \rightarrow \mathsf{PLS}$, takes as input the priority n of the root configuration of the tree, the label lab of the first edge of the tree and the pl-structure s of the subtree (or subtrees) and returns a new pl-structure s'. We define $update(n, lab, s)$ as follows:

- If $s = \bot$ then $update(n, lab, s) = \bot$. This means that a execution tree cannot be scheduled if the subtree cannot.
- Suppose $s = [\![x, y, g_r, g_a, la]\!]$. Then $update(n, lab, s)$ depends on the label of the edge as follows:

- Suppose $lab = \tau$. We update the *lowest transition priority* and the *before priorities* of the locks actions in la. Then $s' = [\![min(x, n), y, g_r, g_a, la']\!]$, where $la' = \{(a, l, min(x, n), y) \mid (a, l, x, y) \in la\}$.
- Suppose $lab = k$, with k a priority. Same as previous case.
- Suppose that $lab = rel\ l$. We update the minimum priorities as previously and we add $(rel, l, n, min(x, y))$ to la'. The lowest before priority is n since, by now, is the unique priority that occurs before the action. The lowest after priority is set to $min(x, y)$ since it is the lowest priority of the tree after the lock action.
- Suppose $lab = acq\ l$ and there is not an initial release of the same lock in la (the acquisition corresponds to a final acquisition). We add $(acq, l, n, min(x, y))$ to la' and for all usages in la we add to g_a an edge from l to its lock: $g'_a = g_a \cup \{l \to l' \mid (usg, l', x', y') \in la\}$.
- Suppose $lab = acq\ l$ and there is an initial release of the same lock (rel, l, x, y) in la (the acquisition corresponds to an usage of the lock l). We remove the matched initial release and we add the usage (usg, l, x, y) to la. Also, we remove the edges from g_r that were pointing to the initial release and we add edges from this usage to all the other initial releases in la. Formally: $g'_r = \{l' \to l'' \mid l' \to l'' \in g_r \wedge l'' \neq l\} \cup \{l \to l' \mid (rel, l', x', y') \in la \wedge l' \neq l\}$.

The **operator** $\oplus$: PLS × PLS → PLS, takes as input two pl-structures s_1, s_2 and returns another one, s', the *composition* of them:

1. If $s_1 = \bot$ or $s_2 = \bot$ then $s_1 \oplus s_2 = \bot$. This means that if one of the execution hedges does not have a schedule then the composition of them is not schedulable.
2. Suppose $s_1 = [\![x_1, y_1, g_{r_1}, g_{a_1}, la_1]\!]$ and $s_2 = [\![x_2, y_2, g_{r_2}, g_{a_2}, la_2]\!]$.
   (a) If $x_1 \geq x_2 \geq y_1 \vee x_2 \geq x_1 \geq y_2$ is not satisfied then the execution hedges cannot be scheduled together because the last priority of one tree will block some transitions in the other one. Then, in this case $s' = \bot$.
   (b) If there is a final acquisition (or initial release) of the same lock in both la_1 and la_2, then $s' = \bot$, since this is forbidden by the lock rules.
   (c) Otherwise, $s' = [\![min(x_1, x_2), max(y_1, y_2), g'_r, g'_a, la']\!]$, where la', g'_r, g'_a are defined as follows:
      i. The lowest priority of the left branch is $lp_1 = min(x_1, y_1)$, and of the right branch is $lp_2 = min(x_2, y_2)$. Then we update the information on each lock action, setting la' as follows:
      $la' = \{(a, l, x, max(lp_2, y)) \mid (a, l, x, y) \in la_1\}$
      $\cup \{(a, l, x, max(lp_1, y)) \mid (a, l, x, y) \in la_2\}$.
      ii. Let $g_r{}' = g_{r_1} \cup g_{r_2}$
      $\cup \{l_2 \to l_1 \mid (usg, l_2, x_2, y_2) \in la_2, (rel, l_1, x_1, y_1) \in la_1, x_2 > x_1\}$
      $\cup \{l_1 \to l_2 \mid (usg, l_1, x_1, y_1) \in la_1, (rel, l_2, x_2, y_2) \in la_2, x_1 > x_2\}$.
      iii. Let $g_a{}' = g_{a1} \cup g_{a2} \cup \{l_1 \to l_2 \mid (acq, l_1, x_1, y_1) \in la_1, (usg, l_2, x_2, y_2) \in la_2, x_1 = x_2 \wedge x_1 < y_2\} \cup \{l_2 \to l_1 \mid (acq, l_2, x_2, y_2) \in la_2, (usg, l_1, x_1, y_1) \in la_1, x_1 = x_2 \wedge x_2 < y_1\}$.

The core of the algorithm consist of items (i), (ii) and (iii) of the operator $\oplus$ definition. Item (i) of the algorithm means that priorities of threads created in the path from the common ancestor of two lock actions to one of the lock actions can block the execution of the other lock action. So when we compute the *lowest after priority* of a lock action we must take into account the priorities of these threads. Item (ii) means that an usage with a higher *lowest before priority* than an initial release will be executed before the initial release (see Fig. 5). This condition does not need to be checked for final acquisitions and usages since the subtree of a final acquisition cannot change priorities, therefore in this case the execution tree cannot be scheduled and will be detected by the equation of (a). Item (iii) has similar reasoning as (ii).

Once we have the pl-structure of the execution hedge computed we can have two possible results. If it is bottom, then the hedge cannot be scheduled. If the pl-structure is not bottom, we still have to check that it is *consistent* in order to get that the execution hedge is schedulable.

Definition 5. *A pl-structure* $s = [\![x, y, g_r, g_a, la]\!]$ *is* consistent *with respect to a set of locks* X *iff it satisfies* $X \setminus \{l \mid (rel, l, x, y) \in la\} \cap \{l \mid (acq, l, x, y) \in la \vee (usg, l, x, y) \in la\} = \emptyset$ *and* g_r, g_a *are acyclic. The bottom pl-structure is not consistent with respect to any set of locks.*

The intuition behind these definitions is as follows:

- The first condition means that the hedge does not acquire a lock that was taken from the beginning of the execution and was not initially released.
- Second, if there is a cycle in one of the graphs, then there is a lock that should be finally acquired before being used, or a lock that should be used before being initially released. Since this is not possible according to the lock semantics, the hedge is not schedulable.

This leads us to the following theorem.

Theorem 2. *An execution hedge* h *is schedulable iff* $\Phi(h)$ *is consistent with respect to the set of locks* $\eta_l(root(h))$.

6.4 Example of Computation of PL-Structure

In Fig. 5 we can observe the computation of the pl-structure for the first tree of the execution hedge of Fig. 3. The computation starts in the leaves of the tree and finishes in the root, with a pl-structure:

$$[\![1, 0, \{l_3 \rightarrow l_2\}, \emptyset, \{(usg, l_3, 2, 0), (rel, l_2, 1, 0)\}]\!]$$

The dependency $l_3 \rightarrow l_2$ is added by the compose operator because the lowest before priority of usg l_3 is higher than the lowest before priority of rel l_2. The pl-structure for the others two execution trees is similar. After composing the pl-structure of all trees using $\oplus$, the resulting pl-structure for the whole hedge of Fig. 4 is: $[\![1, 0, \{l_3 \rightarrow l_2, l_2 \rightarrow l_1, l_1 \rightarrow l_3\}, \emptyset, \{(usg, l_3, 2, 0), (rel, l_2, 1, 0), (usg, l_2, 2, 0), (rel, l_1, 1, 0), (usg, l_1, 2, 0), (rel, l_3, 1, 0)\}]\!]$. Since g_r has a cycle, the pl-structure is not consistent and by Theorem 2, the execution hedge is not schedulable.

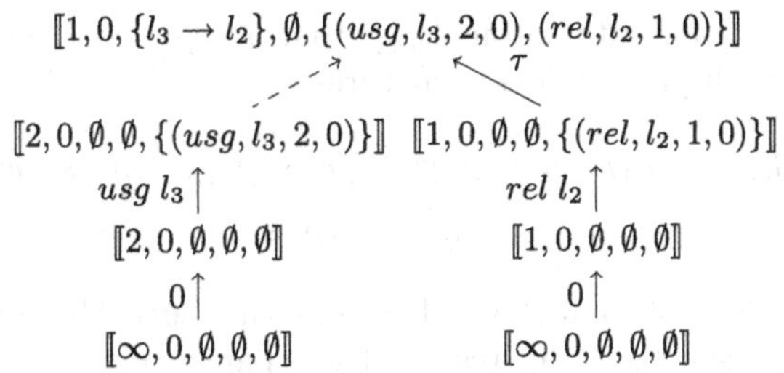

⟦1, 0, {l3 → l2}, ∅, {(usg, l3, 2, 0), (rel, l2, 1, 0)}⟧
τ
⟦2, 0, ∅, ∅, {(usg, l3, 2, 0)}⟧
⟦1, 0, ∅, ∅, {(rel, l2, 1, 0)}⟧
usg l3
rel l2
⟦2, 0, ∅, ∅, ∅⟧
⟦1, 0, ∅, ∅, ∅⟧
0
0
⟦∞, 0, ∅, ∅, ∅⟧
⟦∞, 0, ∅, ∅, ∅⟧

Fig. 5. Example of computation of pl-structure for the rst tree of the execution hedge in Fig. 4. Each node has the pl-structure of the (sub)-tree rooted by himself.

7 Computing pre* Images of PL-DPNs

Following [1], we use finite automata called M-automata to represent regular (possible infinite) sets of configurations of PL-DPNs.

Given a PL-DPN $M = (P, \Gamma, \Delta, \eta_p, \eta_l)$ and a M-automaton $\mathcal{A}$, the main idea of the algorithm consists on computing the predecessors without taking care of the priority and locks semantics, using the algorithm of [1], and then filter out the unreachable configurations using priority-lock structures.

First we modify M' (the DPN of M) and $\mathcal{A}$, as in Sect. 7 of [4], embedding the definition of Φ inside the control states of the configurations:

1. We transform M' into the DPN $M'' = (P', \Gamma, \Delta')$, where $P' = \{(p, s) \mid p \in P, s \in \mathsf{PLS}\}$ and the transition rules of Δ' are:

   $$- \ (p, s_p)\gamma \hookrightarrow (q, s_q)w, \text{ if } p\gamma \xrightarrow{lab} qw \in \Delta \wedge s_p = update(\eta_p(p), lab, s_q),$$
   $$- \ (p, s_p)\gamma \hookrightarrow (q_1, s_{q_1})w_1 \rhd (q_2, s_{q_2})w_2, \text{ if } p\gamma \hookrightarrow q_1w_1 \rhd q_2w_2 \in \Delta \\ \wedge\ s_p = update(\eta_p(p), \tau, s_{q_1} \oplus s_{q_2}),$$

   where $p, q, q_1, q_2 \in \mathcal{P}, \gamma \in \Gamma, w, w_1, w_2 \in \Gamma^*, s_p, s_q, s_{q_1}, s_{q_2} \in \mathsf{PLS}$.
2. We transform $\mathcal{A}$ into $\mathcal{A}'$, that accepts the language:

   $$L(\mathcal{A}') = \{(p_1, [\![\infty, \eta_p(p_1), \emptyset, \emptyset, \emptyset]\!])w_1 \ldots (p_n, [\![\infty, \eta_p(p_n), \emptyset, \emptyset, \emptyset]\!])w_n \\ \mid p_1w_1 \ldots p_nw_n \in L(\mathcal{A})\}.$$

Then, we compute predecessors of $L(\mathcal{A}')$ in M'', using the algorithm of [1], obtaining configurations of the form $(p_1, s_1)w_1 \ldots (p_n, s_n)w_n$, where each s_i is a priority structure. Intuitively, the fact that $(p_1, s_1)w_1 \ldots (p_n, s_n)w_n \in pre^*_{M''}(\mathcal{A}')$ means that $p_1w_1 \ldots p_nw_n \in pre^*_{M'}(L(\mathcal{A}))$ and that $s_1 \oplus \cdots \oplus s_n$ is the priority-lock structure of the hedge rooted at $p_1w_1 \ldots p_nw_n$ and whose yield is in $L(\mathcal{A})$.

Finally, we create an automaton $\mathcal{A}_{pre^*_M}$ that accepts only the configurations of $pre^*_{M''}(L(\mathcal{A}'))$ with priority-lock structures not equal to $\bot$:

$$L(\mathcal{A}_{pre^*_M}) = \{p_1 w_1 \dots p_n w_n \mid (p_1, s_1)w_1 \dots (p_n, s_n)w_n \\ \in L(\mathcal{A}_{pre^*_{M''}}) \wedge s_1 \oplus \dots \oplus s_n \neq \bot\}$$

It is easy to see that is straightforward to construct such M-automata.

In this way we get the main result of the paper that says that backward reachability sets of PL-DPNs are regular and can be effectively computed:

Theorem 3. $L(\mathcal{A}_{pre^*_M}) = pre^*_M(L(\mathcal{A}))$.

8 Implementation and Benchmarks

We implemented our algorithm in a tool called *PL-DPN* [7]. The tool is written in the programming language Python and takes as input programs written in C. We compared our implementation with a tool called i-CBMC [8], an extension of the well known CBMC bounded model checker [9], capable of handling threads with priorities.

The effectiveness of our method is evaluated by using a set of benchmarks derived from real time software, Linux device drivers and a hypervisor. For each benchmark, we have a version where priorities and/or locks correctly protect shared variables from producing data races or deadlocks, and another version where they are incorrectly managed, and hence, safety properties are violated.

In Fig. 6 we can observe the results of running our tool and i-CBMC on the seven benchmark programs. Overall, our tool performs quite well obtaining, in some cases, smaller running times than i-CBMC. Also, our tool found several new data races in the Xvisor program, some of them confirmed and fixed by the author [10]. The bug was caused by an unprotected data structure and was fixed by adding spinlocks.

Program	LOC	Threads	i-CBMC	PL-DPN
Logger (1)	112	2	0.2 sec	2.8 sec
+ incorrect	112	2	0.2 sec	0.6 sec
Logger (2)	172	3	19 sec	34 sec
+ incorrect	172	3	18 sec	8 sec
Blink	2,652	2	8 sec	29 sec
+ incorrect	2,652	2	11 sec	7 sec
Brake (1)	3,938	2	TO	1 sec
+ incorrect	3,938	2	4 sec	0.9 sec
Brake (2)	3,938	3	TO	1 sec
+ incorrect	3,938	3	6 sec	0.9 sec
Brake (3)	3,938	4	TO	1 sec
+ incorrect	3,938	4	8 sec	0.9 sec
Xvisor	108,353	4	TO	15 min
+ incorrect	108,353	4	TO	7 min

Fig. 6. Experimental results.

9 An Undecidability Result

In this section we show that for concurrent programs that allow the synchronization by changing priorities *between lock acquisition and the corresponding release*, the model checking problem for pairwise reachability is undecidable.

Given a concurrent program comprised of two threads T_1 and T_2 communicating via pairwise rendezvous, we construct a new program comprised of two threads T_1' and T_2' simulating rendezvous using changes of priority inside the usages of nested locks. This reduces the decision problem for pairwise reachability for threads communicating by pairwise rendezvous to threads communicating with nested locks and priorities.

We show how to simulate a given pair $a \xrightarrow{m!} b$ and $c \xrightarrow{m?} d$ of send and receive pairwise rendezvous transitions, respectively. Recall that for this rendezvous to be executed, both the send and receive transitions must be simultaneously enabled, else neither transition can fire.

On [3], Kahlon et al. (weakly) simulate pairwise rendezvous by using non-well-nested locks. The main idea for simulating pairwise rendezvous using non-well-nested locks was to create *lock chains*. In a lock chain before releasing a lock a thread is forced to pick up another lock, giving the ability to introduce a relative ordering on the firing of local transitions of T_1' and T_2'.

In this way $a \xrightarrow{m!} b$ becomes: $a \xrightarrow{acq\ l_m} a \xrightarrow{rel\ l_{m?}} a \xrightarrow{acq\ l_{m!}} a \xrightarrow{rel\ l_m} b \xrightarrow{acq\ l_{m?}} b \xrightarrow{l_{m!}} b$ and $c \xrightarrow{m?} d$ becomes $c \xrightarrow{acq\ l_{m?}} c \xrightarrow{rel\ l_{m!}} c \xrightarrow{acq\ l_m} c \xrightarrow{rel\ l_{m?}} d \xrightarrow{acq\ l_{m!}} d \xrightarrow{l_m} d$, where $l_m, l_{m?}, l_{m!}$ are new locks.

Here we simulate their construction using nested locks and priorities. In order to simulate lock chains using nested locks and priorities we can replace each chain link of the form: $c \xrightarrow{acq\ l_1} c \xrightarrow{acql_2} c \xrightarrow{rel\ l_1} c$ by the following sequence: $c_1 \xrightarrow{acq\ l_1} c_1 \xrightarrow{acq\ l_2} c_1 \xrightarrow{2} c_2 \xrightarrow{rel\ l_2} c_2 \xrightarrow{rel\ l_1} c_2 \xrightarrow{acq\ l_2} c_2 \xrightarrow{1} c_1$, where the subindex number denotes the priority of the configuration.

Theorem 4. *The model checking problem for pairwise reachability is undecidable for concurrent programs communicating using nested locks and priorities.*

References

1. Bouajjani, A., Müller-Olm, M., Touili, T.: Regular symbolic analysis of dynamic networks of pushdown systems. In: Abadi, M., Alfaro, L. (eds.) CONCUR 2005. LNCS, vol. 3653, pp. 473–487. Springer, Heidelberg (2005). doi:10.1007/11539452_36
2. Lammich, P., Müller-Olm, M., Wenner, A.: Predecessor sets of dynamic pushdown networks with tree-regular constraints. In: Bouajjani, A., Maler, O. (eds.) CAV 2009. LNCS, vol. 5643, pp. 525–539. Springer, Heidelberg (2009). doi:10.1007/978-3-642-02658-4_39
3. Kahlon, V., Ivančić, F., Gupta, A.: Reasoning about threads communicating via locks. In: Etessami, K., Rajamani, S.K. (eds.) CAV 2005. LNCS, vol. 3576, pp. 505–518. Springer, Heidelberg (2005). doi:10.1007/11513988_49

4. Diaz, M., Touili, T.: Reachability analysis of dynamic pushdown networks with priorities. In: El Abbadi, A., Garbinato, B. (eds.) NETYS 2017. LNCS, vol. 10299, pp. 288–303. Springer, Cham (2017). doi:10.1007/978-3-319-59647-1_22
5. Kidd, N., Jagannathan, S., Vitek, J.: One stack to run them all. In: van de Pol, J., Weber, M. (eds.) SPIN 2010. LNCS, vol. 6349, pp. 245–261. Springer, Heidelberg (2010). doi:10.1007/978-3-642-16164-3_18
6. Atig, M.F., Bouajjani, A., Touili, T.: Analyzing asynchronous programs with preemption. In: FSTTCS, pp. 37–48 (2008)
7. PL-DPN tool website: https://github.com/marcio-diaz/pl-dpn-tool
8. Kroening, D., et al.: Effective verification of low-level software with nested interrupts. In: Design, Automation and Test in Europe Conference and Exhibition (DATE) (2015)
9. Clarke, E., Kroening, D., Lerda, F.: A tool for checking ANSI-C programs. In: Jensen, K., Podelski, A. (eds.) TACAS 2004. LNCS, vol. 2988, pp. 168–176. Springer, Heidelberg (2004). doi:10.1007/978-3-540-24730-2_15
10. Commit message fixing issue found: https://github.com/xvisor/xvisor/commit/e5dd8291b5e3f0c552b9aacc73ef2f000ae14c09

Knowledge Transfer and Information Leakage in Protocols

Abdullah Abdul Khadir, Madhavan Mukund(✉), and S.P. Suresh

Chennai Mathematical Institute and UMI RELAX, Chennai, India
{abdullah,madhavan,spsuresh}@cmi.ac.in

Abstract. A protocol defines a structured conversation aimed at exchanging information between two or more parties. Complete confidentiality is virtually impossible so long as useful information needs to be transmitted. A more useful approach is to quantify the amount of information that is leaked. Traditionally, information flow in protocols has been analyzed using notions of entropy. We move to a discrete approach where information is measured in terms of propositional facts. We consider protocols involving agents holding numbered cards who exchange information to discover each others' private hands. We define a transition system that searches the space of all possible announcement sequences made by such a set of agents and tries to identify a subset of announcements that constitutes an informative yet safe protocol.

1 Introduction

A protocol defines a structured conversation aimed at exchanging information between two or more parties. In a computational setting, there is a natural tension between transmitting relevant information to a trusted partner and leaking confidential data to an intruder.

This has led to the study of security in protocols from the perspective of information flow. Complete confidentiality is virtually impossible so long as useful information needs to be transmitted. For instance, rejecting an invalid password reveals indirectly what the password is *not*. Hence, a more useful approach is to quantify the amount of information that is made available to an eavesdropper and use this as a basis for evaluating the security of protocols.

Several proposals have been made over the past decade to model quantitative information flow [1–4,6–8]. The general consensus has been to use ideas from information theory, primarily the notion of entropy, as a basis for measuring information leakage. Starting with the classical notion of entropy proposed by Shannon, some of this work has moved towards analyzing alternative notions of entropy. These choices are often motivated by ad hoc synthetic scenarios that bear no clear relationship to protocols in actual use.

We move away from this continuous measurement of information content to a discrete approach in terms of knowledge. To start with, we regard information as consisting of propositional facts, representing knowledge that has to be shared amongst agents. Initially, the eavesdropper does not know any of these facts.

D. D'Souza and K. Narayan Kumar (Eds.): ATVA 2017, LNCS 10482, pp. 225–240, 2017.
DOI: 10.1007/978-3-319-68167-2_16

As the protocol evolves and the honest agents participating in the conversation learn facts about each other, the eavesdropper also comes to know certain facts about the system. The goal is to have *informative* protocols that share knowledge effectively, but are still *safe* in terms of leaking this knowledge to an intruder.

Concretely, we focus on problems involving sets of agents holding cards on which distinct numbers are written. Each hand is initially known only to the agent who holds it. The agents' aim is to learn about each others' hands through public announcements, while revealing as little as possible to an eavesdropper.

An example is the Russian Cards problem with distribution $\langle k_1|k_2|k_3\rangle$, denoting that A and B get k_1, k_2 cards respectively while the third player C gets k_3 cards. The objective of A and B is to communicate with each other so that they both eventually learn each other's cards, while C remains ignorant of **every** card. An in-depth analysis of this problem in terms of the logic of public announcements can be found in [9].

One generalization of the Russian Cards setting is the Secure Aggregation of Distributed Information (SADI) problem, where there are k agents and an eavesdropper $\mathcal{E}$. The distribution of cards is then given by $\langle n_1|\ldots|n_k\rangle$, with n_i denoting the number of cards that honest agent i holds. The eavesdropper $\mathcal{E}$ does not receive any cards. The objective is to come up with protocols such that all the honest agents learn each others' cards while $\mathcal{E}$ remains ignorant of the location of at least some, if not all, cards. The SADI problem is analyzed in [5].

We present an approach to the SADI problem based on searching through the state space of a transition system. Each state of the transition system describes the knowledge of the individual agents, in terms of atomic propositions of the form *A knows that B has card i* and *A knows that B does not have card i*. Each announcement updates these knowledge propositions. To effect this update, we set up rules linking the propositions and use a SAT solver to compute the set of possible states after each announcement.

The updates we compute are *first order*—that is, they calculate the knowledge that has been revealed through the current sequence of announcements. However, we also need to capture *second order* knowledge—for instance, the given sequence should be compatible with more than one starting distribution of cards to prevent the eavesdropper from indirectly inferring the cards held by the honest agents from the choice of the announcement sequence. Using the formulation from [5], we show that such second order knowledge can also be captured using our transition system framework.

The paper is organized as follows. We set the framework for the SADI problem in Sect. 2. In the next section, we describe how we set up a transition system to analyze this problem. Section 4 describes how we can formulate and answer questions about information flow using our transition system. In Sect. 5 we describe some experimental results. We conclude with a discussion of future directions.

2 Preliminaries

Recalling the definitions from [5], the setting we consider involves a finite set of agents, Ag, with information distributed amongst them. Apart from the (*honest*) agents in Ag, there is also the *eavesdropper*. For convenience, if Ag consists of k honest agents, we assume that they are named $\{0, 1, \ldots, k-1\}$.

For our purposes, the information that the agents hold consists of a set of cards numbered $0, 1, \ldots, n-1$. These cards are distributed amongst the honest agents. In what follows, if X is a set and m is a natural number, then $\binom{X}{m}$ denotes the subsets of X of cardinality m. The cardinality of X is denoted by $\#X$.

It is assumed that there is a mechanism to distribute the cards initially, at the end of which each agent knows his own hand and the number of cards that everyone has been dealt, but nothing more. The problem is for the honest agents to learn each other's hands via public announcements without leaking information to the eavesdropper.

Definition 1. *The distribution type is a vector $\bar{s} = (s_p)_{p \in Ag}$ of natural numbers, where s_p denotes the number of cards dealt initially to agent p. We denote by $|\bar{s}|$ the total number of cards, $\Sigma_{p \in Ag} s_p$.*

A deal of type $\bar{s}$ is a partition $H = (H_p)_{p \in Ag}$ of $\{0, \ldots, |\bar{s}| - 1\}$ such that $\#H_p = s_p$ for each agent p. We say H_p is the hand of p. Further, we denote the set of all deals over $\bar{s}$ by $Deals(\bar{s})$.

Given two deals H and H' of type $\bar{s}$, and an agent p, we say that H and H' are indistinguishable *for p (in symbols: $H \sim_p H'$) if $H_p = H'_p$.*

The agents try to learn each other's hand by publicly (and truthfully) announcing information about their own cards. Consider an agent A holding the cards $\{1, 2, 3\}$. One announcement he might make is "My hand is either $\{1, 2, 3\}$ or $\{1, 4, 6\}$ or $\{2, 3, 5\}$." Any other agent who holds 4 and 5, on hearing this announcement, will immediately know that A's hand is $\{1, 2, 3\}$. But the eavesdropper still has uncertainty about A's hand, since he doesn't have any cards of his own. Another possible announcement is "My cards are among $\{1, 2, 3, 4, 6, 7\}$." Yet another announcement is "The sum of the numbers on my cards is 6." All these announcements can be encoded as a disjunction of hands. For instance, the last announcement above is the disjunction "My hand is either $\{1, 2, 3\}$ or $\{0, 2, 4\}$."

Definition 2 (Actions). *Fix a distribution type $\bar{s}$, and let $\mathsf{Cards} = \{0, \ldots, |\bar{s}| - 1\}$. An announcement by agent p is a disjunction of possible hands. Since he has s_p cards, the announcement can be thought of as a subset of $\binom{\mathsf{Cards}}{s_p}$. Thus we can define Act_p, the set of p-announcements to be $\mathcal{P}(\binom{\mathsf{Cards}}{s_p})$, where $\mathcal{P}(X)$ denotes the powerset of X. The set of actions is defined to be $Act = \bigcup_{p \in Ag} Act_p$.*

We assume a situation in which agents take turns to make announcements, starting from 0 and proceeding in cyclic order, till they achieve a certain goal. This is formalized by the following definition.

Definition 3 (Runs). *Fix a distribution type $\bar{s}$ as before, with m agents. An* execution *is a (finite or infinite) sequence of actions $\alpha_0\alpha_1\cdots$ such that $\alpha_i \in Act_p$ whenever $i \bmod m = p$. A finite execution is also called a* run. *Given a run $\rho = \alpha_0\alpha_1\ldots\alpha_n$ and two indices $i \leq j$, $\alpha[i\ldots j]$ denotes the segment $\alpha_i\alpha_{i+1}\ldots\alpha_j$. We denote the length of a run ρ by $|\rho|$. The set of runs is denoted by Runs.*

A protocol describes a strategy for each agent to make announcements given the current history. We constrain each announcement to be truthful. We also insist that a protocol depend only on the local information available to the agent—any two situations that are the same from the agent's point of view must elicit the same response. In other words, if the agent holds the same hand in two different deals and sees the same sequence of announcements, he must respond identically in both situations.

Definition 4 (Protocol). *Fix a distribution type $\bar{s}$, with m agents. A* ***protocol*** *(for $\bar{s}$) is a function π assigning to every deal $H \in Deals(\bar{s})$, and every run $\rho \in Runs$ with $|\rho| \bmod m = p$, a non-empty set of p-actions $\pi(H, \rho) \subseteq Act_p$ such that:*

- *$H_p \in \alpha$ for all $\alpha \in \pi(H, \rho)$ (the announcement is* truthful*), and*
- *if $H \sim_p H'$, then $\pi(H, \rho) = \pi(H', \rho)$ (the announcement is* view-based*).*

A run of a protocol π is a pair (H, ρ) where $H \in Deals(\bar{s})$ and $\rho = \alpha_0\alpha_1\ldots\alpha_m$ is a run such that $\alpha_{i+1} \in \pi(H, \rho[0\ldots i])$ for every $i < m$. The set of runs of π is denoted by $Runs(\pi)$.

We are interested in protocols that are *informative* (all honest agents learn the whole deal) and *safe* (the eavesdropper is uncertain about the deal even after listening to all the announcements). We formalize these notions below.

Definition 5. *A run (H, ρ) of a protocol π is informative for an agent p if there is no execution (H', ρ) of π with $H \sim_p H'$ and $H \neq H'$. (i.e., there is no other starting deal that is consistent with p's hand and the subsequent announcements.) A protocol π is*

- ***weakly informative (WI):*** *if every run of π is informative for some agent.*
- ***informative (I):*** *if every run of π is informative for every agent.*

The eavesdropper does not have any information about the deal to begin with. Hence, the actual deal could be any deal of the correct distribution type. As the honest agents communicate amongst themselves, the eavesdropper uses the information in the announcements to eliminate various deals from contention. At the end of a sequence of announcements, he will be left with a set of deals that are consistent with this sequence. This set must have at least one element, namely the actual deal. This set is formally defined below.

Definition 6. *Given a protocol π and a run ρ, define the (eavesdropper's) ignorance set $I_\pi(\rho)$ to be $\{H \mid (H, \rho) \in Runs(\pi)\}$.*

$I_\pi(\rho)$ is can be used to determine what the eavesdropper knows at the end of ρ.

Consider a situation where agent 0 holds the card 5 in every deal in $I_\pi(\rho)$. This means that the eavesdropper has ruled out all deals where agent 0 does not hold card 5 as being inconsistent with ρ. Hence, the run ρ has leaked information about the location of card 5 to the eavesdropper.

Consider another situation involving card 5, where agent 1 holds card 5 in some of the deals in $I_\pi(\rho)$, and agent 2 holds card 5 in the rest of the deals in $I_\pi(\rho)$. Here, even though the eavesdropper does not know exactly who holds the card 5, he is certain that no agent other than $\{1, 2\}$ holds card 5.

This leads us to the following two notions of safety of a card (at the end of a run).

Definition 7 (Safety of cards). *A run (H, ρ) of a protocol π is safe for the card c if for every agent p, there is a deal $G \in I_\pi(\rho)$ such that $c \notin G_p$.*

A run (H, ρ) of a protocol π is strongly safe for the card c if for every agent p, there are two deals $F, G \in I_\pi(\rho)$ such that $c \in F_p$ and $c \notin G_p$.

Thus, safety of a run means that the eavesdropper does not know for certain that an agent p has card c, but the eavesdropper may have concluded that p definitely does not have c. On the other hand, strong safety requires that the eavesdropper cannot conclude whether p holds c or p does not hold c.

We can lift the notion of safety from runs to protocols as follows.

Definition 8 (Safety of Protocols). *A protocol π is*

- ***deal safe:*** *if every run of π is safe for some card c. Equivalently, deal safety means that the eavesdropper does not learn the deal at the end of any run of π.*
- ***p-safe (for an agent p):*** *if every run of π is safe for all cards in H_p.*
- ***safe:*** *if every execution of π is safe for every card c.*
- ***strongly safe:*** *if every execution of π is strongly safe for every card c.*

In the rest of the paper, we will examine an approach to synthesize informative and safe protocols based on these definitions. Equivalently, our approach can be used to validate if a given protocol is informative and safe.

We assume that there are at least three honest agents, so that negative information of the form p *does not hold card* c does not automatically imply positive information of the form q *holds card* c.

3 Implementation

In this section, we describe a tool written in Python to search for informative and safe runs of a particular distribution type. Before presenting the details of the tool, we present an abstract transition system model for protocols.

3.1 Defining the Transition System

Fix a distribution type $\bar{s}$ with k agents $\{0, 1, \ldots, k-1\}$. For convenience, we assume that the eavesdropper is agent k, with the understanding that agent k possesses no cards. Let $\{0, 1, \ldots, n-1\}$ be the set of cards dealt. We describe a transition system that tracks the uncertainty of every agent about the actual deal. Essentially, each agent implicitly stores a set of *valuations* that represent all deals that are compatible with the information that he has seen so far.

Definition 9 (Valuations). *The set of* knowledge propositions *for an agent* $p \leq k$*, denoted* $\mathcal{K}(p)$*, is the set*

$$\{K_{pq}(c), K_{pNq}(c) \mid q < k, q \neq p, c < n\}.$$

The proposition $K_{pq}(c)$ describes the fact that agent p knows that agent q has card c, while the proposition $K_{pNq}(c)$ says that p knows that q does not have card c.

Definition 10 *A* valuation *for agent p (with respect to an initial deal H) is a function $v : \mathcal{K}(p) \to \{\top, \bot\}$ satisfying the following conditions, where we write $v \models \ell$ to mean $v(\ell) = \top$ and $v \not\models \ell$ to mean $v(\ell) = \bot$.*

- ***consistency with the deal:*** *For all $0 \leq c < n$, if $c \in H_p$ then for all $0 \leq q < k$, $p \neq q$, $v \models K_{pNq}(c)$.*
- ***consistency of knowledge propositions:*** *For all $0 \leq q < k$ and $0 \leq c < n$, either $v \not\models K_{pq}(c)$ or $v \not\models K_{pNq}(c)$.*
- ***ownership of cards:*** *For all $0 \leq q < k$ and $0 \leq c < n$, $v \models K_{pq}(c)$ iff for all $r \notin \{p, q\}$, $v \models K_{pNr}(c)$.*
- ***consistency with the distribution type:*** *For each $q \neq p$, there are at most s_q propositions of the form $K_{pq}(c)$ such that $v \models K_{pq}(c)$.*
- ***complete knowledge:*** *For each $q \neq p$, there are exactly s_q propositions of the form $K_{pq}(c)$ such that $v \models K_{pq}(c)$ iff there are exactly $(n-s_q)$ propositions of the form $K_{pNq}(c)$ such that $v \models K_{pNq}(c)$.*

We denote the set of all valuations for agent p by $Vals_p$, and let $Vals = \bigcup_{p \leq m} Vals_p$.

A valuation for p is supposed to capture p's information state. If v maps $K_{pq}(c)$ to $\top$, it means that p believes, in this information state, that q has card c. If v maps $K_{pNq}(c)$ to $\top$, it means that p believes that q does not have card c. If v maps both $K_{pq}(c)$ and $K_{pNq}(c)$ to $\bot$, this means that p is uncertain about whether or not q holds card c.

Assuming three agents $\{0, 1, 2\}$, an example valuation for agent 0 is given in Fig. 1. This corresponds to the initial deal $(\{0, 1\}, \{2, 3, 4\}, \{5, 6, 7, 8\})$.

Each agent has a valuation describing the initial state according to his perspective, but as he hears more and more announcements (which are all disjunctions), it might not be possible to represent the information he has by means of one valuation. Each disjunct in the announcement he hears might lead him

	0	1	2	3	4	5	6	7	8
K_{01}	$\bot$	$\bot$	$\bot$	$\bot$	$\bot$	$\bot$	$\bot$	$\bot$	$\bot$
K_{02}	$\bot$	$\bot$	$\bot$	$\bot$	$\bot$	$\bot$	$\bot$	$\bot$	$\bot$
K_{0N1}	$\top$	$\top$	$\bot$	$\bot$	$\bot$	$\bot$	$\bot$	$\bot$	$\bot$
K_{0N2}	$\top$	$\top$	$\bot$	$\bot$	$\bot$	$\bot$	$\bot$	$\bot$	$\bot$

Fig. 1. Valuation for agent 0 at initial deal $\langle 0,1|2,3,4|5,6,7,8\rangle$

to consider a new valuation as a possible world. Thus each agent might need to store a set of valuations as a run progresses. This leads to the following definition of *states*.

Definition 11 (States). *A state is an $k+1$-tuple $(V_0,\ldots,V_k)$ where each $V_p \subseteq Vals_p$.*

Definition 12 (X-extension). *Let v be a q-valuation and X be an s_p-sized subset of $\{0,\ldots,n-1\}$. We say that a q-valuation v' is a X-extension of v if $v \leq v'$ and $v' \models K_{qp}(c)$ for all $c \in X$.*

Note that for a given v and X, it is possible that there is no X-extension of v.

Definition 13 (State updates). *Given a state $\mathbf{s} = (V_0,\ldots,V_k)$ and a p-announcement α, we define update$(\mathbf{s},\alpha)$ to be $\mathbf{s}' = (V'_0,\ldots,V'_k)$ such that:*

- $V'_p = V_p$
- *for* $q \neq p$, $V'_q = \bigcup_{v\in V_q, X \text{ is a disjunct of } \alpha} \{v' \mid v' \text{is an} X - \text{extension of}\, v\}$.

The core component of our tool computes the updated state at the end of a sequence of announcements, starting from an initial deal. The final state encapsulates a nontrivial amount of information, from which one can test whether the honest agents have complete knowledge of the deal, and also whether the eavesdropper knows the original deal. Furthermore, we can also generate the uncertainty set of the eavesdropper, namely, the set of all deals that are compatible with the given announcement sequence. We can use this information in a variety of ways, as detailed in Sect. 4.

The important point to note is that the tool computes the updated state *implicitly*. Rather than explicitly maintain a set of valuations after each announcement, the tool just collects all the announcements, and invokes the SAT solver to determine the certain knowledge of the agents.

3.2 A High-Level Description of the Tool

In this section, we describe in more detail some key components of our tool. In the interests of space, we present a high-level overview[1]. The tool is written in

[1] Please check http://www.cmi.ac.in/~spsuresh/projects/russian-cards-z3/ for the full code.

Python, and implements the system described in the previous section. It interacts with the SAT solver Z3 to compute the updated state after each announcement. As detailed in the definition of valuations, each valuation has to satisfy a lot of constraints. These are coded as system invariants. A solver instance is created and formulas corresponding to the constraints are added to the solver, as shown in the following snippet.

```
solvR = Solver()
solvR.push()
vD,oW,hK = self.validDeal(), self.ownership(), self.hand2K()
kC,oK,dK = self.kConsistency(), self.ownershipK(), self.dealK()
solvR.add(vD)
solvR.add(oW)
solvR.add(hK)
solvR.add(kC)
solvR.add(oK)
solvR.add(dK)
solvR.push()
return solvR
```

For instance, `validDeal` corresponds to the constraint that if $c \in H_p$ then $v \models KpNq(c)$, while `ownershipK` corresponds to the constraint that $v \models K_{pq}(c)$ iff $v \models K_{pNr}(c)$ for all $r \neq q$. Similarly for the other constraints.

Given any announcement as a tuple consisting of the speaker as well as the DNF formula, the `updateAnn` procedure produces a new state with the appropriate update to the knowledge of each agent. Essentially, it translates the announcement to an appropriate formula denoting how each agent other than the speaker would perceive it and this is appended to the knowledge of each listener.

To process a sequence of announcements, the tool does not calculate the set of valuations at each intermediate state. Rather, repeated calls to `updateAnn` are made, which builds a conjunction of the initial knowledge, the constraints, and all the announcements. Now we can call the SAT solver to check what all propositions are consequences of this formula, and thus determine all the propositions that each agent is certain about.

The tool is meant to go through a set of runs of bounded length, each run consisting of announcements of a specific structure (typically a bound on the number of disjunctions in the announcement), and compute various statistics at the end of each run. For instance, we might want to know how many propositions of the form $K_{mp}(c)$ is definitely known to m (remember $\{0, \ldots, m-1\}$ is the set of honest agents and m is the eavesdropper) at the end of a run. This measures the amount of positive knowledge leaked. We might also want to check how many propositions of the form $K_{mNp}(c)$ is definitely known to m (i.e., for every valuation $v \in V_m$ in the final state, $v \models K_{mNp}(c)$). This measures the amount of negative knowledge leaked. We can use this tool to either discover protocols or check whether a purported protocol is informative and safe, as elaborated in Sect. 4.

3.3 An Example

In this example, we illustrate the functioning of our tool with the $\langle 2|3|4\rangle$ SADI problem detailed in [5]. Recall that the initial deal is $\langle 0,1|2,3,4|5,6,7,8\rangle$, and an informative and safe announcement sequence is the announcement $\{01,08,18\}$ by A, followed by the announcement $\{0234,1237,5678\}$ by C. (B passes its turn – by announcing **true**, for instance).

First, we need to create and initialize the problem instance

```
In [1]: from cpState import *
In [2]: deal = {'a':[0,1],'b':[2,3,4],'c':[5,6,7,8],'e':[]};
In [3]: infAgts, eaves = ['a','b','c'],'e';
In [4]: agts = infAgts + [eaves]
In [5]: s0 = cpState([2, 3, 4, 0], agts, deal, infAgts, eaves)
```

At the end of the above commands, we obtain the initial state s_0 initialized with the deal $\langle 0,1|2,3,4|5,6,7,8\rangle$. Having obtained the initial state, we now need to update it with the announcements ann_1 of A followed by ann_2 of C.

```
In [6]: ann1 = ('a', [[0, 1], [0, 8], [1, 8]])
In [7]: ann2 = ('c', [[0, 2, 3, 4], [1, 2, 3, 7], [5, 6, 7, 8]])
In [8]: s1 = s0.updateAnn(ann1)
In [9]: s2 = s1.updateAnn(ann2)
```

Now that we have the resulting state s_2 alongwith the intermediate state s_1, we can actually analyze the states and query them to obtain further information about the states of any agent in each of the states.

We can obtain the set of all positive knowledge propositions for any agent

```
In [10]: %time s2.getPosK('a')
CPU times: user 3.42 s, sys: 32 ms, total: 3.45 s
Wall time: 3.45 s
Out[10]: ['Kab__2','Kab__3','Kab__4','Kac__5','Kac__6',
                  'Kac__7','Kac__8']

In [11]: %time s2.getPosK('b')
CPU times: user 2.95 s, sys: 0 ns, total: 2.95 s
Wall time: 2.95 s
Out[11]: ['Kba__0','Kba__1','Kbc__5','Kbc__6',
                  'Kbc__7','Kbc__8']

In [12]: %time s2.getPosK('c')
CPU times: user 2.46 s, sys: 4 ms, total: 2.47 s
Wall time: 2.47 s
Out[12]: ['Kca__0','Kca__1','Kcb__2','Kcb__3','Kcb__4']

In [13]: %time s2.getPosK('e')
CPU times: user 4.43 s, sys: 16 ms, total: 4.44 s
```

```
Wall time: 4.45 s
Out[13]: []
```

As observed, the above queries take about 3 to 4 seconds even for this simple example. However, if all we are interested is in the informativity property, we can reduce the time taken by using `isInfAgt` or `isInformative` as shown below,

```
In [14]: %time s2.isInfAgt(a)
CPU times: user 472 ms, sys: 0 ns, total: 472 ms
Wall time: 480 ms
Out[14]: True

In [15]: %time s2.isInfAgt(b)
CPU times: user 468 ms, sys: 0 ns, total: 468 ms
Wall time: 471 ms
Out[15]: True

In [16]: %time s2.isInfAgt(c)
CPU times: user 472 ms, sys: 0 ns, total: 472 ms
Wall time: 476 ms
Out[16]: True

In [17]: %time s2.isInformative(infAgts)
CPU times: user 1.48 s, sys: 0 ns, total: 1.48 s
Wall time: 1.48 s
Out[15]: True

In [16]: %time s2.isInformative([eaves])
CPU times: user 508 ms, sys: 0 ns, total: 508 ms
Wall time: 509 ms
Out[16]: False
```

Hence, we've ascertained that the state s_2 is informative to a, b and c but e doesn't learn the owner of any card. This tallies with the analysis in [5]. However, we can also query the states for negative propositions revealed to `e`,

```
In [17]: %time s1.getNegK('e')
CPU times: user 8.93 s, sys: 0 ns, total: 8.93 s
Wall time: 8.97 s
Out[17]: ['KeNa__2','KeNa__3','KeNa__4','KeNa__5',
                    'KeNa__6','KeNa__7']

In [18]: %time s2.getNegK('e')
CPU times: user 8.86 s, sys: 4 ms, total: 8.87 s
Wall time: 8.89 s
Out[18]: ['KeNa__2','KeNa__3','KeNa__4','KeNa__5',
'KeNa__6','KeNa__7','KeNb__0','KeNb__1','KeNb__8']
```

From the above, it is clear that even though e doesn't know any of the owners of any cards, he does know 9 propositions of negative information involving cards [0, 8]. In fact, for each of the cards, he knows at least one agent that *does not own the card*. Thus, for any card, e initially did not know which of the 3 agents it belonged to, but at the end, his uncertainty is restricted to 2 of the 3 agents.

4 Formulating Information Leakage Problems

We can use the transition system defined in the previous section in two ways: to search for an informative and safe protocol, and to validate if a given protocal is informative and safe.

4.1 Synthesis of Protocols

We can characterize informative states based on the knowledge propositions of the agents—in an informative state, each agent should know completely all the cards of the agents.

Likewise, safety can be described in terms of the knowledge propositions of the eavesdropper. Unlike the classical SADI problem, we can *quantify* the level of safety we tolerate by placing a threshold on the knowledge revealed to the eavesdropper.

Our first task is to identify a set of runs that lead to informative and safe states. We call such a run a first-order informative run. It suffices to start the search at a fixed initial state corresponding a canonical distribution of cards. Every other deal is a permutation of this deal. If we can find a protocol for this starting deal, we can construct a symmetric protocol for every other deal by permuting all announcements in the same manner as the initial deal.

Having identified first order informative runs (through depth-first search, say) we have to check if they satisfy *second order safety* and if they meet the view-based criterion laid down for protocols.

First order safety guarantees that the eavesdropper has at least two possible deals in his ignorance set at the end of each such run. However, this does not guarantee that the *same* run, starting from one of the alternative states, achieves informativeness and safety. This is what we call second order safety. Our first task, therefore, is to identify a set of first order informative runs that is closed with respect to this pairing: for every run ρ starting from the initial deal H, there is another deal H' such that ρ from H' is informative and safe.

Having identified such a set of runs closed with respect to second order safety, we then ensure that there is a subset that is view-based—that is, if $H \sim_p H'$, then the choice made after any sequence of announcements ρ starting from H matches that made after ρ starting from H'.

After these two stages of pruning, any first order informative runs that survive constitute a protocol that solves the given problem.

4.2 Verification of Protocols

Conversely, we can use our transition system to verify a given protocol. This follows conventional lines, where we search for a state that is reachable with respect to the protocol that violates the given safety requirement.

5 Experimental Results

In this section, we document some experiments with our tool on a 3 agent SADI system. To assist readability, we refer to the 3 honest agents as $\{A, B, C\}$ rather than $\{0, 1, 2\}$. The eavesdropper is denoted $\mathcal{E}$.

5.1 Need for Second Order Safety

To illustrate the inadequacy of direct first order reasoning, we consider an example with deal type $\langle 2, 3, 4 \rangle$. Suppose the initial deal is $d_0 = \langle 0, 1|2, 3, 4|5, 6, 7, 8 \rangle$. Let the first announcement (ann_1) by A be $\{01, 12, 23\}$. This would result in B obtaining complete knowledge of the deal (as he has card 2). B could then make the second announcement (ann_2) as $\{234, 056, 178\}$ to inform the others.

The only alternative deals compatible with the above announcements are

(a) $d_1 = (\{1, 2\}, \{0, 5, 6\}, \{3, 4, 7, 8\})$
(b) $d_2 = (\{2, 3\}, \{1, 7, 8\}, \{0, 4, 5, 6\})$
(c) $d_3 = (\{2, 3\}, \{0, 5, 6\}, \{1, 4, 7, 8\})$

One may check that none of these deals are completely informative to all three agents A, B and C when using the run ρ consisting of exactly the two announcements above. For the first deal, A's announcment is not informative to B and the run itself is not informative to any of the agents. So, (d_1, ρ) is not even weakly informative. The runs (d_2, ann_1) as well as (d_3, ann_1) are informative to exactly B and C respectively (the agent that has card 1) but, (d_2, ρ) is not informative to A and (d_3, ρ) is informative to neither A nor C.

Currently, our tool can evaluate announcement sequences for first order safety. It is straightforward to extend it to check for second order safety as defined above. However, one would need to check what one could handle with a naïve implementation of second order safety. In the next section, we describe experiments using our tool for first order safety of larger instances with varying parameters.

5.2 Hand Size and Informativity

For a particular deal type (say $\langle 4, 4, 4, 0 \rangle$), and a particular initial deal (say $\langle \{0, 1, 2, 3\}|\{4, 5, 6, 7\}|\{8, 9, 10, 11\} \rangle$), we generate random truthful announcement sequences using the function `genRun` defined in `cpState`. Though an announcement is simply a disjunction of hands, it makes sense for an agent to reveal only partial information in every announcement. This can be done by uniformly restricting the size of each set in the announcement. We call this the size of the hand (*hSize*) revealed in the announcement. The function **genRun** accepts the following arguments

a) The size of each set in the announcement (*hSize*).
b) The number of sets (or disjuncts) in an announcement (*annLen*).
c) The number of announcements for each run (*runLen*).

The executions were generated for the deal type $\langle 4,4,4,0\rangle$, varying *hSize* in the range $\{1,2,3\}$. Furthermore, we also varied *annLen* to take values in $\{3,5,7\}$. The results obtained are presented in Tables 1, 2 and 3. We also ran some experiments for the deal type $\langle 8,8,8,0\rangle$—the results are tabulated in Table 4. For all runs, we have fixed *runLen* as 6, denoting sequences of 6 announcements, corresponding to exactly 2 rounds across the 3 agents. Our eventual goal is to move beyond the 1 round protocols studied in the literature [5,9].

The *hSize* column denotes the hand size used in the announcements. The other columns are labeled by sets of agents. The entries in the matrix denote the number of runs which were informative for the corresponding set of agents.

If we look at the tables for $\langle 4,4,4,0\rangle$, (that is, Tables 1, 2 and 3) we notice that, as we increase *hSize*, the number of runs which are informative for any agent increases. This reflects our intuition that more information is transferred when each part of the announcment reveals more details about the hand. Another expected outcome is that the number of cards revealed to $\mathcal{E}$ also increases with

Table 1. Executions with $annLen = 3$ for $\langle 4,4,4,0\rangle$ (500 per entry).

hSize	$\emptyset$	A	B	C	A,B	A,C	B,C	A,B,C	A,B,C,E
1	500	0	0	0	0	0	0	0	0
2	355	24	27	34	17	19	22	1	1
3	9	2	6	1	36	30	35	0	381

Table 2. Executions with $annLen = 5$ for $\langle 4,4,4,0\rangle$ (500 per entry).

hSize	$\emptyset$	A	B	C	A,B	A,C	B,C	A,B,C	A,B,C,E
1	500	0	0	0	0	0	0	0	0
2	434	23	19	16	0	4	3	1	0
3	12	2	8	8	41	38	42	4	345

Table 3. Executions with $annLen = 7$ for $\langle 4,4,4,0\rangle$ (500 per entry).

hSize	$\emptyset$	A	B	C	A,B	A,C	B,C	A,B,C	A,B,C,E
1	500	0	0	0	0	0	0	0	0
2	480	7	8	5	0	0	0	0	0
3	12	12	13	10	55	59	55	20	264

Table 4. Executions with *annLen* = 3 for ⟨8, 8, 8, 0⟩ (250 per entry)

hSize	∅	*C*	*A*, *B*	*A*, *C*	*B*, *C*	*A*, *B*, *C*, *E*
2	250	0	0	0	0	0
4	243	0	4	2	1	0
6	38	1	30	19	31	131

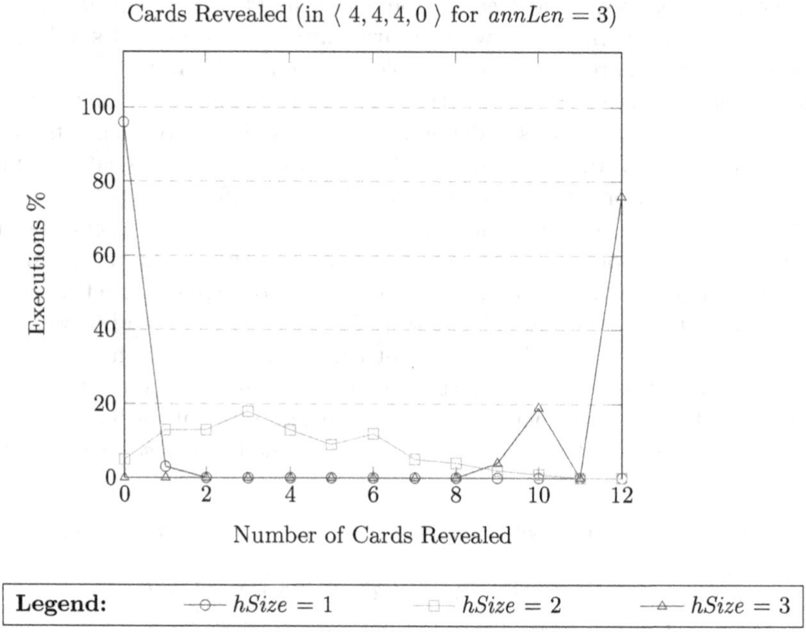

Fig. 2. Infomation leakage to $\mathcal{E}$

increasing *hSize*, as observed in Fig. 2. Note that the number of cards revealed to $\mathcal{E}$ is not represented in the tables but was computed independently using the same set of runs.

Notice that for ⟨4, 4, 4, 0⟩, setting *annLen* = 7 and *hSize* = 3, we obtained about 20 runs that were informative and safe. For the same configuration, we obtained a larger number of runs (about 169 runs or about 33% of the runs) that were informative for 2 of the agents.

One motivation for running these experiments is to identify parameters for which the probability of hitting an informative run is high. Once we identify informative runs, the next step would be to validate these runs with respect to second order reasoning of $\mathcal{E}$ in order to design or search for informative and safe protocols. We can also use these experiments to guide us towards impossibility proofs when a protocol does not exist.

6 Discussion

We have attempted to describe a framework for quantifying information flow in protocols in terms of discrete items of knowledge. We have used card playing protocols because the cards themselves act as natural units of knowledge.

We have identified two kinds of knowledge propositions: *A knows that B has card i* and *A knows that B does not have card i*. In the Russian Cards Problem where there are only two honest agents, these two are dual to each other. However, in the SADI framework, the second type of knowledge is strictly weaker than the first. Positive information about where a card is implies negative information about where the card is not to be found, but not vice versa.

We can thus impose a partial order on different knowledge states of the eavesdropper and use this to rank different protocols according the amount of information that they reveal. A challenge would then be to synthesize an optimal protocol with respect to this information ordering.

A more ambitious extension would be to extend our analysis to settings such as bidding in the game of bridge. In the bridge bidding process, each pair tries to understand the strength of the team's hand without revealing too much to the opponent. Bids are restricted to be an ascending sequence of announcements and the number of such announcements is fixed a priori. Hence, the goal is to maximize the information shared between partners while minimizing the information revealed to the opponents.

References

1. Chatzikokolakis, K., Palamidessi, C., Panangaden, P.: Probability of error in information-hiding protocols. In: 20th IEEE Computer Security Foundations Symposium, CSF 2007, Venice, Italy, 6–8 July 2007, pp. 341–354. IEEE Computer Society (2007)
2. Clark, D., Hunt, S., Malacaria, P.: Quantitative information flow, relations and polymorphic types. J. Log. Comput. **15**(2), 181–199 (2005)
3. Clark, D., Hunt, S., Malacaria, P.: A static analysis for quantifying information flow in a simple imperative language. J. Comput. Secur. **15**(3), 321–371 (2007)
4. Clarkson, M.R., Myers, A.C., Schneider, F.B.: Belief in information flow. In: 18th IEEE Computer Security Foundations Workshop, (CSFW-18 2005), Aix-en-Provence, France, 20–22 June 2005, pp. 31–45. IEEE Computer Society (2005)
5. Fernández-Duque, D., Goranko, V.: Secure aggregation of distributed information: how a team of agents can safely share secrets in front of a spy. Discrete Appl. Math. **198**, 118–135 (2016)
6. Köpf, B., Basin, D.A.: An information-theoretic model for adaptive side-channel attacks. In: Ning, P., De Capitani di Vimercati, S., Syverson, P.F. (eds.) Proceedings of the 2007 ACM Conference on Computer and Communications Security, CCS 2007, Alexandria, Virginia, USA, 28–31 October 2007, pp. 286–296. ACM (2007)
7. Lowe, G.: Quantifying information flow. In: 15th IEEE Computer Security Foundations Workshop (CSFW-15 2002), Cape Breton, Nova Scotia, Canada, 24–26 June 2002, pp. 18–31 (2002)

8. Di Pierro, A., Hankin, C., Wiklicky, H.: Approximate non-interference. In: 15th IEEE Computer Security Foundations Workshop (CSFW-15 2002), Cape Breton, Nova Scotia, Canada, 24–26 June 2002, pp. 3–17 (2002)
9. van Ditmarsch, H.P., van der Hoek, W., van der Meyden, R., Ruan, J.: Model checking russian cards. Electr. Notes Theor. Comput. Sci. **149**(2), 105–123 (2006)

Concurrent Program Verification with Invariant-Guided Underapproximation

Sumanth Prabhu[1(✉)], Peter Schrammel[2], Mandayam Srivas[1], Michael Tautschnig[3], and Anand Yeolekar[4]

[1] Chennai Mathematical Institute, Chennai, India
sumanths1988@gmail.com
[2] University of Sussex, Brighton, UK
[3] Queen Mary University of London, London, UK
[4] Tata Research Development and Design Centre, Pune, India

Abstract. Automatic verification of concurrent programs written in low-level languages like ANSI-C is an important task as multi-core architectures are gaining widespread adoption. Formal verification, although very valuable for this domain, rapidly runs into the state-explosion problem due to multiple thread interleavings. Recently, Bounded Model Checking (BMC) has been used for this purpose, which does not scale in practice. In this work, we develop a method to further constrain the search space for BMC techniques using underapproximations of data flow of shared memory and lazy demand-driven refinement of the approximation. A novel contribution of our method is that our underapproximation is guided by *likely data-flow invariants* mined from dynamic analysis and our refinement is based on proof-based learning. We have implemented our method in a prototype tool. Initial experiments on benchmark examples show potential performance benefit.

1 Introduction

Automatic verification of concurrent programs written in low-level languages like ANSI-C is an important task as multi-core architectures are gaining widespread adoption. Difficulty in development of programs due to concurrency and different memory models of processors underlines the need for tool support. *Bounded Model Checking* (BMC) has been proposed as a solution for this purpose which tries to ferret shallow bugs limiting unwinding depth [1], number of context-switches [2], or number of writes [3,4] as a bounding parameter to restrict search space and manage complexity. In these techniques, the control flow of the concurrent program is sequentialized by choosing an arbitrary thread order, and then modeling the effect of all interleavings by symbolically encoding the possible read-write partial orders as non-deterministic data-flow constraints on all behaviors up to the chosen BMC bounding parameter.

Contributions. In this work, we develop a method to further restrict proof search space by using semantic underapproximations of possible data flow (i.e., write-to-read relations in happens-before orders) of shared memory accesses and

D. D'Souza and K. Narayan Kumar (Eds.): ATVA 2017, LNCS 10482, pp. 241–248, 2017.
DOI: 10.1007/978-3-319-68167-2_17

lazy, on-demand refinement of the approximation. The novel contributions of our work are the following:

1. Our underapproximation is guided by likely data-flow invariants for the program mined from dynamic analysis.
2. We perform automatic refinement of the approximation based on learning from partial proofs.
3. We present an implementation of the method in a prototype tool inside CBMC[1]. The tool fully automates extraction of likely invariants, construction of the underapproximations and the refinement loop.
4. We report results of experiments we have run on a set of benchmarks.

2 The Method

In practice concurrent programs are developed with synchronization techniques such as locks to protect shared memory. Even when explicit locks are not used, the program semantics may constrain data flow. The search space considered by BMC techniques considered earlier should thus be restricted to the feasible data flow. To illustrate this problem and our method we use an example program shown in Fig. 1.

```
1 void* t1() {
2   while(read_y()<NUM) {
3     int tmp1, tmp2;
4     tmp1=read_y();
5     write_y(tmp1+1); // y=y+1
6     tmp1=read_x();
7     tmp2=read_y(); // x=x+y
8     write_x(tmp1+tmp2);
9 }}
```

```
1 void* t2() {
2   int t, tmp1, tmp2;
3   while(read_y()<NUM) { }
4   t=read_y();
5   tmp1=read_x();
6   tmp2=read_y();
7   write_y(tmp1+tmp2); // y=x+y;
8   assert(read_y()==t+read_x());
9 }}
```

Fig. 1. Motivating example

Here two threads are executing functions $t1, t2$ and x, y are global variables initialized to 0. This program is not safe as the following execution violates the asserted condition: y is NUM -1; $t1_2, t1_3, t1_4, t1_5, t2_3, t2_4, t2_5, t2_6, t1_6, t1_7, t1_8, t1_2, t2_7, t2_8$. For this program the encodings of [1] and [4] consider two writes ($t1_5$ and $t2_7$) for reads at $t1_4$ and $t1_7$. However, by considering only local writes ($t1_5$) we can still find the assertion violation in a more constrained model as shown in the previous execution trace. If we were unable to detect an error then we would have to refine the model. Now suppose we modify the program by swapping lines $t1_6$–$t1_8$ with lines $t1_4$–$t1_5$, then it is indeed a true invariant that $t1_4$ and $t1_7$ will always read from the local write. In this case we can complete

[1] http://www.cprover.org/cbmc/.

verification without refining, if we are able to detect that they are true invariants or the underapproximation is sufficient for verifying the property at hand. We use dynamic analysis for this purpose. In particular we extract likely invariants on data flow following [6]. For instance, in most executions of the program in Fig. 1, reads at $t1_4$ and $t1_7$ will refer only to the local write ($t1_5$) due to the spin-lock like condition in $t2_3$.

If the set of possible executions of a given program is represented as $L_C \cap L_D$, where L_C is the set of executions from the control-flow graph and L_D is the allowed data flow in underlying memory model, then our tool starts with $L_C \cap L_{D'}$, where $L_{D'} \subseteq L_D$. It either proves that $L_D \setminus L_{D'}$ is irrelevant to the property or unfeasible, or refines $L_{D'}$ towards L_D. This has the advantage that if the program is unsafe in the restricted model (as shown on Fig. 1) then we can find a counterexample earlier; otherwise we explore data flows which are only relevant to the property. To construct an initial $L_{D'}$ such that $L_{D'} \subseteq L_D$ we use likely invariants on data flow following [6].

We use unsatisfiable cores produced by a SAT solver for refinement of our data-flow invariants on a demand-driven basis. Our refinement algorithm works as shown in Fig. 2. We start with a Boolean formula, which is constructed by converting the conjunction of given program (P), negation of a property (ϕ) and a set of constraints ($Inv := I_1 \wedge \cdots \wedge I_n$) to Boolean form (CNF) using an appropriate method (like bit-blasting). This yields an underapproximation of the original formula ($P \wedge \neg\phi$), which is passed to a SAT solver. If the formula is satisfiable then we deduce that the input program is unsafe. If, however, the formula is unsatisfiable then we check whether any of $I_1 \ldots I_n$ from Inv are part of the unsatisfiability proof (unsatisfiable core) C. If none of the clauses originating from $I_1 \ldots I_n$ are present in C then we decide that the input program is safe. Otherwise we consider $Inv := \{I_1, \ldots, I_n\} \setminus C$ for the next iteration.

Lemma 1. Soundness: *If our algorithm terminates with the outcome "Safe", then the property ϕ is guaranteed to hold; if it terminates with "Unsafe" then ϕ is violated.*

Proof. In symbolic BMC, the program and the assert predicate is converted to a Boolean formula of the form $P \wedge \phi$, where ϕ is the negation of the asserted predicate. To this formula we conjoin additional constraints $I_1 \wedge \cdots \wedge I_n$ to get a Boolean formula $\underline{P} := P \wedge \phi \wedge I_1 \wedge \cdots \wedge I_n$. Here P, ϕ and $I_1 \ldots I_n$ are in CNF. We declare a given program as *Unsafe* when $\underline{P}$ is satisfiable. It is easy to see that if $\underline{P}$ is satisfiable then so is $P \wedge \phi$. This implies that $P \wedge \phi$ is also satisfiable and hence program is unsafe as ϕ is the negation of the asserted predicate. We mark a given program as *Safe* when $C \cap \{I_1 \ldots I_n\} = \emptyset$, where C is an unsatisfiable core. By definition, C is unsatisfiable and $C \subseteq \underline{P}$. Therefore we conclude that $C \subseteq (P \wedge \phi)$ as $C \subseteq \underline{P}$ and $C \cap \{I_1 \ldots I_n\} = \emptyset$. Since C is unsatisfiable $P \wedge \phi$ is also unsatisfiable as P and ϕ are in CNF.

This proves the soundness of our algorithm.

Lemma 2. Completeness: *Our algorithm always terminates for a finite-state concurrent program.*

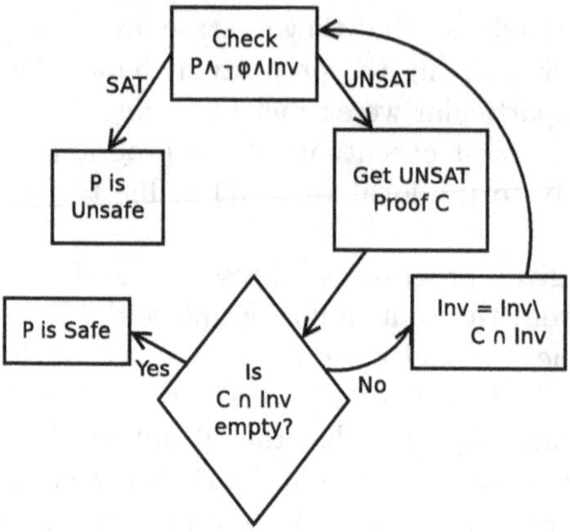

Fig. 2. Refinement flowchart

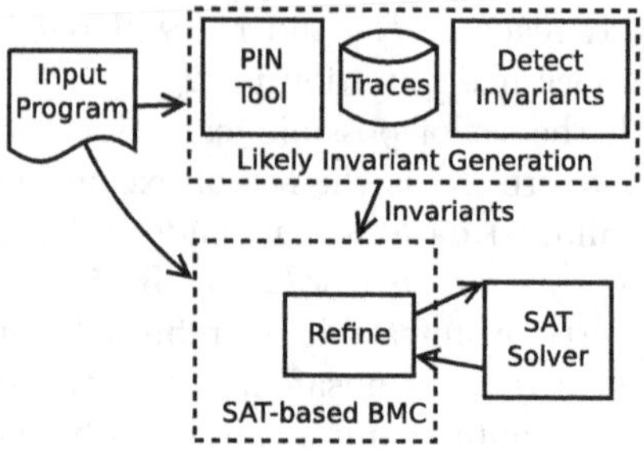

Fig. 3. Design of the tool

Proof. We start with $\underline{P} := P \wedge \phi \wedge I_1 \wedge \cdots \wedge I_n$. At each iteration we either decide safety of a program or consider $\{I_1 \ldots I_n\} \setminus (C \cap \{I_1 \ldots I_n\})$, where C is an unsatisfiable core. If we proceed without deciding about safety of the given program we will have $\underline{P} := P \wedge \phi$ after a maximum of n iterations. This formula is the original formula which can be decided. Hence, we always terminate in at most $n + 1$ iterations.

3 Implementation

Our tool operates in two stages, shown in Fig. 3. First, likely invariants are generated by dynamic analysis, which are used to construct an underapproximation of the input program. In the second stage the tool performs SAT-based bounded model checking and refinement on the underapproximated input program. In subsequent sections we provide details of each stage.

3.1 Likely Invariant Generation and Constraints

The compiled input program is passed to binary instrumentation built using PIN [5]. We instrument shared memory instructions to collect execution traces, which are analyzed to detect three classes of likely invariants following [6]. The generated invariants are sequences of tuples where each tuple consists of a location of the instruction in the source code, the name of the variable on which the instruction operates, and the type of instruction (read or write).

These invariants are passed to CBMC, together with the input program and unwinding depth, via newly added options. Option *--refine-cpu* indicates to CBMC to invoke our changed code path. Options *--invariant-strategy l* and *--invariant-file file-name* specify that likely invariants are to be read from *file-name* for underapproximation. These likely invariants are considered while constructing the *rf* relation: for reads appearing as likely invariants only writes that are present in the corresponding definition set are considered. In order to fall back to the original *rf* relation during refinement we add a switch variable while constructing the *rf* relation, which, when disabled, yields the original *rf* relation. For example, we construct the following formula: $switch_{v_1} \Rightarrow (r_{v_1} = w_{v_1}^{i_1} \vee w_{v_1}^{i_2} \vee \ldots w_{v_1}^{i_m}) \wedge \neg switch_{v_1} \Rightarrow (r_{v_1} = w_{v_1}^{1} \vee w_{v_1}^{2} \vee \ldots w_{v_1}^{n})$, where $r_{v_1} = w_{v_1}^{1} \vee w_{v_1}^{2} \vee \ldots w_{v_1}^{n}$ is the original *rf* relation, $w_{v_1}^{i_1} \ldots w_{v_1}^{i_m}$ are writes corresponding to r_{v_1} in the definition set and $w_{v_1}^{1} \ldots w_{v_1}^{n}$ is the actual set of writes in the program. These constraints along with the unwound program and property are converted to a Boolean formula [1].

3.2 Refinement

We have implemented the refinement algorithm of Fig. 3 in CBMC. Initially, all switch variables $switch_{v_i}$ are true. These constrain the *rf* relation as seen in Sect. 3.1, and will act as constraints $I_1 \ldots I_n$. We pass the Boolean formula constructed above to a SAT solver, which has the capability of generating an unsatisfiability proof. If the program is decided to be unsafe, a counterexample is returned. Otherwise we perform refinement as explained earlier.

4 Experiments

Our experiments address the following questions:

1. How effective are likely data-flow invariants in reducing the proof search space for verification? We measured the number of considered writes with our approach relative to the total possible writes of an unconstrained proof.
2. Does such a reduction in search space translate to a reduction in verification run time? We measure the SAT solver's time spent on a proof.

A reasonable question to ask related to the second item above is why can one expect SAT solver time to reduce by constraining proof search space. Note that we constrain search space by adding additional constraints (invariants) to the formula sent to the solver. Typically the distribution of solving times over degrees of constraining has a peak in the middle of the spectrum. That is, problems that are either under-constrained or over-constrained are easy because solvers encounter few conflicts. The latter because solver gets a solution mostly by propagation, the former because you get a solution mostly by making decisions only. The idea of adding additional constraints is to get us out of the middle of the peak towards the over-constrained side, which should make it easier for the solver although the formula is larger in size.

We ran our tool on a set of targeted benchmark programs as well as benchmark programs from SV-COMP (*pthread* and *pthread-atomic* directories). The targeted benchmarks were constructed based on concurrent algorithms that had interesting data-flow invariants, e.g., programs that exhibited a large number of writes in possible atomic sections and different properties. Our experiments were run on a system with an i3 CPU (1.70 GHz) and 4 GB RAM, running GNU/Linux OS. Our tool, the benchmark programs, and instructions to repeat our experiments are available in public [7]. For mining invariants, every program was executed to completion on random inputs and random interleaving for up to 50 execution traces. Since invariants were mined on limited runs there is no a-priori guarantee that they were true invariants. Table 1 shows the results corresponding to the targeted benchmark programs. We have experimented with both safe and unsafe programs and different unwindings as shown in columns labeled *Type* and *U*. The column *Writes Saved* indicates the total number of writes that were not considered when compared to the original encoding of CBMC. This is measured by taking the difference between the total number of writes that is considered in CBMC and the total number of writes considered with constraints for all reads. This will be 0 if we fall back to the original model after refinement (for example, *7.c*). The *Refinement* columns indicate the number of constraints added in the beginning, the number of constraints remaining when a decision was taken, and the total number of iterations completed. The overall time taken by the SAT solver for CBMC and our tool with likely invariants encoded as constraints, as explained in Sect. 3.1, are shown in columns *CBMC* and *LI*, respectively.

Our main observations are:

1. In all our targeted cases the mined invariants have been effective in reducing the proof search required to be considered as indicated by the numbers in the *Writes Saved* column. This shows that use of good invariants can have a potential impact in reducing proof complexity.
2. There has been a gain in speed in roughly half the number of cases (shown as bold face entries in *File* in Table 1).
3. However, the effect of the underapproximations on the reduction of the SAT solver time has been less significant. In some cases, we have observed that the SAT solver is slowed down even when there has been a significant reduction in the number of writes.

How can one explain observations 2 and 3, especially 3? SAT solver time is function of size of the formula as well as the number of variables. The formula representing the underapproximation is usually much larger (in terms of number of clauses) than the original model, which is one possible explanation for observation 3. To get evidence in support of this explanation, we constructed the underapproximated model more directly by eliminating the unnecessary writes at the partial-encoding itself (instead of adding them as clauses) resulting in smaller formulas. The *NoR* column shows the SAT numbers when run on this directly encoded model. As the numbers indicate this method of encoding reduces SAT time in most cases. There were a few exceptions shown by numbers in italics font. (*TO* indicates more than 200s.) One disadvantage of using this encoding is that it is not amenable for easy refinement.

Our results [8] on the SV-COMP benchmarks were mixed and not as good as for the targeted set. Since most SV-COMP benchmarks are stripped down to their minimal functionality, (1) the total number of memory accesses themselves were very small in most examples and (2) our dynamic analysis step produced very few invariants that could be used to cut down the partial read-write orders.

Table 1. Result of experiment on targeted benchmarks

File	Type	U	CBMC	LI	Refinement	Writes saved	NoR
1.c	Unsafe	10	14.06s	13.541s	87 to 87 in 1	1235/2390	*21.719s*
2.c	Unsafe	10	2.835s	2.034s	28 to 28 in 1	450/912	1.734s
3.c	Unsafe	20	21.127s	10.359s	58 to 58 in 1	1900/3727	*16.87s*
4.c	Safe	16	39.633s	23.987s	107 to 88 in 5	1266/4489	6.818s
5.c	Unsafe	16	28.273s	34.923s	93 to 93 in 1	2415/3710	5.813s
6.c	Unsafe	21	15.984s	11.416s	42 to 42 in 1	1720/3144	*12.832s*
7.c	Safe	6	48.716s	44.519s	22 to 0 in 4	0/599	0.598s
8.c	Unsafe	11	4.567s	5.909s	32 to 32 in 1	685/1194	5.41s
9.c	Unsafe	10	31.835s	17.196s	76 to 76 in 1	2115/3060	8.553s
10.c	Unsafe	10	101.484s	29.699s	76 to 76 in 1	1935/3060	*TO*
11.c	Unsafe	9	38.624s	20.81s	83 to 83 in 1	1744/2868	16.439s
12.c	Unsafe	9	62.895s	155.681s	68 to 68 in 1	1935/3060	3.03s
13.c	Safe	10	7.392s	10.993s	22 to 8 in 3	144/736	8.4s

5 Conclusions and Future Work

We have developed a sound and complete tool to formally verify concurrent ANSI-C programs by automatically constructing underapproximations using likely data-flow invariants and incrementally refining them to get efficient proofs.

Our experimental results show that the tool can lead to reductions in proof search space and verification time on programs the synchronized behaviors of which significantly constrain the possible read-write-orders that can be captured in the form of data-flow invariants. Producer-consumer-like programs, where consumers can only read from producers on a priority-based schedule, is one example that exhibits this characteristic. Our future work is aimed at eliminating some of the bottlenecks: (1) Alternate methods to encode the invariants without increasing size of the formulas, (2) Integrate an overapproximation step during refinement. (3) Interface with proficient open-source invariant mining tools. In related work, the use of underapproximations using number of interleavings as a refinement metric was proposed in [9]. Distinction of our work is in the use likely invariants for this purpose.

References

1. Alglave, J., Kroening, D., Tautschnig, M.: Partial orders for efficient bounded model checking of concurrent software. In: CAV (2013)

2. Qadeer, S., Wu, D.: KISS: keep it simple and sequential. ACM SIGPLAN (2004)
3. Tomasco, E., Inverso, O., Fischer, B., Torre, S., Parlato, G.: Verifying concurrent programs by memory unwinding. In: Baier, C., Tinelli, C. (eds.) TACAS 2015. LNCS, vol. 9035, pp. 551–565. Springer, Heidelberg (2015). doi:10.1007/978-3-662-46681-0_52
4. Yeolekar, A., Madhukar, K., Bhutada, D., Venkatesh, R.: Sequentialization using timestamps. In: Gopal, T.V., Jäger, G., Steila, S. (eds.) TAMC 2017. LNCS, vol. 10185, pp. 684–696. Springer, Cham (2017). doi:10.1007/978-3-319-55911-7_49
5. Luk, C.K., Cohn, R., Muth, R., Patil, H., Klauser, A., Lowney, G., Wallace, S., Reddi, V.J., Hazelwood, K.: Pin: Building customized program analysis tools with dynamic instrumentation. ACM SIGPLAN (2005)
6. Shi, Y., Park, S., Yin, Z., Lu, S., Zhou, Y., Chen, W., Zheng, W.: Do I use the wrong definition?: DeFuse: definition-use invariants for detecting concurrency and sequential bugs. ACM SIGPLAN (2010)
7. https://github.com/sumanthsprabhu/atva_tool
8. http://www.cmi.ac.in/%7Esumanth/dokuwiki/doku.php?id=invariants:underapproximation:experiments#sv-comp
9. Grumberg, O., Lerda, F., Strichman, O., Theobald, M.: Proof-guided underapproximation-widening for multi-process systems. ACM SIGPLAN (2005)

Neural Networks

Maximum Resilience of Artificial Neural Networks

Chih-Hong Cheng(✉), Georg Nührenberg(✉), and Harald Ruess

fortiss - An-Institut Technische Universität München,
Guerickestr. 25, 80805 Munich, Germany
{cheng,nuehrenberg,ruess}@fortiss.org

Abstract. The deployment of Artificial Neural Networks (ANNs) in safety-critical applications poses a number of new verification and certification challenges. In particular, for ANN-enabled self-driving vehicles it is important to establish properties about the resilience of ANNs to noisy or even maliciously manipulated sensory input. We are addressing these challenges by defining resilience properties of ANN-based classifiers as the maximum amount of input or sensor perturbation which is still tolerated. This problem of computing maximum perturbation bounds for ANNs is then reduced to solving mixed integer optimization problems (MIP). A number of MIP encoding heuristics are developed for drastically reducing MIP-solver runtimes, and using parallelization of MIP-solvers results in an almost linear speed-up in the number (up to a certain limit) of computing cores in our experiments. We demonstrate the effectiveness and scalability of our approach by means of computing maximum resilience bounds for a number of ANN benchmark sets ranging from typical image recognition scenarios to the autonomous maneuvering of robots.

1 Introduction

The deployment of Artificial Neural Networks (ANNs) in safety-critical applications such as medical image processing or semi-autonomous vehicles poses a number of new assurance, verification, and certification challenges [2,5]. For ANN-based end-to-end steering control of self-driving cars, for example, it is important to know how much noisy or even maliciously manipulated sensory input is tolerated [12]. Here we are addressing these challenges by establishing maximum and verified bounds for the resilience of given ANNs on these kinds of input disturbances.

More precisely, we are defining and computing safe perturbation bounds for multi-class ANN classifiers. This measure compares the relative ratio-ordering of multiple, so-called *softmax* output neurons for capturing scenarios where one only wants to consider inputs that classify to a certain class with high probability. The problem of finding minimal perturbation bounds is reduced to solving a corresponding *mixed-integer programming* (MIP). In particular, the encoding of some non-linear functions such as *ReLU* and *max-pooling* nodes require the

D. D'Souza and K. Narayan Kumar (Eds.): ATVA 2017, LNCS 10482, pp. 251–268, 2017.
DOI: 10.1007/978-3-319-68167-2_18

introduction of integer variables. These integer constraints are commonly handled by off-the-shelf MIP-solvers such as CPLEX[1] which are based on branch-and-bound algorithms. In the MIP reduction, a number of nonlinear expressions are linearized using a variant of the well-known *big-M* [8] encoding strategy. We also define a dataflow analysis [6] for generating relatively small big-M as the basis for speeding up MIP solving. Other important heuristics in encoding the MIP problem include the usage of solving several substantially simpler MIP problems for speeding up the overall generation of satisfying instances by the solver. Lastly, branch-and-bound is run in parallel on a number of computing cores.

We demonstrate the effectiveness and scalability of our approach and encoding heuristics by computing maximum perturbation bounds for benchmark sets such as MNIST [13] and agent games [14]. These cases studies include ANNs for image recognition and for high-level maneuver decisions for autonomous control of a robot. Using the heuristic encodings outlined above we experienced a speed-up of about two orders of magnitude compared with vanilla MIP encodings. Moreover, parallelization of branch-and-bound [23] on different computing cores can yield, up to a certain threshold, linear speed-ups using a high-performance parallelization framework.

The practical advantages of our approach for validating and qualifying ANNs for safety-relevant applications are manifold. First, perturbation bounds provide a formal interface between sensor sets and ANNs in that they provide a maximum tolerable bound on possible sensor errors. These *assume-guarantee* interfaces therefore form the basis for decoupling the design of sensor sets from the design of the classifier itself. Second, our method also computes minimally perturbed inputs of different classification, which might be included into ANN training sets for potentially improving classification results. Third, maximum perturbation bounds are a useful measure of the resilience of an ANN towards (adversarial) perturbation, and also for objectively comparing different ANNs. Last, large perturbation bounds are intuitively inversely related with the problem of *overfitting*, that is poor generalization to new inputs, which is a common issue with ANNs.

An overview of concrete problems and various approaches to the safety of machine learning is provided in [2]. We compare our results only with work that is most closely related to ours. Techniques including the generation of test cases [7,15,16] or strengthening the resistance of a network with respect to adversarial perturbation [17] are used for validating and improving ANNs. In contrast to our work, these methods do not actually establish verified properties on the input-output behavior of ANNs. Formal methods-based approaches for verifying ANNs include abstraction-refinement based approaches [18], bounded model checking for neural network for control problems [21] and neural network verification using SMT solvers or other specialized solvers [9,11,19]. Instead we rely on solving MIP problems and parallelization of branch-and-bound algorithms. In contrast to previous approaches we also go beyond verification and solve

[1] https://www-01.ibm.com/software/commerce/optimization/cplex-optimizer/.

optimization problems for ANNs for establishing maximum perturbation bounds. These kinds of problems might also be addressed in SMT-based approaches either by using binary search over SMT or by using SMT solvers that support optimization such as νZ [4], but it is not clear how well these approaches scale to complex ANNs. Recent work also targets ReLU [11] or application of a single image [3,9] (point-wise robustness or computing measures by taking samples). Our proposed resilience measure for ANNs goes beyond [3,9,11] in that it applies to multi-classification network using the softmax descriptor. Moreover, our proposed measure is a property of the classification network itself rather than just a property of a single image (as in [9]) or by only taking samples from the classifier without guarantee (as in [3]).

The paper is structured as follows. Section 2 reviews the foundations of feed-forward ANNs. Section 3 presents an encoding of various neurons in terms of linear constraints. Section 4 defines our measure for quantifying the resilience of an ANN, that is, its capability to tolerate random or even adversarial input perturbations. Section 5 summarizes our MIP encoding heuristics for substantially increasing the performance of the MIP-solver in establishing in minimal perturbation bounds of ANN. Finally, we present the results of some of our experiments in Sect. 6, and we describe possible improvements and extensions in Sect. 7.

2 Preliminaries

We introduce some basic concepts of *feed-forward artificial neural networks* (ANN) [1]. These networks consist of a sequence of layers labeled from $l = 0, 1, \ldots, L$, where 0 is the index of the *input layer*, L is the *output layer*, and all other layers are so-called *hidden layers*. For the purpose of this paper we assume that each input is of bounded domain. Superscripts $^{(l)}$ are used to index layer l-specific variables, but these superscripts may be omitted for input layers. Layers l are comprised of *nodes* $n_i^{(l)}$ (so-called neurons), for $i = 0, 1, \ldots, d^{(l)}$, where $d^{(l)}$ is the *dimension* of the layer l. By convention nodes of index 0 have a constant output 1; these *bias nodes* are commonly used for encoding activation thresholds of neurons. In a feed-forward net, nodes $n_j^{(l-1)}$ of layer $l-1$ are connected with nodes $n_i^{(l)}$ in layer l by means of directed edges of *weight* $w_{ji}^{(l)}$. For the purpose of this paper we are assuming that all weights in a network have fixed values, since we do not consider re-learning. Figure 1 illustrates a small feed-forward network structure with four layers, where each layer comes with a different type of node functions, which are also main ingredients of *convolutional neural networks*. These node functions are specified in Fig. 2. The first hidden layer of the network in Fig. 1 is a *fully-connected ReLU layer*. Node $n_2^{(1)}$, for example, computes the weighted linear sum of all inputs from the previous layer as $\mathsf{im}_2^{(1)}$, and outputs the maximum of 0 and this weighted sum. The second hidden layer is using *max-pooling* for down-sampling an input representation by reducing its dimensionality; node $n_1^{(2)}$, for example, just outputs the maximum of its inputs. Node $n_1^{(3)}$ in the output layer applies the sigmoid-shaped tan^{-1} on the weighted linear input sum.

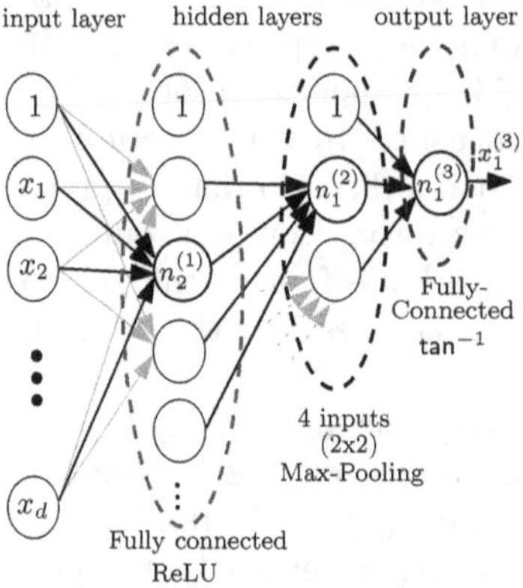

Fig. 1. An illustration of how a neural network is defined.

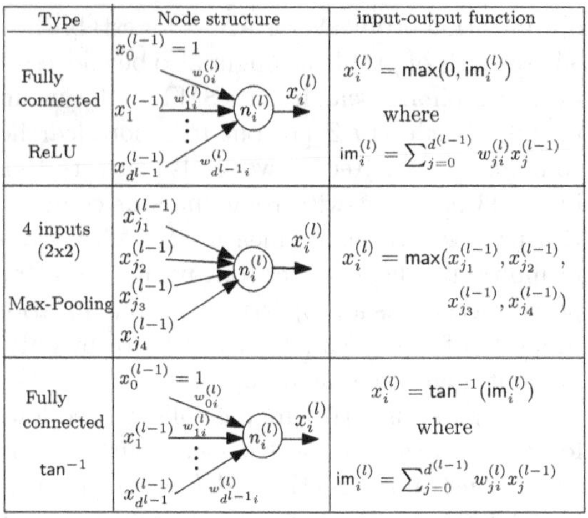

Type
Node structure
input-output function
Fully connected ReLU
$x_i^{(l)} = \max(0, \mathrm{im}_i^{(l)})$
where
$\mathrm{im}_i^{(l)} = \sum_{j=0}^{d^{(l-1)}} w_{ji}^{(l)} x_j^{(l-1)}$
4 inputs (2x2) Max-Pooling
$x_i^{(l)} = \max(x_{j_1}^{(l-1)}, x_{j_2}^{(l-1)}, x_{j_3}^{(l-1)}, x_{j_4}^{(l-1)})$
Fully connected tan^{-1}
$x_i^{(l)} = \tan^{-1}(\mathrm{im}_i^{(l)})$
where
$\mathrm{im}_i^{(l)} = \sum_{j=0}^{d^{(l-1)}} w_{ji}^{(l)} x_j^{(l-1)}$

Fig. 2. Input-output function neurons.

Given an input to the network these node functions are applied successively from layer 0 to $L - 1$ for computing the corresponding network output at layer L. For $l = 1$ to L we use $x_i^{(l)}$ to denote the output value of node $n_i^{(l)}$ and $x_i^{(l)}(a_1, \ldots, a_d)$ denotes the output value $x_i^{(l)}$ for the input $a_1, \ldots, a_d$, sometimes abbreviated by $x_i^{(l)}(a)$.

For the purpose of multi-class classification, outputs in layer L are often transformed into a *probability distribution* by means of the softmax function

$$\frac{\mathrm{e}^{x_i^{(L-1)}}}{\sum_{j=1,\ldots,d^L} \mathrm{e}^{x_j^{(L-1)}}}.$$

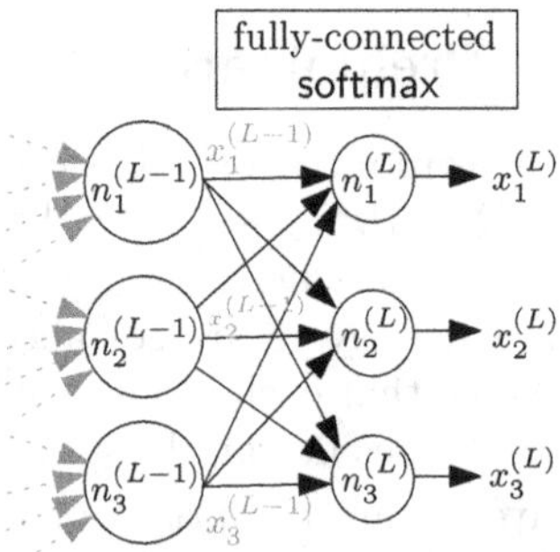

Fig. 3. Topological structure for an output layer with 3 neurons using softmax.

In this way, the output $x_i^{(L)}$ is interpreted as the probability of the input to be in class i. For the inputs $x_1^{(L-1)} = -1$, $x_2^{(L-1)} = 2$, $x_3^{(L-1)} = 3$ of the nodes in Fig. 3, for example, the corresponding outputs $(0.0132, 0.2654, 0.7214)$ for $(x_1^{(L)}, x_2^{(L)}, x_3^{(L)})$ sum up to 1.

3 Arithmetic Encoding of Artificial Neural Networks

In a first step, we are encoding the behavior of ANNs in terms of linear arithmetic constraints. In addition to [11] we are also considering tan^{-1}, max-pooling and softmax nodes as commonly found in many ANNs in practice. These encodings are based on the input-output behavior of every node in the network, and the main challenge is to handle the non-linearities, which are arising from non-linear activation functions (e.g., ReLU and tan^{-1}), max-pooling and softmax nodes.

Constraints for ReLU and tan^{-1} nodes as defined in Fig. 2 are separated into, first, an equality constraint (1) for the intermediate value $\mathsf{im}_i^{(l)}$ and, second, several linear constraints for encoding the non-linear behavior of these nodes.

$$\mathsf{im}_i^{(l)} = \sum_{j=0,\dots,d^{(l-1)}} w_{ji}^{(l)} x_j^{(l-1)} \tag{1}$$

We now describe the encoding of the non-linear functions ($x_i^{(l)} = \mathsf{max}(0, \mathsf{im}_i^{(l)})$ or $x_i^{(l)} = \mathsf{tan}^{-1}(\mathsf{im}_i^{(l)})$).

Encoding ReLU activation function. The non-linearity in ReLU constraints $x_i^{(l)} = \mathsf{max}(0, \mathsf{im}_i^{(l)})$ is handled using the well-known big-M method [8], which introduces a binary integer variable $b_i^{(l)}$ together with a positive constant $M_i^{(l)}$ such that $-M_i^{(l)} \leq \mathsf{im}_i^{(l)}$ and $x_i^{(l)} \leq M_i^{(l)}$ for all possible values of $\mathsf{im}_i^{(l)}$ and $x_i^{(l)}$. A derivation of the following reduction is listed in the appendix.

Proposition 1. *$x_i^{(l)} = \mathsf{max}(0, \mathsf{im}_i^{(l)})$ iff the constraints* (2a) *to* (4b) *hold.*

$$x_i^{(l)} \geq 0 \tag{2a}$$
$$x_i^{(l)} \geq im_i^{(l)} \tag{2b}$$

$$im_i^{(l)} - b_i^{(l)} M_i^{(l)} \leq 0 \tag{3a}$$
$$im_i^{(l)} + (1 - b_i^{(l)}) M_i^{(l)} \geq 0 \tag{3b}$$

$$x_i^{(l)} \leq im_i^{(l)} + (1 - b_i^{(l)}) M_i^{(l)} \tag{4a}$$
$$x_i^{(l)} \leq b_i^{(l)} M_i^{(l)} \tag{4b}$$

The efficiency of a MIP-solver via big-M encoding heavily depends on the size of $M_i^{(l)}$, because MIP-solvers typically relax binary integer variables to real-valued variables, resulting in a weak LP-relaxation for large big-Ms. It is therefore essential to choose relatively small values for $M_i^{(l)}$. We apply static analysis [6] based on interval arithmetic for propagating the bounded input values through the network, as the basis for generating "good" values for $M_i^{(l)}$.

Max-Pooling. The output $x_i^{(l)}$ of a max-pooling node is rewritten as $x_i^{(l)} = \mathsf{max}(\mathsf{im}_1, \mathsf{im}_2)$, where $\mathsf{im}_1 = \mathsf{max}(x_{j_1}^{(l-1)}, x_{j_2}^{(l-1)})$ and $\mathsf{im}_2 = \mathsf{max}(x_{j_3}^{(l-1)}, x_{j_4}^{(l-1)})$. Encoding the $\mathsf{max}(x_1, x_2)$ function into MIP constraints is accomplished by introducing three binary integer variables to encode $y = \mathsf{max}(x_1, x_2)$ using the big-M method.

Property-directed encoding of softmax. The exponential function in the definition of softmax, of course, can not be encoded into a linear MIP constraint. However, using the proposition below, one confirms that if the property to be analyzed does not consider the concrete value of output values from neurons but only the ratio ordering, then (1) it suffices to omit the construction of the output layer, and (2) one may rewrite the property by replacing each $x_i^{(L)}$ by $x_i^{(L-1)}$.

Proposition 2. *Given a feed-forward ANN with* softmax *output layer and a constant $\alpha > 0$, then for all $i, j \in \{1, \ldots, d^{(L)}\}$:*

$$x_{i_1}^{(L)} \geq \alpha\, x_{i_2}^{(L)} \Leftrightarrow x_{i_1}^{(L-1)} \geq \ln(\alpha) + x_{i_2}^{(L-1)}.$$

This equivalence is simply derived by using the definition of softmax, multiplying by the positive denominator, and by applying the logarithm and the resulting inequality. The derivation is listed in the appendix.

Encoding tan^{-1} *with error bounds.* The handling of non-linearity in $\mathsf{tan}^{-1}(\mathsf{im})$ is based on results in digital signal processing for piece-wise approximating $\mathsf{tan}^{-1}(\mathsf{im})$ with quadratic constraints and error bounds. In case $-1 \leq \mathsf{im} \leq 1$ the quadratic approximation methods (Eq. (7) of [20]) are used, and $\mathsf{tan}^{-1}(\mathsf{im})$ is approximated by $\frac{\pi}{4}\mathsf{im} + 0.273\,\mathsf{im}(1 - |\mathsf{im}|)$ with a maximum error smaller than 0.0038. The absolute value $|\mathsf{im}|$ in the formula is removed by encoding case splits between $\mathsf{im} \geq 0$ and $\mathsf{im} < 0$ using big-M methods. Otherwise, when considering the case $\mathsf{im} > 1$ or $\mathsf{im} < -1$, the symmetry condition of tan^{-1} [22] states that (1) if $\mathsf{im} > 0$ then $\mathsf{tan}^{-1}(\mathsf{im}) + \mathsf{tan}^{-1}(\frac{1}{\mathsf{im}}) = \frac{\pi}{2}$, and (2) if $\mathsf{im} < 0$ then $\mathsf{tan}^{-1}(\mathsf{im}) + \mathsf{tan}^{-1}(\frac{1}{\mathsf{im}}) = -\frac{\pi}{2}$. This implies that we can create a variable im_{inv} with a constraint that $\mathsf{im}_{inv}\,\mathsf{im} = 1$, i.e., variable im_{inv} is the inverse of im. By utilizing the fact that $-1 \leq \mathsf{im}_{inv} \leq 1$, the value of $\mathsf{tan}^{-1}(\mathsf{im}_{inv})$ can be computed by the formula in (i).

Moreover, case splits are encoded using the big-M method as outlined above. Since quadratic terms are used, our approach for handling tan^{-1} nodes requires solving *mixed integer quadratic constraint problem* (MIQCP) problems.

Using these approximations for $\mathsf{tan}^{-1}(\mathsf{im}_i)$, we obtain lower and upper bounds for the value of the node variable x_i, where the interval between lower and upper bound is determined by the approximation error of tan^{-1}. Since the approximation error propagates through the network and using lower and upper bounds instead of an equality constraint relaxes the problem, our method computes approximations for the measure when it is used for ANNs with tan^{-1} as activation function.

Pre-processing based on dataflow analysis. We use interval arithmetic to obtain relatively small values for big-M, in order to avoid a weak LP-relaxation of the MIP. Interval bounds for the values of $x_i^{(l)}$ are denoted by $[\mathsf{Lo}(x_i^{(l)}), \mathsf{Up}(x_i^{(l)})]$. We are assuming that all input values (at layer $l = 0$) are bounded, and the output of bias nodes is restricted by the singleton $[1, 1]$ (the value of the bias is given by the weight of a bias node). Interval bounds for the values of node outputs

$x_i^{(l)}$ are obtained from the interval bounds of connected nodes from the previous layers by means of interval arithmetic.

The output $x_i^{(l)}$ of ReLU nodes is defined by $\mathsf{im}_i^{(l)} = \sum_{j=0,\ldots,d^{(l-1)}} w_{ji}^{(l)} x_j^{(l-1)}$ and the ReLU function $\mathsf{max}(0, \mathsf{im}_i^{(l)})$. Therefore, interval bounds for $x_i^{(l)}$ are computed by first considering the interval bounds $\mathsf{Lo}(\mathsf{im}_i^{(l)})$ and $\mathsf{Up}(\mathsf{im}_i^{(l)})$, which are determined by weights of the linear sum and the bounds on $x_j^{(l-1)}$. The bounds $\mathsf{Lo}(\mathsf{im}_i^{(l)})$ and $\mathsf{Up}(\mathsf{im}_i^{(l)})$ are obtained from interval arithmetic as follows:

$$\mathsf{Lo}(\mathsf{im}_i^{(l)}) = \sum_{j=0,\ldots,d^{(l-1)}} \mathsf{min}\left(w_{ij}^{(l)} \cdot \mathsf{Lo}(x_j^{(l-1)}), w_{ij}^{(l)} \cdot \mathsf{Up}(x_j^{(l-1)})\right)$$

$$\mathsf{Up}(\mathsf{im}_i^{(l)}) = \sum_{j=0,\ldots,d^{(l-1)}} \mathsf{max}\left(w_{ij}^{(l)} \cdot \mathsf{Lo}(x_j^{(l-1)}), w_{ij}^{(l)} \cdot \mathsf{Up}(x_j^{(l-1)})\right).$$

Given $\mathsf{Lo}(\mathsf{im}_i^{(l)})$ and $\mathsf{Up}(\mathsf{im}_i^{(l)})$ the bounds on $x_j^{(l)}$ are derived using the definition of ReLU, i.e.,

$$[\mathsf{Lo}(x_i^{(l)}), \mathsf{Up}(x_i^{(l)})] = [\mathsf{max}(0, \mathsf{Lo}(\mathsf{im}_i^{(l)})), \mathsf{max}(0, \mathsf{Up}(\mathsf{im}_i^{(l)}))].$$

Note that if $\mathsf{Lo}(x_i^{(l)}) \geq 0$ or $\mathsf{Up}(x_i^{(l)}) \leq 0$ these bounds suffice to determine which case of the piece-wise linear ReLU function applies. In this way, the constraints (2)–(4) maybe dropped and the value of $x_i^{(l)}$ is directly encoded using linear constraints, which reduces the number of binary variables. See Fig. 4 for an example of dataflow analysis.

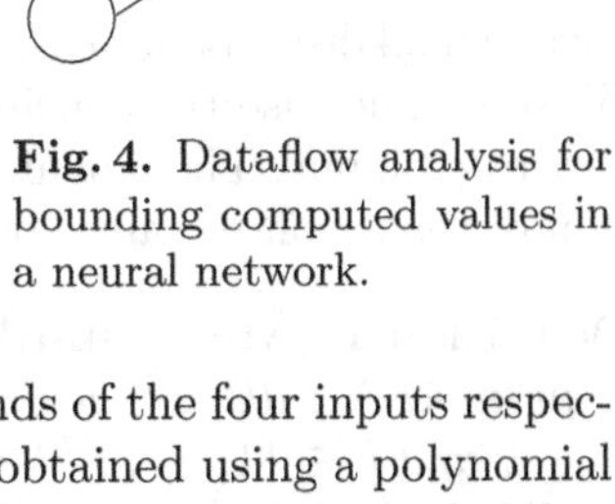

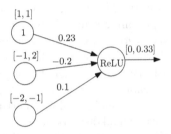

Fig. 4. Dataflow analysis for bounding computed values in a neural network.

In the case of max-pooling nodes, the output $x_i^{(l)}$ is simply the maximum $\mathsf{max}(x_{j_1}^{(l-1)}, x_{j_2}^{(l-1)}, x_{j_3}^{(l-1)}, x_{j_4}^{(l-1)})$ of its four inputs. Therefore, the bounds $\mathsf{Lo}_{x_i^{(l)}}$ and $\mathsf{Up}_{x_i^{(l)}}$ on the output are given by the maximum of the lower and uppers bounds of the four inputs respectively. Interval bounds of the outputs for tan^{-1} are obtained using a polynomial approximation for tan^{-1}. Finally, the output of $\mathsf{softmax}$ nodes is a probability in $[0, 1]$ which might also be further refined using interval arithmetic. These bounds on $\mathsf{softmax}$ nodes, however, are not used in our encodings, because of the property-driven encoding of $\mathsf{softmax}$ output layers as described previously.

4 Perturbation Bounds

We define concrete measures for quantifying the resilience of multi-classification neural networks with $\mathsf{softmax}$ output neurons. This measure for resilience is defined over all possible inputs of the network. In particular, our developments

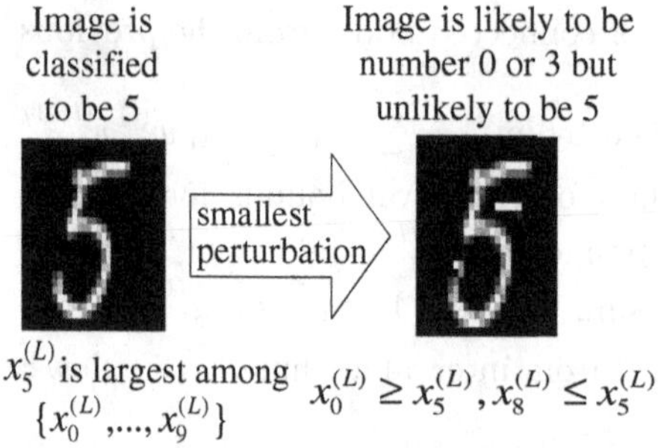

Fig. 5. Finding the smallest possible perturbation for a multi-class classifier to loose confidence.

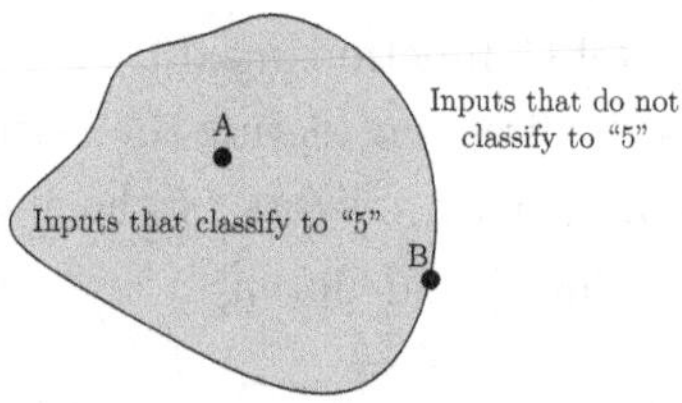

Fig. 6. Two images A, B that both classify to number 5.

do not depend on probability distributions of training and test data as in previous work [3]. Maximum resilience of these ANNs is obtained by means of solving corresponding MIP problems (or MIQCPs in the case of $\tan^{-1}$ activation functions).

We illustrate the underlying principles of maximum resilience using examples from the MNIST database [13] for digit recognition of input images (see Fig. 5). Input images in MNIST are of dimension 24×24 and are represented as a vector $a_1, \ldots, a_{576}$. Input layers of ANN-based multi-digit classifiers for MNIST therefore consist of 576 input neurons, and the output layer is comprised of 10 softmax neurons. Let the output $x_0^{(L)}, \ldots, x_9^{(L)}$ at the last layer be the computed probabilities for an input image to be classified to characters '0' to '9'.

To formally define a perturbation, we allow each input a_i $(i = 1, \ldots, d)$ to have a small disturbance ϵ_i, so the input after perturbation is $(a_1+\epsilon_1, \ldots, a_d+\epsilon_d)$. We sometimes use the concise notation of $a + \epsilon := (a_1 + \epsilon_1, \ldots, a_d + \epsilon_d)$ for the perturbed input. The global value of the perturbation is obtained by taking the sum of the absolute values of each disturbance ϵ_i, i.e., $|\epsilon_1| + |\epsilon_2| + \ldots + |\epsilon_d|$.

Definition 1 (Maximum Perturbation Bound for m-th classifier). *For a given ANN with $d^{(L)}$ neurons in a* softmax *output layer and given constants $\alpha \geq 1$ and $k \in \{1, \ldots, d^{(L)} - 1\}$, we define the* maximum perturbation bound for the m-th classifier, *denoted by Φ_m,*[2] *to be the maximum value such that:*

> *For all inputs $a = (a_1, \ldots, a_d)$ where $x_m^{(L)}(a) \geq \alpha \cdot x_j^{(L)}(a)$ on all other classes $j \in \{1, \ldots, d^{(L)}\} \setminus \{m\}$, we have that for all perturbations $\epsilon = (\epsilon_1, \epsilon_2, \ldots, \epsilon_d)$ where $|\epsilon_1|+|\epsilon_2|+\ldots+|\epsilon_d| < \Phi_m$, there exist at most $k - 1$ classes $j' \in \{0, 1 \ldots, d^{(L)}\}$ such that $x_m^{(L)}(a+\epsilon) \leq x_{j'}^{(L)}(a+\epsilon)$.*

Intuitively, the bound Φ_m guarantees that for all inputs that strongly (defined by α) classify to class m, if the total amount of perturbation is limited to a value

[2] For clarity, we usually omit the dependency of Φ_m from α.

strictly below Φ_m, then either (1) the perturbed input can still be classified as m, or (2) the probability of classifying to m is among the k highest probabilities. Dually, Φ_m is the smallest value such that there exists an input that originally classifies to m, for which the computed probability for class m may *not be among the k highest* after being perturbed with value greater than or equal to Φ_m. Figure 5 illustrates an example of an MNIST image being perturbed, where the neural network considers the perturbed image to be '0' or '3' with at least the probability of being a '5'. The "not among the k highest" property is an indicator that the confidence of classifying to class m has decreased under perturbation, as the perturbed input can be interpreted as at least k other classes. In our experiment evaluations below we used the fixed value $k = 2$.

Constant $\alpha \geq 1$ may be interpreted as indicating the level of confidence of being classified to a class m. When setting α to 1, the analysis takes all inputs for which the probability of class m is greater than or equal to the probabilities of the other classes. Since there might exist an image that has the same probability for all classes, setting $\alpha = 1$ may result in a maximum perturbation of zero. Increasing k helps to avoid this effect, because it requires that at most $k - 1$ other classes have probabilities greater than or equal to the probility of m. By picking an $\alpha > 1$ low-confidence inputs are removed and part (II) of Definition 1 forces the perturbation to be greater than zero. E.g., assume if point B in Fig. 6 is classified to '5' with probability 0.35 and to '0' with probability 0.34, then even by setting $\alpha = 1.1$, point B will not be considered in the analysis. By setting α to 25 one already only considers inputs that classifies to m with probability higher than 0.95.

Provided that Φ_m can be computed for each class m (as shown below), one defines a measure for safe perturbation by taking the minimum of all Φ_m, and the measure is computed by computing each Φ_m independently.

Definition 2 (Perturbation Bound for ANN). *For an ANN with L layers and $d^{(L)}$* softmax *neurons in the output layer, a given $\alpha \geq 1$, $k \in \{1, \ldots, d^{(L)} - 1\}$, and Φ_m the perturbation bound for the m-th classifier of this ANN from Definition 1, the* perturbation bound for ANN *is defined as $\Xi :=$ min$(\Phi_1, \ldots, \Phi_{d^L})$.*

Based on the dual interpretation above of Definition 1 we are now ready to encode the problem of finding Φ_m in terms of the following optimization problem, where $a = (a_1, \ldots, a_d)$ and $a + \epsilon = (a_1 + \epsilon_1, \ldots, a_d + \epsilon_d)$.

$$\text{minimize} \sum_{i=1,\ldots,d} |\epsilon_i|$$

subject to

$$x_m^{(L)}(a) \geq \alpha x_i^{(L)}(a) \qquad \forall i \in \{1, \ldots, d^L\} \setminus m$$

$$\bigvee_{\substack{I \subseteq \{1,\ldots,d^L\} \setminus m \\ |I| = k}} \quad \bigwedge_{\forall i \in I} x_m^{(L)}(a + \epsilon) \leq x_i^{(L)}(a + \epsilon)$$

and subject to constraints (1)–(4) for ANN encoding.

(5)

Proposition 3. *For a given $\alpha \geq 1$ and $k \in \{1, \ldots, d^{(L)} - 1\}$, the optimal value of the optimization problem (5) as stated above equals Φ_m. For ANNs using tan^{-1} problem (5) yields an under-approximation $\Phi'_m \leq \Phi_m$, because the feasible region is relaxed due to the approximation of tan^{-1}.*

The first set of conjunctive constraints specifies that the input $a = (a_1, \ldots, a_d)$ strongly classifies to m (i.e., satisfies condition I in Definition 1), while the second set of disjunctive constraints specifies that by feeding the image after perturbation, the neural network outputs that at least k classes in I are more likely (or equally likely) than class m (i.e., the second condition in Definition 1 is violated). Therefore, for input $a = (a_1, \ldots, a_d)$ and its associated perturbation $\epsilon = (\epsilon_1, \ldots, \epsilon_d)$, we have that $\sum_{i=1,\ldots,d} |\epsilon_i| \geq \Phi_m$. By computing the minimum objective of $\sum_{i=1,\ldots,d} |\epsilon_i|$ satisfying the constraints we obtain $\sum_{i=1,\ldots,d} |\epsilon_i| = \Phi_m$.

We now address the following issues in order to transform optimization problem (5) into a MIP: (1) the objective is not linear due to the introduction of the absolute value function, (2) the non-linearity of $\mathsf{softmax}$ due to the function $x_i^{(L)} = \mathrm{e}^{x_i^{(L-1)}} / \sum_{j=1,\ldots,d^L} \mathrm{e}^{x_j^{(L-1)}}$, and (3) the disjunction in the second set of constraints.

(i) Transforming objectives. Since the objective $|\epsilon_1| + |\epsilon_2| \ldots, |\epsilon_d|$ in problem (5) is not linear, we create new variables $\epsilon_i^{\mathsf{abs}}$ in optimization problem (6), where $i \in \{1, \ldots, d\}$, such that every $\epsilon_i^{\mathsf{abs}}$ is greater than ϵ_i and $-\epsilon_i$. Whenever the value is minimized, we have that $\epsilon_i^{\mathsf{abs}} = |\epsilon_i|$.

(ii) Removing $\mathsf{softmax}$ *output layer.* Optimization problem (5) contains the inequality $x_m^{(L)}(a_1, \ldots, a_d) \geq \alpha x_i^{(L)}(a_1, \ldots, a_d)$. It follows from Proposition 2 that replacing this inequality with $x_m^{(L-1)}(a_1, \ldots, a_d) \geq \ln(\alpha) + x_i^{(L-1)}(a_1, \ldots, a_d)$ is sufficient, thereby omitting the exponential function.

(iii) Transforming disjunctive constraints. The disjunctive constraint in problem (5) guarantees at least k classifications with probability equal or higher as m. We rewrite it by introducing a binary variable c_i for each class $i \neq m$. Then we use (1) an integer constraint $\sum_{i=1,\ldots,d, i \neq m} c_i \geq k$ to select k classifications and (2) the big-M method to enforce that if classification i is selected (i.e., $c_i = 1$), the probability of classifying to i is higher or equal to the probability of classifying to m.

By applying the transformations (i)–(iii) to the optimization problem (5) we obtain problem (6), which is a MIP, and it follows from Proposition 3 that maximum perturbations bounds can be obtained by solving the MIP in (6).

Theorem 1. *For a given $\alpha \geq 1$ and $k \in \{1, \ldots, d^{(L)} - 1\}$, the optimum of the MIP in (6) equals Φ_m for ANNs with ReLU nodes and* $\mathsf{softmax}$ *output layer. For ANNs using tan^{-1} it yields an under-approximation.*

$$\begin{aligned}
&\text{minimize} \quad \Phi_m := \textstyle\sum_{i\in\{1,\dots,d\}} \epsilon_i^{\mathsf{abs}} \\
&\text{subject to} \\
&x_m^{(L-1)}(a) \geq \ln(\alpha) + x_i^{(L-1)}(a) && \forall i \in \{1,\dots,d^L\}\setminus m \\
&\sum_{i\in\{1,\dots,d^L\}\setminus m} c_i \geq k \\
&x_i^{(L-1)}(a+\epsilon) \geq x_m^{(L-1)}(a+\epsilon) - M(1-c_i) && \forall i \in \{1,\dots,d^L\}\setminus m \\
&\epsilon_i^{\mathsf{abs}} \geq \epsilon_i && \forall i \in \{1,\dots,d\} \\
&\epsilon_i^{\mathsf{abs}} \geq -\epsilon_i && \forall i \in \{1,\dots,d\} \\
&c_i \in \{0,1\} && \forall i \in \{1,\dots,d^L\}\setminus m
\end{aligned}$$

and subject to constraints (1)–(4) for ANN encoding.

(6)

5 Heuristic Problem Encodings

We list some simple but essential heuristics for efficiently solving MIP problems for the verification of ANNs. Notice that these heuristics are not restricted to computing the resilience of ANNs, and may well be applicable for other verification tasks involving ANNs.

1. Smaller big-M s by looking back at multiple layers. The dataflow analysis in Sect. 3 essentially views neurons at the same layer to be independent. Here we propose a more fine-grained analysis by considering a fixed number of predecessor layers at once. Finding the bound for the output of a neuron $x_i^{(l)}$, for example, can be understood as solving a substantially smaller MIP problem by considering neurons from layer $l-1$ and $l-2$ when considering two preceding layers. These MIP problems are independent for each node in these layers and can therefore be solved in parallel. For each node, we first set the upper bound as a variable to be maximized in the objective, and trigger the MIP-solver to find such a value. Relations over integer binary variables can be derived by applying similar techniques. Notice that these MIPs only generate correct lower and upper bounds if they can be solved to optimality.

2. Branching priorities. This encoding heuristics uses the given structure of feed-forward ANNs in that binary integer variables originating from lower layers are prioritized for branching. Intuitively, variables from the first hidden layer only depend on the input and it influences all other binary integer variables corresponding to neurons in deeper layers.

3. Constraint generation from samples and solver initialization. For computing Φ_m on complex systems via MIP, we use the following three-step process. First, find an input assignment $(a_1^{\mathsf{ini}}, \ldots, a_d^{\mathsf{ini}})$ such that the probability of classifying to m is α times larger, i.e., $x_m^{(L)}(a_1^{\mathsf{ini}}, \ldots, a_d^{\mathsf{ini}}) \geq \alpha x_j^{(L)}(a_1^{\mathsf{ini}}, \ldots, a_d^{\mathsf{ini}})$ for all $j = 1, \ldots, d^{(L)}, j \neq m$. Finding $(a_1^{\mathsf{ini}}, \ldots, a_d^{\mathsf{ini}})$ is equivalent to solving a substantially simpler MIP problem without introducing variables $\epsilon_1, \ldots, \epsilon_d$ and $\epsilon_1^{\mathsf{abs}}, \ldots, \epsilon_d^{\mathsf{abs}}$. Second, use Eq. (6) to compute the minimum perturbation by considering the domain to be size 1, i.e., $\{(a_1^{\mathsf{ini}}, \ldots, a_d^{\mathsf{ini}})\}$. As the domain is restricted to a single input, all variables $a_1^{\mathsf{ini}}, \ldots, a_d^{\mathsf{ini}}$ in Eq. (6) are replaced by constants $a_1^{\mathsf{ini}}, \ldots, a_d^{\mathsf{ini}}$. This also yields substantially simpler MIP problems, and the computed bound is denoted by Φ_m^{ini}. Third, and finally, initialize the MIP-solver by using the computed values from steps 1 and 2, such that the search directly starts with a feasible solution with objective Φ_m^{ini}. Also, the constraint $-\Phi_m^{\mathsf{ini}} \leq \sum_{i=1,\ldots,d} \epsilon_i \leq \Phi_m^{\mathsf{ini}}$, as $\sum_{i=1,\ldots,d} \epsilon_i \leq \sum_{i=1,\ldots,d} |\epsilon_i| = \Phi_m \leq \Phi_m^{\mathsf{ini}}$, can be further added to restrict the search space.

6 Implementation and Evaluation

We implemented an experimental platform in C++ for verifying and computing perturbation bounds for neural networks, which is based on IBM CPLEX Optimization Studio 12.7 (academic version) for MIP solving. We used three different benchmark sets as the basis for our evaluations: (1) MNIST[3] for number characterization, (2) agent games[4], and (3) deeptraffic for simulating highway overtaking scenarios[5]. These benchmarks are denoted by $\mathrm{I}_{\mathrm{MNIST}}$, $\mathrm{I}_{\mathrm{Agent}}$, and $\mathrm{I}_{\mathrm{deeptraffic}}$ respectively, in the following. For each of the benchmarks we created neural networks with different numbers of hidden layers and numbers of neurons, which are shown in Tables 1 and 2. All the networks were trained using ConvNetJS [10].

- Agents in agent games have 9 sensors, each pointing into a different direction and returning the distances to an apple, poison or a wall, which amounts to the 27 inputs. Neural networks of various size were trained for an agent that gets rewarded for eating red things (apples) and gets negative reward when it eats green things (poison).
- deeptraffic is used as a gamified simulation environment for highway traffic. The controller is trained based on a grid sensor map, and it outputs high-level driving decisions to be taken such as switch lane, accelerate or decelerate.
- For MNIST digit recognition [13] has 576 input nodes for the pixels of a gray-scale image, where we trained three networks with different numbers of neurons in the hidden layers.

[3] http://cs.stanford.edu/people/karpathy/convnetjs/demo/mnist.html.
[4] http://cs.stanford.edu/people/karpathy/convnetjs/demo/rldemo.html.
[5] http://selfdrivingcars.mit.edu/deeptrafficjs/.

Table 1. Execution time for verifying perturbation problem over a single input instance. Time out (`t.o.`) is set to be 1 h. Agent games turn out to be quite simple to solve, therefore no heuristics are being applied (`n.a.`).

ID	Instance & output m	# inputs; # neurons in hidden layers	δ	Status	Time(s) $M = 10^4$	Time(s) dataflow	Time(s) heuristic 1.+2.
0	I_{Agent} m=0	27; 300	0.025	`inf`	1.9	0.1	`n.a.`
			0.05	`feas`	7.2	26.9	`n.a.`
1	$I^{2\times 50}_{\text{MNIST}}$ m=0	576; 100	0.075	`inf`	477.8	186.8	35.1
2			0.1	`inf`	`t.o.`	`t.o.`	2015.9
3	$I^{2\times 50}_{\text{MNIST}}$ m=1	576; 100	0.025	`inf`	516.8	763.9	40.5
4			0.05	`feas`	0.5	0.3	328.3
5	$I^{2\times 50}_{\text{MNIST}}$ m=3	576; 100	0.025	`inf`	0.3	0.3	18.7
6			0.05	`inf`	303.9	405.1	68.9
7			0.075	`feas`	0.3	0.4	151.6
8	$I^{2\times 50}_{\text{MNIST}}$ m=8	576; 100	0.025	`inf`	0.3	0.3	16.5
9			0.05	`inf`	146.0	193.5	37.2
10			0.075	`feas`	1.1	1.2	185.3
11	$I^{4\times 50}_{\text{MNIST}}$ m=0	576; 200	0.025	`inf`	464.7	489.4	38.08
12			0.05	`inf`	`t.o.`	`t.o.`	65.5
13	$I^{4\times 50}_{\text{MNIST}}$ m=1	576; 200	0.025	`inf`	`t.o.`	`t.o.`	128.21
14			0.05	`feas`	`t.o.`	261.4	3197.6
15	$I^{4\times 50}_{\text{MNIST}}$ m=2	576; 200	0.025	`inf`	`t.o.`	`t.o.`	54.32
16			0.05	`unkown`	`t.o.`	`t.o.`	`t.o.`
17	$I^{4\times 50}_{\text{MNIST}}$ m=3	576; 200	0.025	`feas`	2.7	2.7	45.88
18			0.05	`feas`	12.5	18.8712	115.1
19	$I^{4\times 50}_{\text{MNIST}}$ m=4	576; 200	0.025	`inf`	`t.o.`	`t.o.`	66.43
20			0.05	`unkown`	`t.o.`	`t.o.`	`t.o.`

In our experimental validation we focus on efficiency gains of our MIP encodings and parallelization for verifying neural networks, and the computation of perturbation bound by means of the optimization problem stated in Eq. (6).

Evaluation of MIP Encodings. To understand how dataflow analysis and our heuristic encodings reduce the overall execution time, we have created synthetic benchmarks where for each example, we only ask for a given input instance (e.g., an image) that classifies to m, whether the perturbation bound is below δ. By restricting ourselves to only verify a single input instance and by not minimizing δ, the problem under verification (*local robustness* related to an input) is substantially simpler and is similar to those stated in [3,11]. Table 1 gives a summary over results being evaluated using Google Computing Engine (16 CPU and 60 GB RAM) by only allowing 12 threads to be used. Compared to a naïve approach that sets $M_i^{(l)}$ uniformly to a large constant, applying dataflow analysis can bring benefits for instances that take a longer time to solve. The first two heuristics we have implemented are useful for solving some very difficult problems. Admittedly, it can also result in longer solutions times for simpler instances, but as our ultimate goal is for scalability such an issue is currently minor. More difficult instances (see $\mathrm{I}_{\mathrm{MNIST}}^{4\times 50}$ in Table 1) could only be solved using heuristic 1. for preprocessing.

Effects of Parallelization. For $\mathrm{I}_{\mathrm{MNIST}}$ we further measured the solution time for local robustness with $\epsilon = 0.01$ for 10 test inputs using 8, 16, 24, 32 and 64 threads on machines that have at least as many CPUs as we allow CPLEX to have threads. The results are shown in Fig. 7. It is clearly visible that using more threads can bring a significant speed-up till 32 cores, especially for instances that cannot be solved fast with few threads. Interestingly, one can also observe that for this particular problem (200 neurons in hidden layers), increasing the number of threads from 32 to 64 does not improve performance (many lines just flatten from 32 cores onwards). However, for some other problems (e.g., 400 neurons in hidden layers in hidden layers or computing resilience), the parallelization effect can last longer to some larger number of threads. We suspect that for problems that have reached a certain level of simplicity, adding additional parallelization may not further help.

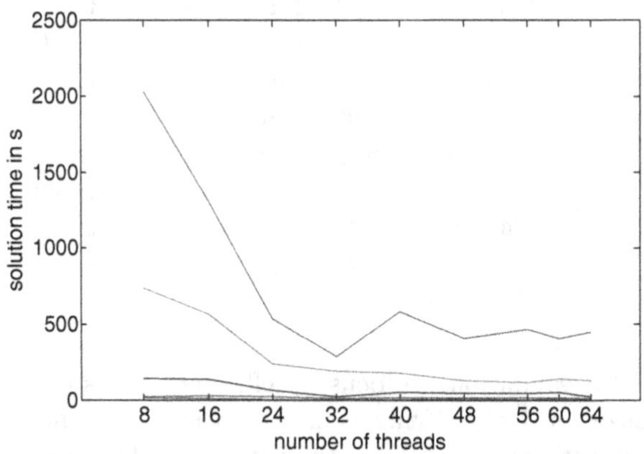

Fig. 7. Execution time vs. the number of threads of five test inputs for $\mathrm{I}_{\mathrm{MNIST}}$ with $\epsilon = 0.01$.

ComputingΦ_m by solving problem (6). Table 2 shows the result of computing precise Φ_m. For simpler problems, we can observe from the first 4 rows of Table 2 that the computed Φ_m increases, when the value of the parameter α increases. This is a natural consequence - for inputs being classified with higher confidence, it should allow for more perturbation to bring to ambiguity. Notably, using a value of α above its maximum makes the problem infeasible, because there does not exist an input for which the neural network has such high confidence. For complex problems, by setting α is closer to its maximum (which can be computed

Table 2. Computation time and results for computing the maximum resilience Φ_m.

Net: # input; # neurons in hidden layers, output m	α	# of parallelization	Φ_m	Time (s)
I_{RL}: 27;15 $m := 0$	1.1	12	0.1537	0.4
	1.2	12	0.3006	0.3
	1.5	12	0.7666	0.1
	1.7	12	1.2730	0.1
I_{RL} 27;15 $m := 3$	1.3	12	0.6904	1.5
$I_{deeptraffic}$: 30;70 $m := 0$	4.022	360	11.3475	421.58
$I_{deeptraffic}$: 30;70 $m := 3$	78.0305	360	69.9109	86.40
$I_{deeptraffic}$: 45;70 $m := 2$	13.5258	360	7.6226	124.46
$I_{deeptraffic}$: 60;70 $m := 2$	2.2704	360	0.8089	2246.8

by solving another substantially simpler MIP that maximizes α for all inputs that classify to class m), one shrinks the complete input space to inputs with high confidence. Currently, scalability of our approach relies on sometimes setting a high value of α, as can be observed in the lower part of Table 2.

7 Concluding Remarks

Our definition and computation of maximum perturbation bounds for ANNs using MIP-based optimization is novel. By developing specialized encoding heuristics and using parallelization we demonstrate the scalability and possible applicability of our verification approach for neural networks in real-world applications. Our verification techniques also allow to formally and quantitatively compare the resilience of different neural networks. Also, perturbation bounds provide a formal assume-guarantee interface for decoupling the design of sensor sets from the design of the neural network itself. In our case, the network assumes a maximum sensor input error for resilience, and the input sensor sets need to be designed to guarantee the given error bound. These kinds of contract-based interfaces may form the basis for constructing more modularized safety cases for autonomous systems.

Nevertheless, we consider the developments in this paper as only a first tiny step towards realizing the full potential of formal verification techniques for artificial neural networks and their deployment for realizing new safety-critical functionalities such as self-driving cars. For simplicity we have restricted ourselves to 1-norms for measuring perturbations but other vector norms may, of course, also be used depending on the specific needs of the application context. Also, the development of specialized MIP solving strategies for verifying ANNs, which go beyond the encoding heuristics provided in this paper, may result in considerable efficiency gains. Notice also that the offline verification approach as presented here is applied *a posteriori* to fixed and "fully trained" networks, whereas real-world networks are usually trained and improved in the field and during operation. Furthermore, the exact relationship of our perturbation bounds with the common phenomena of over-fitting in a neural network classifier deserves a closer examination, since perturbation may also be viewed as generalization from samples. And, finally, investigation of further measures of the resilience of ANNs is needed, as perturbation bounds do not generally cover the resilience of ANNs to input transformations such as scaling or rotation.

Appendix

Proposition 1. $x_i^{(l)} = \mathsf{max}(0, \mathsf{im}_i^{(l)})$ *iff constraints* (2a) *to* (4b) *hold.*

First we establish a lemma to assist the proof.

Lemma 1. $b_i^{(l)} = 1 \Leftrightarrow \mathsf{im}_i^{(l)} \geq 0$.

Proof. ($\Rightarrow$) Assume $b_i^{(l)} = 1$, then (3a) holds trivially and (3b) implies $\mathsf{im}_i^{(l)} \geq 0$. ($\Leftarrow$) Assume $\mathsf{im}_i^{(l)} \geq 0$, then (3b) holds trivially and (3a) only holds if $b_i^{(l)} = 1$.

Proof (Proposition 1).
First we rewrite the condition $x_i^{(l)} = \mathsf{max}(0, \mathsf{im}_i^{(l)})$ to allow further processing.

$$
\begin{aligned}
& x_i^{(l)} = \mathsf{max}(0, \mathsf{im}_i^{(l)}) \\
\xLeftrightarrow{\text{definition of max}} \quad & (\mathsf{im}_i^{(l)} \geq 0 \Rightarrow x_i^{(l)} = \mathsf{im}_i^{(l)}) \wedge (\mathsf{im}_i^{(l)} < 0 \Rightarrow x_i^{(l)} = 0) \\
\xLeftrightarrow{\text{Replace } \mathsf{im}_i^{(l)} \text{ by } b_i^{(l)} = 1 \text{ using lemma 1}} \quad & (b_i^{(l)} = 1 \Rightarrow x_i^{(l)} = \mathsf{im}_i^{(l)}) \wedge (b_i^{(l)} = 0 \Rightarrow x_i^{(l)} = 0)
\end{aligned}
$$

($\Rightarrow$) If $(b_i^{(l)} = 1 \Rightarrow x_i^{(l)} = \mathsf{im}_i^{(l)}) \wedge (b_i^{(l)} = 0 \Rightarrow x_i^{(l)} = 0)$ holds, as $b_i^{(l)}$ is a $0-1$ integer variable, we consider both cases:

(case $b_i^{(l)} = 1$) From the left clause we derive $x_i^{(l)} = \mathsf{im}_i^{(l)}$. From Lemma 1 we have $\mathsf{im}_i^{(l)} \geq 0$. By injecting $b_i^{(l)} = 1$, $x_i^{(l)} = \mathsf{im}_i^{(l)}$, and $\mathsf{im}_i^{(l)} \geq 0$ to constraints (2a) to (4b), all constraints hold due to very large $M_i^{(l)}$.

(case $b_i^{(l)} = 0$) From the right clause we derive $x_i^{(l)} = 0$. From Lemma 1 we have $\mathsf{im}_i^{(l)} < 0$. By injecting $b_i^{(l)} = 0$, $x_i^{(l)} = 0$, and $\mathsf{im}_i^{(l)} < 0$ to constraints (2a) to (4b), all constraints hold due to very large $M_i^{(l)}$.

($\Leftarrow$) If all constraints in (2a) to (4b) hold, we do case split to consider cases $b_i^{(l)} = 0$ and $b_i^{(l)} = 1$, and how they make $(b_i^{(l)} = 1 \Rightarrow x_i^{(l)} = \mathsf{im}_i^{(l)}) \wedge (b_i^{(l)} = 0 \Rightarrow x_i^{(l)} = 0)$ hold.

(case $b_i^{(l)} = 1$) From (2b) and (4a) we know that $x_i^{(l)} = \mathsf{im}_i^{(l)}$.
(case $b_i^{(l)} = 0$) From (2a) and (4b) we know that $x_i^{(l)} = 0$.

In both cases, $(b_i^{(l)} = 1 \Rightarrow x_i^{(l)} = \mathsf{im}_i^{(l)}) \wedge (b_i^{(l)} = 0 \Rightarrow x_i^{(l)} = 0)$ holds.

Proposition 2. *Given a feed-forward ANN with* **softmax** *output layer and a constant $\alpha > 0$, then for all $i, j \in \{1, \ldots, d^{(L)}\}$:*

$$x_{i_1}^{(L)} \geq \alpha\, x_{i_2}^{(L)} \Leftrightarrow x_{i_1}^{(L-1)} \geq \ln(\alpha) + x_{i_2}^{(L-1)}.$$

Proof.

$$\begin{aligned} & x_{i_1}^{(L)} \geq && \alpha\, x_{i_2}^{(L)} \\ \Leftrightarrow\; & \frac{\mathsf{e}^{x_{i_1}^{(L-1)}}}{\sum_{j=1,\ldots,d^L} \mathsf{e}^{x_j^{(L-1)}}} \geq && \alpha \frac{\mathsf{e}^{x_{i_2}^{(L-1)}}}{\sum_{j=1,\ldots,d^L} \mathsf{e}^{x_j^{(L-1)}}} \\ \Leftrightarrow\; & x_{i_1}^{(L-1)} \geq && \ln(\alpha) + x_{i_2}^{(L-1)} \end{aligned}$$

References

1. Abu-Mostafa, Y.S., Magdon-Ismail, M., Lin, H.-T.: Learning from Data, vol. 4. AMLBook, New York (2012)
2. Amodei, D., Olah, C., Steinhardt, J., Christiano, P., Schulman, J., Mané, D.: Concrete problems in Ai safety. arXiv preprint arXiv:1606.06565 (2016)
3. Bastani, O., Ioannou, Y., Lampropoulos, L., Vytiniotis, D., Nori, A., Criminisi, A.: Measuring neural net robustness with constraints. CoRR, abs/1605.07262 (2016)
4. Bjørner, N., Phan, A.-D., Fleckenstein, L.: νZ-an optimizing SMT solver. In: Baier, C., Tinelli, C. (eds.) TACAS 2015. LNCS, vol. 9035, pp. 194–199. Springer, Heidelberg (2015). doi:10.1007/978-3-662-46681-0_14
5. Bhattacharyya, S., Cofer, D., Musliner, D., Mueller, J., Engstrom, E.: Certification considerations for adaptive systems. In ICUAS, pp. 270–279. IEEE (2015)
6. Cousot, P., Cousot, R.: Abstract interpretation: a unified lattice model for static analysis of programs by construction or approximation of fixpoints. In POPL, pp. 238–252. ACM (1977)
7. Goodfellow, I.J., Shlens, J., Szegedy, C.: Explaining and harnessing adversarial examples. arXiv preprint arXiv:1412.6572 (2014)
8. Grossmann, I.E.: Review of nonlinear mixed-integer and disjunctive programming techniques. Optim. Eng. **3**(3), 227–252 (2002)
9. Huang, X., Kwiatkowska, M., Wang, S., Wu, M.: Safety verification of deep neural networks. CoRR, abs/1610.06940 (2016)
10. Karpathy, A.: ConvNetJS: deep learning in your browser (2014). URL http://cs.stanford.edu/people/karpathy/convnetjs
11. Katz, G., Barrett, C.W., Dill, D.L., Julian, K., Kochenderfer, M.J.: Reluplex: an efficient SMT solver for verifying deep neural networks. CoRR, abs/1702.01135 (2017)
12. Kurakin, A., Goodfellow, I., Bengio, S.: Adversarial examples in the physical world. arXiv preprint arXiv:1607.02533 (2016)
13. LeCun, Y., Cortes, C., Burges, C.J.: The MNIST database of handwritten digits (1998)

14. Mnih, V., Kavukcuoglu, K., Silver, D., Graves, A., Antonoglou, I., Wierstra, D., Riedmiller, M.: Playing atari with deep reinforcement learning. arXiv preprint arXiv:1312.5602 (2013)
15. Nguyen, A., Yosinski, J., Clune, J.: Deep neural networks are easily fooled: high confidence predictions for unrecognizable images. In CPVR, pp. 427–436 (2015)
16. Papernot, N., McDaniel, P., Goodfellow, I., Jha, S., Celik, Z.B., Swami, A.: Practical black-box attacks against deep learning systems using adversarial examples. arXiv preprint arXiv:1602.02697 (2016)
17. Papernot, N., McDaniel, P., Wu, X., Jha, S., Swami, A.: Distillation as a defense to adversarial perturbations against deep neural networks. In: Oakland, pp. 582–597. IEEE (2016)
18. Pulina, L., Tacchella, A.: An abstraction-refinement approach to verification of artificial neural networks. In: Touili, T., Cook, B., Jackson, P. (eds.) CAV 2010. LNCS, vol. 6174, pp. 243–257. Springer, Heidelberg (2010). doi:10.1007/978-3-642-14295-6_24
19. Pulina, L., Tacchella, A.: Challenging SMT solvers to verify neural networks. AI Commun. **25**(2), 117–135 (2012)
20. Rajan, S., Wang, S., Inkol, R., Joyal, A.: Efficient approximations for the arctangent function. IEEE Signal Process. Mag. **23**(3), 108–111 (2006)
21. Scheibler, K., Winterer, L., Wimmer, R., Becker, B.: Towards verification of artificial neural networks. In: MBMV, pp. 30–40 (2015)
22. Ukil, A., Shah, V.H., Deck, B.: Fast computation of arctangent functions for embedded applications: a comparative analysis. In ISIE, pp. 1206–1211. IEEE (2011)
23. Xu, Y., Ralphs, T.K., Ladányi, L., Saltzman, M.J.: Computational experience with a software framework for parallel integer programming. INFORMS J. Comput. **21**(3), 383–397 (2009)

Formal Verification of Piece-Wise Linear Feed-Forward Neural Networks

Rüdiger Ehlers(✉)

University of Bremen and DFKI GmbH, Bremen, Germany
ruediger.ehlers@uni-bremen.de

Abstract. We present an approach for the verification of feed-forward neural networks in which all nodes have a piece-wise linear activation function. Such networks are often used in deep learning and have been shown to be hard to verify for modern satisfiability modulo theory (SMT) and integer linear programming (ILP) solvers.

The starting point of our approach is the addition of a global linear approximation of the overall network behavior to the verification problem that helps with SMT-like reasoning over the network behavior. We present a specialized verification algorithm that employs this approximation in a search process in which it infers additional node phases for the non-linear nodes in the network from partial node phase assignments, similar to unit propagation in classical SAT solving. We also show how to infer additional conflict clauses and safe node fixtures from the results of the analysis steps performed during the search. The resulting approach is evaluated on collision avoidance and handwritten digit recognition case studies.

1 Introduction

Many tasks in computing are prohibitively difficult to formalize and thus hard to get right. A classical example is the recognition of digits from images. Formalizing what exactly distinguishes the digit *2* from a *7* is in a way that captures all common handwriting styles is so difficult that this task is normally left to the computer. A classical approach for doing so is to learn a *feed-forward neural network* from pre-classified example images. Since the advent of *deep learning* (see, e.g., [1]), the artificial intelligence research community has learned a lot about engineering these networks, such that they nowadays achieve a very good classification precision and outperform human classifiers on some tasks, such as sketch recognition [2]. Even safety-critical applications such as obstacle detection in self-driving cars nowadays employ neural networks.

But if we do not have formal specifications, how can we assure the safety of such a system? The classical approach to tackle this problem is to construct *safety cases* [3]. In such a safety case, we characterize a set of environment

This work was supported by the Institutional Strategy of the University of Bremen, funded by the German Excellence Initiative.

D. D'Souza and K. Narayan Kumar (Eds.): ATVA 2017, LNCS 10482, pp. 269–286, 2017.
DOI: 10.1007/978-3-319-68167-2_19

conditions under which a certain output is desired and then test if the learned problem model ensures this output under all considered environment conditions. In a self-driving car scenario, we can define an abstract obstacle appearance model all of whose concretizations should be detected as obstacles. Likewise, in a character recognition application, we can define that all images that are *close* to a given example image (by some given metric) should be detected as the correct digit. The verification of safety cases somewhat deviates from the classical aim of formal methods to verify correct system behavior in all cases, but the latter is unrealistic due to the absence of a complete formal specification. Yet, having the means to test neural networks on safety cases would help with certification and also provides valuable feedback to the system engineer.

Verifying formal properties of feed-forward neural networks is a challenging task. Pulina and Tacchella [4] present an approach for neurons with non-linear activation functions that only scales to small networks. In their work, they use networks with 6 nodes, which are far too few for most practical applications. They combine counterexample-triggered abstraction-refinement with *satisfiability modulo theory* (SMT) solving. Scheibler et al. [5] consider the bounded model checking problem for an inverse pendulum control scenario with non-linear system dynamics and a non-linear neuron activation function, and despite employing the state-of-the-art SMT solver iSAT3 [6] and even extending this solver to deal better with the resulting problem instances, their experiments show that the resulting verification problem is already challenging for neural networks with 26 nodes.

In *deep learning* [1], many works use networks whose nodes have piece-wise linear activation functions. This choice has the advantage that they are more amenable to formal verification, for example using SMT solvers with the theory of linear real arithmetic, without the need to perform abstract interpretation. In such an approach, the solver chooses the *phases* of (some of) the nodes, and then applies a linear-programming-like sub-solver to check if there exist concrete real-valued inputs to the network such that all nodes have the selected phases. The node phases represent which part of the piece-wise linear activation functions are used for each node. It has been observed that the SMT instances stemming from such an encoding are very difficult to solve for modern SMT solvers, as they need to iterate through many such phase combinations before a problem instance is found to be satisfiable or unsatisfiable [7,8]. Due to the practical importance of verifying piecewise-linear feed-forward neural networks, this observation asks for a specialized approach for doing so.

Huang et al. [9] describe such an approach that is based on propagating constraints through the layers of a network. The constraints encode regions of the input space of each layer all of whose points lead to the same overall classification in the network. Their approach is partially based on discretization and focusses on robustness testing, i.e., determining the extent to which the input can be altered without changing the classification result. They do not support general verification properties. Bastiani et al. [10] also target robustness testing and define an abstraction-refinement constraint solving loop to test a network's robustness against adversarial pertubations. They also employ the counter-examples that their approach finds to learning more robust networks. Katz et al. [7] provide an alternative approach that allows to check the input/output behavior of a neural network with linear and so-called *ReLU* nodes against convex specifications. Many modern network architectures employ these nodes. They present a modification of the *simplex algorithm* for solving linear programs that can also deal with the constraints imposed by ReLU nodes, and they show that their approach scales orders of magnitudes better than when applying the SMT solvers `MathSAT` or `Yices` on SMT instances generated from the verification problems.

Modern neural network architectures, especially those for image recognition, however often employ another type of neural network node that the approach by Katz et al. does not support: *MaxPool* nodes. They are used to determine the strongest signal from their input neurons, and they are crucial for *feature detection* in complex machine learning tasks. In order to support the verification of safety cases for machine learning applications that make use of this node type, it is thus important to have verification approaches that can efficiently operate on networks that have such nodes, without the need to simulate MaxPool nodes by encoding their behavior into a much larger number of ReLU nodes.

In this paper, we present an approach to verify neural networks with piece-wise linear activation functions against convex specifications. The approach supports all node types used in modern network, network architectures that only employ piece-wise linear activation functions (such as MaxPool and ReLU nodes). The approach is based on combining satisfiability (SAT) solving and linear programming and employs a novel linear approximation of the overall network behavior. This approximation allows the approach to quickly rule out large search space parts for the node phases from being considered during the verification process. While the approximation can also be used as additional constraints in SMT solving and improves the computation times of the SMT solver, we apply it in a customized solver that uses the *elastic filtering* algorithm from [11] for minimal infeasible linear constraint set finding in case of conflicts, and combine it with a specialized procedure for inferring implied node phases. Together, these components lead to much shorter verification times. We apply the approach on two cases studies, namely collision avoidance and character recognition, and report on experimental results. We also provide the resulting solver and the complete tool-chain to generate verifiable models using the Deep Learning framework `Caffe` [12] as open-source software.

2 Preliminaries

Feed-Forward Neural Networks: We consider *multi-layer* (*Perceptron*) networks with *linear*, *ReLU*, and *MaxPool* nodes in this paper. Such networks are formally defined as directed acyclic weighted graphs $G = (V, E, W, B, T)$, where V is a set of nodes, $E \subset V \times V$ is a set of edges, $W : E \to \mathbb{R}$ assigns a weight to each edge of the network, $B : V \to \mathbb{R}$ assigns a *node bias* to each node, and T assigns a *type* to each node in the network from a set of available types $T \in \{input, linear, ReLU, MaxPool\}$. Nodes without incoming edges are called *input nodes*, and we assume that $T(v) = input$ for every such node v. Vertices that have no outgoing edge are also called *output nodes*.

A feed-forward neural network with n input nodes and m output nodes represents a function $f : \mathbb{R}^n \rightarrow \mathbb{R}^m$. Given assignments $in : \{1, \ldots, n\} \rightarrow V$ and $out : \{1, \ldots, m\} \rightarrow V$ that define the orders of the input and output nodes (so that we can feed elements from $\mathbb{R}^n$ to the network to obtain an output from $\mathbb{R}^m$), and some input vector $(x_1, \ldots, x_n) \in \mathbb{R}^n$, we can define the network's behavior by a node value assignment function $a : V \rightarrow \mathbb{R}$ that is defined as follows:

- For every node v with $T(v) = input$, we set $a(v) = x_j$ for $j = in^{-1}(v)$,
- For every node v with $T(v) = linear$, we set $a(v) = \sum_{v' \in V, (v',v) \in E} W((v', v)) \cdot a(v') + B(v)$.
- For every node v with $T(v) = ReLU$, we set $a(v) = \max(B(v) + \sum_{v' \in V, (v',v) \in E} W((v', v)) \cdot a(v'), 0)$.
- For every node v with $T(v) = MaxPool$, we set $a(v) = \max_{v' \in V, (v',v) \in E} a(v')$.

Function f's output for $(x_1, \ldots, x_n)$ is defined to be $(a(out(1)), \ldots, a(out(m)))$. Note that the weights of the edges leading to *MaxPool* nodes and their bias values are not used in the definition above. Given a node value assignment function $a : V \rightarrow \mathbb{R}$, we also simply call $a(v)$ the *value* of v. If for a ReLU node v, we have $s(v) < 0$ for $s(v) = B(v) + \sum_{v' \in V, (v',v) \in E} W((v, v')) \cdot a(v')$, and hence $a(v) = 0$, we say that node n is in the ≤ 0 phase, and for $s(v) \geq 0$, and hence $a(v) \geq 0$, we say that it is in the ≥ 0 phase. If we have $s(v) = 0$, then it can be in either phase. For a *MaxPool* node v, we define it to be in phase $e \in E \cap (V \times \{v\})$ if $a(v) = a(v')$ for $e = (v', v)$. If multiple nodes with edges to v have the same values, then node v can have any of the respective phases.

Modern neural network architectures are *layered*, i.e., we have that every path from an input node to an output node has the same length. For the verification techniques given in this paper, it does however not matter whether the network is layered. Networks can also be used to *classify* inputs. In such a case, the network represents a function $f' : \mathbb{R}^n \rightarrow \{1, \ldots, m\}$ (for some numbering of the classes), and we define $f'(x_1, \ldots, x_n) = \arg\max_{i \in \{1, \ldots, m\}} y_i$ for $(y_1, \ldots, y_m) = f(x_1, \ldots, x_n)$.

We do not discuss here how neural networks are learned, but assume networks to be given with all their edge weights and node bias values. Frameworks such as `Caffe` [12] provide ready-to-use functionality for learning edge weights and bias values from databases of examples, i.e., tuples $(x_1, \ldots, x_n, y_1, \ldots, y_m)$ such that we want the network to induce a function f with $(x_1, \ldots, x_n) = (y_1, \ldots, y_m)$. Likewise, for classification problems, the databases consist of tuples $(x_1, \ldots, x_n, c)$ such that we want the network to induce a function f' with $f'(x_1, \ldots, x_n) = c$. When using a neural network learning tool, the architecture of the network, i.e., everything except for the weights and the node bias values, is defined up-front, and the framework automatically derives suitable edge weights and node bias values. There are other node types (such as *Softmax* nodes) that are often used during the learning process, but removed before the deployment of the trained network, and hence do not need to be considered in this work. Also, there are network layer types such as *convolutional layers* that have special structures. From a verification point of view, these are however just sets of linear nodes whose edges share some weights, and thus do not have to be treated differently.

Satisfiability Solvers: Satisfiability (SAT) solvers check if a Boolean formula has a satisfying assignment. The formula is normally required to be in conjunctive normal form, and thus consists of *clauses* that are connected by *conjunction*. Every clause is a disjuction of one of more *literals*, which are Boolean variables or their negation. A SAT solver operates by successively building a valuation of the Boolean variables and *backtracking* whenever a conflict of the current *partial valuation* and a clause has been found. To achieve a better performance, SAT solvers furthermore perform *unit propagation*, where the partial assignment is extended by literals that are the only remaining ones not yet violated by the partial valuation in some clause. Additionally, modern solvers perform *clause learning*, where clauses that are implied by the conjunction of some other clauses are lazily inferred during the search process, and select variables to branch on using a *branching heuristic*. Most modern solvers also perform *random restarts*. For more details on SAT solving, the interested reader is referred to [13].

Linear Programming: Given a set of linear inequalities over real-valued variables and a linear optimization function (which together are called a *linear program*), the linear programming problem is to find an assignment to the variables that minimizes the objective function and fulfills all constraints. Even though linear programming was shown to have polynomial-time complexity, it has been observed that in practice [14], it is often faster to apply the *Simplex algorithm*, which is an exponential-time algorithm.

Satisfiability Modulo Theory Solving: SAT solvers only support Boolean variables. For problems that can be naturally represented as a Boolean combination of constraints over other variable types, Satisfiability Modulo Theory (SMT) solvers are normally applied instead. An SMT solver combines a SAT solver with specialized decision procedures for other theories (such as, e.g., the theory of linear arithmetic over real numbers).

3 Efficient Verification of Feed-Forward Neural Networks

In this paper, we deal with the following verification problem:

Definition 1. *Given a feed-forward neural network G that implements a function $f : \mathbb{R}^n \rightarrow \mathbb{R}^m$, and a set of linear constraints ψ over the real-valued variables $V = \{x_1, \ldots, x_n, y_1, \ldots, y_m\}$, the neural net (NN) verification problem is to find a node value assignment function a for V that fulfils ψ over the input* *and output nodes of G and for which we have $f(x_1, \ldots, x_n) = (y_1, \ldots, y_m)$, or to conclude that no such node value assignment function exists.*

The restriction to conjunctions of linear properties in Definition 1 was done for simplicity. Verifying arbitrary Boolean combinations of linear properties can be fitted into Definition 1 by encoding them into the structure of the network itself, so that an additional output neuron y_{add} outputs a value ≥ 0 if and only if the property is fulfilled. In this case, ψ is then simply $y_{add} \geq 0$.

There are multiple ways to solve the neural network (NN) verification problem. The encoding of an NN verification problem to an SMT problem instance is straight-forward, but yields instances that are difficult to solve even for modern SMT solvers (as the experiments reported on in Sect. 4 show). As an alternative, we present a new approach that combines (1) linear approximation of the overall NN behavior, (2) irreducible infeasible subset analysis for linear constraints based on elastic filtering [11], (3) inferring possible safe node phase choices from feasibility checking of partial node phase valuations, and (4) performing unit-propagation-like reasoning on node phases. We describe these ideas in this section, and present experimental results on a tool implementing them in the next section.

Starting point is the combination of a linear programming solver and a satisfiability solver. We let the satisfiability solver guide the search process. It determines the phases of the nodes and maintains a set of constraints over node phase combinations. On a technical level, we allocate the SAT variables $x_{(v,\leq 0)}$ and $x_{(v,\geq 0)}$ for every ReLU node v, and also reserve variables $x_{(v,e)}$ for every MaxPool node v and every edge e ending in v. The SAT solver performs unit propagation, clause learning, branching, and backtracking as usual, but whenever the solver is about to branch, we employ a linear programming solver to check a linear approximation of the network behavior (under the node phases already fixed) for feasibility. Whenever a conflict is detected, the SAT solver can then learn a conflict clause. Additionally, we infer implied node phases in the search process.

We describe the components of our approach in this section, and show how they are combined at the end of it.

3.1 Linear Approximation of Neural Network Value Assignment Functions

Let $G = (V, E, W, B, T)$ be a network representing a function $f : \mathbb{R}^n \to \mathbb{R}^m$. We want to build a system of linear constraints using V as the set of variables that closely approximates f, i.e., such that every node value assignment function a is a correct solution to the linear constraint system, and the constraints are as tight as possible. The main difficulty in building such a constraint system is that the *ReLU* and *MaxPool* nodes do not have linear input-output behavior (until their phases are fixed), so we have to approximate them linearly.

Figure 1 shows the activation function of a *ReLU* node, where we denote the weighted sum of the input signals to the node (and its bias) as variable c. The output of the node is denoted using the variable d. If we have upper and lower

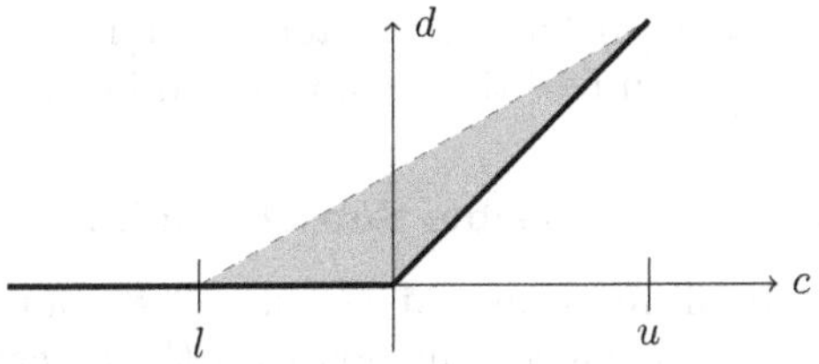

Fig. 1. The activation function of a *ReLU* node, with a linear over-approximation drawn as filled area.

bounds $[l, u]$ of c, then we can approximate the relationship between c and d by the constraints $d \geq 0$, $d \geq c$, and $d \leq \frac{u \cdot (c-l)}{u-l}$, all of which are linear equations for constant u and l. This yields the set of allowed value combinations for c and d drawn as the filled area in Fig. 1.

Obviously, this approach requires that we know upper and lower bounds on c. However, even though neural networks are defined as functions from $\mathbb{R}^n$, bounds on the input values are typically known. For example, in image processing networks, we know that the input neurons receive values from the range $[0, 1]$. In other networks, it is common to *normalize* the input values before learning the network, i.e., to scale them to the same interval or to $[-1, 1]$. This allows us to use classical *interval arithmetic* on the network to obtain basic lower and upper bounds $[l, u]$ on every node's values.

For the case of *MaxPool* nodes, we can approximate the behavior of the nodes linearly similarly to the ReLU case, except that we do not need upper bounds for the nodes' values. Let $c_1, \ldots, c_k$ be the values of nodes with edges leading to the *MaxPool* node, $l_1, \ldots, k_k$ be their lower bounds, and d be the output value of the node. We instantiate the following linear constraints:

$$\bigwedge_{i \in \{1,\ldots,k\}} (d \geq c_i) \wedge (c_1 + \ldots + c_k \geq d + \sum_{i \in \{1,\ldots,k\}} l_i - \max_{i \in \{1,\ldots,k\}} l_i)$$

Note that these are the tightest linear constraints that can be given for the relationship between the values of the predecessor nodes of a *MaxPool* node and the node value of the *MaxPool* node itself.

After a linear program that approximates the behavior of the overall network has been built, we can use it to make all future approximations even tighter. To achieve this, we add the problem specification ψ as constraints and solve, for every variable $v \in V$, the resulting linear program while minimizing first for the objective functions $1 \cdot v$, and then doing the same for the objective function $-1 \cdot v$. This yields new tighter lower and upper bounds $[l, u]$ for each node (if the network has any ReLU nodes), which can be used to obtain a tighter linear program. Including the specification in the process allows us to derive tighter bounds than we would have found without the specification. The whole process can be repeated several times: whenever new upper and lower bounds have been obtained, they can be used to build a tighter linear network approximation, which in turn allows to obtain new tighter upper and lower bounds.

3.2 Search Process and Infeasible Subset Finding

Given a phase fixture for all ReLU and MaxPool nodes in a network, checking if there exists a node value assignment function with these phases (and such that the verification constraint ψ is fulfilled) can be reduced to a linear programming problem. For this, we extend the linear program built with the approach from the previous subsection (with V as the variable set for the node values) by the following constraints:

- For every ≤ 0 phase selected for a ReLU node v, we add the constraints $v = 0$ and $\sum_{(v',v)\in E} W((v',v)) \cdot v' + B(v) \leq 0$.
- For every ≥ 0 phase selected for a ReLU node v, we add the constraint $v \geq \sum_{(v',v)\in E} W((v',v)) \cdot v' + B(v)$.
- For every phase (v',v) selected for a MaxPool node v, we add the constraint $v = v'$.

If we only have a partial node phase selection, we add these constraints only for the fixed nodes. If the resulting linear program is infeasible, then we can discard all extensions to the partial valuation from consideration in the search process. This is done by adding a *conflict* clause that rules out the Boolean encoding of this partial node phase selection, so that even after restarts of the solver, the reason for infeasibility is retained.

However, the reasons for conflicts often involve relatively few nodes, so shorter conflict clauses can also be learned instead (which makes the search process more efficient). To achieve this, we employ *elastic filtering* [11]. In this approach, all of the constraints added due to node phase selection are weakened by *slack variables*, where there is one slack variable for each node. So, for example a constraint $\sum_{(v',v)\in E} W((v',v)) \cdot v' + B(v) \leq 0$ becomes $\sum_{(v',v)\in E} W((v',v)) \cdot v' + B(v) - s_v \leq 0$. When running the linear programming solver again with the task of minimizing a weighted sum of the slack variables, we get a ranking of the nodes by how much they contributed to the conflict, where some of them did not contribute at all (since their slack variable had a 0 value). We then fix the slack variable with the highest value to be 0, hence making the corresponding constraints strict, and repeat the search process until the resulting LP instance becomes infeasible. We then know that the node phase fixtures that were made strict during this process are together already infeasible, and build conflict clauses that only contain them. We observed that these conflict clauses are much shorter than without applying elastic filtering.

Satisfiability modulo theory solvers typically employ cheaper procedures to compute *minimal infeasible subsets* of linear constraints, such as the one by Duterte and de Moura [15], but the high number of constraints in the linear approximation of the network behavior that are independent of node phase selections seems to make the approach less well-suited, as our experiments with the SMT solver `Yices` that uses this approach suggest.

3.3 Implied Node Phase Inference During Partial Phase Fixture Checking

In the partial node fixture feasibility checking step from Sect. 3.2, we employ a linear programming solver. However, except for the elastic filtering step, we did not employ an optimization function yet, as it was not needed for checking the feasibility of a partial node fixture.

For the common case that the partial node fixture *is* feasible (in the linear approximation), we define an optimization function that allows us to infer additional infeasible *and* feasible partial node fixtures when checking some other partial node fixture for feasibility. The feasible fixtures are cached so that if it or a partial fixture of it is later evaluated, no linear programming has to be performed. Given a partial node fixture to the nodes $V' \subset V$, we use $-1 \cdot \sum_{v \in V \setminus V', T(v)=ReLU} v - \frac{1}{10} \sum_{v \in V \setminus V', T(v)=MaxPool} v$ as optimization function. This choice asks the linear programming solver to minimize the error for the ReLU nodes, i.e., the difference between $a(v)$ and $\max(\sum_{v' \in V, (v',v) \in E} W((v',v)) \cdot a(v') + B(v), 0)$ for every assignment a computed in the linear approximation of the network behavior and every ReLU-node v. While this choice only minimizes an approximation of the error sum of the nodes and thus does not guarantee that the resulting variable valuation denotes a valid node value assignment function, it often yields assignments in which a substantial number of nodes v *have* a tight value, i.e., have $a(v) = \max(\sum_{v' \in V, (v',v) \in E} W((v',v)) \cdot a(v') + B(v), 0)$.

If tight is the set of nodes with tight values, p is the partial SAT solver variable valuation that encodes the phase fixtures for the nodes V', and if p' is the (partial) valuation of the SAT variables that encodes the phases of the tight nodes, we can then cache that $p \cup p'$ is a partial assignment that is feasible in the linear approximation. So when the SAT solver adds literals from p' to the partial valuation, there is no need to let the linear programming solver run again.

At the same time, the valuation a (in the linear approximation) can be used to derive an additional clause for the SAT solver. Let $\mathsf{unfixed}$ be the ReLU nodes whose values are not fixed by p. If for any node $v \in \mathsf{unfixed}$, we have $a(v) > 0$, then we know by the choice of optimization function and the fact that we performed the analysis in a linear approximation of the network behavior, that some node in v needs to be in the ≥ 0 phase (under the partial valuation p). Thus, we can learn the additional clause $\left(\bigvee_{l \in p} \neg l\right) \vee \bigvee_{v \in V, T(v)=ReLU, ((v,\leq 0) \mapsto \mathbf{true}) \notin p} (v, \geq 0)$ for the SAT solver, provided that the values of the MaxPool nodes are valid, i.e., for all MaxPool nodes v we have $a(v) = a(v')$ for some $(v, v') \in E$. This last restriction is why we also included the MaxPool nodes in the optimization function above (but with lower weight).

3.4 Detecting Implied Phases

Whenever the SAT solver has fixed a new node phase, the selected phases together may imply other node phases. Take for example the net excerpt from Fig. 2. There are two ReLU nodes, named r_1 and r_2, and one MaxPool node.

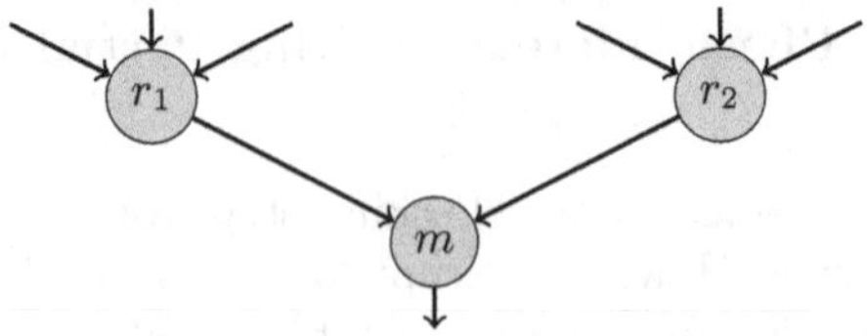

Fig. 2. An example neural network part, used in Subsect. 3.4.

Assume that during the initial analysis of the network (Sect. 3.1), it has been determined that the value of node r_1 is between 0.0 and 1.5, and the value of node r_2 is between 0.1 and 2.0. First of all, the SAT solver can unconditionally detect that node r_2 is in the ≥ 0 phase. Then, if at some point, the SAT solver decides that node r_1 should be in the ≤ 0 phase, this fixes the value of r_1 to 0. Since the flow out of r_2 has a lower bound >0, we can then deduce that m's phase should be set to (r_2, m).

Similar reasoning can also be performed for flow leading into a node. If we assume that the analysis of the initial linear approximation of the network's node functions yields that the outgoing flow of m needs to be between 0.5 and 0.7, and the phase of r_1 is chosen to be ≤ 0, then this implies that the phase of r_2 must be ≥ 0, as otherwise m would be unable to supply a flow of >0.

Both cases can be detected without analyzing the linear approximation of the network. Rather, we can just propagate the lower and upper bounds on the nodes' outgoing flows through the network and detect implied phases. Doing so takes time linear in the size of the network, which is considerably faster than making an LP solver call. This allows the detection of implied phases to be applied in a way similar to classical unit propagation in SAT solving: whenever a decision has been made by the solver, we run implied phase detection to extend the partial valuation of the SAT solver by implied choices (which allows to make the linear approximation tighter for the following partial node fixture feasibility checks).

3.5 Overview of the Integrated Solver

To conclude this section, let us discuss how the techniques presented in it are combined. Algorithm 1 shows the overall approach. In the first step, upper and lower bounds for all nodes' values are computed. The solver then prepares an empty partial valuation to the SAT variables and an empty list *extra* in which additional clauses generated by the LP instance analysis steps proposed in this section are stored. The SAT instance is initialized with clauses that enforce that every ReLU node and every MaxPool node has exactly one phase selected (using a *one-hot encoding*).

In the main loop of the algorithm, the first step is to perform most steps of SAT solving, such as unit propagation, conflict detection & analysis, and others. We assume that the partial valuation is always labelled by *decision levels* so that backtracking can also be performed whenever needed. Furthermore, additional clauses from *extra* are mixed to the SAT instance ψ. This is done on a step-by-step basis, as the additional clauses may trigger unit propagation and even conflicts, which need to be dealt with eagerly. After all clauses from *extra* have been mixed into ψ, and possibly the partial valuation p has been extended by implied literals, in line 12, the approach presented in Sect. 3.4 is applied. If it returns new implied literals (in the form of additional clauses), they are taken care of by the SAT solving steps in line 11 next. This is because the clauses already in ψ may lead to unit propagation on the newly inferred literals, which makes sense to check as every additional literal makes the linear approximation of the network behavior tighter (and can lead to additional implied literals being detected). Only when all node phases have been inferred, p is checked for feasibility in the linear approximation (line 14).

There are two different outcomes of this check: if the LP instance is infeasible, a new conflict clause is generated, and hence the condition in line 15 is not satisfied. The algorithm then continues in line 11 in this case. Otherwise, the branching step of the SAT solver is executed. If p is already a complete valuation, we know at this point that the instance is *satisfiable*, as then the CheckForFeasibility function just executed operated on an LP problem that is not approximate, but rather captures the precise behavior of the network. Otherwise, p is extended by a decision to set a variable b to **true** (for some variable chosen by the SAT solver's variable selection heuristics). Whenever this happens, we employ a plain SAT solver for checking if the partial valuation can be extended to one that satisfies ψ. This not being the case may not be detected by unit propagation in line 11 and hence it makes sense to do an eager SAT check. In case of conflict, the choice of b's value is inverted, and in any case, the algorithm continues with the search.

4 Experiments

We implemented the approach presented in the preceding section in a tool called `Planet`. It is written in C++ and bases on the linear programming toolkit `GLPK` 4.61[1] and the SAT solver `Minisat 2.2.0` [16]. While we use `GLPK` as it is, we modified the main search procedure of `Minisat` to implement Algorithm 1. We repeat the initial approximation tightening process from Sect. 3.1 until the cumulative changes in $\overrightarrow{min}$ and $\overrightarrow{max}$ fall below 1.0. We also abort the process if 5000 node approximation updates have been performed (to not spend too much time in the process for very large nets), provided that for every node, its bounds have been updated at least three times.

All numerical computations are performed with `double` precision, and we did not use any compensation for numerical imprecision in the code apart from using a fixed safety margin $\epsilon = 0.0001$ for detecting node assignment values $a(v)$ to be greater or smaller than other node assignment values $a(v')$, i.e., we actually check if $a(v) \leq a(v') - \epsilon$ to conclude $a(v) \leq a(v')$, whenever such a comparison is

[1] GNU Linear Programming Kit, http://www.gnu.org/software/glpk/glpk.html.

Algorithm 1. Top-level view onto the neural network verification algorithm.

function VERIFYNN(V, E, T, B, W)
  $(\overrightarrow{min}, \overrightarrow{max}) \leftarrow$ ComputeInitialBounds(V, E, T, B, W) ▷ Section 3.1
  $(\overrightarrow{min}, \overrightarrow{max}) \leftarrow$ RefineBounds$(V, E, T, B, W, \overrightarrow{min}, \overrightarrow{max})$ ▷ Section 3.1
  $p \leftarrow \emptyset$, $extra \leftarrow \emptyset$
  $\psi \leftarrow \bigwedge_{v \in V, T(v)=MaxPool} \bigvee_{v' \in V, (v',v) \in E} x_{v,(v',v)}$
  $\psi \leftarrow \psi \wedge \bigwedge_{v \in V, T(v)=MaxPool, v', v'' \in V, v' \neq v'', (v',v) \in E, (v'',v) \in E} (\neg x_{v,(v',v)} \vee \neg x_{v,(v'',v)})$
  $\psi \leftarrow \psi \wedge \bigwedge_{v \in V, T(v)=ReLU} (x_{v,\leq 0} \vee x_{v,\geq 0}) \wedge (\neg x_{v,\leq 0} \vee \neg x_{v,\geq 0})$
  while ψ has a satisfying assignment **do**
    while *extra* is non-empty **do**
      Perform unit propagation, conflict detection, backtracking, and clause learning for p on ψ, while moving the clauses from *extra* to ψ one-by-one.
    $extra \leftarrow$ InferNodePhases$(V, E, T, B, W, p, \overrightarrow{min}, \overrightarrow{max})$ ▷ Section 3.4
    if $extra = \emptyset$ **then**
      $extra \leftarrow$ CheckForFeasibility$(V, E, T, B, W, p, \overrightarrow{min}, \overrightarrow{max})$ ▷ Section 3.2–3.3
      if $p \models c$ for all clauses $c \in extra$ **then**
        if p is a complete assignment to all variables **then**
          return Satisfiable
        Add a new variable assignment $b \mapsto$ **true** to p for some variable b in ψ.
        if p cannot be extended to a satisfying valuation to ψ **then**
          $p = p \setminus \{b \mapsto \textbf{true}\} \cup \{b \mapsto \textbf{false}\}$
  return Unsatisfiable

made in the verification algorithm steps described in Sects. 3.2 and 3.3. Since the neural networks learned using the `Caffe` [12] deep learning framework (which we employ for our experiments in this paper) tend not to degenerate in the node weights, this is sufficient for the experimental evaluation in this paper. Also, we did not observe any differences in the verification results between the SMT solver `Yices` [17] on the SMT instances that we computed from the verification problems and the results computed by our tool. The tool is available under the GPLv3 license and can be obtained from https://github.com/progirep/planet along with all scripts & configuration files needed to learn the neural networks used in our experiments with the `Caffe` framework and to translate them to input files for our tool.

All computation times given in the following were obtained on a computer with an Intel Core i5-4200U 1.60 GHz CPU and 8 GB of RAM running an x64 version of GNU/Linux. We do not report memory usage, as it was always <1 GB. All tools run with a single computation thread.

4.1 Collision Avoidance

As a first example, we consider the problem of predicting collisions between two vehicles that follow curved paths at different speeds. We learned a neural network that processes tuples (x, y, s, d, c_1, c_2) and classifies them into whether they represent a colliding or non-colliding case. In such a tuple,

- the x and y components represent the relative distances of the vehicles in their workspace in the X- and Y-dimensions,
- the speed of the second vehicle is s,
- the starting direction of the second vehicle is d, and
- the rotation speed values of the two vehicles are c_1 and c_2.

The data is given in normalized (scaled) form to the neural network learner, so that all tuple components are between 0 and 1 (or between -1 and 1 for c_1 and c_2). We wrote a tool that generates a few random tuples (within some intervals of possible values) along with whether they represent a colliding or non-colliding case, as determined by simulation. The vehicles are circle-shaped, and we defined a safety margin and only consider tuples for which either the safety margins around the vehicles never overlap, or the vehicles themselves collide. So when only the safety margins overlap, this represents a "don't care" case for the learner. The tool also visualizes the cases, and we show two example traces in Fig. 3. The tool ensures that the number of colliding cases and non-colliding ones are the same in the case list given to the neural network learner (by discarding tuples whenever needed). We generated 3000 tuples in total as input for `Planet`.

We defined a neural network architecture that consists of 40 linear nodes in the first layer, followed by a layer of MapPool nodes, each having 4 input edges, followed by a layer of 19 ReLU nodes, and 2 ReLU nodes for the output layer. Since `Caffe` employs randomization to initialize the node weights, the accuracy of the computed network is not constant. In 86 out of 100 tries, we were able to learn a network with an accuracy of 100%, i.e., that classifies all example tuples correctly.

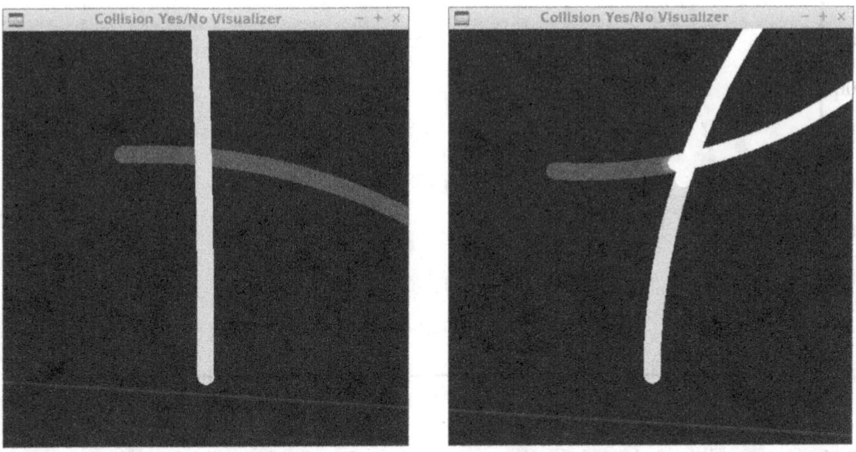

Fig. 3. Two pairs of vehicle trajectories, where the first one is non-colliding, and the second one is colliding. The lower vehicle starts roughly in north direction, whereas the other one starts roughly in east direction. The first trajectory is non-colliding as the two vehicles pass through the trajectory intersection point at different times.

We want to find out the *safety margin* around the tuples, i.e., the highest value of $\epsilon > 0$ such that for every tuple (x, y, s, d, c_1, c_2) that is classified to $b \in \{colliding, notColliding\}$, we have that all other tuples $(x \pm \epsilon, y \pm \epsilon, s \pm \epsilon, d \pm \epsilon, c_1 \pm \epsilon, c_2 \pm \epsilon)$ are classified to b by the network as well. We perform this check for the first 100 tuples in the list, use *bisection search* to test this for $\epsilon \in [0, 0.05]$, and abort the search process if ϵ has been determined with a precision of 0.002.

We obtained 500 NN verification problem instances from this safety margin exploration process. Figure 4 shows the distribution of the computation times of our tool on the problem instances, with a timeout of 1 h. For comparison, we show the computation times of the SMT solver `Yices 2.5.2` and the (I)LP solver `Gurobi 7.02` on the problem instances. The SMT solver `z3` was observed to perform much worse than `Yices` on the verification problems, and is thus not shown. The choice of these comparison solvers was rooted in the fact that they performed best for verifying networks without MaxPool nodes in [7]. We also give computation times for `Gurobi` and `Yices` after adding additional linear approximation constraints obtained with the approach in Sect. 3.1. The computation times include the time to obtain them with our tool.

It can be observed that the computation times of `Gurobi` and `Yices` are too long for practical verification, except if the linear approximation constraints from our approach in this paper are added to the SMT and ILP instances to help

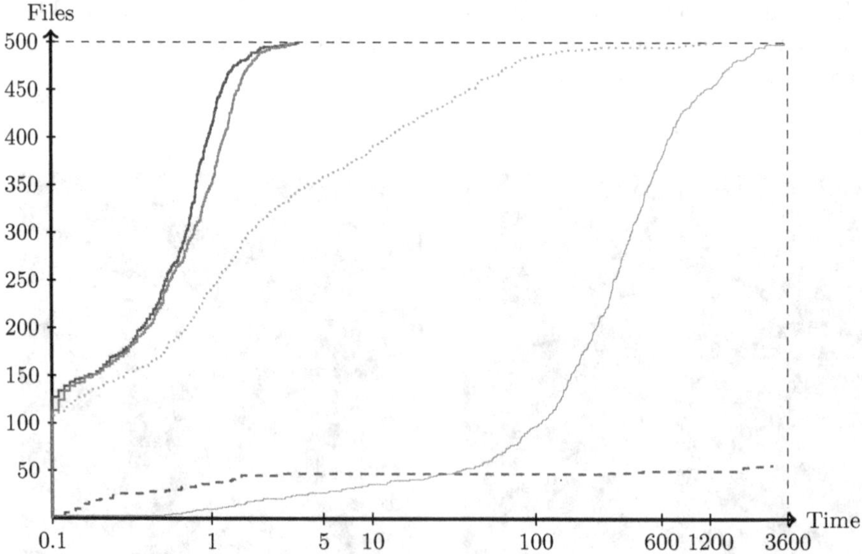

Fig. 4. Cactus plot of the solver time comparison for the 500 vehicle collision benchmarks. Time is given in seconds (on a log-scale), and the lines, from bottom right to top left, represent `Gurobi` without linear approximation (dashed), `Yices` without linear approximation (solid), `Yices` with linear approximation (dotted), `Planet` (solid), and `Gurobi` with linear approximation (solid).

the solvers. While Yices is then still slower than our approach, Gurobi actually becomes a bit faster in most cases, which is not surprising, given that it is a highly optimized commercial product that employs many sophisticated heuristics under-the-hood, whereas we use the less optimized GLPK linear programming framework. Planet spends most time on LP solving. It should be noted that the solver comparison is slightly skewed, as Yices employs arbitrary precision arithmetic whereas the other tools do not.

4.2 MNIST Digit Recognition

As a second case study, we consider handwritten digit recognition. This is a classical problem in machine learning, and the MNIST dataset [18] is the most commonly used benchmark for comparing different machine learning approaches. The Caffe framework comes with some example architectures, and we use a simplified version of Caffe's version of the lenet network [19] for our experiments. The Caffe version differs from the original network in that is has piecewise linear node activation functions.

Figure 5(a)–(b) shows some example digits from the MNIST dataset. All images are in gray-scale and have 28×28 pixels. Our simplified network uses the following layers:

- One input layer with 28×28 nodes,
- one convolutional network layer with $3 \times 13 \times 13$ nodes, where every node has 16 incoming edges,
- one pooling layer with $3 \times 4 \times 4$ nodes, where each node has 16 incoming edges,
- one ReLU layer with 8 nodes, and
- one ReLU output layer with 10 nodes

The ReLU layers are fully connected. Overall, the network has 1341 nodes, the search space for the node phases is of size $16^{3 \cdot 4 \cdot 4} \cdot 2^8 \cdot 2^{10} = 2^{162}$, and the network has 9344 edges.

We used this architecture to learn a network from the 100000 training images of the dataset, and the resulting network has an accuracy of 95.05% on a separate testing dataset. Note that an accuracy of 100% cannot be expected from any machine learning technique, as the dataset also contains digits that are even hardly identifiable for humans (as shown in Fig. 5(b)).

We performed a few tests with the resulting network. First we wanted to see an input image that is classified strongly as a 2. More formally, we wanted to obtain an input image $(x_{1,1}, \ldots, x_{28,28})$ for which the network outputs a vector $(y_0, \ldots, y_9)$ for which $y_2 \geq y_i + \delta$ for all $i \in \{0, 1, 3, 4, 5, 6, 7, 8, 9\}$ for a large value of δ. We found that for values of $\delta = 20$ and $\delta = 30$, such images can be found in 4 min 25 s and 32 min 35 s, respectively. The two images are shown in Fig. 5(c) and (d). For $\delta = 50$, no such image can be found (4 min 41 s of computation time), but for $\delta = 35$, Planet times out after 4 h. Gurobi (with the added linear approximation constraints) could not find a solution in this time frame, either.

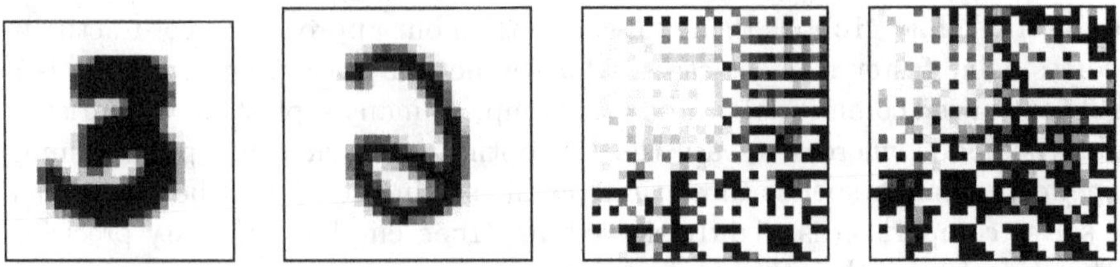

(a) '3' digit from the MNIST dataset (b) '2' digit from the MNIST dataset (c) Image classified as digit 2 with $\delta = 20$ (d) Image classified as digit 2 with $\delta = 30$

Fig. 5. Example digit images from Sect. 4.2

Then, we are interested in how much noise can be added to images before they are not categorized correctly anymore. We start with the digit given in Fig. 5(a), which is correctly categorized by the learned network as digit 3. We ask whether there is another image that is categorized as a 4, but for which each pixel has values that are within an absolute range of $\pm 8\%$ of color intensity of the original image's pixels, where we keep the pixels the same that are at most three pixels away from the boundaries. To determine that this is not the case, `planet` requires 1 min 46.8 s. For a range of ± 0.12, `planet` times out after four hours. The output of `planet` shows that long conflict clauses are learned in the process, which suggests that we applied it to a difficult verification problem.

We then considered an error model that captures noise that is likely to occur in practice (e.g., due to stains on scanned paper). It excludes sharp noise edges such as the ones in Fig. 5(d). Instead of restricting the amplitude of noise, we restrict the noise value differences in adjacent pixels to be ≤ 0.05 (i.e., 5% of color density). This constraint essentially states that the noise must pass through a linearized low-pass filter unmodified. We still exclude the pixels from the image boundaries from being modified. Our tool concludes in 9 min 2.4 s that the network never misclassifies the image from Fig. 5(a) as a 4 under this noise model. Since the model allows many pixels to have large deviations, we can see that including a linear noise model can improve the computation time of `planet`.

5 Conclusion

In this paper, we presented a new approach for the verification of feed-forward neural networks with piece-wise linear activation functions. Our main idea was to generate a linear approximation of the overall network behavior that can be added to SMT or ILP instances which encode neural network verification problems, and to use the approximation in a specialized approach that features multiple additional techniques geared towards neural network verification, which are grouped around a SAT solver for choosing the node phases in the network. We considered two case studies from different application domains. The approach allows arbitrary convex verification conditions, and we used them to define a noise model for testing the robustness of a network for recognizing handwritten digits.

We made the approach presented in this paper available as open-source software in the hope that it fosters the co-development of neural network verification tools and neural network architectures that are easier to verify. While our approach is limited to network types in which all components have piece-wise linear activation functions, they are often the only ones used in modern network architectures anyway. But even if more advanced activation functions such as *exponential linear units* [20] shall be used in learning, they can still be applied to learn an initial model, which is then linearly approximated with ReLU nodes and fine-tuned by an additional learning process. The final model is then easier to verify. Such a modification of the network architecture during the learning process is not commonly applied in the artificial intelligence community yet, but while verification becomes more practical, this may change in the future.

Despite the improvement in neural network verification performance reported in this paper, there is still a lot to be done on the verification side: we currently do not employ specialized heuristics for node phase branching selection, and while our approach increases the scalablity of neural network verification substantially, we observed it to still be quite fragile and prone to timeouts for difficult verification properties (as we saw in the MNIST example). Also, we had to simplify the LeNet architecture for digit recognition in our experiments, as the original net is so large that even obtaining a lower bound for a single variable in the network (which we do for all network nodes before starting the actual solution process as explained in Sect. 3.1) takes more than 30 min otherwise, even though this only means solving a single linear program. While the approach by Huang et al. [9] does not suffer from this limitation, it cannot handle general verification properties, which we believe to be important. We plan to work on tackling the network size limitation of the approach presented in this paper in the future.

References

1. Schmidhuber, J.: Deep learning in neural networks: an overview. Neural Netw. **61**, 85–117 (2015)
2. Yu, Q., Yang, Y., Song, Y., Xiang, T., Hospedales, T.M.: Sketch-a-net that beats humans. In: British Machine Vision Conference (BMVC), pp. 7.1–7.12 (2015)
3. Wagner, M., Koopman, P.: A philosophy for developing trust in self-driving cars. In: Meyer, G., Beiker, S. (eds.) Road Vehicle Automation 2. LNMOB, pp. 163–171. Springer, Cham (2015). doi:10.1007/978-3-319-19078-5_14
4. Pulina, L., Tacchella, A.: An abstraction-refinement approach to verification of artificial neural networks. In: Touili, T., Cook, B., Jackson, P. (eds.) CAV 2010. LNCS, vol. 6174, pp. 243–257. Springer, Heidelberg (2010). doi:10.1007/978-3-642-14295-6_24
5. Scheibler, K., Winterer, L., Wimmer, R., Becker, B.: Towards verification of artificial neural networks. In: 2015 MBMV Workshop, Chemnitz, Germany, pp. 30–40 (2015)

6. Scheibler, K., Neubauer, F., Mahdi, A., Fränzle, M., Teige, T., Bienmüller, T., Fehrer, D., Becker, B.: Accurate ICP-based floating-point reasoning. In: Formal Methods in Computer-Aided Design (FMCAD), pp. 177–184 (2016)
7. Katz, G., Barrett, C.W., Dill, D.L., Julian, K., Kochenderfer, M.J.: Reluplex: an efficient SMT solver for verifying deep neural networks. In: Majumdar, R., Kunčak, V. (eds.) CAV 2017. LNCS, vol. 10426, pp. 97–117. Springer, Cham (2017). doi:10.1007/978-3-319-63387-9_5
8. Pulina, L., Tacchella, A.: Challenging SMT solvers to verify neural networks. AI Commun. **25**(2), 117–135 (2012)
9. Huang, X., Kwiatkowska, M., Wang, S., Wu, M.: Safety verification of deep neural networks. In: Majumdar, R., Kunčak, V. (eds.) CAV 2017. LNCS, vol. 10426, pp. 3–29. Springer, Cham (2017). doi:10.1007/978-3-319-63387-9_1
10. Bastani, O., Ioannou, Y., Lampropoulos, L., Vytiniotis, D., Nori, A.V., Criminisi, A.: Measuring neural net robustness with constraints. In: Annual Conference on Neural Information Processing Systems (NIPS), pp. 2613–2621 (2016)
11. Chinneck, J.W., Dravnieks, E.W.: Locating minimal infeasible constraint sets in linear programs. INFORMS J. Comput. **3**(2), 157–168 (1991)
12. Jia, Y., Shelhamer, E., Donahue, J., Karayev, S., Long, J., Girshick, R., Guadarrama, S., Darrell, T.: Caffe: convolutional architecture for fast feature embedding. arXiv/CoRR 1408.5093 arXiv:1408.5093 (2014)
13. Franco, J., Martin, J.: A history of satisfiability. In: Handbook of Satisfiability. Frontiers in Artificial Intelligence and Applications, vol. 185, pp. 3–74. IOS Press, February 2009
14. Kroening, D., Strichman, O.: Decision Procedures - An Algorithmic Point of View. Springer, Heidelberg (2008)
15. Dutertre, B., de Moura, L.: A fast linear-arithmetic solver for DPLL(T). In: Ball, T., Jones, R.B. (eds.) CAV 2006. LNCS, vol. 4144, pp. 81–94. Springer, Heidelberg (2006). doi:10.1007/11817963_11
16. Eén, N., Sörensson, N.: An extensible SAT-solver. In: Giunchiglia, E., Tacchella, A. (eds.) SAT 2003. LNCS, vol. 2919, pp. 502–518. Springer, Heidelberg (2004). doi:10.1007/978-3-540-24605-3_37
17. Dutertre, B.: Yices 2.2. In: Biere, A., Bloem, R. (eds.) CAV 2014. LNCS, vol. 8559, pp. 737–744. Springer, Cham (2014). doi:10.1007/978-3-319-08867-9_49
18. Lecun, Y., Cortes, C.: The MNIST database of handwritten digits (2009)
19. Lecun, Y., Bottou, L., Bengio, Y., Haffner, P.: Gradient-based learning applied to document recognition. Proc. IEEE **86**(11), 2278–2324 (1998)
20. Clevert, D., Unterthiner, T., Hochreiter, S.: Fast and accurate deep network learning by exponential linear units (ELUs). arXiv/CoRR 1511.07289 arXiv:1511.07289 (2015)

Learning and Invariant Synthesis

Liquid Types for Array Invariant Synthesis

Manuel Montenegro(✉), Susana Nieva, Ricardo Peña, and Clara Segura

Universidad Complutense de Madrid, Madrid, Spain
montenegro@fdi.ucm.es, nieva@ucm.es, {ricardo,csegura}@sip.ucm.es

Abstract. Liquid types qualify ordinary Hindley-Milner types by predicates expressing properties. The system infers the types of all the variables and checks that the verification conditions proving correctness hold. These predicates are currently expressed in a quantifier free decidable logic.

Here, we extend Liquid types with quantified predicates of a decidable logic for arrays, propose a concept of an array refinement type, and present an inference algorithm for this extension, that we have implemented. By applying our tool to several imperative algorithms dealing with arrays, we have been able to infer complex invariants.

1 Introduction

Liquid types [10,13,17–19] are a variant of dependent types which have been successfully used for automatically verifying a number of non trivial properties of programs. Recently they have also been used as a guide for synthesizing correct programs [12]. They have been mainly applied to functional languages. A liquid type is a refinement of an ordinary type, defined by restricting the set of possible values to those satisfying a predicate. This predicate may have as free variables some variables in scope. In this way, the type depends on the values computed by the program.

The original idea [13] has been extended to recursive data structures [10], and it is possible for instance to define a list whose tail values depend on the value at the head, or a tree whose children values depend on the value at the root. This captures in a natural way invariants of sorted lists, binary search trees, binary heaps and many other interesting data structures. Once the programmer has written the invariant, the system assists the programmer in verifying that the functions manipulating the data structure actually preserve the invariant. This saves most of the verification effort that would be needed by doing it manually.

The underlying machinery is a type inference algorithm which tries to prove a set of logical implications, which in essence are the verification conditions that a human programmer would try to prove manually. The system does it

Work partially supported by the Spanish MINECO project CAVI-ART (TIN2013-44742-C4-3-R), Madrid regional project N-GREENS Software-CM (S2013/ICE-2731) and UCM grant GR3/14-910502.

D. D'Souza and K. Narayan Kumar (Eds.): ATVA 2017, LNCS 10482, pp. 289–306, 2017.
DOI: 10.1007/978-3-319-68167-2_20

automatically with the aid of a SMT solver. In order that the solver never fails to prove a formula, the logic of the predicates used in liquid types must be decidable. In its current state, the logic, and hence the liquid types one can infer, does not include quantifiers. It supports however linear integer arithmetic, equality, algebraic types and uninterpreted functions (this logic is known as QF-EUFLIA).

Our contribution here is extending the liquid types to properties on arrays, which very frequently need predicates universally quantified over the array indices. Nevertheless, we still remain in the safe side by only allowing formulas in a decidable theory of arrays, which is a fragment of Bradley and colleagues' [2].

Additionally, we extend the type inference algorithm to quantified formulas, and also use SMTs to automatically discharge them. This extension includes two novelties: (a) new liquid variables are created dynamically in order to split a quantified formula over an array segment into two or more formulas over smaller segments; and (b) these variables occur in negative positions of the formula. Even though, our domain is still a finite one, and our abstract interpretation is monotonic in this domain. This ensures that the inference algorithm always terminates without the need of a widening operator.

Another contribution is that we apply the liquid type technology to imperative programming languages dealing with arrays such as C++ and Java. This is possible thanks to our verification platform [11] that transforms programs into an *intermediate representation* (IR) common to all these languages. In essence, this IR is a desugared functional language, where state updating has been replaced by dynamic creation of variables, and iteration has been transformed into recursion.

Our inference algorithm has been integrated in that platform. With this new tool, we have inferred complex invariants on arrays, as for instance those occurring in the imperative sorting algorithms. We think that this opens the door to the use of liquid types in verifying non trivial properties of programs written in conventional imperative languages.

The plan of the paper is as follows: after this introduction, Sect. 2 explains some fundamentals about liquid types and their inference algorithm; then, Sect. 3 reviews the decidable theories about arrays; inspired in those theories, Sect. 4 contains our proposal for an array refinement, whose aim is to capture as many properties about arrays as possible out of those arising in imperative algorithms; Sect. 5 presents our type inference algorithm, and Sect. 6 shows a number of meaningful examples to which the algorithm has been applied. Sect. 7 relates our approach to other works in the literature, and Sect. 8 draws some conclusions.

2 Liquid Types

The Liquid type system [13] extends the polymorphic Hindley-Milner type system by decorating types with *refinement predicates* constraining the values represented by them. A refined type has the form $\{\nu : \tau \mid e\}$, where τ is a Hindley-Milner type and e is a boolean expression which may name the ν variable and other program variables. This type represents the values b of type τ such that $e[b/\nu]$ evaluates to *true*. For instance, the type $\{\nu : int \mid \nu \geq 0\}$ represents the type of nonnegative integers. Another example is the following declaration, which specifies the type of a function `get` for array indexing,

$$\texttt{get} :: \forall\alpha.(a : array\ \alpha) \rightarrow i : \{\nu : int \mid 0 \leq \nu \land \nu < len\ a\} \rightarrow \{\nu : \alpha \mid \nu = a[i]\} \tag{1}$$

where *len a* represents the length of the array a. The type *array* α abbreviates the refined type $\{\nu : array\ \alpha \mid true\}$.

In their most general form, type checking and type inference of refined types is undecidable. However, in the Liquid type system inference becomes decidable by restricting the boolean expressions to the logic of linear arithmetic, equality and uninterpreted functions (QF-EUFLIA), and by bounding the search space of refinements with the help of logical qualifiers.

A *logical qualifier* q is a predicate which depends on ν and a placeholder variable denoted by $\star$. The set $\mathbb{Q}$ of qualifiers to be used is given by the programmer. The larger this set, the more complex refinements can be specified, but the larger the search space becomes. An *instance* of a logical qualifier q is another qualifier obtained by replacing each placeholder in q by a program variable. We denote by $\mathbb{Q}^*$ the set of qualifiers that are instances of $\mathbb{Q}$. Since $\mathbb{Q}$ is finite, so is $\mathbb{Q}^*$. A *liquid type* is a refined type in which the refinement predicates are conjunctions of elements in $\mathbb{Q}^*$. For instance, if $\mathbb{Q} = \{\nu \geq 0, \nu < len\ \star, \nu = \star[\star]\}$, the type (1) is a liquid type.

The inference algorithm, which will be detailed in Sect. 2.1 transforms subtyping relations between liquid types into boolean formulas which are subsequently sent to a SMT solver. The variables occurring in these formulas are assumed to be universally quantified at the outermost level. However, in some cases we need nested quantification: assume a function that initializes all the positions of an array with a given element x. The type of the resulting array have the refinement $\forall i. 0 \leq i < n \rightarrow \nu[i] = x$. As another example, a function that sorts an array would have the refinement $\forall i.\forall j. 0 \leq i \leq j < len\ \nu \rightarrow \nu[i] \leq \nu[j]$ in the type of the output. These types are not liquid types, since their refinements are not conjunctions of qualifiers, but universally quantified formulas.

The original work of [13] summarized above only manages quantifier-free refinements in order to make inference decidable. In further work [10,17], the authors extend the Liquid type system in order to allow parametricity on the refinement predicates. This is achieved by including *refinement predicate variables*. For instance, if p denotes a predicate variable, the type *int* $\langle p \rangle$ stands for the set of integers x such that $p\ x$ holds. This type can be instantiated, for instance, to $int\langle \lambda x.x\ mod\ 2 = 0\rangle$, which denotes the set of even integers. This idea is also applied to arrays by including two refinement predicate variables into the *array* data type. The first one (*dom*) constraints the set of valid indexes, whereas the second one (*rng*) specifies the property that must hold for each element stored in the array. This property may also, in turn, depend on the element index. Therefore we would have the type $array\ \alpha\langle dom, rng\rangle$ with the following signatures for accessing and modifying arrays:

$$\begin{aligned}
\texttt{get} &:: \forall\alpha.\forall(dom :: int \rightarrow bool).\forall(rng :: int \rightarrow \alpha \rightarrow bool).\\
&\quad (i : int\langle dom\rangle) \rightarrow array\ \alpha\langle dom, rng\rangle \rightarrow \alpha\langle rng\ i\rangle\\
\texttt{set} &:: \forall\alpha.\forall(dom :: int \rightarrow bool).\forall(rng :: int \rightarrow \alpha \rightarrow bool).\\
&\quad (i : int\langle dom\rangle) \rightarrow array\ \alpha\langle dom', rng\rangle \rightarrow \alpha\langle rng\ i\rangle \rightarrow array\ \alpha\langle dom, rng\rangle
\end{aligned}$$

where dom' abbreviates $\lambda k.dom\ k \wedge k \neq i$. These parametric arrays allow one to express properties on the elements of an array while still avoiding quantified formulas in the refinements. However, this approach has some drawbacks. In principle we would be tempted to think that the type $array\ \alpha\langle dom, rng\rangle$ is semantically equivalent to the refined type $\{\nu : array\ \alpha \mid \forall i.dom\ i \rightarrow rng\ i\ \nu[i]\}$. However, there is a difference: in presence of refinement variables, the subtyping relation is defined covariantly. That is, in order to prove that $array\ \alpha\langle dom, rng\rangle$ is a subtype of $array\ \alpha\langle dom', rng'\rangle$ the condition $\forall i.\forall z.(dom\ i \wedge rng\ i\ z \Rightarrow dom'\ i \wedge rng'\ i\ z)$ is sent to an SMT solver. We cannot justify covariance in the dom variable, as this implies, for instance, that an array whose indices are in $[0..3]$ is a subtype of an array whose indices range over the interval $[0..5]$. On the other hand, if we allow quantifiers in refinement types, proving that $\{\nu : array\ \alpha \mid \forall i.dom\ i \rightarrow rng\ i\ \nu[i]\}$ is a subtype of $\{\nu : array\ \alpha \mid \forall i.dom'\ i \rightarrow rng'\ i\ \nu[i]\}$ amounts to prove the assertion $(\forall i.dom\ i \rightarrow rng\ i\ \nu[i]) \Rightarrow (\forall i.dom'\ i \rightarrow rng'\ i\ \nu[i])$. This kind of assertions can be managed by some SMTs under some conditions which will be explained in Sect. 3.

Another drawback of the type $array\langle dom, rng\rangle$ is that properties involving two quantifiers, such as the one shown above for the sort function, cannot be expressed. Our main technical contribution in this work is the extension of the Liquid type system in order to be able to infer properties involving quantification on the indices of the array in order to overcome the limitations explained above.

2.1 Features of the Type System and Inference

As mentioned above, there is a subtyping relation between refined types. This relation is defined by a set of rules of the form $\Gamma \vdash \tau_1 <: \tau_2$, meaning that τ_1 is a subtype of τ_2 under an environment Γ. The type system is path-sensitive, so the type environment does not only contain the types of the variables in scope, but also the conditions that are satisfied in the context of an expression (these are gathered, for example, when traversing `if` expressions). Among the typing rules of the system (see [13]), the most relevant one specifies that, under Γ, the type $\{\nu : B \mid e_1\}$ is a subtype of $\{\nu : B \mid e_2\}$ whenever B is a basic type and the formula $[\![\Gamma]\!] \wedge e_1 \Rightarrow e_2$ is valid. The notation $[\![\Gamma]\!]$ is a logical characterization of the environment in which each binding of the form $x : \{\nu : B \mid e\}$ is translated into the formula $e[x/\nu]$.

The inference algorithm assumes that a standard Hindley-Milner inference has been applied previously. After this, each type τ in the typing derivation is refined with a fresh template variable κ so as to obtain $\{\nu : \tau \mid \kappa\}$. Type inference consists in finding a substitution A from variables κ to conjunctions of $\mathbb{Q}^*$ such that, when applied to the typing derivation, the expression type checks. This solution is obtained by a standard fixpoint algorithm. Initially all refinement templates are mapped to $\bigwedge_{q \in \mathbb{Q}^*} q$, which is the strongest refinement. If it is a valid solution, the algorithm terminates. Otherwise, the subtyping rules must have generated an assertion $A([\![\Gamma]\!]) \wedge A(\kappa_1) \Rightarrow A(\kappa_2)$ that is not proven valid by the SMT. In this case the algorithm modifies the substitution A by removing from $A(\kappa_2)$ the qualifiers not being satisfied in the formula. Then, program is type checked again with the new substitution. This process is repeated until a solution is found. Since the set of conjunctions of elements of $\mathbb{Q}^*$ is finite, the algorithm is guaranteed to terminate.

3 Decidable Theories on Arrays

As explained before, when working with liquid types, refinements should be formalized using formulas whose satisfiability could be provable. Therefore, it is important to know which theories concerning arrays are decidable, in order to use formulas of such theories to specify array properties. First studies involving satisfiability decision procedures for array theories have focused on quantifier-free fragments [16], as the full theories are undecidable. Later, an extensional theory of arrays with equality between unbounded arrays has been formalized as a decidable fragment [15]. An extension of these theories is studied in [2]. The motivation is that most assertions and invariants of programs related to arrays require at least a universal quantifier over index variables. Usual array properties can be formalized by formulas having the form $(\forall \overline{j}.\varphi_I(\overline{j}) \rightarrow \varphi_V(\overline{j}))$ where $\overline{j}$ is a vector of index variables, the guard $\varphi_I(\overline{j})$ delimits the segment of the array we are interested in, while $\varphi_V(\overline{j})$ refers to the value constraint. Both the guard and the value constraint involve predicates referring to program variables.

In order to have a satisfiability procedure for universal quantified formulas with that shape, some limitations are imposed to the syntax of $\varphi_I(\overline{j})$ and $\varphi_V(\overline{j})$. These limitations restrict the set of predicates that can be used to build those formulas, but most of the common program invariants referring arrays can be expressed with the restricted set, as we will see. The form of an index guard $\varphi_I(\overline{j})$ is constrained according to the grammar:

$$\begin{aligned}
guard &::= guard \wedge guard \mid guard \vee guard \mid atom \\
atom &::= expr \leq expr \mid expr = expr \\
expr &::= uvar \mid pexpr \\
pexpr &::= z \mid z * evar \mid pexpr + pexpr
\end{aligned}$$

where z stands for Presburger arithmetic basic terms (i.e. terms built up from the constants 0, 1 and the functions + and −), *uvar* represents variables that will occur universally quantified, and *evar* represents integer variables that will occur existentially quantified. Notice that the relations $\neq$ and $<$ are not allowed between quantified indices, and that they cannot be simulated by using $\leq$ because terms like $j + 1$ are not valid in *pexpr* if j is a universally quantified variable. However, we will write $j < b$, where j is quantified and b is in *pexpr*, as an abbreviation of $j \leq b - 1$, which is allowed if b is not quantified.

The formula $\varphi_V(\overline{\jmath})$ is constrained in such a way that any occurrence of a quantified variable $j \in \overline{\jmath}$ must be as a read into an array, $a[j]$, for array term a, and nested array reads are not allowed. Other program variables and terms can occur everywhere in the formula. A formula of the form $(\forall \overline{\jmath}.\varphi_I(\overline{\jmath}) \rightarrow \varphi_V(\overline{\jmath}))$ with the previous constraints for $\varphi_I(\overline{\jmath})$ and $\varphi_V(\overline{\jmath})$ is called an *array property.*

The theory consisting in all existentially-closed Boolean combinations of array properties, and quantifier-free formulas built from program variables and terms is decidable. However, when considering existentially-closed $\forall$-$\exists$-fragments, even with syntactic restrictions like those in the array property, the satisfiability problem becomes undecidable. Other theories also proved undecidable are the following extensions of the array property formulas: If the formula contains nested reads as $a_1[a_2[j]]$ and j is universally quantified, or if $a[j]$ appears in the guard and j is universally quantified, or if the formula includes general Presburger arithmetic expressions over universally quantified index variables (e.g., $j + 1$) in the index guard or in the value constraint.

4 Array Refinements

In order to bound the decidable fragment of the array theory, we realize that most of the array properties fall in some of the following categories:

- Some elements of an array satisfy individually a property. For example:

$$\forall j.0 \leq j < \mathit{len}\ v \wedge j\%2 = 0 \rightarrow v[j] > 0 \tag{2}$$

$$\forall j.a \leq j \leq b \rightarrow x < v[j] \wedge v[j] \leq y \tag{3}$$

- Some pairs of elements in a segment of an array satisfy a binary relation:

$$\forall j_1, j_2.a \leq j_1 < j_2 \leq b \rightarrow v[j_1] \neq v[j_2] \tag{4}$$

$$\forall j_1, j_2.a \leq j_1 \leq p \wedge p \leq j_2 \leq b \rightarrow v[j_1] \leq v[j_2] \tag{5}$$

  Property (5) holds after partition in *quicksort*, being p the pivot position. Sometimes the binary relation concerns two different arrays. For example:

$$\forall j_1, j_2.a \leq j_1 \leq k - 1 \wedge i \leq j_2 \leq m \rightarrow v[j_1] \leq w[j_2] \tag{6}$$

  is a property that holds while merging the two sorted halves $[a, m]$ and $[m + 1, b]$ of an array w into an ordered array v (see Example 3).
- Usually we also need properties related to the length of the array in order to guarantee that the array accesses are well defined. For instance, the property (3) can be completed with $(0 \leq a < \mathit{len}\ v) \wedge (0 \leq b < \mathit{len}\ v)$.

Some formulas listed above do not belong to the decidable fragment mentioned in the previous section. In particular, (2) is not in the fragment because operators over the quantified variables are not allowed, and (4) is not an array property, because relation $<$ is not allowed over the quantified indices. The remaining formulas are allowed[1], even more, they belong to a subset of the fragment that we are going to characterize in our formalization of array refinements.

[1] We consider $\mathit{len}\ v$ to be a fixed integer rather than a function applied to v.

$\{0 \le n < len\ v \wedge ord(v, 0, n-1)\}$

```
i = n-1; x = v[n];
while (i >= 0 && x < v[i])
   {v[i+1] = v[i]; i = i-1;}
v[i+1] = x;
```

$\{ord(v, 0, n)\}$

Fig. 1. *insert* algorithm

$\{ord(v, 0, len\ v - 1)\}$

```
a = 0; b = (len v) - 1;
while (a<=b)
 { m = (a+b)/2;
   if (v[m] < x) {a = m+1;}
   else {b = m-1;}  }
```

$\{lt(v, x, 0, a) \wedge geq(v, x, a, len\ v)\}$

Fig. 2. *binSearch* algorithm

$\{0 \le a \le m \le b < len\ v\ \wedge ord(w, a, m) \wedge ord(w, m+1, b)\}$

```
i = a; j = m+1;k = a;
while (i <= m && j <= b)
  { if (w[i] <= w[j]) { v[k] = w[i]; i=i+1; }
    else  { v[k] = w[j]; j=j+1; }
    k=k+1; }
while (i <= m) {v[k]=w[i]; i=i+1; k=k+1;}
while (j <= b) {v[k]=w[j]; j=j+1; k=k+1;}
```

$\{ord(v, a, b)\}$

Fig. 3. *merge* algorithm

Considering these three kinds of array properties, we establish three kinds of refinements with the aim of inferring automatically array properties. We consider that they widely cover many of the invariants needed to verify programs dealing with arrays, including the most known sorting algorithms, as we will show in Sect. 6. We will call them respectively *simple* array refinements (denoted as ρ), *double* array refinements (denoted as $\rho\!\!\rho$) and *length* refinements (denoted as ψ).

Simple refinements have the shape $\rho(w) \equiv \forall j.I(j) \rightarrow E(w[j])$, where w is an array. In the liquid type this will be the array being refined, i.e. ν. Predicate I restricts the values of the indices whose elements satisfy the property, and E expresses the individual property satisfied by each considered element. The qualifiers allowed in both of them are constrained as explained in Sect. 3 to ensure decidability, and belong to the sets of qualifiers which are provided by the programmer. As we may have several simple refinements, we can consider predicate I to be just a conjunction of qualifiers due to the logical equivalence $(A \vee B) \rightarrow C \Leftrightarrow (A \rightarrow C) \wedge (B \rightarrow C)$. In order to reduce the search space in the inference process we have decided E to be a conjunction of qualifiers[2]. Due to the logical equivalence $A \rightarrow (B \wedge C) \Leftrightarrow (A \rightarrow B) \wedge (A \rightarrow C)$, we can consider that in fact E is a single qualifier. Note that the previous predicate (3) is a valid simple refinement.

[2] This does not preclude that a qualifier could be a disjunction of atomic properties.

Double refinements have the shape $\wp(v,w) \equiv \forall j_1, j_2. II(j_1,j_2) \rightarrow EE(v[j_1], w[j_2])$, where v, w are array variables. In the liquid type, at least one of them will be the refined array ν, and in case the other is not, it has to be a free in scope variable. Predicate II restricts the values of the pairs of indices, and EE expresses the relation satisfied by each considered pair. Both of them must meet the constraints of the array property formulas. Similarly to simple refinements, II is a conjunction of qualifiers and EE is a single qualifier. Note that examples (5) and (6) are valid double refinements.

Length refinements are qualifiers relating the length of the array to other values or program variables, such as $a < len\ \nu$ or $len\ \nu = len\ w$.

Definition 1. *A* refined array type *has the following shape:*

$$\{\nu : array\ \tau \mid (\bigwedge_i \psi_i(\nu)) \wedge (\bigwedge_j \rho_j(\nu)) \wedge (\bigwedge_k \wp_k(\nu, v_k))\}$$

where each v_k may be ν itself or a free array variable.

Example 1. Figure 1 shows the specification and the imperative code corresponding to the algorithm *insert* used in the insertion sort, where $ord(v,l,r) \equiv \forall j_1, j_2. l \leq j_1 \leq j_2 \leq r \rightarrow v[j_1] \leq v[j_2]$. The property $\forall j. i+2 \leq j \leq n \rightarrow x < \nu[j]$ is part of the refinement of array v in line 2, i.e. it is an invariant property of the loop. □

Example 2. Figure 2 shows the specification and the imperative code corresponding to the binary search algorithm, where $lt(v,x,l,r) \equiv \forall j. l \leq j < r \rightarrow v[j] < x$ and $geq(v,x,l,r) \equiv \forall j. l \leq j < r \rightarrow x \leq v[j]$. The property $geq(v,x,b+1, len\ v)$ is part of the refinement of array v in line 2, i.e. it is an invariant property of the loop. □

Example 3. In Fig. 3 we show the specification and the imperative code corresponding to the algorithm *merge* used in the mergesort algorithm. The property

$$(\forall j_1, j_2 \,.\, a \leq j_1 \leq k-1 \wedge i \leq j_2 \leq m \rightarrow \nu[j_1] \leq w[j_2]) \wedge$$
$$(\forall j_1, j_2 \,.\, a \leq j_1 \leq k-1 \wedge j \leq j_2 \leq b \rightarrow \nu[j_1] \leq w[j_2])$$

is part of the refinement of array v in line 2, i.e. it is an invariant property of the first loop. It is also part of v's refinement in the second and third loops. □

5 The Type Inference Algorithm

The inference algorithm has the following phases:

1. A standard type checking algorithm decorates every variable with its conventional type. Our IR includes types at every defining occurrence. The type checking propagates this information to every applied variable occurrence.
2. Each type occurrence is then refined with a *liquid template* (see below) of the appropriate type. The template refining a type occurrence introduces a fresh liquid variable. The purpose of the inference algorithm is to find appropriate substitutions for these liquid variables.

3. The syntax-driven liquid typing rules of the IR are applied, and a set of *constraints* is obtained. These are to be satisfied in order the program be correctly typed in the liquid type sense. A constraint has the form $[\![\Gamma]\!] \wedge \theta_1.\iota_1 \Rightarrow \theta_2.\iota_2$, where ι_1 and ι_2 are liquid variables and θ_1, θ_2 *pending substitutions*, as in [13]. The purpose of the pending substitutions is to replace formal arguments by actual ones in function applications. In our IR, actual arguments are always variables. The liquid typing rule for application is as follows:

$$\frac{\Gamma \vdash e : (x : T_x \to T) \qquad \Gamma \vdash y : T_x}{\Gamma \vdash e\ y : T[y/x]}$$

4. The constraints are solved by an *iterative weakening* algorithm. The algorithm starts with the strongest possible mapping A for all the liquid variables, and at each step, a variable assignment is weakened in order to satisfy a constraint. If a fixpoint is reached, then the final mapping obtained, when applied to all the templates, gives us the liquid types for all the variables.

5.1 Liquid Templates

The liquid types of the variables x that are not arrays are represented by a liquid variable κ with pending substitutions θ, as usual: $x : \{\nu : \tau \mid \theta.\kappa\}$. The range of $A(\kappa)$ are conjunctions of qualifiers taken from the set $\mathbb{Q}^*$, which is obtained from $\mathbb{Q}$ at each program location by substituting program variables in scope of the appropriated type for the wildcard $\star$. After applying A, the pending substitution θ is applied to the result.

The liquid types of the variables a of array type are dealt with similarly, except for the fact that we denote the liquid variable by μ, $a : \{\nu : \mathit{array}\ \tau \mid \theta.\mu\}$. In this case we assume that the programmer provides several qualifier sets $\mathbb{Q}_E$, $\mathbb{Q}_{EE}$, $\mathbb{Q}_I$, $\mathbb{Q}_{II}$ and $\mathbb{Q}_{len}$, explained in detail below. The range of $A(\mu)$ are *array refinements* obtained from conjunctions of *array refinements templates* by substitution. These templates may be:

- Simple array refinement templates, $\rho \stackrel{\text{def}}{=} (\forall j.\eta \to q)$, where q is a qualifier taken from the set $\mathbb{Q}^*_E$, and η is a liquid variable.
- Double array refinement templates, $\rho\!\rho \stackrel{\text{def}}{=} (\forall j_1, j_2.\eta\!\eta \to q)$, where q is a qualifier taken from the set $\mathbb{Q}^*_{EE}$ and $\eta\!\eta$ is a liquid variable.
- An array length refinement template ζ. This liquid variable represents properties restricting the length of the array.

We will use ξ to denote both a simple and a double array refinement template, so $A(\mu) = (\bigwedge_{i=1}^{n} A(\xi_i)) \wedge A(\zeta)$, where $A(\rho) = \forall j.A(\eta) \to q$, and $A(\rho\!\rho) = \forall j_1, j_2.A(\eta\!\eta) \to q$. The range of $A(\eta)$, $A(\eta\!\eta)$ and $A(\zeta)$ are conjunctions of qualifiers taken respectively from the sets $\mathbb{Q}^*_I$, $\mathbb{Q}^*_{II}$, and $\mathbb{Q}^*_{len}$. Only variables in scope are considered on these instances of the respective qualifier sets $\mathbb{Q}_E$, $\mathbb{Q}_{EE}$, $\mathbb{Q}_I$, $\mathbb{Q}_{II}$, $\mathbb{Q}_{len}$. These sets meet several constraints which guarantee that, when wildcards are instantiated, then the obtained qualifiers satisfy the restrictions imposed on the array property formulas, e.g. $\mathbb{Q}_I$ and $\mathbb{Q}_E$ use $\star$ and # as wildcards in the qualifiers, and only the bound variable j can be substituted for the wildcard #.

From now on, we will consider fixed the sets $\mathbb{Q}$, $\mathbb{Q}_I$, $\mathbb{Q}_{II}$, $\mathbb{Q}_E$, $\mathbb{Q}_{EE}$ and $\mathbb{Q}_{len}$ and we denote by $\mathcal{Q}$ the collection of these six sets.

Definition 2. *A mapping A is* suitable to $\mathcal{Q}$ *if it assigns a value of their respective ranges to each κ, μ, ζ, η, and $\eta\!\!\eta$ variables, and for each η variable of a ρ template, $A(\eta)$ contains $0 \le j < len\ \nu$, where j is the universal quantified variable in ρ, and for each $\eta\!\!\eta$ variable of a $\rho\!\!\rho$ template, $A(\eta\!\!\eta)$ contains $0 \le j_1 < len\ a \wedge 0 \le j_2 < len\ b$, where j_1, j_2 are the universal quantified variables in $\rho\!\!\rho$, a and b are either ν, or the free array variable in scope substituted for $\star$ in the qualifier at the right-hand side of $\rho\!\!\rho$. We denote by $\mathcal{A}_{\mathcal{Q}}$ the set of all the mappings suitable to $\mathcal{Q}$.*

The κ, μ, ζ variables occur in logically positive positions in the templates, while η, and $\eta\!\!\eta$ variables occur in negative ones. As a consequence, weakening A may consist of weakening the assignment to a κ, a μ, or a ζ variable, or strengthening the assignment to a η or a $\eta\!\!\eta$ variable.

For any liquid variable ι, if Q is a set of qualifiers, or a set of array refinements, when we write $A(\iota) = Q$, Q denotes the conjunction of its elements. In the examples, we omit the component $0 \le j < len\ \nu$ of $A(\eta)$ when it is not relevant (analogously for $A(\eta\!\!\eta)$).

Example 4. In the *insert* algorithm of Fig. 1, from the template $(\forall j_1, j_2.\eta\!\!\eta \rightarrow q)$, and the sets $\mathbb{Q}_{II} = \{0 \le \#_1, \star + 2 \le \#_2, \#_1 \le \star, \#_2 \le \star\}$, and $\mathbb{Q}_{EE} = \{\nu[\#_1] \le \nu[\#_2]\}$, the predicate $\forall j_1, j_2. 0 \le j_1 \le i \wedge i+2 \le j_2 \le n \rightarrow \nu[j_1] \le \nu[j_2]$ can be obtained. It is part of the refinement type for v. □

5.2 The Iterative Weakening Algorithm

Given a set C of constraints, and a collection $\mathcal{Q} = \{\mathbb{Q}, \mathbb{Q}_I, \mathbb{Q}_{II}, \mathbb{Q}_E, \mathbb{Q}_{EE}, \mathbb{Q}_{len}\}$, the purpose of the algorithm is to find a solution to C, in accordance to the following definition:

Definition 3. *Given $A \in \mathcal{A}_{\mathcal{Q}}$, we say that A* satisfies *$c \in C$ if $A(c)$ is a valid formula. We say that A is a* solution *of C, if the set $A(C)$ is a set of valid formulas, abbreviated $A(C)$ valid.*

Below we describe the steps of the weakening algorithm. It starts with the strongest possible mapping A suitable to $\mathcal{Q}$. This consists of:

1. For a κ variable, $A(\kappa)$ is the conjunction of all the well-typed qualifiers of $\mathbb{Q}^*$ containing variables in scope.
2. For a μ variable, $A(\mu)$ is the conjunction of as many instances $A(\rho)$ of ρ templates as well-typed qualifiers in $\mathbb{Q}^*_E$, and as many instances $A(\rho\!\!\rho)$ of $\rho\!\!\rho$ templates as well-typed qualifiers in $\mathbb{Q}^*_{EE}$. There is also an additional conjunction $A(\zeta)$ for qualifying the array length (with variables in scope in each case).

- For a ζ variable, $A(\zeta)$ is the conjunction of all the well-typed qualifiers of $\mathbb{Q}^*_{len}$ containing variables in scope.
- For the η variable of a ρ template, $A(\eta)$ is the weakest possible predicate, $0 \leq j < len\ \nu$, where j is the universally quantified variable in ρ.
- For the $\eta\!\!\eta$ variable of a $\rho\!\!\rho$ template, $A(\eta\!\!\eta)$ is the weakest possible predicate, $0 \leq j_1 < len\ a \wedge 0 \leq j_2 < len\ b$, where j_1, j_2 are the universally quantified variables in $\rho\!\!\rho$, a and b are either ν, or the free array variable in scope substituted for $\star$ in the qualifier at the right-hand side of $\rho\!\!\rho$.

Example 5. In the *binSearch* algorithm of Fig. 2, we have $\mathbb{Q}^*_E = \{x \leq \nu[j], x > \nu[j]\}$, $\mathbb{Q}^*_I = \{j \leq a-1,\ b+1 \leq j\}$ for the μ_3 variable corresponding to the array v at the beginning of each iteration. Then the refinement:

$$(\forall j\,.\,0 \leq j \wedge j < len\ \nu \rightarrow x \leq \nu[j]) \wedge (\forall j\,.\,0 \leq j \wedge j < len\ \nu \rightarrow x > \nu[j]) \quad (7)$$

will be included in the strongest assignment to μ_3. □

At each iteration, the algorithm arbitrarily chooses a constraint $c \in C$ not satisfied by A. Then, A is *weakened* in order to make the constraint valid. If this is not possible, then the algorithm ends up with **failure**. If this is possible, A is replaced by its weakened form A', and the set C of constraints is inspected again looking for a new unsatisfied constraint. Because A has changed, some prior satisfied constraints may have turned into unsatisfied ones. If no unsatisfied constraint remains, then the algorithm ends up with **success**. The final mapping A, when applied to all the templates, and then applying the pending substitutions, gives the liquid type of each program variable.

The crucial step is then how to weaken the mapping A in order to satisfy a constraint c. Differently to the standard algorithm of [13], weakening A in our case may change the constraints themselves, and may introduce new liquid variables. Let us see the process in detail:

1. If c has the form $[\Gamma] \wedge \theta_1.\iota \Rightarrow \theta_2.\kappa$, where ι denotes either a κ or a μ variable, and $A(\kappa) = q_1 \wedge \cdots \wedge q_r$, then the weakening removes from $A(\kappa)$ all the qualifiers q_i such that the formula $A([\Gamma]) \wedge \theta_1.A(\iota) \Rightarrow \theta_2.q_i$ is not valid. This approach corresponds to the standard weakening of [13]. The ζ variable of an array refinement is dealt with exactly in the same way as a κ variable, so in what follows we will not insist in these ζ variables.
2. If c has the form $[\Gamma] \wedge \theta_1.\iota \Rightarrow \theta_2.\mu$, and $A(\mu) = A(\xi_1) \wedge \cdots \wedge A(\xi_r)$, in a first step the weakening removes from $A(\mu)$ all the refinements $A(\xi_i)$ such that the formula $A([\Gamma]) \wedge \theta_1.A(\iota) \Rightarrow \theta_2.A(\xi_i)$ is not valid and cannot not be made valid. If the formula is not valid, then it is tested whether it can be made valid by strengthening the antecedent of $A(\xi_i)$. To do this, the η or $\eta\!\!\eta$ variable of ξ_i is assigned the strongest possible value, i.e. the conjunction of all the qualifiers of its respective $\mathbb{Q}^*_I$ or $\mathbb{Q}^*_{II}$ set. This assignment makes the instance of ξ_i as weak as possible. If, in spite of being that weak, the formula is not valid, then $A(\xi_i)$ is discarded from $A(\mu)$.

3. For each not valid $A(\xi_i)$ in $A(\mu)$ which can be made valid by strengthening its antecedent as explained before, a search for the strongest possible valid forms of the ξ_i instance is performed. Let us assume for a moment that ξ_i is a simple refinement template ρ_1 of the form $\forall j.\eta_1 \rightarrow q$, and $A(\eta_1) = Q_1 \subseteq \mathbb{Q}_I^*$. The discussion would be similar for a double one. Conjunctions m_j of $|Q_1| + 1$, $|Q_1| + 2$, $|Q_1| + 3$, etc. qualifiers from $\mathbb{Q}_I^*$, all of them supersets of Q_1, are tried in this order as possible mappings for the η_1 variable of ρ_1, until one of them, let us call it m_1, makes the formula valid. Then the algorithm refrains from trying any superset of m_1, instead, it continues the search by trying the rest of the conjunctions. It may be the case that more than one conjunction (excluding their respective supersets) succeeds. Let them be $m_2, \ldots, m_s$. Then, fresh copies of ρ_1, call them $\rho_2, \ldots, \rho_s$, of the form $\forall j.\eta_l \rightarrow q$, with η_l fresh variables $l = 2..s$, are created. Now A' is defined from A changing the component $A(\xi_i)$ of $A(\mu)$ by the conjunction $A'(\rho_1) \wedge \cdots \wedge A'(\rho_s)$, where $A'(\eta_1) = m_1, \ldots, A'(\eta_s) = m_s$.

Example 6. In the *binSearch* algorithm, the following constraint establishes the correctness of the initial iteration:

$$x : \kappa_1 \wedge v : \mu_1 \wedge a = 0 \wedge b = (\mathit{len}\ \ v) - 1 \Rightarrow v : \mu_3$$

This constraint is not valid under the initial assignment to μ_3 given in (7), but it can be made valid by strenghtening its antecedent, since for instance the first conjunct of (7) becomes:

$$(\forall j\,.\,0 \le j \wedge j \le a - 1 \wedge b + 1 \le j \wedge j < \mathit{len}\ \ \nu \rightarrow x \le \nu[j])$$

The search for supersets refines this predicate into the following two:

$$(\forall j\,.\,0 \le j \wedge j \le a - 1 \rightarrow x \le \nu[j]) \wedge (\forall j\,.\,b + 1 \le j \wedge j < \mathit{len}\ \ \nu \rightarrow x \le \nu[j])$$

which are both valid because the j ranges over two empty sets. The first conjunct will disappear from the μ_3 assignment in subsequent weakenings. □

5.3 Soundness and Completeness

We have proven the following properties of the inference algorithm:

1. The algorithm always terminates.
2. If the algorithm terminates with **failure**, there exists no mapping A satisfying all the constraints.
3. If the algorithm terminates with **success**, the result mapping A satisfies all the constraints and it is the strongest possible mapping satisfying them.

The proof starts by showing that the search space, i.e the set $\mathcal{A}_Q$ of mappings, is a complete lattice, with the following definition of $\sqsubseteq$.

Definition 4. *Let $A, A' \in \mathcal{A}_Q$. We say that $A \sqsubseteq A'$ if for all κ, $A(\kappa) \Rightarrow A'(\kappa)$ and for all μ, $A(\mu) \Rightarrow A'(\mu)$.*

Theorem 1. The partial ordered set $(\mathcal{A}_Q, \sqsubseteq)$ is a (finite) complete lattice.

Sketch of the Proof: Since the liquid variables are mapped to conjunctions of formulas, the empty conjunction *true* is the weakest one, corresponding to the $\top$ of the lattice. The strongest possible mapping is the initial one A_0, i.e. $\bot = A_0$. It is easy to prove that the following definition $(A_1 \sqcap A_2)(\iota) = A_1(\iota) \cup A_2(\iota)$ makes $\sqcap$ a greatest lower bound, and the lowest upper bound can be defined in terms of $\sqcap$ in a standard way. Since all the $\mathbb{Q}^*$ sets are finite, so it is the set of formulas, and also the set $\mathcal{A}_Q$ of mappings. □

Moreover, the following theorem shows that each step of the weakening algorithm produces an output mapping weaker than the input one.

Theorem 2. Let $A \in \mathcal{A}_Q$. If A' is obtained from A by one step of the inference algorithm, then $A' \in \mathcal{A}_Q$ and $A \sqsubseteq A'$. □

The following two theorems allow to prove that, if a solution exists for C, then the algorithm terminates in a finite number of steps, and gives the strongest mapping A^s as a result.

Theorem 3. Given a set C of constraints, if there exists a mapping $A \in \mathcal{A}_Q$ such that A is a solution of C, then there exists a minimum mapping $A^s \in \mathcal{A}_Q$ such as $A^s(C)$ is valid.

Sketch of the Proof: As the set of mappings making C valid is finite, it is enough to show that for every pair of mappings A_1, A_2 making C valid, their greatest lower bound $A_1 \sqcap A_2$ is also a solution of C. □

Theorem 4. If the set C of constraints has a strongest solution $A^s \in \mathcal{A}_Q$, and A is a mapping produced by the inference algorithm, then $A \sqsubseteq A^s$.

Proof: By induction on the number of weakening steps of the algorithm. □

6 Implementation and Results

We have implemented our tool in two separated phases. The first one, called *Template Generator*, traverses the program text previously transformed to the platform IR, applies the typing rules, and generates the set of relevant constraints that should be valid in order the program to be well-typed in the liquid-type sense. These constraints contain κ and μ variables for respectively the unknown basic and array types. The second phase is properly the type inference algorithm explained in Sect. 5.2. It searches for a substitution of the κ and μ variables that will make all the constraints valid. It uses the Why3 platform [5] and its SMT solvers as the underlying proving machinery.

We have applied the tool to an assorted set of array algorithms, including several sorting ones, or pieces of them, the binary search in a sorted array, a simple linear search, the Dutch National Flag algorithm [4, pp. 111–116], and the *fill* algorithm filling an array with a fixed value. Some of them are iterative,

Function	Array	Inferred liquid type	#C	#F
fill	v (loop)	$\{\nu : \mathit{array}\ \alpha \mid (\forall j\,.\,0 \leq j < i \rightarrow \nu[j] = x) \wedge (i \leq \mathit{len}\ \nu)$	13	49
insert	v (loop)	$\{\nu : \mathit{array}\ \alpha \mid (\forall j\,.\,i+2 \leq j \leq n \rightarrow x < \nu[j])$ $\wedge(\forall j_1, j_2\,.\,0 \leq j_1 \leq j_2 \leq i \rightarrow \nu[j_1] \leq \nu[j_2])$ $\wedge(\forall j_1, j_2\,.\,i+2 \leq j_1 \leq j_2 \leq n \rightarrow \nu[j_1] \leq \nu[j_2])$ $\wedge(\forall j_1, j_2\,.\,0 \leq j_1 \leq i \wedge i+2 \leq j_2 \leq n \rightarrow \nu[j_1] \leq \nu[j_2])$ $\wedge(n < \mathit{len}\ \nu)\}$	30	593
merge	v (1st loop)	$\{\nu : \mathit{array}\ \alpha \mid (\forall j_1, j_2\,.\,a \leq j_1 \leq k-1 \wedge i \leq j_2 \leq m \rightarrow \nu[j_1] \leq w[j_2])$ $\wedge(\forall j_1, j_2\,.\,a \leq j_1 \leq k-1 \wedge j \leq j_2 \leq b \rightarrow \nu[j_1] \leq w[j_2])$ $\wedge(\forall j_1, j_2\,.\,a \leq j_1 \leq j_2 \leq k-1 \rightarrow \nu[j_1] \leq \nu[j_2])$ $\wedge(a < \mathit{len}\ \nu) \wedge (b < \mathit{len}\ \nu)\}$	88	1.278
partition	v (loop)	$\{\nu : \mathit{array}\ \alpha \mid (\forall j_1, j_2\,.\,a+1 \leq j_1 \leq i-1 \wedge j_2 = a \rightarrow \nu[j_1] \leq \nu[j_2])$ $\wedge(\forall j_1, j_2\,.\,j_1 = a \wedge j+1 \leq j_2 \leq b \rightarrow \nu[j_1] \leq \nu[j_2]$ $\wedge(a < \mathit{len}\ \nu) \wedge (b < \mathit{len}\ \nu)\}$	44	287
quicksort	v (before 2nd call)	$\{\nu : \mathit{array}\ \alpha \mid (\forall j_1, j_2\,.\,a \leq j_1 \leq p-1 \wedge j_2 = p \rightarrow \nu[j_1] \leq \nu[j_2])$ $\wedge(\forall j_1, j_2\,.\,j_1 = p \wedge p+1 \leq j_2 \leq b \rightarrow \nu[j_1] \leq \nu[j_2])$ $\wedge(\forall j_1, j_2\,.\,a \leq j_1 \leq j_2 \leq p-1 \rightarrow \nu[j_1] \leq \nu[j_2])$ $\wedge(a < \mathit{len}\ \nu) \wedge (b < \mathit{len}\ \nu)\}$	18	203
selsort	v (outer loop)	$\{\nu : \mathit{array}\ \alpha \mid (\forall j_1, j_2\,.\,0 \leq j_1 \leq j_2 < i \rightarrow \nu[j_1] \leq \nu[j_2])$ $\wedge(\forall j_1, j_2\,.\,0 \leq j_1 < i \wedge i \leq j_2 < \mathit{len}\ \nu \rightarrow \nu[j_1] \leq \nu[j_2])$ $\wedge(i \leq \mathit{len}\ \nu)\}$	30	233
selsort	v (inner loop)	$\{\nu : \mathit{array}\ \alpha \mid (\forall j_1, j_2\,.\,j_1 = \mathit{min} \wedge i \leq j_2 < j \rightarrow \nu[j_1] \leq \nu[j_2])$ $\wedge(i \leq \mathit{len}\ \nu) \wedge (j \leq \mathit{len}\ \nu)\}$		
binSearch	v (loop)	$\{\nu : \mathit{array}\ \alpha \mid (\forall j_1, j_2\,.\,0 \leq j_1 \leq j_2 < \mathit{len}\ \ \nu \rightarrow \nu[j_1] \leq \nu[j_2])$ $\wedge(\forall j\,.\,0 \leq j \leq a-1 \rightarrow x > \nu[j]) \wedge (\forall j\,.\,b+1 \leq j < \mathit{len}\ \ \nu \rightarrow x \leq \nu[j])\}$ $\wedge 0 \leq a \leq b+1 \leq \mathit{len}\ \ v$	25	206
linSearch	v (loop)	$(i \leq \mathit{len}\ \nu) \wedge (\forall j\,.\,0 \leq j \leq i-1 \rightarrow \nu[j] \neq x)$	19	193
DutchFlag	v (loop)	$\{\nu : \mathit{array}\ \alpha \mid (\forall j\,.\,0 \leq j < \mathit{len}\ \ \nu \rightarrow \nu[j] = R \vee \nu[j] = W \vee \nu[j] = B)$ $\wedge(\forall j\,.\,0 \leq j < a \rightarrow \nu[j] = R) \wedge (\forall j\,.\,a \leq j < b \rightarrow \nu[j]) = W)$ $\wedge(\forall j\,.\,c < j < \mathit{len}\ \ \nu \rightarrow \nu[j] = W) \wedge c < \mathit{len}\ \ v\}$	40	2.935

Fig. 4. Some of the liquid types inferred for assorted examples of array algorithms

and some other are recursive. As explained in the introduction section, after transformed to our IR, all of them are recursive. In some cases, they call to an external function that has been separately inferred. This poses no special problems to the inference algorithm.

We have provided the liquid types of the arguments and the results, i.e. the equivalent to the preconditions and the postconditions of the algorithms, and left the system to infer all the intermediate types. The *quicksort* algorithm does not include the code of *partition*. The qualifier sets used for inferring the types of these algorithms are variants of the following ones:

$$
\begin{aligned}
\mathbb{Q} &= \{\mathit{constant} \leq \nu,\ \star \leq \nu,\ \nu \leq \star,\ \nu < \star\} \\
\mathbb{Q}_E &= \{\star < \nu[\#],\ \mathit{constant} = \nu[\#], \star \neq \nu[\#]\} \\
\mathbb{Q}_I &= \{\star \leq \#,\ \# \leq \star,\ \star < \#,\ \# < \star\} \\
\mathbb{Q}_{EE} &= \{\nu[\#_1] \leq \nu[\#_2],\ \nu[\#_1] \leq \star[\#_2]\} \\
\mathbb{Q}_{II} &= \{\star \leq \#_1,\ \#_1 \leq \star,\ \star \leq \#_2,\ \#_2 \leq \star,\ \#_1 \leq \#_2,\ \#_1 = \star,\ \#_2 = \star\} \\
\mathbb{Q}_{len} &= \{\star < \mathit{len}\ \nu,\ \star \leq \mathit{len}\ \nu,\ \star < \mathit{len}\ \star,\ \star \leq \mathit{len}\ \star\}
\end{aligned}
$$

For the sets $\mathbb{Q}_I$ and $\mathbb{Q}_{II}$, the qualifiers $0 \leq \#$, $\# < len\ \nu$, $0 \leq \#_1$, $\#_1 < len\ \nu$, $0 \leq \#_2$, and $\#_2 < len\ \nu$ are automatically introduced by the tool, so programmers do not need to provide them. Also, the algorithm removes fake formulas (e.g. $\forall j \,.\, a \leq j < a \rightarrow v[j] > x$) that it can prove equivalent to *true*.

Some of the relevant types obtained are shown in Fig. 4. There, we have observed the types in text positions corresponding to entering a loop iteration, or entering a recursive call, which amounts to inferring the relevant invariants of the respective programs. With these inferred invariants all the algorithms have been proven correct by our tool.

Column $\#C$ records the number of constraints generated for the example, and column $\#F$ the number of formulas sent to the SMT solvers. Our current prototype is extremely slow: in order to prove a formula, two processes (Why3 and Z3) are, each time, started and stopped. Due to that, we can only process 10–12 formulas per second. This leads to times of up to 4 min in one of the examples. We are improving the tool by implementing a direct interface to Z3 via its API, which will process 500–1000 formulas per second. Then, the most complex example of Fig. 4 could be solved in about 5 s.

We make note that the properties inferred are in general far from being trivial. Up to five array refinements are needed in some cases to completely express the property kept invariant by a loop. We believe that these results are encouraging enough to continue exploring the power of liquid types to assist the programmer in the verification of complex array manipulating algorithms.

7 Related Work

The nearest works related to this paper are those about liquid types. These have been already reviewed in Sect. 2, and we have explained their limitations regarding universally quantified formulas.

A related technique to infer invariants of imperative programs is *predicate abstraction*, a variant of abstract interpretation which is also part of the liquid type approach. This was applied by [1,6]. The starting point is to have a finite set $Q = \{p_1, \ldots, p_n\}$ of atomic predicates in a decidable logic, from which more complex predicates can be built. In [6], the domain contains all combinations of the p_i by $\wedge$ and $\vee$, i.e. the set of all boolean functions with n boolean arguments, that is 2^{2^n} functions. The abstract interpretation of a loop proceeds in the forward direction, by using a strongest postcondition semantics. After each loop iteration, the predicate obtained is joined by $\vee$ to the one obtained in the prior iteration, and the result is abstracted by the abstraction function to that domain. Since this one is finite, a least fixpoint is always reached, provided the loop invariant can be effectively expressed by combinations of the given atomic predicates. If the algorithm succeeds, it obtains the strongest invariant belonging to the domain. They report experimenting their system with a Java program consisting of 520 loops, and were able to infer invariants for 98% of these loops.

In [8], they propose an abstract interpretation domain with universally quantified predicates. In prior attempts, quantification was introduced by rather *ad-hoc* means, but the abstract domain did not contain quantified formulas. After looking at the shape of many invariants, the authors propose the general form $E \wedge \bigwedge_{j=1}^{n} \forall U_j(F_j \Rightarrow e_j)$ where E, all the F_j, and all the e_j, are formulas belonging to non-quantified domains. Both E and the F_j are conjunctions of atomic predicates, and the e_j are just atomic ones. Each U_j is a tuple of (quantified) variables occurring free in F_j and e_j. An example of invariant is $1 \leq i \leq n \wedge \forall k(0 \leq k < i \Rightarrow a[k] = 0)$. The authors define an infinite lattice where the elements are formulas with this shape, define widening and narrowing operators to ensure termination, and also give some heuristics in order to convert non-quantified facts into quantified ones, when at least two iterations have been done during the interpretation of a loop. They infer invariants for most of the usual sorting algorithms, for finding an element in an array, and for other similar examples. The main differences with our approach are that our lattice is finite, so termination is guaranteed, and that we need neither widening nor heuristics.

In [14], the user gives a *template* formula for each particular invariant. In the template, the predicates are represented by unknowns that the system must guess. For instance, in $a \wedge \forall k(b \Rightarrow c)$ the system must find a substitution of concrete predicates for the variables a, b and c. The user must also supply a set Q of atomic predicates, conjunctions of which will replace the template unknowns. If an invariant exists having the template shape and formed by conjunctions of predicates from Q, then the algorithm finds the strongest one. The reported examples include invariants for all the sorting algorithms, the binary search in an array, list insertion, and list deletion. A difference with our approach is that decidability of the formulas is not guaranteed. The authors recognize that they sometimes provide their SMT solver with additional hints (triggers) in order to deal with undecidable quantified formulas. Additionally, they need to give a template with the exact number of quantified conjuncts, which is sometimes difficult to guess. Our algorithm generates as many conjuncts as needed to prove the correctness of the input program.

A last group of related papers is the temporal sequence [3,7,9] based on abstract interpretation. The main insight is the definition of an abstract domain for arrays, where they are considered to be split into a finite number of slices, and each slice satisfies a possibly different property. Its contents is represented by a single abstract variable that is updated as long as the algorithm progresses. They succeed in obtaining invariants for some array processing algorithms, the most complex of which is insertion sort. The approach is limited to single **for** loops, and to slices described by a predicate with only one universally quantified index. Also, they would be forced to change the abstract domain each time they wish to infer a different property. All the reported examples can be dealt with by our approach, and they admit that, at present, they cannot infer *quicksort*.

8 Conclusions

We have presented an extension of the Liquid type approach to universally quantified formulas about arrays. Arrays are non-recursive data structures and cannot be dealt with by using the recursive refinements introduced in [10]. Additionally, arrays are normally updated in-place and so used in imperative languages, while the Liquid type approach seems to fit better with functional ones. We have circumvented both obstacles: the first one, by allowing predicates on arrays where the indices can be universally quantified, and the second one, by using our verification platform which transform imperative programs into functional ones. The array refinements introduced in this paper try to cover properties satisfied for all the elements of an array segment and properties between pair of elements, either of the same array, or of two different ones. Algorithms searching arrays for a certain property are also covered, since their invariant can usually be expressed by a universal quantification (saying that no element of the array segment currently explored satisfies the property). As future work, we would like to generate at least a part of the qualifiers directly from the code, so liberating the programmer from most of this task.

We believe that other general refinements for arrays could be defined in order to cover programs in which certain elements of an array segment are counted or operated in some way. The resulting constraints should still be automatically proved valid by the current SMT solver technology. In this way, more decidable array invariants could be rescued from the general undecidable problem of invariant synthesis.

References

1. Ball, T., Majumdar, R., Millstein, T.D., Rajamani, S.K.: Automatic predicate abstraction of C programs. In: ACM SIGPLAN Conference on Programming Language Design and Implementation (PLDI 2001), pp. 203–213 (2001)
2. Bradley, A.R., Manna, Z., Sipma, H.B.: What's decidable about arrays? In: Emerson, E.A., Namjoshi, K.S. (eds.) VMCAI 2006. LNCS, vol. 3855, pp. 427–442. Springer, Heidelberg (2006). doi:10.1007/11609773_28
3. Cousot, P., Cousot, R., Logozzo, F.: A parametric segmentation functor for fully automatic and scalable array content analysis. In: ACM SIGPLAN Symposium on Principles of Programming Languages, POPL 2011, pp. 105–118 (2011)
4. Dijkstra, E.W.: A Discipline of Programming. Prentice-Hall, Englewood Cliffs (1976)
5. Filliâtre, J.-C., Paskevich, A.: Why3 — where programs meet provers. In: Felleisen, M., Gardner, P. (eds.) ESOP 2013. LNCS, vol. 7792, pp. 125–128. Springer, Heidelberg (2013). doi:10.1007/978-3-642-37036-6_8
6. Flanagan, C., Qadeer, S.: Predicate abstraction for software verification. In: Launchbury, J., Mitchell, J.C. (eds.) 29th SIGPLAN-SIGACT Symposium on Principles of Programming Languages, POPL 2002, pp. 191–202. ACM (2002)
7. Gopan, D., Reps, T.W., Sagiv, S.: A framework for numeric analysis of array operations. In: 32nd ACM SIGPLAN-SIGACT Symposium on Principles of Programming Languages, POPL 2005, pp. 338–350 (2005)
8. Gulwani, S., McCloskey, B., Tiwari, A.: Lifting abstract interpreters to quantified logical domains. In: POPL 2008, pp. 235–246 (2008)

9. Halbwachs, N., Péron, M.: Discovering properties about arrays in simple programs. In: Gupta, R., Amarasinghe, S.P. (eds.) Proceedings of the ACM SIGPLAN 2008 Conference on Programming Language Design and Implementation, Tucson, AZ, USA, June 7–13, 2008, pp. 339–348. ACM (2008)
10. Kawaguchi, M., Rondon, P.M., Jhala, R.: Type-based data structure verification. In: Hind, M., Diwan, A. (eds.) PLDI, pp. 304–315. ACM (2009)
11. Montenegro, M., Peña, R., Sánchez-Hernández, J.: A generic intermediate representation for verification condition generation. In: Falaschi, M. (ed.) LOPSTR 2015. LNCS, vol. 9527, pp. 227–243. Springer, Cham (2015). doi:10.1007/978-3-319-27436-2_14
12. Polikarpova, N., Kuraj, I., Solar-Lezama, A.: Program synthesis from polymorphic refinement types. In: ACM SIGPLAN Conference on Programming Language Design and Implementation, PLDI 2016, pp. 522–538 (2016)
13. Rondon, P.M., Kawaguchi, M., Jhala, R.: Liquid types. In: Gupta, R., Amarasinghe, S.P. (eds.) PLDI, pp. 159–169. ACM (2008)
14. Srivastava, S., Gulwani, S.: Program verification using templates over predicate abstraction. In: Hind, M., Diwan, A. (eds.) PLDI, pp. 223–234. ACM (2009)
15. Stump, A., Barrett, C.W., Dill, D.L., Levitt, J.R.: A decision procedure for an extensional theory of arrays. In: 16th Annual IEEE Symposium on Logic in Computer Science (LICS 2001), pp. 29–37. IEEE Computer Society Press (2001)
16. Suzuki, N., Jefferson, D.: Verification decidability of presburger array programs. J. ACM **27**(1), 191–205 (1980)
17. Vazou, N., Rondon, P.M., Jhala, R.: Abstract refinement types. In: Felleisen, M., Gardner, P. (eds.) ESOP 2013. LNCS, vol. 7792, pp. 209–228. Springer, Heidelberg (2013). doi:10.1007/978-3-642-37036-6_13
18. Vazou, N., Seidel, E.L., Jhala, R.: LiquidHaskell: experience with refinement types in the real world. In: ACM SIGPLAN Symposium on Haskell 2014, pp. 39–51 (2014)
19. Vazou, N., Seidel, E.L., Jhala, R., Vytiniotis, D., Jones, S.L.P.: Refinement types for Haskell. In: 19th ACM SIGPLAN International Conference on Functional Programming, ICFP 2014, pp. 269–282 (2014)

Lifting CDCL to Template-Based Abstract Domains for Program Verification

Rajdeep Mukherjee[1](✉), Peter Schrammel[2], Leopold Haller[3], Daniel Kroening[1], and Tom Melham[1]

[1] University of Oxford, Oxford, UK
rajdeep.mukherjee@cs.ox.ac.uk
[2] University of Sussex, Brighton, UK
[3] Google Inc., San Francisco, USA

Abstract. The success of Conflict Driven Clause Learning (CDCL) for Boolean satisfiability has inspired adoption in other domains. We present a novel lifting of CDCL to program analysis called *Abstract Conflict Driven Learning for Programs* (ACDLP). ACDLP alternates between *model search*, which performs over-approximate deduction with constraint propagation, and *conflict analysis*, which performs under-approximate abduction with heuristic choice. We instantiate the model search and conflict analysis algorithms with an abstract domain of *template polyhedra*, strictly generalizing CDCL from the Boolean lattice to a richer lattice structure. Our template polyhedra can express intervals, octagons and restricted polyhedral constraints over program variables. We have implemented ACDLP for automatic bounded safety verification of C programs. We evaluate the performance of our analyser by comparing with CBMC, which uses Boolean CDCL, and Astrée, a commercial abstract interpretation tool. We observe two orders of magnitude reduction in the number of decisions, propagations, and conflicts as well as a 1.5x speedup in runtime compared to CBMC. Compared to Astrée, ACDLP solves twice as many benchmarks and has much higher precision. This is the first instantiation of CDCL with a template polyhedra abstract domain.

1 Introduction

Static program analysis with abstract interpretation [10] is widely used to verify properties of safety-critical systems. Static analyses commonly aim to compute program invariants as fixed-points of abstract transformers. Abstract states are chosen from a lattice that has meet ($\sqcap$) and join ($\sqcup$) operations; the meet precisely models set intersection (or conjunction, taking a logical view), and the join over-approximates set union (or disjunction). Over-approximation in the join operation is one of the sources of precision loss, which can cause false alarms. Typical abstract domains are *non-distributive*; suppose a and b together

Supported by ERC project 280053 (CPROVER), the H2020 FET OPEN 712689 SC[2] and SRC contracts no. 2012-TJ-2269 and 2016-CT-2707.

D. D'Souza and K. Narayan Kumar (Eds.): ATVA 2017, LNCS 10482, pp. 307–326, 2017.
DOI: 10.1007/978-3-319-68167-2_21

represent the abstract semantics of a program and c represents a set of abstract behaviours that violate the specification. In a non-distributive domain, $(a \sqcup b) \sqcap c$ can be strictly less precise than $(a \sqcap c) \sqcup (b \sqcap c)$. This means that in typical abstract domains, analysing program behaviours separately can improve the precision of the analysis. Usual means to address false alarms therefore include not only the use of richer abstract domains, but also of refinements that delay joins or perform some form of case-splitting. Such techniques trade off higher precision against lower efficiency and may be susceptible to case enumeration behaviour.

By contrast, Model Checking (MC) [2] can be seen to operate on distributive lattice structures that represent disjunction without loss of precision. Classical MC directly operates on distributive representations, such as BDDs, while more recent implementations use SAT solvers. SAT solvers themselves operate on partial assignments, which are non-distributive structures. To handle disjunction, case-splitting is performed [15]. Propositional SAT solvers solve large formulae, and are often able to avoid enumerating cases. The impressive performance of modern solvers is credited to well-tuned decision heuristics and sophisticated clause learning algorithms. Collectively, these algorithms are referred to as *Conflict Driven Clause Learning* (CDCL) [3]. An appealing idea is to lift CDCL from the domain of partial assignments to other non-distributive domains.

Abstract Conflict Driven Clause Learning (ACDCL) [13] is one such lattice-based generalization of CDCL. ACDCL is a general algorithmic framework, parameterized by a concrete domain C and an abstract domain A. Classical CDCL can be viewed as an instance of ACDCL in which C is the set of propositional truth assignments and A the domain of propositional partial assignments [17]. Since the concrete domain is a parameter to the framework, ACDCL can in principle be used to build both *logical decision procedures* [5] and *program analyzers.* In the former case, the concrete domain is the set of candidate models for the formula; in the latter case, it is the set of program traces that may lead to an error. Haller et al. [5] pursue the first idea by presenting a floating-point decision procedure that uses interval constraint propagation.

In this paper, we explore the second idea by presenting an extension of ACDCL to program analysis. We call our framework *Abstract Conflict Driven Learning for Programs* (ACDLP). The key insight of ACDLP is to use decisions and learning to reason precisely about disjunctions in non-distributive domains, thereby automatically refining the precision of analysis for safety checking of C programs. We introduce two central components of our framework: an abstract model search algorithm that uses decisions and propagations to search for counterexample trace and an abstract conflict analysis procedure that approximates a set of unsafe traces through transformer learning. We illustrate the application of our framework to program analysis using a *template polyhedra abstract domain* [26], which includes most of the commonly used abstract domains, such as boxes, octagons, zones and TCMs.

We give an experimental evaluation of our analyser compared to CBMC [8], which uses propositional solvers, and to Astrée [4], a commercial abstract interpretation tool. In this paper, we make the following contributions.

1. A novel program analysis framework that lifts model search and conflict analysis procedures of CDCL algorithm over a template polyhedra abstract domain. These techniques are embodied in our tool, *ACDLP*, for automatic bounded safety verification of C programs.
2. A parameterized abstract transformer that guides the model search in forward, backward and multi-way direction for counterexample detection.
3. A conflict analysis procedure that performs UIP-based transformer learning over template polyhedra abstract domain through abductive reasoning.

2 Motivating Examples

We present two simple examples to demonstrate the essence of ACDLP for bounded verification. For each one, we apply three analysis techniques: *abstract interpretation* (AI), SAT-based *bounded model checking* (BMC) and ACDLP.

First Example. The simple Control-Flow Graph (CFG) in Fig. 1 squares a machine integer and checks whether the result is positive. To avoid overflow, we assume the input v has an upper bound N. This example shows that (a) interval analysis in ACDLP is more precise than a forward AI in the interval domain, and (b) ACDLP with intervals can achieve a precision similar to that of AI with octagons without employing more sophisticated mechanisms such as trace partitioning [25].

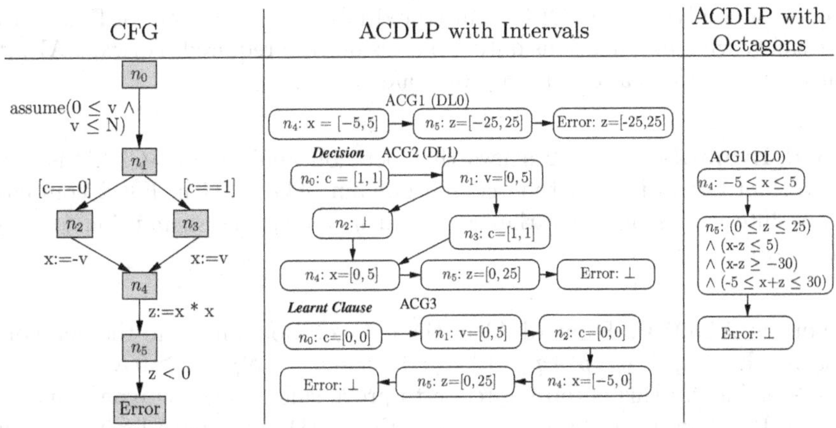

Fig. 1. CFG and corresponding Abstract Conflict Graphs for intervals and octagons

AI versus ACDLP. Conventional forward interval AI is too imprecise to verify safety of this program owing to the control-flow join at node n_4. For example, the state-of-the-art AI tool Astrée requires external hints, provided by manually annotating the code with partition directives at n_1. This tells Astrée to analyse the program paths separately.

ACDLP can be understood as an algorithm to infer such partitions automatically. For the example in Fig. 1, interval analysis with ACDLP is sufficient to prove safety. The analysis records the decisions and deductions in a *trail* data-structure. The trail can be seen to represent a graph structure called the *Abstract Conflict Graph* (ACG) that stores dependencies between decisions and deductions, similar to the way an *Implication Graph* [3] works in a SAT solver. Nodes of the ACG in the second column of Fig. 1 are labelled with the CFG location and the corresponding abstract value. Beginning with the assumption that $v = [0, 5]$ at node n_1, the intervals generated by forward analysis in the initial deduction phase at *decision level* 0 (DL0) are $x = [-5, 5]$ and $z = [-25, 25]$. These do not prove safety, as shown in ACG1. So ACDLP makes a heuristic decision, at DL1, to refine the analysis. With the decision $c = [1, 1]$, interval analysis then concludes $x = [0, 5]$ at node n_4, which leads to (Error: $\bot$) in ACG2, indicating that the error location is unreachable and that the program is safe when $c = [1, 1]$.

Reaching (Error: $\bot$) is analogous to reaching a conflict in a propositional SAT solver. At this point, a clause-learning SAT solver learns a reason for the conflict and backtracks to a level such that the learnt clause is *unit*. By a similar process, ACDLP learns that $c = [0, 0]$. That is, all error traces must satisfy $c \neq 1$. The analysis discards all interval constraints that lead to the conflict and backtracks to DL0. ACDLP then performs interval analysis with the learnt clause $c \neq 1$. This also leads to a conflict, as shown in ACG3. The analysis cannot backtrack further and so terminates, proving the program safe. Thus, *decision* and *clause learning* are used to infer the partitions necessary for a precise analysis. Alternatively, the octagon analysis in ACDLP—illustrated in the third column of Fig. 1—can prove safety with propagations only. No decisions are required. Forward AI with octagons in Astrée is also able to prove safety.

Second Example. Figure 2 shows that octagon analysis in ACDLP is more precise than forward AI in the octagon domain. The CFG in Fig. 2 computes the absolute values of two variables, x and y, under the assumption $(x = y) \vee (x = -y)$.

AI versus ACDLP. Forward AI in the octagon domain infers the octagonal constraint Error: $p \geq 0 \wedge p + q \geq 0 \wedge q \geq 0 \wedge p + x \geq 0 \wedge p - x \geq 0 \wedge q + y \geq 0 \wedge q - y \geq 0$. Clearly this is too imprecise to prove safety. The octagonal analysis in ACDLP is illustrated by the ACGs in Fig. 2. (Due to space limitations, we elide intermediate deductions.) The decision $x = y$ at DL1 is not sufficient to prove safety, as shown in ACG1. So a new decision $x < 0$ is made at DL2, followed by forward propagation that infers $y < 0$ at node n_5. This subsequently leads to safety (Error: $\bot$), as shown in ACG2. The analysis learns the reason for the conflict, discards all deductions in ACG2 and backtracks to DL1. Octagon analysis is run with the learnt constraint $x \geq 0$ and this infers $y \geq 0$ at node n_5, as shown in ACG3. This also leads to safety (Error: $\bot$). The analysis now makes

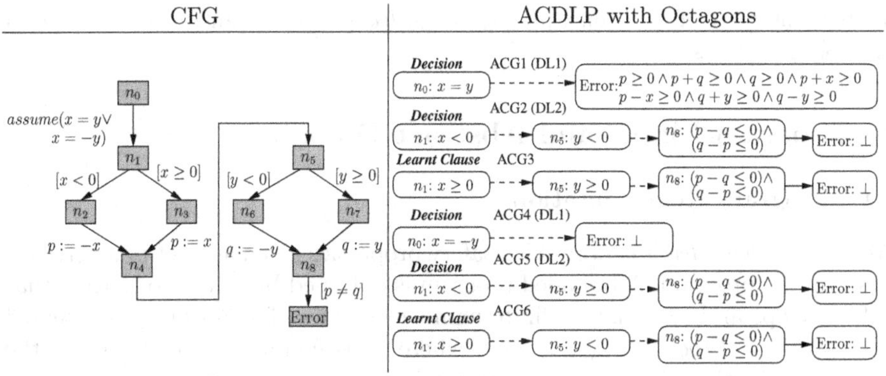

Fig. 2. CFG and corresponding Abstract Conflict Graphs for octagon analysis

a new decision $x = -y$ at DL1. The procedure is repeated leading to results shown in ACG4, ACG5, and ACG6. Clearly, the decisions $x = -y$ and $x < 0$ also lead to safety. The analysis backtracks to DL0 and returns *safe*. Note that the specific decision heuristic we use in this case exploits the control structure of the program to infer partitions that are sufficient to prove safety.

ACDLP versus BMC. ACDLP can require many fewer iterations than SAT-based BMC due to its ability to reason over much richer lattice structures. A SAT-based BMC converts the program into a bit-vector formula and passes it to a CDCL-based SAT solver for proving safety. Table 1 compares the statistics for BMC with MiniSAT [21] solver to those for interval and octagon analysis in ACDLP. In the column labelled Domains, *BVars* is the set of propositional variables; each of these is mapped to *true* (t), *false* (f) or *unknown* (?). *NVars* is the set of numerical variables; *Itvs*[*NVars*] and *Octs*[*NVars*] are the Interval and Octagon domains over *NVars*. As can be seen, ACDLP outperforms BMC in

Table 1. SAT-based BMC versus ACDLP for verification of programs in Figs. 1 and 2

Solver	Domain	Decisions	Propagations	Conflicts	Conflict literals	Restarts
Solver statistics for Fig. 1 (for N = 46000)						
MiniSAT	$BVars \rightarrow \{t, f, ?\}$	233	36436	162	2604	2
ACDLP	$Itvs[NVars]$	1	17	1	1	0
ACDLP	$Octs[NVars]$	0	7	0	0	0
Solver statistics for Fig. 2						
MiniSAT	$BVars \rightarrow \{t, f, ?\}$	4844	32414	570	4750	5
ACDLP	$Octs[NVars]$	4	412	2	2	0

the total number of *decisions*, *propagations*, *learnt clauses* and *restarts* for both example programs.

3 Program Model and Abstract Domain

3.1 Program Representation

We consider *bounded programs* with safety properties given as a set of assertions, *Assn*, in the program. A bounded program is obtained by a transformation that unfolds loops and recursions a finite number of times. The result is represented by a set $\Sigma = Prog \cup \{\neg \bigwedge_{a \in Assn} a\}$, where *Prog* contains an encoding of the statements in the program as constraints, obtained after translating the program into single static assignment (SSA) form via a data flow analysis. The representation Σ for the program in Fig. 1 is

$$\begin{array}{l}\{g_0 = (0 \leq v \leq N),\ g_1 = (g_0 \wedge c),\ x_0 = v,\ x_1 = -v, \\ \ x_2 = g_1 ? x_0 : x_1,\ g_2 = (g_1 \vee g_0 \wedge \neg c),\ z = x_2 {\cdot} x_2,\ g_2 \wedge z < 0\}\end{array} \quad (1)$$

Assignments such as x:=v become equalities $x_1 = v$, where the left-hand side variable gets a subscripted fresh name. Control flow is encoded using guard variables, e.g. $g_1 = g_0 \wedge c$. Data flow joins become conditional expressions, e.g. $x_3 = g_1 ? x_1 : x_2$. The assertions in *Assn* are constraints such as $g_2 \Rightarrow z \geq 0$, meaning that if g_2 holds (i.e., the assertion is reachable), then $z \geq 0$ must hold. We write *Vars* for the set of variables occurring in Σ. Based on this representation, we define a *safety formula* (φ) as the conjunction of everything in Σ, i.e. $\varphi := \bigwedge_{\sigma \in \Sigma} \sigma$. The formula φ is unsatisfiable if and only if the program is safe.

3.2 Abstract Domain

In this paper, we instantiate ACDLP over a reduced product domain [11] $D[Vars] = \mathcal{B}^{|BVars|} \times \mathcal{TP}[NVars]$ where $\mathcal{B}$ is the Boolean domain that permits abstract values $\{\mathsf{true}, \mathsf{false}, \bot, \top\}$ over boolean variables *BVars* in the program, and $\mathcal{TP}$ is a *template polyhedra* [26] domain over the numerical (bit-vector) variables *NVars*. Our template polyhedra domain can express various relational and non-relational templates over *NVars*, as given in Table 2.

Template Polyhedra Abstract Domain. An abstract value of the template polyhedra domain [26] represents a set X of values of the vector $\boldsymbol{x}$ of

Table 2. Template instances in the template polyhedra domain

Interval	Octagons	Zones	Equality	Fixed-coef. polyhedra
$a \leq x_i \leq b$	$\pm x_i \pm x_j \leq d$	$x_i - x_j \leq d$	$x_i = x_j$	$a_1 x_1 + \ldots + a_n x_n \leq d$

numerical (bit-vector) variables *NVars* of their respective data types. (Currently, signed and unsigned integers are supported.) For example, in the program given by Eq. (1), we have four numerical variables, written as the vector $\boldsymbol{x} = (x_0, x_1, x_2, z)$. An abstract value is a constant vector $\boldsymbol{d}$ that represents sets of values for $\boldsymbol{x}$ for which $\boldsymbol{C}\boldsymbol{x} \leq \boldsymbol{d}$, for a fixed coefficient matrix $\boldsymbol{C}$. The domain containing $\boldsymbol{d}$ is augmented by a special element $\bot$ to denote the minimal element of the lattice. There are several optimisation techniques [26] for computing the domain operations, such as meet ($\sqcap$) and join ($\sqcup$), in the template polyhedra domain. In our implementation, we use the strategy iteration approach of [6]. The abstraction function is $\alpha(X) = min\{\boldsymbol{d} \mid \boldsymbol{C}\boldsymbol{x} \leq \boldsymbol{d}, \boldsymbol{x} \in X\}$, where *min* is applied component-wise. The concretisation $\gamma(\boldsymbol{d})$ is the set $\{\boldsymbol{x} \mid \boldsymbol{C}\boldsymbol{x} \leq \boldsymbol{d}\}$ and $\gamma(\bot) = \emptyset$, i.e., the empty polyhedron.

For notational convenience we will use conjunctions of linear inequalities, for example $x_1 \geq 0 \wedge x_1 - z \leq 30$, to write the abstract domain value $\boldsymbol{d} = \begin{pmatrix} 0 \\ 30 \end{pmatrix}$, with $\boldsymbol{C} = \begin{pmatrix} -1 & 0 \\ 1 & -1 \end{pmatrix}$ and $\boldsymbol{x} = \begin{pmatrix} x_1 \\ z \end{pmatrix}$; true corresponds to abstract value $\top$ and false to abstract value $\bot$. For a program with $N = |NVars|$ variables, the template matrix $\boldsymbol{C}$ for the interval domain *Itvs*[*NVars*], has $2N$ rows. Hence, it generates at most $2N$ inequalities, one for the upper and lower bounds of each variable. For octagons *Octs*[*NVars*], we have at most $2N^2$ inequalities, one for the upper and lower bounds of each variable and sums and differences for each pair of variables. Unlike a non-relational domain, a relational domain such as octagons requires the computation of a *closure* to obtain a normal form, necessary for precise domain operation. The closure computes all implied domain constraints. An example of a closure computation for octagonal inequalities is $closure((x - y \leq 4) \wedge (y - z \leq 5)) = ((x - y \leq 4) \wedge (y - z \leq 5) \wedge (x - z \leq 9))$. For octagons, closure is the most critical and expensive operator; it has cubic complexity in the number of program variables. We therefore compute closure lazily in template polyhedra domain in our abstract model search procedure, which is described in Sect. 5.3.

Abstract Transformers. An abstract transformer $[\![\sigma]\!]_D$ transforms an abstract value a through a constraint σ; it *deduces* information from a and σ. The best transformer is

$$[\![\sigma]\!]_D(a) = a \sqcap \alpha(\{u \mid u \in \gamma(a), u \models \sigma\}) \tag{2}$$

where we write $u \models \sigma$ if the concrete value u satisfies the constraint σ. Any abstract transformer that over-approximates the best abstract transformer is a sound transformer and can be used in our algorithm. For example, we can deduce $[\![x = 2(y + z)]\!]_D(a) = (0 \leq y \leq 2 \wedge 1 \leq y - z \leq 1 \wedge -2 \leq x \leq 6)$ for the abstract value $a = (0 \leq y \leq 2 \wedge 1 \leq y - z \leq 1)$. We denote the set of abstract transformers for a safety formula φ using the abstract domain D by $\mathcal{A} = \{[\![\sigma]\!]_D \mid \sigma \in \Sigma\}$.

3.3 Precise Complementation in Abstract Domains

An important property of a clause-learning SAT solver is that each non-singleton element of the partial assignment domain can be decomposed into a set of *precisely complementable* singleton elements [13]. This property is necessary to learn elements that guide the model search away from the conflicting region of the search space. Most numerical abstract domains, such as intervals and octagons, lack complements in general: not every domain element has a precise complement. But these domain elements can be represented as intersections of half-spaces, each of which admits a precise complement. We formalise this in the sequel.

Definition 1. *A* meet irreducible *m in a complete lattice structure A is an element with the following property.*

$$\forall m_1, m_2 \in A : m_1 \sqcap m_2 = m \implies (m = m_1 \vee m = m_2), m \neq \top \quad (3)$$

The meet irreducibles in the Boolean domain $\mathcal{B}$ for a variable x are x and $\neg x$. The meet irreducibles in the template polyhedra domain are all elements that concretise to half-spaces; i.e., they can be represented by a single inequality. For the interval domain, these are $x \leq d$ or $x \geq d$ for constants d.

Definition 2. *A* meet decomposition *$decomp(a)$ of an abstract element $a \in D$ is a set of meet irreducibles $M \subseteq D$ such that $a = \bigsqcap_{m \in M} m$.*

For polyhedra this means that each polyhedron can be written as an intersection of half-spaces. For example, the meet decomposition of the interval domain element $decomp(2 \leq x \leq 4 \wedge 3 \leq y \leq 5)$ is the set $\{x \geq 2, x \leq 4, y \geq 3, y \leq 5\}$.

Definition 3. *An element $a \in D$ is called* precisely complementable *iff there exists $\bar{a} \in D$ such that $\neg\gamma(\bar{a}) = \gamma(a)$. That is, there is an element whose complemented concretisation equals the concretisation of a.*

The precise complementation property of a partial assignment lattice can be generalised to other lattice structures. For example, the precise complement of a meet irreducible $(x \leq 2)$ in the interval domain over integers is $(x \geq 3)$, or the precise complement of the meet irreducible $(x + y \leq 1)$ in the octagon domain over integers is $(x + y \geq 2)$. Our domain implementation supports a precise complementation operation. Standard abstract interpretation does not require a complementation operator, so abstract domain libraries, such as APRON [19], do not provide it. But it can be implemented with the help of a meet decomposition as explained above.

4 Abstract Conflict Driven Learning for Programs

Figure 3 presents our framework called *Abstract Conflict Driven Learning for Programs* that uses abstract model search and abstract conflict analysis procedures for safety verification of C programs. The model search procedure operates on an over-approximate domain of program traces through repeated application of abstract deduction transformer, *ded*, and decisions in order to search for a counterexample trace. If the model search finds a satisfying assignment (corresponding deduction transformer is γ-complete), then ACDLP terminates with a counterexample trace, and the program is *unsafe*. Else, if a conflict is encountered, then it implies that the corresponding program trace is either not valid or safe. ACDLP then moves to the conflict analysis phase where it learns the reason for the conflict from partial safety proof using an abstract abductive transformer, *abd*, followed by a heuristic choice of conflict reason. Similar to a SAT solver, ACDLP picks one conflict reason from multiple incomparable reasons for conflict for efficiency reasons. Hence, it operates over an under-approximate domain of conflict reasons. A conflict reason under-approximates a set of invalid or safe traces. The conflict analysis returns a learnt transformer (negation of conflict reason) that over-approximates a set of valid and unsafe traces. Model search is repeated with this new transformer. Else, if no further backtracking is possible, then ACDLP terminates and returns *safe*. We present the ACDLP algorithm in the subsequent section.

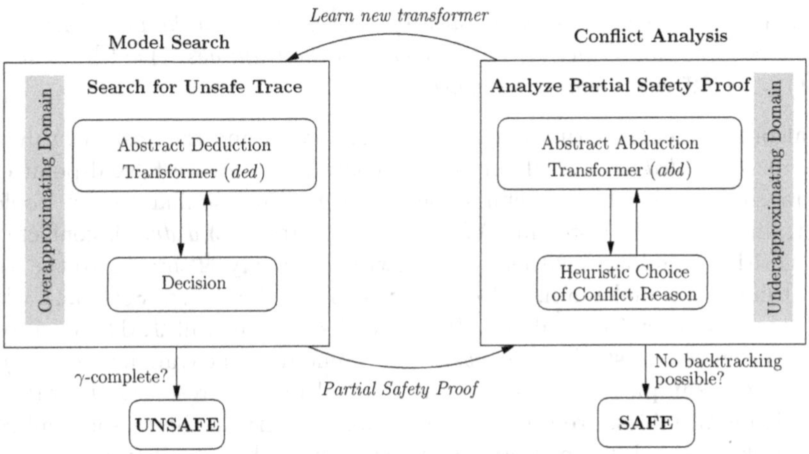

Fig. 3. Architectural view of ACDLP

The input to ACDLP (Algorithm 1) is a program in the form of a set of abstract transformers $\mathcal{A} = \{[\![\sigma]\!]_D | \sigma \in \Sigma\}$ w.r.t. an abstract domain D. Recall that the safety formula $\bigwedge_{\sigma \in \Sigma} \sigma$ is unsatisfiable if and only if the program is safe. The algorithm is parametrised by heuristics for propagation (H_P), decisions (H_D), and conflict analysis (H_C). The algorithm maintains a propagation trail $\mathfrak{T}$ and a reason trail $\mathfrak{R}$. The propagation trail stores all meet irreducibles inferred by the abstract model search phase (deductions and decisions). The reason trail maps the elements of the propagation trail to the transformers $ded \in \mathcal{A}$ that were used to derive them.

Algorithm 1. Abstract Conflict Driven Learning $ACDLP_{H_P,H_D,H_C}(\mathcal{A})$

```
   input : A program in the form of a set of abstract transformers 𝒜.
   output: The status safe or unsafe.
1  𝒯 ← ⟨⟩, ℛ ← []
2  result ← deduce_{H_P}(𝒜, 𝒯, ℛ)
3  if result = conflict then return safe
4  while true do
5      if result = sat then return unsafe
6      q ← decide_{H_D}(abs(𝒯))
7      𝒯 ← 𝒯 · q
8      ℛ[|𝒯|] ← ⊤
9      result ← deduce_{H_P}(𝒜, 𝒯, ℛ)
10     do
11         if ¬analyzeConflict_{H_C}(𝒜, 𝒯, ℛ) then return safe
12         result ← deduce_{H_P}(𝒜, 𝒯, ℛ)
13     while result = conflict
14 end
```

Definition 4. *The* abstract value $abs(\mathcal{T})$ *corresponding to the propagation trail* $\mathcal{T}$ *is the conjunction of the meet irreducibles on the trail:* $abs(\mathcal{T}) = \bigsqcap_{m \in \mathcal{T}} m$ *with* $abs(\mathcal{T}) = \top$ *if* $\mathcal{T}$ *is the empty sequence.*

The algorithm begins with an empty $\mathcal{T}$, an empty $\mathcal{R}$, and the abstract value $\top$. The procedure *deduce* (details in Sect. 5) computes a greatest fixed-point over the transformers in $\mathcal{A}$ that refines the abstract value, similar to the Boolean Constraint Propagation step in SAT solvers. If the result of *deduce* is conflict ($\bot$), the algorithm terminates with safe. Otherwise, the analysis enters into the while loop at line 4 and makes a new decision by a call to *decide* (see Sect. 5.4), which returns a new meet irreducible q. We append q to the trail $\mathcal{T}$. The decision q refines the current abstract value $abs(\mathcal{T})$ represented by the trail, i.e., $abs(\mathcal{T} \cdot q) \sqsubseteq abs(\mathcal{T})$. For example, a decision in the interval domain restricts the range of intervals for variables. We set the corresponding entry in the reason trail $\mathcal{R}$ to $\top$ to mark it as a decision. Here, the index of $\mathcal{R}$ is the size of trail $\mathcal{T}$, denoted by $|\mathcal{T}|$. The procedure *deduce* is called next to infer new meet irreducibles based on the current decision. The model search phase alternates between the decision and deduction until *deduce* returns either sat or conflict.

If *deduce* returns sat, then we have found an abstract value that represents models of the safety formula, which are counterexamples to the required safety property, and so ACDLP returns unsafe. If *deduce* returns conflict, the algorithm enters in the *analyzeConflict* phase (see Sect. 6) to learn the reason for the conflict. There can be multiple incomparable reasons for conflict. ACDLP heuristically chooses one reason C and learns it by adding it as an abstract transformer to $\mathcal{A}$. The analysis backtracks by removing the content of $\mathcal{T}$ up to a point where it does not conflict with C. ACDLP then performs deductions with the learnt transformer. If *analyzeConflict* returns false, then no further backtracking

Algorithm 2. Abstract Model Search $deduce_{H_P}(\mathcal{A}, \mathcal{T}, \mathcal{R})$

input : A program in the form of a set of abstract transformers $\mathcal{A}$, a propagation trail $\mathcal{T}$, and a reason trail $\mathcal{R}$.
output: sat or conflict or unknown

```
worklist ← initWorklist_{H_P}(A)
while !worklist.empty() do
    ded^L ← worklist.pop()
    a ← ded^L(abs(T))
    if a = ⊥ then
        R[⊥] ← ded^L
        worklist.clear()
        return conflict
    else
        v = onlyNew(a)
        T ← T · decomp(v)
        R[|T|] ← ded^L
        updateWorklist_{H_P}(worklist, v, ded^L, A)
end
if A is γ-complete at abs(T) then return sat
return unknown
```

is possible. Thus, the safety formula is unsatisfiable and ACDLP returns safe. An example demonstrating step-by-step execution of the ACDLP algorithm is available at [23].

5 Abstract Model Search for Template Polyhedra

Model search in a SAT solver has two steps: *deductions*, which are repeated application of the unit rule (also called Boolean Constraint Propagation, or BCP), to refine current partial assignments, and *decisions* to heuristically guess a value for an unassigned literal. BCP can be seen to compute the greatest fixed point over the partial assignment domain [13]. Below, we present an abstract model search procedure that computes a greatest fixed point over abstract transformers $[\![\sigma]\!]_D$.

5.1 Parametrised Abstract Transformers

The key considerations for an abstract transformer are precision and efficiency. A precise transformer is usually less efficient than a more imprecise one. In this paper, we present a specialised variant of the abstract transformer to compute deductions called *Abstract Deduction Transformer* (ADT), which is parametrised by a given *subdomain* $L \subseteq D$. A subdomain contains a chosen subset of the elements in D including $\bot$ and $\top$ that forms a lattice. The use of a subdomain serves two purposes: (a) It allows us elegantly and flexibly to guide the deductions in *forward*, *backward* or *multi-way* direction, which in turn affects the analysis precision, and (b) it makes deductions more efficient, for example by performing lazy closure in template polyhedra domain.

An ADT is defined formally as follows.

$$[\![\sigma]\!]^L_D(a) = a \sqcap_D \alpha_L(\{u \mid u \in \gamma_D(a), u \models \sigma\}) \tag{4}$$

For $L = D$, the ADT is identical to the abstract transformer defined in Eq. (2) in Sect. 3. Note that a restricted subdomain makes a transformer less precise but more efficient. Conversely, an unrestricted subdomain make a transformer more precise, but less efficient. Therefore, we have the property $[\![\sigma]\!]^D_D(a) \sqsubseteq [\![\sigma]\!]^L_D(a)$. To illustrate point (1), we give examples that demonstrate how the choice of subdomain influences the propagation direction:

Forward Transformer. For an abstract value $a = (0 \le y \le 1 \wedge 5 \le z)$, $\sigma = (x = y + z)$, and $L = \mathit{Itvs}[\{x\}]$, we have $[\![x = y + z]\!]^{\mathit{Itvs}[\{x\}]}_{\mathit{Itvs}[\{x,y,z\}]}(a) = a \sqcap (x \ge 6)$. Assuming that the equality $x = y + z$ originated from an assignment to x, this performs a right-hand side (rhs) to left-hand side (lhs) propagation and hence emulates a forward analysis.

Backward Transformer. For an abstract value $a = (0 \le x \le 10 \wedge 0 \le y \le 1 \wedge 5 \le z)$, $\sigma = (x = y + z)$, and $L = \mathit{Itvs}[\{y, z\}]$, we have $[\![x = y + z]\!]^{\mathit{Itvs}[\{y,z\}]}_{\mathit{Itvs}[\{x,y,z\}]} = a \sqcap (z \le 10)$. This performs an lhs-to-rhs propagation and hence emulates a backward analysis.

Multi-way Transformer. For an abstract value $a = (c \le 1 \wedge c \ge 1 \wedge x \le 5 \wedge x \ge 5)$, $\sigma = ((c = (x = y)) \wedge y = y + 1)$ and $L = \mathit{Itvs}[\{c, x, y\}]$, we have $[\![\sigma]\!]^{\mathit{Itvs}[\{c,x,y\}]}_{\mathit{Itvs}[\{c,x,y\}]} = a \sqcap (y \le 6 \wedge y \ge 6)$. This performs an lhs-to-rhs propagation for $c = (x = y)$ and rhs to lhs propagation for $y = y + 1$ and hence emulates a multi-way analysis.

5.2 Algorithm for the Deduction Phase

Algorithm 2 presents the deduction phase *deduce* in our abstract model search procedure. The input to *deduce* is the set of abstract transformers, a propagation trail ($\mathcal{T}$) and a reason trail ($\mathcal{R}$). Additionally, the procedure *deduce* is parametrised by a propagation heuristic (H_P). We write the ADT $[\![\sigma]\!]^L_D$ as ded^L in Algorithm 2. The algorithm maintains a *worklist*, which is a queue that contains ADTs. The propagation heuristics provides two functions *initWorklist* and *updateWorklist*. The order of the elements in the worklist and the subdomain L associated with each ADT (ded^L) determine the propagation strategy (forward, backward, multi-way). These two functions construct a subdomain (L) for ded^L by calling the function *MakeL* such that $L = \mathit{MakeL}_D(V)$, where V are the variables that appear in ded^L. The abstract value a is updated upon the application of ded^L in line 4 in Algorithm 2. The function $\mathit{onlyNew}(a) = \bigsqcap(\mathit{decomp}(a) \setminus \mathit{decomp}(\mathit{abs}(\mathcal{T})))$ is used to filter out all meet irreducibles that are already on the trail in order to obtain only new deductions

(v) when applying the ADT (shown in line 10). Depending on the propagation heuristics, *updateWorklist* adds ADTs ded^L to the worklist that contain variables that appear in v, and updates the subdomains of the ADTs in the worklist to include the variables in v (shown in line 13).

If ded^L deduces $\bot$, then the procedure *deduce* returns conflict (shown in line 8). Otherwise, when a fixed-point is reached, i.e., the worklist is empty, we check whether the abstract transformers $\mathcal{A}$ are γ-complete [13] for the current abstract value $abs(\mathfrak{T})$ (shown in line 15). Intuitively, this checks whether all concrete values in $\gamma(abs(\mathfrak{T}))$ satisfy the safety formula φ, where $\varphi := \bigwedge_{\sigma \in \Sigma} \sigma$ is obtained from the program transformation (as defined in Sect. 3.1). If it is indeed γ-complete, then *deduce* returns sat. Otherwise, the algorithm returns unknown and ACDLP makes a new decision.

5.3 Computing Lazy Closure for Template Polyhedra

An advantage of our formalism in Eq. (4) is that the *closure* operation for relational domains can be computed in a lazy manner through the construction of a subdomain, L. The construction of L allows us to perform one step of the closure operation when ded^L is applied. For example, let us consider $D = Octs[\{x, y, z\}]$ and $V = \{y\}$. An octagonal inequality relates at most two variables. Thus it is sufficient to consider the subdomain $MakeL_D(\{y\}) = Octs[\{y\}] \cup Octs[\{x, y\}] \cup Octs[\{y, z\}]$, which will compute the one-step transitive relations of y with each of the other variables. Only if any subsequent abstract deduction transformer makes new deductions on x or z, then the next step of the closure will be computed through the subdomain $Octs[\{x, z\}]$. Hence, an application of each abstract deduction transformer does not compute the full closure in the full domain, but compute only a single step of the closure in a subdomain. This makes each deduction step more efficient but may require more steps to reach the fixed point.

5.4 Decisions

A decision q is a meet irreducible that refines the current abstract value $abs(\mathfrak{T})$, when the result of the fixed-point computation through deduction is neither a *conflict* nor a *satisfiable model* of φ. A decision must always be consistent with respect to the trail $\mathfrak{T}$, i.e., $abs(\mathfrak{T} \cdot q) \neq \bot$. A new decision increases the decision level by one. Given the current abstract value $abs(\mathfrak{T})$, the procedure *decide* in Algorithm 1 heuristically returns a meet irreducible.

For example, a decision in the interval domain can be of the form xRd where $R \in \{\leq, \geq\}$, and d is the bound. A decision in the octagon domain can specify relations between variables, and can be of the form $ax - by \leq d$, where x and y are variables, $a, b \in \{-1, 0, 1\}$ are coefficients, and d is a constant. The detailed description of the different decision heuristics in ACDLP is available at [23].

6 Abstract Conflict Analysis for Template Polyhedra

Propositional conflict analysis with FIRST-UIP [3] can be seen as abductive reasoning that under-approximates a set of models that do not satisfy a formula [13,15]. Thus, we view abduction as De Morgan dual of deduction whose result does not need to be consistent with respect to a background theory. Below, we present an abstract conflict analysis procedure, *analyzeConflict* of Algorithm 1, that uses a domain-specific abductive transformer for effective learning. A conflict analysis procedure involves two steps: *abduction* and *heuristic choice for generalisation*. Abduction infers possible generalised reasons for a conflict, which is followed by heuristically selecting a generalisation. Below, we define a global conflict transformer that gives a set of models that do not satisfy a formula.

Definition 5. *Given a formula φ, a downwards closed set of abstract elements Q, and domain D, $conf_{\varphi}^{D}(Q) = \{u \in D \mid u \in Q \vee u \not\models \varphi\}$, that is, it returns the set of abstract models that do not satisfy φ or are approximated by Q. An abstract abductive transformer, $abd_{\varphi}^{D}(Q)$, corresponds to the under-approximation of the global conflict transformer, $conf_{\varphi}^{D}(Q)$.*

For example, given a formula $\varphi = (x = y + 1 \ \wedge \ x \geq 0)$ and an interval abstract element $Q = (y \leq -5 \wedge x \leq -4)$, $conf_{\varphi}^{Itvs}(Q) = \{(y \leq -5 \wedge x \leq -4), (y \leq -2 \wedge x < 0), \ldots, (y \leq 2 \wedge x \leq 10), \ldots\}$. Now, an abstract abductive transformer for φ is given by $abd_{\varphi}^{Itvs}(Q) = (y \leq -2 \wedge x < 0)$, which clearly underapproximates $conf_{\varphi}^{Itvs}$ as well as strictly generalizes the reason for Q.

The main idea of abductive reasoning is to iteratively replace an abstract element s in the conflict reason by a partial assignment that is sufficient to infer s. Conflict abduction is performed by obtaining cuts through markings in the trail $\mathfrak{T}$ using an abstract Unique Implication Point (UIP) search algorithm [3]. Every cut is a reason for a conflict. The UIP search can be understood as graph cutting in an Abstract Conflict Graph, which is defined next.

Definition 6. *An Abstract Conflict Graph (ACG) is a directed acyclic graph in which the vertices are defined by deduced elements (including a special conflict node ($\perp$)) or a decision node in the trail $\mathfrak{T}$. The edges in ACG are obtained from the reason trail $\mathfrak{R}$ that maps pairs of elements in $\mathfrak{T}$ to the abstract transformers that are used to derive the deduced elements.*

Abstract UIP Search. An abstract UIP is a node in the ACG that must be traversed on every path between a decision node and the conflict. An abstract UIP cut is necessary to ensure that the learnt clauses are asserting after backtracking and prevent cyclic algorithm behavior. An abstract UIP algorithm [5] traverses the trail $\mathfrak{T}$ starting from the conflict node and computes a cut that suffices to produce a conflict. For example, consider a formula $\varphi := (x + 4 = z \wedge x + z = 2y \wedge z + y > 10)$. As before, the trail can be viewed to represent an ACG, given in Fig. 4, that records the sequence of deductions

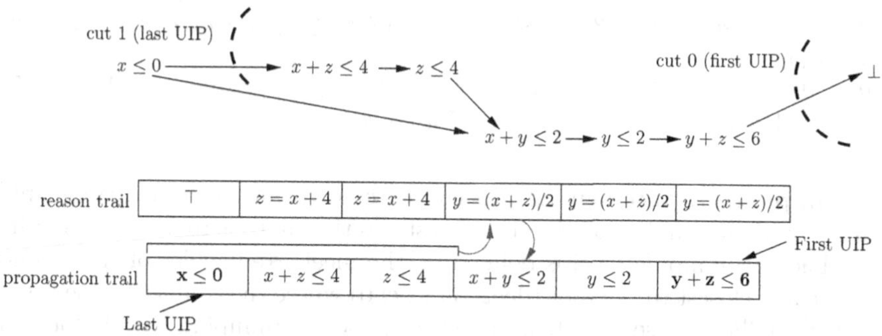

Fig. 4. Finding the Abstract UIP in the octagon domain (Color figure online)

in the octagon domain that are inferred from a decision $x \leq 0$ for the formula φ. The arrows (in red) indicate the relationship between the reason trail and propagation trail at the bottom of Fig. 4. For the partial abstract value, $a = (x \leq 0 \wedge x+z \leq 4 \wedge z \leq 4)$, obtained from the trail, the result of the abstract deduction transformer is $[\![y = (x+z)/2]\!]_{Octs}(a) = (x+y \leq 2 \wedge y \leq 2 \wedge y+z \leq 6)$. A conflict ($\bot$) is reached for the decision $x \leq 0$. Note that there exist multiple incomparable reasons for the conflict, marked as *cut 0* and *cut 1* in Fig. 4. Here, cut 0 is the first UIP (node closest to conflict node). Choosing cut 0 yields a learnt clause $y + z > 6$, which is obtained by negating the reason for the conflict. The abstract UIP algorithm returns a learnt transformer *AUnit*, which is described next.

Learning in Template Polyhedra Domain. Learning in a propositional solvers yields an asserting clause [3] that expresses the negation of the conflict reasons. We present a lattice-theoretic generalisation of the *unit rule* for template-based abstract domains that learns a new transformer called *abstract unit transformer* (*AUnit*). We add *AUnit* to the set of abstract transformers $\mathcal{A}$. *AUnit* is a generalisation of the propositional unit rule to numerical domains. For an abstract lattice D with complementable meet irreducibles and a set of meet irreducibles $C \subseteq D$ such that $\bigsqcap C$ does not satisfy φ, $AUnit_C : D \to D$ is formally defined as follows.

$$AUnit_C(a) = \begin{cases} \bot & \text{if } a \sqsubseteq \bigsqcap C & (1) \\ \bar{t} & \text{if } t \in C \text{ and } \forall t' \in C \setminus \{t\}. a \sqsubseteq t' & (2) \\ \top & \text{otherwise} & (3) \end{cases}$$

Rule (1) shows *AUnit* returns $\bot$ when $a \sqsubseteq \bigsqcap C$ is conflicting. Rule (2) of *AUnit* infers a valid meet irreducible, which implies that C is unit. Rule (3) of *AUnit* returns $\top$ which implies that the learnt clause is not *asserting* after backtracking. This would prevent any new deductions from the learnt clause. Progress is then made by decisions. An example of *AUnit* for $C = \{x \geq 2, x \leq 5, y \leq 7\}$ is below.

Rule 1: For $a = (x \geq 3 \wedge x \leq 4 \wedge y \geq 5 \wedge y \leq 6)$, $AUnit_C(a) = \bot$, since $a \sqsubseteq \bigsqcap C$.
Rule 2: For $a = (x \geq 3 \wedge x \leq 4)$, $AUnit_C(a) = (y \geq 8)$, since $a \sqsubseteq (2 \leq x \leq 5)$.
Rule 3: For $a = (x \geq 1 \wedge y \leq 10)$, $AUnit_C(a) = \top$.

Backjumping. A backjumping procedure removes all the meet irreducibles from the trail up to a decision level that restores the analysis to a non-conflicting state. The backjumping level is defined by the meet irreducibles of the conflict clause that is closest to the root (decision level 0) where the conflict clause is still unit. If a conflict clause is globally unit, then the backjumping level is the root of the search tree and *analyzeConflict* returns false, otherwise it returns true.

7 Experimental Results

We have implemented ACDLP for bounded safety verification of C programs. ACDLP is implemented in C++ on top of the CPROVER [12] framework as an extension of 2LS [27] and consists of around 9 KLOC. The template polyhedra domain is implemented in C++ in 10 KLOC. Templates can be intervals, octagons, zones, equalities, or restricted polyhedra. Our domain handles all C operators, including bit-wise ones, and supports precise complementation of meet irreducibles, which is necessary for conflict-driven learning. Our tool and benchmarks are available at http://www.cprover.org/acdcl/.

We verified a total of 85 ANSI-C benchmarks. These are derived from: (1) the bit-vector regression category in SV-COMP'16; (2) ANSI-C models of hardware circuits auto-generated by v2c [24] from VIS Verilog models and opencores.org; (3) controller code with varying loop bounds auto-generated from Simulink model and control intensive programs with nested loops containing relational properties. All the programs with bounded loops are completely unrolled before analysis.

We compare ACDLP with the state-of-the-art SAT-based bounded model checker CBMC ([7], version 5.5) and a commercial static analysis tool, Astrée ([1], version 14.10). CBMC uses MiniSAT 2.2.1 in the backend. Astrée uses a range of abstract domains, which includes interval, bit-field, congruence, trace partitioning, and relational domains (octagons, polyhedra, zones, equalities, filter). To enable fair comparison using Astrée, all bounded loops in the program are completely unwound up to a given bound before passing to Astrée. This prevents Astrée from widening loops. ACDLP is instantiated to a product of the Booleans and the Interval or Octagon domain. ACDLP is also configured with a decision heuristic (ordered, random, activity-based), propagation (forward, backward and multi-way), and conflict-analysis (learning UIP, DPLL-style). The timeout for our experiments is set to 200 s.

ACDLP versus CBMC. Figure 5 presents a comparison between CBMC and ACDLP. Figure 5(a) clearly shows that the SAT-based analysis makes significantly more decisions than ACDLP for all the benchmarks. The points on the

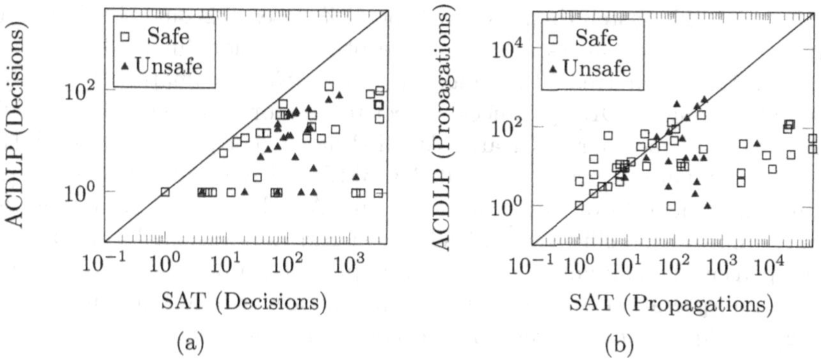

Fig. 5. Comparing SAT-based BMC and ACDLP: number of decisions and propagations

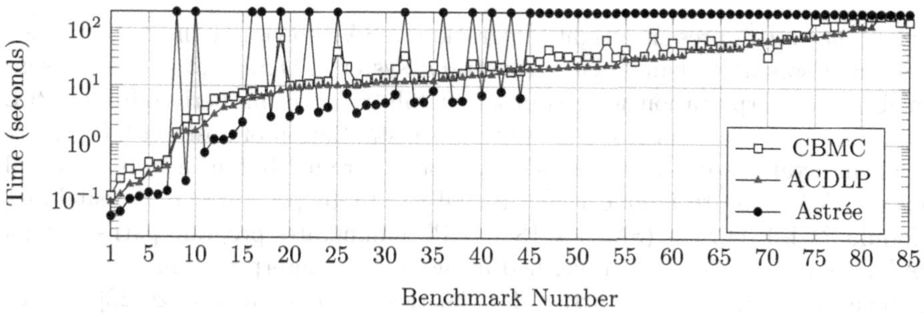

Fig. 6. Runtime comparison between CBMC, Astrée and ACDLP

extreme right below the diagonal in Fig. 5(b) show that the number of propagations in the SAT-based analysis is maximal for benchmarks that exhibit relational behaviour. These benchmarks are solved by the octagon domain in ACDLP. We see a reduction of at least two orders of magnitude in the total number of decisions, propagations and conflicts compared to analysis using CBMC.

Out of 85 benchmarks, SAT-based analysis could prove only 26 benchmarks without any restarts. The solver was restarted in the other 59 cases to avoid spending too much time in "hopeless" branches. By contrast, ACDLP solved all 85 benchmarks without restarts. The runtime comparison between ACDLP and CBMC is shown in Fig. 6. ACDLP is 1.5X faster than CBMC. The superior performance of ACDLP is attributed to the decision heuristics, which exploit the high-level structure of the program, combined with the precise deduction by multi-way transformer and stronger learnt clauses aided by the abstract domains.

ACDLP versus Astrée. To enable precise analysis with Astrée, we manually instrument the benchmarks with partition directives `__ASTREE_partition_control` at various control-flow joins. These directives provide external hints to Astrée to guide its internal trace partitioning domain. Figure 6 demonstrates that Astrée is 2X faster than ACDLP for 37% cases (32 out of 85); but the analysis using Astrée shows a high degree of imprecision (marked as timeout in Fig. 6). Astrée reported 53 false alarms among 85 benchmarks. By contrast, the analysis using ACDLP produces correct results for 81 benchmarks. ACDLP times out for 4 benchmarks. Clearly, ACDLP has higher precision than Astrée. A detailed comparison between ACDLP, CBMC and Astrée is available at [23].

Our experimental evaluation suggests that ACDLP can be seen as a technique to improve the efficiency of SAT-based BMC. Additionally, ACDLP can also be perceived as an automatic way to improve the precision of conventional abstract interpretation over non-distributive lattices through automatic partitioning techniques such as decisions and transformer learning.

8 Related Work

Fränzle et al. [16] present a tight integration of SAT solving with interval-based constraint solving to handle large constraint systems. D'Silva et al. [15] present an abstract interpretation account of satisfiability algorithms derived from DPLL procedures. The work of [14] is a very early instantiation of abstract CDCL [15] as an interval-based decision procedure for programs, but in a purely logical setting. A similar technique that lifts DPLL(T) to programs is Satisfiability Modulo Path Programs (SMPP) [18]. SMPP enumerates program paths using a SAT formula, which are then verified using abstract interpretation.

The lifting of CDCL to first-order theories is proposed in [9,20,22]. Unlike previous work that operates on a fixed first-order lattice, ACDLP can be instantiated with different abstract domains as well as product domains. This involves model search and learning in abstract lattices. A similar technique that lifts decisions, propagations and learning to theory variables is Model-Constructing Satisfiability Calculus (mcSAT) [22].

ACDLP is not, however, similar to abstraction refinement. ACDLP works on a fixed abstraction. Also, transformer learning in ACDLP does not soundly overapproximate the existing program transformers. Hence, transformer learning in ACDLP is distinct from transformer refinement in classical CEGAR.

9 Conclusions

We present a general algorithmic framework for lifting the model search and conflict analysis procedures in DPLL-style satisfiability solvers to program analysis. We embody these techniques in a tool, ACDLP, for automatic bounded safety verification of C programs over a template polyhedra abstract domain.

We present an *abstract model search* procedure that uses a parameterised abstract transformer to flexibly control the precision and efficiency of the deductions in the template polyhedra abstract domain. The underlying expressivity of the abstract domain helps our decision heuristics to exploit the high-level structure of the program for making effective decisions. Our *abstract conflict analysis* learns abstract transformers over a given template following a UIP computation.

Experimental evaluation over a range of benchmarks shows a 20× reduction in the total number of *decisions*, *propagations*, *conflicts* and *backtracking* iterations compared to CBMC. Moreover, ACDLP is 1.5× faster than CBMC. Compared to Astrée, ACDLP solves twice as many benchmarks and has much higher precision. In the future, we plan to extend our framework to unbounded verification through invariant generation.

References

1. Astrée. https://www.absint.com/astree/index.htm
2. Baier, C., Katoen, J.P.: Principles of Model Checking. The MIT Press, Cambridge (2008)
3. Biere, A., Heule, M., Van Maaren, H., Walsh, T.: Handbook of Satisfiability. IOS, Amsterdam (2009)
4. Blanchet, B., Cousot, P., Cousot, R., Feret, J., Mauborgne, L., Miné, A., Monniaux, D., Rival, X.: A static analyzer for large safety-critical software. In: Programming Language Design and Implementation (PLDI), pp. 196–207. ACM (2003)
5. Brain, M., D'Silva, V., Griggio, A., Haller, L., Kroening, D.: Deciding floating-point logic with abstract conflict driven clause learning. Form. Methods Syst. Des. **45**(2), 213–245 (2014)
6. Brain, M., Joshi, S., Kroening, D., Schrammel, P.: Safety verification and refutation by k-invariants and k-induction. In: Blazy, S., Jensen, T. (eds.) SAS 2015. LNCS, vol. 9291, pp. 145–161. Springer, Heidelberg (2015). doi:10.1007/978-3-662-48288-9_9
7. CBMC. http://www.cprover.org/cbmc/
8. Clarke, E., Kroening, D., Lerda, F.: A tool for checking ANSI-C programs. In: Jensen, K., Podelski, A. (eds.) TACAS 2004. LNCS, vol. 2988, pp. 168–176. Springer, Heidelberg (2004). doi:10.1007/978-3-540-24730-2_15
9. Cotton, S.: Natural domain SMT: a preliminary assessment. In: Chatterjee, K., Henzinger, T.A. (eds.) FORMATS 2010. LNCS, vol. 6246, pp. 77–91. Springer, Heidelberg (2010). doi:10.1007/978-3-642-15297-9_8
10. Cousot, P., Cousot, R.: Abstract interpretation: a unified lattice model for static analysis of programs by construction or approximation of fixpoints. In: Principles of Programming Languages (POPL), pp. 238–252. ACM (1977)
11. Cousot, P., Cousot, R.: Systematic design of program analysis frameworks. In: Principles of Programming Languages (POPL), pp. 269–282. ACM (1979)
12. CPROVER verification framework. http://www.cprover.org/
13. D'Silva, V., Haller, L., Kroening, D.: Abstract conflict driven learning. In: Principles of Programming Languages (POPL), pp. 143–154. ACM (2013)
14. D'Silva, V., Haller, L., Kroening, D., Tautschnig, M.: Numeric bounds analysis with conflict-driven learning. In: Flanagan, C., König, B. (eds.) TACAS 2012. LNCS, vol. 7214, pp. 48–63. Springer, Heidelberg (2012). doi:10.1007/978-3-642-28756-5_5
15. D'Silva, V., Haller, L., Kroening, D.: Satisfiability solvers are static analysers. In: Miné, A., Schmidt, D. (eds.) SAS 2012. LNCS, vol. 7460, pp. 317–333. Springer, Heidelberg (2012). doi:10.1007/978-3-642-33125-1_22
16. Fränzle, M., Herde, C., Teige, T., Ratschan, S., Schubert, T.: Efficient solving of large non-linear arithmetic constraint systems with complex Boolean structure. J. Satisf. Boolean Model. Comput. **1**, 209–236 (2007)
17. Haller, L.C.R.: Abstract satisfaction. Ph.D. thesis, University of Oxford, UK (2013)

18. Harris, W.R., Sankaranarayanan, S., Ivančić, F., Gupta, A.: Program analysis via satisfiability modulo path programs. In: Principles of Programming Languages (POPL), pp. 71–82. ACM (2010)
19. Jeannet, B., Miné, A.: Apron: a library of numerical abstract domains for static analysis. In: Bouajjani, A., Maler, O. (eds.) CAV 2009. LNCS, vol. 5643, pp. 661–667. Springer, Heidelberg (2009). doi:10.1007/978-3-642-02658-4_52
20. McMillan, K.L., Kuehlmann, A., Sagiv, M.: Generalizing DPLL to richer logics. In: Bouajjani, A., Maler, O. (eds.) CAV 2009. LNCS, vol. 5643, pp. 462–476. Springer, Heidelberg (2009). doi:10.1007/978-3-642-02658-4_35
21. MiniSAT. http://minisat.se/
22. de Moura, L., Jovanović, D.: A model-constructing satisfiability calculus. In: Giacobazzi, R., Berdine, J., Mastroeni, I. (eds.) VMCAI 2013. LNCS, vol. 7737, pp. 1–12. Springer, Heidelberg (2013). doi:10.1007/978-3-642-35873-9_1
23. Mukherjee, R., Schrammel, P., Haller, L., Kroening, D., Melham, T.: Lifting CDCL to template-based abstract domains for program verification (extended version). arXiv Computing Research Repository [cs.LO], July 2017. arXiv:1707.02011
24. Mukherjee, R., Tautschnig, M., Kroening, D.: v2c – A verilog to C translator. In: Chechik, M., Raskin, J.-F. (eds.) TACAS 2016. LNCS, vol. 9636, pp. 580–586. Springer, Heidelberg (2016). doi:10.1007/978-3-662-49674-9_38
25. Rival, X., Mauborgne, L.: The trace partitioning abstract domain. ACM TOPLAS **29**(5), 26 (2007)
26. Sankaranarayanan, S., Sipma, H.B., Manna, Z.: Scalable analysis of linear systems using mathematical programming. In: Cousot, R. (ed.) VMCAI 2005. LNCS, vol. 3385, pp. 25–41. Springer, Heidelberg (2005). doi:10.1007/978-3-540-30579-8_2
27. Schrammel, P., Kroening, D.: 2LS for program analysis. In: Chechik, M., Raskin, J.-F. (eds.) TACAS 2016. LNCS, vol. 9636, pp. 905–907. Springer, Heidelberg (2016). doi:10.1007/978-3-662-49674-9_56

Synthesizing Invariants by Solving Solvable Loops

Steven de Oliveira[1(✉)], Saddek Bensalem[2], and Virgile Prevosto[1]

[1] CEA, LIST, Software Safety and Security Laboratory, P.C. 174, 91191 Gif-sur-Yvette, France
{steven.deoliveira,virgile.prevosto}@cea.fr
[2] Verimag, Université Grenoble Alpes, Grenoble, France
saddek.bensalem@imag.fr

Abstract. Formal program verification faces two problems. The first problem is related to the necessity of having automated solvers that are powerful enough to decide whether a formula holds for a set of proof obligations as large as possible, whereas the second manifests in the need of finding sufficiently strong invariants to obtain correct proof obligations. This paper focuses on the second problem and describes a new method for the automatic generation of loop invariants that handles polynomial and non deterministic assignments. This technique is based on the eigenvector generation for a given linear transformation and on the polynomial optimization problem, which we implemented on top of the open-source tool PILAT.

1 Introduction

Program verification relies on different mathematical foundations to let users prove that a piece of code behaves as intended. The problem is however undecidable for any Turing complete language, partly because of loops. This is one of the reasons why loop analysis is a highly studied topic in the field of verification. Let us take for example linear filters, whose purpose are to apply a linear constraint to input signals. Such programs are heavily used in embedded software for analyzing sensors' data and are thus critical for the correction of the system. Yet, linear filters are difficult to verify because of the non-determinism induced by the unknown input signal and the use of floating-point computations. This lack of precision forbids the direct use of exact mathematical techniques.

Figure 1 presents an example of program inspired by linear filters [21]. We claim that loop invariants are a good way to obtain general information about such a loop. In this particular case, the loop admits the invariant $x^2 + y^2 \leqslant 14.9$, bounding the maximal value of $|x|$ and $|y|$ to 3.9: this is an infinite loop. More generally, if we can infer bounds for the value of the loop variables or for polynomial expressions of these variables, we are then able to perform precise

This work has been partially conducted within the VESSEDIA project, that has received funding from the European Union's Horizon 2020 research and innovation programme under grant agreement No. 731453.

D. D'Souza and K. Narayan Kumar (Eds.): ATVA 2017, LNCS 10482, pp. 327–343, 2017.
DOI: 10.1007/978-3-319-68167-2_22

analyses, such as reachability. In this paper, we aim at facing two major problems of numeric invariant generation, namely the generation of polynomial relations between variables and the search of inductive spaces to which variables of a program belong, in the context of simple (i.e. non-nested) loops composed of polynomial and non deterministic assignments. In particular, linear filters are encompassed in such context. The relations we generate have the advantage to be completely independent from the initial state of the loop, making them fully generic, as opposed to full-program based techniques that start from a specific initial state. This work is an extension of the algorithm PILA [11], which generates polynomial equalities between variables manipulated by a simple deterministic loop. We show in this paper that a refined version of this algorithm can also produce inductive inequality invariants and tackle non-deterministic assignments as well as deterministic ones. Moreover, we add to this analysis an optimization algorithm enabling us to minimize the inductive set described by invariants of non deterministic loops.

```
x = non_det(-1,1);
y = non_det(-1,1);
while(x < 4) do
 N = non_det(-0.1,0.1);
  (x,y) = (0.68 * (x-y) + N,\
     0.68 * (x+y) + N);
done
```

Fig. 1. Example of linear filter

Contributions. The original PILA approach generates inductive invariants as equality relations of the form $P(X) = 0$ with P a polynomial. This paper extends this method (Sect. 2) to generate new kinds of inductive invariants of the form $|P(X)| \leqslant k$ and $|P(X)| \geqslant k$. It is mostly based on linear algebra and is applicable to C programs manipulating integers and floating point numbers. To simplify the presentation, we describe the method on a simple imperative language (Sect. 3). The two main results of this extension are the treatment of loops with deterministic (Sect. 4.1) and non-deterministic assignments (Sect. 4.2). Finally, we explain how to manage imprecision in floating point computations (Sect. 4.3). In the latter cases, we reduce the problem of generating invariants to the polynomial optimization problem. An algorithm for solving this problem is given. The proposed method in this paper is correct, fully implemented in PILAT and is currently part of the Frama-C suite [17] as an external open-source plug-in, available at [3]. We show its efficiency by applying it on several examples from related literature in Sect. 6. Due to space constraints, proofs have been omitted. They are available in a separate report [12].

2 Overview

When synthesizing invariants, three ingredients are required:

1. what kind of invariants are computed;
2. what will be their most useful shape;
3. how strong they will be.

In abstract interpretation for example, we first choose the type of invariant that will be computed, i.e. the abstract domain, then a symbolic execution of properties of this domain will shape the initial state into an invariant that we will try to keep as strong as possible by applying appropriate widening and narrowing operators.

Overview of the PILA Algorithm. Let us first recall how PILA works on a simple example. Consider the loop of Fig. 2 for which we want to generate all invariants (polynomials P such that $P(x, y) = 0$) of degree 2. By enhancing the loop expressiveness with new variables representing the value of the monomials of variables used in the loop, namely x_2 for x^2, y_2 for y^2 and xy for $x * y$, it first creates linear variables representing monomials.

Let us take for instance x_2. As the new value of x is $0.68.(x - y)$, the new value of x^2 is $0.68^2.(x^2 - 2.x.y + y^2)$. x_2 can then be expressed as a linear application of x_2, xy and y_2. More generally, any monomial of variables of the loop in Fig. 2 evolves linearly along the execution of the enhanced loop.

```
x = non_det(-1,1);
y = non_det(-1,1);
while(*) do
  (x,y) = (0.68 * (x-y),\
   0.68 * (x+y));
done
```

Fig. 2. Simple affine loop

Next, PILA starts generating invariants. Instead of starting with an initial state, which is not assumed to be known, it generates relations that are preserved by each step of the loop. Let f be the loop transformation, (here $f(x, y) = (0.68 * (x - y), 0.68 * (x + y))$. A linear application φ is a semi-invariant if, given any valuation of the variables, it stays constant through one iteration of f. In other words, it must respect the following property:

$$\text{If } \varphi(X) = 0 \text{ then } \varphi(f(X)) = 0$$

In linear algebra, this is strictly equivalent to the following:

$$\text{If } \varphi(X) = 0 \text{ then } f^*(\varphi)(X) = 0$$

where $f^*(\varphi) = \varphi \circ f$ is the dual application of f. If there exists a scalar λ such that $f^*(\varphi) = \lambda.\varphi$ (i.e. φ an eigenvector of f^* associated to the eigenvalue λ) the criterion becomes obviously true, thus φ is a semi-invariant.

In fact, it is shown in [11] that eigenvectors of f^* are exactly the set of such invariants bound to the transformation f. More precisely, when an eigenvector φ is associated to the eigenvalue 1 (i.e. $f^*(\varphi) = \varphi$), it represents an affine invariant of f ($\varphi.X = k$). When the associated eigenvalue is not 1, the PILA algorithm is not always capable of lifting the semi-invariant into a proper invariant. In the example of Fig. 2, the associated eigenvalue of the only semi-invariant $x^2 + y^2$ is 0.9248. PILAT concludes that $x^2 + y^2 = 0$ is inductive but if it does not respect the initial state, this is not an invariant.

The key idea of this paper is to consider not only equalities, but also inequalities. If the left eigenvector φ is associated to an eigenvalue λ such that $0 < \lambda \leqslant 1$ then $\lambda.\varphi(X)$ will necessarily be smaller than $\varphi(X)$. Thus for any $k \geqslant 0$, the following proposition holds:

$$\text{If } \varphi(X) \leqslant k \text{ then } f^*(\varphi)(X) \leqslant k$$

$\varphi(X) \leqslant k$ is thus inductive. In our example, the relation $x^2 + y^2 \leqslant k$ is inductive, and contrarily to $x^2 + y^2 = 0$ it can be made an invariant even if the initial values of x and y are not 0: we just have to choose $k = x_{init}^2 + y_{init}^2$.

Non Determinism. The same reasoning can be applied to treat non deterministic values in assignments. By setting the non deterministic values to a random value, e.g. 0, we are left to find inductive inequality relations, which can be easily performed as we just saw. In the deterministic case, generated formulas are inductive because the set of possible values for x and y that respects the formula gets bigger by applying the loop transformation once. Adding the non deterministic noise may lead to non inductive formulas. A solution consists in finding upper and lower bounds for this noise and check if the set obtained in deterministic case stays stable under this new transformation. If this is not the case, we must consider a weaker invariant.

3 Setting

Mathematical Background. We work in the real field $\mathbb{R}$. Let $(\mathbb{R}^n, \|.\|)$ the normed vector space of dimension n associated to the usual euclidean norm $\|.\|$. Elements of $\mathbb{R}^n$ are denoted $x = (x_1, \ldots, x_n)^t$ a column vector. The variables vector of a mapping f is denoted X. $\mathcal{M}_n(\mathbb{R})$ is the set of matrices of size $n * n$ and $\mathbb{R}[X]$ is the set of polynomials with coefficients in $\mathbb{R}$. The complex field $\mathbb{C}$ is the algebraic closure of $\mathbb{R}$. Let $|.|$ be the euclidian norm on $\mathbb{C}$. We use $\langle .,. \rangle$ the linear algebra standard notation, $\langle u, v \rangle = u^t.v$, with . the usual dot product (i.e. the sum of the product of each component of u and v). For a linear mapping $f(X) = A.X$, we define its *dual* $f^*(X) = A^t X$. The kernel of a matrix $A \in \mathcal{M}_n(\mathbb{R})$, denoted $\ker(A)$, is the vectorial space defined as $\ker(A) = \{x \in \mathbb{R}^n, Ax = 0\}$. Every matrix of $\mathcal{M}_n(\mathbb{R})$ admits a finite set of eigenvalues $\lambda \in \mathbb{C}$ and their associated eigenspaces E_λ, defined as $E_\lambda = \ker(A - \lambda Id)$, where Id is the identity matrix and $E_\lambda \neq \{0\}$. Similarly, every matrix A admits *left-eigenspaces*, i.e. eigenspaces of A^t. The limit of a multivariate function $f : \mathbb{R}^n \to \mathbb{R}$ for $\|X\| \to l$ is defined by the maximal value of $f(X)$ with $\|X\|$ in the neighborhood of $l \in \mathbb{R} \cup \{+\infty\}$ and is denoted $\lim\limits_{\|X\| \to l} f(X)$.

Invariants. A formula requires two canonical properties to be a loop invariant: it must be true at the beginning of the loop (initialization); it must be preserved by a loop step (inductivity). Similarly to [11], we define the inductive relation φ by the following constraint.

Definition 1 *(Exact).*
$\varphi \in \mathbb{R}^n$ *is an* exact inductive invariant *for a linear mapping f iff*

$$\forall X \in \mathbb{R}^n, |\langle \varphi, X \rangle| = 0 \Rightarrow |\langle \varphi, f(X) \rangle| = 0 \tag{1}$$

In the present paper, we add to this definition the concept of convergent and divergent inductive relation.

Definition 2 *(Convergence).*
$\varphi \in \mathbb{R}^n$ *is a* convergent inductive invariant *for a linear mapping f iff*

$$\forall X \in \mathbb{R}^n, \forall k \in \mathbb{R}, |\langle \varphi, X \rangle| \leqslant k \Rightarrow |\langle \varphi, f(X) \rangle| \leqslant k \tag{2}$$

Definition 3 *(Divergence).*
$\varphi \in \mathbb{R}^n$ *is a* divergent inductive invariant *for a linear mapping f iff*

$$\forall X \in \mathbb{R}^n, \forall k \in \mathbb{R} |\langle \varphi, X \rangle| \geqslant k \Rightarrow |\langle \varphi, f(X) \rangle| \geqslant k \tag{3}$$

The convergent invariant definition could have been written equivalently $|\langle \varphi, X \rangle| \leqslant |\langle \varphi, f(X) \rangle|$. We choose the other notation as the idea of the technique is to find a suitable value of k such that $|\langle \varphi, X \rangle| \leqslant k$ is an invariant of the loop. A vector φ satisfying the inductive relation is called a *semi-invariant* in contrast with *invariants* that also verify the initialization criterion, denoted $\langle \varphi, X_{init} \rangle$ with X_{init} the variables' initial values. The exact semi-invariants set of a linear mapping f is the union of all eigenspaces of f^* as proven in [11]. Also, we define the solvability of a mapping introduced in [27].

Definition 4. *Let $g \in (\mathbb{R}[X])^m$ be a polynomial mapping. g is solvable if there exists a partition of X into sub-vectors of variables $x = w_1 \uplus \ldots \uplus w_k$ and we can divide g into different mappings g_{w_j} manipulating variables of w_j such that*

$$g_{w_j}(x) = M_j w_j^t + P_j(w_1, \ldots, w_{j-1}, N)$$

with P_j a polynomial and N eventual non deterministic parameters.

For example, the mapping $g_N(x, y) = (x + y^2, y + N)$ depending on the parameter N is solvable because we can set $w_1 = \{y\}$ and $w_2 = \{x\}$. $g_y(x, y) = y + P_1(N)$, where $P_1 = N$ and $g_x(x, y) = x + P_2(y)$ where $P_2(y) = y^2$. We also can write $g_N(x, y) = (g_x(x, y), g_y(x, y))$.

Remark. As shown in [11], deterministic solvable assignments are linearizable, i.e. they can be replaced by equivalent linear mappings. This allows to consider deterministic linear mappings $X' = A.X$ with X a vector containing both variables and monomials of those variables to represent deterministic solvable assignments.

Programming Model. We use a basic programming language whose syntax is given in Fig. 3. Var is the set of variables used by the program. Variables take their value in $\mathbb{R}$. A program state is then a partial mapping $Var \rightharpoonup \mathbb{R}$. Any given program only uses a finite number n of variables, thus program states can be represented as vectors $X = (x_1, \ldots, x_n)^t$. Finally, we assume that for all programs, there exists $x_{n+1} = \mathbb{1}$ a constant variable always equal to 1. This allows to represent any affine assignment by a matrix. The expression $non\_det(exp_1, exp_2)$ returns a random value between the valuation of exp_1 and exp_2 when the program reaches this location. Multiple variables assignments occur simultaneously within a single instruction. We say an assignment $X = exp$ is affine (resp. solvable) when exp is an affine (resp. solvable) combination. Also, we say that an instruction is non-deterministic when it is an assignment in which the right value contains the expression non_det.

$i ::=$	skip	$exp ::=$	$cst \in \mathbb{R}$
	$\mid i; i$		$\mid x \in Var$
	$\mid (x_1, .., x_n) := (exp_1, ..., exp_n)$		$\mid exp + exp$
	$\mid$ while $*$ do i done		$\mid exp * exp$
			$\mid non\_det(exp, exp)$

Fig. 3. Code syntax

4 Convergent and Divergent Linear Applications

4.1 Deterministic Assignments

Being an inductive invariant requires for a formula F to be true after an iteration of the loop under the hypothesis that F holds before the iteration. The left eigenspace of a linear transformation (i.e. the eigenspace of the dual transformation) is exactly its set of exact invariants as defined in Definition 1.

Convergence. By linear algebra, $|\langle\varphi, X\rangle| \leqslant k \Rightarrow |\langle f^*(\varphi), X\rangle| \leqslant k$ is strictly equivalent to the Definition 2 of convergent semi-invariants. The formula $|\langle\varphi, X\rangle| \leqslant k$ represents what we call a *domain described by* φ, i.e. a polynomial relation over the variables of the program. The previous constraint specify that the domain described by φ is stable by f. The loop in Fig. 2 admits the invariant $x^2 + y^2 \leqslant 2$, a domain described by $\varphi = (0, 0, 0, 1, 0, 1)^t$ in the base $(\mathbb{1}, x, xy, x_2, y, y_2)$ where x_2 represents x^2, xy represents $x * y$ and y_2 represents y^2. We can check with the PILA algorithm that φ is an exact semi-invariant of the loop as it is a left eigenvector of the transformation performed by the loop. As such, it generates a vectorial space of exact semi-invariants $I = \{k.(x^2 + y^2) = 0 \mid k \in \mathbb{R}\}$, which is a very poor result as

$x^2 + y^2$ is constant only if it starts at 0 (else, $k = 0$ and we don't know anything about $x^2 + y^2$). We focus now on the eigenvalue associated to φ on f^*, which is 0.9248. Thus, we can replace $|\langle f^*(\varphi), X\rangle|$ by $|\lambda|.|\langle\varphi, X\rangle|$, which returns $|\langle\varphi, X\rangle| \leqslant k \Rightarrow |\lambda|.|\langle\varphi, X\rangle| \leqslant k$. As $|\lambda| < 1$, the vector φ satisfies the equation, thus φ is a convergent semi-invariant. Knowing the maximal initial value of $x^2 + y^2$ allows to determine the value of k, which is 2.

More generally, the set of convergent semi-invariants is exactly the set of eigenvectors bound to an eigenvalue λ such that $|\lambda| < 1$. The proof of this assertion requires the following lemma:

Lemma 1. $(\forall k, |\langle\varphi, X\rangle| \leqslant k \Rightarrow |\langle\varphi, f(X)\rangle| \leqslant k) \Rightarrow f^*(\varphi) = \lambda.\varphi$

In other words, convergent invariants are eigenvectors. The goal of the following property is to characterize the associated eigenvalue.

Property 1. *φ is a convergent semi-invariant* $\Leftrightarrow \exists\lambda, |\lambda| \leqslant 1, f^*(\varphi) = \lambda.\varphi$.

Proof. If $|\lambda| \leqslant 1$, then φ is a convergent semi-invariant (see introduction of Sect. 4.1). As the exact semi-invariants set of f is the union of the eigenspaces of f^*, we can deduce that this set is a superset of all the relations satisfying the Definition 2. Moreover by the Lemma 1, we have

$$(|\langle\varphi, X\rangle| \leqslant k \Rightarrow |\langle\varphi, f(X)\rangle| \leqslant k) \Rightarrow (|<\varphi, X>| \leqslant k \Rightarrow |\lambda|.|<\varphi, X>| \leqslant k)$$

For $k = |<\varphi, X>|$ it is true if and only if $|\lambda| \leqslant 1$. □

Divergence. The same reasoning applies to the generation of divergent invariants. For example, an eigenvalue λ such that $|\lambda| > 1$ associated to a semi-invariant φ implies that $|\langle\varphi, X\rangle| \geqslant k$ is an inductive invariant.

Property 2. $\exists\lambda, |\lambda| > 1, f^*(\varphi) = \lambda.\varphi \Rightarrow$ *φ is a divergent semi-invariant.*

Proof. If there exists λ such that $f^*(\varphi) = \lambda.\varphi$, then we have that being a divergent semi invariant is equivalent to

$$|<\varphi, X>| \geqslant k \Rightarrow |\lambda|.|<\varphi, X>| \geqslant k$$

If we also have that $|\lambda| > 1$, then the previous equation is true. □

Note that this time, we only have an implication. For example, the transformation $f(x, \mathbb{1}) = (x + \mathbb{1}, \mathbb{1})$ admits $x \geqslant x_{init}$ as a divergent invariant but the only left eigenvector of f is $(0, 1)$, which correspond to the invariant "$\mathbb{1}$ *is constant*". Moreover, not all invariants of the form $P(X) \leqslant k$ are generated : the loop with the only assignment $x = x - 1$ admits the (non-convergent) invariant $x \leqslant x_{init}$. This invariant does not enter the scope of our setting as $|x| \leqslant x_{init}$ is false for $2x_{init} + 1$ iterations of $x = x - 1$.

4.2 Non-deterministic Assignments

Some programs depend on inputs given all along their execution, for example linear filters. More generally, an important part of program analysis consists in studying non-deterministic assignments. As an example let us consider the program in Fig. 4, a slightly modified version of the program in Fig. 2. Our previous reasoning is not applicable now because, due to the non-determinism of N, the loop is no longer a linear mapping.

```
while (*) do
  N = non_det(-0.1,0.1);
  (x,y) = (0.68 * (x-y) + N, \
    0.68(x+y) + N);
done
```

Fig. 4. Non deterministic variant of the Fig. 2

Idea. Intuitively, we will represent this loop by a matrix parametrized by N. For that purpose we use the concept of abstract mapping introduced in [15].

Definition 5. *An abstract linear mapping* $f : \mathbb{R}^q \mapsto \mathcal{M}_n(\mathbb{R})$ *is a mapping associating a vector* $N \in \mathbb{R}^q$ *to a matrix. We call* f^* *the dual mapping of* f *(i.e. the mapping such that* $f^*(N) = (f(N))^T$*). The expression of the parametrized matrix with respect to an abstract linear mapping will be called the* abstract matrix.

In our setting, the parameters are the non-deterministic values. For example, the previous loop can be represented by the abstract matrix M_N:

$$\begin{pmatrix} 1 & 0 & 0 & 0 & 0 & 0 \\ N & 0.68 & 0 & 0 & -0.68 & 0 \\ N^2 & 1.36N & 0 & 0.462 & 0 & -0.462 \\ N^2 & 1.36N & 0.925 & 0.462 & -1.36N & 0.462 \\ N & 0.68 & 0 & 0 & 0.68 & 0 \\ N^2 & 1.36N & 0.925 & 0.462 & 1.36N & 0.462 \end{pmatrix}$$

Remark. Similarly to deterministic solvable mappings defined in Sect. 3, non deterministic solvable mappings can be linearized to an abstract matrix. By considering non deterministic parameters as constants, the problem is reduced to the linearization of deterministic solvable mappings.

We have shown in Sect. 4.1 that M_0 admits the invariant $e_0 = (0,0,0,1,0,1)$ associated to the eigenvalue $\lambda_0 = 0.9248$. By decomposing M_N as the sum of M_0 and $(M_N - M_0)$, we also have $e_0.M_N = e_0.M_0 + e_0.(M_N - M_0) = \lambda_0.e_0 + \delta_0^N$, where $\delta_0^N = e_0.(M_N - M_0) = (2N^2, 2.72N, 0, 0, 0, 0)$. As the eigenvalue λ_0 is smaller than 1, we are looking for relations φ such that $\forall X, |\langle\varphi, X\rangle| \leqslant k \Rightarrow |\langle M_N^T.\varphi, X\rangle| \leqslant k$. We will call e_0 a *candidate invariant* for M_N. For e_0 to be a proper invariant for this transformation, the following property must hold:

$$\forall X, |\langle e_0, X\rangle| \leqslant k \Rightarrow |\lambda_0\langle e_0, X\rangle + \langle\delta_0^N, X\rangle| \leqslant k \tag{4}$$

Intuitively, multiplying $\langle e_0, X\rangle$ by λ_0 reduces its norm strictly under k. We need to make sure that adding $\langle \delta_0^N, X\rangle$ does not contradict the induction criterion by increasing the result over k. The variables of the program depend on k, as does $\langle \delta_0^N, X\rangle$. If it increases faster than $|\lambda_0\langle e_0, X\rangle|$ when k is increased, then no value of k will make the candidate invariant inductive. In particular, if $\langle e_0, X\rangle$ is a polynomial P of degree d, we need to be able to give an upper bound of $\langle \delta_0^N, X\rangle$ knowing that $|P(X)| < k$. If the degree of $\langle \delta_0^N, X\rangle$ is strictly smaller than d, then it will grow asymptotically slower than $|P(X)|$, thus for a big enough k the induction criterion is respected.

Property 3.

$$\left(\forall X, |\langle e_0, X\rangle| \leqslant k \Rightarrow |\langle \delta_0^N, X\rangle| \leqslant (1 - |\lambda_0|).k\right) \Rightarrow \tag{5}$$

$$|\langle e_0, X\rangle| \leqslant k \textit{ is an invariant of the loop.}$$

In our example, $\langle \delta_0^N, X\rangle = 2.72 * N * x + 2 * N^2$. The polynomial x is of degree 1 while $< e_0, X >= x^2 + y^2$ is of degree 2. We need to find a k such that

$$-0.0752 * k \leqslant 2.72 * N * x + 2 * N^2 \leqslant 0.0752 * k \tag{6}$$

Optimizing Expressions. We will now maximize and minimize $2.72 * N * x + 2 * N^2$, knowing that $x^2 + y^2 \leqslant k$ and $-0.1 \leqslant N \leqslant 0.1$. Solving this problem is very close to solving a constrained polynomial optimization (CPO) problem [7]. CPO techniques provide ways to find values minimizing and maximizing expressions under a set of inequalities constraints. Our main issue is related to the parameter k that must be known in order to use CPO directly. We will not investigate in this article how CPO works in detail, but how we can reduce the problem of finding an optimal k to the CPO problem.

Assuming we have a function *min* computing the minimum, if it exists, of an expression under polynomial constraints, we propose an algorithm that refines the value of k in Fig. 5. The idea is to find k by dichotomy.

- If k doesn't satisfy the constraints, we try a bigger one.
- If we find a k satisfying the two conditions, then it is a potential candidate. We can still try to refine it by searching for a smaller k.

We can improve this algorithm by guessing an upper value of k instead of taking an arbitrary maximal value *MAX_INT*. For our example, we started at $k = 50$ and found that $k = 14.9$ respects all the constraints.

- $x^2 + y^2 \leqslant 14.9 \Rightarrow |x| \leqslant 3.9$
- $|N| \leqslant 0.1$
- $|2.72 * x * N + 2 * N^2| \leqslant 1.08$, and $k * (1 - |\lambda|) = 1.12$.

```
Data:
λ : float
Q : objective function
P : polynomial constraint
non_det_c : non deterministic constraints
N : int
Result: k such that ∀X, P(X) ⩽ k ⇒ f(X) ⩽ (1 − |λ|).k
low_k = 0;
up_k = MAX_INT;
k = MAX_INT / 2;
i = 0;
while i<N ∧ up_k = MAX_INT do
    i = i+1;
    Pk = function (x → P(x) + k);
    min = min(Q,[Pk] ∪ non_det_c);
    max = min(-1*Q,[Pk] ∪ non_det_c);
    if min > (-1+|λ|) * k and max < (1-|λ|)*k then
        up_k = k;
    else
        low_k = k;
    end
    k = (low_k + up_k) / 2;
end
```

Fig. 5. Dichotomy search of a k satisfying the condition (6)

Convergence. Note however that the existence of a k satisfying (6) is not guaranteed. For example, the set $S = \{(x, y, N)|x^2 + y^2 \leqslant k \wedge -0.1 \leqslant N \leqslant 0.1\}$ is a compact set for any value of k, which means that x, y and N have maximum and minimum values. This implies the existence of a lower and an upper bound for every expression composed with x, y and N, but the value of those expressions may be always higher than k such as for $x^2 + y^2 + 1$ bounded by $k + 1$.

Property 4. *Let P and Q two polynomials and $M > 0 \in \mathbb{R}$.*
If $\lim_{\|X\| \to +\infty} |\frac{Q(X)}{P(X)}| < M$, then there exists $k \in \mathbb{R}$ such that for all $k' \geqslant k$

$$|P(X)| \leqslant k' \Rightarrow |Q(X)| \leqslant M.k'$$

By taking $M = (1 - |\lambda_0|)$, this theorem gives us a sufficient condition to guarantee the convergence of the algorithm in Fig. 5.

Corollary. *If the objective has a lower degree in the deterministic variables than the candidate invariant, then the algorithm converges. If it has the same degree, then it depends on the main coefficients.*

As we are dealing with two polynomials P and Q, then if P (the candidate invariant) has a higher degree than Q (the objective function) in all its variables, the limit of $\frac{Q(X)}{P(X)}$ will be 0, which is enough to ensure the convergence of the method. If we come back to the objective function for the loop of Fig. 2, $Q(X) = 2.72.x.N + 2.N^2$ is a polynomial of degree 1 in x and 0 in y, thus $\lim_{\|X\| \to +\infty} |\frac{Q(X,N)}{P(X)}| = 0$ and we can be sure that the optimization will converge.

On the other hand, if we have $X = (x, y)$, $P(X) = x^2 + y^2$ and $Q(X, N) = 10.N(x^2 + y^2 + 1)$, with $|N| \leqslant 0.1$, the optimization procedure may not produce a result by Theorem 4 because $\lim_{\|X\| \to +\infty} |\frac{Q(X,N)}{P(X)}| = 10\,N$ is higher than $1 - |\lambda|$ for $N = 0.1$.

Initial State. The knowledge of the initial state is not one of our hypotheses yet, but the previous theorem provides the necessary information we need to treat the case where the initial state is strictly higher than the minimal k we found. The previous theorem tells us that there exists a k such that for all $k' \geqslant k$, k' is a solution to the optimization problem. Our optimization algorithm is searching for a value of k for which the set is inductive, though, and this solution may be only local: there may be a $k' > k$ which is not a solution of the optimization procedure. If the value of $P(X_{init})$ is strictly higher than k, there are two possibilities:

- it satisfies the objective (6), optimization is then not necessary as $k = P(X_{init})$ is correct, and we directly have a solution.
- it doesn't satisfy the objective, we have to find a $k > P(X_{init})$ satisfying it.

In both cases, we can enhance the optimization algorithm by first testing the objective (6) with $k = P(X_{init})$. If it does not respect the objective, then starting the dichotomy with $low\_k = P(X_{init})$ will return a solution (guaranteed by the property 4) strictly higher than $P(X_{init})$.

4.3 Rounding Error

When dealing with real life programs, performing floating point arithmetic generates rounding error. As for an input signal abstracted by a non deterministic value, we can add to every computation that may lead to a rounding error a non deterministic value whose bounds are determined by the variables types and values.

Addition. Addition over two floating-point values lose some properties like associativity. For example, $(2^{64} - 2^{64}) + 2^{-64}$ will be strictly equal to 2^{-64} but $2^{64} + (-2^{64} + 2^{-64})$ will be equal to 0. To deal with addition, we can consider the highest possible error between a real value and its floating point representation, a.k.a. the machine epsilon. It is completely dependent of the C type used: for *float* (single precision) it corresponds to 2^{-23}; for *double* (double precision) it is 2^{-52}. More generally, let x and y be two reals, with $\tilde{x}$ and $\tilde{y}$ their respective C representation. The IEEE model [2] says that an operation on floating point numbers must be equivalent to an operation on the reals, and then round the result to one of the nearest[1] floating point number. In this case, the relative error $|(\tilde{x} + \tilde{y}) - (x + y)| = (x + y) * \varepsilon$ where ε is the highest machine epsilon between the machine epsilon of the type of x, y and $(x + y)$. The error is relative to the value of x and y. This is not a problem, as we authorize in our setting non deterministic calls with expressions as argument.

Multiplication. A similar approximation happens during a multiplication of two floating point values. The relative error $|(\tilde{x} * \tilde{y}) - (x * y)| = x * y * \varepsilon$. Thus for every multiplication, we can add a non deterministic value between $-x * y * \varepsilon$ and $x * y * \varepsilon$.

With these considerations, we are able to provide precise bounds for rounding error for every operation performed in the loop.

Remark. Note that we can also deal with value casting. For example, when a cast from a floating point value to a integer is performed, the maximal error is bounded by 1 which can be abstracted in our setting by a non deterministic assignment.

5 Related Work

There exist mainly two kinds of polynomial invariants: equality relations between variables, representing precise relations, and inequality relations, providing bounds over the different values of the variables. After the results of Karr in [16,22] on the complete search of affine equality relations between variables of an affine program, Müller-Olm and Seidl [23] have proposed an inter-procedural method for computing polynomial equalities of bounded degree as invariants. For linear programs, *Farkas' lemma* can be used to encode the invariance condition [9] under non linear constraints. Similarly, for polynomial programs, Gröbner bases have been shown to be an efficient way to compute the exact relation set of minimal polynomial loop invariants composed of *solvable assignments* by computing the intersection of polynomial ideals [26,27]. Even if this algorithm is known to be EXP-TIME complete in the degree of the invariant searched, high degree invariants are very rare for common loops and the tool ALIGATOR [18], inspired from this technique for *P-solvable loops*[19,20], is very efficient for low degree loops. Finally, [8] presents a technique that avoids the combination problem by using abstract interpretation to generate *abstract invariants*. This technique is implemented in the tool FASTIND. The main issue is the completion loss: some invariants are missed and a maximal degree must be provided. The direct use of exact mathematical techniques is also not very efficient for the analysis of non-deterministic assignments.

[1] Depending on rounding mode, this may be the floating point value immediately below or above the result.

Synthesis of inequality invariants has become a growing field [21,29], for example in linear filters analysis and automatic verification in general as it provides good knowledge of the variables bounds when computing floating point operations. Abstract interpretation [10] with widening operators allows good approximation of loops with the desired format. A recent work [14] mixes abstract interpretation and loop acceleration (i.e. the precise computation of the transitive closure of a loop) to extend the framework and obtain precise upper and lower bounds on variables in the polyhedron domain. Very precise and computing non-trivial relations for complex loops and conditions, it has the drawback to be applicable to a very restricted type of transformations (linear transformation with eigenvalues λ such that $|\lambda| = 0$ or 1). We see this technique as complementary to ours as it generates invariants we do not find (such as $k \leqslant k_{init}$ for loop counters) and conversely. In order to treat non-deterministic loops, [21] refines as precisely as possible the set of reachable states for linear filters, harmonic oscillators and similar loops manipulating floating point numbers using a very specific abstract domain. A specific domain of polynomial inequalities have been implemented by [5], allowing conditions in the form $P(X) \leqslant 0$.

Dynamic analysis is also widely used in the detection of invariants. Daikon [13] infers linear *likely invariants*, i.e. candidate invariants, by confronting a given property pattern against a large number of executions. By expanding the pattern to more expressive terms with polynomial and array expressions, [24,25] infers general and disjunctive polynomial and array invariants.

6 Application and Results

The plug-in PILAT, written in OCaml as a Frama-C plug-in (compatible with the latest stable release, Aluminium) and originally generating exact relations for deterministic C loops, has been extended with convergent invariant generation and non deterministic loop treatment for simple C loops. It implements our main algorithm of invariant generation in addition to the optimization algorithm of Fig. 5, and generates invariants as ACSL [6] annotations, making them readily understandable by other Frama-C plugins. The tool is available at [3].

Let us now detail the work performed by PILAT over the example of Fig. 6 (taken from [21]). First, our tool generates the *shape* of the invariant, i.e. the polynomial P such that $|P(X)| \leqslant k$ is inductive for a certain k of the loop by setting the non deterministic choice to 0. We know by Property 1 that such an invariant is an eigenvector of the transformation. By expressing $s_0^2, s_0 * s_1$ and s_1^2 as linear variables, we find the eigenvector $e_0 = (1.42857, -2.14285, 1)$ (in the base $(s_0^2, s_0 s_1, s_1^2)$) associated to the eigenvalue 0.7. Thus, $P_0(s_0, s_1) = 1.42857 * s_0^2 - 2.14285 * s_0 * s_1 + s_1^2 \leqslant k$ is an invariant of the loop *when N is set to 0.* The error made between the deterministic transformation (with $N = 0$) and the non deterministic one (with $N \in [-0.1, 0.1]$) is given by $Q(s_0, s_1, N) = 2 * N * s_1 - 2.142 * N * s_0 - 1.428 * N^2$. Q has a lower degree than P for a fixed N, so we have that $\lim_{\|(s0,s1)\| \to +\infty} \frac{Q(s0,s1,N)}{P(s0,s1)} = 0 < 1 - \lambda$. The optimization procedure is now certain to converge, thus we minimize and maximize $Q(X, N)$

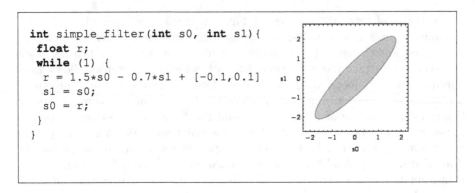

```
int simple_filter(int s0, int s1){
 float r;
 while (1) {
  r = 1.5*s0 - 0.7*s1 + [-0.1,0.1]
  s1 = s0;
  s0 = r;
 }
}
```

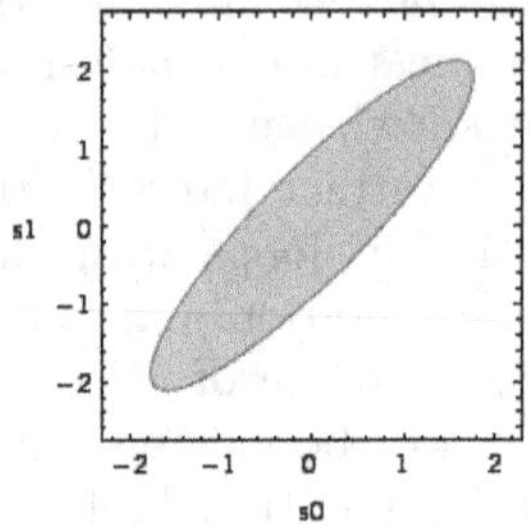

Fig. 6. Generation of one of the smallest polynomial invariant of degree 2 for a linear filter [21,31]

Table 1. Performance results with our implementation PILAT. Tests have been performed on a Dell Precision M4800 with 16 GB RAM and 8 cores. The first part represents deterministic loops (thus, no optimization is necessary). The second part of the benchmark are non deterministic loops. Tests with abstract interpretation have been performed with the fixpoint solver described in [21] by attempting to prove goals implied by the invariants our tool synthesizes when they were compatible. Details and benchmark are available in [1]

Program	PILAT	Input	Results			Abs. Int. [21]
	Var	Degree	# invariants	Generation (in s)	Optimization (in s)	Proof (in s)
Deterministic						
Example 1	2	2	1	0.003	–	1.6
Dampened oscillator	2	2	1	0.007	–	0.036
Harmonic oscillator	2	2	1	0.004	–	0.035
Sympletic oscillator	2	2	1	0.002	–	0.008
[4] filter	2	1	1	0.0035	–	0.0017
Non deterministic						
Simple linear filter	2	2	1	0.0015	1.3	6.5
Example 3	2	2	1	0.003	1.7	4.3
Linear filter	2	2	1	0.0019	1	1
Lead-lag controller	2	1	2	0.002	2.5	6
Gaussian regulator	3	2	1	0.007	2.5	–
Controller	4	2	5	0.066	14	–
Low-pass filter	5	2	2	0.06	7	–

with the hypothesis $P(s0, s1) \leqslant k$. By starting the procedure with $k = 50$ (which is usually a good heuristic) and performing 10 iterations the optimization procedure returns $k = 0.87891$, thus $1.42857 * s_0^2 - 2.14285 * s_0 s_1 + s_1^2 \leqslant 0.87891$

is an inductive invariant represented in Fig. 6. This is a real invariant, *assuming the initial state satisfies the relation.*

Let us now consider that the initial state of the loop is $(s_0, s_1) = (2, 1)$. Then at the beginning of the loop, $1.42857 * s_0^2 - 2.14285 * s_0 s_1 + s_1^2 = 2.42858 > 0.87891$, which does not respect the invariant. In this case the procedure starts by testing the optimization criterion with $k = 2.14285$. This choice of k is correct. In conclusion, we know that $1.42857 * s_0^2 - 2.14285 * s_0 s_1 + s_1^2 \leqslant 2.42858$ is an invariant of the loop.

More generally, we evaluated our method over the benchmark used in [28] for which we managed to find an invariant for every program containing no conditions. Though this benchmark has been built to test the effectiveness of a specific abstract domain, we managed to find similar results with a more general technique. Our results are given in Table 1. As ellipsoids are a suitable representation for those examples, we have choosen 2 as the input degree of almost all our examples. The optimization script is based on SAGE [30]. Note that the candidate generation is a lot faster than the optimization technique, mainly because of two reasons: computing *min* is time consuming for a large number of constraints; it is imprecise and its current implementation is incorrect (outputs an under approximation of the answer), we have to approximate its results to get a correct over approximation.

7 Conclusion and Future Work

Invariant generation for non deterministic linear loop is known to be a difficult problem. We provide to this purpose a surprisingly fast technique generating inductive relations that mostly relies on linear algebra algorithms widely used in many fields of computer science. Also, the optimization procedure for the non determinism treatment returns strong results. These invariants will be used in the scope of Frama-C [17] as a help to static analyzers, weakest precondition calculators and model-checkers.

We are currently facing three major issues that we intend to address in the future. The current optimization algorithm is assumed to have an exact *min* function. However, such function is both time consuming and imprecise. In addition, conditions are treated non deterministically, which reduces the strength of our results and limits the size of our benchmark to simple loops (linear filters with saturation are not included in our setting). Finally, the search of invariants for nested loops is a complex problem on which we are currently focusing.

References

1. Benchmark for the invariant generation. http://steven-de-oliveira.fr/content/bench/pilat_nd.pdf
2. IEEE Standard for Floating-Point Arithmetic. IEEE 754-2008
3. PILAT. https://github.com/Stevendeo/Pilat

4. Adjé, A., Gaubert, S., Goubault, E.: Coupling policy iteration with semi-definite relaxation to compute accurate numerical invariants in static analysis. Log. Methods Comput. Sci. **8**(1), 23–42 (2012)
5. Bagnara, R., Rodríguez-Carbonell, E., Zaffanella, E.: Generation of basic semi-algebraic invariants using convex polyhedra. In: Hankin, C., Siveroni, I. (eds.) SAS 2005. LNCS, vol. 3672, pp. 19–34. Springer, Heidelberg (2005). doi:10.1007/11547662_4
6. Baudin, P., Filliâtre, J.-C., Marché, C., Monate, B., Moy, Y., Prevosto, V.: ACSL: ANSI C Specification Language (2008)
7. Bertsekas, D.P.: Constrained Optimization and Lagrange Multiplier Methods. Academic Press, Cambridge (2014)
8. Cachera, D., Jensen, T., Jobin, A., Kirchner, F.: Inference of polynomial invariants for imperative programs: a farewell to Gröbner bases. SCP **93**, 89–109 (2014)
9. Colón, M.A., Sankaranarayanan, S., Sipma, H.B.: Linear invariant generation using non-linear constraint solving. In: Hunt, W.A., Somenzi, F. (eds.) CAV 2003. LNCS, vol. 2725, pp. 420–432. Springer, Heidelberg (2003). doi:10.1007/978-3-540-45069-6_39
10. Cousot, P., Cousot, R.: Abstract interpretation: a unified lattice model for static analysis of programs by construction or approximation of fixpoints. In: Proceedings of 4th ACM SIGACT-SIGPLAN Symposium on Principles of Programming Languages, pp. 238–252. ACM (1977)
11. Oliveira, S., Bensalem, S., Prevosto, V.: Polynomial invariants by linear algebra. In: Artho, C., Legay, A., Peled, D. (eds.) ATVA 2016. LNCS, vol. 9938, pp. 479–494. Springer, Cham (2016). doi:10.1007/978-3-319-46520-3_30
12. de Oliveira, S., Bensalem, S., Prevosto, V.: Synthesizing invariants by solving solvable loops. Technical report, CEA (2016). http://steven-de-oliveira.fr/content/publis/2017_atva.pdf
13. Ernst, M.D., Perkins, J.H., Guo, P.J., McCamant, S., Pacheco, C., Tschantz, M.S., Xiao, C.: The Daikon system for dynamic detection of likely invariants. Sci. Comput. Program. **69**(1), 35–45 (2007)
14. Gonnord, L., Schrammel, P.: Abstract acceleration in linear relation analysis. Sci. Comput. Program. **93**, 125–153 (2014)
15. Jeannet, B., Schrammel, P., Sankaranarayanan, S.: Abstract acceleration of general linear loops. ACM SIGPLAN Not. **49**(1), 529–540 (2014)
16. Karr, M.: Affine relationships among variables of a program. Acta Informatica **6**(2), 133–151 (1976)
17. Kirchner, F., Kosmatov, N., Prevosto, V., Signoles, J., Yakobowski, B.: Frama-C: a software analysis perspective. Form. Asp. Comput. **27**(3), 573–609 (2015)
18. Kovács, L.: Aligator: a mathematica package for invariant generation (system description). In: Armando, A., Baumgartner, P., Dowek, G. (eds.) IJCAR 2008. LNCS, vol. 5195, pp. 275–282. Springer, Heidelberg (2008). doi:10.1007/978-3-540-71070-7_22
19. Kovács, L.: Reasoning algebraically about P-solvable loops. In: Ramakrishnan, C.R., Rehof, J. (eds.) TACAS 2008. LNCS, vol. 4963, pp. 249–264. Springer, Heidelberg (2008). doi:10.1007/978-3-540-78800-3_18
20. Kovács, L.: A complete invariant generation approach for P-solvable loops. In: Pnueli, A., Virbitskaite, I., Voronkov, A. (eds.) PSI 2009. LNCS, vol. 5947, pp. 242–256. Springer, Heidelberg (2010). doi:10.1007/978-3-642-11486-1_21

21. Miné, A., Breck, J., Reps, T.: An algorithm inspired by constraint solvers to infer inductive invariants in numeric programs. In: Thiemann, P. (ed.) ESOP 2016. LNCS, vol. 9632, pp. 560–588. Springer, Heidelberg (2016). doi:10.1007/978-3-662-49498-1_22
22. Müller-Olm, M., Seidl, H.: A note on Karr's algorithm. In: Díaz, J., Karhumäki, J., Lepistö, A., Sannella, D. (eds.) ICALP 2004. LNCS, vol. 3142, pp. 1016–1028. Springer, Heidelberg (2004). doi:10.1007/978-3-540-27836-8_85
23. Müller-Olm, M., Seidl, H.: Precise interprocedural analysis through linear algebra. In: ACM SIGPLAN Notices, vol. 39. ACM (2004)
24. Nguyen, T., Kapur, D., Weimer, W., Forrest, S.: Using dynamic analysis to discover polynomial and array invariants. In: 2012 34th International Conference on Software Engineering (ICSE), pp. 683–693. IEEE (2012)
25. Nguyen, T., Kapur, D., Weimer, W., Forrest, S.: Using dynamic analysis to generate disjunctive invariants. In: Proceedings of 36th International Conference on Software Engineering, pp. 608–619. ACM (2014)
26. Rodríguez-Carbonell, E., Kapur, D.: Automatic generation of polynomial invariants of bounded degree using abstract interpretation. Sci. Comput. Program. **64**(1), 54–75 (2007)
27. Rodríguez-Carbonell, E., Kapur, D.: Generating all polynomial invariants in simple loops. J. Symb. Comput. **42**(4), 443–476 (2007)
28. Roux, P.: Analyse statique de systèmes de contrôle commande: synthèse d'invariants non linéaires. Ph.D. thesis, Toulouse, ISAE (2013)
29. Roux, P., Jobredeaux, R., Garoche, P.-L., Féron, É.: A generic ellipsoid abstract domain for linear time invariant systems. In: Proceedings of 15th ACM International Conference on Hybrid Systems: Computation and Control, pp. 105–114. ACM (2012)
30. Stein, W., et al.: Sage: Open Source Mathematical Software. 7 December 2009 (2008)
31. Wolfram—Alpha. Polynomial invariant for the simple_filter function, http://www.wolframalpha.com/input/?i=(-2.14285714286*(s1*s0)%2B1.42857142857*(s0*s0))%2B1.*(s1*s1)+%3C%3D++0.87891

Exploiting Partial Knowledge for Efficient Model Analysis

Nuno Macedo(✉), Alcino Cunha, and Eduardo Pessoa

INESC TEC & Universidade do Minho, Braga, Portugal
nfmmacedo@di.uminho.pt

Abstract. The advancement of constraint solvers and model checkers has enabled the effective analysis of high-level formal specification languages. However, these typically handle a specification in an opaque manner, amalgamating all its constraints in a single monolithic verification task, which often proves to be a performance bottleneck.

This paper addresses this issue by proposing a solving strategy that exploits user-provided partial knowledge, namely by assigning symbolic bounds to the problem's variables, to automatically decompose a verification task into smaller ones, which are prone to being independently analyzed in parallel and with tighter search spaces. An effective implementation of the technique is provided as an extension to the Kodkod relational constraint solver. Evaluation shows that, in average, the proposed technique outperforms the regular amalgamated verification procedure.

1 Introduction

The steady advancement of constraint solvers and model checkers renders the automatic analysis of software models increasingly efficient. Thus, high-level formal specification languages – like Alloy [9], B [1] or TLA$^+$ [10] – are currently backed up by effective tool support that promotes the effortless specification and analysis of complex systems. In fact, such frameworks have reached a level of maturity that enables their application in industrial scenarios [16].

Nonetheless, such tools are still affected by scalability issues. One approach to tackle this issue is to allow the user to provide additional *a priori* knowledge about the problem's domain, thus reducing its search space. For this effect, the Kodkod [21] model finder supports the definition of *partial instances*, obtaining impressive performance gains. Its language, based on relational logic, is sufficiently simple, yet powerful, to be used directly by end users, but its relevance also lies in its usage by the Alloy Analyzer to automate the analysis of Alloy specifications, and as an alternative back-end for ProB, B's model checker and animator.

Kodkod's partial instances define lower- and upper-bounds for the problem's variables, concretely stating which values must and may be assigned to a variable, respectively. While useful, such bounds are rather inflexible and often do not allow the user to specify all available partial knowledge. In this paper we

D. D'Souza and K. Narayan Kumar (Eds.): ATVA 2017, LNCS 10482, pp. 344–362, 2017.
DOI: 10.1007/978-3-319-68167-2_23

advocate the support for richer partial instances by allowing the user to declare *symbolic* bounds for the problem's variables. We then show how such partial knowledge can be exploited to improve the performance of automated analysis procedures. Verification is typically handled opaquely by solvers, resulting in the "*amalgamation*" of the variables and constraints into a single search problem. Symbolic bounds give rise to dependencies that can be used to automatically decompose the amalgamated problem into smaller ones. The first portion of one such decomposed problem can be used to generated candidate *partial solutions*, which are further refined in independent solving tasks taking into account the remainder problem. This strategy can lead to better scalability since these independent solving tasks (*i*) have smaller search spaces (in particular once the symbolic bounds are factored in) and (*ii*) are prone to being executed in parallel.

Consider the analysis of a hotel room locking system [9]. The specification of this system in Kodkod, `Hotel`, consists of a set of `Rooms`, a set of `Keys` (assigned to rooms through a relation `keys`) and a set of potential `Guests`, restricted by appropriate constraints (e.g., the same key cannot be assigned to different rooms). These elements are static components of the problem, in the sense that, although several assignments are possible, once defined they remain frozen. Other parts of the system are dynamic and evolve over time (explicitly modeled in Kodkod by the set of `Time` instants under analysis). This is the case, for example, of the keys registered at the rooms (relation `r_keys`) or assigned to guests (relation `g_keys`) at any given instant of time. The possible assignments to those relations depend on values assigned to the static ones (e.g., `g_keys` must only relate existing `Keys` to potential `Guests` inside the `Time` period under analysis).

Unfortunately, in Kodkod this inclusion dependency cannot be captured by the bounds defined in partial instances, requiring the user to express it in a regular logical constraint. Using the extension proposed in this paper, such dependencies can be explicitly declared using symbolic bounds in the partial instance definition (in this case setting the upper-bound to the cross product of the static relations). For our example, this would result in the dependency graph depicted in Fig. 1, where, e.g., the dependency of `g_keys` on the sets of available `Keys`, `Guests` and `Time` instants becomes explicit. Using information from the dependency graph (in particular the number of dependencies), our proposed solving strategy will split the problem, first generating candidate partial solutions for a subset of variables. These partial solutions will then be incorporated into new problems extended with the remaining variables and the respective constraints,

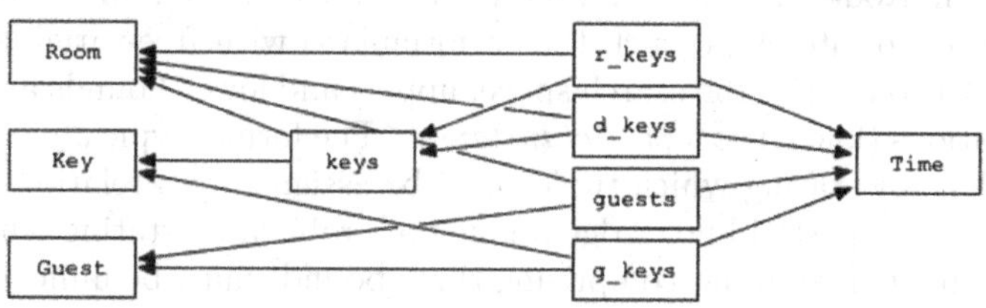

Fig. 1. Dependency graph for the hotel room locking system.

to be solved in parallel and with tighter bounds once the dependencies are resolved. Naturally, not all of these candidate partial solutions can be extended to full satisfiable instances, meaning that many of them can be discarded in this process.

This paper formalizes the strategy described above and implements the parallel solving procedure as an extension to Kodkod. Kodkod is well-suited to deploy such strategy due to: (*i*) its native support for partial instances, that will allow an efficient embedding of the partial solutions into the remainder problem; (*ii*) its ability to incrementally generate solutions, that will allow the efficient iterative generation of the partial solutions; and (*iii*) its powerful symmetry breaking mechanism, that will avoid the generation of isomorphic candidate partial solutions. The parallel implementation of the strategy both relies and preserves these distinctive features. Experimental evaluation of this extension shows that it can indeed outperform Kodkod amalgamated execution for complex problems, particularly for satisfiable (SAT) problems. To balance the performance of the technique for unsatisfiable (UNSAT) problems, we propose a hybrid technique that minimizes performance deterioration in such scenarios, preserving the benefits of the decomposed solving strategy otherwise.

Section 2 formalizes symbolic partial instances and the decomposed solving strategy. Section 3 presents its implementation as a parallel extension to Kodkod, which is then evaluated in Sect. 4. Section 5 compares this work with previously proposed techniques. Section 6 wraps up and points directions for future work.

2 From Symbolic Bounds to Decomposed Model Finding

The proposed strategy is formalized over *relational model finding* problems as embodied by Kodkod [21]. Although simple, this formalization is sufficiently powerful and flexible to express general analysis procedures as model finding, including model checking and animation.

2.1 Relational Model Finding with Symbolic Bounds

Model finders search for variable bindings that satisfy certain problem constraints. In Kodkod, problems are represented by a set of *relations* $\mathcal{R}$ with the associated constraints specified in relational logic (a flavor of first-order logic enhanced with transitive closure). A valid *binding* $b : \mathcal{R} \rightarrow \mathcal{T}$, denoted by problem instance in Kodkod, assigns to each relation a tuple set from $\mathcal{T}$, constructed from a universe of atoms $\mathcal{A}$, such that a formula ϕ with free-variables from $\mathcal{R}$ holds. In order to restrict the search space, upper- and lower-bounds are imposed to these relations (known as a *partial instance*). The former typically encode typing restrictions by stating which tuples may be assigned to a relation, while the latter may encode partial knowledge about the problem by stating which tuples must be assigned. The tuples comprising these bounds must be uniform on their arity.

```
A= {R1,R2,K1,K2,G1,G2,T1,T2}
R= Time   : [{T1,T2},{T1,T2}]
   Key    : [{K1,K2},{K1,K2}]
   Room   : [{},{R1,R2}]
   Guest  : [{},{G1,G2}]
   keys   : [{},{(R1,K1),(R2,K1),
                 (R1,K2),(R2,K2)}]
   guests : [{},{(R1,G1,T1),(R2,G1,T1),...,
                 (R1,G2,T2),(R2,G2,T2)}]
   g_keys : [{},{(G1,K1,T1),(G2,K1,T1),...,
                 (G1,K2,T2),(G2,K2,T2)}]
   ...
φ= keys in Room → Key &&
   guests in Room → Guest → Time &&
   g_keys in Guest → Key → Time &&
   all t:Time,r:Room | one r.r_keys.t &&
   all k:Key | one keys.k && ...
```

(a) The `Hotel` problem in normal Kodkod.

```
A= {R1,R2,K1,K2,G1,G2,T1,T2}
R= Room   : [{},{R1,R2}]
   Key    : [{K1,K2},{K1,K2}]
   Guest  : [{},{G1,G2}]
   keys   : [{},Room → Key]
   Time   : [{T1,T2},{T1,T2}]
   guests : [{},Room → Guest → Time]
   g_keys : [{},Guest → Key → Time]
   ...
φ= all t:Time,r:Room | one r.r_keys.t &&
   all k:Key | one keys.k && ...
```

(b) The `Hotel` problem with symbolic bounds.

Fig. 2. Hotel room locking system problem for $n = 2$.

Definition 1. *A (relational) model finding problem* P *is a tuple* $\langle \mathcal{A}, l, u, \phi \rangle$ *where* $\mathcal{A}$ *is a universe of atoms,* $l, u : \mathcal{R} \to \mathcal{T}$ *assign to each relation variable* $r \in \mathcal{R}$ *lower- and upper-bounds, respectively, with* $l(r) \subseteq u(r)$*, and* ϕ *is a relational logic formula over* $\mathcal{R}$ *variables. A binding* $b : \mathcal{R} \to \mathcal{T}$ *is a* solution *of* P *if* ϕ *holds and* $b(r) \subseteq u(r) \backslash l(r)$ *for every* $r \in \mathcal{R}$.

For simplicity, components of P are denoted as $\mathcal{A}_P$, l_P, u_P and ϕ_P, respectively.

Figure 2a depicts part of the encoding of the `Hotel` specification in Kodkod, for a problem of size $n = 2$ (n is the maximum size of `Room` and `Guest` and the exact size of `Time` and `Key`). The lower- and upper-bounds appear between square brackets in the declaration of the variables. Notice how constant tuple sets are assigned to these bounds using the atoms available in the universe $\mathcal{A}$. Equal lower- and upper-bounds fix a relation *exactly*, as in `Key` and `Time`. Relational logic formula ϕ is presented in Kodkod's notation, which includes logical (`&&` for conjunction and `all` for universal quantification) and relational operators ($\to$ denotes the Cartesian product, `in` relational inclusion, . relational composition, and `one` a multiplicity restriction). The five presented formulas specify, respectively, the `keys`, `guests`, and `g_keys` typing restrictions, the requirement that at each time instant a single `Key` is registered in every `Room`, and that every `Key` must be assigned to a `Room`. The model finding procedure, denoted by $[\![P]\!] : \mathcal{R} \to \mathcal{T}$, searches for an instance for a problem P. Kodkod does so by encoding relations into boolean matrices, creating a boolean variable for each tuple between the lower- and upper-bounds. A propositional formula is then computed by converting relational operators into matrix operations, which is passed to an off-the-shelf SAT solver. If there is no satisfying solution, an empty binding $\perp : \emptyset \to \mathcal{T}$ is assumed to be returned (this is not the same as an empty model that binds every $\mathcal{R}$ variable to an empty tuple set).

Kodkod allows users to iterate through valid instances. This can be embodied by a scenario exploration operation [13] next, that given the previous problem and the last known solution, generates a novel problem to be solved:

$$\mathsf{next}(\langle \mathcal{A}, l, u, \phi \rangle, b) = \langle \mathcal{A}, l, u, \phi \wedge \neg \overline{b} \rangle$$

For a binding b, $\overline{b}$ denotes its encoding into a predicate that exactly characterizes it [13]: by adding the negation of this predicate to the iterated problem's constraints, only different instances will be generated. To avoid the generation of isomorphic solutions, Kodkod's symmetry breaking algorithm introduces additional restrictions during translation (see Sect. 3.2).

Kodkod problems allow relations to be bound by constant tuple sets, as depicted in Fig. 2a for `Hotel`. As mentioned above, upper-bounds usually encode typing restrictions. For instance, a valid binding for `g_keys` must be included in the Cartesian product of `Room`, `Key` and `Time`. However, since we are forced to use constants in the declarations, the upper-bound must be approximated by the Cartesian product of the upper-bounds of those sets, and a constraint must be explicitly included in the problem to enforce the desired typing restriction. A similar situation occurs with relations `keys` and `guests`. The latter records which `Guest` is in each `Room` at any `Time` instant.

In this paper we propose to extend Kodkod problems with a notion of *symbolic bounds*, allowing users to bound relations with Kodkod relational expressions that explicitly refer other relations rather than using just constant tuple sets. A symbolic bound for a relation expresses some sort of conditional partial knowledge, in the sense that once you know the value of the relations on which it depends, you will know which tuples may or must appear in it. Although such symbolic bounds bring no additional expressiveness, they can reduce the verbosity of the declarations and constraints without any additional burden from the user, since it only requires certain (already existing) constraints to be moved from the problem's formula to the bounds. Most importantly, it will expose the dependencies between the declarations of relations, information that will be later exploited by the decomposed solving strategy presented in Sect. 2.2. Using this extension, the upper-bound of relations `keys`, `guests`, and `g_keys` can now be declared directly as the desired Cartesian product, as depicted in Fig. 2b, avoiding the extra constraints in $\phi_{\texttt{Hotel}}$.

Naturally, symbolic bounds must be *resolved* (i.e., converted into concrete tuple sets) prior to solving. This action, denoted by $\lfloor P \rfloor$ for a problem P, is achieved by iteratively expanding the binding relational expressions, replacing each relation reference with its respective lower- or upper-bound. This process must eventually result in constant bounds for every relation, thus the dependency graph must be acyclic. That is the case of the `Hotel` example, whose dependency graph is shown in Fig. 1. If the relations referred in a symbolic bound are not bound exactly, the respective expression cannot be exactly evaluated, and thus the symbolic bound must also be included as an explicit constraint in problem formula that will be solved. For instance, if one resolves directly the problem depicted in Fig. 2b we would end up with the problem in Fig. 2a, having no gains whatsoever when solving. However, if meanwhile we found out the exact value of `Room` then the binding expression of `keys` could be resolved exactly, reducing the search space and avoiding the additional constraint in the solving stage. This latter insight is exploited by the decomposed solving strategy presented in the next section.

Input: A model finding problem $P = \langle \mathcal{A}, \mathcal{R}, l, u, \phi \rangle$ and a variable set $\mathcal{R}_p \subseteq \mathcal{R}$.
Output: A solution for the problem P or $\perp$, and the updated formula for the partial problem.

```
P↓ ← ⟨A, l|R_p, u|R_p, φ|R_p⟩
repeat
    p ← [[⌊P↓⌋]];
    b ← [[⌊P ⊕ p⌋]];
    if b = ⊥ then
        P↓ ← next(P↓, p);
    end
until b ≠ ⊥ ∨ p = ⊥;
return ⟨b, φ_{P↓}⟩;
```

Algorithm 1. Algorithm for decomposed model finding.

2.2 Decomposed Model Finding

Given a subset of variables $\mathcal{R}_p \subseteq \mathcal{R}$, the decomposed strategy will first search for valid bindings for those variables, which will improve the solving of the remainder depending variables. A binding over $\mathcal{R}_p$ is a candidate *partial solution* of a problem if it is within the bounds defined for $\mathcal{R}_p$ variables and the constraint conjuncts defined exclusively over $\mathcal{R}_p$ hold. Let $b|_A$ denote the domain restriction of mapping b to set A, and through an abuse of notation, $\phi|_{\mathcal{R}_p}$ denote the conjuncts of ϕ that refer exclusively to $\mathcal{R}_p$.

Definition 2. *A binding* $b : \mathcal{R}_p \to \mathcal{T}$ *is a* candidate partial solution *of a model finding problem* $P = \langle \mathcal{A}, l, u, \phi \rangle$ *with symbolic bounds if* $\mathcal{R}_p \subseteq \mathcal{R}$ *for* $l, u : \mathcal{R} \to \mathcal{T}$*, and it is a solution of the* partial (model finding) problem $P{\downarrow} = \lfloor \langle \mathcal{A}, l|_{\mathcal{R}_p}, u|_{\mathcal{R}_p}, \phi|_{\mathcal{R}_p} \rangle \rfloor$.

This definition assumes the empty binding $\perp$ to be a candidate partial solution of every problem. Partial solutions can be embedded into the bounds of the original problem, binding $\mathcal{R}_p$ relations exactly, leaving only $\mathcal{R}_r = \mathcal{R} \backslash \mathcal{R}_p$ to be solved. Moreover, symbolic bounds in $\mathcal{R}_r$ referring to $\mathcal{R}_p$ variables will be assigned stricter tuple sets after resolution. For relations depending uniquely on $\mathcal{R}_p$ (or other exactly bound relations) resolution will exactly calculate the value of the relational expressions in the symbolic bounds, avoiding the need for additional constraints in ϕ, as in Fig. 2b. Let $\oplus$ denote the overriding of mappings.

Definition 3. *A candidate partial solution* $b : \mathcal{R}_p \to \mathcal{A}$ *can be* integrated *into a model finding problem* $P = \langle \mathcal{A}, l, u, \phi \rangle$ *as* $\lfloor \langle \mathcal{A}, l \oplus b, u \oplus b, \phi \rangle \rfloor$*, denoted by* $P \oplus b$.

By overriding the lower- and upper-bounds with the concrete valuation from the partial solution, $\mathcal{R}_p$ become exactly bound. The integration of a candidate partial solution b does not entail a SAT problem by itself, since there may not exist an extension to b for which ϕ holds.

The decomposed model finding strategy will generate candidate partial solutions until an instance is found to an integrated problem. This strategy is encoded

```
Room  : [{R1},{R1}]
Key   : [{K1,K2},{K1,K2}]
Guest : [{G1},{G1}]
keys  : [{(R1,K1),(R1,K2)},
         {(R1,K1),(R1,K2)}]
```

(a) Candidate partial solution p obtained from $\lfloor$`Hotel`$\downarrow\rfloor$.

```
Room   : [{R1},{R1}]
Key    : [{K1,K2},{K1,K2}]
Guest  : [{G1},{G1}]
keys   : [{(R1,K1),(R1,K2)},{(R1,K1),(R1,K2)}]
Time   : [{T1,T2},{T1,T2}]
guests : [{},{(R1,G1,T1),(R1,G1,T2)}]
...
g_keys : [{},{(G1,K1,T1),(G1,K1,T1),(G1,K2,T2),(G1,K2,T2)}]
```

(b) Result of integrating and resolving p into `Hotel`, i.e. $\lfloor$`Hotel`$\oplus p\rfloor$.

Fig. 3. Decomposed model finding for `Hotel`.

in Algorithm 1, relying only on regular model finding procedures. Essentially, given the current state of the partial problem $P\downarrow$, the procedure successively generates candidate partial solutions p, that are integrated into the full problem until a full solution is found or $\perp$ is returned, rendering P UNSAT. Suppose P to be the `Hotel` problem in Fig. 2b and $\mathcal{R}_p$ to include `Room`, `Key`, `Guest` and `keys`. Solving $\lfloor P\downarrow\rfloor$ could produce the candidate partial solution in Fig. 3a. Integration into P and symbolic bound resolution ($\lfloor P \oplus p\rfloor$) results in the constant bounds in Fig. 3b. Since there `Room` and `Guest` are now exactly bound, the bounds of the remainder variables are considerable smaller than in the amalgamated problem defined in regular Kodkod (Fig. 2a), potentially speeding up the solving of the integrated problem. This algorithm is prone to being parallelized on the exploration of the integrated problems, as will be shown in Sect. 3.

The procedure is complete, since every partial solution may be eventually explored. To speed up the process, the current state of the partial problem, embodied by $\phi_{P\downarrow}$, is also returned by the algorithm. This avoids the redundant generation, at each iteration, of candidate partial solutions p that have already been fully explored (i.e., for which $[\![\lfloor P \oplus p\rfloor]\!]$ has already returned $\perp$). The discarding of partial solutions cannot be performed externally by next since the current partial solution extended by b may still produce additional full solutions. Given the output of Algorithm 1, iteration of decomposed problems is defined as follows, resulting in an iterated problem to be inputed back into the algorithm:

$$\mathsf{next}(\langle\mathcal{A},\mathcal{R},l,u,\phi\rangle,\langle b,\phi_{P\downarrow}\rangle) = \langle\mathcal{A},\mathcal{R},l,u,\phi\wedge\neg\bar{b}\wedge\phi_{P\downarrow}\rangle$$

2.3 Criterion for Decomposing Problems

The previous section has shown how to decompose the model finding of a problem given a subset of variables $\mathcal{R}_p$. This subset can be defined manually, but ideally, it should be derived automatically, and several criteria can be proposed to do so. The usage of symbolic bounds enabled us to define a simple criterion that lead to substantial gains in efficiency in most examples in our evaluation.

Looking at the entailed dependency graph and given a threshold t, relations with outdegree (number of dependencies) bigger than t, or that depend directly or indirectly from one of those, are left out of $\mathcal{R}_p$. The intuition behind this criterion is that variables with more dependencies benefit more from prior solving. If more than a single connected component is left, only the largest one is kept in $\mathcal{R}_p$. The number of candidate partial solutions should be manageable, and such disconnected components usually give rise to an explosion of non-symmetric solutions, unlike connected relations whose valuations are most likely restricted by the constraints. We also found that setting t to the maximum outdegree typically provides optimal performance. In our running example, this would assign to $\mathcal{R}_p$ `Room`, `Key`, `Guest` and `keys`, resulting in a behavior similar to that of Fig. 3. The criterion was applied to all examples considered in Sect. 4.

3 Decomposed Kodkod

This section describes a concrete implementation of the decomposed strategy described in the previous section as an extension to Kodkod [11].

3.1 Implementation Overview

The decomposed solver implements the strategy presented in Sect. 2.2: given a problem P and a set of $\mathcal{R}_p$ variables, the procedure automatically extracts $\phi_P|_{\mathcal{R}_p}$ depending on the occurrence of $\mathcal{R}_p$ variables, and then solves the problem following the general idea behind Algorithm 1. $P\downarrow$ is deployed as a regular Kodkod problem and generates candidate partial solutions p_i, and for each p_i, an integrated problem $P \oplus p_i$ is created that can also be deployed under regular Kodkod. To avoid unnecessary translations, $\phi_P|_{\mathcal{R}_p}$ is not included in the integrated problem, since it is already known to hold for p_i. However, unlike the abstract formalization from Sect. 2.2, these integrated problems are launched in parallel rather than explored sequentially. The number i of candidate partial solutions is unknown *a priori*, so a (configurable) threshold is imposed on the number of launched parallel threads. The state of $P\downarrow$ is also internally preserved, rather than being constructed at each iteration, benefiting from the performance gains of incremental SAT solving. When one of the $P \oplus p_i$ procedures finishes and is SAT, the full solution s_{i_k} is pushed into a blocking queue that the user can inspect. UNSAT integrated problem are discarded. Remainder integrated problems keep being solved and launched in the background until the blocking queue fills up, providing a buffer of full solutions.

When the user asks for another solution succeeding s_{i_k}, the system iterates the $P \oplus p_i$ problem (by negating the full solution s_{i_k} into it), and pushes it to the execution queue (which is LIFO since it is cheaper to solve iterated problems). Nonetheless, other integrated problems executing in the background could have already pushed solutions into the queue, so there is no guarantee that succeeding full solutions will share the same partial solution. Thus, although the set of candidate partial solutions explored is identical, iteration order differs from that of Algorithm 1. The set of solutions returned by each of the integrated problem is disjoint since partial solutions are unique. Moreover, SAT integrated problems are directly and independently iterated (unlike the sequential Algorithm 1 that iterated the overall decomposed problem).

For UNSAT problems, every candidate partial solution must be explored, which may entail an overwhelming number of integrated problems to solve. As will be evident in Sect. 4, this may be a bottleneck for the decomposed strategy. To address this issue, a *hybrid* strategy is proposed where the integrated problems are paired with a thread solving the amalgamated problem P. In the worst case, P will finish first and be handled as a regular model finding problem (terminating the running integrated problems); in the best case a SAT (or *every* UNSAT) integrated problem will finish before P, terminating it. This guarantees no repeated full solutions are returned. This strategy resembles portfolio parallel SAT solving [8], where identical solvers with different parameters competitively solve the same problem. Nonetheless, the hybrid approach is expected to have slightly deteriorated performance due to cache interference.

3.2 Symmetry Breaking

Symmetry breaking greatly reduces the number of generated solutions by determining equivalences between atoms and avoiding the generation of instances considered isomorphic. This is particularly relevant when solving partial problems as it determines the number of integrated problems that will be launched. Kodkod's symmetry breaking procedure starts by detecting the symmetries of a problem based on its bounds [21], and then generates a symmetry breaking predicate [6] that is added to the problem's constraint. This section describes how these procedures were adapted in order to be sound in the decomposed scenario. Symbolic bounds are assumed to be resolved at this point.

Symmetry detection searches for atom permutations that map valid bindings to valid bindings and invalid to invalid based on the declared bounds. For instance, a problem with a single relation `s : [{},{(A1,B1),(A2,B1)}]` induces a symmetry `{A1,A2}`, since permuting these two atoms results in identical bounds (see [21] for technical details). Thus, solutions `s = {(A1,B1)}` and `s = {(A2,B1)}` are considered isomorphic. Clearly, the fixed valuation for $\mathcal{R}_p$ relations in integrated problems cannot be considered as these would break potential symmetries: for example, assuming $\mathcal{R}_r$= `s` and $\mathcal{R}_p$= `r :[{},{(A1,B1),(A2,B1)}]`, candidate partial solution `r = {(A1,B1)})` would break the symmetry between `A1` and `A2`, distinguishing `s = {(A1,B1)}` from `s = {(A2,B1)}`. The bounds of $P{\downarrow}$ may also cause incongruences if considered independently. For example, if we have `r :[{},{(A1,B1),(A2,B1)}]` and `s : [{},{(A1,B1),(A1,B2)}]` in the amalgamated problem no symmetries should be detected, but if $\mathcal{R}_p$= `r` and $P{\downarrow}$ considers only `r`, symmetry `{A1,A2}` would be detected, meaning that the solving procedure could return only solution `r = {(A2,B1)}` and not `r = {(A1,B1)}`, the only candidate that could be extended to a full instance. The issue persists in integrated problems, as considering only `s` would result in the symmetry `{B1,B2}`. To preserve the soundness of the symmetry detection procedure, the original bounds P_l and P_u of every relation $\mathcal{R}$ must be considered in both the partial and integrated problems. Relations not relevant to each problem should then be ignored when generating the symmetry breaking predicate. Our extension implements this strategy.

The generation of the symmetry breaking predicate imposes an ordering on the boolean variables resulting from the translation of the relations $\mathcal{R}$ into SAT, constructs a lexicographical order over them, and generates predicates that force minimal valuations (see [6] for details). The main insight is that the variable ordering must be preserved between the partial problem and the integrated problems, otherwise the procedure will not be sound. Consider an example with `r : [{},{A1,A2}]` and `s : [{},{A1,A2}]`, producing 4 boolean variables, $\mathtt{r}_{\mathtt{A1}}, \mathtt{r}_{\mathtt{A2}}, \mathtt{s}_{\mathtt{A1}}$ and $\mathtt{s}_{\mathtt{A2}}$, denoting whether `A1` and `A2` belong to `r` and `s`, respectively. Since `A1` and `A2` are symmetric, a lexicographical order $[\mathtt{r}_{\mathtt{A1}}, \mathtt{s}_{\mathtt{A1}}] \leq [\mathtt{r}_{\mathtt{A2}}, \mathtt{s}_{\mathtt{A2}}]$ will be constructed, allowing 10 different valuations for the boolean variables. Now, if $\mathcal{R}_p$= `s`, 3 partial solutions will be generated, `s = {}`, `s = {A2}` and `s = {A1,A2}`, giving rise to 3 integrated problems with $[\mathtt{r}_{\mathtt{A1}}, \mathsf{F}] \leq [\mathtt{r}_{\mathtt{A2}}, \mathsf{F}], [\mathtt{r}_{\mathtt{A1}}, \mathsf{F}] \leq [\mathtt{r}_{\mathtt{A2}}, \mathsf{T}]$ and $[\mathtt{r}_{\mathtt{A1}}, \mathsf{T}] \leq [\mathtt{r}_{\mathtt{A2}}, \mathsf{T}]$. These allow only 9 valuations: solution `r = {A2}` and `s = {A1}` will be disregarded. If the ordering is preserved, problems with $[\mathsf{F}, \mathtt{r}_{\mathtt{A1}}] \leq [\mathsf{F}, \mathtt{r}_{\mathtt{A2}}], [\mathsf{F}, \mathtt{r}_{\mathtt{A1}}] \leq [\mathsf{T}, \mathtt{r}_{\mathtt{A2}}]$ and $[\mathsf{T}, \mathtt{r}_{\mathtt{A1}}] \leq [\mathsf{T}, \mathtt{r}_{\mathtt{A2}}]$ allow the expected 10 solutions. Our implementation guarantees that the ordering is preserved between partial and integrated problems by prioritizing $\mathcal{R}_p$ variables.

4 Empirical Evaluation

To evaluate the performance of the procedure, several Kodkod problems with scalability problems were collected. `Hotel(1)` is a SAT version of the `Hotel` specification where a counter-example is found, and `Hotel(2)` is a fixed UNSAT version. `RBT(1)` is a structural problem that generates red-black trees (SAT) with n nodes, while `RBT(2)` checks whether every red-black tree is balanced (UNSAT). `Hand` is a structural problem that models the Halmos handshake puzzle for n persons: `Hand(1)` generates instances of the puzzle (SAT) and `Hand(2)` checks whether the answer to the puzzle holds (UNSAT). Regarding dynamic problems, `Dijk` models Dijkstra's mutual exclusion algorithm for n processes and mutexes: `Dijk(1)` searches for a valid instance (SAT) while `Dijk(2)` checks whether deadlocks may occur (UNSAT). `Ring` models a leader election algorithm over ring network topologies: `Ring(1)` checks a liveness property that fails (SAT), in `Ring(2)` the liveness property holds (UNSAT), and `Ring(3)` checks a safety property that holds (UNSAT). Finally, `Span` models a distributed algorithm that calculates the spanning tree of a graph, with `Span(1)` and `Span(2)` searching for instances with different properties (both SAT). For `Ring` and `Span`, n denotes the number of nodes in the network. Since Kodkod may only perform bounded model checking, trace length t of 15 was imposed on `Dijk`, 20 on `Hotel` and `Ring`, and 9 on `Span`. These problems, available in the code repository [11], range from very few candidate partial solutions to tens of thousands, as well as from low to high satisfiability ratios. All were modeled with symbolic bounds, which have a larger impact in the search space of `Dijk` and `Hotel`, and decomposed according to the criterion from Sect. 2.3.

4.1 Setup

Tests were run in amalgamated, purely parallel and hybrid mode, with and without symbolic bounds, for increasing n sizes, with a timeout (TO) of 10000 seconds. Problems solved under a second are not presented since performance differences would be negligible. The most efficient SAT solvers supported by the latest version of Kodkod [20] were used to solve the partial and integrated problems, namely Glucose [2] and MiniSat [7]. The performance tests were run on commodity hardware, namely in a quad core 4 GHz Intel Core i7 with hyper-threading, with 8 GB memory and running OS X 10.10.

Decomposed problems were solved with 4 parallel integrated problems (3 in hybrid mode). Our tests show that, as expected, the performance of the purely parallel approach increases with the number of threads. However, in hybrid mode, the performance is deteriorated when the amalgamated problem terminates first, due to cache interference. For instance, in `RBT(1)` for $n = 10$, an integrated problem terminates first, at 3.8 s, 4.0 s and 4.3 s for 2, 4 and 6 threads, respectively. In contrast, in `RBT(2)` at $n = 8$ the amalgamated problem terminates first, at 1.3 s, 1.5 s and 1.8 s for 2, 4 and 6 threads, respectively. The 4 threads provide a reasonable balance between the benefits of the decomposition while still relying on the amalgamated problem in the worst case scenario.

Since the parallelization of the solving process is at the core of our approach, its performance was also compared with that of state-of-the-art parallel SAT solvers over amalgamated problems. Both Syrup [2] (Glucose's parallel version) and Plingeling [5] (Lingeling's parallel version), which ranked at the top of the most recent SAT race[1], were considered in our evaluation and used to solve the selected tests. Although Plingeling is the only parallel SAT solver currently distributed with Kodkod, we also implemented support for Syrup, which was straightforward since its sequential version Glucose is already supported. It should be noted, however, that, unlike our technique, these parallel SAT solvers do not yet support incremental executions, and as such cannot be used to efficiently iterate through alternative solutions.

The results of the proposed strategy for the SAT and UNSAT problems using Glucose are summarized in Tables 1 and 2, respectively. For each problem, the tables present the number of candidate partial solutions ($p_{\#}$), the satisfiability ratio ($p_{\%}$, estimated for larger $p_{\#}$ values), the performance of the amalgamated (T_0), the performance of the purely parallel procedure with regular (T_p) and symbolic bounds (T_s) and the performance of the hybrid procedure with symbolic bounds (T_h). The performance gain between the regular amalgamated approach T_0 and the proposed hybrid approach with symbolic bound T_h is also presented (G). The results are further detailed in Fig. 4 for `RBT` and `Hotel`.

4.2 Satisfiable Problems

For most problems (`Dijk(1)`, `Hand(1)`, `Hotel(1)` and `RBT(1)`) the hybrid approach considerably outperforms the amalgamated execution, even for problems

[1] http://baldur.iti.kit.edu/sat-race-2015/.

with a large number of candidate partial solutions and reduced satisfiability ratio, like RBT(1). In fact, the speedup may reach orders of magnitude, like Hand(1) at $n = 16$, Hotel(1) at $n = 11$ and RBT(1) at $n = 12$, with speedups of 916×, 1086× and 118×, respectively. At larger n values, several amalgamated problems timeout while the decomposed procedure still takes few seconds to execute. As Fig. 4a and c show, for SAT problems the performance of amalgamated executions tends to increase exponentially, unlike the decomposed strategy. For Span(2) speedups are less significant, going up to 4.6×. Finally, for Ring(1) and Span(1), results range from slowdowns of 0.5× to speedups of 1.2×. Here, it can be seen that the purely parallel approach would actually be outperformed by the amalgamated procedure, but the hybrid mode balances the losses. However, these problems were solved below 6 s, thus these differences are not very significant. For the specifications for which symbolic bounds impact the search space, (Dijk(1) and Hotel(1)) the purely parallel approach shows in average a 4× speedup. For the other specifications, performance differences are marginal, as expected.

Results with MiniSat (not shown in the table) in general mirror those obtained with Glucose. For instance, Hand(1) at $n = 14$, Hotel(1) at $n = 9$ and RBT(1) at $n = 10$, have speedups of 528×, 376× and 14×, respectively. Regarding the comparison with parallel SAT solvers, Syrup follows the tendency of Glucose, as hinted by Fig. 4a and c, albeit with considerably improved performance. Thus, problems that were considerably outperformed by the decomposed strategy remain so: Hand(1) at $n = 16$, Hotel(1) at $n = 11$ and RBT(1) at $n = 12$, have speedups of 650×, 255× and 7×, respectively. For Ring(1), Span(1) and Span(2), which are solved below 6 s, Syrup actually performs slightly worse than Glucose. For the considered specifications, Plingeling is usually outperformed by Syrup, so the same conclusions apply. For this reason Plingeling's results are omitted in Fig. 4.

4.3 Unsatisfiable Problems

Although, as expected, the purely parallel execution is often outperformed by the amalgamated execution, the hybrid execution is able to compensate the losses. In fact, results show that the amalgamated approach is never more than 2× faster than the hybrid approach for the considered specifications under considerable n sizes. Figure 4b and d depict the overall tendency, with the hybrid execution mostly accompanying the performance of the amalgamated execution.

Specifications where the amalgamated execution outperforms the hybrid strategy are usually balanced by the results of their SAT counter-part. For instance, for the UNSAT Dijk(2), the hybrid approach is about 1.5× slower than the amalgamated approach for every n size; however, for the SAT Dijk(1), the speedup of the hybrid approach ranges from 20× to 30×. Thus, in average, the performance of the decomposed strategy outperforms the amalgamated approach. Interestingly, for RBT(2) and Ring(2), the hybrid approach actually outperforms amalgamated execution: for RBT(2) at $n = 11$ there is a 6× speedup, and for Ring(2) at $n = 5$ a 553× speedup. For larger n values the amalgamated

Table 1. Summary of the SAT performance tests.

Model	n	$p_{\#}$ ($p_{\%}$)	T_O	T_p	T_s	T_h	G
Dijk(1)	27	28 (0.93)	25.3	4.8	1.1	**1.1**	23.3
Dijk(1)	28	29 (0.93)	30.6	4.8	1.2	**1.2**	26.4
Dijk(1)	29	30 (0.93)	43.9	5.4	1.3	**1.3**	32.7
Dijk(1)	30	31 (0.94)	28.3	5.7	1.4	**1.4**	20.1
Hand(1)	14	1 (1.00)	81.5	0.6	0.6	**0.6**	127.3
Hand(1)	15	0 (0.00)	2.1	0.1	0.1	**0.1**	14.3
Hand(1)	16	1 (1.00)	1496.2	1.6	1.6	**1.6**	916.3
Hand(1)	17	0 (0.00)	40.6	0.1	0.1	**0.2**	240.7
Hand(1)	18	1 (1.00)	TO	4.7	4.7	**5.1**	$+\infty$
Hand(1)	19	0 (0.00)	2724.8	0.2	0.2	**0.2**	13910.2
Hand(1)	20	1 (1.00)	TO	874.5	871.3	**1047.2**	$+\infty$
Hotel(1)	8	12833 (0.60)	64.1	2.9	1.0	**0.9**	71.6
Hotel(1)	9	211470 (>0.6)	216.0	3.4	1.0	**0.9**	236.5
Hotel(1)	10	>999999 (>0.6)	224.4	4.0	1.1	**0.9**	237.2
Hotel(1)	11	>999999 (>0.6)	1106.1	4.5	1.2	**1.0**	1086.3
Hotel(1)	12	>999999 (>0.6)	184.8	4.9	1.3	**1.0**	178.2
RBT(1)	9	4862 (0.01)	1.6	0.5	0.5	**0.5**	2.9
RBT(1)	10	16796 (0.00)	55.8	3.1	3.3	**4.0**	13.9
RBT(1)	11	58786 (0.00)	240.8	1.6	1.6	**2.0**	121.6
RBT(1)	12	208012 (0.00)	2350.5	17.0	17.3	**19.9**	118.2
RBT(1)	13	>999999 (0.00)	TO	133.3	133.5	**164.6**	$+\infty$
Ring(1)	8	16072 (>0.1)	**1.9**	193.8	196.2	4.2	0.5
Ring(1)	9	125673 (>0.1)	1.5	1.1	1.2	**1.2**	1.2
Ring(1)	10	>999999 (>0.1)	**1.6**	2.2	2.1	2.0	0.8
Ring(1)	11	>999999 (>0.1)	**2.6**	61.8	62.1	5.1	0.5
Ring(1)	12	>999999 (>0.1)	**3.4**	20.4	19.1	5.4	0.6
Span(1)	14	>999999 (1.00)	**1.1**	1.7	2.0	1.8	0.6
Span(1)	15	>999999 (1.00)	**1.3**	2.4	2.4	2.2	0.6
Span(1)	16	>999999 (1.00)	**2.0**	2.6	2.7	2.7	0.7
Span(2)	14	>999999 (1.00)	15.1	3.5	3.5	**3.3**	4.6
Span(2)	15	>999999 (1.00)	9.2	4.2	4.0	**4.0**	2.3
Span(2)	16	>999999 (1.00)	6.4	4.4	4.5	**5.0**	1.3

execution times out, while the hybrid approach still terminates within reasonable time. Using symbolic bounds and the decomposed parallel solving strategy can also lead to speedups in the UNSAT scenarios.

Likewise the SAT case, MiniSat results are similar to those of Glucose. For instance, Dijk(2) preserves the 1.5× slowdown in average, albeit at slightly higher performance times, while Ring(2) at $n = 5$ the amalgamated execution times out while the hybrid takes 18 s. Comparing with parallel SAT solvers, the results are also similar to those obtained for the SAT problems. For instance, for Ring(2) at $n = 5$ the speedup persists but reduced to 244×, while the slowdown at Dijk(2) is in average increased to 2×. This phenomenon is hinted in Fig. 4b and d, where Syrup has a similar growth curve to that of Glucose but with better performance. Plingeling continues to be in general outperformed by Syrup.

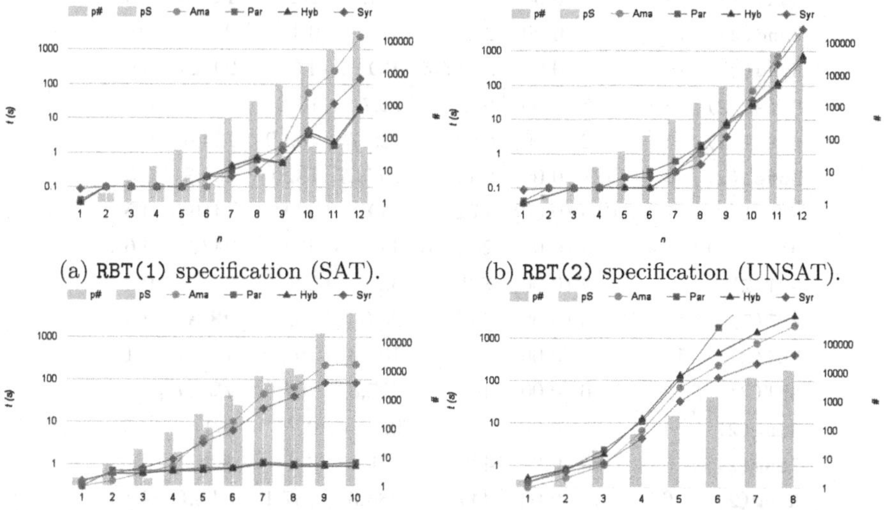

(a) RBT(1) specification (SAT). (b) RBT(2) specification (UNSAT).

(c) Hotel(1) specification (SAT). (d) Hotel(2) specification (UNSAT).

Fig. 4. Performance times for the RBT and Hotel specifications.

4.4 Threats to Validity

The performance of the decomposed strategy is highly dependent on the order on which the candidate partial solutions are generated, since they determine the satisfiability of the integrated problems. However, since the generation of partial solutions is extremely efficient, and the UNSAT integrated problems are often quickly discharged, our technique has been able to handle problems with very large number of partial solutions and very small satisfiability ratio, like RBT(1).

The partition criteria automatically inferred from the symbolic bounds is not necessarily optimal. However, manual experiments have not found any better partition for the considered problems. Nonetheless, the soundness of the decomposed strategy would be preserved by alternative partition criteria, and since our tool accepts the set $\mathcal{R}_p$ of variables that will determine the partial problem, the user is free to manually define the decomposition or experiment with other automated criteria.

Table 2. Summary of the UNSAT performance tests.

Model	n	$p_{\#}$ ($p_{\%}$)	T_O	T_p	T_s	T_h	G
Dijk(2)	27	28 (0.00)	**23.9**	79.0	55.2	37.6	0.6
Dijk(2)	28	29 (0.00)	**24.7**	98.7	67.8	37.1	0.7
Dijk(2)	29	30 (0.00)	**31.1**	115.4	80.4	47.2	0.7
Dijk(2)	30	31 (0.00)	**32.0**	132.8	93.7	49.6	0.6
Hand(2)	12	1 (0.00)	**5.0**	6.6	6.9	**5.1**	1.2
Hand(2)	13	0 (0.00)	0.2	0.1	0.1	**0.1**	1.8
Hand(2)	14	1 (0.00)	**127.3**	724.2	162.7	**122.9**	1.0
Hand(2)	15	0 (0.00)	2.5	0.1	0.1	**0.1**	16.8
Hand(2)	16	1 (0.00)	**2537.5**	TO	TO	2912.8	0.9
Hotel(2)	4	75 (0.00)	**6.5**	12.7	10.8	12.3	0.5
Hotel(2)	5	312 (0.00)	**68.2**	128.7	109.9	134.6	0.5
Hotel(2)	6	1421 (0.00)	**234.7**	1973.7	1820.5	460.3	0.5
Hotel(2)	7	7016 (0.00)	**772.1**	TO	TO	1416.5	0.5
Hotel(2)	8	12833 (0.00)	**2023.6**	TO	TO	3432.4	0.6
RBT(2)	9	4862 (0.00)	**7.3**	6.7	6.8	7.9	0.9
RBT(2)	10	16796 (0.00)	70.1	25.0	25.4	**28.8**	2.4
RBT(2)	11	58786 (0.00)	721.7	100.3	102.8	**118.1**	6.1
RBT(2)	12	58786 (0.00)	TO	567.8	564.9	**721.7**	$+\infty$
Ring(2)	4	24 (0.00)	10.8	0.7	0.7	**3.1**	3.5
Ring(2)	5	89 (0.00)	4486.8	6.6	6.6	**8.1**	552.8
Ring(2)	6	415 (0.00)	TO	238.3	237.1	**318.0**	$+\infty$
Ring(3)	5	89 (0.00)	**1.4**	2.5	2.4	2.8	0.5
Ring(3)	6	415 (0.00)	**4.9**	13.4	13.3	8.9	0.6
Ring(3)	7	2372 (0.00)	**14.6**	105.8	104.8	24.4	0.6
Ring(3)	8	16072 (0.00)	**76.1**	1100.5	1098.1	134.7	0.6
Span(1)	5	58 (0.00)	**0.2**	7.6	1.2	0.3	0.7
Span(1)	6	457 (0.00)	**0.6**	342.9	7.8	1.0	0.6
Span(1)	7	5777 (0.00)	**4.4**	663.4	337.2	9.0	0.5
Span(2)	5	58 (0.00)	**0.4**	3.1	2.9	0.7	0.6
Span(2)	6	457 (0.00)	**0.6**	30.0	30.1	1.1	0.5
Span(2)	7	5777 (0.00)	**1.9**	786.9	780.4	4.2	0.5

5 Related Work

The decomposition of Alloy models into smaller problems to improve the performance of the solving process has been previously explored [22], a work from which we drew inspiration. Likewise our technique, constraints are split in two, and solutions to the first are fed as partial information to the second. The best partition criteria is chosen by testing candidates at small scopes. In contrast, our partition criteria is automatically calculated from the partial knowledge provided by the user. The proposed solving process was purely sequential but already showed performance gains. Our technique takes this one step further by parallelizing the process and exploiting additional partial knowledge to reduce the search space. Moreover, the iteration of solutions was not addressed, and thus symmetry breaking issues were not raised. Evaluation mainly focuses on the small scope tests for SAT problems, with speedups not reaching an order of magnitude, rendering direct performance comparisons unfeasible.

The partitioning and parallelization of Alloy analysis procedures has also been proposed [18]. Here, each parallel problem solves the same constraints but within a restricted search space, defined by a range of solutions. Ranges are derived from the structure of the models, disregarding the constraints, resulting in unpredictable complexity. A relevant difference is that, unlike our approach, the number of partitions calculated is exactly that of the parallel processes available. Since the range partitioning does not guarantee problems with similar complexity, some process may become idle while others are encumbered with more complex tasks. This issue is tamed by allowing the dynamic partition of problems. In our approach there are usually much more partitions, with reduced complexity, than available processes, so processes rarely become idle. In general, this renders their approach more suitable for UNSAT problems (where the complete search space must be searched) and ours for SAT problems. It could be interesting to see how our hybrid approach would fare replacing the amalgamated process by their approach. In a different study [17], the same authors explore a technique to infer partitions on the SAT propositional variables from high-level Alloy models with small scopes. Likewise our strategy, both techniques obtain speedups up to two orders of magnitude before the amalgamated analyses timeout, but since evaluation is performed in clusters direct comparisons should be read with care. By allowing the definition of symbolic bounds, our approach is able to explore additional knowledge about the problem's domain without burdening the user, since that information would still have to be integrated in the constraints otherwise. The proposed hybrid approach, with a thread solving the worst case scenario amalgamated problem, is also novel.

Techniques have been proposed to extract finer Kodkod partial instances from high-level specifications, still relying on its constant tuple set bounds. In [15] an extension to the Alloy language for the specification of instances is proposed, that can be mapped into Kodkod bounds. Our approach extends the expressiveness of partial instances at the Kodkod level. Since Alloy natively support binding expressions in the declaration of the relations, symbolic bounds could easily be retrieved from regular Alloy specifications without any extension to the language.

Many techniques have been proposed for parallelizing SAT solvers [8,14], most based on the *Conflict-Driven Clause Learning* (CDCL) algorithm and exploiting clause learning and sharing. In general, these fit into two families [8]: competitive (or portfolio) approaches, where the solvers explore the same search space, the fastest returning the solution; and cooperative approaches, following a divide and conquer strategy, where the search space is split and the solution is built from the results of the solvers. Focusing on top ranking solvers from the latest SAT competitions, Plingeling [4] falls in the former category, deploying solvers with different configurations, with minimal clause sharing, while Syrup [3] follows an hybrid approach, with an initial portfolio phase that switches to cooperative after a certain threshold. These solvers, however, do not support incremental solving, and thus cannot be used to effectively iterate solutions. Moreover, our technique could be adapted to run in a distributed environment, unlike modern solvers based on clause sharing.

A parallel SAT solving approach that is more closely related to ours is the one followed by JaCk-SAT [19]. Here, the set of boolean variables is split through heuristics, and the clauses are divided accordingly. Problems are then deployed in parallel to solve the two sets of variables independently; solutions are then checked over the clauses referring to both sets of variables, and are rejected if not. This process can be repeated recursively. This technique, however, is not able to compete with the performance of modern parallel SAT solvers. Rather than acting on the SAT level, our technique exploits higher-level domain knowledge provided in the problem definition.

6 Conclusions

This paper proposes the usage of symbolic partial knowledge to enhance the analysis of declarative specifications through their automatic decomposition into partial solutions and subsequent parallelization of the solving process with tighter search spaces. This strategy is formalized and an effective parallel implementation for the Kodkod constraint solver is provided. This extension exploits symbolic partial knowledge for increased efficiency, being able to automatically analyze relational model finding problems without any additional burden to the user, while still preserving the ability to iterate over solutions and the soundness of the symmetry breaking algorithm.

Our evaluation has shown that, even in commodity hardware, the technique is able to outperform amalgamated problems for most satisfiable specifications; the hybrid approach addressed the worst case scenarios, providing balanced results in comparison with the amalgamated execution. In fact, it rivals with state-of-the-art parallel SAT solvers. We also show that decomposing the problems based on the dependency degree of the problem's variables is a suitable partition criteria.

Although we believe Kodkod to be powerful enough to be used by end users, we expect the extension presented to be exploited by analyzers for high-level specifications. In the future we intend to derive symbolic bounds directly from the binding expressions of Alloy's declarations, thus benefiting the large community of Alloy users. The decomposed strategy is already being used in the back-end of Electrum [12], a temporal extension to Alloy. As in `Hotel`, in such scenarios the partition criteria naturally degenerates into a division between the static and dynamic variables. To support full (non-bounded) model checking for such problems, we are currently exploring a generalization where Kodkod is used for the generation of the static partial solutions, while the integrated dynamic problems are checked in parallel by off-the-shelf model checkers, such as NuSMV.

Acknowldgements. This work is financed by the ERDF – *European Regional Development Fund* through the *Operational Programme for Competitiveness and Internationalisation* - COMPETE 2020 Programme and by National Funds through the Portuguese funding agency, FCT - *Fundação para a Ciência e a Tecnologia* within project POCI-01-0145-FEDER-016826.

References

1. Abrial, J.: The B-book - Assigning Programs to Meanings. Cambridge University Press, Cambridge (2005)
2. Audemard, G., Simon, L.: Glucose, version 4.0, October 2014. http://alloy.mit.edu/kodkod/download.html
3. Audemard, G., Simon, L.: Lazy clause exchange policy for parallel SAT solvers. In: Sinz, C., Egly, U. (eds.) SAT 2014. LNCS, vol. 8561, pp. 197–205. Springer, Cham (2014). doi:10.1007/978-3-319-09284-3_15
4. Biere, A.: Lingeling, Plingeling, PicoSAT and PrecoSAT at SAT race 2010. Technical report 10/1, FMV Reports Series, Institute for Formal Models and Verification, Johannes Kepler University (2010)
5. Biere, A.: Plingeling, version ayv-86bf266-140429, April 2014. http://fmv.jku.at/lingeling/
6. Crawford, J.M., Ginsberg, M.L., Luks, E.M., Roy, A.: Symmetry-breaking predicates for search problems. In: KR 1996, pp. 148–159. Morgan Kaufmann (1996)
7. Eén, N., Sörensson, N.: MiniSat, version 2.2.0, July 2010. http://minisat.se/MiniSat.html
8. Hölldobler, S., Manthey, N., Nguyen, V.H., Stecklina, J., Steinke, P.: A short overview on modern parallel SAT-solvers. In: AICACSIS 2011, pp. 201–206. IEEE (2011)
9. Jackson, D.: Software Abstractions: Logic, Language, and Analysis, revised edition. MIT Press, Cambridge (2012)
10. Lamport, L.: Specifying Systems, The TLA$^+$ Language and Tools for Hardware and Software Engineers. Addison-Wesley, Boston (2002)
11. Macedo, N.: Pardinus, version 0.3, September 2016. https://github.com/nmacedo/Pardinus/
12. Macedo, N., Brunel, J., Chemouil, D., Cunha, A., Kuperberg, D.: Lightweight specification and analysis of dynamic systems with rich configurations. In: FSE 2016. ACM (2016)
13. Macedo, N., Cunha, A., Guimarães, T.: Exploring scenario exploration. In: Egyed, A., Schaefer, I. (eds.) FASE 2015. LNCS, vol. 9033, pp. 301–315. Springer, Heidelberg (2015). doi:10.1007/978-3-662-46675-9_20
14. Martins, R., Manquinho, V.M., Lynce, I.: An overview of parallel SAT solving. Constraints **17**(3), 304–347 (2012)
15. Montaghami, V., Rayside, D.: Extending alloy with partial instances. In: Derrick, J., Fitzgerald, J., Gnesi, S., Khurshid, S., Leuschel, M., Reeves, S., Riccobene, E. (eds.) ABZ 2012. LNCS, vol. 7316, pp. 122–135. Springer, Heidelberg (2012). doi:10.1007/978-3-642-30885-7_9

16. Newcombe, C., Rath, T., Zhang, F., Munteanu, B., Brooker, M., Deardeuff, M.: How Amazon web services uses formal methods. Commun. ACM **58**(4), 66–73 (2015)
17. Rosner, N., López Pombo, C.G., Aguirre, N., Jaoua, A., Mili, A., Frias, M.F.: Parallel bounded verification of alloy models by transcoping. In: Cohen, E., Rybalchenko, A. (eds.) VSTTE 2013. LNCS, vol. 8164, pp. 88–107. Springer, Heidelberg (2014). doi:10.1007/978-3-642-54108-7_5
18. Rosner, N., Siddiqui, J.H., Aguirre, N., Khurshid, S., Frias, M.F.: Ranger: parallel analysis of alloy models by range partitioning. In: ASE 2013, pp. 147–157. IEEE (2013)
19. Singer, D., Monnet, A.: JaCk-SAT: a new parallel scheme to solve the satisfiability problem (SAT) based on join-and-check. In: Wyrzykowski, R., Dongarra, J., Karczewski, K., Wasniewski, J. (eds.) PPAM 2007. LNCS, vol. 4967, pp. 249–258. Springer, Heidelberg (2008). doi:10.1007/978-3-540-68111-3_27
20. Torlak, E.: Kodkod, version 2.1, September 2015. http://alloy.mit.edu/kodkod/download.html
21. Torlak, E., Jackson, D.: Kodkod: a relational model finder. In: Grumberg, O., Huth, M. (eds.) TACAS 2007. LNCS, vol. 4424, pp. 632–647. Springer, Heidelberg (2007). doi:10.1007/978-3-540-71209-1_49
22. Uzuncaova, E., Khurshid, S.: Constraint prioritization for efficient analysis of declarative models. In: Cuellar, J., Maibaum, T., Sere, K. (eds.) FM 2008. LNCS, vol. 5014, pp. 310–325. Springer, Heidelberg (2008). doi:10.1007/978-3-540-68237-0_22

A Language-Theoretic View on Network Protocols

Pierre Ganty[1], Boris Köpf[1], and Pedro Valero[1,2(✉)]

[1] IMDEA Software Institute, Madrid, Spain
{pierre.ganty,boris.koepf,pedro.valero}@imdea.org
[2] Universidad Politécnica de Madrid, Madrid, Spain

Abstract. Input validation is the first line of defense against malformed or malicious inputs. It is therefore critical that the validator (which is often part of the parser) is free of bugs.

To build dependable input validators, we propose using parser generators for context-free languages. In the context of network protocols, various works have pointed at context-free languages as falling short to specify precisely or concisely common idioms found in protocols. We review those assessments and perform a rigorous, language-theoretic analysis of several common protocol idioms. We then demonstrate the practical value of our findings by developing a modular, robust, and efficient input validator for HTTP relying on context-free grammars and regular expressions.

1 Introduction

Input validation, often carried out during parsing, is the first line of defense against malformed or maliciously crafted inputs. As the following reports demonstrate, bugs make parsers vulnerable, hence prone to attacks: a bug in the URL parser enabled attackers to recover user credentials from a widely used password manager [14], a bug in the RTF parser led to a vulnerability in Word 2010 [19], and a lack of input validation in the Bash shell has been used for privilege escalation by a remote attacker [13] just to cite a few. To stop the flow of such reports improved approaches for building input validators are needed.

To build dependable input validators, an approach is to rely on mature parsing technologies. As a candidate, consider parser generators for context-free languages (hereafter CFLs). Their main qualities are:

1. The code for parsing is synthesized automatically from a grammar specification, shifting the risk of programming errors away from the architect of the validator to the designer of the parser generator;
2. CFL is the most expressive class of languages supported by trustworthy implementation of parser generators. Here by trustworthy we mean an implementation that either stood the test of time like Flex, Bison, or ANTLR, or that has been formally verified like the certified implementations of Valiant's [3] and CYK [11] algorithms.

D. D'Souza and K. Narayan Kumar (Eds.): ATVA 2017, LNCS 10482, pp. 363–379, 2017.
DOI: 10.1007/978-3-319-68167-2_24

Relying on established CFL technology is an asset compared to existing solutions which are either programmed from scratch [8] or generated from ad hoc parser generators [2,21].

However, even though CFL is the most expressive language class with trustworthy parser generators, previous works suggest CFLs are not enough for network messages. Specifically, they claim the impossibility or difficulty to specify precisely the various idioms found in network messages using CFLs. For example, some authors argue that CFL are insufficiently expressive because "data fields that are preceded by their actual length (which is common in several network protocols) cannot be expressed in a context-free grammar" [7]. Yet other authors suggest that going beyond CFLs is merely required for conciseness of expression, because "it is possible to rewrite these grammars to [...] be context-free, but the resulting specification is much more awkward" [4]. Surprisingly, the arguments made are not backed up by any formalization or proof.

In this paper we formally analyze which idioms can and which cannot be (concisely) specified using CFLs, and we turn the results into practice by building an input validator for HTTP messages entirely based on CFL technology.

As the main contributions of our analysis we find out that:

- Length fields of *bounded size* are finite and hence form a regular language. However, while they can be concisely represented in terms of a context-free grammar, every finite automaton that recognizes them grows exponentially with the bound. In contrast, length fields of *unbounded size* cannot even be expressed as a finite intersection of CFLs.
- Equality tests between words of *bounded size* again form a regular language but, as opposed to length fields, they cannot be compactly represented in terms of a context-free grammar. They do, however, allow for a concise representation in terms of a finite intersection of context-free grammars. Specifically, we show that both the grammar and the number of membership checks grows only linearly with the size bound, which has interesting practical implications, see below. As in the case of length fields, equality checks between words of *unbounded size* cannot be expressed as a finite intersection of CFLs.

We consider finite intersections of CFLs because they are (a) strictly more expressive than CFLs, and (b) checking membership in the intersection of CFLs is equivalent to checking membership in each individual CFL.

These results lead to a principled and modular approach to input validation: several CFL parsers are run on the input and their boolean results (whether the input belongs or not to the CFL) are combined following a predefined logic to decide whether or not the input message conforms to the standard (that specifies what valid messages are).

We demonstrate that this approach is practical by implementing a proof of concept input validator for a large subset of the HTTP protocol, covering a significant number of the idioms found in network messages. Our input validator, called HTTPValidator [24] draws inspiration from HTTPolice [8], a state of the art input validator for HTTP messages built from scratch by the open source community. HTTPValidator is close to achieve feature parity (in terms of checks) with HTTPolice and offers competitive performance.

Summary of Contributions. In summary, our contributions are both foundational and applied. On the foundational side we perform a language-theoretic analysis of important protocol idioms, making a step towards more rigor in the field. On the applied side we show how to implement an input validator for HTTP using off-the-shelf parser generators.

Paper Structure. Section 2 introduces basic language-theoretic and input validation concepts, Sect. 3 discusses the case of length fields, including the chunked messages, whereas Sect. 4 considers the case of comparisons. We show the practicality of our approach in Sect. 5, before concluding with related work (Sect. 6), conclusions and future work (Sect. 7). Due to the lack of space, some proofs are deferred to a long version [25].

2 Preliminaries

Language Theory. We begin by introducing the language-theoretic context needed for our development. An *alphabet* Σ is a nonempty finite set of *symbols*. A *word* w is a finite sequence of symbols of Σ where the empty sequence is denoted ε. A *language* is a set of words and the set of all words over Σ is denoted Σ^*. We denote by $|w|$ the *length* of w. Further define $(w)_i$ as the i-th symbol of w if $1 \leq i \leq |w|$ and ε otherwise. Given a nonempty subset X of Σ and $i \in \mathbb{N}$ define X^i as $\{w \in X^* \mid |w| = i\}$.

We assume the reader is familiar with common operations on languages such as concatenation and boolean combinations. Likewise, we count on the reader's familiarity with regular languages and finite-state automata. Yet we next give a description of context-free grammars, which are the formal basis of our work.

A *context-free grammar* (or grammar for short) is a tuple $G = (V, \Sigma, S, R)$ where V is a finite set of *variables* (or *non-terminals*) including the *start variable* S; Σ is an alphabet (or set of *terminals*), $R \subseteq V \times (\Sigma \cup V)^*$ is a finite set of *rules*. We often write $X \to w$ for a rule $(X, w) \in R$. We define a *step* as the binary relation $\Rightarrow$ on $(V \cup \Sigma)^*$ given by $u \Rightarrow v$ if there exists a rule $X \to w$ of G such that $u = \alpha\, X\, \beta$ and $v = \alpha\, w\, \beta$ for some $\alpha, \beta \in (V \cup \Sigma)^*$. Define $u \Rightarrow^* v$ if there exists a $n \geq 0$ steps sequence $u_0 \Rightarrow u_1 \Rightarrow \ldots \Rightarrow u_n$ such that $u_0 = u$ and $u_n = v$. A step sequence $u \Rightarrow^* w$ is called a *derivation* whenever $u = S$ and $w \in \Sigma^*$. Define $L(G) = \{w \in \Sigma^* \mid S \Rightarrow^* w\}$ and call it the language generated by G. A language L is said to be *context-free*, or *CFL*, if there exists a grammar G such that $L = L(G)$. The *size* of a grammar is the sum of the sizes of its production rules R, that is, it is given by $\sum_{(X,w)\in R} 1+|w|$.

Input Validation. In this paper, validating an input means checking whether it belongs to a language. In particular, no data structure is filled and no information is extracted from the input other than its membership status. Thus, validating an input w for a language L means deciding whether w is a member of L which is also known as the *membership problem*. To specify L, we use context-free grammars or regular expressions.

3 Formal Analysis of Length Fields

Length fields, whose role is to specify the length of subsequent fields, are commonly found in network protocols such as HTTP [9], SIP [23], DNS [20] and UDP [22]. As an example, consider the following HTTP POST message:

```
POST /1/notification/list HTTP/1.1\r\n
Content-Length: 47\r\n\r\n
{"header":{},"query":{"count":100},"answer":{}}
```

The length field begins after the keyword `Content-Length` and terminates before the carriage return/newline `\r\n`. Its content, i.e. 47, describes the length of the message body, which is the string coming after the double `\r\n`.

In this section, we characterize length fields from the point of view of formal language theory. We begin with a formalization aiming to capture their essence, and then characterize the class of languages specifying them in the bounded and unbounded cases. We consider both cases because some protocols, such as DNS and UDP, require length fields to have fixed size, while others, such as HTTP and SIP, have no such restriction. We conclude by leveraging these results to analyze chunked transfer encoding.

3.1 Modeling Length Fields

To model length fields, we will work with formal languages over an alphabet Σ. For the example of HTTP, Σ would be the ASCII character set.

Fixed Size. To describe length fields of finite size $n > 0$ we define the language $L_{len}(n)$ over $\Sigma = B \cup W$ as follows:

$$L_{len}(n) \stackrel{\text{def}}{=} \{x\, w \mid x \in B^n, w \in W^*, |w| = \textstyle\sum_{i=0}^{n-1} (x)_{i+1} \cdot b^i\}$$

where $B = \{0, \ldots, b-1\}$ for an integer $b > 1$. Intuitively, $L_{len}(n)$ represents the same number twice, using two different encodings: first b-ary as x and then unary as w, where the relationship between both encodings is given by $|w| = \sum_{i=0}^{n-1} (x)_{i+1} \cdot b^i$. For example, let $n = 3$, $B = \{\mathtt{0}, \mathtt{1}\}$ and $W = \{\mathtt{a}, \mathtt{b}, \mathtt{c}\}$ the word $\mathtt{110abc}$ consists of the binary representation of $3 = (1 \cdot 2^0) + (1 \cdot 2^1) + (0 \cdot 2^2)$ followed by a word ($\mathtt{abc}$) of length 3 and, therefore, $\mathtt{110abc} \in L_{len}(3)$. We choose this unconventional "least significant digit first" to keep notation simple. The results of this section stay valid for the "most significant digit first" convention.

Unbounded Size. For describing length fields of unbounded size, observe that any overlap between the alphabets W and B for describing the body of the message and its length, respectively, introduces ambiguity as to where the length field ends. A common approach to remove such ambiguities is to use a *delimiter*, which is a special symbol $\sharp$ not occurring in x whose aim is to separate explicitly the length field from the body of the message. We extend the definition of $L_{len}(n)$ to account for such delimiters:

$$L^{\sharp}_{len}(n) \stackrel{\text{def}}{=} \{x \sharp w \mid x \in B^n, w \in W^*, |w| = \textstyle\sum_{i=0}^{n-1} (x)_{i+1} \cdot b^i\}.$$

We are now in position to define a language for describing length fields of arbitrary and unbounded size:

$$L^{\sharp}_{len} \stackrel{\text{def}}{=} \textstyle\bigcup_{i>0} L^{\sharp}_{len}(i).$$

Results shown in this section remain valid when there is no overlap between alphabets W and B. In such case the delimiter is no longer needed and removing it from the results in Sect. 3.2 has no effect on them.

3.2 Unbounded Length Fields

The following theorem shows that length fields of unbounded size cannot be specified using intersection of finitely many CFLs. This means that we need to impose restrictions, such as size bounds, in order to specify length fields using CFLs. We will study fixed size length fields in Sect. 3.3.

Theorem 1. *$L^{\sharp}_{len}$ is not a finite intersection of CFLs.*

To prove this result, we begin by defining the following subset of $L^{\sharp}_{len}$:

$$L_{\angle} \stackrel{\text{def}}{=} L^{\sharp}_{len} \cap 1^* \sharp^* a^*.$$

Lemma 2. *$L_{\angle}$ is not a finite intersection of CFLs. Moreover, no infinite subset of $L_{\angle}$ is a finite intersection of CFLs.*

The proof argument relies on semilinear sets which we recall next: a subset of $\mathbb{N}^k$, with $k > 0$, is called *semilinear*, if it can be specified as a finite union of linear sets. A set $S \subseteq \mathbb{N}^k$ is called *linear* if there exists $\boldsymbol{b} \in \mathbb{N}^k$ and a finite subset $\{\boldsymbol{p}_1, \ldots, \boldsymbol{p}_m\}$ of $\mathbb{N}^k$ such that $S = \{\boldsymbol{b} + \lambda_1 \boldsymbol{p}_1 + \ldots + \lambda_m \boldsymbol{p}_m \mid \lambda_1, \ldots, \lambda_m \in \mathbb{N}\}$.

Let $\bar{w} = \langle w_1, \ldots, w_k \rangle$ be a tuple of $k > 0$ words, define a mapping $f_{\bar{w}} \colon \mathbb{N}^k \to w_1^* \ldots w_k^*$ by $f_{\bar{w}}(i_1, \ldots, i_k) = w_1^{i_1} \ldots w_k^{i_k}$, that is, the output of $f_{\bar{w}}$ is a word in which the i-th component of $\bar{w}$ is repeated a number of times that corresponds to the i-th input to $f_{\bar{w}}$. We define the preimage of $f_{\bar{w}}$ and liftings of $f_{\bar{w}}$ from elements to subsets of $\mathbb{N}^k$ in the natural way.

The following result by Latteux [15] establishes a fundamental correspondence between languages given by finite intersection of CFLs and semilinear sets.

Proposition 3 ([15, Proposition 7]). *Let $\bar{w} = \langle w_1, \ldots, w_k \rangle$, $k > 0$, and $L \subseteq w_1^* \ldots w_k^*$: $f_{\bar{w}}^{-1}(L)$ is semilinear if and only if L is a finite intersection of CFLs.*

Now we meet the requirements to prove Lemma 2.

Proof (Sketch). The proof of Lemma 2 relies on the observation that

$$L_\angle = \{1^n \sharp a^{val} \mid val = \sum_{i=0}^{n-1} b^i\}.$$

Let $\bar{w} = \langle 1, \sharp, a \rangle$, since $\sum_{i=0}^{n-1} b^i = \frac{b^n - 1}{b-1}$ for all $b > 1$, we obtain:

$$f_{\bar{w}}^{-1}(L_\angle) = \left\{ \left(i, 1, \tfrac{b^i - 1}{b-1}\right) \mid i \in \mathbb{N} \right\}. \tag{1}$$

Next, we show this set is not semilinear using the facts that (a) the third component grows exponentially in i, and $f_{\bar{w}}^{-1}(L_\angle)$ is an infinite set. The definition of semilinear set then shows that by taking two elements in (b) we can obtain a third one. We then show that those three elements violate (a) unless they all coincide. The same reasoning remains valid when considering an infinite subset of $L_\angle$. □

Once Lemma 2 is proved, the proof of Theorem 1 easily follows.

Proof (of Theorem 1). Assume $L_{len}^\sharp$ is a finite intersection of CFLs. Since $1^* \sharp^* a^*$ is a CFL, $L_\angle$ is also a finite intersection of CFLs contradicting Lemma 2. □

Our definitions of $L_{len}(n)$ and $L_{len}^\sharp$ do not put any constraints on the structure of the word w that follows the length field and the delimiter (if any). In practice, however, the word w may need to satisfy constraints beyond those on its length, such as containment in a specific language.

Theorem 4. *The language $L_{len}^\sharp \cap \{x \sharp w \mid x \in B^*,\ w \in L_C\}$ is a finite intersection of CFLs for* **no** *infinite CFL $L_C \subseteq W^*$.*

The proof of this Theorem follows the same argument used to prove Theorem 1. Hence, we begin by defining a subset of $L_{len}^\sharp \cap \{x \sharp w \mid x \in B^*,\ w \in L_C\}$ for which Proposition 3 holds.

Let S be the start symbol of the grammar generating language L_C. Since language L_C is infinite the following must hold: for some non terminal A and $a_i \in W^*$, we have $S \Rightarrow^* a_1 A a_5$; $A \Rightarrow^* a_2 A a_4$; $A \Rightarrow^* a_3$ with $a_2 \neq \varepsilon$ or $a_4 \neq \varepsilon$.

It follows that $\{a_1 a_2^i a_3 a_4^i a_5 \mid i \geq 0\} \subseteq L_C$ and, thus,

$$L_\measuredangle \stackrel{\text{def}}{=} L_{len}^\sharp \cap \{x \sharp w \mid x \in B^*,\ w \in L_C\} \cap 1^* \sharp^* a_1^* a_2^* a_3^* a_4^* a_5^*$$

is an infinite language contained in $1^* \sharp^* a_1^* a_2^* a_3^* a_4^* a_5^*$.

Lemma 5. *Language $L_\measuredangle$ is not a finite intersection of CFLs. Moreover, no infinite subset of $L_\measuredangle$ is a finite intersection of CFLs.*

This Lemma is similar to Lemma 2 and so is the proof. Finally, we proceed to prove Theorem 4 by contradiction.

Proof (of Theorem 4). Assume that $L_{len}^\sharp \cap \{x \sharp w \mid x \in B^*,\ w \in L_C\}$ is a finite intersection of CFLs. Since $1^* \sharp^* a_1^* a_2^* a_3^* a_4^* a_5^*$ is context-free, $L_\measuredangle$ is also a finite intersection of CFLs, which contradicts Lemma 5. □

3.3 Fixed Size Length Fields

In this section we sidestep the negative results of Sect. 3.2 by assuming an upper bound on the length field which indeed occurs in some network protocols. Such is the case of the IP, UDP and DNS protocols, whose specifications [1,20,22] define 16-bit fields containing the length of the data in terms of bytes. In some cases, assuming an upper bound on the length field, even if it is not defined by the standard, yields no loss of generality for all practical purposes. It is the case for HTTP where the majority of implementations do assume a bound on the size of length fields (e.g. major web browsers all do).

We start with the family of languages $L_{len}(n)$ where the length field is n symbols long. It is easy to see that each language of this family is finite, hence regular. Now we turn to the size of specifications for $L_{len}(n)$. In terms of finite state automata, all automata specifying $L_{len}(n)$ grow exponentially in n. Let $b > 1$ be the base in which the length is encoded, then there are b^n possible encodings for the length. By the pigeonhole principle, having less than b^n reachable states after reading the first n symbols implies that two distinct length encodings end up in the same state, making them indistinguishable for the automaton. Hence, it cannot decide $L_{len}(n)$. However, when $L_{len}(n)$ is specified using context-free grammars, we show that it admits a more compact description.

Theorem 6. *Let Σ be fixed alphabet and $n > 0$, there exists a context-free grammar $G_{len}(n)$ of size $\mathcal{O}(n)$ such that $L(G_{len}(n)) = L_{len}(n)$.*

Proof. For simplicity of presentation we assume that length fields are encoded in binary, i.e. $b = 2$ in the definition of $L_{len}(n)$. The generalization to any $b > 2$ is tedious but straightforward.

The grammar $G_{len}(n)$ is defined by the alphabet Σ, variables $\{S\} \cup \{X_i \mid 0 \leq i \leq n\} \cup \{F_i \mid 0 \leq i \leq n-1\}$ and the following rules:

$$\begin{array}{ll} \{S \to X_0\} & \{X_n \to \varepsilon\} \\ \{X_i \to 0\ X_{i+1} \mid 0 \leq i < n\} & \{X_i \to 1\ X_{i+1}\ F_i \mid 0 \leq i < n\} \\ \{F_j \to F_{j-1}\ F_{j-1} \mid 1 \leq j \leq n-1\} & \{F_0 \to c \mid c \in W\} \end{array}$$

It follows by construction that $L(G_{len}(n)) = L_{len}(n)$. A closer look reveals that, since the alphabet is fixed and therefore so is $|\Sigma| \geq |W|$, the size of the rules of each set is bounded and independent from n while there are $3n+2+|W|$ rules so the size of $G_{len}(n)$ is $\mathcal{O}(n)$. □

Next, we show that $110abc \in L_{len}(3)$ is also contained in $L(G_{len}(3))$.

$$\begin{aligned} S &\Rightarrow X_0 \Rightarrow 1X_1F_0 \Rightarrow 11X_2F_1F_0 \Rightarrow 110X_3F_1F_0 \\ &\Rightarrow 110F_1F_0 \Rightarrow 110F_0F_0F_0 \Rightarrow^* 110abc \end{aligned}$$

3.4 Chunked Messages

Closely related to length fields are chunked messages, a feature found in the HTTP protocol. According to the standard, the header `Transfer-Encoding:`

`chunked` signals that the body of the message is divided into chunks, each of which has its size defined by a variable size length field as shown below:

```
HTTP/1.1 200 OK\r\n
Transfer-Encoding: chunked\r\n\r\n
12\r\nThe file is \r\n
16\r\n3,400 bytes long\r\n
0\r\n\r\n
```

Relying on previous definitions we model chunked messages by defining the languages $L^{\sharp}_{chunk} \stackrel{\text{def}}{=} (L^{\sharp}_{len}\ \{\sharp\})^{+}$ and $L^{\sharp}_{chunk}(n) \stackrel{\text{def}}{=} (L_{len}(n)\ \{\sharp\})^{+}$ for unbounded and fixed (given by n) length field size, respectively. We further assume $\sharp \notin W$ and $\Sigma = B \cup W \cup \{\sharp\}$ to recognize the end of each chunk and thus avoid ambiguity.

Next, we turn to the claims found in the literature [7] about the impossibility of specifying chunked messages using CFLs.

Theorem 7. *$L^{\sharp}_{chunk}$ is not a finite intersection of CFLs.*

Theorem 8. *Let Σ be a fixed alphabet and $n > 0$. The language $L^{\sharp}_{chunk}(n)$ is regular and can be specified by a context-free grammar of size $\mathcal{O}(n)$.*

4 Formal Analysis of (In)equalities

Input validation sometimes requires comparing different parts of a message, e.g., to check that two subwords are identical or that the first one represents a number or a date that is greater than the second one. For instance, an HTTP GET message is valid only if the field `last-byte-pos` is greater than `first-byte-pos`.

4.1 Equality Check

Consider the case of HTTP when a client is asking for a transition to some other protocol. As the standard of mandates, equality should hold between the `Upgrade` fields of the request and its response.

```
======== REQUEST ========      ======== RESPONSE ========
GET /example HTTP/1.1\r\n      HTTP/1.1 101 Switching Protocols\r\n
Upgrade: h2c\r\n               Connection: Upgrade\r\n
                               Upgrade: h2c\r\n
```

Modeling Equality Check. We begin our study of comparisons with the case of two contiguous subwords compared for equality. To this end consider the following language over alphabet Σ given by

$$L^{\sharp}_{=} \stackrel{\text{def}}{=} \{x \sharp y \mid x = y\}.$$

This language consists of twice the same word with '$\sharp$' in between. Again, we assume $\sharp$ occurs in x for no x.

When the size of the words x and y is fixed, the delimiter is no longer needed. Thus, we define $L_{=}(n)$

$$L_{=}(n) \stackrel{\text{def}}{=} \{x\, y \mid x, y \in \Sigma^{n}\ \wedge\ x = y\}.$$

Unbounded Size. We now consider the case where the length of the subwords to compare is unbounded. The example at the top of the section requires, when validating a request-response pair of HTTP messages, to check equality across `Upgrade` fields.

This situation is described by the language $L^{\sharp}_{=}$. Next, we recall results by Liu and Weiner [17] and Brough [5] enabling us to show that $L^{\sharp}_{=}$ is not a finite intersection of context-free languages.

Proposition 9 ([5, Proposition 2.1]). *For every $k > 0$, the set of languages that are an intersection of k CFLs is closed under (i) inverse GSM mappings, and (ii) union with context-free languages.*

Theorem 10 ([17, Theorem 8]). *Let $a_1, \dots a_k$ be $k > 0$ distinct symbols. Then $L_{(k)} \stackrel{\text{def}}{=} \{a_1^{i_1}a_2^{i_2}\dots a_k^{i_k}a_1^{i_1}a_2^{i_2}\dots a_k^{i_k} \mid i_j \geq 0 \text{ for all } j\}$ is an intersection of ℓ context-free languages for* ***no*** *$\ell < k$.*

We are now in position to prove our impossibility result about $L^{\sharp}_{=}$.

Theorem 11. *$L^{\sharp}_{=}$ is not a finite intersection of CFLs.*

Proof (Sketch.). For the proof sketch we deliberately ignore the delimiter.

Assume $L_{=}$ (the delimiterless version of $L^{\sharp}_{=}$) is an intersection of m CFLs. Now observe that $L_{(k)} = L_{=} \cap a_1^* a_2^* \dots a_k^* a_1^* a_2^* \dots a_k^*$ This implies $L_{(k)}$ is an intersection of $m+1$ context-free languages, which contradicts Theorem 10 for $k > m+1$. □

Fixed Size. Because of the negative result of Theorem 11 we turn back again to the restriction assuming an upper bound on the length of the subwords to compare. We argue next that, in practice, such a restriction is reasonable.

Consider the following HTTP message.

```
HTTP/1.1 200 OK\r\n
Date: Sat, 25 Aug 2012 23:34:45 GMT\r\n
Warning: 112 -"Net down" "Sat, 25 Aug 2012 23:34:45 GMT"\r\n
```

The RFC mandates that the date in the `Warning` header be equal to `Date`. Since date formats have bounded length we immediately have an upper bound of the length of the subwords to compare.

Another example is given by the MIME protocol which allows to split messages into multiple parts provided they are flanked by a user-defined delimiter string. Let us consider an example:

```
MIME-Version: 1.0\r\n
Content-type: multipart/mixed; boundary="Mydelimiter"\r\n\r\n
PREAMBLE to be ignored\r\n--Mydelimiter\r\n
Plain ASCII text.\r\n--Mydelimiter\r\n
Plain ASCII text.\r\n--Mydelimiter--\r\n
EPILOGUE to be ignored.\r\n
```

Observe that the delimiter is first declared, `boundary="Mydelimiter"`, and then `Mydelimiter` is used three times, the first two times as `--Mydelimiter` the last time as `--Mydelimiter--`.

Equality checks can ensure each part is flanked with the same delimiter. In the case of MIME, the standard [12] imposes a maximum length of 69 symbols for the delimiter giving us an upper bound.

Equality checks for a fixed number n of symbols are specified by $L_{=}(n)$. For every n, the language $L_{=}(n)$ is finite, hence regular. Nonetheless Theorem 12, due to Filmus [10], states that this language has no "compact" specification as a grammar.[1] Still it can be represented "compactly" as a finite intersection of CFLs, as shown by Theorem 13. In this section we will study the size of different grammars assuming the alphabet Σ is fixed and, thus, $|\Sigma|$ is a constant.

Theorem 12 ([10, Theorem 7]). *Let $|\Sigma| > 2$, every context-free grammar for $L_{=}(n)$ has size*

$$\Omega\left(\frac{|\Sigma|^{n/4}}{\sqrt{2n}}\right).$$

Recall that $f(n) = \Omega(g(n))$ means that f is bounded from below[2] by g for sufficiently large n, which implies that context-free grammars for $L_{=}(n)$ exhibit exponential growth in n.

Our next theorem based on the observation that $x = y$ iff $(x)_i = (y)_i$ for all i allows to capture $L_{=}(n)$ as a intersection of n CFLs.

Theorem 13. *Let the alphabet Σ be fixed, the language $L_{=}(n)$ is an intersection of n CFLs, each of which is specified by a grammar of size $\mathcal{O}(n)$.*

Proof. Given $i \in \{1, \ldots, n\}$, define the language $L_{=_i}(n)$ over the alphabet Σ given by

$$L_{=_i}(n) \stackrel{\text{def}}{=} \{x\, y \mid x, y \in \Sigma^n,\ (x)_i = (y)_i\}.$$

Clearly, for every word u we have $u \in L_{=}(n)$ iff $u \in L_{=_i}(n)$ for all $i \in \{1, \ldots, n\}$. Next, define $G_{=_i}$ as the grammar for $L_{=_i}(n)$ with variables S and T, alphabet Σ and the rules: $\{S \to T^{i-1}\, c\, T^{n-1}\, c\, T^{n-i} \mid c \in \Sigma\}$, $\{T \to c \mid c \in \Sigma\}$. It is routine to check that the size of the grammar is $\mathcal{O}(n)$. □

Above, we studied specification of equality checks for two contiguous subwords. In practice, however, comparisons are often more general. In the previous HTTP example, the dates to compare for equality are not necessarily contiguous. Also, to specify the split messages of MIME using equality checks we need to generalize to the cases where equality covers more than two subwords (each of the multiple parts is flanked with the same delimiter) and those are not necessarily contiguous (some parts are non empty).

We show this generalization of equality checks can still be specified concisely by a finite intersection of CFLs.

[1] This implies it has no "compact" specification by a finite state automaton either.
[2] $f(n) = \Omega(g(n))$ iff $\exists$ positive c, n_0 s.t. $\forall n > n_0,\ f(n) \geq c \cdot g(n)$.

4.2 Inequality Checks

Thus far, we have focused on languages whose words consist of two equal subwords. However, comparisons sometimes require that the first subword represents a lower number than the second or an earlier date. The following request is asking for bytes of `BigBuckBunny.mp4` between offsets `2833` and `7026`. To be valid the requested range should describe a non empty set.

```
GET /BigBuckBunny.mp4\r\n
Range: bytes=2833-7026\r\n
```

Modeling Inequality Checks. Let $\preceq$ define a total order on Σ. We extend $\preceq$ to Σ^* and denote it $\preceq^*$ as follows. We first define $\preceq^*$ when its arguments have equal length, then we proceed with the general case.

Given $x, y \in S^*$ of equal length, let p be the least position such that $(x)_p \neq (y)_p$. Then $(x)_p \preceq (y)_p$ iff $x \preceq^* y$. Otherwise (no such position p exists) we also have $x \preceq^* y$ since the two words are equal.

Let us now proceed to the case where x and y have different length and assume x is the shortest of the two words (the other case is treated similarly). Then we have $x \preceq^* y$ iff $x' \preceq^* y$ where $x' = \min_{\preceq}(\Sigma)^{|y|-|x|}x$, that is x' is the result of padding x with the minimal element of Σ so that the resulting word and y have equal length. For instance, $5 \preceq^* 21$ because $05 \preceq^* 21$ where Σ is the set of all digits and $\preceq$ is defined as expected. It is an easy exercise to check that $\preceq^*$ is a total order (hint: $\preceq$ is a total order).

Unbounded Size. Let us turn back to the `Range` field example at the top of the section. To specify the language of valid ranges, since the two subwords are unbounded, a delimiter is needed to indicate the end of the first word. In our example the delimiter is the dash symbol.

Next we define $L^{\sharp}_{\preceq}$, the language deciding unbounded size inequality check using $\sharp$ as a delimiter, as follows:

$$L^{\sharp}_{\preceq} \stackrel{\text{def}}{=} \{x \sharp y \mid x, y \in \Sigma^*,\ x \preceq^* y\}.$$

Theorem 14. *The language $L^{\sharp}_{\preceq}$ is not a finite intersection of CFLs.*

Proof. We begin by defining the order $\succeq$ over Σ as $\preceq^{-1}$ and define $\succeq^*$ by replacing $\preceq$ with $\succeq$ in the definition of $\preceq^*$. Clearly $a \preceq b$ iff $b \succeq a$ holds, hence there exists a permutation γ on Σ. Indeed, we can write Σ as the set $\{a_1, \ldots, a_n\}$ such that $a_i \preceq a_j$ iff $i \leq j$. Now define $\gamma\colon a_i \mapsto a_{n+1-i}$. It follows that $a \preceq b$ iff $\gamma(a) \succeq \gamma(b)$. The previous equivalence naturally lifts to words ($\preceq^*$ and $\succeq^*$), e.g. $v \preceq^* w$ iff $\gamma(v) \succeq^* \gamma(w)$.

Next define

$$L^{\sharp}_{\succeq} \stackrel{\text{def}}{=} \{x \sharp y \mid x, y \in \Sigma^*,\ x \succeq^* y\}.$$

Notice that the following equality holds: $L^{\sharp}_{\succeq} = \{\gamma(x) \sharp \gamma(y) \mid x \sharp y \in L^{\sharp}_{\preceq}\}$. Stated equivalently, $\gamma(L^{\sharp}_{\preceq}) = L^{\sharp}_{\succeq}$ where γ is lifted to be a language homomorphism and also $L^{\sharp}_{\preceq} = \gamma^{-1}(L^{\sharp}_{\succeq})$ since γ is a bijection.

Following Proposition 9 (i) finite intersections of CFLs are closed under inverse GSM mapping. This implies that they are also closed under inverse homomorphism such as γ^{-1}.

Assume $L^{\sharp}_{\preceq}$ is a finite intersection of CFLs. It follows from above that so is $L^{\sharp}_{\succeq}$. Finally, consider the equivalence $v = w$ iff $v \preceq^* w$ and $v \succeq^* w$. Lifted to the languages the previous equivalence becomes: $L^{\sharp}_{=} = L^{\sharp}_{\preceq} \cap L^{\sharp}_{\succeq}$.

Since both $L^{\sharp}_{\preceq}$ and $L^{\sharp}_{\succeq}$ are finite intersection of CFLs we conclude that so is $L^{\sharp}_{=}$ which contradicts Theorem 11. □

Fixed Size. With the same motives as for equality checks we turn to the case in which the size of the words to be compared is fixed, say n. As opposed to the unbounded case, we can discard the delimiter because n – the last position of the first word – is known. The message below illustrates an inequality check between fixed size subwords.

```
HTTP/1.1 304 Not Modified\r\n
Date: Tue, 29 Mar 2016 09:05:57 GMT\r\n
Last-Modified: Wed, 24 Feb 2016 15:23:38 GMT\r\n
```

To ensure that this response is valid the `Last-Modified` field must contain a date earlier than the `Date` field.

Let $n > 0$, we define $L_{\preceq}(n)$ to be:

$$L_{\preceq}(n) \stackrel{\text{def}}{=} \{x\, y \mid x, y \in \Sigma^n,\ x \preceq^* y\}.$$

Theorem 15. *Let the alphabet Σ be fixed and $n > 0$, $L_{\preceq}(n)$ is a boolean combination of $2n$ languages each one specified by a grammar of size $\mathcal{O}(n)$.*

Proof. Let $G_{=_i}$ be the grammars used in the proof of Theorem 13 and let $G_{\preceq_i}$ a grammar for the language $L_{\preceq_i}(n) \stackrel{\text{def}}{=} \{x\, y \mid x, y \in \Sigma^n,\ (x)_i \preceq (y)_i\}$. Then, by definition of the order $\preceq$ over Σ^n, we write

$$w \in L_{\preceq}(n) \Leftrightarrow w \in L_{=_{1..n}}(n) \bigvee_{i=1}^{n} \left(w \in L_{=_{1..i-1}}(n) \wedge w \notin L_{=_i}(n) \wedge w \in L_{\preceq_i}(n)\right)$$

where $w \in L_{=_{1..i}}(n)$ is equivalent to $w \in \bigcap_{j=1}^{i} L_{=_j}(n)$.

The size of each grammar $G_{=_i}$ was shown to be $\mathcal{O}(n)$. On the other hand, each grammar $G_{\preceq_i}$ is defined by the alphabet Σ, variables S, T and $\{T_a \mid a \in \Sigma\}$ and the rules:

$$\{S \to T^{i-1}\, a\, T^{n-1}\, T_a\, T^{n-i} \mid a \in \Sigma\} \quad \{T_a \to c \mid c \in \Sigma, a \preceq c\} \quad \{T \to c \mid c \in \Sigma\}.$$

It is routine to check that the size of the grammar is $\mathcal{O}(n)$. □

The language $L_{\preceq}(n)$ can be extended to describe the situation in which x and y represent dates and $\preceq$ means "earlier than". To this end, whenever the month is given by its name instead of the number thereof we should read it as a single symbol, considering each one as an element of the alphabet. Otherwise, a comparison between numbers as described in proof of Theorem 15 will work. Once we know how to compare the years, months, and days of two dates, combining them to construct the language comparing two dates is straightforward.

5 Practical Evaluation

The results given in Sects. 3 and 4 characterize the extent to which (intersections of) CFL can be used to specify common idioms of network protocols. In this section, we demonstrate that the positive theoretical results can be turned into practical input validators for real-world network protocols. We begin by discussing practical encoding issues, before we present an input validator for HTTP.

5.1 Encoding Real-World Protocols as CFG

Encoding Effort. The manual effort of translating protocol specification into grammars is facilitated by the RFC format: Protocol RFCs usually consist of a grammar accompanied by a list of additional constraints written in English. This grammar is typically given in ABNF format [6] which easily translates to a context-free grammar. The additional constraints translate to regular expressions or CFGs, along the lines described in this paper. Then the set of valid messages of the protocol is described by a boolean combination of small CFLs.

Encoding Size. The grammars required to perform the validation against the idioms discussed in this paper remain small even for real-world protocols:

Length Fields. The CFG for $L_{len}(n)$ consists of $3n+2$ rules, i.e. it grows linearly in the size of the length field. This implies that it grows only *logarithmically* with the size of the message body, which makes the CFG encoding practical for real-world scenarios.

Comparisons. To compare two strings of length n we need $2n$ grammars each with no more than $3|\Sigma|$ rules where $|\Sigma|$ is the size of the alphabet. In practice, n is small because it is the length of the encoding of a position within a file, a timestamp, a hash value,...

5.2 An Input Validator for HTTP

Next we report on HTTPValidator [24], a proof of concept implementation to validate HTTP messages based on mere CFGs and regular expressions, without using attributes nor semantic actions.

Why HTTP? First, HTTP contains almost all of the features that have been used in the literature [4,21] to dispute the suitability of CFLs for parsing network protocols. Second, HTTP is a widely used and complex protocol, making it an ideal testbed for our approach. Finally, HTTPolice [8] is a lint for HTTP messages which checks them for conformance to standards and best practices and provides a reference for comparison.

HTTP as CFG. The ABNF described by the standard [9] is translated into a single CFG while constraints such as "A client MUST send a Host header field in all HTTP/1.1 request messages." and "A client MUST NOT send the chunked transfer coding name in TE" are translated into regular expressions and CFGs.

Implementation. Regular expressions and grammars are compiled with Flex and Bison respectively. We avoid conflicts altogether by relying on the `%glr-parser` declaration, which forces Bison to produce a generalized LR parser[3] that copes with unresolved conflicts without altering the specified language. Finally, a script runs all these validators sequentially and combines their boolean outputs to conclude the validation. Table 1 describes the sizes of each separate element of our validator. Further details can be found in the repository [24].

Table 1. Sizes of the formal languages required to validate an HTTP message

Feature	Size
HTTP ABNF as a CFG	1013 grammar rules
Decimal length field of size up to 80	871 grammar rules
Comparison of version numbers	3 grammars with 13 grammar rules each
Constraints (91 different ones)	260 regular expressions

Evaluation. We evaluate HTTPValidator on messages obtained from real-world traffic (using Wireshark) and on messages provided with HTTPolice as test cases. In total we thus obtain 239 test cases of which HTTPolice classifies 116 as valid and 123 as invalid HTTP. We run HTTPValidator on these test cases obtaining the same classification as HTTPolice but for two false positives. These errors are due to well-formedness checks on message bodies in JSON and XML format, which we currently do not consider in HTTPValidator but HTTPolice does.

The time required for evaluating all test cases[4] is 16.1 s for HTTPValidator and 60 s for HTTPolice, i.e. we achieve a 4-fold speedup. Note that this comparison is slightly biased towards HTTPValidator because HTTPolice relies on interpreted Python code whereas the parsers in HTTValidator are compiled to native code. Moreover, we store each of the test cases in a single file, forgoing HTTPolice's ability to process several HTTP messages in a single file. On

[3] https://www.gnu.org/software/bison/manual/html_node/GLR-Parsers.html.

[4] We run our experiments on an Intel Core i5-5200U CPU 2.20 GHz with 8 GB RAM.

the other hand, we have put ease of implementation before performance so no parallelization has been implemented so far.

Overall, the experimental evaluation shows that, on our testbed, HTTPValidator achieves coverage and performance that is competitive with the state-of-the-art in the field, thereby demonstrating the practicality of our approach.

6 Related Work

We discussed related work on language theory and input validation in the paper body. Here we focus on discussing recent efforts for building parser generators for network protocols.

In recent years, a number of parser generators for network protocols have emerged. They are often parts of larger projects, but can be used in a stand-alone fashion. Important representatives are BinPac [21], which is part of the Bro Network Security Monitor[5], UltraPac [16], which is part of the NetShield Monitor, Gapa [4], FlowSifter [18], and Nail [2]. The difference to our approach is that they are all are built from scratch, whereas we rely on established CFG parsing technology. Moreover, they rely on user-provided code for parsing idioms such as length fields, whereas we specify everything in terms of (intersections of) CFG. However, we emphasize that the focus of our approach lies on the task of *input validation*, whereas those approaches deal with *parsing*, i.e. they additionally fill a data structure.

Among the previous parser generators, Gapa and Nail stand out in terms of their safety features. Gapa achieves a degree of safety by generating parsers in a memory-safe language. Note that this does not prevent runtime error, e.g., dividing by zero still remains possible. Nail also aims at safety by providing some automated support for filling user-defined data structure therefore reducing the risk of errors introduced by user-defined code. In contrast, we do not rely on any user-provided code.

Another line of work [7] relies on the use of the so-called attribute grammars, an extension of context-free grammar that equips rules with attributes that can be accessed and manipulated. For the parser generator, the authors use Bison and encode the attribute aspect of grammars through user-defined C code annotating the grammar rules which, as we argued before, augments the risk of errors.

7 Conclusions and Future Work

Input validation is an important step for defending against malformed or malicious inputs. In this paper we perform the first rigorous, language theoretic study of the expressiveness required for validating a number of common protocol idioms. We further show that input validation based on formal languages is practical and build a modular input validator for HTTP from dependable

[5] https://www.bro.org/.

software components such as off-the-shelf parser generators for context-free languages. Our experimental result shows that our approach is competitive with the state-of-the-art input validator for HTTP in terms of coverage and speed.

There are some promising avenues for extending our work. For instance our approach can be generalized to boolean closures of CFLs, which are known to be strictly more expressive than the finite intersection we deal with in this paper [5]. Besides, our approach can be extended with a notion of state that is shared between protocol participants which will allow us to implement, e.g., stateful firewalls using our approach.

Acknowledgments. We thank Juan Caballero for feedback on an early version of this paper. This work was supported by Ramón y Cajal grant RYC-2014-16766, Spanish projects TIN2015-70713-R DEDETIS, TIN2015-71819-P RISCO, TIN2012-39391-C04-01 StrongSoft, and Madrid regional project S2013/ICE-2731 N-GREENS.

References

1. Internet Protocol. RFC 791 (Proposed Standard), September 1981
2. Bangert, J., Zeldovich, N.: Nail: a practical tool for parsing and generating data formats. In: 11th USENIX Symposium on Operating Systems Design and Implementation (2014)
3. Bernardy, J.-P., Jansson, P.: Certified context-free parsing: a formalisation of valiant's algorithm in agda. Logical Methods Comput. Sci. **12**(2) (2016)
4. Borisov, N., Brumley, D., Wang, H.J., Dunagan, J., Joshi, P., Guo, C.: Generic application-level protocol analyzer and its language. In: NDSS 2007 (2007)
5. Brough, T.: Groups with poly-context-free word problem. Groups Complexity Cryptol. **6**(1) (2014)
6. Crocker, P.D. (ed.): Brandenburg InternetWorking. Augmented BNF for Syntax Specifications: ABNF. RFC 5234 (Proposed Standard), January 2008
7. Davidson, D., Smith, R., Doyle, N., Jha, S.: Protocol normalization using attribute grammars. In: Backes, M., Ning, P. (eds.) ESORICS 2009. LNCS, vol. 5789, pp. 216–231. Springer, Heidelberg (2009). doi:10.1007/978-3-642-04444-1_14
8. Faronov, V.: HTTPolice (2017). https://github.com/vfaronov/httpolice
9. Fielding, R., Reschke, J.: Hypertext Transfer Protocol (HTTP/1.1): Message Syntax and Routing. RFC 7230 (Proposed Standard), June 2014
10. Filmus, Y.: Lower bounds for context-free grammars. Inf. Process. Lett. **111**(18) (2011)
11. Firsov, D., Uustalu, T.: Certified CYK parsing of context-free languages. J. Logical Algebraic Methods Program. **83**(5–6) (2014)
12. Freed, N., Borenstein, N.: Multipurpose internet mail extensions (MIME). RFC 1341 (Proposed Standard), November 1996
13. Graham-Cumming, J.: Inside shellshock: How hackers are using it to exploit systems. https://blog.cloudflare.com/inside-shellshock/
14. Lastpass security updates. https://blog.lastpass.com/2016/07/lastpass-security-updates.html/
15. Latteux, M.: Intersections de langages algébriques bornés. Acta Informatica **11**(3) (1979)

16. Li, Z., Xia, G., Gao, H., Tang, Y., Chen, Y., Liu, B., Jiang, J., Lv, Y.: NetShield: massive semantics-based vulnerability signature matching for high-speed networks. In: ACM SIGCOMM 2010 (2010)
17. Liu, L.Y., Weiner, P.: An infinite hierarchy of intersections of context-free languages. Math. Syst. Theory **7**(2) (1973)
18. Meiners, C.R., Norige, E., Liu, A.X., Torng, E.: Flowsifter: a counting automata approach to layer 7 field extraction for deep flow inspection. In: IEEE INFOCOM 2012 (2012)
19. Microsoft releases security advisory 2953095. https://technet.microsoft.com/library/security/2953095
20. Mockapetris, P.: Domain Names - Implementation and Specification. RFC 1035 (Proposed Standard), November 1987
21. Pang, R., Paxson, V., Sommer, R., Peterson, L.L.: Binpac: a Yacc for writing application protocol parsers. In: ACM SIGCOMM IMC 2006 (2006)
22. Postel, J.: User Datagram Protocol. RFC 768 (Proposed Standard), August 1980
23. Rosenberg, J., Schulzrinne, H., Camarillo, G., Johnston, A., Peterson, J., Sparks, R., Handley, M., Schooler, E.: SIP: Session Initiation Protocol. RFC 3261 (Proposed Standard), June 2002
24. Valero, P.: HTTPValidator, April 2017. https://github.com/pevalme/HTTPValidator
25. Ganty, P., Köpf, B., Valero, P.: A Language-theoretic View on Network Protocols (2016). (long version). Pre-print arXiv: https://arxiv.org/abs/1610.07198

Efficient Strategy Iteration for Mean Payoff in Markov Decision Processes

Jan Křetínský and Tobias Meggendorfer(✉)

Technical University of Munich, Munich, Germany
tobias.meggendorfer@in.tum.de

Abstract. Markov decision processes (MDPs) are standard models for probabilistic systems with non-deterministic behaviours. Mean payoff (or long-run average reward) provides a mathematically elegant formalism to express performance related properties. Strategy iteration is one of the solution techniques applicable in this context. While in many other contexts it is the technique of choice due to advantages over e.g. value iteration, such as precision or possibility of domain-knowledge-aware initialization, it is rarely used for MDPs, since there it scales worse than value iteration. We provide several techniques that speed up strategy iteration by orders of magnitude for many MDPs, eliminating the performance disadvantage while preserving all its advantages.

1 Introduction

Markov decision processes (MDPs) [19,28,34] are a standard model for analysis of systems featuring both probabilistic and non-deterministic behaviour. They have found rich applications, ranging from communication protocols to biological systems and robotics. A classical objective to be optimized in MDPs is *mean payoff* (or *long-run average reward*). It captures the reward we can achieve on average per step when simulating the MDP. Technically, one considers partial averages (average over the first n steps) and let the time n go to infinity. This objective can be used to describe performance properties of systems, for example, average throughput, frequency of errors, average energy consumption, etc.

Strategy (or *policy*) *iteration* (or *improvement*) (SI) is a dynamic-programming technique applicable in many settings, including optimization of mean payoff in MDPs [28,34], but also mean payoff games [6,9], parity games [17,33,35,38], simple stochastic games [11], concurrent reachability games [25], or stochastic parity games [24]. The main principle of the technique is to start with an arbitrary strategy (or policy or controller of the system) and iteratively improve it locally in a greedy fashion until no more improvements can be done. The resulting strategy is guaranteed to be optimal.

SI has several advantages compared to other techniques used in these contexts. Most interestingly, domain knowledge or heuristics can be used to *initialize*

This work is partially supported by the German Research Foundation (DFG) project "Verified Model Checkers" and the Czech Science Foundation grant No. 15-17564S.

D. D'Souza and K. Narayan Kumar (Eds.): ATVA 2017, LNCS 10482, pp. 380–399, 2017.
DOI: 10.1007/978-3-319-68167-2_25

with a reasonable strategy, thus speeding up the computation to a fraction of the usual analysis time. Further, SI is conceptually simple as it boils down to a search through a *finite space* of memoryless deterministic strategies, yielding arguments for correctness and termination of the algorithm.

More specifically, in the context of MDPs, it has advantages over the other two standard techniques. Firstly, compared to *linear programming* (LP), SI *scales* much better. LP provides a rich framework, which is able to encode many optimization problems on MDPs and in particular mean payoff. However, although the linear programs are typically of polynomial size and can be also solved in polynomial time, such procedures are not very useful in practice. For larger systems the solvers often time out or run out of memory already during the construction of the linear program. Furthermore, SI ensures that the current lower bounds on the mean payoff is *monotonically improving*. Consequently, the iteration can be stopped at any point, yielding a strategy at least as good as all previous iterations.

Secondly, compared to *value iteration* (VI), SI provides a *precise solution*, whereas VI is only optimal in the limit and the number of iterations before the numbers can be rounded in order to obtain a precise solution is very high [10]. Furthermore, stopping criteria for VI are limited to special cases or are very inefficient. Consequently, VI is practically used to produce results that may be erroneous even for simple, realistic examples in verification, see e.g. [23].

On the other hand, the main disadvantage of SI, in particular for mean payoff, is its *scalability*. Although SI scales better than LP, it is only rarely the case that SI is faster than VI. Firstly, in the worst case, we have to examine *exponentially* many strategies [15], in contrast to the discounted case, which is polynomial (for a fixed discount factor) [39] even for games [26]. However, note that even for parity games it was for long not known [21] whether all SI algorithms exhibit this property since the number of improvements is only rarely high in practice. Secondly, and more importantly, the *evaluation* of each strategy necessary for the greedy improvement takes enormous time since large systems of linear equations have to be solved. Consequently, VI typically is much faster than SI to obtain a similar precision, although it may also need an exponential number of updates.

This scalability limitation is even more pronounced by the following contrast. On the one hand, mean payoff games, parity games, and simple stochastic games are not known to be solvable in polynomial time, hence the exponential-time SI is an acceptable technique for these models. On the other hand, for problems on MDPs that are solvable in polynomial time, such as mean payoff, the exponential-time SI becomes less appealing. In summary, we can only afford to utilize the mentioned advantages of SI for MDPs if we make SI perform well in practice.

This paper suggest several heuristics and opens new directions to increase performance of SI for MDPs, in particular in the setting of mean payoff. Our contribution is the following:

- We present several techniques to significantly speed up SI in many cases, most importantly the evaluation of the current strategy. The first set of techniques (in Sect. 4) is based on maximal end component decomposition of the

MDP and strongly connected component decomposition of the Markov chain induced by the MDP and the currently considered strategy. The second class (in Sect. 5) is based on approximative techniques to compute mean payoff in these Markov chains. Both variants reduce the time taken by the strategy evaluation. Finally, we combine the two approaches in a non-trivial way in Sect. 5.1, giving rise to synergic optimizations and opening the door for approximation techniques.
- We provide experimental evaluation of the proposed techniques and compare to the approaches from literature. We show experimental evidence that our techniques are speeding up SI by orders of magnitude and make its performance (i) on par with VI, the prevalent technique which, however, only provides approximate solutions, and (ii) incomparably more scalable than the precise technique of LP.

Further related work. Strategy iteration for MDPs has been extensively studied [16,28,34]. Performance of SI for MDPs has been mainly improved in the discounted total reward case by, e.g., approximate evaluation of the strategy using iterative methods of linear algebra [36], model reduction by adaptive state-space aggregation [1] or close-to-optimal initialization [20]; for an overview see [5]. The treatment of the undiscounted case has focused on unichain MDPs [27,34]. Apart from solving the MDPs modelling probabilistic systems, the technique has found its applications in other domains, too, for example program analysis [22].

2 Preliminaries

In this section, we introduce some central notions. Furthermore, relevant technical notions from linear algebra can be found in [30, Appendix A].

A *probability distribution* on a finite set X is a mapping $\rho : X \to [0,1]$, such that $\sum_{x \in X} \rho(x) = 1$. Its *support* is denoted by $supp(\rho) = \{x \in X \mid \rho(x) > 0\}$. $\mathcal{D}(X)$ denotes the set of all probability distributions on X.

Definition 1. *A* Markov chain (MC) *is a tuple* $\mathsf{M} = (S, s_{init}, \Delta, r)$, *where* S *is a finite set of* states, $s_{init} \in S$ *is the* initial *state,* $\Delta : S \to \mathcal{D}(S)$ *is a* transition function *that for each state* s *yields a probability distribution over successor states and* $r : S \to \mathbb{R}^{\geq 0}$ *is a* reward function, *assigning rewards to states.*

Definition 2. *A* Markov decision process (MDP) *is a tuple of the form* $\mathcal{M} = (S, s_{init}, Act, \mathsf{Av}, \Delta, r)$, *where* S *is a finite set of* states, $s_{init} \in S$ *is the* initial *state,* Act *is a finite set of* actions, $\mathsf{Av} : S \to 2^{Act}$ *assigns to every state a set of* available *actions,* $\Delta : S \times Act \to \mathcal{D}(S)$ *is a* transition function *that for each state* s *and action* $a \in \mathsf{Av}(s)$ *yields a probability distribution over successor states and* $r : S \times Act \to \mathbb{R}^{\geq 0}$ *is a* reward function, *assigning rewards to state-action pairs.*

Furthermore, we assume w.l.o.g. that actions are unique for each state, i.e. $\mathsf{Av}(s) \cap \mathsf{Av}(s') = \emptyset$ *for* $s \neq s'$.[1]

[1] The usual procedure of achieving this in general is to replace Act by $S \times Act$ and adapting Av, Δ, and r appropriately.

For ease of notation, we overload functions mapping to distributions $f : Y \to \mathcal{D}(X)$ by $f : Y \times X \to [0,1]$, where $f(y,x) := f(y)(x)$. For example, instead of $\Delta(s)(s')$ and $\Delta(s,a)(s')$ we write $\Delta(s,s')$ and $\Delta(s,a,s')$, respectively. Further, given some MC M, a function $f : S \to \mathbb{R}$ and set of states $C \subseteq S$, we define $\mathbb{E}^C_\Delta(f,s) := \sum_{s' \in C} \Delta(s,s') f(s')$, i.e. the weighted sum of f over all the successors of s in C. Analogously, for some MDP $\mathcal{M}$, we set $\mathbb{E}^C_\Delta(f,s,a) := \sum_{s' \in C} \Delta(s,a,s') f(s')$. Further, we define $\mathbb{E}_\Delta(f,s) := \mathbb{E}^S_\Delta(f,s)$ and $\mathbb{E}_\Delta(f,s,a) := \mathbb{E}^S_\Delta(f,s,a)$.

An *infinite path* ρ in a Markov chain is an infinite sequence $\rho = s_0 s_1 \cdots \in S^\omega$, such that for every $i \in \mathbb{N}$ we have that $\Delta(s_i, s_{i+1}) > 0$. A *finite path* $w = s_0 s_1 \ldots s_n \in S^*$ is a finite prefix of an infinite path. Similarly, an *infinite path* in an MDP is some infinite sequence $\rho = s_0 a_0 s_1 a_1 \cdots \in (S \times Act)^\omega$, such that for every $i \in \mathbb{N}$, $a_i \in \mathsf{Av}(s_i)$ and $\Delta(s_i, a_i, s_{i+1}) > 0$. *Finite paths* are defined analogously as elements of $(S \times Act)^* \times S$.

A Markov chain together with a state s induces a unique probability distribution $\mathbb{P}_s$ over measurable sets of infinite paths [3, Chapter 10]. For some $C \subseteq S$, we write $\Diamond C$ to denote the set of all paths which eventually reach C, i.e. $\Diamond C = \{\rho = s_0 s_1 \cdots \mid \exists i \in \mathbb{N}.\ s_i \in C\}$, which is measurable [3, Sect. 10.1.1].

A *strategy* on an MDP is a function $\pi : (S \times Act)^* \times S \to \mathcal{D}(Act)$, which given a finite path $w = s_0 a_0 s_1 a_1 \ldots s_n$ yields a probability distribution $\pi(w) \in \mathcal{D}(\mathsf{Av}(s_n))$ on the actions to be taken next. We call a strategy *memoryless randomized* (or *stationary*) if it is of the form $\pi : S \to \mathcal{D}(Act)$, and *memoryless deterministic* (or *positional*) if it is of the form $\pi : S \to Act$. We denote the set of all strategies of an MDP by Π, and the set of all memoryless deterministic strategies as Π^{MD}. Note that Π^{MD} is finite, since at each state there exist only finitely many actions to choose from. Fixing any positional strategy π induces a Markov chain where $\Delta(s,s') = \sum_{s \in \mathsf{Av}(s)} \pi(s,a) \cdot \Delta(s,a,s')$ and $r(s) = \sum_{a \in \mathsf{Av}(s)} \pi(s,a) \cdot r(s,a)$.

Fixing a strategy π and an initial state s on an MDP $\mathcal{M}$ also gives a unique measure $\mathbb{P}^\pi_s$ over infinite paths [34, Sect. 2.1.6]. The expected value of a random variable F then is defined as $\mathbb{E}^\pi_s[F] = \int F \, d\mathbb{P}^\pi_s$.

Strongly Connected Components and End Components. A non-empty set of states $C \subseteq S$ in a Markov chain is *strongly connected* if for every pair $s, s' \in C$ there is a path from s to s', possibly of length zero. Such a set C is a *strongly connected component* (SCC) if it is inclusion maximal, i.e. there exists no strongly connected C' with $C \subsetneq C'$. Note that each state of an MC belongs to exactly one SCC[2]. An SCC is called *bottom strongly connected component* (BSCC) if additionally no path leads out of it, i.e. for $s \in C, s' \in S \setminus C$ we have $\Delta(s,s') = 0$. The set of (B)SCCs in an MC M is denoted by $\mathsf{SCC}(\mathsf{M})$ and $\mathsf{BSCC}(\mathsf{M})$, respectively.

The concept of SCCs is generalized to MDPs by so called *(maximal) end components*. A pair (T, A), where $\emptyset \neq T \subseteq S$ and $\emptyset \neq A \subseteq \bigcup_{s \in T} \mathsf{Av}(s)$, is an *end*

[2] Some authors deliberately exclude so called "trivial" or "transient" SCCs, which are single states without a self-loop.

component of an MDP $\mathcal{M}$ if (i) for all $s \in T, a \in A \cap \mathsf{Av}(s)$ we have $supp(\Delta(s,a)) \subseteq T$, and (ii) for all $s, s' \in T$ there is a finite path $w = sa_0 \dots a_n s' \in (T \times A)^* \times T$, i.e. the path stays inside T and only uses actions in A. Note that we assumed actions to be unique for each state.

Intuitively, an end component describes a set of states for which a particular strategy exists such that all possible paths remain inside these states. An end component (T, A) is a *maximal end component (MEC)* if there is no other end component (T', A') such that $T \subseteq T'$ and $A \subseteq A'$. Given an MDP $\mathcal{M}$, the set of its MECs is denoted by $\mathsf{MEC}(\mathcal{M})$.

Finally, given an MDP $\mathcal{M}$ let $(T, A) \in \mathsf{MEC}(\mathcal{M})$ some MEC in it. By picking some initial state $s'_{\text{init}} \in T$, defining the straightforward restrictions of Av and Δ by $\mathsf{Av}' : T \to 2^A$, $\mathsf{Av}'(s) := \mathsf{Av}(s) \cap A$ and $\Delta' : T \times A \to \mathcal{D}(T)$, $\Delta'(s,a) := \Delta(s,a)$ one obtains the *restricted MDP* $\mathcal{M}' = (T, s'_{\text{init}}, A, \mathsf{Av}', \Delta')$.

Remark 1. For a Markov chain M, the computation of $\mathsf{SCC}(\mathsf{M})$, $\mathsf{BSCC}(\mathsf{M})$ and a topological ordering of the SCCs can be achieved in linear time w.r.t. the number of states and transitions by, e.g., Tarjan's algorithm [37]. Similarly, the MEC decomposition of an MDP can be computed in polynomial time [12].

Long-Run Average Reward. (also called *mean payoff*) of a strategy π intuitively describes the optimal reward we can expect on average per step when simulating the MDP according to π. In the following, we will only consider the case of maximizing the average reward, but the presented methods easily can be transferred to the minimization case.

Formally, let R_i be a random variable which given an infinite path returns the reward obtained at step $i \geq 0$, i.e. for $\rho = s_0 a_0 s_1 a_1 \dots$ we have $R_i(\rho) = r(s_i, a_i)$. Given a strategy π, the n-step (maximal) average reward then is defined as $g_n^\pi(s) = \mathbb{E}_s^\pi(\frac{1}{n}\sum_{i=0}^{n-1} R_i)$. The *long-run average reward* (in this context also traditionally called *gain* [34]) of the strategy π is $g^\pi(s) = \liminf_{n\to\infty} g_n^\pi(s)$.[3] Consequently, the *long-run average reward* (or *gain*) of a state s is defined as

$$g^*(s) := \sup_{\pi \in \Pi} g^\pi(s) = \sup_{\pi \in \Pi} \liminf_{n\to\infty} \mathbb{E}_s^\pi\left(\frac{1}{n}\sum_{i=0}^{n-1} R_i\right).$$

For finite MDPs $g^*(s)$ in fact is attained by a memoryless deterministic strategy $\pi^* \in \Pi^{\mathsf{MD}}$ and it further is the *limit* of the n-step average reward [34]. Formally,

$$g^*(s) = \max_{\pi \in \Pi^{\mathsf{MD}}} g^\pi(s) = \lim_{n\to\infty} g_n^{\pi^*}(s).$$

With this in mind, we now only consider memoryless deterministic strategies.

3 Strategy Iteration

One way of computing the optimal gain of an MDP (i.e. determining the optimal gain of each state) is *strategy iteration* (or *policy iteration* or *strategy*

[3] The lim inf is used since the limit may not exist in general for an arbitrary strategy.

improvement). The general approach of strategy iteration is to (i) fix a strategy, (ii) evaluate it and (iii) improve each choice greedily, repeating the process until no improvement is possible any more. For an in depth theoretical exposé of strategy iteration for MDPs, we refer to e.g. [34, Sect. 9.2]. We briefly recall the necessary definitions.

Gain and Bias. As mentioned, the second step of strategy iteration requires to evaluate a given strategy. By investigating the Markov chain $\mathsf{M} = (S, s_{\text{init}}, \Delta, r)$ induced by the MDP $\mathcal{M}$ together with a strategy $\pi \in \Pi^{\mathsf{MD}}$, one can employ the following system of linear equations characterizing the gain g [34]:

$$g(s) = \sum_{s' \in S} \Delta(s, s') \cdot g(s') = \mathbb{E}_\Delta(g, s) \quad \forall s \in S,$$
$$b(s) = \sum_{s' \in S} \Delta(s, s') \cdot b(s') + r(s) - g(s) = \mathbb{E}_\Delta(b, s) + r(s) - g(s) \quad \forall s \in S.$$

A solution (g, b) to these *gain/bias equations* yields the gain g and the so called *bias* b of the induced Markov chain, which we also refer to as gain g_π and bias b_π of the corresponding strategy π. Intuitively, the bias relates to the total expected deviation from the gain until the obtained rewards "stabilize" to the gain. Note that the equations uniquely determine the gain but not the bias. We refer the reader to [34, Sects. 9.1.1 and 9.2.1] for more detail but highlight the following result. A unique solution can be obtained by adding the constraints $b(s_i) = 0$ for one arbitrary but fixed state s_i in each BSCC [34, Condition 9.2.3]. Note this condition requires to fix the bias of the "first" state in the BSCC to zero. But, as the states can be numbered arbitrarily, any state of the BSCC is eligible. This is also briefly touched upon in the corresponding chapter of [34]. Unfortunately, this results in a non-square system matrix.

With these results, the strategy iteration for the average reward objective on MDPs is defined in Algorithm 1[4]. Reasoning of [34, Sect. 9.2.4] yields correctness.

Theorem 1. *The strategy iteration presented in Algorithm 1 terminates with a correct result for any input MDP.*

It might seem unintuitive why the bias improvement in Line 6 is necessary, since we are only interested in the gain after all. Intuitively, when optimizing the bias the algorithm seeks to improve the expected "bonus" until eventually stabilizing without reducing the obtained gain. This may lead to actually improving the overall gain, as illustrated in [30, Appendix C].

[4] Note that the procedure found in [34, Sect. 9.2.1] differs from our Algorithm in Line 6. There, the bias is improved over all available actions instead of the gain-optimal ones, which is erroneous. The proofs provided in the corresponding chapter actually prove the correctness of the algorithm as presented here.

Algorithm 1. SI

Input: MDP $\mathcal{M} = (S, s_{\text{init}}, Act, \mathsf{Av}, \Delta, r)$.
Output: (g^*, π^*), s.t. g^* is the optimal gain of the MDP and is obtained by π^*.
1: Set $n = 0$ and pick an arbitrary strategy $\pi_0 \in \Pi^{\mathsf{MD}}$.
2: Obtain g_n and b_n which satisfy the gain/bias equations.
3: Let ▷ Gain improvement

$$\mathsf{Av}_{g_n}(s) = \arg\max_{a \in \mathsf{Av}(s)} \mathbb{E}_\Delta(g_n, s, a),$$

all actions maximizing the successor gains.
4: Pick $\pi_{n+1} \in \Pi^{\mathsf{MD}}$ s.t. $\pi_{n+1}(s) \in \mathsf{Av}_{g_n}(s)$, setting $\pi_{n+1}(s) = \pi_n(s)$ if possible.
5: **if** $\pi_{n+1} \neq \pi_n$ **then** increment n by 1 and go to Line 2.
6: Pick $\pi_{n+1} \in \Pi^{\mathsf{MD}}$ which satisfies ▷ Bias improvement

$$\pi_{n+1}(s) \in \arg\max_{a \in \mathsf{Av}_{g_n}(s)} r(s, a) + \mathbb{E}_\Delta(b_n, s, a),$$

again setting $\pi_{n+1}(s) = \pi_n(s)$ if possible.
7: **if** $\pi_{n+1} \neq \pi_n$ **then** increment n by 1 and go to Line 2.
8: **return** (g_{n+1}, π_{n+1}).

Advantages and Drawbacks of Strategy Iteration. Compared to other methods for solving the average reward objective, e.g. value iteration [2,10], strategy iteration offers some advantages:

(i) A *precise solution* can be obtained, compared to value iteration which is only optimal in the limit.
(ii) The gain of the strategy is *monotonically improving*, the iteration can be stopped at any point, yielding a strategy at least as good as the initial one.
(iii) It therefore is easy to *introduce knowledge* about the model or results of some pre-computation by initializing the algorithm with a sensible strategy.
(iv) On some models, strategy iteration performs *significantly faster* than value iteration, as outlined in [30, Appendix B].
(v) The algorithm searches through the *finite space* of memoryless deterministic strategies, simplifying termination and correctness proofs.

But on the other hand, the naive implementation of strategy iteration as presented in Algorithm 1 has several drawbacks:

(i) In order to determine the precise gain by solving the gain/bias equations, one necessarily has to determine the bias, too. Therefore, the algorithm has to determine *both gain and bias* in each step, while often only the gain is actually used for the improvement.
(ii) For reasonably sized models the equation system becomes *intractably large*. In the worst case, it contains $2n^2 + n$ non-zero entries and even for standard models there often are significantly more than n non-zero entries.

(iii) Furthermore, the gain/bias equation system is under-determined, ruling out a lot of fast solution methods for linear equation systems. Uniqueness can be introduced by adding several rows, which results in the matrix being non-square, again ruling out a lot of solution methods. Experimental results suggest that this equation system furthermore has rather large condition numbers (see [30, Appendix A]) even for small, realistic models, leading to numerical instabilities[5].

(iv) Lastly, the equation system is solved *precisely* for every improvement step, which often is unnecessary. To arrive at a precise solution, we often only need to identify states in which the strategy is not optimal, compared to having a precise measure of how non-optimal they are.

In the following two sections, we present approaches and ideas tackling each of the mentioned problems, arriving at procedures which perform orders of magnitude faster than the original approach.

4 Topological Optimizations

Our first set of optimizations is based on various topological arguments about both MDPs and MCs. They are used to eliminate unnecessary redundancies in the equation systems and identify sub-problems which can be solved separately, eventually leading to small, full-rank equation systems. Reduction in size and removal of redundancies naturally lead to significantly better condition numbers, which we also observed in our experiments.

Proofs of our claims can be found in [30, Appendix E].

4.1 MEC Decomposition

We presented a variant of this method in our previous work [2] in the context of value iteration. Due to space constraints we only give a short overview of the idea.

The central idea is that all states in a MEC of some MDP have the same optimal gain [34, Sect. 9.5][6]. Intuitively this is the case since any state in a particular MEC can reach every other state of the MEC almost surely. For some MEC M we define $g^*(M)$ to be this particular optimal value and call it the *gain of the MEC*. The optimal gain of the whole MDP then can be characterized by

$$g^*(s) = \max_{\pi \in \Pi^{\mathsf{MD}}} \sum_{M \in \mathsf{MEC}(\mathcal{M})} \mathbb{P}_s^{\pi}[\Diamond\Box M] \cdot g^*(M)$$

where $\Diamond\Box M$ denotes the measurable set of paths that eventually remain within M. This leads to a divide-and-conquer procedure for determining the gain of an

[5] On crafted models with less than 10 states we observed numerical errors leading to non-convergence and condition numbers of up to 10^5.

[6] Restricting a general MDP to a MEC results in a "communicating" MDP.

Algorithm 2. MEC-SI

Input: MDP $\mathcal{M} = (S, s_{\text{init}}, Act, \mathsf{Av}, \Delta, r)$.
Output: The optimal gain g^* of the MDP.
1: $f \leftarrow \emptyset$, $r_{\max} \leftarrow \max_{s \in S, a \in \mathsf{Av}(s)} r(s, a)$.
2: **for** $M_i = (T_i, A_i) \in \mathsf{MEC}(\mathcal{M})$ **do**
3: Compute $g^*(M_i)$ of the MEC by applying Algorithm 1 on the restricted MDP.
4: Set $f(M_i) \leftarrow g^*(M_i)/r_{\max}$.
5: Compute the weighted MEC quotient $\mathcal{M}^f$.
6: Compute $p \leftarrow \mathbb{P}^{\max}_{\mathcal{M}^f}(\Diamond\{s_+\})$.
7: **return** $r_{\max} \cdot p$

MDP. Conceptually, the algorithm first computes the MEC decomposition [12], then for each MEC M determines its gain $g^*(M)$ by strategy iteration and finally solves a reachability query on the *weighted MEC quotient* $\mathcal{M}^f$ by, e.g., strategy iteration or (interval) value iteration [7,23].

The weighted MEC quotient $\mathcal{M}^f$ is a modification of the standard *MEC quotient* of [13], which for each MEC M introduces an action leading from the collapsed MEC M to a designated target sink s_+ with probability $f(M)$ (which is proportional to $g^*(M)$) and a non-target sink s_- with the remaining probability. With this construction, we can relate the maximal probability of reaching s_+ to the maximal gain in the original MDP. For a formal definition, see [30, Appendix D].

Using this idea, we define the first optimization of strategy iteration in Algorithm 2. Its correctness follows from [2, Theorem 2]. Since we are only concerned with the average reward and each state in the restriction can reach any other (under some strategy), the initial state we pick for the restriction in Line 3 is irrelevant. Note that while the restricted MDP consists of a single MEC, an induced Markov chain may still contain an arbitrary number of (B)SCCs.

This algorithm already performs significantly better on a lot of models, as shown by our experimental evaluation in Sect. 6. But, as to be expected, on models with large MECs this algorithm still is rather slow compared to, e.g., VI and may even add additional overhead when the whole model is a single MEC. To this end, we will improve strategy iteration in general. To combine these optimized variants with the ideas of Algorithm 2, one can simply apply them in Line 3.

4.2 Using Strongly Connected Components

The underlying ideas of the previous approach are independent of the procedure used to determine $g^*(M)$. Naturally, this optimization does not exploit any specific properties of strategy iteration to achieve the improvement. In this section, we will therefore focus on improving the core principle of strategy iteration, namely the evaluation of a particular strategy π on some MDP $\mathcal{M}$. As explained in Sect. 3, this problem is equivalent to determining the gain and bias of some

Markov chain M. Hence we fix such a Markov chain M throughout this section and present optimized methods for determining the required values precisely.

BSCC Compression. In this approach, we try to eliminate superfluous redundancies in the equation system. The basic idea is that all states in some BSCC have the same optimal gain. Moreover, the same gain is achieved in the *attractor* of B, i.e. all states from which almost all runs eventually end up in B.

Definition 3 (Attractor). *Let* M *be some Markov chain and* $C \subseteq S$ *some set of states in* M. *The* attractor *of* C *is defined as*

$$\mathsf{prob1}(C) := \{s \in S \mid \mathbb{P}_s[\Diamond C] = 1\},$$

i.e. the set of states which almost surely eventually reach C.

Lemma 1. *Let* M *be a Markov chain and* B *a BSCC. Then* $g(s) = g(s')$ *for all* $s, s' \in \mathsf{prob1}(B)$.

Proof. When interpreting the MC as a degenerate MDP with $|\mathsf{Av}(s)| = 1$ for all s, the gain of the MC coincides with the optimal gain of this MDP and each BSCC in the original MC is a MEC in the MDP. Using the reasoning from Sect. 4.1 and [34, Sect. 9.5], we obtain that all states in $\mathsf{prob1}(B)$ have the same gain. □

Therefore, instead of adding one gain variable per state to the equation system, we "compress" the gain of all states in the same BSCC (and its attractor) into one variable. Formally, the reduced equation system is formulated as follows.

Let $\{B_1, \dots, B_n\} = \mathsf{BSCC}(\mathsf{M})$ be the BSCC decomposition of the Markov chain. Further, define $A_i := \mathsf{prob1}(B_i)$ the attractors of each BSCC and $T := \bigcup_{i=1}^{n} A_i$ the set of all states which don't belong to any attractor. The *BSCC compressed gain/bias equations* then are defined as

$$\begin{aligned} g(s) &= \mathbb{E}_{\Delta}^{T'}(g, s) + \sum\nolimits_{A_i} \mathbb{E}_{\Delta}^{A_i}(g_i, s) \quad \forall s \in T, \\ b(s) &= \mathbb{E}_{\Delta}^{A_i}(b, s) + r(s) - g_i \quad \forall 1 \leq i \leq n, s \in A_i, \\ b(s) &= \mathbb{E}_{\Delta}(b, s) + r(s) - g(s) \quad \forall s \in T, \\ b(s_i) &= 0 \quad \text{for one arbitrary but fixed } s_i \in B_i, \forall 1 \leq i \leq n. \end{aligned} \tag{1}$$

Applying the reasoning of Lemma 1 immediately gives us correctness.

Corollary 1. *The values* $g_1, \dots, g_n$, $g(s)$ *and* $b(s)$ *are a solution to the equation system (1) if and only if*

$$g'(s) := \begin{cases} g_i & if\ s \in A_i, \\ g(s) & otherwise. \end{cases}$$

and $b(s)$ *are a solution to the gain/bias equations.*

Algorithm 3. SCC-SI

Input: MC $\mathsf{M} = (S, s_{\text{init}}, \Delta, r)$.
Output: (g, b), s.t. g and b are solutions to the gain/bias equations.

1: Obtain $\mathsf{BSCC}(\mathsf{M}) = \{B_1, \ldots, B_n\}$ and $\mathsf{SCC}(\mathsf{M}) \setminus \mathsf{BSCC}(\mathsf{M}) = \{S_1, \ldots, S_m\}$ with S_i in reverse topological order.
2: **for** $B_i \in \mathsf{BSCC}(\mathsf{M})$ **do** ▷ Obtain gain and bias of BSCCs
3: Obtain g_i and $b(s)$ for all $s \in B_i$ by solving the equations

$$b(s) = \mathbb{E}_{\Delta}^{B_i}(b, s) + r(s) - g_i \quad \forall s \in B_i,$$
$$b(s_i) = 0 \quad \text{for one arbitrary but fixed } s_i \in B_i.$$

4: Set $g(s) \leftarrow g_i$ for all $s \in B_i$.
5: **for** i from 1 to m **do** ▷ Obtain gain and bias of non-BSCC states
6: Let $S^{<} := \bigcup_{j=1}^{i-1} S_j \cup \bigcup_{j=1}^{n} B_j$
7: Compute $\mathsf{succ}(\mathsf{g}) \leftarrow \{s' \in S^{<} \mid \exists s \in S_i.\ \Delta(s, s') > 0 \wedge g(s') = \mathsf{g}\}$.
8: Set $\mathsf{succg} = \{\mathsf{g} \mid \mathsf{succ}(\mathsf{g}) \neq \emptyset\}$.
9: For each $\mathsf{g} \in \mathsf{succg}$, obtain p_{g} by solving the equations

$$p_{\mathsf{g}}(s) = \mathbb{E}_{\Delta}^{S_i}(p_{\mathsf{g}}, s) + \sum_{s' \in \mathsf{succg}} \Delta(s, s') \quad \forall s \in S_i.$$

10: Set $g(s) \leftarrow \sum_{\mathsf{g} \in \mathsf{succg}} p_{\mathsf{g}}(s) \cdot \mathsf{g}$ for all $s \in S_i$.
11: Obtain $b(s)$ for all $s \in S_i$ by solving the equations

$$b(s) = \mathbb{E}_{\Delta}^{S_i}(b, s) + \mathbb{E}_{\Delta}^{S^{<}}(b, s) + r(s) - g(s) \quad \forall s \in S_i.$$

12: **return** (g, b).

This equation system is significantly smaller for Markov chains which contain large BSCC-attractors. Furthermore, observe that the resulting system matrix also is square. We have $|\mathsf{BSCC}(\mathsf{M})| + |T|$ gain and $|S|$ bias variables but also $|T|$ gain and $|S| + |\mathsf{BSCC}(\mathsf{M})|$ bias equations. Additionally, by virtue of Corollary 1 and [34, Condition 9.2.3], the system has a unique solution. Together, this allows the use of more efficient solvers. Especially when combined with the previous MEC decomposition approach, significant speed-ups can be observed.

SCC Decomposition. The second approach extends the BSCC compression idea by further decomposing the problem into numerous sub-problems. A formal definition of the improved evaluation algorithm is given in Algorithm 3.

As with the compression approach, we exploit the fact that all states in some BSCC have the same gain. But instead of encoding this information into one big linear equation system, we use it to obtain multiple sub-problems.

First, we obtain gain and bias for each BSCC separately in Line 3. Note that there are only $|B_i| + 1$ variables and equations, since there only is a single gain variable. The last equation, setting bias to zero for some state of the BSCC, again induces a unique solution.

Now, these values are back-propagated through the MC. As mentioned, we can obtain a topological ordering of the SCCs, where a state s in a "later" SCC cannot reach any state s' in some earlier SCC. By processing the SCCs in reverse topological order, we can successively compute values of all states as follows.

Since the gain actually is only earned in BSCCs, the gain of some non-BSCC state naturally only depends on the probability of ending up in some BSCC. More generally, by a simple inductive argument, the gain of such a non-BSCC state only depends on the gains of the states it ends up in after moving to a later SCC. In other words, the gain only depends on the reachability of the successor gains. So, instead of constructing a linear equation system involving both gain and bias for each SCC, we determine the different "gain outcomes" in Line 8 and then compute the probability of these outcomes in Line 9, i.e. the probability of reaching a state obtaining some particular successor gain. Finally, we simply set the gain of some state as the expected outcome in Line 10. Only then the bias is computed in Line 11 by solving the bias equation with the computed gain values inserted as constants.

At first glance, this might seem rather expensive, as there are $|\mathsf{succg}|+1$ linear equation systems instead of one. But the corresponding matrices of the systems in Lines 9 and 11 actually are (i) square with a unique solution, allowing the use of LU decomposition; and (ii) are the same for a particular SCC, enabling reuse of the obtained decomposition.

Note how this in fact generalizes the idea of computing attractors in the BSCC-compression approach. Suppose a non-BSCC state $s \in S_j$ is in the attractor of a particular BSCC B_i. Since moving to B_i is the only possible outcome, succg as computed in Line 8 actually is a singleton set containing only the gain g_i of the BSCC. Then $p_{g_i}(s) = 1$ for all states in S_j and we can immediately set $g(s) = g_i$.

5 Approximation-Guided Solutions

This section introduces another idea to increase efficiency of the strategy iteration. Section 5.1 then combines this method with optimizations of the previous section in a non-trivial way, yielding a super-additive optimization effect. Our new approach relies on the following observation. In order to improve a strategy, it is not always necessary to know the exact gain in each state; sufficiently tight bounds are enough to decide that the current action is sub-optimal. To this end, we assume that we are given an approximative oracle for the gain of any state under some strategy[7]. Formally, we require a function $g^{\approx} : \Pi^{\mathsf{MD}} \times S \to \mathbb{R}^{\geq 0} \times \mathbb{R}^{\geq 0}$ and call it *consistent* if for $g^{\approx}(\pi, s) = (g_L(\pi, s), g_U(\pi, s))$ we have that $g^{\pi}(s) \in [g_L(\pi, s), g_U(\pi, s)]$. For readability, we write $g_L(\pi)$ and $g_U(\pi)$ for the functions $s \mapsto g_L(\pi, s)$ and $s \mapsto g_U(\pi, s)$, respectively.

In Algorithm 4, we define a variant of strategy iteration, which incorporates this approximation for gain improvement. Let us focus on this improvement in

[7] We will go into detail why we do not deal with bias later on.

Algorithm 4. Approx-SI

Input: MDP $\mathcal{M} = (S, s_{\text{init}}, Act, \mathsf{Av}, \Delta, r)$ and consistent gain approximation $g^{\approx}$.
Output: (g^*, π^*), s.t. g^* is the optimal gain of the MDP and is obtained by π^*.

1: Set $n \leftarrow 0$, and pick an arbitrary strategy $\pi_0 \in \Pi^{\mathsf{MD}}$.
2: Set $\pi_{n+1} = \pi_n$
3: **for** $s \in S$ **do** ▷ Approximate gain improvement
4: **if** $g_U(\pi_n, s) < \max_{a \in \mathsf{Av}(s)} \mathbb{E}_\Delta(g_L(\pi_n), s)$ **then**
5: Pick $\pi_{n+1} \in \arg\max_{a \in \mathsf{Av}(s)} \mathbb{E}_\Delta(g_L(\pi_n), s, a)$.
6: **if** $\pi_{n+1} \neq \pi_n$ **then** increment n by 1, go to Line 2.
7: Obtain g_{n+2} and π_{n+2} by one step of precise SI. ▷ Precise improvement
8: **if** $\pi_{n+2} \neq \pi_{n+1}$ **then** increment n by 2, go to Line 2.
9: **return** (g_{n+2}, π_{n+2})

Line 5. There are three cases to distinguish. (1) If the test on Line 4 holds, i.e. the upper bound on the gain in the current state is smaller than the lower bound under some other action a, then a definitely gives us a better gain. Therefore, we switch the strategy to this action. If the test does not hold, there are two other cases to distinguish: (2) If in contrast, the lower bound on the gain in the current state is bigger than the upper bound under any other action, the current gain definitely is better than the gain achievable under any other action. Hence the current action is optimal and the strategy should not be changed. (3) Otherwise, the approximation does not offer us enough information to conclude anything. The current action is neither a clear winner nor a clear loser compared to the other actions. In this case we also refrain from changing the strategy. Intuitively, if there are any changes to be done in Case (3), we postpone them until no further improvements can be done based solely on the approximations. They will be dealt with in Line 7, where we determine the gain precisely.

Theorem 2. *Algorithm 4 terminates for any MDP and consistent gain approximation function. Furthermore, the gain and corresponding strategy returned by the algorithm is optimal.*

Implementing Gain Approximations. In order to make Algorithm 4 practical, we provide a prototype for such a gain approximation. To this end, we can again interpret the MC M as a degenerate MDP $\mathcal{M}$ and apply variants of the value iteration methods of [2, Algorithm 2]. We want to emphasize that there are no restrictions on the oracle except consistency, hence there may be other, faster methods applicable here. This also opens the door for more fine-tuning and optimizations. For instance, instead of "giving up" on the estimation and solving the equations precisely, the gain approximation could be asked to refine the estimate for all states where there is uncertainty and Case (3) occurs.

Difficulties in Using Bias Estimations. One may wonder why we did not include a bias estimation function in the previous algorithm. There are two

Procedure 5. MEC-APPROX

1: Set $g_L^{\max}(\pi_n) \leftarrow \max_{s \in M} g_L(\pi_n, s)$, $S_- \leftarrow \{s \mid g_U(\pi_n, s) < g_L^{\max}(\pi_n)\}$, $S_+ = M \setminus S_-$.
2: **if** $S_- = \emptyset$ **then** Continue with precise improvement.
3: **else**
4:     **while** $S_- \neq \emptyset$ **do**
5:         Obtain $s \in S_-$ and $a \in \mathsf{Av}(s)$ such that $\sum_{s' \in S_+} \Delta(s, a, s') > 0$.
6:         Set $\pi_{n+1}(s) \leftarrow a$, $S_+ \leftarrow S_+ \cup \{s\}$, $S_- \leftarrow S_- \setminus \{s\}$.
7:     Increment n by 1, go to Line 1.

main reasons for this, namely (i) by naively using the bias approximation, the algorithm may not converge any more (even with ε-precise approximations) and (ii) it seems rather difficult to efficiently obtain a reasonable bias estimate. We provide more detail and intuition in [30, Appendix F].

5.1 Synergy of the Approaches

In order to further improve the approximation-guided approach, we combine it with the idea of MEC decomposition, which in turn allows for even more optimizations. As already mentioned, each state in a MEC has the same optimal gain. In combination with the idea of the algorithm in [34, Sect. 9.5.1], this allows us to further enhance the gain improvement step as follows.

The gain $g^*(M)$ of some MEC M certainly is higher than the lower bound achieved through some strategy in any state of the MEC, which is $g_L^{\max}(\pi_n) := \max_{s \in M} g_L(\pi_n, s)$. Hence, any state of the MEC which has an upper bound less than $g_L^{\max}(\pi_n)$ is suboptimal, as we can adapt the strategy such that it achieves at least this value in every state of the MEC. With this, the gain improvement step can be changed to (i) determine the maximal lower bound $g_L^{\max}(\pi_n)$, (ii) identify all states S_+ which have an upper bound greater than this lower bound and (iii) update the strategy in all other states S_- to move to this "optimal" region. Algorithm 5 then is obtained by replacing the approximate gain improvement in Lines 3 to 2 of Algorithm 4 by Procedure 5.

Theorem 3. *Algorithm 5 terminates for any MDP and consistent gain approximation function. Furthermore, the gain and corresponding strategy returned by the algorithm indeed is optimal.*

6 Experimental Evaluation

In this section, we compare the presented approaches to established tools.

Implementation Details. We implemented our constructions[8] in the PRISM Model Checker [31]. We also added several general purpose optimizations to

[8] Accessible at https://www7.in.tum.de/~meggendo/artifacts/2017/atva_si.txt.

PRISM, improving the used data structures. This may influence the comparability of these results to other works implemented in PRISM.

In order to solve the arising systems of linear equations, we used the `ojAlgo` Java library[9]. Whenever possible, we employed LU decomposition to solve the equation systems and SVD otherwise. We use `double` precision for all computations, which implies that results are only precise modulo numerical issues. The implementation can easily be extended to arbitrary precision, at the cost of performance. Further, our implementation only uses the parallelization of `ojAlgo`. Since the vast majority of computation time is consumed by solving equation systems, we did not implement further parallelization.

Experimental Setup. All benchmarks have been run on a `4.4.3-gentoo` x64 virtual machine with 16 cores of 3.0 GHz each, a time limit of 10 min and memory limit of 32 GB, using the 64-bit Oracle JDK version `1.8.0_102-b14`. All time measurements are given in seconds and are averaged over 10 executions. Instead of measuring the time which is spent in a particular algorithm, we decide to measure the overall *user CPU time* of the PRISM process using the UNIX tool `time`. This metric has several advantages. It allows for an easy and fair comparison between, e.g., multithreaded executions, symbolic methods or implementations which do not construct the whole model. Further, it reduces variance in measurements caused by the operating system through, e.g., the scheduler. Note that this also allows for measurements larger than the specified timeout, as the process may spend this timeout on each of the 16 cores.

6.1 Models

We briefly explain the examples used for evaluation. **virus** [32] models a *virus spreading through a network*. We reward each attack carried out by an infected machine. **cs_nfail** [29] models a *client-server mutual exclusion protocol* with probabilistic failures of the clients. A reward is given for each successfully handled connection. **phil_nofair** [14] represents the (randomised) *dining philosophers* without fairness assumptions. We use two reward structures, rewarding "thinking" and "eating", respectively. **sensor** [29] models a *network of sensors* sending values to a central processor over a lossy connection. Processing received data is rewarded. **mer** [18] captures the behaviour of a *resource arbiter* on a Mars exploration rover. We reward each time some user is granted access to a resource by the arbiter.

6.2 Tools

Since we are unaware of other implementations, we implemented standard SI as in Algorithm 1 by ourselves. We compare the following variants of SI.

[9] http://ojalgo.org/.

- SI: Standard SI as presented in Algorithm 1.
- BSCC: SI with BSCC compression gain/bias equations.
- SCC: The SCC decomposition approach of Algorithm 3.
- $\texttt{SCC}_A$: The SCC decomposition approach combined with the approximation methods from Sect. 5.

Further, a "M" superscript denotes use of the MEC decomposition approach as in Algorithm 2. In the case of $\texttt{SCC}_A^M$, we use the improved method of Sect. 5.1. More details and evaluation of some further variants can be found in [30, Appendix G]. During our experiments, we observed that the algorithm used to solve the resulting reachability problem did not influence the results significantly, since the weighted quotients are considerably simpler than the original models.

We compare our methods to the value iteration approach we presented in [2, Algorithm 2] with a required precision of 10^{-8} (VI). This comparison has to be evaluated with care, since (i) value iteration inherently is only ε-precise and (ii) it needs a MEC decomposition for soundness. Note that topological optimizations for value iteration as suggested by, e.g., [4] are partially incorporated by VI, since each MEC is iterated separately.

We also provide a comparison to the LP-based MultiGain [8] in [30, Appendix G]. In summary, the LP approach is soundly beaten by our optimized approaches. A more detailed comparison can be found in [2].

We are unaware of other implementations capable of solving the mean payoff objective for MDPs. Neither did we find a mean payoff solver for stochastic games which we could easily set up to process the PRISM models.

6.3 Results

We will highlight various conclusions to be drawn from Table 1. Comparing the naive SI with our enhanced versions BSCC and SCC, the number of strategy improvements does not differ, but the evaluation of each strategy is significantly faster, yielding the differences displayed in the table.

On the smaller models (**cs_nfail** and **virus**) nearly all of the optimized methods perform comparable, a majority of the runtime actually is consumed by the start-up of PRISM. Especially on **virus**, all the MEC-decomposition approaches have practically the same execution time due to the model only having a single MEC with a single state, which the problem trivial for these approaches.

The results immediately show how intractable naive strategy iteration is. On models with only a few hundred states, the computation already times out. The BSCC compression approach BSCC suffers from the same issues, but already performs significantly better than SI. In particular, when combined with MEC decomposition, it is able to solve more models within the given time.

Further, we see immense benefits of using the SCC approach, regularly beating even the quite performant (and imprecise) value iteration approach. Interestingly, the variants using approximation often perform worse than the "pure" SCC method. We conjecture that this is due the gain approximation function we used. It computes the gain up to some adaptively chosen precision instead of

Table 1. Comparison of various variants on the presented models. Timeouts and memo-outs are denoted by a hyphen. The best results in each row are marked in bold, excluding VI. The number of states and MECs are written next to the model.

Model	SI	SI^M	BSCC	$BSCC^M$	SCC	SCC_A	SCC_A^M	VI
cs_nfail3 (184, 38)	17	**4**	**4**	**4**	**4**	**4**	**4**	4
cs_nfail4 (960, 176)	1129	6	16	**5**	**5**	**5**	6	5
virus (809, 1)	–	**4**	10	**4**	5	5	**4**	4
phil_nofair3 (856, 1)	–	–	112	112	**6**	10	7	5
phil_nofair4 (9440, 1)	–	–	–	–	**15**	310	107	18
sensors1 (462, 132)	–	13	23	**4**	**4**	6	**4**	5
sensors2 (7860, 4001)	–	89	–	14	13	168	**11**	15
sensors3 (77766, 46621)	–	–	–	78	**40**	–	46	72
mer3 (15622, 9451)	–	21	–	26	**16**	244	22	15
mer4 (119305, 71952)	–	58	–	281	**42**	–	84	64
mer5 (841300, 498175)	–	–	–	–	**474**	–	–	–

computing up to a certain number of iterations. Changing this precision bound gave mixed results, on some models performance increased, on some it decreased. Comparing the two approximation-based approaches SCC_A and SCC_A^M, we highlight the improvements of Algorithm 5, speeding up convergence even though a MEC decomposition is computed.

Finally, we want to emphasize the mer results. Here, our SCC approach manages to obtain a solution within the time- and memory-bound, while all other approaches, including VI, fail due to a time-out.

7 Conclusion

We have proposed and evaluated several techniques to speed up strategy iteration. The combined speed ups are in orders of magnitude. This makes strategy iteration competitive even with the most used and generally imprecise value iteration and shows the potential of strategy iteration in the context of MDPs.

In future work, we will further develop this potential. Firstly, building upon the *SCC decomposition*, we can see opportunities to interleave the SCC computation and the improvements of the current strategy. Secondly, the *gain approximation* technique used is quite naive. Here we could further adapt our recent results on VI [2], in order to improve the performance of the approximation. Besides, we suggest to use simulations to evaluate the strategies. Nevertheless, the incomplete confidence arising form stochastic simulation has to be taken into account here. Thirdly, techniques for efficient *bias* approximation and algorithms to utilize it would be desirable. Finally, a fully configurable tool would be helpful to find the sweet-spot combinations of these techniques and useful as the first scalable tool for mean payoff optimization in MDPs.

Acknowledgments. We thank the anonymous reviewers for their insightful comments and valuable suggestions. In particular, a considerable improvement to the BSCC compression approach of Sect. 4.2 has been proposed.

References

1. Abate, A., Češka, M., Kwiatkowska, M.: Approximate policy iteration for Markov Decision Processes via quantitative adaptive aggregations. In: Artho, C., Legay, A., Peled, D. (eds.) ATVA 2016. LNCS, vol. 9938, pp. 13–31. Springer, Cham (2016). doi:10.1007/978-3-319-46520-3_2
2. Ashok, P., Chatterjee, K., Daca, P., Křetínský, J., Meggendorfer, T.: Value iteration for long-run average reward in Markov Decision Processes. In: CAV (2017). To appear
3. Baier, C., Katoen, J.-P.: Principles of Model Checking (2008)
4. Baier, C., Klein, J., Leuschner, L., Parker, D., Wunderlich, S.: Ensuring the reliability of your model checker: Interval iteration for Markov Decision Processes. In: CAV (2017). To appear
5. Bertsekas, D.P.: Approximate policy iteration: a survey and some new methods. J. Control Theor. Appl. **9**(3), 310–335 (2011)
6. Björklund, H., Vorobyov, S.G.: A combinatorial strongly subexponential strategy improvement algorithm for mean payoff games. DAM **155**(2), 210–229 (2007)
7. Brázdil, T., Chatterjee, K., Chmelík, M., Forejt, V., Křetínský, J., Kwiatkowska, M., Parker, D., Ujma, M.: Verification of Markov Decision Processes using learning algorithms. In: Cassez, F., Raskin, J.-F. (eds.) ATVA 2014. LNCS, vol. 8837, pp. 98–114. Springer, Cham (2014). doi:10.1007/978-3-319-11936-6_8
8. Brázdil, T., Chatterjee, K., Forejt, V., Kučera, A.: MultiGain: a controller synthesis tool for MDPs with multiple mean-payoff objectives. In: Baier, C., Tinelli, C. (eds.) TACAS 2015. LNCS, vol. 9035, pp. 181–187. Springer, Heidelberg (2015). doi:10.1007/978-3-662-46681-0_12
9. Brim, L., Chaloupka, J.: Using strategy improvement to stay alive. IJCSIS **23**(3), 585–608 (2012)
10. Chatterjee, K., Henzinger, T.: Value iteration. 25 Years of Model Checking, pp. 107–138 (2008)
11. Condon, A.: On algorithms for simple stochastic games. In: Advances in Computational Complexity Theory, pp. 51–72 (1990)
12. Courcoubetis, C., Yannakakis, M.: The complexity of probabilistic verification. J. ACM **42**(4), 857–907 (1995)
13. de Alfaro, L.: Formal verification of probabilistic systems. Ph.D thesis (1997)
14. Duflot, M., Fribourg, L., Picaronny, C.: Randomized dining philosophers without fairness assumption. Distrib. Comput. **17**(1), 65–76 (2004)
15. Fearnley, J.: Exponential lower bounds for policy iteration. In: Abramsky, S., Gavoille, C., Kirchner, C., Meyer auf der Heide, F., Spirakis, P.G. (eds.) ICALP 2010. LNCS, vol. 6199, pp. 551–562. Springer, Heidelberg (2010). doi:10.1007/978-3-642-14162-1_46
16. Fearnley, J.: Strategy iteration algorithms for games and Markov Decision Processes. Ph.D thesis, University of Warwick (2010)
17. Fearnley, J.: Efficient parallel strategy improvement for parity games. In: CAV (2017). To appear

18. Feng, L., Kwiatkowska, M., Parker, D.: Automated learning of probabilistic assumptions for compositional reasoning. In: Giannakopoulou, D., Orejas, F. (eds.) FASE 2011. LNCS, vol. 6603, pp. 2–17. Springer, Heidelberg (2011). doi:10.1007/978-3-642-19811-3_2
19. Filar, J., Vrieze, K.: Competitive Markov Decision Processes. Springer, New York (1997)
20. Frausto-Solis, J., Santiago, E., Mora-Vargas, J.: Cosine policy iteration for solving infinite-horizon Markov Decision Processes. In: Aguirre, A.H., Borja, R.M., Garciá, C.A.R. (eds.) MICAI 2009. LNCS, vol. 5845, pp. 75–86. Springer, Heidelberg (2009). doi:10.1007/978-3-642-05258-3_7
21. Friedmann, O.: An exponential lower bound for the parity game strategy improvement algorithm as we know it. In: LICS, pp. 145–156 (2009)
22. Gawlitza, T.M., Schwarz, M.D., Seidl, H.: Parametric strategy iteration. arXiv preprint arXiv:1406.5457 (2014)
23. Haddad, S., Monmege, B.: Reachability in MDPs: refining convergence of value iteration. In: Ouaknine, J., Potapov, I., Worrell, J. (eds.) RP 2014. LNCS, vol. 8762, pp. 125–137. Springer, Cham (2014). doi:10.1007/978-3-319-11439-2_10
24. Hahn, E.M., Schewe, S., Turrini, A., Zhang, L.: Synthesising strategy improvement and recursive algorithms for solving 2.5 player parity games. In: Bouajjani, A., Monniaux, D. (eds.) VMCAI 2017. LNCS, vol. 10145, pp. 266–287. Springer, Cham (2017). doi:10.1007/978-3-319-52234-0_15
25. Hansen, K.A., Ibsen-Jensen, R., Miltersen, P.B.: The complexity of solving reachability games using value and strategy iteration. Theor. Comput. Syst. **55**(2), 380–403 (2014)
26. Hansen, T.D., Miltersen, P.B., Zwick, U.: Strategy iteration is strongly polynomial for 2-player turn-based stochastic games with a constant discount factor. J. ACM **60**(1), 1:1–1:16 (2013)
27. Hordijk, A., Puterman, M.L.: On the convergence of policy iteration in finite state undiscounted Markov Decision Processes: the unichain case. MMOR **12**(1), 163–176 (1987)
28. Howard, R.A.: Dynamic Programming and Markov Processes (1960)
29. Komuravelli, A., Păsăreanu, C.S., Clarke, E.M.: Assume-guarantee abstraction refinement for probabilistic systems. In: Madhusudan, P., Seshia, S.A. (eds.) CAV 2012. LNCS, vol. 7358, pp. 310–326. Springer, Heidelberg (2012). doi:10.1007/978-3-642-31424-7_25
30. Křetínský, J., Meggendorfer, T.: Efficient strategy iteration for mean payoff in Markov Decision Processes. Technical report abs/1707.01859. arXiv.org (2017)
31. Kwiatkowska, M., Norman, G., Parker, D.: PRISM 4.0: verification of probabilistic real-time systems. In: Gopalakrishnan, G., Qadeer, S. (eds.) CAV 2011. LNCS, vol. 6806, pp. 585–591. Springer, Heidelberg (2011). doi:10.1007/978-3-642-22110-1_47
32. Kwiatkowska, M., Norman, G., Parker, D., Vigliotti, M.G.: Probabilistic mobile ambients. Theoret. Comput. Sci. **410**(12–13), 1272–1303 (2009)
33. Luttenberger, M.: Strategy iteration using non-deterministic strategies for solving parity games. CoRR, abs/0806.2923 (2008)
34. Puterman, M.L.: Markov Decision Processes: Discrete Stochastic Dynamic Programming. Wiley (2014)
35. Schewe, S.: An optimal strategy improvement algorithm for solving parity and payoff games. In: Kaminski, M., Martini, S. (eds.) CSL 2008. LNCS, vol. 5213, pp. 369–384. Springer, Heidelberg (2008). doi:10.1007/978-3-540-87531-4_27
36. Shlakhter, O., Lee, C.-G.: Accelerated modified policy iteration algorithms for Markov Decision Processes. MMOR **78**(1), 61–76 (2013)

37. Tarjan, R.: Depth-first search and linear graph algorithms. SICOMP **1**(2), 146–160 (1972)
38. Vöge, J., Jurdziński, M.: A discrete strategy improvement algorithm for solving parity games. In: Emerson, E.A., Sistla, A.P. (eds.) CAV 2000. LNCS, vol. 1855, pp. 202–215. Springer, Heidelberg (2000). doi:10.1007/10722167_18
39. Ye, Y.: The simplex and policy-iteration methods are strongly polynomial for the Markov decision problem with a fixed discount rate. MMOR **36**(4), 593–603 (2011)

Finding Polynomial Loop Invariants for Probabilistic Programs

Yijun Feng[1(✉)], Lijun Zhang[2,3], David N. Jansen[2(✉)], Naijun Zhan[2], and Bican Xia[1]

[1] LMAM and School of Mathematical Sciences, Peking University, Beijing, China
fyj_jyf9225@pku.edu.cn, xbc@math.pku.edu.cn

[2] State Key Laboratory of Computer Science, Institute of Software, CAS, Beijing, China
{zhanglj,dnjansen,znj}@ios.ac.cn

[3] University of Chinese Academy of Sciences, Beijing, China

Abstract. Quantitative loop invariants are an essential element in the verification of probabilistic programs. Recently, multivariate Lagrange interpolation has been applied to synthesizing polynomial invariants. In this paper, we propose an alternative approach. First, we fix a polynomial template as a candidate of a loop invariant. Using Stengle's Positivstellensatz and a transformation to a sum-of-squares problem, we find sufficient conditions on the coefficients. Then, we solve a semidefinite programming feasibility problem to synthesize the loop invariants. If the semidefinite program is unfeasible, we backtrack after increasing the degree of the template. Our approach is semi-complete in the sense that it will always lead us to a feasible solution if one exists and numerical errors are small. Experimental results show the efficiency of our approach.

1 Introduction

Probabilistic programs extend standard programs with probabilistic choices and are widely used in protocols, randomized algorithms, stochastic games, etc. In such situations, the program may report incorrect results with a certain probability, rendering classical program specification methods [10,18] inadequate. As a result, formal reasoning about the correctness needs to be based on quantitative specifications. Typically, a probabilistic program consists of steps that choose probabilistically between several states, and the specification of a probabilistic program contains constraints on the probability distribution of final states, e.g. through the expected value of a random variable. Therefore the expected value is often the object of correctness verification [14,21,23].

To reason about correctness for probabilistic programs, quantitative annotations are needed. Most importantly, correctness of while loops can be proved by inferring special bounds on expectations, usually called *quantitative loop invariants* [23]. As in the classical setting, finding such invariants is the bottleneck of proving program correctness. For some restricted classes, such as linear loop invariants, some techniques have been established [4,21,24]. To use them to synthesize polynomial loop invariants, so-called linearization can be used [1],

D. D'Souza and K. Narayan Kumar (Eds.): ATVA 2017, LNCS 10482, pp. 400–416, 2017.
DOI: 10.1007/978-3-319-68167-2_26

a technique widely applied in linear algebra. It views higher-degree monomials as new variables, establishes their relation with existing variables, and then exploits linear loop invariant generation techniques. However, the number of monomials is exponential in the degree. Rodríguez-Carbonell and Kapur [28] introduce solvable mappings, which are a generalization of affine mappings, to avoid non-polynomial effects generated by polynomial programs. Recently, Chen et al. [7] applied multivariate Lagrange interpolation to synthesize polynomial loop invariants directly.

Another important problem for probabilistic programs is the *almost-sure termination problem,* answering whether the program terminates almost surely. Fioriti and Hermanns [13] argued that Lyapunov ranking functions, used in non-probabilistic termination analysis, cannot be extended to probabilistic programs. Instead, they extended ranking supermartingales [3] to the bounded probabilistic case and provided a compositional and sound proof method for the almost-sure termination problem. Kaminski and Katoen [20] investigated the computational complexity of computing expected outcomes (including lower bounds, upper bounds and exact expected outcomes) and of deciding almost-sure termination of probabilistic programs. Further, Chatterjee et al. [6] investigated termination problems for affine probabilistic programs. Recently, they also presented a method [5] to efficiently synthesize ranking supermartingales by Putinar's Positivstellensatz [27] and used it to prove the termination of probabilistic programs. Their method is sound and semi-complete over a large class of programs.

In this paper, we develop a technique exploiting *semidefinite programming* through another Positivstellensatz to synthesize the quantitative loop invariants. Positivstellensätze are essential theorems in real algebra to describe the structure of polynomials that are positive (or non-negative) on a *semialgebraic set.* While our approach shares some similarities with the one in [5], the difference to the termination problem requires a variation of the theorem. In detail, Putinar's Positivstellensatz deals with the situation when the polynomial is strictly positive on a quadratic module, which is not enough for quantitative loop invariants. In the program correctness problem, equality constraints are taken into consideration as well as inequalities. Therefore in our method, Stengle's Positivstellensatz [29] dealing with general real semi-algebraic sets is being used.

As previous results [7,15,21], our approach is *constraint-based* [8]. We fix a polynomial template for the invariants with a fixed degree and generate constraints from the program. The constraints can be transformed into an emptiness problem of a semialgebraic set. By Stengle's Positivstellensatz [29], it suffices to solve a semidefinite programming feasibility problem, for which efficient solvers exist. From a feasible solution (which need not be tight) we can then obtain the corresponding template coefficients. If the solver does not provide a feasible solution or a verification shows that the coefficients are not correct, we refine the analysis by adding constraints to block the undesired solutions or by increasing the template degree, which will always lead us to a feasible solution if one exists.

The method is applied to several case studies taken from [7]. Our technique usually solves the problem within one second, which is about one tenth of the time taken by the tool of [7]. Our tool supports real variables rather than discrete ones and can generate polynomial invariants. We illustrate these features by analyzing a non-linear perceptron program and a model for airplane delay with continuous distributions. Moreover, we conduct a sequence of trials on parameterized probabilistic programs to show that the main influence factor on the running time of our method is the degree of the invariant template. We compare our results on these examples with the Lagrange Interpolation Prototype (LIP) in [7], PRINSYS [15] and the tool for super-martingales (TM) [3].

2 Preliminaries

In this section we introduce some notations. We use $\mathbf{X}_n$ to denote an n-tuple of variables $(X_1, \ldots, X_n)$. For a vector $\alpha = (\alpha_1, \ldots, \alpha_n) \in \mathbb{N}^n$, $\mathbf{X}_n^\alpha$ denotes the monomial $X_1^{\alpha_1} \cdots X_n^{\alpha_n}$, and $d = \sum_i \alpha_i$ is its degree.

Definition 1. *A polynomial f in variables $X_1, \ldots, X_n$ is a finite linear combination of monomials: $f = \sum_\alpha c_\alpha \mathbf{X}_n^\alpha$ where finitely many $c_\alpha \in \mathbb{R}$ are non-zero.*

The degree of a polynomial is the highest degree of its component monomials. Extending the notation, for a sequence of polynomials $\mathcal{F} = (f_1, \ldots, f_s)$ and a vector $\alpha = (\alpha_1, \ldots, \alpha_s) \in \mathbb{R}^s$, we let $\mathcal{F}^\alpha$ denote $\prod_{i=1}^s f_i^{\alpha_i}$. The polynomial ring with n variables is denoted with $\mathbb{R}[\mathbf{X}_n]$, and the set of polynomials of degree at most d is denoted with $\mathbb{R}^{\leq d}[\mathbf{X}_n]$. For $f \in \mathbb{R}[\mathbf{X}_n]$ and $\mathbf{z}_n = (z_1, \ldots, z_n) \in \mathbb{R}^n$, $f(\mathbf{z}_n) \in \mathbb{R}$ is the value of f at $\mathbf{z}_n$.

A *constraint* is a quantifier-free formula constructed from (in)equalities of polynomials. It is *linear* if it contains only linear expressions. A semialgebraic set is a set described by a constraint:

Definition 2. *A semialgebraic set in $\mathbb{R}^k$ is a finite union of sets of the form $\{x \in \mathbb{R}^k | f(x) = 0 \wedge \bigwedge_{g \in \mathcal{G}} g > 0\}$, where f is a polynomial and $\mathcal{G}$ is a finite set of polynomials.*

A polynomial $p(\mathbf{X}_n) \in \mathbb{R}[\mathbf{X}_n]$ is a *sum of squares* (or SOS, for short), if there exist polynomials $f_1(x), \ldots, f_m(x) \in \mathbb{R}[\mathbf{X}_n]$ such that $p(\mathbf{X}_n) = \sum_{i=1}^m f_i^2(\mathbf{X}_n)$. Chapters 2 and 3 of [2] introduce a way to transform the problem whether a given polynomial is an SOS into a *semidefinite programming problem* (or SDP, for short), which is a generalization of linear programming problem. We introduce the transformation and SDP problems briefly in our technical report [12].

2.1 Probabilistic Programs

We use a simple *probabilistic guarded-command language* to construct *probabilistic programs* with the grammar:

$$P ::= \mathsf{skip} \mid \mathsf{abort} \mid x := E \mid P; P \mid P\ [p]\ P \mid \mathsf{if}\ (G)\ \mathsf{then}\ \{P\}\ \mathsf{else}\ \{P\} \mid \mathsf{while}(G)\{P\}$$

where E is a real-valued expression and G is a Boolean guard defined by the grammar:

$E ::= c \mid \mathbf{x}_n \mid r \mid$	constant/variable/random variable
$E + E \mid E \cdot E \mid$	arithmetic
$G ::= E < E \mid G \wedge G \mid \neg G$	guards

Random variable r follows a given probability distribution, discrete or continuous. For $p \in [0, 1]$, the *probabilistic choice command* P_0 $[p]$ P_1 executes P_0 with probability p and P_1 with probability $1 - p$.

Example 3. The following probabilistic program P describes a simple game:

$$z := 0;\ \mathsf{while}(0 < x < y)\ \{x := x + 1[0.5]x := x - 1;\ z := z + 1\}.$$

The program models a game where a player has x dollars at the beginning and keeps tossing a coin with probability 0.5. The player wins one dollar if he tosses a head and loses one dollar for a tail. The game ends when the player loses all his money, or he wins $y - x$ dollars for a predetermined y. The variable z records the number of tosses made by the player during this game.

We assume that the reader is familiar with the basic concepts of probability theory and in particular expectations, see e.g. [11] for details. Expectations are typically functions from program states (i.e. the real-valued program variables) to $\mathbb{R}$. An expectation is called a *post-expectation* when it is to be evaluated on the final distribution, and it is called a *pre-expectation* when it is to be evaluated on the initial distribution. Let *preE*, *postE* be expectations and *prog* a probabilistic program. We say that the sentence $\langle preE \rangle$ *prog* $\langle postE \rangle$ *holds* if the expected value of *postE* after executing *prog* is equal to or greater than the expected value of *preE*. When *postE* and *preE* are functions, the comparison is executed pointwise.

Classical programs can be viewed as special probabilistic programs in the following sense. For classical precondition *pre* and postcondition *post*, let the characteristic function χ_{pre} equal 1 if the precondition is true and 0 otherwise, and define χ_{post} similarly. If one considers a Hoare triple $\{pre\}$ *prog* $\{post\}$ where *prog* is a classical program, then it holds if and only if $\langle \chi_{pre} \rangle$ *prog* $\langle \chi_{post} \rangle$ holds in the probabilistic sense.

2.2 Probabilistic Predicate Transformers

Let P_0, P_1 be probabilistic programs, E an expression, *post* a post-expectation, *pre* a pre-expectation, G a Boolean expression, and $p \in (0, 1)$. The probabilistic predicate transformer *wp* can be defined as follows [16]:

$$wp(\mathsf{skip}, post) = post$$
$$wp(\mathsf{abort}, post) = 0$$
$$wp(x := E, post) = post[x/\mathbb{E}_S(E)]$$
$$wp(P;\ Q, post) = wp(P, wp(Q, post))$$
$$wp(\mathsf{if}(G)\ \mathsf{then}(P)\ \mathsf{else}(Q), post) = \chi_G \cdot wp(P, post) + (1 - \chi_G) \cdot wp(Q, post)$$
$$wp(P\ [p]\ Q, post) = p \cdot wp(P, post) + (1 - p) \cdot wp(Q, post)$$
$$wp(\mathsf{while}(G)\ \{P\}, post) = \mu X.(\chi_G \cdot wp(P, X) + (1 - \chi_G) \cdot post)$$

Here $post[x/\mathbb{E}_S(E)]$ denotes the formula obtained by replacing free occurrences of x in *post* by the expectation of E over state space S. The least fixed point operator μ is defined over the domain of expectations [23, 24], and it can be shown that $\langle pre\rangle\ P\ \langle post\rangle$ holds if and only if $pre \leq wp(P, post)$. Thus, $wp(P, post)$ is the greatest lower bound of precondition expectation of P with respect to *post*, and we say $wp(P, post)$ is the *weakest pre-expectation of P w.r.t. post.*

2.3 Positivstellensatz

Hilbert's Nullstellensatz is very important in algebra, and its real version, known as Positivstellensatz, is crucial to our method. First, some concepts are needed to introduce the theorem.

- The set $P \subseteq \mathbb{R}[\mathbf{X}_n]$ is a *positive cone* if it satisfies: (i) If $a \in \mathbb{R}[\mathbf{X}_n]$, then $a^2 \in P$, and (ii) P is closed under addition and multiplication.
- The set $M \subseteq \mathbb{R}[\mathbf{X}_n]$ is a *multiplicative monoid with 0* if it satisfies: (i) $0, 1 \in M$, and (ii) M is closed under multiplication.
- The set $I \subseteq \mathbb{R}[\mathbf{X}_n]$ is an *ideal* if it satisfies: (i) $0 \in I$, (ii) I is closed under addition, and (iii) If $a \in I$ and $b \in \mathbb{R}[\mathbf{X}_n]$, then $a \cdot b \in I$.

We are interested in finitely generated positive cones, multiplicative monoids with 0, and ideals. Let $\mathcal{F} = \{f_1, \dots, f_s\}$ be a finite set of polynomials. We recall that

- Any element in the positive cone generated by $\mathcal{F}$ (i.e., the smallest positive cone containing $\mathcal{F}$) is of the form
$$\sum_{\alpha\in\{0,1\}^s} k_\alpha \mathcal{F}^\alpha \quad \text{where } k_\alpha \text{ is a sum of squares for all } \alpha \in \{0,1\}^s$$
In the sum, α denotes an s-length vector with each element 0 or 1.
- Any nonzero element in the multiplicative monoid with 0 generated by $\mathcal{F}$ is of the form $\mathcal{F}^\alpha$, where $\alpha = (\alpha_1, \dots, \alpha_s) \in \mathbb{N}^s$.
- Any element in the ideal generated by $\mathcal{F}$ is of the form $k_1 f_1 + k_2 f_2 + \cdots + k_s f_s$, where $k_1, \dots, k_s \in \mathbb{R}[\mathbf{X}_n]$.

The Positivstellensatz due to Stengle states that for a system of real polynomial equalities and inequalities, either there exists a solution, or there exists a certain polynomial which guarantees that no solution exists.

Theorem 4 (Stengle's Positivstellensatz [29]). *Let $(f_j)_{j=1}^s, (g_k)_{k=1}^t, (h_l)_{l=1}^w$ be finite families of polynomials in $\mathbb{R}[\mathbf{X}_n]$. Denote by P the positive cone generated by $(f_j)_{j=1}^s$, by M the multiplicative monoid with 0 generated by $(g_k)_{k=1}^t$, and by I the ideal generated by $(h_l)_{l=1}^w$. Then the following are equivalent:*

1. *The set*
$$\left\{ \mathbf{z}_n \in \mathbb{R}^n \,\middle|\, \begin{array}{l} f_j(\mathbf{z}_n) \geq 0,\ j = 1, \dots, s \\ g_k(\mathbf{z}_n) \neq 0,\ k = 1, \dots, t \\ h_l(\mathbf{z}_n) = 0,\ l = 1, \dots, w \end{array} \right\} \tag{1}$$
is empty.
2. *There exist $f \in P, g \in M, h \in I$ such that $f + g^2 + h = 0$.*

3 Problem Formulation

The question that concerns us here is to verify whether the loop sentence

$$\langle preE \rangle \ \mathsf{while}(G)\ \{body\}\ \langle postE \rangle$$

holds, when given the pre-expectation *preE*, post-expectation *postE*, a Boolean expression G, and a loop-free probabilistic program *body*. One way to solve this problem is to calculate the weakest pre-expectation $wp(\mathsf{while}(G, \{body\}), postE)$ and to check whether it is not smaller than *preE*. However, the weakest pre-expectation of a while statement requires a fixed-point computation, which is not trivial. To avoid the fixed point, the problem can be solved through a quantitative loop invariant.

Theorem 5 [15]. *Let preE be a pre-expectation, postE a post-expectation, G a Boolean expression, and body a loop-free probabilistic program. To show*

$$\langle preE \rangle \ \mathit{while}(G)\ \{body\}\ \langle postE \rangle,$$

it suffices to find a loop invariant I which is an expectation such that

1. *(boundary)* $preE \leq I$ *and* $I \cdot (1 - \chi_G) \leq postE$;
2. *(invariant)* $I \cdot \chi_G \leq wp(body, I)$;
3. *(soundness) the loop terminates with probability 1 from any state that satisfies G, and*
   (a) *the number of iterations is finite, or*
   (b) *I is bounded from above by some fixed constant, or*
   (c) *the expected value of* $I \cdot \chi_G$ *tends to zero as the number of iterations tends to infinity.*

Since soundness of a loop invariant is not related to pre- and postconditions and can be verified from its type before any specific invariants are found, we focus on the boundary and invariant conditions in Theorem 5. The soundness property is left to be verified manually in case studies.

For pre-expectation *preE* and post-expectation *postE*, the boundary and invariant conditions in Theorem 5 provide the following requirements for a loop invariant I:

$$\begin{aligned} preE &\leq I \\ I \cdot (1 - \chi_G) &\leq postE \\ I \cdot \chi_G &\leq wp(body, I). \end{aligned} \tag{2}$$

The inequalities induced by the boundary and invariant conditions contain indicator functions, which may be difficult to analyze if they appear multiple times. So we rewrite them to a standard form. For a Boolean expression F, we use $[F]$ to represent its integer value, i.e. $[F] = 1$ if F is true, and $[F] = 0$ otherwise. An expectation is in *disjoint normal form* (DNF) if it is of the form

$$f = [F_1] \cdot f_1 + \cdots + [F_k] \cdot f_k$$

where the F_i are disjoint expressions, which means any two of the expressions cannot be true simultaneously, and the f_i are polynomials.

Lemma 6 [21]. *Suppose* $f = [F_1]\cdot f_1 + \cdots + [F_k]\cdot f_k$ *and* $g = [G_1]\cdot g_1 + \cdots + [G_l]\cdot g_l$ *are expectations over* $\mathbf{X}_n$ *in DNF. Then,* $f \leq g$ *if and only if (pointwise)*

$$\bigwedge_{i=1}^{k}\bigwedge_{j=1}^{l}\left[F_i \wedge G_j \Rightarrow f_i \leq g_j\right] \wedge \bigwedge_{i=1}^{k}\left[F_i \wedge \left(\bigwedge_{j=1}^{l}\neg G_j\right) \Rightarrow f_i \leq 0\right] \wedge \bigwedge_{j=1}^{l}\left[\left(\bigwedge_{i=1}^{k}\neg F_i\right) \wedge G_j \Rightarrow 0 \leq g_j\right]. \tag{3}$$

Example 7. Consider the following loop sentence for our running example:

$\langle xy - x^2\rangle\ z := 0;\ \mathsf{while}(0 < x < y)\{x := x + 1\ [0.5]\ x := x - 1; z := z + 1;\}\ \langle z\rangle$

For this case, the following must hold for any loop invariant I.

$$\begin{aligned} xy - x^2 &\leq I \\ I\cdot[x \leq 0 \vee y \leq x] &\leq z \\ I\cdot[0 < x < y] &\leq 0.5\cdot I(x+1, y, z+1) + 0.5\cdot I(x-1, y, z+1) \end{aligned}$$

By Lemma 6, these requirements can be written as

$$xy - x^2 \leq I \wedge \tag{4}$$

$$x \leq 0 \vee y \leq x \Rightarrow I \leq z \wedge \tag{5}$$

$$0 < x < y \Rightarrow 0 \leq z \wedge \tag{6}$$

$$0 < x < y \Rightarrow I \leq 0.5\cdot I(x+1, y, z+1) + 0.5\cdot I(x-1, y, z+1) \wedge \tag{7}$$

$$x \leq 0 \vee y \leq x \Rightarrow 0 \leq 0.5\cdot I(x+1, y, z+1) + 0.5\cdot I(x-1, y, z+1) \tag{8}$$

The program in this example originally served as a running example in [7]. There, after transforming the constraints into the form above, Lagrange interpolation was applied to synthesize the template coefficients. Our approach asserts the correctness of each conjunct in (4–8) by checking the nonnegativity of the polynomial on the right side over a semialgebraic set related to polynomials on the left side. In this way, we use the Positivstellensatz to synthesize the coefficients.

4 Constraint Solving by Semidefinite Programming

Our aim is to synthesize coefficients for the fixed invariant template for simple (Subsect. 4.1) and nested (Subsect. 4.2) programs. Checking the validity of constraints can be transformed into checking the emptiness of a semialgebraic set. Then, we show that the emptiness problem can be turned into sum-of-squares constraints using Stengle's Positivstellensatz.

Our Approach in a Nutshell. For a given polynomial template as a candidate quantitative loop invariant, it needs to satisfy *boundary* and *invariant* conditions. Our goal is to synthesize the coefficients in the template. These conditions describe a semialgebraic set, and the satisfiability of the constraints is equivalent to the non-emptiness of the corresponding semialgebraic set. Applying the Positivstellensatz (see Sect. 2.3), we will transform the problem to an equivalent semidefinite programming problem using Lemma 8. Existing efficient solvers can be used to solve the problem. A more efficient yet sufficient way is to transform the problem into a *sum-of-squares problem* using Lemma 9 and then to solve it by semidefinite programming. After having synthesized the coefficients of the template, we verify whether they are valid. In case of a negative answer, which may happen due to numerical errors, some amendments can be made by adding further constraints, which is described in Sect. 4.3. If the problem is still unsolved, we try raising the degree of the template and reiterate the procedure.

4.1 Synthesis Algorithm for Simple Loop Programs

Now we are ready for the transformation method. Each conjunct obtained in Lemma 6 is of the form $F \Rightarrow G$, where F is a quantifier-free formula constructed from (in)equalities between polynomials in $\mathbb{R}^{\leq d}[\mathbf{X}_n]$, and G is of the form $f \leq g$, $f \leq 0$ or $0 \leq g$, with $f, g \in \mathbb{R}^{\leq d}[\mathbf{X}_n]$. If F contains negations, we use De Morgan's laws to eliminate them. If there is a disjunction in F, we split the constraints into sub-constraints as $\varphi \vee \psi \Rightarrow \chi$ is equivalent to $(\varphi \Rightarrow \chi) \wedge (\psi \Rightarrow \chi)$. After these simplifications, $F \Rightarrow G$ can be written in the form $\bigwedge_i (f_i \trianglerighteq_i 0) \Rightarrow g \geq 0$ where $\trianglerighteq_i \in \{\geq, =\}$. Observe that a constraint $\bigwedge_i (f_i \trianglerighteq_i 0) \Rightarrow g \geq 0$ is satisfied if and only if the set $\{x | f_i(x) \trianglerighteq_i 0 \text{ for all } i;\ -g(x) \geq 0; \text{ and } g(x) \neq 0\}$ is empty. In this way, we transform our constraint into the form required by Theorem 4.

Summarizing, Constraint (2) (the main condition of Theorem 5) is satisfied if and only if all semialgebraic sets created using the procedure above are empty. Now we are ready to transform this constraint to an SDP problem.

Lemma 8 [9,25]. *The emptiness of* (1) *is equivalent to the feasibility of an SDP problem.*

This and the following results are proven in the technical report [12] accompanying this publication. Although the transformation in Lemma 8 is effective, it is complicated in practice. In the following lemma we present a simpler yet sufficient procedure.

Lemma 9. *The following statements hold (with* $\trianglerighteq_i \in \{\geq, =\}$*):*

1. $f(\mathbf{X}_n) \geq 0 \Rightarrow g(\mathbf{X}_n) \geq 0$ *holds if* $g(\mathbf{X}_n) - u \cdot f(\mathbf{X}_n)$ *is a sum of squares for some* $u \in \mathbb{R}_{\geq 0}$.
2. $f(\mathbf{X}_n) = 0 \Rightarrow g(\mathbf{X}_n) \geq 0$ *holds if* $g(\mathbf{X}_n) - v \cdot f(\mathbf{X}_n)$ *is a sum of squares for some* $v \in \mathbb{R}$.
3. $f_1(\mathbf{X}_n) \trianglerighteq_1 0 \wedge f_2(\mathbf{X}_n) \trianglerighteq_2 0 \Rightarrow g(\mathbf{X}_n) \geq 0$ *holds if* $g(\mathbf{X}_n) - r_1 \cdot f_1(\mathbf{X}_n) - r_2 \cdot f_2(\mathbf{X}_n)$ *is a sum of squares for some* $r_1, r_2 \in \mathbb{R}$*; if* $\trianglerighteq_i$ *is* $\geq$*, it is additionally required that* $r_i \geq 0$.

Note that Item (3) can be strengthened slightly by adding a cross product $r_{12} f_1(\mathbf{X}_n) f_2(\mathbf{X}_n)$ and squares of the $f_i(\mathbf{X}_n)$.

Example 10. Applying the above procedure, Constraint (5) in Example 7 is split into $(x \leq 0 \Rightarrow I \leq z) \wedge (y \leq x \Rightarrow I \leq z)$ and then normalized to $(-x \geq 0 \Rightarrow z - I \geq 0) \wedge (x - y \geq 0 \Rightarrow z - I \geq 0)$. This holds if $z - I + u_1 x$ is a SOS for some $u_1 \in \mathbb{R}_{\geq 0}$ and $z - I + u_2(y - x)$ is a SOS for some $u_2 \in \mathbb{R}_{\geq 0}$. The other constraints can be handled in a similar way.

After applying the Positivstellensatz and Lemma 8, template coefficients for the loop invariant can be synthesized efficiently by semidefinite programming. See our technical report [12] for details on the corresponding technique.

Algorithm 1. Loop Invariant Generation with Refinement

Input: *sentence* := $\langle preE \rangle$ while$(G)\{body\}$ $\langle postE \rangle$ with program variables $\mathbf{X}_n$
Output: a loop invariant satisfying the boundary and invariant conditions

loop
  $d := 2$
  Choose a template for $I \in \mathbb{R}^{\leq d}[\mathbf{X}_n]$
  Let f be Constraint (2), i.e. the boundary and invariant conditions from Theorem 5, for *sentence*
  Let *constraints* be the SDP problem equivalent to f according to Lemma 8
  while *constraints* is feasible **do**
    Set the coefficients in the template for I
    Round the coefficients of I into rational numbers
    if I satisfies the boundary and invariant conditions **then**
      Output I and terminate
    end if
    Refine *constraints*
  end while
  $d := d + 2$
end loop

We summarize our approach in Algorithm 1. The aim is to synthesize the coefficients of template I. The terms in I are all terms with degree $\leq d$ from variables in $\mathbf{X}_n$. Algorithm 1 is semi-complete in the sense that it will generate an invariant if there exists one. Its termination is guaranteed in principle by Theorem 4 and the equivalence between SOS and SDP in Lemma 8, though due to numerical errors, the algorithm may fail to find I in practice.

For efficiency, Lemma 9 is often used instead of Lemma 8. Step 5 in Algorithm 1 is replaced by: "Let *constraints* be the relaxation of f to an SOS problem according to Lemma 9"; this can be translated to an equivalent SDP problem, which is simpler than the direct translation of Lemma 8.

Example 11. We extend Example 7 using Lemma 9. To illustrate our solution method, we choose Constraints (4), (5), and (7). The initial condition $z = 0$ is not included in these constraints, so (4) needs to be refined to $z = 0 \Rightarrow xy - x^2 \leq I$.

First, we set a template for I. Assume I as a quadratic polynomial with three variables x, y, z:

$$I = c_0 + c_1x + c_2y + c_3z + c_{11}x^2 + c_{12}xy + c_{13}xz + c_{22}y^2 + c_{23}yz + c_{33}z^2$$

where $c_0, \ldots, c_{33} \in \mathbb{R}$ are coefficients that remains to be determined.

For Constraint (4) with initial constraint $z = 0$, we get the following corresponding constraint:

$$I - (xy - x^2) - v \cdot z \geq 0 \tag{4'}$$

For (5), the antecedens is a conjunction of two constraints. As in Example 10, (5) is split into two constraints and transformed into

$$\begin{aligned} z - I + u_1 \cdot x \geq 0 \quad \text{and} \\ z - I - u_2 \cdot (x - y) \geq 0 \end{aligned} \tag{5'}$$

For (7), the constraint $0 < x < y$ needs to be split into two inequalities $x > 0 \wedge y - x > 0$. Similarly to (5), we transform (7) to

$$0.5 \cdot I(x+1, y, z+1) + 0.5 \cdot I(x-1, y, z+1) - I - u_3 \cdot x - u_4 \cdot (y - x) \geq 0 \tag{7'}$$

In this way the example can be transformed into an SDP problem with constraints (4′), (5′), and (7′), and positivity constraints on the multipliers $u_1 \geq 0, \ldots, u_4 \geq 0$. (For v, an arbitrary real value is allowed.) Then the resulting SDP problem can be submitted to any SOS solver.

The result using solver SeDuMi [30] is shown below.

$$\begin{aligned} I = &-7.1097 \cdot 10^{-10} - 3.8818 \cdot 10^{-10}x - 0.4939 \cdot 10^{-10}y + z - x^2 + xy + \\ &2.7965 \cdot 10^{-10}xz + 0.97208 \cdot 10^{-10}y^2 + 4.4656 \cdot 10^{-10}yz - 0.28694 \cdot 10^{-10}z^2 \end{aligned}$$

If we ignore the amounts smaller than the order of magnitude of 10^{-6}, we get $I = z - x^2 + xy$. This I satisfies all constraints (including (6) and (8), which are similar to (5) and (7)), so it is correct.

4.2 Synthesis Algorithm for Nested Loop Programs

We are now turning to programs containing nested loops. To simplify our discussion, we assume the program only contains a single, terminating inner loop, i.e. it can be written as

$$\begin{aligned} P &= \mathsf{while}(G)\{\mathit{body}\} \\ &= \mathsf{while}(G)\{\mathit{body1};\ \mathsf{while}(G_{\text{inn}})\{\mathit{body}_{\text{inn}}\};\ \mathit{body2}\} \end{aligned}$$

where *body1*, $\mathit{body}_{\text{inn}}$, and *body2* are loop-free program fragments. (If the inner loop is placed within an if statement, one can transform it to the above form by strengthening G.) For a given *preE* and *postE*, we need to verify whether there exists an invariant I that satisfies Constraint (2) (the boundary and invariant conditions of Theorem 5). We denote the inner loop by $P_{\text{inn}} = \mathsf{while}(G_{\text{inn}})\{\mathit{body}_{inn}\}$.

For such a program, the main difficulty is how to deal with $wp(\mathit{body}, I)$ in Constraint (2). We propose a method here that takes the inner and outer iteration into consideration together and uses the verified pre-expectation of the inner loop to relax the constraint.

Fix templates for the polynomial invariants: I for the outer loop and I_{inn} for the inner loop P_{inn}, both with degree d. Since *body2* is loop-free, it is easy to obtain $\tilde{I} := wp(\mathit{body2}, I)$. We use $\tilde{I}$ as post-expectation $\mathit{postE}_{\text{inn}}$ for the inner loop. Note that (2) for the inner loop requires $\mathit{preE}_{\text{inn}} \leq I_{\text{inn}}$, so we can use the template I_{inn} also as template for $\mathit{preE}_{\text{inn}}$. Then the constraints for loop invariants I and I_{inn} are

$$\begin{aligned} \mathit{preE} &\leq I \\ I \cdot [1 - \chi_G] &\leq \mathit{postE} \\ I \cdot \chi_G &\leq \widetilde{wp}(\mathit{body}, I) := wp(\mathit{body1}, \mathit{preE}_{\text{inn}}) \\ \mathit{preE}_{\text{inn}} &= I_{\text{inn}} \\ I_{\text{inn}} \cdot [1 - \chi_{G_{\text{inn}}}] &\leq \mathit{postE}_{\text{inn}} = wp(\mathit{body2}, I) \\ I_{\text{inn}} \cdot \chi_{G_{\text{inn}}} &\leq wp(\mathit{body}_{\text{inn}}, I_{\text{inn}}) \end{aligned} \tag{9}$$

The first three equations are almost Constraint (2) for the outer loop, except that $\widetilde{wp}$ is the strengthening of the weakest pre-expectation using $\mathit{preE}_{\text{inn}} = I_{\text{inn}}$ in the *wp*-calculation instead of $wp(P_{\text{inn}}, \tilde{I})$. The last three equations are Constraint (2) for the inner loop, except that we require equality in $\mathit{preE}_{\text{inn}} \leq I_{\text{inn}}$.

Then we have the following lemma, proven in our technical report [12].

Lemma 12. *An invariant I that satisfies Constraint* (9) *also satisfies* (2), *therefore it is a loop invariant for program P.*

4.3 Handling Numerical Error

In practice, it sometimes happens that numerical errors lead to wrong or trivial coefficients in the templates. We suggest several methods to refine the constraints and avoid these errors.

Due to the inaccuracy of floating-point calculations, it is hard for a software to check equations and inequalities like $x = 0$ or $x \neq 0$. A common trick to avoid this problem is to turn the equality constraint into $x \geq 0 \wedge x \leq 0$. As for inequalities, taking $x \neq 0$ as an example, a way to solve the problem is adding a new variable y to transform the constraint into $xy \geq 1$, since $xy \geq 1$ implies $x \neq 0$ for any value of y. The new constraints are in the form required by Theorem 4.

Numerical errors may also lead to an unsound invariant: we may get some coefficients with a small magnitude, which often result from floating-point inaccuracies. A common solution for this problem is to ignore those small numbers, usually smaller than 10^{-6} in practice, which means that if r is presented as $\frac{a_0}{a_1}$ with $a_1 > 0$, then it is the closest to r in all rational numbers having smaller denominator. In Example 11, eliminating the terms with a small order of magnitude was successful, but we cannot be sure whether the resulting invariant is correct if the remaining coefficients are approximate. We propose to check the soundness of such solutions symbolically as follows. Checking whether the generated invariant satisfies Constraint (2) is a special case of quantifier elimination $\forall \mathbf{x}_n \in \mathbb{R}^n,\ f(\mathbf{x}_n) \geq 0$. Such problem can be solved efficiently using an improved Cylindrical Algebraic Decomposition (CAD) algorithm implemented in [17]. In our experiments in Sect. 5, the found solutions are obtained by ignoring small numbers, and we verified they are correct by running CAD in a separate tool.

If the invariant still violates some of the constraints, we can try to strengthen the constraint (e. g., change $x \geq 0$ to $x \geq 0.1$) and repeat our method.

5 Experimental Results

We have implemented a prototype in Python to test our technique. We call the MATLAB toolbox YALMIP [22] with the SeDuMi solver [30] to solve the SDP feasibility problem. We use the math software Maple to verify the correctness of the constraints through CAD. The experiments were done on a computer with Intel(R) Core(TM) i7-4710HQ CPU and 16 GiB of RAM. The operating system is Window 7 (32bit). Constraint refinement cannot be handled automatically in the current version, but we plan to add it together with projection for rounding solutions in a future version.

Our prototype and the detailed experimental results can be found at http://iscasmc.ios.ac.cn/ppsdp. For each probabilistic program, we give the pre- and post-expectations in Table 1. The annotated pre-expectation serves as an exact estimate of the annotated post-expectation at the entrance of the loop. We apply the method to several different types of examples. A summary of the results is shown in Table 1. The first eleven probabilistic programs are benchmarks taken from paper [7]. We have further constructed three case studies to illustrate continuous distributions, polynomial probabilistic programs and nested loop programs. Detailed descriptions and the code of all examples are available from [12]. After generating an invariant, we ran CAD in Maple manually to verify its feasability.

Table 1. The column "Name" shows the name of each experiment. The annotated pre- and post-expectations are shown in the columns "*preE*" and "*postE*". The inferred quantitative loop invariant for each example is given in the column "Invariant". The column "Time" gives the running time needed of our tool: the first one is the total running time, and the second one is the time used in the SeDuMi solver.

Name	*preE*	*postE*	Invariant	Time (s)
ruin	$xy - x^2$	z	$z + xy - x^2$	0.4/0.3
bin1	$x + \frac{1}{4}ny$	x	$x + \frac{1}{4}ny$	0.4/0.2
bin2	$\frac{1}{8}n^2 - \frac{1}{8}n + \frac{3}{4}ny$	x	$x + \frac{1}{8}n^2 - \frac{1}{8}n + \frac{3}{4}ny$	0.7/0.3
bin3	$\frac{1}{8}n^2 - \frac{1}{8}n + \frac{3}{4}ny^2$	x	$x - 0.0057n - 0.0014x^2 + 0.1763xn + 712.909n^2 + 0.0014x^2n + 0.4114xn^2 + 0.4188ny^2 - 0.0178n^3$	0.7/0.3
geo	$x + 3zy$	x	$x + 3zy$	0.2/0.2
geo2	$x + \frac{15}{2}$	x	$x + 30.2312y + 3.4699z - 12.6648y^2 - 44.6591yz - 35.5112z^2 - 22.8807$	0.2/0.1
sum	$\frac{1}{4}n^2 + \frac{1}{4}n$	x	$x + \frac{1}{4}n^2 + \frac{1}{4}n$	0.3/0.1
prod	$\frac{1}{4}n^2 - \frac{1}{4}n$	xy	$-\frac{1}{4}n + xy + \frac{1}{2}xn + \frac{1}{2}yn + \frac{1}{4}n^2$	0.3/0.1
fair coin1	$\frac{1}{2} - \frac{1}{2}x$	$1 - x + xy$	$0.7130 - 0.5622x + 0.3364y + 0.8564n - 1.2740x^2 + 07610xy - 1.4572xn - 1.2208y^2 + 1.4572yn - 0.1366n^2$	0.2/0.1
fair coin2	$\frac{1}{2} - \frac{1}{2}y$	$x + xy$	$1.1941 + 1.6157x + 0.6387y + 7.9774n - 14.6705x^2 + 9.7904xy - 14.9948xn - 14.6457y^2 + 14.9948yn - 1.4058n^2$	0.3/0.1
fair coin3	$\frac{8}{3} - \frac{8}{3}x - \frac{8}{3}y + \frac{1}{3}n$	n	$6.0556 + 2.5964x + 3.2468y + 39.2052n - 69.9038x^2 + 44.0224xy - 72.1408xn - 69.8067y^2 + 72.1408yn - 6.7632n^2$	0.2/0.1
simple perceptron	$-2b$	n	$n - 2b$	0.3/0.1
airplane delay	$106.548x$	h	$106.548x - 106.548n + h$	0.4/0.2
airplane delay2	$282.507x$	h	$282.507(x - n) + h$	0.5/0.2
nested loop	$20(m - x)$	k	$k + 20(m - x)$	1.6/1.1

As we can see from Table 1, the running time of our method is within one second. There are some notes when calculating the examples. We relax the loop condition $z \neq 0$ in example geo2 into $z \geq 0.5$. Also in the fair coin example, we relax the loop condition $x \neq y$ into $x - y \geq 0.5 \vee y - x \geq 0.5$. Since variables in those two examples are integers, the relaxation is sound.

5.1 Evaluation

Other approaches to compute loop invariants in probabilistic programs are the Lagrange Interpolation Prototype (LIP) in [7], the tool for martingales (TM) in [3] and PRINSYS in [15]. The tools are executed on the same computer, LIP and TM under Linux and the other two under Windows. In Table 2, we compare the features supported by the four tools.

Table 2. Comparison of the features supported by 4 tools

	PRINSYS	LIP	TM	Our tool
Type of program	Linear	Cubic	Linear	Polynomial
Type of invariant	Linear	Polynomial	Linear	Polynomial
Computation method	Symbolic	Symbolic	Numerical	Numerical
Distribution of variable	Discrete	Discrete	Continuous	Continuous

We have tested the examples in Table 1 on these four tools. PRINSYS takes the longest time and fails to verify any of non-linear examples presented. LIP fails to verify any examples that include a continuous variable or have a degree larger than 3; additionally it is always about 10 times slower than our tool. TM fails to verify examples ruin, bin3 and geo directly. We observe that it cannot treats constraints of the form $x = y$ or $x \neq y$ (where x and y might be variables or constants). However, by transforming $x = y$ into $x \geq y \wedge y \geq x$, TM can synthesize a supermartingale for the program. Also, it cannot verify the simple perceptron, as it is a non-linear program. Furthermore, TM cannot deal with nested loop programs.

A weakness of our approach is that it depends heavily on the number of variables. We have constructed an artificial example to expose this: a parametric linear program that repeats t times the probabilistic assignment

$$h := h + x_1 + \cdots + x_n \ [0.5] \ h := h + x_1 + \cdots + x_n + \text{UnifDist}(0, 2n)$$

This program has $n + 2$ variables. Table 3 compares the time consumption of the main technical step in our prototype. Adding five variables leads to a solver time that is about 2.5 times higher, showing that the measured solver time is exponential in the number of variables. The full description and code are, again, in our report [12].

Table 3. Comparison of running time (in seconds) of the parameterized linear example

Number of variables	$n = 15$	$n = 20$	$n = 25$	$n = 30$	$n = 35$	$n = 40$
Solver time of our tool	0.41	1.30	2.44	8.30	20.56	46.62

6 Conclusion

In this paper, we propose a method to synthesize polynomial quantitative invariants for recursive probabilistic programs by semialgebraic programming via a Positivstellensatz. First, a polynomial template is fixed whose coefficients remain to be determined. The loop and its pre- and post-expectation can be transformed into a semialgebraic set, of which the emptiness can be decided by finding a counterexample satisfying the condition of the Positivstellensatz. Semidefinite programming provides an efficient way to synthesize such a counterexample. The method can be applied to polynomial programs containing continuous or discrete variables, including those with nested loops. When numerical errors prevent finding a loop invariant polynomial right away, we currently can correct them *ad hoc* (by deleting terms with very small coefficients and sometimes strengthening the constraints), but we would like to develop a more systematic treatment.

As future improvement, we are working on the handling of numerical errors. A better approximation can be found by projecting $\tilde{I}(x)$ onto a rational subspace defined by SDP constraints [19,26]. There are also acceleration methods for different types of probabilistic programs: For *linear* programs, Handelman's Positivstellensatz describes a faster way to synthesize SOS constraints, and for *Archimedean* programs, [9] describes a faster way to apply Stengle's Positivstellensatz.

Acknowledgement. This work has been supported by the National Natural Science Foundation of China (Grants 61532019 and 61472473), the CAS/SAFEA International Partnership Program for Creative Research Teams, and the Sino-German CDZ project CAP (GZ 1023).

References

1. Barthe, G., Espitau, T., Ferrer Fioriti, L.M., Hsu, J.: Synthesizing probabilistic invariants via Doob's decomposition. arXiv preprint arXiv:1605.02765 (2016)
2. Blekherman, G., Parrilo, P.A., Thomas, R.R. (eds.): Semidefinite Optimization and Convex Algebraic Geometry. SIAM, Philadelphia (2012). doi:10.1137/1.9781611972290
3. Chakarov, A., Sankaranarayanan, S.: Probabilistic program analysis with martingales. In: Sharygina, N., Veith, H. (eds.) CAV 2013. LNCS, vol. 8044, pp. 511–526. Springer, Heidelberg (2013). doi:10.1007/978-3-642-39799-8_34
4. Chakarov, A., Sankaranarayanan, S.: Expectation invariants for probabilistic program loops as fixed points. In: Müller-Olm, M., Seidl, H. (eds.) SAS 2014. LNCS, vol. 8723, pp. 85–100. Springer, Cham (2014). doi:10.1007/978-3-319-10936-7_6
5. Chatterjee, K., Fu, H., Goharshady, A.K.: Termination analysis of probabilistic programs through positivstellensatz's. In: Chaudhuri, S., Farzan, A. (eds.) CAV 2016. LNCS, vol. 9779, pp. 3–22. Springer, Cham (2016). doi:10.1007/978-3-319-41528-4_1

6. Chatterjee, K., Fu, H., Novotný, P., Hasheminezhad, R.: Algorithmic analysis of qualitative and quantitative termination problems for affine probabilistic programs. In: Bodik, R., Majumdar, R. (eds.) POPL'16, pp. 327–342. ACM, New York (2016). doi:10.1145/2837614.2837639
7. Chen, Y.-F., Hong, C.-D., Wang, B.-Y., Zhang, L.: Counterexample-guided polynomial loop invariant generation by lagrange interpolation. In: Kroening, D., Păsăreanu, C.S. (eds.) CAV 2015. LNCS, vol. 9206, pp. 658–674. Springer, Cham (2015). doi:10.1007/978-3-319-21690-4_44
8. Colón, M.A., Sankaranarayanan, S., Sipma, H.B.: Linear invariant generation using non-linear constraint solving. In: Hunt Jr., W.A., Somenzi, F. (eds.) CAV 2003. LNCS, vol. 2725, pp. 420–432. Springer, Berlin (2003). doi:10.1007/978-3-540-45069-6_39
9. Dai, L., Xia, B., Zhan, N.: Generating non-linear interpolants by semidefinite programming. In: Sharygina, N., Veith, H. (eds.) CAV 2013. LNCS, vol. 8044, pp. 364–380. Springer, Heidelberg (2013). doi:10.1007/978-3-642-39799-8_25
10. Dijkstra, E.: A Discipline of Programming, vol. 4. Prentice-Hall, Englewood Cliffs (1976)
11. Feller, W.: An Introduction to Probability Theory and Its Applications, vol. 1. Wiley, Hoboken (1968)
12. Feng, Y., Zhang, L., Jansen, D.N., Zhan, N., Xia, B.: Finding polynomial loop invariants for probabilistic programs. arXiv:1707.02690 (2017)
13. Ferrer Fioriti, L.M., Hermanns, H.: Probabilistic termination: soundness, completeness, and compositionality. In: POPL 2015, Principles of Programming Languages, pp. 489–501. ACM, New York (2015). doi:10.1145/2775051.2677001
14. Gordon, A.D., Henzinger, T.A., Nori, A.V., Rajamani, S.K.: Probabilistic programming. In: Dwyer, M.B., Herbsleb, J. (eds.) Future of Software Engineering (FOSE 2014), pp. 167–181. ACM, New York (2014). doi:10.1145/2593882.2593900
15. Gretz, F., Katoen, J.-P., McIver, A.: PRINSYS—on a quest for probabilistic loop invariants. In: Joshi, K., Siegle, M., Stoelinga, M., D'Argenio, P.R. (eds.) QEST 2013. LNCS, vol. 8054, pp. 193–208. Springer, Heidelberg (2013). doi:10.1007/978-3-642-40196-1_17
16. Gretz, F., Katoen, J.-P., McIver, A.: Operational versus weakest pre-expectation semantics for the probabilistic guarded command language. Perf. Eval. **73**, 110–132 (2014). doi:10.1016/j.peva.2013.11.004
17. Han, J., Jin, Z., Xia, B.: Proving inequalities and solving global optimization problems via simplified CAD projection. J. Symb. Comput. **72**, 206–230 (2016). doi:10.1016/j.jsc.2015.02.007
18. Hoare, C.A.R.: An axiomatic basis for computer programming. Commun. ACM **12**(10), 576–580 (1969). doi:10.1145/363235.363259
19. Kaltofen, E.L., Li, B., Yang, Z., Zhi, L.: Exact certification in global polynomial optimization via sums-of-squares of rational functions with rational coefficients. J. Symb. Comput. **47**(1), 1–15 (2012). doi:10.1016/j.jsc.2011.08.002
20. Kaminski, B.L., Katoen, J.-P.: On the hardness of almost–sure termination. In: Italiano, G.F., Pighizzini, G., Sannella, D.T. (eds.) MFCS 2015. LNCS, vol. 9234, pp. 307–318. Springer, Heidelberg (2015). doi:10.1007/978-3-662-48057-1_24
21. Katoen, J.-P., McIver, A.K., Meinicke, L.A., Morgan, C.C.: Linear-invariant generation for probabilistic programs: In: Cousot, R., Martel, M. (eds.) SAS 2010. LNCS, vol. 6337, pp. 390–406. Springer, Berlin (2010). doi:10.1007/978-3-642-15769-1_24

22. Löfberg, J.: YALMIP: a toolbox for modeling and optimization in MATLAB. In: 2004 IEEE International Symposium on Computer Aided Control Systems Design (CACSD), pp. 284–289. IEEE, Piscataway (2004). doi:10.1109/CACSD.2004.1393890
23. McIver, A., Morgan, C.C.: Abstraction, Refinement and Proof for Probabilistic Systems. Springer, New York (2005). doi:10.1007/b138392
24. Morgan, C., McIver, A., Seidel, K.: Probabilistic predicate transformers. ACM Trans. Progr. Lang. Syst. **18**(3), 325–353 (1996). doi:10.1145/229542.229547
25. Parrilo, P.A.: Semidefinite programming relaxations for semialgebraic problems. Math. Program. Ser. B **96**(2), 293–320 (2003). doi:10.1007/s10107-003-0387-5
26. Peyrl, H., Parrilo, P.A.: Computing sum of squares decompositions with rational coefficients. Theoret. Comput. Sci. **409**(2), 269–281 (2008). doi:10.1016/j.tcs.2008.09.025
27. Putinar, M.: Positive polynomials on compact semi-algebraic sets. Indiana Univ. Math. J. **42**(3), 969–984 (1993)
28. Rodríguez-Carbonell, E., Kapur, D.: Generating all polynomial invariants in simple loops. J. Symb. Comput. **42**(4), 443–476 (2007). doi:10.1016/j.jsc.2007.01.002
29. Stengle, G.: A nullstellensatz and a positivstellensatz in semialgebraic geometry. Math. Ann. **207**(2), 87–97 (1974). doi:10.1007/BF01362149
30. Sturm, J.F.: Using SeDuMi 1.02, a MATLAB toolbox for optimization over symmetric cones. Optim. Methods Softw. **11**(1–4), 625–653 (1999). doi:10.1080/10556789908805766

Synthesis of Optimal Resilient Control Strategies

Christel Baier[1], Clemens Dubslaff[1(✉)], L'uboš Korenčiak[2(✉)], Antonín Kučera[2], and Vojtěch Řehák[2]

[1] TU Dresden, Dresden, Germany
{christel.baier,clemens.dubslaff}@tu-dresden.de
[2] Masaryk University, Brno, Czech Republic
{korenciak,kucera,rehak}@fi.muni.cz

Abstract. Repair mechanisms are important within resilient systems to maintain the system in an operational state after an error occurred. Usually, constraints on the repair mechanisms are imposed, e.g., concerning the time or resources required (such as energy consumption or other kinds of costs). For systems modeled by Markov decision processes (MDPs), we introduce the concept of *resilient schedulers*, which represent control strategies guaranteeing that these constraints are always met within some given probability. Assigning rewards to the operational states of the system, we then aim towards resilient schedulers which maximize the long-run average reward, i.e., the expected mean payoff. We present a pseudo-polynomial algorithm that decides whether a resilient scheduler exists and if so, yields an optimal resilient scheduler. We show also that already the decision problem asking whether there exists a resilient scheduler is PSPACE-hard.

1 Introduction

Computer systems are resilient when they incorporate mechanisms to adapt to changing conditions and to recover rapidly or at low costs from disruptions. The latter property of resilient systems is usually maintained through repair mechanisms, which push the system towards an operational state after some error occurred. Resilient systems and repair mechanisms have been widely studied in the literature and are an active field of research (see, e.g., [2] for an overview). Errors such as measurement errors, read/write errors, connection errors do not necessarily impose a system error but may be repaired to foster the system to be operational. Examples of repair mechanisms include rejuvenation procedures that face the degradation of software over time [13], the evaluation of checksums to repair communication errors, or methods to counter an attack from outside a security system. The repair of a degraded software system could be achieved, e.g., by clearing caches (fast, very good availability), by running maintenance

The authors are partly supported by the Czech Science Foundation, grant No. 15-17564S, by the DFG through the Collaborative Research Center SFB 912 – HAEC, the Excellence Initiative by the German Federal and State Governments (cluster of excellence cfAED), and the DFG-projects BA-1679/11-1 and BA-1679/12-1.

D. D'Souza and K. Narayan Kumar (Eds.): ATVA 2017, LNCS 10482, pp. 417–434, 2017.
DOI: 10.1007/978-3-319-68167-2_27

methods (more time, less availability, but higher success), or by a full restart (slow, cutting off availability, but guaranteed success). Depending on the situation the system faces, there is a trade-off between these characteristics and a choice has to be made, which of the repair mechanisms should be executed to fulfill further constraints on the repair, which errors should be avoided, and to optimize an overall goal. Usually, finding suitable control strategies performing the choices for repair is done in an ad-hoc manner and requires a considerable engineering effort.

In this paper, we face the question of an automated synthesis of *resilient control strategies* that maximize the long-run average availability of the system. Inspired by the use of probabilistic response patterns to describe resilience [8], we focus on control strategies that are *probabilistically resilient*, i.e., with high probability repair mechanisms succeed within a given amount of time or other kinds of costs. Our formal model we use to describe resilient systems is provided by Markov decision processes (MDPs, see, e.g., [17,19]). That is, directed graphs over states with edges annotated by actions that stand for non-deterministic choices and stochastic information about the probabilistic choices resolved after taking some action. Following [3,16], we distinguish between three kinds of states: error, repair and operational states. Error states stand for states where a disruption of the system is discovered, initiating a repair mechanism modeled by repair states. Operational states are those states where the system is available and no repair is required. To reason about the trade-off between choosing control strategies, we amend error and repair states with cost values, and operational states with payoff values, respectively. Assigned costs formalize, e.g., the time required or the energy consumed for leaving an error or repair state. Likewise, assigned payoff values quantify the benefit of some operational state, e.g., stand for the number of successfully completed tasks while being operational. We define the long-run average availability as the mean-payoff. Control strategies in MDPs are provided by (randomized) schedulers that, depending on the history of the system execution, choose the probability of the next action to fire. When the probabilities for action choices are Dirac, i.e., exactly one action is chosen almost surely, the scheduler is called deterministic. Schedulers which select an action only depending on the current state, i.e., do not depend on the history, are called memoryless. For a given cost bound R and a probability threshold $\wp$, we call a scheduler *resilient* if the scheduler ensures for every error a recovery within at most R costs with probability at least $\wp$.

Our Contribution. We show that if the cost bound R is represented in *unary*, the existence of a resilient scheduler is solvable in polynomial time. Further, we show that if there is at least one resilient scheduler, then there also exists an *optimal* resilient scheduler $\mathfrak{R}$ computable in polynomial time. Here, optimality means that $\mathfrak{R}$ achieves the maximal long-run average availability among all resilient schedulers. The constructed scheduler $\mathfrak{R}$ is randomized and uses finite memory. The example below illustrates that deterministic or memoryless randomized schedulers are less powerful. If R is encoded in binary, our algorithms are exponential, and we show that deciding the existence of a resilient scheduler

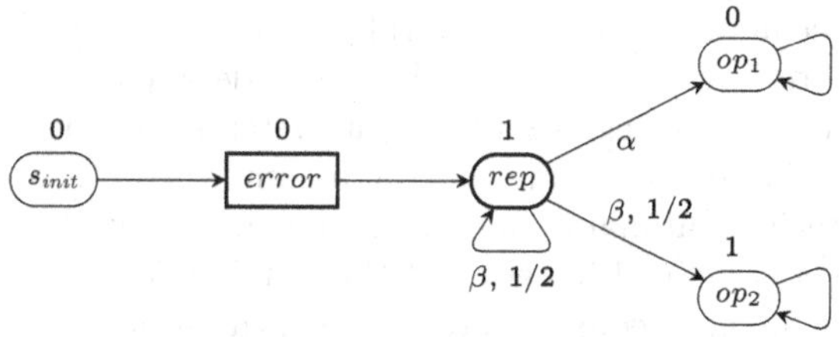

Fig. 1. Optimal resilient schedulers might require finite memory and randomization

becomes PSPACE-hard. Let us note that all numerical constants (such as $\wp$ or MDP transition probabilities) except for R are represented as fractions of binary numbers. The key technical ingredients of our results are non-trivial observations about the structure of resilient schedulers, which connect the studied problems to the existing works on MDPs with multiple objectives and optimal strategy synthesis [7,11,17]. The PSPACE-hardness result is obtained by a simple reduction of the cost-bounded reachability problem in acyclic MDPs [15]. More details are given at appropriate places in Sect. 3. Due to space constraints, full proofs can be found in the full version of this paper [4].

Example. As a simple example, consider an MDP model of a resilient system depicted in Fig. 1. Operational states are depicted by thin rounded boxes, error states are shown as rectangles and repair states are depicted by thick-rounded boxes. Assigned cost and payoff values are indicated above the nodes of the MDP. For edges without any action name or probability, we assume one action with probability one. The system starts its execution in the operational state s_{init}, from which it reaches the error state *error* and directly invokes a repair mechanism by switching to the repair state *rep*, where either action α or β can be chosen. After taking α, an operational state op_1 is reached that, however, does not grant any payoff. When choosing β, a fair coin is flipped and either the repair mechanism has to be tried again or the operational state op_2 is reached, while providing the payoff value 1 for each visit of op_2. Assume that we have given the cost bound $R = 2$ and probability threshold $\wp = 4/5$. The memoryless deterministic strategy always choosing β yields the maximal possible mean payoff of 1, but is not resilient as $\wp > 1 - 1/2^R = 3/4$. The memoryless randomized scheduler that chooses β with probability $2/\sqrt{5}$ is resilient and achieves the maximal mean payoff of $1/(\sqrt{5} - 1) \approx 0.809$, when ranging over all memoryless randomized schedulers. Differently, the finite-memory randomized scheduler playing β with probability 4/5 in the second step and with probability 1 in all other steps yields the mean payoff of 0.9, which is optimal within all resilient schedulers. As this example shows, optimal resilient schedulers might require randomization and finite memory in terms of remembering the accumulated costs spent so far after an error occurred.

Related work. Concerning the analysis of resilient systems, [3] presented algorithms to reason about trade-offs between costs and payoffs using (probabilistic) model-checking techniques. In [18], several metrics to quantify resiliency and their applications to large scale systems has been detailed.

Synthesis of control strategies for resilient systems have been mainly considered in the non-probabilistic setting. In [16], a game-theoretic approach towards synthesizing strategies that maintain a certain resilience level has been presented. The resilience level is defined in terms of the number of errors from which the system can recover simultaneously. Automatic synthesis of Pareto-optimal implementations of resilient systems were detailed in [10]. Robust synthesis procedures with both, qualitative and mean-payoff objectives have been presented in [6]. In [14], the authors present algorithms to synthesize controllers for fault-tolerant systems compliant to constraints on power consumption.

Optimization problems for MDPs with mean-payoff objectives and constraints on cost structures have been widely studied in the field of constrained Markov decision processes (see, e.g., [19] and [1] for an overview). MDPs with multiple constraints on the probabilities for satisfying ω-regular specifications were studied in [11]. This work has been extended to also allow for (multiple) constraints on the expected total reward in MDPs with rewards in [12]. Synthesis of optimal schedulers with multiple long-run average objectives in MDPs has been considered in [7,9]. All of the mentioned approaches have in common that they adapt well-known linear programs to synthesize optimal memoryless randomized schedulers (see, e.g., [17,19]). We also use combinations of similar techniques to find optimal resilient schedulers. As far as we know, we are the first to consider mean-payoff optimization problems under cost-bounded reachability probability constraints. Although we investigate these problems in the context of resilient systems, they are interesting by its own.

2 Notations and Problem Statement

Given a finite set X, we denote by $\mathrm{Dist}(X)$ the set of *probability distributions* on X, i.e., the set of functions $\mu\colon X \to [0,1]$ where $\sum_{x\in X} \mu(x) = 1$. By X^∞ we denote finite or infinite sequences of elements of X. We assume that the reader is familiar with principles about probabilistic systems, logics, and model-checking techniques and refer to [5] for an introduction in these subjects.

2.1 Markov Decision Processes

A *Markov decision process (MDP)* is a triple $\mathcal{M} = (S, Act, P, s_{init})$, where S is a finite state space, $s_{init} \in S$ an initial state, Act a finite set of actions, and $P\colon S \times Act \times S \to [0,1]$ a transition probability function, i.e., a function where $\sum_{s'\in S} P(s,\alpha,s') \in \{0,1\}$ for all $s \in S$ and $\alpha \in Act$. For $s \in S$, let $Act(s)$ denote the set of actions $\alpha \in Act$ that are enabled in s, i.e., $\alpha \in Act(s)$ iff $P(s,\alpha,\cdot)$ is a probability distribution over S. Unless stated differently, we suppose that any MDP does not have any trap states, i.e., states s where $Act(s) = \varnothing$. *Paths* in $\mathcal{M}$ are alternating sequences $s_0\alpha_0 s_1\alpha_1 \ldots \in S \times (Act{\times}S)^\infty$ of states and actions, such that $P(s_i,\alpha_i,s_{i+1}) > 0$ for all $i \in \mathbb{N}$. The set of all finite paths starting in state $s \in S$ is denoted by $FinPaths(s)$, where we omit s when all finite paths from any state are issued.

A *(randomized, history-dependent) scheduler* for $\mathcal{M}$ is a function $\mathfrak{S}\colon FinPaths \to \mathrm{Dist}(Act)$. A $\mathfrak{S}$*-path* in $\mathcal{M}$ is a path $\pi = s_0\alpha_0 s_1\alpha_1\dots$ in $\mathcal{M}$ where for all $n \in \mathbb{N}$ we have that $\mathfrak{S}(s_0\alpha_0 s_1\alpha_1\dots\alpha_{n-1}s_n)(\alpha_n) > 0$. We write $\Pr^{\mathfrak{S}}_{\mathcal{M},s}$ for the probability measure on infinite paths of $\mathcal{M}$ induced by a scheduler $\mathfrak{S}$ and starting in s. For a scheduler $\mathfrak{S}$ and $\pi \in FinPaths$, $\mathfrak{S} \uparrow \pi$ denotes the *residual scheduler* $\mathfrak{T}$ given by $\mathfrak{T}(\pi') = \mathfrak{S}(\pi;\pi')$ for each finite path π' where the first state of π' equals the last state of π. Here ; is used for the concatenation operator on finite paths. $\mathfrak{S}$ is called *memoryless* if $\mathfrak{S}(s) = \mathfrak{S}(\pi)$ for all $s \in S$ and all finite paths $\pi \in FinPaths$ where the last state of π is s. We abbreviate memoryless (randomized) schedulers as *MR-schedulers.*

2.2 Markov Decision Processes with Repair

Let $\mathcal{M} = (S, Act, P, s_{init})$ be an MDP and suppose that we have given two disjoint sets of states $Err, Op \subseteq S$. Intuitively, Err stands for the set of states where an error occurs, and Op stands for the set of states where the system modeled is operational. In all other states, we assume that a repair mechanism is running, triggered directly within the next transition after some error occurred. We formalize the latter assumption by

$$e \models \forall\bigcirc\forall(\neg Err\,\mathsf{W}\,Op) \qquad \text{for all states } e \in Err \tag{$*$}$$

where $\bigcirc$ and W stand for the standard next and weak-until operator, respectively, borrowed from computation tree logic (CTL, see, e.g., [5]). Assumption (*) also asserts that as soon as a repair protocol has been started, the system does not enter a new error state before a successful repair, i.e., until the system switches to its operational mode.

Further, we suppose that states in $\mathcal{M}$ are amended with non-negative integer values, i.e., we are given a non-negative integer reward function $rew\colon S \to \mathbb{N}$. For an operational state $s \in Op$, the value $rew(s)$ is viewed as the *payoff* value of state s, while for the non-operational states $s \in S\backslash Op$, the value $rew(s)$ is viewed as the repairing *costs* caused by state s. To reflect this intuitive meaning of the reward values, we shall write $payoff(s)$ instead of $rew(s)$ for $s \in Op$ and $cost(s)$ instead of $rew(s)$ for $s \in S\backslash Op$. Furthermore, we assume $payoff(s) = 0$ if $s \in S\backslash Op$ and $cost(s) = 0$ if $s \in Op$. For a finite path $\pi = s_0\alpha_0 s_1\dots\alpha_{n-1}s_n$, let $cost(\pi)$ and $payoff(\pi)$ be $\sum_{i=0}^{n} cost(s_i)$ and $\sum_{i=0}^{n} payoff(s_i)$, respectively.

An *MDP with repair* is formally defined as a tuple $(\mathcal{M}, Err, Op, rew)$, where assumption (*) is satisfied and the transition probability function of $\mathcal{M}$ is rational, assuming representation of probabilities as fractions of binary numbers.

2.3 Long-Run Availability and Resilient Schedulers

Given an MDP with repair $(\mathcal{M}, Err, Op, rew)$ and a scheduler $\mathfrak{S}$ for $\mathcal{M}$, we define the *long-run availability* of $\mathfrak{S}$, denoted by $\mathrm{Avail}^{\mathfrak{S}}_{\mathcal{M},s_{init}}$, as the expected long-run average (mean-payoff) of the payoff function. That is, for any $s_0 \in S$, $\mathrm{Avail}^{\mathfrak{S}}_{\mathcal{M},s_0}$ agrees with the expectation of the random variable X under $\mathrm{Pr}^{\mathfrak{S}}_{\mathcal{M},s_0}$ that assigns to each infinite path $\zeta = s_0\, \alpha_0\, s_1\, \alpha_1\, s_2\, \alpha_2 \ldots$ the value

$$X(\zeta) \;=\; \liminf_{n\to\infty} \frac{1}{n} \sum_{i=0}^{n-1} \mathit{payoff}(s_i).$$

Let us further assume that we have given a rational probability threshold $\wp \in (0,1]$ and a cost bound $R \in \mathbb{N}$. The threshold $\wp$ is always represented as a fraction of two binary numbers. The bound R is represented either in binary or in unary, which significantly influences the (computational) complexity of the studied problems.

Definition 1 (Resilient schedulers). *A scheduler $\mathfrak{S}$ is said to be* probabilistically resilient *with respect to $\wp$ and R if the following conditions (Res) and (ASRep) hold for all finite $\mathfrak{S}$-paths π from s_{init} to an error state s:*

$$Pr^{\mathfrak{S}\uparrow\pi}_{\mathcal{M},s}(\ \Diamond^{\leqslant R}\, Op\ ) \geqslant \ \wp \qquad \text{(Res)}$$

$$Pr^{\mathfrak{S}\uparrow\pi}_{\mathcal{M},s}(\ \Diamond\, Op\ ) = \ 1 \qquad \text{(ASRep)}$$

Here, $\Diamond\, Op$ denotes the set of infinite paths ζ for which there exist a finite path π' and an infinite path ϱ such that $\zeta = \pi'; \varrho$ and the last state of π' is in Op. Further, $\Diamond^{\leqslant R}\, Op$ denotes the set $\Diamond\, Op$ restricted to paths satisfying $cost(\pi') \leqslant R$.

The task addressed in this paper is to check the existence of resilient schedulers (i.e., schedulers that are probabilistically resilient w.r.t. $\wp$ and R), and if so, construct an *optimal* resilient scheduler $\mathfrak{R}$ that has maximal long-run availability amongst all resilient schedulers, i.e., $\mathrm{Avail}^{\mathfrak{R}}_{\mathcal{M},s_{init}} = \mathrm{Avail}^{\max}_{\mathcal{M},s_{init}}$, where

$$\mathrm{Avail}^{\max}_{\mathcal{M},s_{init}} \;=\; \sup \left\{ \mathrm{Avail}^{\mathfrak{R}'}_{\mathcal{M},s_{init}} \;:\; \mathfrak{R}' \text{ is a resilient scheduler} \right\}.$$

3 The Results

In the following, we present and prove our main result of this paper:

Theorem 1. *Let $(\mathcal{M}, Err, Op, rew)$ be an MDP with repair, $\wp \in (0,1]$ a rational probability threshold, and $R \in \mathbb{N}$ a cost bound encoded in unary. The existence of a probabilistically resilient scheduler w.r.t. $\wp$ and R is decidable in polynomial time. If such a scheduler exists, then an* optimal *probabilistically resilient scheduler $\mathfrak{R}$ (w.r.t. $\wp$ and R) is computable in polynomial time.*

If R is encoded in binary, our algorithms are exponential, and we show that even the existence of a probabilistically resilient scheduler w.r.t. $\wp$ and R becomes PSPACE-hard. The optimal scheduler $\mathfrak{R}$ is randomized and history dependent, which is unavoidable (see the example in the introduction). More precisely, the memory requirements of $\mathfrak{R}$ are finite with at most $|Err| \cdot R$ memory elements, and this memory is only used in the repairing phase where the scheduler needs to remember the error state and the total costs accumulated since visiting this error state.

For the rest of this section, we fix an MDP with repair $(\mathcal{M}, Err, Op, rew)$ where $\mathcal{M} = (S, Act, P, s_{init})$, a rational probability threshold $\wp \in (0,1]$, and a cost bound $R \in \mathbb{N}$. We say that a scheduler is *resilient* if it is probabilistically resilient w.r.t. $\wp$ and R.

The proof of Theorem 1 is obtained in two steps. First, the MDP $\mathcal{M}$ is transformed into a suitable MDP $\hat{\mathcal{M}}$ where the total costs accumulated since the last error are explicitly remembered in the states. Hence, the size of $\hat{\mathcal{M}}$ is polynomial in the input size if R is encoded in unary. We will show that the problem of computing an optimal resilient scheduler can be safely considered in $\hat{\mathcal{M}}$ instead of $\mathcal{M}$. In the second step, it is shown that there exists an optimal *memoryless* resilient scheduler for $\hat{\mathcal{M}}$ computable in time polynomial in the size of $\hat{\mathcal{M}}$. This is the very core of our paper requiring non-trivial observations and constructions. Roughly speaking, we start by connecting our problem to the problem of multiple mean-payoff optimization, and use the results and algorithms presented in [7] to analyze the limit behavior of resilient schedulers. First, we show how to compute the set of end components such that resilient schedulers can stay only in these end components without loosing availability. We also compute memoryless schedulers for these end components that can safely be adopted by resilient schedulers. Then, we show that the behavior of a resilient scheduler prior entering an end component can also be modified so that it becomes memoryless and the achieved availability does not decrease. After understanding the structure of resilient schedulers, we can compute an optimal memoryless resilient scheduler for $\hat{\mathcal{M}}$ by solving suitable linear programs.

The first step (i.e., the transformation of $\mathcal{M}$ into $\hat{\mathcal{M}}$) is described in Sect. 3.1, and the second step in Sect. 3.2.

3.1 Transformation

Let $(\hat{\mathcal{M}}, \hat{Err}, \hat{Op}, \hat{rew})$ be an MDP with repair where $\hat{\mathcal{M}}$ is an MDP $(\hat{S}, \hat{Act}, \hat{P}, s_{init})$ such that $\hat{S} = S \cup Rep$ with

$$Rep \;=\; Err \times S \times \{0, 1, \ldots, R\}.$$

Intuitively, state $\langle e, s, r\rangle \in Rep$ indicates that the system is in state s executing a repair procedure that has been triggered by visiting $e \in Err$ somewhen in the past and with accumulated costs r so far. For technical reasons, we also include triples $\langle e, s, r\rangle$ with $s \in Op$ in which case a repair mode with total cost r has just finished. The sets of error and operational states in $\hat{\mathcal{M}}$ are:

$$\hat{Err} \;=\; Err \quad \text{and} \quad \hat{Op} \;=\; Op \cup \big\{ \langle e, s, r\rangle \in Rep : s \in Op \big\}.$$

The action set of $\hat{\mathcal{M}}$ is the same as for $\mathcal{M}$. In what follows, we write $\hat{Act}(\hat{s})$ for the set of actions that are enabled in state $\hat{s}$ of $\hat{\mathcal{M}}$. Then, $\hat{Act}(s) = \hat{Act}(\langle e, s, r\rangle) = Act(s)$. Let $s, s' \in S$ and $\alpha \in Act$. Then, $\hat{P}(s, \alpha, s') = P(s, \alpha, s')$ if $s \notin Err$. If $e \in Err$ and $\alpha \in Act(e)$, then

$$\hat{P}(e, \alpha, \langle e, s, cost(e)\rangle) \;=\; P(e, \alpha, s)$$

For, $e \in Err$, $r \in \{0, 1, \ldots, R\}$, and $\alpha \in Act(s)$ we have:

$$\begin{aligned} \hat{P}(\langle e, s, r\rangle, \alpha, \langle e, s', r{+}cost(s)\rangle) &= P(s, \alpha, s') && \text{if } r{+}cost(s) \leqslant R \text{ and } s \notin Op \\ \hat{P}(\langle e, s, r\rangle, \alpha, s') &= P(s, \alpha, s') && \text{if } r{+}cost(s) > R \text{ or } s \in Op \end{aligned}$$

In all remaining cases, we set $\hat{P}(\cdot) = 0$. The reward function $\hat{rew}$ of $\hat{\mathcal{M}}$ is given by $\hat{cost}(s) = \hat{cost}(\langle e, s, r\rangle) = cost(s)$ and $\hat{payoff}(s) = \hat{payoff}(\langle e, s, r\rangle) = payoff(s)$. Note that assumption (*) ensures that $s \notin Err$ for all states $\langle e, s, r\rangle$.

There is a one-to-one correspondence between the paths in $\mathcal{M}$ and in $\hat{\mathcal{M}}$. More precisely, given a (finite or infinite) path $\hat{\pi}$ in $\hat{\mathcal{M}}$, let $\hat{\pi}|_{\mathcal{M}}$ denote the unique path in $\mathcal{M}$ that arises from $\hat{\pi}$ by replacing each repair state $\langle e, s, r\rangle$ with s. Vice versa, each path π in $\mathcal{M}$ can be lifted to a path $\pi|^{\hat{\mathcal{M}}}$ in $\hat{\mathcal{M}}$ such that $(\pi|^{\hat{\mathcal{M}}})|_{\mathcal{M}} = \pi$. Next lemmas follow directly from definitions of $\hat{cost}$ and $\hat{payoff}$.

Lemma 1. *For each finite path $\hat{\pi}$ in $\hat{\mathcal{M}}$ starting in some state $e \in \hat{Err}$ we have $\hat{cost}(\hat{\pi}) = cost(\hat{\pi}|_{\mathcal{M}})$.*

Lemma 2. *For each infinite path $\hat{\zeta}$ in $\hat{\mathcal{M}}$, $\hat{payoff}(\hat{\zeta}) = payoff(\hat{\zeta}|_{\mathcal{M}})$.*

The one-to-one correspondence between the paths in $\mathcal{M}$ and in $\hat{\mathcal{M}}$ carries over to the schedulers for $\mathcal{M}$ and $\hat{\mathcal{M}}$. Given a scheduler $\mathfrak{S}$ for $\mathcal{M}$, let $\mathfrak{S}|^{\hat{\mathcal{M}}}$ denote the scheduler for $\hat{\mathcal{M}}$ given by $\mathfrak{S}|^{\hat{\mathcal{M}}}(\hat{\pi}) = \mathfrak{S}(\hat{\pi}|_{\mathcal{M}})$ for all finite paths $\hat{\pi}$ of $\hat{\mathcal{M}}$. This yields a scheduler transformation $\mathfrak{S} \mapsto \mathfrak{S}|^{\hat{\mathcal{M}}}$ that maps each scheduler for $\mathcal{M}$ to a scheduler for $\hat{\mathcal{M}}$. Vice versa, given a scheduler $\hat{\mathfrak{S}}$ for $\hat{\mathcal{M}}$ there exists a scheduler $\hat{\mathfrak{S}}|_{\mathcal{M}}$ such that $\hat{\mathfrak{S}} = (\hat{\mathfrak{S}}|_{\mathcal{M}})|^{\hat{\mathcal{M}}}$.

Due to assumption (*) we have that $s \notin Err$ for all repair states $\langle e, s, r\rangle$ that are reachable from e in $\hat{\mathcal{M}}$. Thus, with Lemmas 1 and 2, we obtain:

Lemma 3. *Let $\mathfrak{S}$ be a scheduler for $\mathcal{M}$ and $\hat{\mathfrak{S}}$ a scheduler for $\hat{\mathcal{M}}$ such that $\mathfrak{S} = \hat{\mathfrak{S}}|_{\mathcal{M}}$. Then:*

(a) For each state $e \in Err$: $Pr^{\mathfrak{S}}_{\mathcal{M},e}(\Diamond\, Op) \;=\; Pr^{\hat{\mathfrak{S}}}_{\hat{\mathcal{M}},e}(\Diamond\, \hat{Op})$ *and*

$$Pr^{\mathfrak{S}}_{\mathcal{M},e}(\Diamond^{\leqslant R}\, Op) \;=\; Pr^{\hat{\mathfrak{S}}}_{\hat{\mathcal{M}},e}(\Diamond^{\leqslant R}\, \hat{Op}) \;=\; Pr^{\hat{\mathfrak{S}}}_{\hat{\mathcal{M}},e}(\bigcirc(Rep \cup Op_e))$$

where $Op_e = \{\, \langle e, s, r\rangle \in Rep : s \in Op \,\}$.

(b) $\mathrm{Avail}^{\mathfrak{S}}_{\mathcal{M},s_{init}} \;=\; \mathrm{Avail}^{\hat{\mathfrak{S}}}_{\hat{\mathcal{M}},s_{init}}$

Corollary 1. $\mathrm{Avail}^{\max}_{\mathcal{M},s_{init}} \;=\; \mathrm{Avail}^{\max}_{\hat{\mathcal{M}},s_{init}}$

Proof. The above transformations $\pi \mapsto \pi|^{\hat{\mathcal{M}}}$ and $\mathfrak{S} \mapsto \mathfrak{S}|^{\hat{\mathcal{M}}}$ for paths and schedulers of $\mathcal{M}$ to paths and schedulers of $\hat{\mathcal{M}}$, and the inverse mappings $\hat{\pi} \mapsto \hat{\pi}|_{\mathcal{M}}$ and $\hat{\mathfrak{S}} \mapsto \hat{\mathfrak{S}}|_{\mathcal{M}}$ for paths and schedulers of $\hat{\mathcal{M}}$ to paths and schedulers of $\mathcal{M}$ are compatible with the residual operator for schedulers in the following sense:

$$(\mathfrak{S} \uparrow \pi)|^{\hat{\mathcal{M}}} = (\mathfrak{S}|^{\hat{\mathcal{M}}}) \uparrow (\pi|^{\hat{\mathcal{M}}}) \quad \text{and} \quad (\hat{\mathfrak{S}} \uparrow \hat{\pi})|_{\mathcal{M}} = (\hat{\mathfrak{S}}|_{\mathcal{M}}) \uparrow (\hat{\pi}|_{\mathcal{M}})$$

Thus, part (a) of Lemma 3 yields that $\hat{\mathfrak{S}}$ is resilient for $\hat{\mathcal{M}}$ if and only if $\mathfrak{S}$ is resilient for $\mathcal{M}$. Part (b) of Lemma 3 then yields the claim. □

The following mainly technical lemma shows that residual schedulers arising from resilient schedulers maintain the resilience property.

Lemma 4. *Let $\mathfrak{S}$ be a resilient scheduler for $\hat{\mathcal{M}}$, and let s be a state of $\hat{\mathcal{M}}$ such that $s \notin Rep$. Let $\mathcal{P}$ be a set of finite $\mathfrak{S}$-paths initiated in s_{init} and terminating in s, and let $\mathfrak{S}'$ be a scheduler for $\hat{\mathcal{M}}$ resilient for the initial state changed to s. Consider the scheduler $\mathfrak{S}[\mathcal{P}, \mathfrak{S}']$ which is the same as $\mathfrak{S}$ except that for every finite path w such that $w = w'; w''$ where $w' \in \mathcal{P}$ we have that $\mathfrak{S}[\mathcal{P}, \mathfrak{S}'](w) = \mathfrak{S}'(w'')$. Then $\mathfrak{S}[\mathcal{P}, \mathfrak{S}']$ is resilient (for the initial state s_{init}).*

3.2 Solving the Resilience-Availability Problem for $\hat{\mathcal{M}}$

In this section, we analyze the structure of resilient schedulers for $\hat{\mathcal{M}}$ and prove the following proposition:

Proposition 1. *The existence of a resilient scheduler for $\hat{\mathcal{M}}$ can be decided in polynomial time. The existence of some resilient scheduler for $\hat{\mathcal{M}}$ implies the existence of an optimal memoryless resilient scheduler for $\hat{\mathcal{M}}$ computable in polynomial time.*

Note that Theorem 1 follows immediately from Proposition 1 and Corollary 1.

We start by introducing some notions. A *fragment* of $\hat{\mathcal{M}} = (\hat{S}, \hat{Act}, \hat{P}, s_{init})$ is a pair $(F, \mathcal{A})$ where $F \subseteq \hat{S}$ and $\mathcal{A}: F \to 2^{\hat{Act}}$ is a function such that $\mathcal{A}(s) \neq \emptyset$ and $\mathcal{A}(s) \subseteq \hat{Act}(s)$ for every $s \in F$. An *MR-scheduler for* $(F, \mathcal{A})$ is a function $\mathfrak{S}_F$ assigning a probability distribution over $\mathcal{A}(s)$ to every $s \in F$. We say that a scheduler $\mathfrak{S}$ for $\hat{\mathcal{M}}$ is *consistent* with $\mathfrak{S}_F$ if for every $\pi \in FinPaths$ ending in a state of F we have that $\mathfrak{S}(\pi) = \mathfrak{S}_F(\pi)$.

An *end component* of $\hat{\mathcal{M}}$ is a fragment $(E, \mathcal{A})$ of $\hat{\mathcal{M}}$ such that

- $(E, \mathcal{A})$ is strongly connected, i.e., for all $s, s' \in E$ there is a finite path $s_0 \alpha_0 s_1 \ldots \alpha_{n-1} s_n$ from $s = s_0$ to $s' = s_n$ such that $s_i \in E$ and $\alpha_i \in \mathcal{A}(s_i)$ for all $0 \leq i < n$;
- for all $s \in E$, $\alpha \in \mathcal{A}(s)$, and $s' \in \hat{S}$ such that $\hat{P}(s, \alpha, s') > 0$ we have $s' \in E$.

Let $\mathfrak{S}$ be a scheduler for $\hat{\mathcal{M}}$ (not necessarily resilient). For every infinite path ζ, let F_ζ be the set of states occurring infinitely often in ζ. For every $s \in F_\zeta$, let $\mathcal{A}_\zeta(s)$ be the set of all actions executed infinitely often from s along ζ. For a fragment $(F, \mathcal{A})$, let $Path(F, \mathcal{A})$ be the set of all infinite paths ζ such that $F_\zeta = F$ and $\mathcal{A}_\zeta = \mathcal{A}$, and let $\Pr^{\mathfrak{S}}_{\hat{\mathcal{M}}, s_{init}}(F, \mathcal{A})$ be the probability of all $\zeta \in Path(F, \mathcal{A})$ starting in s_{init}. If $(F, \mathcal{A})$ is *not* an end component, then clearly $\Pr^{\mathfrak{S}}_{\hat{\mathcal{M}}, s_{init}}(F, \mathcal{A}) = 0$. Hence, there are end components $(F_1, \mathcal{A}_1), \ldots, (F_m, \mathcal{A}_m)$ such that:

$$\Pr^{\mathfrak{S}}_{\hat{\mathcal{M}}, s_{init}}(F_i, \mathcal{A}_i) > 0 \text{ for all } i \leq m, \text{ and } \sum_{i=1}^{m} \Pr^{\mathfrak{S}}_{\hat{\mathcal{M}}, s_{init}}(F_i, \mathcal{A}_i) = 1$$

We say that $\mathfrak{S}$ *stays* in these end components.

Proposition 1 is proved as follows. We show that there is a set $\mathcal{E}$, computable in time polynomial in $|\hat{\mathcal{M}}|$, consisting of triples of the form $(E, \mathcal{A}, \mathfrak{S}_E)$ such that $(E, \mathcal{A})$ is an end component of $\hat{\mathcal{M}}$ and $\mathfrak{S}_E$ is an MR-scheduler for $(E, \mathcal{A})$, satisfying the following conditions (E1) and (E2):

(E1) If $(E, \mathcal{A}, \mathfrak{S}_E), (E', \mathcal{A}', \mathfrak{S}_{E'}) \in \mathcal{E}$, then the two triples are either the same or $E \cap E' = \varnothing$.

(E2) Every $(E, \mathcal{A}, \mathfrak{S}_E) \in \mathcal{E}$ is *strongly connected*, i.e., the directed graph $(E, \rightarrow)$, where $s \rightarrow s'$ iff there is some $\alpha \in \mathcal{A}(s)$ such that $\mathfrak{S}_E(s)(\alpha) > 0$ and $\hat{P}(s, \alpha, s') > 0$, is strongly connected. (In this case, E is a bottom strongly connected component of the Markov chain induced by $\mathfrak{S}_E$.)

Further, we can safely restrict ourselves to resilient schedulers whose long-run behavior is captured by some subset $\mathcal{E}' \subseteq \mathcal{E}$ in the following sense:

Lemma 5. *Given the set $\mathcal{E}$, for every resilient scheduler $\mathfrak{R}$ there exist a set $\mathcal{E}' \subseteq \mathcal{E}$ and a resilient scheduler $\mathfrak{R}'$ such that*

- *almost all $\mathfrak{R}'$-paths starting in s_{init} visit a state of $\bigcup_{(E, \mathcal{A}, \mathfrak{S}_E) \in \mathcal{E}'} E$,*
- *$\mathfrak{R}'$ is consistent with $\mathfrak{S}_E$ for every $(E, \mathcal{A}, \mathfrak{S}_E) \in \mathcal{E}'$,*
- $\mathrm{Avail}^{\mathfrak{R}}_{\hat{\mathcal{M}}, s_{init}} \leq \mathrm{Avail}^{\mathfrak{R}'}_{\hat{\mathcal{M}}, s_{init}}$.

Using Lemma 5, we prove the following:

Lemma 6. *Given the set $\mathcal{E}$, there is a linear program $\mathcal{L}$ computable in time polynomial in $|\hat{\mathcal{M}}|$ satisfying the following: If $\mathcal{L}$ is not feasible, then there is no resilient scheduler for $\hat{\mathcal{M}}$. Otherwise, there is a subset $\mathcal{E}' \subseteq \mathcal{E}$ and an MR-scheduler $\mathfrak{S}_F$ for the fragment $(F, \mathcal{A})$ with $F = \hat{S} \setminus \bigcup_{(E, \mathcal{A}, \mathfrak{S}_E) \in \mathcal{E}'} E$ and $\mathcal{A}(s) = \hat{Act}(s)$ for every $s \in F$ such that*

- *$\mathcal{E}'$ and $\mathfrak{S}_F$ are computable in time polynomial in $|\hat{\mathcal{M}}|$,*
- *the scheduler $\mathfrak{R}$ consistent with $\mathfrak{S}_F$ and $\mathfrak{S}_E$ for every $(E, \mathcal{A}, \mathfrak{S}_E) \in \mathcal{E}'$ is resilient, and*
- *for every resilient scheduler $\mathfrak{R}'$ we have that* $\mathrm{Avail}^{\mathfrak{R}}_{\hat{\mathcal{M}}, s_{init}} \geq \mathrm{Avail}^{\mathfrak{R}'}_{\hat{\mathcal{M}}, s_{init}}$.

In the next subsections, we show how to compute the set $\mathcal{E}$ satisfying conditions (E1) and (E2) in polynomial time and provide proofs for Lemmas 5 and 6. Note that Proposition 1 then follows from Lemma 6 and the polynomial-time computability of $\mathcal{E}$.

Constructing the Set $\mathcal{E}$. For each $e \in Err$, we define the weight function $wgt_e \colon \hat{S} \to \mathbb{Q}$ given by

$$wgt_e(\langle e,s,r\rangle) = 1-\wp \quad \text{if } s \in Op$$
$$wgt_e(\langle e,s,r\rangle) = -\wp \quad \text{if } s \notin Op \text{ and } r+cost(s) > R$$

and $wgt_e(\hat{s}) = 0$ otherwise (in particular, for all states in $\hat{s} \in \hat{S}$ that do not have the form $\langle e,s,r\rangle$). For every scheduler $\mathfrak{S}$, let $\mathrm{MP}_e^{\mathfrak{S}}$ be the expected value (under $\Pr^{\mathfrak{S}}_{\hat{\mathcal{M}},s_{init}}$) of the random variable X_e assigning to each infinite $\mathfrak{S}$-path $\zeta = s_0\,\alpha_0\,s_1\,\alpha_1\,s_2\,\alpha_2\ldots$ the value

$$X_e(\zeta) \quad = \quad \liminf_{n\to\infty} \tfrac{1}{n} \sum_{i=0}^{n-1} wgt_e(s_i).$$

We say that a scheduler $\mathfrak{S}$ for $\hat{\mathcal{M}}$ is *average-resilient* if $\mathrm{MP}_e^{\mathfrak{S}} \geq 0$ for all $e \in Err$. Note that if $\mathfrak{R}$ is a resilient scheduler for $\hat{\mathcal{M}}$, then $X_e(\zeta) \geq 0$ for almost all ζ (this follows by a straightforward application of the strong law of large numbers). Thus, we obtain:

Lemma 7. *Every resilient scheduler for $\hat{\mathcal{M}}$ is average-resilient.*

Although an average-resilient scheduler for $\hat{\mathcal{M}}$ is not necessarily resilient, we show that the problems of maximizing the long-run availability under resilient and average-resilient schedulers are to some extent related. The latter problem can be solved by the algorithm of [7]. More precisely, by Theorem 4.1 of [7], one can compute a linear program $\mathcal{L}_{\hat{\mathcal{M}}}$ in time polynomial in $|\hat{\mathcal{M}}|$ such that:

- if $\mathcal{L}_{\hat{\mathcal{M}}}$ is not feasible, then there is no average-resilient scheduler for $\hat{\mathcal{M}}$;
- otherwise, there is a 2-memory stochastic update scheduler $\mathfrak{H}$ for $\hat{\mathcal{M}}$, constructible in time polynomial in $|\hat{\mathcal{M}}|$, which is average-resilient and achieves the maximal long-run availability among all average-resilient schedulers.

The scheduler $\mathfrak{H}$ almost surely "switches" from its initial mode to its second mode where it behaves memoryless. Hence, there is a set $\mathcal{E}_{\mathfrak{H}}$ (computable in time polynomial in $|\hat{\mathcal{M}}|$) comprising triples $(E, \mathcal{A}, \mathfrak{H}_E)$ that enjoy the following properties (H1) and (H2):

- **(H1)** $(E, \mathcal{A})$ is an end component of $\hat{\mathcal{M}}$ and $\mathfrak{H}_E$ is an MR-scheduler for $(E, \mathcal{A})$ achieving the *maximal* long-run availability among all average-resilient schedulers for every initial state $s \in E$.
- **(H2)** If $(E, \mathcal{A}, \mathfrak{H}_E), (E', \mathcal{A}', \mathfrak{H}_{E'}) \in \mathcal{E}_{\mathfrak{H}}$, then the two triples are either the same or $E \cap E' = \varnothing$. Further, every $(E, \mathcal{A}, \mathfrak{H}_E) \in \mathcal{E}_{\mathfrak{H}}$ is strongly connected.

We show that for every $(E, \mathcal{A}, \mathfrak{H}_E) \in \mathcal{E}_{\mathfrak{H}}$ and every $s \in E$, the scheduler $\mathfrak{H}_E$ is *resilient* when the initial state is changed to s (see Lemma 10). So, $\mathfrak{H}$ starts to behave like a resilient scheduler after a "switch" to some $(E, \mathcal{A}, \mathfrak{H}_E) \in \mathcal{E}_{\mathfrak{H}}$. However, in the initial transient phase, $\mathfrak{H}$ may violate the resilience condition, which may disallow a resilient scheduler $\mathfrak{R}$ to enter some of the end components

Algorithm 1. Computing the set $\mathcal{E}$.

input : the transformed MDP $\hat{\mathcal{M}}$
output: the set $\mathcal{E}$ satisfying (E1) and (E2)

$\mathcal{Q} := \hat{\mathcal{M}}$, $s := s_{init}$, $\mathcal{E} := \emptyset$
repeat
  Compute the linear program $\mathcal{L}_{\mathcal{Q}}$
  if $\mathcal{L}_{\mathcal{Q}}$ *is feasible* **then**
    compute the scheduler $\mathfrak{H}$ and the set $\mathcal{E}_{\mathfrak{H}}$ satisfying (H1) and (H2)
    $\mathcal{E} := \mathcal{E} \cup \mathcal{E}_{\mathfrak{H}}$
    $\mathcal{Q} := \mathcal{Q} \ominus \mathcal{E}_{\mathfrak{H}}$
  else
    $\mathcal{Q} := \mathcal{Q} \ominus \{s\}$
  if s *is not a state of* $\mathcal{Q}$ **then**
    $s :=$ some state of $\mathcal{Q}$
until $\mathcal{Q}$ *becomes empty*
return $\mathcal{E}$

of $\mathcal{E}_{\mathfrak{H}}$. Thus, a resilient scheduler $\mathfrak{R}$ can in general be forced to stay in an end component that does not appear in $\mathcal{E}_{\mathfrak{H}}$. So, the set $\mathcal{E}$ needs to be *larger* than $\mathcal{E}_{\mathfrak{H}}$, and we show that a sufficiently large $\mathcal{E}$ is computable in polynomial time by Algorithm 1.

Algorithm 1 starts by initializing $\mathcal{Q}$ to $\hat{\mathcal{M}}$, s to s_{init}, and $\mathcal{E}$ to $\emptyset$. Then, it computes the linear program $\mathcal{L}_{\mathcal{Q}}$ and checks its feasibility. If $\mathcal{L}_{\mathcal{Q}}$ is not feasible, the initial state s of $\mathcal{Q}$ is removed from $\mathcal{Q}$ in the way described below. Otherwise, the algorithm constructs the scheduler $\mathfrak{H}$, adds $\mathcal{E}_{\mathfrak{H}}$ to $\mathcal{E}$, and "prunes" $\mathcal{Q}$ into $\mathcal{Q} \ominus \mathcal{E}_{\mathfrak{H}}$. If the state s is deleted from $\mathcal{Q}$, some state of $\mathcal{Q}$ is chosen as a new initial state. This goes on until $\mathcal{Q}$ becomes empty. Here, the MDP $\mathcal{Q} \ominus X$ is the largest MDP subsumed by $\mathcal{Q}$ which does not contain the states in $X \subseteq \hat{S}$. Note that when a state of $\mathcal{Q}$ is deleted, all actions leading to this state must be disabled; and if all outgoing actions of a state s are disabled, then s must be deleted. Hence, deleting the states appearing in $\mathcal{E}_{\mathfrak{H}}$ may enforce deleting additional states and disabling further actions. Note that every $(E, \mathcal{A}, \mathfrak{H}_E) \in \mathcal{E}$ is obtained in some iteration of the repeat-until cycle of Algorithm 1 by constructing the scheduler $\mathfrak{H}$ for the current value of $\mathcal{Q}$. We denote this MDP $\mathcal{Q}$ as $\mathcal{Q}_E$ (note that $\mathcal{Q}_E$ is not necessarily connected). The set $\mathcal{E}$ returned by Algorithm 1 indeed satisfies conditions (E1) and (E2). The outcome $\mathcal{E} = \varnothing$ is possible, in which case there is no resilient scheduler for $\hat{\mathcal{M}}$ as the linear program $\mathcal{L}$ of Lemma 6 is not feasible for $\mathcal{E} = \varnothing$.

An immediate consequence of property (H1) is the following:

Lemma 8. *Let* $(E, \mathcal{A}, \mathfrak{H}_E) \in \mathcal{E}$ *and* $s \in E$. *Then* $\mathfrak{H}_E$ *achieves the* maximal *long-run availability for the initial state* s *among all average-resilient schedulers for* $\mathcal{Q}_E$.

The next lemma follows easily from the construction of $\mathcal{E}$.

Lemma 9. *Let $\mathfrak{S}$ be a scheduler for $\hat{\mathcal{M}}$ (not necessarily resilient) and let $(F, \mathcal{B})$ be an end component where $\mathfrak{S}$ stays with positive probability. Then there is $(E, \mathcal{A}, \mathfrak{H}_E) \in \mathcal{E}$ such that $(F, \mathcal{B})$ is an end component of $\mathcal{Q}_E$ and $F \cap E \neq \varnothing$.*

Let $(E, \mathcal{A}, \mathfrak{H}_E) \in \mathcal{E}$. Since $\mathfrak{H}_E$ is an MR-scheduler, the behavior of $\mathfrak{H}_E$ in an error state $f \in E$ (for an arbitrary initial state $s \in E$) is independent of the history. That is, the resilience condition is either simultaneously satisfied or simultaneously violated for all visits to f. However, if the second case holds, $\mathfrak{H}_E$ is not even average-resilient, what is a contradiction. Thus, we obtain:

Lemma 10. *Let $(E, \mathcal{A}, \mathfrak{H}_E) \in \mathcal{E}$, and let $s \in E$. Then the scheduler $\mathfrak{H}_E$ is* resilient *when the initial state is changed to s. Further, if $\mathfrak{R}$ is a resilient scheduler for $\mathcal{Q}_E$ with the initial state s, then* $\text{Avail}_{\mathcal{Q}_E,s}^{\mathfrak{H}_E} \geq \text{Avail}_{\mathcal{Q}_E,s}^{\mathfrak{R}}$.

Proof of Lemma 5. Let $\mathfrak{R}$ be a resilient scheduler for $\hat{\mathcal{M}}$. We show that there is another resilient scheduler $\mathfrak{R}'$ satisfying the conditions of Lemma 5. First, let us consider the end components $(F_1, \mathcal{B}_1), \ldots, (F_m, \mathcal{B}_m)$ where $\mathfrak{R}$ stays. For every $(F_i, \mathcal{B}_i)$, let $(E, \mathcal{A}, \mathfrak{H}_E) \in \mathcal{E}$ be a triple with the maximal $\text{Avail}(E)$ such that $F_i \cap E \neq \varnothing$ (such a triple exists due to Lemma 9). We say that $(E, \mathcal{A}, \mathfrak{H}_E)$ is *associated* to $(F_i, \mathcal{B}_i)$. Let $\text{Avail}(F_i, \mathcal{B}_i)$ be the *conditional availability* w.r.t. scheduler $\mathfrak{R}$ under the condition that an infinite path initiated in s_{init} stays in $(F_i, \mathcal{B}_i)$. Given a triple $(E, \mathcal{A}, \mathfrak{H}_E) \in \mathcal{E}$, we use $\text{Avail}(E)$ to denote the availability achieved by scheduler $\mathfrak{H}_E$ for s. Note that $\text{Avail}(E)$ is independent of s.

Lemma 11. $\text{Avail}(F_i, \mathcal{B}_i) \leq \text{Avail}(E)$, *where $(E, \mathcal{A}, \mathfrak{H}_E) \in \mathcal{E}$ is the triple associated to $(F_i, \mathcal{B}_i)$.*

Further, we say that $(F_i, \mathcal{B}_i)$ is *offending* if there is a finite $\mathfrak{R}$-path π initiated in s_{init} ending in a state $s \in E$, where $(E, \mathcal{A}, \mathfrak{H}_E)$ is associated to $(F_i, \mathcal{B}_i)$, such that $s \notin \mathit{Rep}$ and the availability achieved by the scheduler $\mathfrak{R} \uparrow \pi$ in s is *strictly larger* than $\text{Avail}(E)$. Note that if no $(F_i, \mathcal{B}_i)$ is offending, we can choose $\mathcal{E}'$ as the set of triples associated to $(F_1, \mathcal{B}_1), \ldots, (F_m, \mathcal{B}_m)$, and redefine the scheduler $\mathfrak{R}$ into a resilient scheduler $\mathfrak{R}'$ as follows: $\mathfrak{R}'$ behaves exactly like $\mathfrak{R}$ until a state s of some $(E, \mathcal{A}, \mathfrak{H}_E) \in \mathcal{E}'$ is visited. Then, $\mathfrak{R}'$ switches to $\mathfrak{H}_E$ immediately. The scheduler $\mathfrak{R}'$ is resilient because $s \notin \mathit{Rep}$ (a visit to a repair state is preceded by a visit to the associated fail state which also belongs to E) and hence we can apply Lemma 4. Clearly, $\mathfrak{R}'$ is consistent with every $\mathfrak{H}_E$ such that $(E, \mathcal{A}, \mathfrak{H}_E) \in \mathcal{E}'$. It remains to show that the availability achieved by $\mathfrak{R}'$ in s_{init} is not smaller than the one achieved by $\mathfrak{R}$. This follows immediately by observing that whenever $\mathfrak{R}'$ makes a switch to $\mathfrak{H}_E$ after performing a finite $\mathfrak{R}$-path initiated in s_{init} ending in $s \in E$, the availability achieved by the resilient scheduler $\mathfrak{R} \uparrow \pi$ for the initial state s must be bounded by $\text{Avail}(E)$, because otherwise some $(F_i, \mathcal{B}_i)$ would be offending. So, the introduced "switch" can only increase the availability.

Now assume that $(F_m, \mathcal{B}_m)$ is offending, and let $(E, \mathcal{A}, \mathfrak{H}_E)$ be the triple associated to $(F_m, \mathcal{B}_m)$. We construct a resilient scheduler $\tilde{\mathfrak{R}}$ which stays in $(F_1, \mathcal{B}_1), \ldots, (F_{m-1}, \mathcal{B}_{m-1})$ and achieves availability not smaller than the one achieved by $\mathfrak{R}$. This completes the proof of Lemma 5, because we can then successively remove all offending pairs. Since $(F_m, \mathcal{B}_m)$ is offending, there is a finite $\mathfrak{R}$-path π initiated in s_{init} ending in a state $s \in E$ such that $s \notin Rep$ and the availability A achieved by $\mathfrak{R} \uparrow \pi$ in s is larger than $\text{Avail}(E)$. Since $F_m \cap E \neq \emptyset$, there is a state $t \notin Rep$ such that $t \in F_m \cap E$. Note that $\mathfrak{H}_E$ is resilient for the initial state t, and almost all infinite paths initiated in t visit the state s under the scheduler $\mathfrak{H}_E$.

Now, we construct a resilient scheduler $\mathfrak{S}_s$ achieving availability at least A in s such that all components where $\mathfrak{S}_s$ stays (for the initial state s) are among $(F_1, \mathcal{B}_1), \ldots, (F_{m-1}, \mathcal{B}_{m-1})$. Let P_m be the probability that an infinite path initiated in s stays in $(F_m, \mathcal{B}_m)$ under the scheduler $\mathfrak{R} \uparrow \pi$. If $P_m = 0$, we put $\mathfrak{S}_s = \mathfrak{R} \uparrow \pi$. Now assume $P_m > 0$. We cannot have $P_m = 1$, because then A is bounded by $\text{Avail}(E)$ (see Lemma 11). Let B be the conditional availability achieved in s by $\mathfrak{R} \uparrow \pi$ under the condition that an infinite path initiated in s stays in $(F_1, \mathcal{B}_1), \ldots, (F_{m-1}, \mathcal{B}_{m-1})$. Since $A \leq (1-P_m) \cdot B + P_m \cdot \text{Avail}(E)$ and $A > \text{Avail}(E)$, we obtain $B > A$. For every $\varepsilon > 0$, let Π^ε be the set of all finite $(\mathfrak{R} \uparrow \pi)$-paths π' initiated in s and ending in t such that the probability of all infinite paths initiated in t staying in $(F_m, \mathcal{B}_m)$ under the scheduler $\mathfrak{R} \uparrow (\pi; \pi')$ is at least $1-\varepsilon$. Note that each $(\mathfrak{R} \uparrow \pi)$-path initiated in s and staying in $(F_m, \mathcal{B}_m)$ is included in $(\mathfrak{R} \uparrow \pi)$-paths starting with a prefix of Π^ε. Hence, a smart redirection of the strategy after passing via Π^ε can avoid staying in $(F_m, \mathcal{B}_m)$. We use P_m^ε to denote the probability (under the scheduler $\mathfrak{R} \uparrow \pi$) of all infinite paths initiated in s starting with a prefix of Π^ε, and B^ε to denote the conditional availability achieved in s by $\mathfrak{R} \uparrow \pi$ under the condition that an infinite path initiated in s does *not* start with a prefix of Π^ε. Since $\lim_{\varepsilon \to 0} P_m^\varepsilon = P_m$ and $\lim_{\varepsilon \to 0} B^\varepsilon = B$, we can fix a sufficiently small $\delta > 0$ where

I. $\delta \cdot M + (1-\delta) \cdot \text{Avail}(E) < A$, where M is the maximal payoff assigned to a state of $\hat{\mathcal{M}}$.
II. conditional bound $B^\delta > A$.

The scheduler $\mathfrak{S}_s$ is defined in the following way, where Σ denotes the set of all finite paths ϱ initiated in t and ending in s, such that the state s is visited by ϱ only once:

$$\mathfrak{S}_s(\pi') = \begin{cases} \mathfrak{S}_s(\pi'') & \text{if } \pi' = \hat{\pi}; \varrho; \pi'' \text{ where } \hat{\pi} \in \Pi^\delta \text{ and } \varrho \in \Sigma, \\ \mathfrak{H}_E(\pi'') & \text{if } \pi' = \hat{\pi}; \pi'' \text{ where } \hat{\pi} \in \Pi^\delta \text{ and no prefix of } \pi'' \text{ is in } \Sigma, \\ (\mathfrak{R} \uparrow \pi)(\pi') & \text{otherwise.} \end{cases}$$

Intuitively, $\mathfrak{S}_s$ simulates $\mathfrak{R} \uparrow \pi$ unless a path of Π^δ is produced, in which case $\mathfrak{S}_s$ temporarily "switches" to $\mathfrak{H}_E$ until s is revisited and the simulation of $\mathfrak{R} \uparrow \pi$ is restarted. It is easy to verify that $\mathfrak{S}_s$ is a resilient scheduler achieving availability equal to $B^\delta > A$ staying in end components $(F_i, \mathcal{B}_i)$ with $i < m$.

Now we can easily construct the scheduler $\tilde{\mathfrak{R}}$. Let Ξ^δ be the set of all finite paths π initiated in s_{init} and ending in t where the probability of all infinite paths initiated in t staying in $(F_m, \mathcal{B}_m)$ is at least $1-\delta$. The scheduler $\tilde{\mathfrak{R}}$ behaves as $\mathfrak{R}$ unless a path of Ξ^δ is produced, in which case $\tilde{\mathfrak{R}}$ temporarily switches to

$\mathfrak{H}_E$ until the state s is reached, and then it permanently switches to $\mathfrak{S}_s$. The availability achieved by $\tilde{\mathfrak{R}}$ in s_{init} can be only larger that the availability achieved by $\mathfrak{R}$ due to Conditions I and II above.

Proof of Lemma 6. Let $\mathcal{E}$ denote the set of triples computed by Algorithm 1. Due to Lemma 5, we can concentrate on schedulers those paths almost surely reach subsets $\mathcal{E}' \subseteq \mathcal{E}$ and are consistent with the schedulers in $\mathcal{E}'$. Observe that the transient prefix of each path then has no effect on the long-run availability of the path and just influences the reachability probability distribution on $\mathcal{E}$. The resulting availability then is a convex combination of availabilities of the triples in $\mathcal{E}$. Thus, the aim is to find a *resilient* scheduler that maximizes this convex combination. We do so by constructing an MDP $\mathcal{N}$ where the resilient MR-scheduler $\mathfrak{R}_\mathcal{N}$ with optimal reachability reward induces optimal resilient scheduler in $\hat{\mathcal{M}}$. We show that $\mathfrak{R}_\mathcal{N}$ can be obtained from a slightly modified linear program of [17,19].

Let $\mathcal{N} = (S_\mathcal{N}, Act_\mathcal{N}, P_\mathcal{N}, s_{init})$ be an MDP over the state space

$$S_\mathcal{N} \quad = \quad \hat{S} \cup \{\, goal_E \,:\, (E, \mathcal{A}, \mathfrak{H}_E) \in \mathcal{E} \,\} \cup \{goal\}$$

and the action space $Act_\mathcal{N} = \hat{Act} \cup \{\tau\}$, where τ is a fresh action symbol. The transition probabilities $P_\mathcal{N}$ are defined as for $\hat{\mathcal{M}}$, but with additional τ-transitions for each $(E, \mathcal{A}, \mathfrak{H}_E) \in \mathcal{E}$:

- from each state $\hat{s} \in E \cap \hat{Op}$ to $goal_E$, i.e., $P_\mathcal{N}(\hat{s}, \tau, goal_E) = 1$,
- from $goal_E$ to $goal$, i.e., $P_\mathcal{N}(goal_E, \tau, goal) = 1$, and
- from $goal$ to $goal$, i.e., $P_\mathcal{N}(goal, \tau, goal) = 1$.

The reward function in $\mathcal{N}$ is given by $rew(goal_E) = \text{Avail}(E)$ for each $goal_E \in S_\mathcal{N}$ and $rew(s) = 0$ for all the remaining states $s \in \hat{S} \cup \{goal\}$. Given a scheduler $\mathfrak{S}$, the random variable TR assigns to an infinite $\mathfrak{S}$-path $\zeta = s_0\, \alpha_0\, s_1\, \alpha_1\, s_2\, \alpha_2 \ldots$ the total accumulated reward $TR(\zeta) = \sum_{i=0}^{\infty} rew(s_i)$. The expected total accumulated reward from a state $s \in S_\mathcal{N}$ is denoted by $\mathbb{E}^{\mathfrak{S}}_{\mathcal{N},s}[TR]$.

Lemma 12. *Let $\mathfrak{R}'$ be a resilient scheduler for $\hat{\mathcal{M}}$ such that $\mathfrak{R}'$-paths from s_{init} almost surely reach a subset $\mathcal{E}' \subseteq \mathcal{E}$ and is consistent with the schedulers in $\mathcal{E}'$. Then, there is a resilient scheduler $\mathfrak{R}$ for $\mathcal{N}$ where the $\mathfrak{R}$-paths from s_{init} almost surely reach goal and*

$$\text{Avail}^{\mathfrak{R}'}_{\hat{\mathcal{M}},s_{init}} = \mathbb{E}^{\mathfrak{R}}_{\mathcal{N},s_{init}}[TR].$$

From $\mathfrak{R}'$ we can easily construct an equivalent scheduler $\mathfrak{R}$ by redefining $\mathfrak{R}'$ to almost surely perform τ actions in $E \cap \hat{Op}$ for $(E, \mathcal{A}, \mathfrak{H}_E) \in \mathcal{E}'$. From Lemmas 5 and 12 it follows that if there is no resilient scheduler for $\mathcal{N}$ there is no resilient scheduler for $\hat{\mathcal{M}}$. Let $\mathfrak{R}_\mathcal{N}$ be the resilient scheduler that acquires the supremum of the expected total accumulated rewards from s_{init} among all resilient schedulers for $\mathcal{N}$ that reach *goal* almost surely from s_{init}. As we shall see bellow, we can safely assume that $\mathfrak{R}_\mathcal{N}$ is an MR-scheduler. The technical details for proving the following lemma can be found in [4].

Lemma 13. *Let $\mathfrak{R}_{\mathcal{N}}$ be an MR-scheduler that acquires maximal $\mathbb{E}^{\mathfrak{R}'}_{\mathcal{N},s_{init}}[TR]$ within resilient schedulers $\mathfrak{R}'$ for $\mathcal{N}$ such that almost all $\mathfrak{R}'$-paths reach the goal. Let $\mathcal{E}'$ be the set of all $(E, \mathcal{A}, \mathfrak{H}_E) \in \mathcal{E}$ such that $goal_E$ is visited from s_{init} with positive probability under $\mathfrak{R}_{\mathcal{N}}$, and let $\mathfrak{S}_e(s) = \mathfrak{R}_{\mathcal{N}}(s)$ for each $s \in F$ where $F = \hat{S} \setminus \bigcup_{(E,\mathcal{A},\mathfrak{S}_E)\in\mathcal{E}'} E$. Moreover, let $\mathfrak{R}$ be the unique scheduler consistent with $\mathfrak{S}_e$ and $\mathfrak{H}_E$ for each $(E, \mathcal{A}, \mathfrak{H}_E) \in \mathcal{E}'$. It holds that*

$$\mathrm{Avail}^{\mathfrak{R}}_{\hat{\mathcal{M}},s_{init}} = \mathbb{E}^{\mathfrak{R}_{\mathcal{N}}}_{\mathcal{N},s_{init}}[TR].$$

Note that the scheduler $\mathfrak{R}$ of Lemma 13 simulates the scheduler $\mathfrak{R}_{\mathcal{N}}$ only until a state of $\mathcal{E}'$ is visited (not until $\mathfrak{R}_{\mathcal{N}}$ visits a $goal_E$ state). This is the main subtlety hidden in Lemma 13.

A resiliency linear program. To obtain $\mathfrak{R}_{\mathcal{N}}$, let us consider the following linear program clearly constructible in polynomial time in $|\mathcal{N}|$ (and thus also in $|\hat{\mathcal{M}}|$). Intuitively, the variables $y_{t,\alpha}$ stand for the expected number of times an action $\alpha \in Act_{\mathcal{N}}$ is taken from state $t \in S_{\mathcal{N}}$. We set $y_t = \sum_{\alpha\in Act_{\mathcal{N}}(t)} y_{t,\alpha}$ and define

(1) flow equation: for all states $s \in S_{\mathcal{N}} \setminus \{goal\}$

$$y_s \;=\; \delta(s, s_{init}) + \sum_{t\in S_{\mathcal{N}}} \sum_{\alpha\in Act_{\mathcal{N}}(t)} y_{t,\alpha} \cdot P_{\mathcal{N}}(t, \alpha, s)$$

where $\delta(s, s_{init})$ is 1 if $s = s_{init}$, and 0 otherwise.

(2) non-negativeness: $y_{s,\alpha} \geqslant 0$ for all state-action pairs (s, α).

(3) flow equation for the goal state: $y_{goal} \geqslant 1$.

(4) resiliency constraint: for all $e \in Err$

$$\sum_{s\in Op_e} y_s \;\geqslant\; \wp \cdot y_e$$

The next lemma is proven by the methods of [17,19] (the only difference distinguishing our case is Constraint (4), which is easy to handle).

Lemma 14. *Each feasible solution $(z^*_{s,\alpha})_{s\in S_{\mathcal{N}},\alpha\in Act_{\mathcal{N}}(s)}$ of the linear program (1)–(4) under the objective to maximize $\sum_{(E,\mathcal{A},\mathfrak{H}_E)\in\mathcal{E}} y_{goal_E} \cdot \mathrm{Avail}(E)$, induces an MR-scheduler $\mathfrak{R}_{\mathcal{N}}$ that is resilient in $\mathcal{N}$ and can be computed in time polynomial in $|\mathcal{N}|$. If there is no such solution, there is no resilient scheduler in $\mathcal{N}$.*

Conversely, let $\mathfrak{R}$ be a resilient scheduler such that $\mathfrak{R}$-paths almost surely reach goal and the expected number of actions executed before reaching goal is finite. Let $z_{s,\alpha}$ denote the expected number of times an action $\alpha \in Act_{\mathcal{N}}$ is taken in a state $s \in S_{\mathcal{N}}$ using $\mathfrak{R}$. Then, values $z_{s,\alpha} = y_{t,\alpha}$ form a solution of the above linear constraints (1)–(4).

According to the second part of Lemma 14, the scheduler $\mathfrak{R}_{\mathcal{N}}$ achieves the optimal total accumulated reward among all resilient schedulers where the expected number of transitions executed before reaching *goal* is finite. The next lemma shows that $\mathfrak{R}_{\mathcal{N}}$ achieves the optimal total accumulated reward among *all* resilient schedulers, which completes the proof of Lemma 6.

Lemma 15. *$\mathbb{E}^{\mathfrak{R}_{\mathcal{N}}}_{\mathcal{N},s_{init}}[TR] \geq L$ with L being the supremum over all $E^{\mathfrak{R}}_{\mathcal{N},s_{init}}[TR]$ ranging over resilient schedulers $\mathfrak{R}$ in $\mathcal{N}$ those paths almost surely reach goal.*

Proof. First, note that $\mathbb{E}^{\mathfrak{S}}_{\mathcal{N},s_{init}}[TR]$ for an HR-scheduler $\mathfrak{S}$ can be approximated up to an arbitrary small error using a sequence of schedulers $\mathfrak{R}_i$: For each $i \in \mathbb{N}$ we define the scheduler $\mathfrak{R}_i$ by acting as $\mathfrak{S}$ until the i-th step and then continuing as $\mathfrak{R}_{\mathcal{N}}$. The expected number of executed actions before reaching the *goal* state is finite for all $\mathfrak{R}_i$. Clearly, $|\mathbb{E}^{\mathfrak{S}}_{\mathcal{N},s_{init}}[TR] - \mathbb{E}^{\mathfrak{R}_i}_{\mathcal{N},s_{init}}[TR]|$ gets arbitrarily small for increasing i. Towards a contradiction, assume that $L - \mathbb{E}^{\mathfrak{R}_{\mathcal{N}}}_{\mathcal{N},s_{init}}[TR] > \delta > 0$. Then, there is a sequence of schedulers that approximate L arbitrarily close and there is a scheduler $\mathfrak{R}$ such that $\mathbb{E}^{\mathfrak{R}}_{\mathcal{N},s_{init}}[TR] = K$ with $|L-K| < \delta/2$. Moreover, there is sequence of schedulers $\mathfrak{R}_i$ that approximate K arbitrarily close and have a finite expected number of executed actions before reaching *goal*. Hence, there is some $\mathfrak{R}_i$ such that $\left|L - \mathbb{E}^{\mathfrak{R}_i}_{\mathcal{N},s_{init}}[TR]\right| < \delta$, which is in contradiction with the optimality of $\mathfrak{R}_{\mathcal{N}}$ among all schedulers with a finite expected number of actions executed before reaching *goal*. □

3.3 A Lower Complexity Bound

When the bound R is encoded in binary, our algorithms become exponential. Using the PSPACE-hardness result for cost-bounded reachability problems in acyclic MDPs by Haase and Kiefer [15], we show that the question whether there exists a resilient scheduler is PSPACE-hard, even for acyclic MDPs, when R is encoded in binary.

Lemma 16. *If R is encoded in binary, the problem to check the existence of a resilient scheduler and the decision variant of the resilience-availability problem are PSPACE-hard.*

Proof. In [15], the PSPACE-completeness of the following cost-problem has been proven: Given an acyclic MDP $\mathcal{N} = (S, Act, P, s_{init})$ with a cost function and a cost bound R, the task is to check whether there is a scheduler $\mathfrak{S}$ for $\mathcal{N}$ such that $\Pr^{\mathfrak{S}}_{\mathcal{N},s_{init}}(\Diamond^{\leqslant R} T) \geqslant \frac{1}{2}$. Here, T denotes the set of trap states in $\mathcal{N}$ and $s_{init} \notin T$.

We now provide a polynomial reduction from the cost-problem à la Haase and Kiefer [15] to the problem to decide the existence of a resilient scheduler and the decision variant of the resilience-availability problem.

Let $\mathcal{M}$ be the MDP resulting from $\mathcal{N}$ by defining $Err = \{s_{init}\}$ and $Op = T$ and adding a fresh action symbol τ and τ-transitions from the states $t \in T$ to s_{init}. That is, $\mathcal{M}$ has the same state space as $\mathcal{N}$, the action set is $Act_{\mathcal{M}} = Act \cup \{\tau\}$ and the $\mathcal{M}$'s transition probability function extends $\mathcal{N}$'s transition probability function by $P(t, \tau, s_{init}) = 1$ and $P(t, \alpha, s) = 0$ for all states $t \in T$, $\alpha \in Act_{\mathcal{M}}$ and $s \in S$ with $(s, \alpha) \neq (s_{init}, \tau)$. $\mathcal{M}$'s cost function is the same as in $\mathcal{N}$ for all states $s \in S$ and $cost(t) = 0$ for all states $t \in T$. Obviously, each scheduler $\mathfrak{S}$ for $\mathcal{N}$ with $\Pr^{\mathfrak{S}}_{\mathcal{N},s_{init}}(\Diamond^{\leqslant R} T) \geqslant \frac{1}{2}$ can be viewed as a memoryless resilient scheduler for $\mathcal{M}$ with respect to the probability threshold $\wp = \frac{1}{2}$ and cost bound R. Vice versa, given a resilient scheduler $\mathfrak{S}'$ for $\mathcal{M}$, the decisions of $\mathfrak{S}'$ for the paths from s_{init} to a T-state yield a scheduler $\mathfrak{S}$ for $\mathcal{N}$ with $\Pr^{\mathfrak{S}}_{\mathcal{N},s_{init}}(\Diamond^{\leqslant R} T) \geqslant \frac{1}{2}$.

For the decision problem of the resilience-availability problem, we use the same reduction with availability threshold $\vartheta = 0$ and the payoff function that assign 0 to all operational states.

References

1. Altman, E.: Constrained Markov Decision Processes. Chapman and Hall, Boca Raton (1999)
2. Attoh-Okine, N.: Resilience Engineering: Models and Analysis. Resilience Engineering: Models and Analysis. Cambridge University Press, Cambridge (2016)
3. Baier, C., Dubslaff, C., Klüppelholz, S., Leuschner, L.: Energy-utility analysis for resilient systems using probabilistic model checking. In: Ciardo, G., Kindler, E. (eds.) PETRI NETS 2014. LNCS, vol. 8489, pp. 20–39. Springer, Cham (2014). doi:10.1007/978-3-319-07734-5_2
4. Baier, C., Dubslaff, C., Korenčiak, Ľ., Kučera, A., Řehák, V.: Synthesis of optimal resilient control strategies. CoRR, abs/1707.03223 (2017)
5. Baier, C., Katoen, J.-P.: Principles of Model Checking. MIT Press (2008)
6. Bloem, R., Chatterjee, K., Greimel, K., Henzinger, T.A., Hofferek, G., Jobstmann, B., Könighofer, B., Könighofer, R.: Synthesizing robust systems. Acta Inf. **51**(3), 193–220 (2014)
7. Brázdil, T., Brožek, V., Chatterjee, K., Forejt, V., Kučera, A.: Markov decision processes with multiple long-run average objectives. LMCS **10**(1) (2014)
8. Camara, J., de Lemos, R.: Evaluation of resilience in self-adaptive systems using probabilistic model-checking. In: SEAMS, pp. 53–62 (2012)
9. Chatterjee, K.: Markov decision processes with multiple long-run average objectives. In: Arvind, V., Prasad, S. (eds.) FSTTCS 2007. LNCS, vol. 4855, pp. 473–484. Springer, Heidelberg (2007). doi:10.1007/978-3-540-77050-3_39
10. Ehlers, R., Topcu, U.: Resilience to intermittent assumption violations in reactive synthesis. In: HSCC, pp. 203–212. ACM, New York (2014)
11. Etessami, K., Kwiatkowska, M., Vardi, M.Y., Yannakakis, M.: Multi-objective model checking of Markov decision processes. LMCS **4**(4) (2008)
12. Forejt, V., Kwiatkowska, M., Norman, G., Parker, D., Qu, H.: Quantitative multi-objective verification for probabilistic systems. In: Abdulla, P.A., Leino, K.R.M. (eds.) TACAS 2011. LNCS, vol. 6605, pp. 112–127. Springer, Heidelberg (2011). doi:10.1007/978-3-642-19835-9_11
13. German, R.: Performance Analysis of Communication Systems with Non-Markovian Stochastic Petri Nets. Wiley, Hobokon (2000)
14. Girault, A., Rutten, É.: Automating the addition of fault tolerance with discrete controller synthesis. Form. Methods Syst. Des. **35**(2), 190–225 (2009)
15. Haase, C., Kiefer, S.: The odds of staying on budget. In: Halldórsson, M.M., Iwama, K., Kobayashi, N., Speckmann, B. (eds.) ICALP 2015. LNCS, vol. 9135, pp. 234–246. Springer, Heidelberg (2015). doi:10.1007/978-3-662-47666-6_19
16. Huang, C.H., Peled, D.A., Schewe, S., Wang, F.: A game-theoretic foundation for the maximum software resilience against dense errors. IEEE Trans. Software Eng. **42**(7), 605–622 (2016)
17. Kallenberg, L.: Markov Decision Processes. Lect. Notes, University of Leiden (2011)
18. Longo, F., Ghosh, R., Naik, V.K., Rindos, A.J., Trivedi, K.S.: An approach for resiliency quantification of large scale systems. SIGMETRICS **44**(4), 37–48 (2017)
19. Puterman, M.L.: Markov Decision Processes. Wiley (1994)

Hybrid Systems and Control

ForFET: A Formal Feature Evaluation Tool for Hybrid Systems

Antonio Anastasio Bruto da Costa(✉) and Pallab Dasgupta

Department of Computer Science and Engineering,
Indian Institute of Technology Kharagpur, Kharagpur, India
{bruto,pallab}@cse.iitkgp.ernet.in

Abstract. This tool paper discusses the design and implementation of the formal *feature* evaluation tool for hybrid systems, *ForFET*. Features extend the notion of assertions by associating a computable function to the match of an assertion. This paper illustrates the practical utility of feature evaluation through several examples.

1 Introduction

Present day research has focused on assertion languages [7,14] for the model checking of hybrid system. Assertions however, do not give insight into the robustness of systems. *Features* (first introduced in [2]) are richer than assertions and allow assertions to be written in the form of timed sequences of events and predicates over real variables (PORVs) [13]. Features overlay computable functions over assertion matches allowing complex properties such as *rise time*, *overshoot*, *settling times* etc. to be evaluated. Hence, while assertions evaluate to a Boolean outcome, the match of a feature evaluates to a value in the real number domain. Since an assertion can match multiple runs of the hybrid systems, a computable function associated with it can yield multiple results, one for each match of the assertion. All these values contribute to an interval of feature values. The *Feature Indented Assertion* language (FIA), for features, used by ForFET is detailed in [9].

Hybrid Automata (HA) [5] are widely used to model control systems and analog mixed-signal (AMS) designs (including AMS circuits) [3,4,6,10]. Several tools for the reachability analysis of hybrid systems exist, such as PHAVer [11] and SpaceEx [12], to name a few. This paper presents the design of the tool ForFET for the feature analysis of hybrid systems. ForFET transforms the problem of feature computation to a problem of reachability analysis and uses SpaceEx to compute the feature value. An initial attempt to study the formal feature evaluation of HAs was made in [8]. The study therein presented an intuitive approach to the treatment of features for the analysis of HAs. A generalized theory, with a richer feature description language, FIA, and a universal methodology for the evaluation of features for HAs was presented in [9]. ForFET uses techniques of model checking introduced in [9] to evaluate features over runs of the HA model of a hybrid system. The tool ForFET was designed keeping AMS

D. D'Souza and K. Narayan Kumar (Eds.): ATVA 2017, LNCS 10482, pp. 437–445, 2017.
DOI: 10.1007/978-3-319-68167-2_28

designers in mind. Therefore, in this article, we introduce for the first time the *HA Specification Language for AMS Circuits* (HASLAC). HASLAC is designed to be familiar to AMS and digital circuit designers, and is inspired by constructs in Verilog and SystemVerilog Assertions.

2 Tool Design

ForFET[1] is a feature evaluation tool for hybrid systems, subsuming assertion checking tools by also providing a measure of robustness in addition to the notion of assertion match/failure. It does this by delivering an explicit confidence in how well the feature interval fits specification. ForFET is developed in C and uses the reachability analysis tool SpaceEx [12]. The transformations applied to the HA during the reduction of the feature analysis problem to the reachability analysis problem are independent of the underlying reachability analysis tool used and scale well. Therefore as reachability analysis tools improve in accuracy and scalability, ForFET can work with them to improve the accuracy of its feature analysis results. The reader is referred to [9] for a complete description of the underlying theory used for ForFET. The implementation details of the tool will now be outlined. One of the inputs to ForFET is the HA model of the system specified in the language HASLAC[2].

```
module buck(v,i,t)
    output v,i,t;
    parameter
        Vr = 12,
        ...
        b1c = 0,
        T = 1e-05,
        D = 0.51667;
    mode closed
    begin
        ddt t = 1;
        ddt v = (a10c*i + a11c*v + b1c*Vs);
        ddt i = (a00c*i + a01c*v + b0c*Vs);
    end
    ...
    property inv closed
        mode==closed |=> t<=D * T && t>=0;
    endproperty
```

```
    property trans closed_open
        mode==closed && mode'==open &&
        t>=D*T |=> i'==i && t'==0 && v'==v;
    endproperty
    ...
    initial begin
        set begin
            mode == closed;
            i == 0; v == 0; t == 0;
        end
    end
endmodule
```

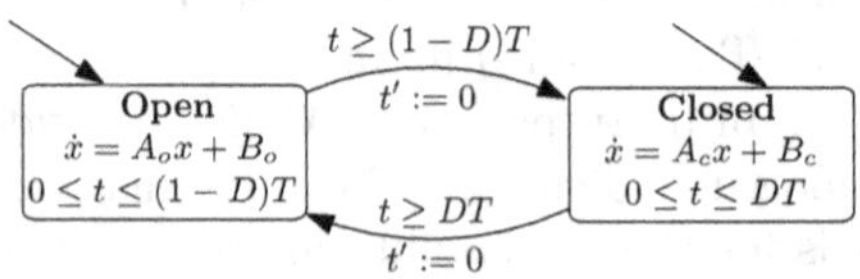

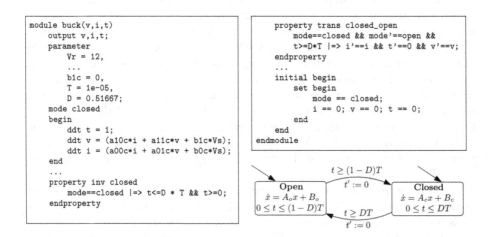

Fig. 1. Code-snippet of the HASLAC model of a buck regulator

A variety of benchmark HA models, including one of a DC-DC buck regulator, are available in Ref. [6]. The HA and a code-snippet of the HASLAC description for a buck regulator model is shown in Fig. 1. In the HA, x is the vector $[v, i]$.

[1] Available at the repository http://cse.iitkgp.ac.in/~bdcaa/ForFET.

[2] ForFET Manual available at http://cse.iitkgp.ac.in/~bdcaa/ForFET/ref.pdf.

The matrices A_o, A_c, B_o and B_c capture the constants of the transfer function. The variables of the HA are `v, i` and `t`. In HASLAC, the mode dynamics are specified using the keyword `ddt`. The invariant of a mode is specified in a `property inv` block, and is written out as a property over the variables of the HA. The interpretation of a property of the form `A |=> B` is, when `A` holds true, then `B` holds true. An invariant property has the following form:

```
property inv ID
      mode==ID |=> CNF_CONSTRAINTS ;
endproperty
```

`ID` is any unique identifier. Within a property, `mode` is a special variable used to indicate the location of the HA for which the property is applicable. `CNF_CONSTRAINTS` is a conjunction of PORVs, indicating the invariant in the location. Similarly, a transition between two modes is also written as a property specified in a `property trans` block, and relates the valuation of variables before and after the transition is taken. A transition property has the following form:

```
property trans ID
      mode==ID && CNF_CONSTRAINTS && mode'==ID |=> RESET_RELATION;
endproperty
```

In a transition property, for any variable `z`, the `RESET_RELATION` relates `z'`, the value of variable `z` after the transition is taken, with values of the HA variables before the transition is taken. Additionally, `mode'` specifies the destination location of the transition. For the transition property `closed_open` described in the example of Fig. 1, the logical comparison `mode'==open` specifies that the next mode is location *open*.

Additionally, a *feature* specifying what is to be measured must be clearly defined. For instance, for the buck regulator circuit, an AMS designer would want to know how fast the regulator's voltage output settles to its stable state value (Vr). This measurement is known as the settling time of the buck regulator. The buck regulator model HA in the hybrid systems benchmarks of [6], has two locations, *open* and *closed*, indicating the state of the switch that charges the capacitor of the regulator. The fact that the output voltage (v) of the regulator has settled can be expressed as an assertion in a SystemVerilog Assertion (SVA) [1] like language as follows:

```
(v>=Vr+E) ##[0:$] @+(state==Open)&&(v<=Vr+E) ##[0:$] @+(state==Open)&&(v<=Vr+E)
```

This assertion is called a sequence expression. Note that the sequence expression presented here and the expressions used to describe invariants and transitions in HASLAC are distinctly different. The later describe the structure of the HA while in general the former describe temporal sequences of PORVs and events. Additionally the artifacts used in a `RESET_RELATION` are not relevant in the former.

In the sequence expression above, the symbol `E` represents the maximum allowed tolerance around the stable state voltage. ($\mathtt{v} >= \mathtt{Vr} + \mathtt{E}$) and ($\mathtt{v} <= \mathtt{Vr} + \mathtt{E}$) are PORVs. `state` is a special variable allowing us to write predicates over the location labels of the HA. The construct `@+(P)` is true only on the positive edge of the predicate `P`. The statement `P ##[a:b] Q` is true whenever

Q occurs within a time interval of a and b from when P is true; a,b $\in \mathbb{R}^+$, b$\geq$a. Observe that P can be true over a dense time interval, and for each point in the interval P ##[a:b] Q can be true yielding an infinite number of matches. P and Q are termed as sub-expressions of the sequence. Sub-expressions are separated by delay constructs of the form ##[a:b]. The symbol $ represents the notion *"anytime after* a". In the above expression, the notable differences with SVA are the following:

- Sequence expressions allows PORVs. Here (v>=Vr+E) and (v<=Vr+E) are PORVs.
- Events of the form @+(P), @−(P) denoting the positive and negative crossing for PORV P are allowed.
- All intervals of the form ##[a:b], a, b $\in \mathbb{R}^{\geq 0}$, are treated as *dense time intervals*, as opposed to intervals countable in terms of the number of clock cycles in SVA semantics.

To understand the semantics of sequence expressions further, the reader may refer to [2]. The assertion above can be interpreted as follows: (v<=Vr+E) *is true and thereafter* v *settles below* (Vr+E) *for two successive openings of the capacitor switch.* This sequence expression captures the notion of settling of the buck regulator voltage, however, in and of itself, the outcome of evaluating a sequence expression is Boolean, that is, it will either yield a match (evaluating to true) or no match (evaluating to false). Therefore, to compute the settling time, a feature uses the sequence expression to define the scenario for measurement, along with other artifacts, associates a computable function with it, and is written as follows:

```
feature settleTime(Vr,E);
begin
  var st;
  (v>=Vr+E) ##[0:$] @+(state==Open) && (v<=Vr+E), st=$time
  ##[0:$] @+(state==Open) && (v<=Vr+E) |-> settleTime = st;
end
```

The feature is named settleTime and has two parameters Vr and E. The variable st is a *local variable* that can hold a value local to a single match of the assertion. In the assertion the variable st is assigned the value of the special variable $time, after the second sub-expressions matches. The construct $time which measures the time elapsed from the initial state and is modeled in ForFET using a clock variable in the HA. When the entire sequence expression matches, the feature is computed by the feature expression settleTime = st. The feature variable settleTime is modeled in ForFET as a variable. More complex feature expressions can be computed as functions over multiple local variables (see footnote 2).

In general, a feature has the following syntax.

```
feature <feature-name> (<list-of-parameters>);
begin
  var <list-of-local-variables>;
  <sequence-expr> |-> <feature-name> = <feature-expr>;
end
```

The sequence expression, <feature-expr>, is of the form s_1 ## τ_1 s_2 ## τ_2... ## τ_{n-1} s_n, where s_1, s_2, ..., s_n are normalized sub-expressions of the form: $D \wedge E$, $\mathcal{A}$, where D is a boolean expression of PORVs in disjunctive normal form, E is an event, and $\mathcal{A}$ is an optional ordered list of comma-separated local variable assignment statements. τ_i represents a time interval and is of the form $[a : b]$, where $a, b \in \mathbb{R}^+$, $a \leq b$, and additionally b can be the symbol $, which represents infinity. The use of local variables in a feature is similar to the use of their counterparts in SVA, with the added fact that for features they are treated as real variables. The local variables are assigned values as the sequence expression matches. <feature-expr> is a linear function over the set of local variables, representing the feature value. For a sequence expression that matches, the computable function, <feature-expr>, is evaluated over the values of the local variables for that match and the computed value is assigned to the special variable <feature-name>. A more detailed discussion on assertions and features, with more elaborate examples, is available in [2,9].

ForFET parses the HASLAC model, $\mathcal{H}$, and the feature specification $\mathcal{F}$, and internally transforms $\mathcal{H}$ so that a reachability analysis on the resulting model computes the feature expression on the runs matching the feature sequence-expression. The model $\mathcal{H}$ and specification $\mathcal{F}$ are maintained in in-memory data structures. $\mathcal{F}$ is internally represented as a monitoring automaton, F, known as the *Feature Automaton*. The feature automaton is in its accepting/final location when a run of the HA has matched the sequence expression for the feature. The problem of computing the feature expression reduces to computing the range of values of the feature variable in the final location of the product of $\mathcal{H}$ and F. The product automaton is computed by the following steps:

- Locations of the model $\mathcal{H}$ are marked as *Level 0* locations.
- Timers/Clocks and Local Variables are added to the model.
- The sequence of locations in the feature automaton, capture the sequence in which sub-expressions match. This sequence is enforced on the model using transitions from HA locations `L` that match the predicate `"state = L"` with transition guards that take the form `"S ∧ level==k ; level:=k+1"`. Here, `S` is the boolean expression over predicates over variables of the model for the $(k+1)^{th}$ sub-expression. The variable `level` is assigned the value `k+1` indicating that the $(k+1)^{th}$ sub-expression has matched.
- Once the last sub-expression has matched, transitions guarded by `level == k+1` lead to the accepting/final location of the product. On these transitions the feature value is computed according to <feature-expr>.
- When an ordering amongst assignments exists, for an individual sub-expression (arising out of assignment dependencies), a set of *urgent/pause* locations is used to impose this ordering.

The product automaton $\mathcal{H}_F$, called a Level Sequenced Hybrid Automaton, is fed to the reachability analysis tool SpaceEx. SpaceEx requires a configuration file containing initial state specifications, error resolution and other parameters. These parameters are specified in an auto-generated configuration file. The model and the configuration are fed to SpaceEx. The SpaceEx analysis proceeds to compute a flow-pipe of the reachable state space for all the variables in $\mathcal{H}_F$. SpaceEx can be queried to produce the reachable set for each location of $\mathcal{H}_F$ in terms of a range of values for a select list of variables. In ForFET, we ask SpaceEx for the range of values reached in the final location for the special feature variable `<feature-name>`. The result of the SpaceEx analysis is interpreted by ForFET as the feature value interval. An outline of ForFET is shown in Fig. 2.

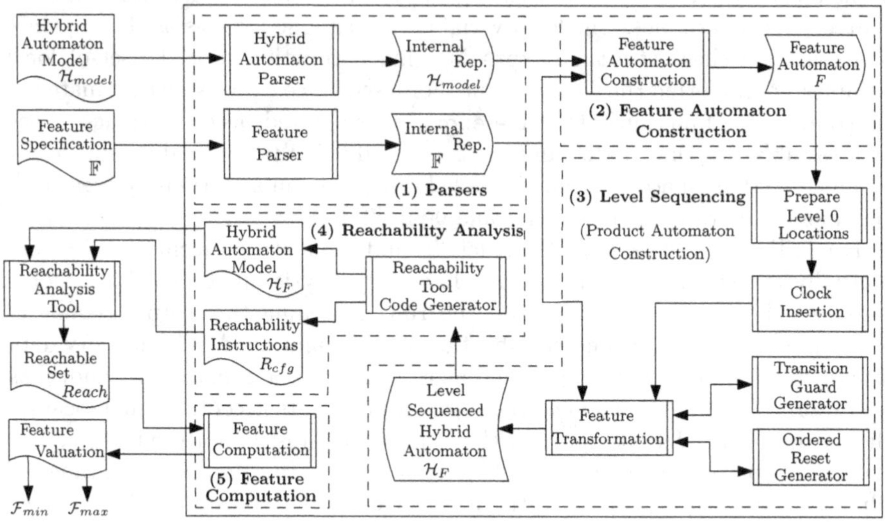

Fig. 2. Design of the ForFET tool for feature analysis of hybrid systems

3 Tool Usage and Evaluation

ForFET is equipped with a library of models covering both the AMS circuit domain and the control domain, including battery charger circuits, buck regulators, a cruise control system and control strategies for nuclear reactor cooling rod controllers, containing both unsafe and safe strategies. The buck regulator and cruise control models are benchmark models from [6]. For each model, example features are provided. Models and features can be added to the library seamlessly, by adding them into the `lib` directory of the tool and ForFET will add them to its library.

ForFET runs in a terminal without any command line parameters. In the tool-flow, the user chooses the model and feature to be used for analysis. The user also chooses the error tolerance and a time bound on path lengths (the length of a run in time). ForFET analyzes the feature and provides a feature value range as output. The tool also indicates if no run matches the feature assertion. We evaluate the following four features spanning three models.

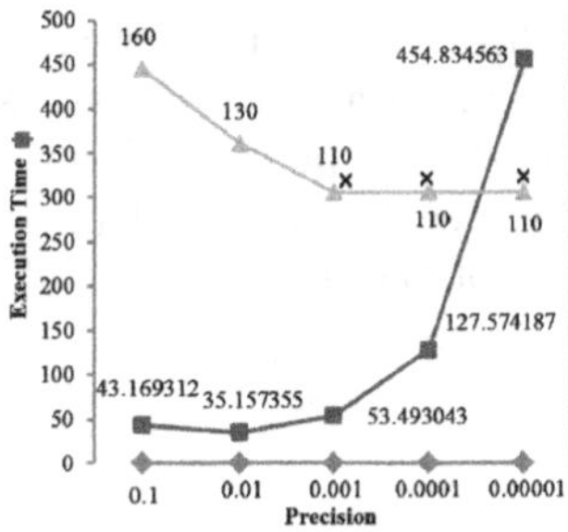

(a) Buck Regulator: **settleTime** ($[135 : 245]\mu s$)

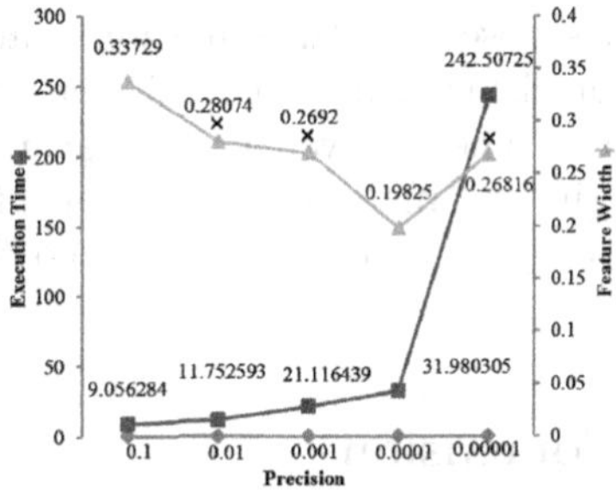

(b) Buck Regulator: **overshoot** ($[6.26 : 6.46]V$)

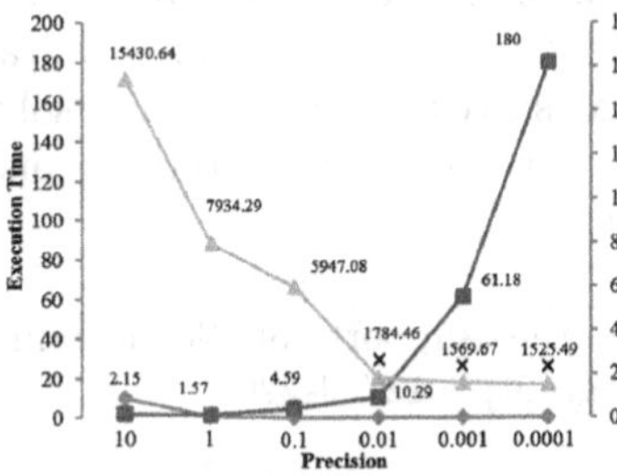

(c) Battery Charger: **chargeTime** ($[7562.75 : 9088.24]s$)

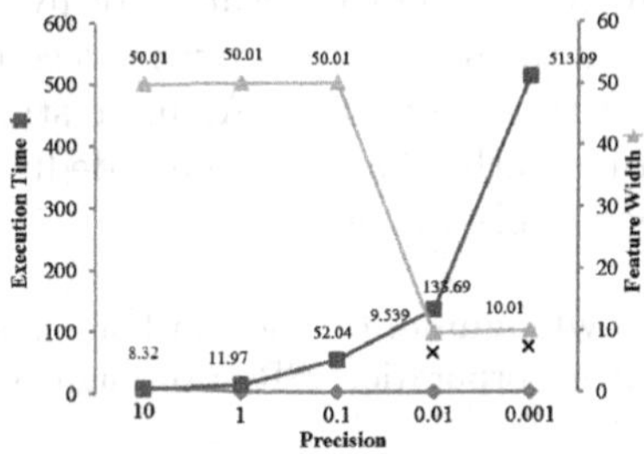

(d) Nuclear Reactor: **unsafe** ($[590 : 600]^{\circ}$)

Fig. 3. ForFET: Observing execution time and feature width versus precision.

- The **buck regulator** switches the capacitor switch between *open* and *closed* very frequently and therefore poses quite a challenge for analysis. We quantify two features of the buck regulator, the time taken for the voltage of the regulator to settle (feature *settleTime*) and the maximum overshoot above the stable state output voltage of 6.3 V of the regulator (feature *overshoot*).
- The **battery charger** model HA has five locations, each indicating where in the charge cycle the charger has reached. We quantify the time taken for the batter to charge (feature *chargeTime*).
- We also analyze a control strategy used for controlling the insertion of cooling rods into a **nuclear reactor**. A variety of such strategies also form part of the example set provided with ForFET. Here we pick the model `nuclearReactor_v2.ha`. The nuclear reactor model switches between three locations, one in which no rod is in the reactor, and two modes each representing the rate of change of temperature when a rod is inserted. Here the feature measures temperatures at which the strategy fails to keep the reaction under control (feature *unsafe*).

The reader may read the tool usage manual (see footnote 2) for more insights into the features and models used. The general trend for feature analysis can be observed in the charts plotted in Fig. 3. Each chart plots the results of feature analysis observing the time for analysis and width of the feature interval for each precision node. For each feature, the most accurate feature interval is in brackets. The interval of the feature becomes narrower as precision improves, while time to analyze grows exponentially. However, a saturation point (marked $\times$) is observed, at which point no further changes of the feature interval are observed.

4 Conclusion

We have demonstrated the utility of a formal feature evaluation tool for hybrid systems specified as HA. We also introduced a Verilog and SVA-like language HASLAC for the specification of hybrid automata. In the future our work will focus on the use of SMT solvers to compute features and produce concrete traces for feature corner points. An interesting challenge is to extend reachability solvers to prune paths that can be decidedly proven to not contribute to the expansion of the feature range.

Acknowledgement. The authors acknowledge the support of Semiconductor Research Corporation (SRC) through the research grant, 2012-TJ-2267.

References

1. 1800–2012 - IEEE Standard for SystemVerilog. http://standards.ieee.org/findstds/standard/1800-2012.html
2. Ain, A., Bruto da Costa, A.A., Dasgupta, P.: Feature indented assertions for analog and mixed-signal validation. IEEE TCAD **35**(11), 1928–1941 (2016)
3. Ain, A., et al.: Chassis: a platform for verifying PMU integration using autogenerated behavioral models. ACM TODAES **16**(3), 33:1–33:30 (2011)
4. Althoff, M., Dolan, J.: Reachability computation of low-order models for the safety verification of high-order road vehicle models. In: ACC, pp. 3559–3566, June 2012
5. Alur, R., et al.: The algorithmic analysis of hybrid systems. Theoret. Comput. Sci. **138**, 3–34 (1995)
6. ARCH: benchmarks for continuous and hybrid system verification. http://cps-vo.org/group/ARCH/benchmarks
7. Bresolin, D.: HyLTL: a temporal logic for model checking hybrid systems. In: Proceedings of Third International Workshop on HAS 2013, pp. 73–84 (2013)
8. Bruto da Costa, A.A., Dasgupta, P.: Formal interpretation of assertion-based features on AMS designs. IEEE Des. Test **32**(1), 9–17 (2015)
9. Bruto da Costa, A.A., Dasgupta, P., Frehse, G.: Formal feature analysis of hybrid automata. In: MEMOCODE (2016)
10. Dang, T., Donzé, A., Maler, O.: Verification of analog and mixed-signal circuits using hybrid system techniques. In: Hu, A.J., Martin, A.K. (eds.) FMCAD 2004. LNCS, vol. 3312, pp. 21–36. Springer, Heidelberg (2004). doi:10.1007/978-3-540-30494-4_3
11. Frehse, G.: PHAVer: algorithmic verification of hybrid systems past HyTech. In: Morari, M., Thiele, L. (eds.) HSCC 2005. LNCS, vol. 3414, pp. 258–273. Springer, Heidelberg (2005). doi:10.1007/978-3-540-31954-2_17

12. Frehse, G., Guernic, C., Donzé, A., Cotton, S., Ray, R., Lebeltel, O., Ripado, R., Girard, A., Dang, T., Maler, O.: SpaceEx: scalable verification of hybrid systems. In: Gopalakrishnan, G., Qadeer, S. (eds.) CAV 2011. LNCS, vol. 6806, pp. 379–395. Springer, Heidelberg (2011). doi:10.1007/978-3-642-22110-1_30
13. Maler, O., Nickovic, D.: Monitoring temporal properties of continuous signals. In: Lakhnech, Y., Yovine, S. (eds.) FORMATS/FTRTFT -2004. LNCS, vol. 3253, pp. 152–166. Springer, Heidelberg (2004). doi:10.1007/978-3-540-30206-3_12
14. Roehm, H., Oehlerking, J., Heinz, T., Althoff, M.: STL model checking of continuous and hybrid systems. In: Artho, C., Legay, A., Peled, D. (eds.) ATVA 2016. LNCS, vol. 9938, pp. 412–427. Springer, Cham (2016). doi:10.1007/978-3-319-46520-3_26

Attacking the V: On the Resiliency of Adaptive-Horizon MPC

Ashish Tiwari[1], Scott A. Smolka[2], Lukas Esterle[3], Anna Lukina[3], Junxing Yang[2(✉)], and Radu Grosu[2,3]

[1] SRI International, Menlo Park, USA
[2] Department of Computer Science, Stony Brook University, New York, USA
junyang@cs.stonybrook.edu
[3] Cyber-Physical Systems Group, Technische Universität Wien, Vienna, Austria

Abstract. Inspired by the emerging problem of CPS security, we introduce the concept of *controller-attacker games*. A controller-attacker game is a two-player stochastic game, where the two players, a controller and an attacker, have antagonistic objectives. A controller-attacker game is formulated in terms of a Markov Decision Process (MDP), with the controller and the attacker jointly determining the MDP's transition probabilities. We also introduce the class of controller-attacker games we call *V-formation games*, where the goal of the controller is to maneuver the plant (a simple model of flocking dynamics) into a V-formation, and the goal of the attacker is to prevent the controller from doing so. Controllers in V-formation games utilize a new formulation of model-predictive control we have developed called *Adaptive-Horizon MPC* (AMPC), giving them extraordinary power: we prove that under certain controllability conditions, an AMPC controller can attain V-formation with probability 1. We evaluate AMPC's performance on V-formation games using statistical model checking. Our experiments demonstrate that (a) as we increase the power of the attacker, the AMPC controller adapts by suitably increasing its horizon, and thus demonstrates resiliency to a variety of attacks; and (b) an intelligent attacker can significantly outperform its naive counterpart.

1 Introduction

Many Cyber-Physical Systems (CPSs) are highly distributed in nature, comprising a multitude of computing agents that can collectively exhibit *emergent behavior*. A compelling example of such a distributed CPS is the *drone swarm*, which are beginning to see increasing application in battlefield surveillance and reconnaissance [3]. The emergent behavior they exhibit is that of *flight formation*.

A particularly interesting form of flight formation is *V-formation*, especially for long-range missions where energy conservation is key. V-formation is emblematic of migratory birds such as Canada geese, where a bird flying in the *upwash region* of the bird in front of it can enjoy significant energy savings. The V-formation also offers a *clear view* benefit, as no bird's field of vision is obstructed

D. D'Souza and K. Narayan Kumar (Eds.): ATVA 2017, LNCS 10482, pp. 446–462, 2017.
DOI: 10.1007/978-3-319-68167-2_29

by another bird in the formation. Because of the V-formation's intrinsic appeal, it is important to quantify the resiliency of the control algorithms underlying this class of multi-agent CPSs to various kinds of cyber-attacks. This question provides the motivation for the investigation put forth in this paper.

Problem Statement and Summary of Results. Inspired by the emerging problem of CPS security, we introduce the concept of *controller-attacker games*. A controller-attacker game is a two-player stochastic game, where the two players, a controller and an attacker, have antagonistic objectives. A controller-attacker game is formulated in terms of a Markov Decision Process (MDP), with the controller and the attacker jointly determining the MDP's transition probabilities.

We also introduce a class of controller-attacker games we call V-formation games, where the goal of the controller is to maneuver the plant (a simple model of flocking dynamics) into a V-formation, and the goal of the attacker is to prevent the controller from doing so. Controllers in V-formation games utilize a new formulation of model-predictive control we have developed called *Adaptive-Horizon MPC* (AMPC), giving them extraordinary power: we prove that under certain controllability conditions, an AMPC controller can attain V-formation with probability 1.

We define several classes of attackers, including those that in one move can remove a small number R of birds from the flock, or introduce random displacement (perturbation) into the flock dynamics, again by selecting a small number of victim agents. We consider both *naive attackers*, whose strategies are purely probabilistic, and *AMPC-enabled attackers*, putting them on par strategically with the controller. The architecture of a V-formation game with an AMPC-enabled attacker is shown in Fig. 1.

While an AMPC-enabled controller is expected to win every game with probability 1, in practice, it is *resource-constrained*: its maximum prediction horizon and the maximum number of execution steps are fixed in advance. Under these conditions, an attacker has a much better chance of winning a V-formation game.

AMPC is a key contribution of the work presented in this paper. Traditional MPC uses a fixed *prediction horizon* to determine the optimal control action. The AMPC procedure chooses the prediction horizon dynamically. Thus, AMPC can adapt to the severity of the action played by its adversary by choosing its own horizon accordingly. While the concept of MPC with an adaptive horizon has been investigated before [5,9], our approach for choosing the prediction horizon based on the progress toward a fitness goal is entirely novel, and has a more general appeal compared to previous work.

In recent work [10], we presented a procedure for synthesizing plans (sequences of actions) that take an MDP to a desired set of states (defining a V-formation). The procedure adaptively varied the settings of various parameters of an underlying optimization routine. Since we did not consider any adversary or noise in [10], there was no need for a control algorithm. Here we consider V-formation in the presence of attacks, and hence we develop a generic adaptive control procedure, AMPC, and evaluate its resilience to attacks.

Our extensive performance evaluation of V-formation games uses statistical model checking to estimate the probability that an attacker can thwart the controller. Our results show that for the bird-removal game with 1 bird being removed, the controller almost always wins (restores the flock to a V-formation). When 2 birds are removed, the game outcome critically depends on which two birds are removed. For the displacement game, our results again demonstrate that an intelligent attacker, i.e. one that uses AMPC in this case, significantly outperforms its naive counterpart that randomly carries out its attack.

Traditional feedback control is, by design, resilient to noise, and also certain kinds of attacks; as our results show, however, it may not be resilient against smart attacks. Adaptive-horizon control helps to guard against a larger class of attacks, but it can still falter due to limited resources. Our results also demonstrate that statistical model checking represents a promising approach toward the evaluation of CPS resilience against a wide range of attacks.

2 V-Formation

We consider the problem of bringing a flock of birds from a random initial configuration to an organized V-formation. Recently, Lukina et al. [10] have modeled this problem as a deterministic Markov Decision Process (MDP) $\mathcal{M}$, where the goal was to generate actions that caused $\mathcal{M}$ to reach a desired state. In our case $\mathcal{M}$ is an MDP as actions taken lead to probability distributions over the states. The definition of $\mathcal{M}$ is given in Sect. 3. In this section, we present a simple model of flocking dynamics that forms the basis of this definition.

In our flocking model, each bird in the flock is modeled using 4 variables: a 2-dimensional vector $\boldsymbol{x}$ denoting the position of the bird in a 2D space, and a 2-dimensional vector $\boldsymbol{v}$ denoting the velocity of the bird. We use $s = \{\boldsymbol{x}_i, \boldsymbol{v}_i\}_{i=1}^B$ to denote a state of a flock with B birds. The *control actions* of each bird are 2-dimensional accelerations $\boldsymbol{a}$ and 2-dimensional position displacements $\boldsymbol{d}$ (see discussion of $\boldsymbol{a}$ and $\boldsymbol{d}$ below). Both are random variables.

Let $\boldsymbol{x}_i(t), \boldsymbol{v}_i(t), \boldsymbol{a}_i(t)$, and $\boldsymbol{d}_i(t)$ respectively denote the position, velocity, acceleration, and displacement of the i-th bird at time t, $1 \leqslant i \leqslant B$. The behavior of bird i in discrete time is modeled as follows:

$$\begin{aligned} \boldsymbol{x}_i(t+1) &= \boldsymbol{x}_i(t) + \boldsymbol{v}_i(t+1) + \boldsymbol{d}_i(t) \\ \boldsymbol{v}_i(t+1) &= \boldsymbol{v}_i(t) + \boldsymbol{a}_i(t) \end{aligned} \quad (1)$$

The next state of the flock is jointly determined by the accelerations and the displacements based on the current state following Eq. 1.

The problem of whether we can go from a random flock to a V-formation can be posed as a reachability question, where the reachability goal is the set of states representing a V-formation. A key assumption in [10] was that the reachability goal can be specified as $J(s) \leqslant \varphi$, where J is a fitness function that assigns a non-negative real (fitness) value to each state s, and φ is a small positive constant.

The fitness of a state was determined by the following three terms:

- *Clear View.* A bird's visual field is a cone with angle θ that can be blocked by the wings of other birds. The clear-view metric is defined by accumulating the percentage of a bird's visual field that is blocked by other birds. $CV(s)$ for flock state s is the sum of the clear-view metric of all birds. The minimum value of CV is $CV^*=0$, and this value is attained in a perfect V-formation where all birds have clear view.
- *Velocity Matching.* $VM(s)$ for flock state s is defined as the difference between the velocity of a given bird and all other birds, summed up over all birds in the flock. The minimum value for VM is $VM^*=0$, and this value is attained in a perfect V-formation where all birds have the same velocity.
- *Upwash Benefit.* The trailing upwash is generated near the wingtips of a bird, while downwash is generated near the center of a bird. An upwash measure um is defined on the 2D space using a Gaussian-like model that peaks at the appropriate upwash and downwash regions. For bird i with upwash um_i, the upwash-benefit metric UB_i is defined as $1-um_i$, and $UB(s)$ for flock state s is the sum of all UB_i for $1 \leqslant i \leqslant B$. The upwash benefit $UB(s)$ in V-formation is $UB^*=1$, as all birds, except for the leader, have minimum upwash-benefit metric $(UB_i = 0, um_i = 1)$, while the leader has upwash-benefit metric of 1 $(UB_i = 1, um_i = 0)$.

Given the above metrics, the overall fitness (cost) metric J is of a sum-of-squares combination of VM, CV, and UB defined as follows:

$$J(s) = (CV(s) - CV^*)^2 + (VM(s) - VM^*)^2 + (UB(s) - UB^*)^2. \quad (2)$$

A state s^* is considered to be a V-formation whenever $J(s^*) \leqslant \varphi$, for a small positive threshold φ.

3 Controller-Attacker Games

We are interested in games between a controller and an attacker, where the goal of the controller is to take the system to a desired set of states, and the goal of the attacker is to keep the system outside these states. We formulate our problem in terms of Markov Decision Processes for which the controller and the attacker jointly determine the transition probabilities.

Definition 1. *A* ***Markov Decision Process*** *(MDP)* $\mathcal{M} = (S, A, T, J, I)$ *is a 5-tuple consisting of a set* S *of* states, *set* A *of* actions, transition function $T : S \times A \times S \mapsto [0, 1]$, *where* $T(s, a, s')$ *is the probability of transitioning from state* s *to state* s' *under action* a, cost function $J : S \mapsto \mathbb{R}$, *where* $J(s)$ *is the cost associated with state* s, *and* I *is the* initial state distribution.

Our definition of an MDP differs from the traditional one in that it uses a cost function instead of a reward function. We find this definition more convenient for our purposes. Our focus is on continuous-space MDPs; i.e., the state space S is

$\mathbb{R}^n$ and the action space A is in $\mathbb{R}^m$. For the bird-flocking problem, $n = m = 4B$, where B is the number of birds. We have four state variables and four action variables for each bird. The state variables represent the x- and the y-components of the position $\boldsymbol{x}_i$ and velocity $\boldsymbol{v}_i$ of each bird i, whereas the action variables represent the (x- and y-components of the) acceleration $\boldsymbol{a}_i$ and displacement $\boldsymbol{d}_i$ of each bird i. The transition relation for the bird-flocking MDP is given by Eq. 1.

A *randomized strategy* over an MDP is a mapping taking every state s to a probability distribution $P(a \mid s)$ over the (available) actions. We formally define randomized strategies as follows.

Definition 2. *Let $\mathcal{M} = (S, A, T, J, I)$ be an MDP. A* **randomized strategy** *σ over $\mathcal{M}$ is a function of the form $\sigma : S \mapsto PD(A)$, where $PD(A)$ is the set of probability distributions over A. That is, σ takes a state s and returns an action consistent with the probability distribution $\sigma(s)$.*

A *controller-attacker game* is a stochastic game [18], where the transition probability from state s to state s' is controlled jointly by two players, a controller and an attacker in our case. To view an MDP as a stochastic game, we assume that the set of actions A is given as a product $C \times D$, where the controller chooses the C-component of an action $\boldsymbol{a}$ and the attacker chooses the D-component of $\boldsymbol{a}$. We assume that the game is played in parallel by the controller and the attacker; i.e., they both take the state $s(t) \in S$ of the system at time t, compute their respective actions $c(t) \in C$ and $d(t) \in D$, and then use the composed action $(c(t), d(t))$ to determine the next state $s(t+1) \in S$ of the system (based on the transition function T). We formally define a controller-attacker game as follows.

Definition 3. *A* **controller-attacker game** *is an MDP $\mathcal{M} = (S, A, T, J, I)$ with $A = C \times D$, where C and D are action sets of the controller and the attacker, respectively. The transition probability $T(s, c \times d, s')$ is jointly determined by actions $c \in C$ and $d \in D$.*

The actions of the controller and the attacker are determined by their randomized strategies. Once we fix a randomized strategy for the controller, and the attacker, the MDP reduces to a Markov chain on the state space S. Thus, the controller and the attacker jointly fix the probability of transitioning from a state s to a state s'. We refer to the underlying Markov chain induced by σ over $\mathcal{M}$ as $\mathcal{M}_\sigma$.

We define controller-attacker games on the flocking model by considering the scenario where the accelerations are under the control of one agent (the controller), and the displacements (position perturbations) are under the control of the second malicious agent (the attacker).

Definition 4. *A* **V-formation game** *is a controller-attacker game $\mathcal{M} = (S, A, T, J, I)$, where $S = \{s \mid s = \{\boldsymbol{x}_i, \boldsymbol{v}_i\}_{i=1}^{B}\}$ is the set of states for a flock of B birds, $A = C \times D$ with the controller choosing accelerations $\boldsymbol{a} \in C$ and the attacker choosing displacements $\mathbf{d} \in D$, T and J are given in Eqs. 1 and 2, respectively.*

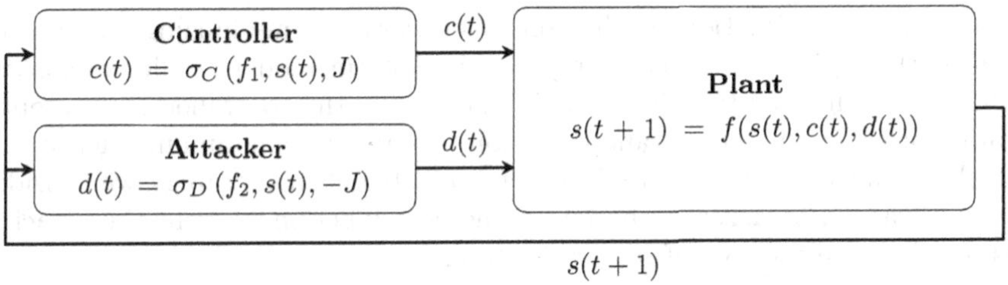

Fig. 1. Controller-attacker game architecture. The controller and the attacker use randomized strategies σ_C and σ_D to choose actions $c(t)$ and $d(t)$ based on dynamics $f_1 = f(s(t), c(t), 0)$ and $f_2 = f(s(t), 0, d(t))$, respectively, where $s(t)$ is the state at time t, and f is the dynamics of the plant model. The controller tries to minimize the cost J, while the attacker tries to maximize it.

In this paper, we consider *reachability games* only. In particular, we are given a set G of *goal states* and the goal of the controller is to reach a state in G. Let $s_0 \rightarrow s_1 \rightarrow s_2 \rightarrow \cdots$ be a sequence of states (a run of the system). The controller wins on this run if $\exists i : s_i \in G$, and the attacker wins otherwise.

A classical problem in the study of games pertains to determining the existence of an optimal winning strategy (e.g. a Nash equilibrium) for a player. We are *not* concerned with such problems in this paper. Due to the uncountably many states in the state- and action-space, solving such problems for our games of interest is extremely challenging. Instead, we focus on the problem of determining the likely winner of a game where the strategy of the two players is fixed. Since we consider randomized strategies, determining the likely winner is a statistical model checking problem, which allows us to evaluate the resilience of certain controllers under certain attack models. We are now ready to formally define the problem we would like to solve.

Definition 5. *Let $\mathcal{M} = (S, A, T, J, I)$ be an MDP, where $A = C \times D$, and let $\sigma_C : S \mapsto PD(C)$ and $\sigma_D : S \mapsto PD(D)$ be randomized strategies over M. Also, let $G \subseteq S$ be the set of* goal states *of $\mathcal{M}$. The* stochastic game verification problem *is to determine the probability of reaching a state in G in m steps, for a given m, starting from an initial state in $\mathcal{M}_{(\sigma_C, \sigma_D)}$.*

Figure 1 shows the architecture of a stochastic game between the controller and the attacker, where at each time step the controller chooses action $c(t)$ as the C-component using strategy σ_C, and the attacker chooses action $d(t)$ as the D-component using strategy σ_D. The next state of the plant is determined by the composed action $(c(t), d(t))$ based on the current state $s(t)$ and the dynamics of the plant model f.

Our main interest is in evaluating the resilience of a control algorithm σ_C (a controller can be viewed as a strategy in our framework) to an attack algorithm σ_D. The key assumption that the controller and the attacker make is the existence of a *cost function* $J : S \mapsto \mathbb{R}^+$ such that

$$G := \{s \mid J(s) \leqslant \varphi \text{ for some very small } \varphi > 0\}.$$

Given such a cost function J, the controller works by minimizing the cost of states reachable in one or more steps, as is done in model predictive control (MPC). Since the cost function is highly nonlinear, the controller uses an optimization procedure based on randomization to search for a minimum. Hence, our controller is a randomized procedure. One possible attack strategy we consider (for an advanced attacker) is based on the cost function as well: the attacker tries to maximize the cost of reachable states.

4 The Adaptive-Horizon MPC Algorithm

We now present our new *adaptive-horizon* MPC algorithm we call AMPC. We will use this algorithm as the controller strategy in the stochastic games we play on MDPs. We will also consider attacker strategies that use AMPC. AMPC is an MPC procedure based on particle-swarm optimization (PSO) [8]. The MPC approach can be used for achieving a V-formation, as was outlined in [19,20]. These earlier works, however, did not use an adaptive dynamic window, and did not consider the adversarial control problem.

The main algorithm of AMPC performs step-by-step control of a given MDP $\mathcal{M}$ by looking h steps ahead—i.e. it uses a *prediction horizon* of length h—to determine the next optimal control action to apply. We use PSO to solve the optimization problem generated by the MPC procedure.

For V-formation, define the cost of $\boldsymbol{a}^h$ as the minimum cost J (Eq. 2) obtained within h steps by applying the sequence $\boldsymbol{a}^h$ of h accelerations on $\mathcal{M}$. Formally, we have

$$\texttt{Cost}(\mathcal{M}, \boldsymbol{a}^h, h) = \min_{1 \leqslant \tau \leqslant h} J(s^{\tau}_{\boldsymbol{a}^h}) \tag{3}$$

where $s^{\tau}_{\boldsymbol{a}^h}$ is the state after applying the τ-th action of $\boldsymbol{a}^h$ to the initial state of $\mathcal{M}$.[1] For horizon h, PSO searches for the best sequence of 2-dimensional acceleration vectors of length h, thus having $2hB$ parameters to be optimized. The number of particles p used in PSO is proportional to the number of parameters to be optimized, i.e., $p = 2\beta hB$, where β is a preset constant.

The AMPC procedure is given in Algorithm 1. A novel feature of AMPC is that, unlike classical MPC which uses a fixed horizon h, AMPC adaptively chooses an h depending on whether it is able to reach a cost that is lower than the current cost by our chosen quanta Δ_i, $0 \leqslant i \leqslant m$, for m steps.

AMPC is hence an adaptive MPC procedure that uses level-based horizons. It employs PSO to identify the potentially best next actions. If the actions $\boldsymbol{a}^h$ improve (decrease) the cost of the state reached within h steps, namely $\texttt{Cost}(\mathcal{M}, \boldsymbol{a}^h, h)$, by the predefined Δ_i, the controller considers these actions to be worthy of leading the flock towards, or keeping it in, a V-formation.[2]

---

[1] The initial state of $\mathcal{M}$ is being used to store the "current" state of the MDP as we execute our algorithm.

[2] We focus our attention on bird flocking, since the details generalize naturally to other MDPs that come with a cost function.

Algorithm 1. AMPC: Adaptive-Horizon Model Predictive Control

Input : $\mathcal{M}, \varphi, h_{max}, m, B, \beta,$ `Cost`
Output: $\{\boldsymbol{a}^i\}_{1 \leqslant i \leqslant m}$ // *optimal control sequence*

Initialize $\ell_0 \leftarrow J(s_0)$; $\widehat{J} \leftarrow \inf$; $i \leftarrow 1$; $h \leftarrow 1$; $p \leftarrow 2\beta h B$; $\Delta_0 \leftarrow (\ell_0 - \varphi)/m$;
while $(\ell_{i-1} > \varphi) \wedge (i < m)$ **do**
  // *find and apply first best action out of the horizon sequence of length h*
  $[\boldsymbol{a}^h, \widehat{J}] \leftarrow$`particleswarm(Cost,`$\mathcal{M}, p, h$`);`
  if $\ell_{i-1} - \widehat{J} > \Delta_i \vee h = h_{max}$ **then**
    // *if a new level or the maximum horizon is reached*
    $\boldsymbol{a}^i \leftarrow \boldsymbol{a}_1^h$; $\mathcal{M} \leftarrow \mathcal{M}^{\boldsymbol{a}^i}$; // *apply the action and move to the next state*
    $\ell_i \leftarrow J(s(\mathcal{M}))$; // *update ℓ_i with the cost of the current state*
    $\Delta_i \leftarrow \ell_i/(m-i)$; // *update the threshold on reaching the next level*
    $i \leftarrow i+1$; $h \leftarrow 1$; $p \leftarrow 2\beta h B$; // *update parameters*
  else
    $h \leftarrow h+1$; $p \leftarrow 2\beta h B$; // *increase the horizon*
  end
end

In this case, the controller applies the first action to each bird and transitions to the next state of the MDP. The threshold Δ_i determines the next level $\ell_i = \texttt{Cost}(\mathcal{M}, \widehat{\boldsymbol{a}}^h, h)$, where $\widehat{\boldsymbol{a}}^h$ is the optimal action sequence. The prediction horizon h is increased iteratively if the cost has not been decreased enough. Upon reaching a new level, the horizon is reset to one (see Algorithm 1).

Having a horizon $h > 1$ means it will take multiple transitions in the MDP to reach a solution with sufficiently improved cost. However, when finding such a solution with $h > 1$, we only apply the first action to transition the MDP to the next state. This is explained by the need to allow the other player (the environment or an adversary) to apply their action before we obtain the actual next state. If no new level is reached within h_{max} horizons, the first action of the best $\boldsymbol{a}^h$ using horizon h_{max} is applied.

The dynamic threshold Δ_i is defined as in [10]. Its initial value Δ_0 is obtained by dividing the cost range to be covered into m equal parts, that is, $\Delta_0 = (\ell_0 - \ell_m) / m$, where $\ell_0 = J(s_0)$ and $\ell_m = \varphi$. Subsequently, Δ_i is determined by the previously reached level ℓ_{i-1}, as $\Delta_i = \ell_{i-1}/(m-i+1)$. This way AMPC advances only if $\ell_i = \texttt{Cost}(\mathcal{M}, \widehat{\boldsymbol{a}}^h, h)$ is at least Δ_i apart from ℓ_{i-1}.

This approach allows us to force PSO to escape from a local minimum, even if this implies passing over a bump, by gradually increasing the exploration horizon h. We assume that the MDP is controllable. A discrete-time system S is said to be *controllable* if for any given states s and t, there exist a finite sequence of control inputs that takes S from s to t [13]. We also assume that the set G of goal states is non-empty, which means that from any state, it is possible to reach a state whose cost decreased by at least Δ_i. Algorithm 1 describes our approach in more detail.

Theorem 1 (AMPC Convergence). *Given an MDP $\mathcal{M} = (S, A, T, J)$ with positive and continuous cost function J, and a nonempty set of target states $G \subset S$ with $G = \{s \mid J(s) \leqslant \varphi\}$. If the transition relation T is controllable with actions in A, then there exists a finite maximum horizon h_{max} and a finite number of execution steps m, such that AMPC is able to find a sequence of actions $a_1, \ldots, a_m$ that brings a state in S to a state in G with probability one.*

Proof. In each (macro-) step of horizon length h, from level ℓ_{i-1} to level ℓ_i, AMPC decreases the distance to φ by $\Delta_i \geqslant \Delta$, where $\Delta > 0$ is fixed by the number of steps m chosen in advance. Hence, AMPC converges to a state in G in a finite number of steps, for a properly chosen m. AMPC is able to decrease the cost in a macro step by Δ_i by the controllability assumption and the fairness assumption about the PSO algorithm. Since AMPC is a randomized algorithm, the result is probabilistic. Note that the theorem is an existence theorem of h_{max} and m whose values are chosen empirically in practice.

The adaptive MPC procedure, AMPC, is a key contribution of our work. Recall that traditional MPC uses a fixed finite horizon to determine the best control action. In contrast, AMPC dynamically chooses the horizon depending on the severity of the action played by the opponent (or environment). AMPC is inspired by the optimal plan synthesis procedure we recently presented in [10], which dynamically configures the amount of the effort it uses to search for a better solution at each step. In [10] the monolithic synthesis procedure was adaptive (and involved dynamically changing several parameters), whereas here the control procedure is adaptive and the underlying optimization is non-adaptive off-the-shelf procedure, and hence the overall procedure here is simpler.

Note that AMPC is a general procedure that performs adaptive MPC using PSO for dynamical systems that are controllable, come with a cost function, and have at least one optimal solution. In an adversarial situation two players have opposing objectives. The question arises what one player assumes about the other when computing its own action, which we discuss next.

5 Stochastic Games for V-Formation

We describe the specialization of the stochastic-game verification problem to V-formation. In particular, we present the AMPC-based control strategy for reaching a V-formation, and the various attacker strategies against which we evaluate the resilience of our controller.

5.1 Controller's Adaptive Strategies

Given current state $(\boldsymbol{x}(t), \boldsymbol{v}(t))$, the controller's strategy σ_C returns a probability distribution on the space of all possible accelerations (for all birds). As mentioned above, this probability distribution is specified implicitly via a randomized algorithm that returns an actual acceleration (again for all birds). This randomized algorithm is the AMPC algorithm, which inherits its randomization from the randomized PSO procedure it deploys.

When the controller computes an acceleration, it assumes that the attacker does *not* introduce any disturbances; i.e., the controller uses the following model:

$$\begin{aligned} \boldsymbol{x}_i(t+1) &= \boldsymbol{x}_i(t) + \boldsymbol{v}_i(t+1) \\ \boldsymbol{v}_i(t+1) &= \boldsymbol{v}_i(t) + \boldsymbol{a}_i(t) \end{aligned} \tag{4}$$

where $\boldsymbol{a}(t)$ is the only control variable. Note that the controller chooses its next action $\boldsymbol{a}(t)$ based on the current configuration $(\boldsymbol{x}(t), \boldsymbol{v}(t))$ of the flock using MPC. The current configuration may have been influenced by the disturbance $\boldsymbol{d}(t-1)$ introduced by the attacker in the previous time step. Hence, the current state need not to be the state predicted by the controller when performing MPC in step $t-1$. Moreover, depending on the severity of the attacker action $\boldsymbol{d}(t-1)$, the AMPC procedure dynamically adapts its behavior, i.e. the choice of horizon h, in order to enable the controller to pick the best control action $\boldsymbol{a}(t)$ in response.

5.2 Attacker's Strategies

We are interested in evaluating the resilience of our V-formation controller when it is threatened by an attacker that can remove a certain number of birds from the flock, or manipulate a certain number of birds by taking control of their actuators (modeled by the displacement term in Eq. 1). We assume that the attack lasts for a limited amount of time, after which the controller attempts to bring the system back into the good set of states. When there is no attack, the system behavior is the one given by Eq. 4.

Bird Removal Game. In a BRG, the attacker selects a subset of R birds, where $R \ll B$, and removes them from the flock. The removal of bird i from the flock can be simulated in our framework by setting the displacement $\boldsymbol{d}_i$ for bird i to ∞. We assume that the flock is in a V-formation at time $t=0$. Thus, the goal of the controller is to bring the flock back into a V-formation consisting of $B-R$ birds. Apart from seeing if the controller can bring the flock back to a V-formation, we also analyze the time it takes the controller to do so.

Definition 6. *In a* Bird Removal Game *(BRG), the attacker strategy σ_D is defined as follows. Starting from a V-formation of B birds, i.e., $J(s_0) \leqslant \varphi$, the attacker chooses a subset of R birds, $R \ll B$, by uniform sampling without replacement. Then, in every round, it assigns each bird i in the subset a displacement $\boldsymbol{d}_i = \infty$, while for all other birds j, $\boldsymbol{d}_j = 0$.*

Random Displacement Game. In an RDG, the attacker chooses the displacement vector for a subset of R birds uniformly from the space $[0, M] \times [0, 2\pi]$ with $R \ll B$. This means that the magnitude of the displacement vector is picked from the interval $[0, M]$, and the direction of the displacement vector is picked from the interval $[0, 2\pi]$. We vary M in our experiments. The subset of R birds that are picked in different steps are not necessarily the same, as the attacker makes this choice uniformly at random at runtime as well.

The game starts from an initial V-formation. The attacker is allowed a fixed number of moves, say 20, after which the displacement vector is identically 0 for all birds. The controller, which has been running in parallel with the attacker, is then tasked with moving the flock back to a V-formation, if necessary.

Definition 7. *In a* Random Displacement Game *(RDG), the attacker strategy* σ_D *is defined as follows. Starting from a V-formation of B birds, i.e.,* $J(s_0) \leqslant \varphi$, *in every round, it chooses a subset of R birds,* $R \ll B$, *by uniform sampling without replacement. It then assigns each bird i in the subset a displacement* $\boldsymbol{d}_i$ *chosen uniformly at random from* $[0, M] \times [0, 2\pi]$, *while for all other birds j,* $\boldsymbol{d}_j = 0$. *After T rounds, all displacements are set to* 0.

AMPC Game. An AMPC game is similar to an RDG except that the attacker does not use a uniform distribution to determine the displacement vector. The attacker is advanced and strategically calculates the displacement using the AMPC procedure. See Fig. 1. In detail, the attacker applies AMPC, but assumes the controller applies zero acceleration. Thus, the attacker uses the following model of the flock dynamics:

$$\begin{aligned} \boldsymbol{x}_i(t+1) &= \boldsymbol{x}_i(t) + \boldsymbol{v}_i(t+1) + \boldsymbol{d}_i(t) \\ \boldsymbol{v}_i(t+1) &= \boldsymbol{v}_i(t) \end{aligned} \tag{5}$$

Note that the attacker is still allowed to have $\boldsymbol{d}_i(t)$ be non-zero for only a small number of birds. However, it gets to choose these birds in each step. It uses the AMPC procedure to simultaneously pick the subset of R birds and their displacements. The objective of the attacker's AMPC is to maximize the cost.

Definition 8. *In an* AMPC game, *the attacker strategy* σ_D *is defined as follows. Starting from a V-formation of B birds, i.e.,* $J(s_0) \leqslant \varphi$, *in every round, it uses AMPC to choose a subset of R birds,* $R \ll B$, *and their displacements* $\boldsymbol{d}_i$ *for bird i in the subset from* $[0, M] \times [0, 2\pi]$; *for all other birds j,* $\boldsymbol{d}_j = 0$. *After T rounds, all displacements are set to* 0.

Theorem 2 (AMPC resilience in a C-A game). *Given a controller-attacker game, there exists a finite maximum horizon* h_{max} *and a finite maximum number of game-execution steps m such that AMPC controller will win the controller-attacker game in m steps with probability 1.*

Proof. Since the flock MDP (defined by Eq. 1) is controllable, the PSO algorithm we use is fair, and the attack has a bounded duration, the proof of the theorem follows from Theorem 1.

Remark 1. While Theorem 2 states that the controller is expected to win with probability 1, we expect winning probability to be possibly lower than one in many cases because: (1) the maximum horizon h_{max} is fixed in advance, and so is (2) the maximum number of execution steps m; (3) the underlying PSO algorithm is also run with bounded number of particles and time. Theorem 2 is an existence theorem of h_{max} and m, while in practice one chooses fixed values of h_{max} and m that could be lower than the required values.

6 Statistical MC Evaluation of V-Formation Games

As discussed in Sect. 3, the stochastic-game verification problem we address in the context of the V-formation-AMPC algorithm is formulated as follows. Given a flock MDP $\mathcal{M}$ (we consider the case of $B = 7$ birds), acceleration actions $\boldsymbol{a}$ of the controller, displacement actions $\boldsymbol{d}$ of the attacker, the randomized strategy $\sigma_C : S \mapsto PD(C)$ of the controller (the AMPC algorithm), and a randomized strategy $\sigma_D : S \mapsto PD(D)$ for the attacker, determine the probability of reaching a state s where the cost function $J(s) \leqslant \varphi$ (V-formation in a 7-bird flock), starting from an initial state (in this case this is a V-formation), in the underlying Markov chain induced by strategies σ_C, σ_D on $\mathcal{M}$.

Since the exact solution to this reachability problem is intractable due to the infinite/continuous space of states and actions, we solve it approximately with classical statistical model-checking (SMC). The particular SMC procedure we use is from [7] and based on an *additive* or *absolute-error* (ε, δ)*-Monte-Carlo-approximation scheme*. This technique requires running N i.i.d. game executions, each for a given maximum time horizon, determining if these executions reach a V-formation, and returning the average number of times this occurs.

Each of the games described in Sect. 5 is executed 2,000 times. For a confidence ratio $\delta = 0.01$, we thus obtain an additive error of $\varepsilon = 0.1$. We use the following parameters in the game executions: number of birds $B = 7$, threshold on the cost $\varphi = 10^{-3}$, maximum horizon $h_{max} = 5$, number of particles in PSO $p = 20hB$. In BRG, the controller is allowed to run for a maximum of 30 steps. In RDG and AMPC game, the attacker and the controller run in parallel for 20 steps, after which the displacement becomes 0, and the controller has a maximum of 20 more steps to restore the flock to a V-formation.

To perform SMC evaluation of our AMPC approach we designed the above experiments in C and ran them on the Intel Core i7-5820K CPU with 3.30 GHz and with 32 GB RAM available.

Table 1. Results of 2,000 game executions for removing 1 bird with $h_{max} = 5$, $m = 40$

	Ctrl. success rate, %	Avg. convergence duration	Avg. horizon
Bird 4	99.9	12.75	3.64
Bird 3	99.8	18.98	4.25
Bird 2	100	10.82	3.45

6.1 Discussion of the Results

To demonstrate the resilience of our adaptive controller, for each game introduced in Sect. 5, we performed a number of experiments to estimate the probability of the controller winning. Moreover, for the runs where the controller wins, the average number of steps required by the controller to bring the flock to a V-formation is reported as *average convergence duration*, and the average length of the horizon used by AMPC is reported as *average horizon.*

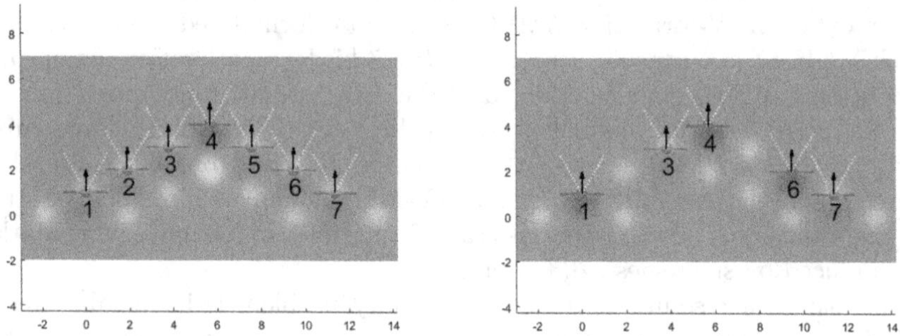

Fig. 2. Left: numbering of the birds. Right: configuration after removing bird 2 and 5. The red-filled circle and two protruding line segments represent a bird's body and wings. Arrows represent bird velocities. Dotted lines illustrate clear-view cones. A brighter/darker background color indicates a higher upwash/downwash.

Table 2. Results of 2,000 game executions for removing 2 birds with $h_{max} = 5$, $m = 30$

	Ctrl. success rate, %	Avg. convergence duration	Avg. horizon
Birds 2 and 3	0.8	25.18	4.30
Birds 2 and 4	83.1	11.11	2.94
Birds 2 and 5	80.3	9.59	2.83
Birds 2 and 6	98.6	7.02	2.27
Birds 3 and 4	2.0	22.86	4.30
Birds 3 and 5	92.8	11.8	3.43

The numbering of the birds in Tables 1 and 2 is given in Fig. 2. Bird-removal scenarios that are symmetric with the ones in the tables are omitted. The results presented in Table 1 are for the BRG game with $R = 1$. In this case, the controller is *almost always* able to bring the flock back to a V-formation, as is evident from Table 1. Note that removing Bird 1 (or 7) is a trivial case that results in a V-formation.

Table 3. Results of 2,000 game executions for random displacement and AMPC attacks with $h_{max} = 5$ and $m = 40$ (attacker runs for 20 steps)

Range of noise	Ctrl. success rate, %	Avg. convergence duration	Avg. horizon
	Random displacement game		
$[0, 0.50] \times [0, 2\pi]$	99.9	3.33	1.07
$[0, 0.75] \times [0, 2\pi]$	97.9	3.61	1.11
$[0, 1.00] \times [0, 2\pi]$	92.3	4.14	1.18
	AMPC game		
$[0, 0.50] \times [0, 2\pi]$	97.5	4.29	1.09
$[0, 0.75] \times [0, 2\pi]$	63.4	5.17	1.23
$[0, 1.00] \times [0, 2\pi]$	20.0	7.30	1.47

In the case when $R = 2$, shown in Table 2, the success rate of the controller depends on *which two birds are removed*. Naturally, there are cases where dropping two birds does not break the V-formation; for example, after dropping Birds 1 and 2, the remaining birds continue to be in a V-formation. Such trivial cases are not shown in Table 2. Note that the scenario of removing Bird 1 (or 7) and one other bird can be viewed as removing one bird in flock of 6 birds, thus not considered in this table. Among the other nontrivial cases, the success rate of controller drops slightly in four cases, and drops drastically in remaining two cases. This suggests that attacker of a CPS system can incur more damage by being prudent in the choice of the attack.

Impressively, whenever the controller wins, the controller needs about the same number of steps to get back to V-formation (as in the one-bird removal case). On average, removal of two birds results in a configuration that has worse cost compared to an BRG with $R = 1$. Hence, the adaptive controller is able to make bigger improvements (in each step) when challenged by worse configurations. Furthermore, among the four cases where the controller win rate is high, experimental results demonstrate that removing two birds positioned asymmetrically with respect to the leader poses a stronger, however, still manageable threat to the formation. For instance, the scenarios of removing birds 2 and 6 or 3 and 5 give the controller a significantly higher chance to recover from the attack, 98.6% and 92.8%, respectively.

Table 3 explores the effect of making the attacker smarter. Compared to an attacker that makes random changes in displacement, an attacker that uses AMPC to pick its action is able to win more often. This again shows that an attacker of a CPS system can improve its chances by cleverly choosing the attack. For example, the probability of success for the controller to recover drops from 92.3% to 20.0% when the attacker uses AMPC to pick displacements with magnitude in $[0, 1]$ and direction in $[0, 2\pi]$. The entries in the other two columns in Table 3 reveal two even more interesting facts.

First, in the cases when the controller wins, we clearly see that the controller uses a longer look-ahead when facing a more challenging attack. This follows from the observation that the average horizon value increases with the strength of attack. This gives evidence for the fact that the adaptive component of our AMPC plays a pivotal role in providing resilience against sophisticated attacks. Second, the average horizon still being in the range 1–1.5, means that the adaptation in our AMPC procedure also helps it perform better than a fixed-horizon MPC procedure, where usually the horizon is fixed to $h \geqslant 2$. When a low value of h (say $h = 1$) suffices, the AMPC procedure avoids unnecessary calculation that using a fixed h might incur.

In the cases where success rate was low (Row 1 and Row 5 in Table 2, and Row 3 of the AMPC game in Table 3), we conducted additional 500 runs for each case and observed improved success rates (2.4%, 9% and 30.8% respectively) when we increased h_{max} to 10 and m to 40. This shows that success rates of AMPC improves when given more resources, as predicted by Theorem 1.

7 Related Work

In the field of CPS security, one of the most widely studied attacks is *sensor spoofing*. When sensors measurements are compromised, state estimation becomes challenging, which inspired a considerable amount of work on attack-resilient state estimation [4,6,14–16]. In these approaches, resilience to attacks is typically achieved by assuming the presence of redundant sensors, or coding sensor outputs. In our work, we do not consider sensor spoofing attacks, but assume the attacker gets control of the displacement vectors (for some of the birds/drones). We have not explicitly stated the mechanism by which an attacker obtains this capability, but it is easy to envision ways (radio controller, attack via physical medium, or other channels [2]) for doing so.

Adaptive control, and its special case of adaptive model predictive control, typically refers to the aspect of the controller updating its process model that it uses to compute the control action. The field of adaptive control is concerned with the discrepancy look aheadand its model used by the controller. In our adaptive-horizon MPC, we adapt the lookahead horizon employed by the MPC, and not the model itself. Hence, the work in this paper is orthogonal to what is done in adaptive control [1,11].

Adaptive-horizon MPC was used in [5] to track a reference signal. If the reference signal is unknown, and we have a poor estimate of its future behavior, then a larger horizon for MPC is not beneficial. Thus, the horizon was determined by the uncertainty in the knowledge of the future reference signal. We consider cost-based reachability goals here, which allows us to choose a horizon in a more generic way based on the progress toward the goal. More recently, adaptive horizons were also used in [9] for a reachability goal. However, they chose a large-enough horizon that enabled the system to reach states from where a pre-computed local controller could guarantee reachability of the goal. This is less practical than our approach for establishing the horizon.

A key focus in CPS security has also been detection of attacks. For example, recent work considers displacement-based attacks on formation flight [12], but it primarily concerned with detecting which UAV was attacked using an unknown-input-observer based approach. We are not concerned with detecting attacks, but establishing that the adaptive nature of our controller provides attack-resilience for free. Moreover, in our setting, for both the attacker the and controller the state of the plant is completely observable. In [17], a control policy based on the robustness of the connectivity graph is proposed to achieve consensus on the velocity among a team of mobile robots, in the present of non-cooperative robots that communicate false values but execute the agreed upon commands. In contrast, we allow the attacker to manipulate the executed commands of the robots. The cost function we use is also more flexible so that we can encode more complicated objectives.

We are unaware of any work that uses statistical model checking to evaluate the resilience of adaptive controllers against (certain classes of) attacks.

8 Conclusions

We have introduced AMPC, a new model-predictive controller that unlike MPC, comes with provable convergence guarantees. The key innovation of AMPC is that it dynamically adapts its receding horizon (RH) to get out of local minima. In each prediction step, AMPC calls PSO with an optimal RH and corresponding number of particles. We used AMPC as a bird-flocking controller whose goal is to achieve V-formation despite various forms of attacks, including bird-removal, bird-position-perturbation, and advanced AMPC-based attacks. We quantified the resiliency of AMPC to such attacks using statistical model checking. Our results show that AMPC is able to adapt to the severity of an attack by dynamically changing its horizon size and the number of particles used by PSO to completely recover from the attack, given a sufficiently long horizon and execution time (ET). The intelligence of an attacker, however, makes a difference in the outcome of a game if RH and ET are bounded before the game begins.

Future work includes the consideration of additional forms of attacks, including: *Energy attack*, when the flock is not traveling in a V-formation for a certain amount of time; *Collisions*, when two birds are dangerously close to each other due to sensor spoofing or adversarial birds; and *Heading change*, when the flock is diverted from its original destination (mission target) by a certain degree.

Acknowledgments. Research supported in part by the Doctoral Program Logical Methods in Computer Science and the Austrian National Research Network RiSE/SHiNE (S11412-N23) project funded by the Austrian Science Fund (FWF) project W1255-N23, AFOSR Grant FA9550-14-1-0261 and NSF Grants CCF-1423296, CNS-1423298, IIS-1447549, CNS-1446832, CNS-1445770, CNS-1445770.

References

1. Adetola, V., DeHaan, D., Guay, M.: Adaptive model predictive control for constrained nonlinear systems. Syst. Control Lett. **58**(5), 320–326 (2009)

2. Checkoway, S., McCoy, D., Kantor, B., Anderson, D., Shacham, H., Savage, S., Koscher, K., an, A.C., Roesner, F., Kohno, T.: Comprehensive experimental analyses of automotive attack surfaces. In: USENIX Security (2011)
3. Condliffe, J.: A 100-drone swarm, dropped from jets, plans its own moves, MIT Technology Review, January 2017
4. Davidson, D., Wu, H., Jellinek, R., Ristenpart, T., Singh, V.: Controlling UAVs with sensor input spoofing attacks. In: Proceedings of 10th USENIX Workshop on Offensive Technologies, WOOT 2016, Austin, TX, August 2016
5. Droge, G., Egerstedt, M.: Adaptive time horizon optimization in model predictive control. In: 2011 American Control Conference (ACC), pp. 1843–1848. IEEE (2011)
6. Fawzi, H., Tabuada, P., Diggavi, S.N.: Secure estimation and control for cyber-physical systems under adversarial attacks. IEEE Trans. Autom. Control **59**(6), 1454–1467 (2014). http://dx.doi.org/10.1109/TAC.2014.2303233
7. Grosu, R., Peled, D., Ramakrishnan, C.R., Smolka, S.A., Stoller, S.D., Yang, J.: Using statistical model checking for measuring systems. In: Margaria, T., Steffen, B. (eds.) ISoLA 2014. LNCS, vol. 8803, pp. 223–238. Springer, Heidelberg (2014). doi:10.1007/978-3-662-45231-8_16
8. Kennedy, J., Eberhart, R.: Particle swarm optimization. In: Proceedings of 1995 IEEE International Conference on Neural Networks, pp. 1942–1948 (1995)
9. Krener, A.J.: Adaptive horizon model predictive control, arXiv preprint (2016). arXiv:1602.08619
10. Lukina, A., et al.: ARES: adaptive receding-horizon synthesis of optimal plans. In: Legay, A., Margaria, T. (eds.) TACAS 2017. LNCS, vol. 10206, pp. 286–302. Springer, Heidelberg (2017). doi:10.1007/978-3-662-54580-5_17
11. Narendra, K.S.: Adaptive control using neural networks. In: Neural Networks for Control, pp. 115–142. MIT Press (1990)
12. Negash, L., Kim, S.H., Choi, H.L.: An unknown-input-observer based approach for cyber attack detection in formation flying UAVs. In: AIAA Infotech (2016)
13. Ogata, K.: Modern Control Engineering: Instrumentation and Controls Series. Prentice Hall, Upper Saddle River (2010)
14. Pajic, M., Weimer, J., Bezzo, N., Tabuada, P., Sokolsky, O., Lee, I., Pappas, G.J.: Robustness of attack-resilient state estimators. In: 5th ACM/IEEE International Conference on Cyber-Physical Systems (ICCPS) (2014)
15. Park, J., Ivanov, R., Weimer, J., Pajic, M., Lee, I.: Sensor attack detection in the presence of transient faults. In: 6th ACM/IEEE International Conference on Cyber-Physical Systems (ICCPS) (2015)
16. Pasqualetti, F., Dorfler, F., Bullo, F.: Attack detection and identification in cyber-physical systems. IEEE Trans. Autom. Control **58**(11), 2715–2729 (2013)
17. Saulnier, K., Saldana, D., Prorok, A., Pappas, G.J., Kumar, V.: Resilient flocking for mobile robot teams. IEEE Robot. Autom. Lett. **2**(2), 1039–1046 (2017)
18. Shapley, L.S.: Stochastic games. Proc. Nat. Acad. Sci. **39**(10), 1095–1100 (1953)
19. Yang, J., Grosu, R., Smolka, S.A., Tiwari, A.: Love thy neighbor: V-formation as a problem of model predictive control. In: LIPIcs-Leibniz International Proceedings in Informatics, vol. 59. Schloss Dagstuhl-Leibniz-Zentrum fuer Informatik (2016)
20. Yang, J., Grosu, R., Smolka, S.A., Tiwari, A.: V-formation as optimal control. In: Proceedings of the Biological Distributed Algorithms Workshop (2016)

The Reach-Avoid Problem for Constant-Rate Multi-mode Systems

Shankara Narayanan Krishna[1], Aviral Kumar[1], Fabio Somenzi[2], Behrouz Touri[2], and Ashutosh Trivedi[2(✉)]

[1] Indian Institute of Technology Bombay, Mumbai, India
[2] University of Colorado Boulder, Boulder, USA
ashutosh.trivedi@colorado.edu

Abstract. A constant-rate multi-mode system is a hybrid system that can switch freely among a finite set of modes, and whose dynamics is specified by a finite number of real-valued variables with mode-dependent constant rates. Alur, Wojtczak, and Trivedi have shown that reachability problems for constant-rate multi-mode systems for open and convex safety sets can be solved in polynomial time. In this paper we study the reachability problem for non-convex state spaces, and show that this problem is in general undecidable. We recover decidability by making certain assumptions about the safety set. We present a new algorithm to solve this problem and compare its performance with the popular sampling based algorithm rapidly-exploring random tree (RRT) as implemented in the Open Motion Planning Library (OMPL).

1 Introduction

Autonomous vehicle planning and control frameworks [15,20] often follow the hierarchical planning architecture outlined by Firby [9] and Gat [11]. The key idea here is to separate the complications involved in low-level hardware control from high-level planning decisions to accomplish the navigation objective. A typical example of such separation-of-concerns is proving the controllability property (vehicle can be steered from any start point to arbitrary neighborhood of the target point) of the motion-primitives of the vehicle followed by the search (path-planning) for an obstacle-free path (called the *roadmap*) and then utilizing the controllability property to compose the low-level primitives to follow the path (path-following). However, in the absence of the controllability property, it is not always possible to follow arbitrary roadmaps with given motion-primitives. In these situations we need to study a motion planning problem that is not opaque to the motion-primitives available to the controller.

This research was supported in part by CEFIPRA project AVeRTS and by DARPA under agreement number FA8750-15-2-0096. All opinions stated are those of the authors and not necessarily of the organizations that have supported this research. The authors would like to thank the anonymous reviewers for their careful reading of the earlier versions of this manuscript and their many insightful comments and suggestions.

D. D'Souza and K. Narayan Kumar (Eds.): ATVA 2017, LNCS 10482, pp. 463–479, 2017.
DOI: 10.1007/978-3-319-68167-2_30

We study this motion planning problem in a simpler setting of systems modeled as constant-rate multi-mode systems [4]—a switched system with constant-rate dynamics (vector) in every mode—and study the reachability problem for the non-convex safety sets. Alur et al. [4] studied this problem for convex safety sets and showed that it can be solved in polynomial time. Our key result is that even for the case when the safety set is defined using polyhedral obstacles, the problem of deciding reachability is undecidable. On a positive side we show that if the safety set is an open set defined by linear inequalities, the problem is decidable and can be solved using a variation of cell-decomposition algorithm [22]. We present a novel bounded model-checking [7] inspired algorithm equipped with acceleration to decide the reachability. We use the Z3-theorem prover as the constraint satisfaction engine for the quadratic formulas in our implementation. We show the efficiency of our algorithm by comparing its performance with the popular sampling based algorithm *rapidly-exploring random tree* (RRT) as implemented in the *Open Motion Planning Library (OMPL)*.

For a detailed survey of motion planning algorithms we refer to the excellent expositions by Latombe [17] and LaValle [18]. The motion-planning problem while respecting system dynamics can be modeled [10] in the framework of hybrid automata [1,12]; however the reachability problem is undecidable even for simple stopwatch automata [14]. There is a vast literature on decidable subclasses of hybrid automata [1,6]. Most notable among these classes are initialized rectangular hybrid automata [14], two-dimensional piecewise-constant derivative systems [5], timed automata [2], and discrete-time control for hybrid automata [13]. For a review of related work on multi-mode systems we refer to [3,4].

Due to lack of space proofs are either sketched or omitted in this extended abstract. A full version including detailed proofs is available at [16].

2 Motivating Example

Let us consider a two-dimensional multi-mode system with three modes m_1, m_2 and m_3 shown geometrically with their rate-vectors in Fig. 1(a). We consider the reach-while-avoid problem in the arena given in Fig. 1(b) with two rectangular obstacles $\mathcal{O}_1$ and $\mathcal{O}_2$ and source and target points x_s and x_t, respectively. In particular, we are interested in the question whether it is possible to move a point-robot from point x_s to point x_t using directions dictated by the multi-mode system given in Fig. 1(a) while avoiding passing through or even grazing any obstacle.

It follows from our results in Sect. 5 that in general the problem of deciding reachability is undecidable even with polyhedral obstacles. However, the example considered in Fig. 1 has an interesting property that the safety set can be represented as a union of finitely many polyhedral open sets (cells). This property, as we show later, makes the problem decidable. In fact, if we decompose the workspace into cells using any off-the-shelf cell-decomposition algorithm, we only need to consider the sequences of obstacle-free cells to decide reachability. In particular, for a given sequence of obstacle-free convex sets such that the

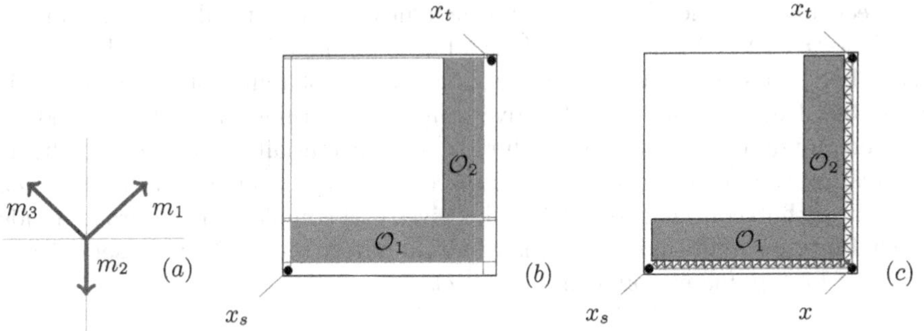

Fig. 1. (a) A multi-mode system, (b) an "L"-shaped arena consisting of obstacles $\mathcal{O}_1$ and $\mathcal{O}_2$ with start and target points x_s and x_t along with the cell-decomposition shown by orange lines, and (c) a safe schedule from x_s to x_t. (Color figure online)

starting point is in the first set, and the target point is in last set, one can write a linear program checking whether there is a sequence of intermediate states, one each in the intersection of successive sets, such that these points are reachable in the sequence using the constant-rate multi-mode system. Our key observation is that one need not to consider cell-sequences larger than the total number of cells since for reachability, it does not help for the system to leave a cell and enter it again.

This approach, however, is not very efficient since one needs to consider all sequences of the cells. However, this result provides an upper bound on sequence of "meta-steps" or "bound" through the cells that system needs to take in order to reach the target and hint towards a bounded model-checking [7] approach. We progressively increase bound k and ask whether there is a sequence of points $x_0, \ldots, x_{k+1}$ such that $x_0 = x_s$, $x_{k+1} = x_t$, and for all $0 \leq i \leq k$ we have that x_i can reach x_{i+1} using the rates provided by the multi-mode system (convex cone of rates translated to x_i contains x_{i+1}) and the line segment $\lambda x_i + (1-\lambda)x_{i+1}$ does not intersect any obstacle. Notice that if this condition is satisfied, then the system can safely move from point x_i to x_{i+1} by carefully choosing a scaling down of the rates so as to stay in the safety set, as illustrated in Fig. 1.

Let us first consider $k = 0$ and notice that one can reach point x_t from x_s using just the mode m_1, however unfortunately the line segment connecting these points passes through both obstacles. In this case we increase the bound by 1 and consider the problem of finding a point x such that the system can reach from x_s to x and also from x to x_t, and the line segment connecting x_s with x, and x with x_t do not intersect any obstacles. It is easy to see from the Fig. 1 that it is indeed the case. We can alternate modes m_1, m_2 from x_s to x, and modes m_1, m_3 from x to x_t. Hence, there is a schedule that steers the system from x_s to x_t as shown in the Fig. 1(c).

The property we need to check to ensure a safe schedule is the following: there exists a sequence of points $x_s = x_0, x_1, x_2, \ldots, x_n = x_t$ such that for all $0 \leq \lambda \leq 1$, and for all i, the line $\lambda x_i + (1-\lambda)x_{i+1}$ joining x_i and x_{i+1} does not intersect any obstacle $\mathcal{O}$. This can be thought of as a first-order formula of the form $\exists X \forall Y F(X,Y)$ where $F(X,Y)$ is a linear formula. By invoking the Tarski-Seidenberg theorem we know that checking the satisfiability of this property is decidable. However, one can also give a direct quantifier elimination based on Fourier-Motzkin elimination procedure to get existentially quantified quadratic constraints that can be efficiently checked using theorem provers such as Z3 (https://github.com/Z3Prover/z3). This gives us a complete procedure to decide reachability for multi-mode systems when the safety set can be represented as a union of finitely many polyhedral open sets.

3 Problem Formulation

Points and Vectors. Let $\mathbb{R}$ be the set of real numbers. We represent the states in our system as points in $\mathbb{R}^n$, which is equipped with the standard *Euclidean norm* $\|\cdot\|$. We denote points in this state space by x, y, vectors by $\boldsymbol{r}, \boldsymbol{v}$, and the i-th coordinate of point x and vector $\boldsymbol{r}$ by $x(i)$ and $\boldsymbol{r}(i)$, respectively. The distance $\|x, y\|$ between points x and y is defined as $\|x - y\|$.

Boundedness and Interior. We denote an *open ball* of radius $d \in \mathbb{R}_{\geq 0}$ centered at x as $B_d(x) = \{y \in \mathbb{R}^n : \|x, y\| < d\}$. We denote a closed ball of radius $d \in \mathbb{R}_{\geq 0}$ centered at x as $\overline{B_d(x)}$. We say that a set $S \subseteq \mathbb{R}^n$ is *bounded* if there exists $d \in \mathbb{R}_{\geq 0}$ such that, for all $x, y \in S$, we have $\|x, y\| \leq d$. The *interior* of a set S, $\text{int}(S)$, is the set of all points $x \in S$, for which there exists $d > 0$ s.t. $B_d(x) \subseteq S$.

Convexity. A point x is a *convex combination* of a finite set of points $X = \{x_1, x_2, \ldots, x_k\}$ if there are $\lambda_1, \lambda_2, \ldots, \lambda_k \in [0,1]$ such that $\sum_{i=1}^{k} \lambda_i = 1$ and $x = \sum_{i=1}^{k} \lambda_i \cdot x_i$. We say that $S \subseteq \mathbb{R}^n$ is *convex* iff, for all $x, y \in S$ and all $\lambda \in [0,1]$, we have $\lambda x + (1-\lambda)y \in S$ and moreover, S is a *convex polytope* if there exists $k \in \mathbb{N}$, a matrix A of size $k \times n$ and a vector $\boldsymbol{b} \in \mathbb{R}^k$ such that $x \in S$ iff $Ax \leq \boldsymbol{b}$. A closed *hyper-rectangle* is a convex polytope that can be characterized as $x(i) \in [a_i, b_i]$ for each $i \leq n$ where $a_i, b_i \in \mathbb{R}$.

Definition 1. *A (constant-rate) multi-mode system (MMS) is a tuple $\mathcal{H} = (M, n, R)$ where: M is a finite nonempty set of* modes, *n is the number of continuous variables, and $R : M \to \mathbb{R}^n$ maps to each mode a rate vector whose i-th entry specifies the change in the value of the i-th variable per time unit. For computation purposes, we assume that the real numbers are rational.*

Example 1. An example of a 2-dimensional multi-mode system $\mathcal{H} = (M, n, R)$ is shown in Fig. 1(a) where $M = \{m_1, m_2, m_3\}$, $n = 2$, and the rate vector is such that $R(m_1) = (1, 1)$, $R(m_2) = (0, -1)$, and $R(m_3) = (-1, 1)$.

A *schedule* of an MMS specifies a timed sequence of mode switches. Formally, a *schedule* is defined as a finite or infinite sequences of *timed actions*, where a timed action $(m, t) \in M \times \mathbb{R}_{\geq 0}$ is a pair consisting of a mode and a time delay. A finite *run* of an MMS $\mathcal{H}$ is a finite sequence of states and timed actions $r = \langle x_0, (m_1, t_1), x_1, \ldots, (m_k, t_k), x_k \rangle$ such that for all $1 \leq i \leq k$ we have that

$x_i = x_{i-1} + t_i \cdot R(m_i)$. For such a run r we say that x_0 is the *starting state*, while x_k is its *terminal state*. An *infinite run* of an MMS $\mathcal{H}$ is similarly defined to be an infinite sequence $\langle x_0, (m_1, t_1), x_1, (m_2, t_2), \ldots \rangle$ such that for all $i \geq 1$ we have that $x_i = x_{i-1} + t_i \cdot R(m_i)$.

Given a finite schedule $\sigma = \langle (m_1, t_1), (m_2, t_2), \ldots, (m_k, t_k) \rangle$ and a state x, we write $Run(x, \sigma)$ for the (unique) finite run $\langle x_0, (m_1, t_1), x_1, (m_2, t_2), \ldots, x_k \rangle$ such that $x_0 = x$. In this case, we also say that the schedule σ steers the MMS $\mathcal{H}$ from the state x_0 to the state x_k.

We consider the problem of MMS reachability within a given *safety set* S. We specify the safety set by a pair $(\mathcal{W}, \mathcal{O})$, where $\mathcal{W} \subseteq \mathbb{R}^n$ is called the *workspace* and $\mathcal{O} = \{\mathcal{O}_1, \mathcal{O}_2, \ldots, \mathcal{O}_k\}$ is a finite set of *obstacles*. In this case the safety set S is characterized as $S_{\mathcal{W} \setminus \mathcal{O}} = \mathcal{W} \setminus \mathcal{O}$. We assume in the rest of the paper that $\mathcal{W} = \mathbb{R}^n$ and for all $1 \leq i \leq k$, $\mathcal{O}_i$ is a *convex* (not necessarily closed) polytope specified by a set of linear inequalities.

We say that a finite run $\langle x_0, (m_1, t_1), x_1, (m_2, t_2), \ldots \rangle$ is S-safe if for all $i \geq 0$ we have that $x_i \in S$ and $x_i + \tau_{i+1} \cdot R(m_{i+1}) \in S$ for all $\tau_{i+1} \in [0, t_{i+1}]$. Notice that if S is a convex set then for all $i \geq 0$, $x_i \in S$ implies that for all $i \geq 0$ and for all $\tau_{i+1} \in [0, t_{i+1}]$ we have that $x_i + \tau_{i+1} \cdot R(m_{i+1}) \in S$. We say that a schedule σ is S-safe from a state x, or is (S, x)-safe, if the corresponding unique run $Run(x, \sigma)$ is S-safe. Sometimes we simply call a schedule or a run safe when the safety set and the starting state are clear from the context. We say that a state x' is S-safe reachable from a state x if there exists a finite schedule σ that is S-safe at x and steers the system from state x to x'.

We are interested in solving the following problem.

Definition 2 (Reachability). *Given a constant-rate multi-mode system* $\mathcal{H} = (M, n, R)$*, safety set* S*, start state* x_s*, and target state* x_t*, the reachability problem* $\text{Reach}(\mathcal{H}, S_{\mathcal{W} \setminus \mathcal{O}}, x_s, x_t)$ *is to decide whether there exists an* S*-safe finite schedule that steers the system from state* x_s *to* x_t*.*

Alur *et al.* [4] gave a polynomial-time algorithm to decide if a state x_t is S-safe reachable from a state x_0 for an MMS $\mathcal{H}$ for a convex safety set S. In particular, they characterized the following necessary and sufficient condition.

Theorem 1 [4]. *Let* $\mathcal{H} = (M, n, R)$ *be a multi-mode system and let* $S \subset \mathbb{R}^n$ *be an open, convex safety set. Then, there is an* S*-safe schedule from* $x_s \in S$ *to* $x_t \in S$*, if and only if there is* $\boldsymbol{t} \in \mathbb{R}^{|M|}_{\geq 0}$ *satisfying:* $x_s + \sum_{i=1}^{|M|} R(m_i) \cdot \boldsymbol{t}(i) = x_t$.

A key property of this result is that if x_t is reachable from x_s without considering the safety set, then it is also reachable inside arbitrary convex set as long as both x_s and x_t are strictly in the interior of the safety set.

We study the extension of this theorem for the reachability problem with non-convex safety sets. A key contribution of this paper is a precise characterization of the decidability of the reachability problem for multi-mode systems.

Theorem 2. *Given a constant-rate multi-mode system* $\mathcal{H}$*, workspace* $\mathcal{W} = \mathbb{R}^n$*, obstacles set* $\mathcal{O}$*, start state* x_s *and target state* x_t*, the reachability problem*

Reach$(\mathcal{H}, S_{\mathcal{W}\setminus\mathcal{O}}, x_s, x_t)$ *is in general undecidable. However, if the obstacle set* $\mathcal{O}$ *is given as finitely many closed polytopes, each defined by a finite set of linear inequalities, then reachability is decidable.*

4 Decidability

We prove the decidability condition of Theorem 2 in this section.

Theorem 3. *For a MMS* $\mathcal{H} = (M, n, R)$*, a safety set* S*, a start state* x_s*, and a target state* x_t*, the problem* Reach$(\mathcal{H}, S_{\mathcal{W}\setminus\mathcal{O}}, x_s, x_t)$ *is decidable if* $\mathcal{O}$ *is given as finitely many closed polytopes.*

For the rest of this section let us fix a MMS $\mathcal{H} = (M, n, R)$, a start state x_s and a target state x_t. Before we prove this theorem, we define cell cover (a notion related to, but distinct from the one of cell decomposition introduced in [17]).

Definition 3 (Cell Cover). *Given a safety set* $S \in \mathbb{R}^n$*, a cell of* S *is an open, convex set that is a subset of* S*. A* cell cover *of* S *is a collection* $\mathcal{C} = \{c_1, \ldots, c_N\}$ *of cells whose union equals* S*. Cells* $c, c' \in \mathcal{C}$ *are* adjacent *if and only if* $c \cap c'$ *is non-empty.*

A *channel* in S is a finite sequence $\langle c_1, c_2, \ldots, c_N\rangle$ of cells of S such that c_i and c_{i+1} are adjacent for all $1 \le i < N$. It follows that $\cup_{1\le i\le N} c_i$ is a path-connected open set. A $\mathcal{C}$-channel is a channel whose cells are in cell cover $\mathcal{C}$.

Given a channel $\pi = \langle c_1, \ldots, c_N\rangle$, a multi-mode system $\mathcal{H} = (M, n, R)$, start and target states $x_s, x_t \in S$, we say that π is a *witness* to reachability if the following linear program is feasible:

$$\exists_{0\le i\le N} x_i . \Big(x_s = x_0 \wedge x_t = x_N\Big) \wedge \Big(1 \le i < N \rightarrow x_i \in (c_i \cap c_{i+1})\Big) \wedge$$
$$\exists_{1\le i\le N, m\in M} t_i^{(m)} . \Big(t_i^{(m)} \ge 0\Big) \wedge \bigwedge_{1\le i\le N} \Big(x_i = x_{i-1} + \sum_{m\in M} R(m) \cdot t_i^{(m)}\Big) . \quad (1)$$

Lemma 1. *If* S *is an open safety set, there exists a finite* S*-safe schedule that solves* Reach$(\mathcal{H}, S, x_s, x_t)$ *if and only if* S *contains a witness channel* $\langle c_1, c_2, \ldots, c_N\rangle$ *for some* $N \in \mathbb{N}$.

Proof. ($\Leftarrow$) If $\langle c_1, c_2, \ldots, c_N\rangle$ is a witness channel, then for $0 < i \le N$, x_{i-1} and x_i are in c_i. Theorem 1 guarantees the existence of a c_i-safe schedule for each i. The concatenation of these schedules is a solution to Reach$(\mathcal{H}, S, x_s, x_t)$.

($\Rightarrow$) The run of a finite schedule that solves Reach$(\mathcal{H}, S, x_s, x_t)$ defines a closed, bounded subset P of S. Since S is open, every point $x \in P$ is contained in a cell of S. Collectively, these cells form an open cover of P. By compactness, then, there is a finite subcover of P. If any element of the subcover is entered by the run more than once, there exists another run that is contained in that cell between the first entry and the last exit. For such a run, if two elements of the subcover are entered at the same time, the one with the earlier exit time is redundant. Therefore, there is a subcover in which no two elements are entered by the run of the schedule at the same time. This subcover can be ordered according to the time at which the run enters each cell to produce a sequence that satisfies the definition of witness channel. □

Lemma 2. *If S is an open safety set and $\mathcal{C}$ a cell cover of S, there exists a witness channel for* $\text{Reach}(\mathcal{H}, S, x_s, x_t)$ *iff there exists a witness $\mathcal{C}$-channel.*

Proof. One direction is obvious. Suppose therefore that there exists a witness channel; let σ be the finite schedule whose existence is guaranteed by Lemma 1. The path that is traced in the MMS $\mathcal{H}$ when steered by σ is a bounded closed subset P of S because it is the continuous image of a compact interval of the real line. (The time interval in which $\mathcal{H}$ moves from x_s to x_t.) Since $\mathcal{C}$ is an open cover of P, there exists a finite subset of $\mathcal{C}$ that covers P; specifically, there is an irredundant finite subcover such that no two cells are entered at the same time during the run of σ. This subcover can be ordered according to entry time to produce a sequence of cells that satisfies the definition of witness channel. □

Lemma 3. *If $\mathcal{O}$ is a finite set of closed polytopes, then a finite cell cover of the safety set S is computable.*

Proof. If $\mathcal{O}$ is a finite set of closed polytopes, one can apply the the vertical decomposition algorithm of [17] to produce a cell *decomposition*. Each cell C in this decomposition of dimension less than n that is not contained in the obstacles (and hence is entirely contained in S) is replaced by a convex open set obtained as follows. Let B be an n-dimensional box around a point of C that is in S. The desired set is the convex hull of the set of vertices of either C or B. □

Proof (of Theorem 3). Lemmas 1–2 imply that $\text{Reach}(\mathcal{H}, S, x_s, x_t)$ is decidable if a finite cell cover of S is available. If $\mathcal{O}$ is given as a finite set of closed polytopes, each presented as a set of linear inequalities, then Lemma 3 applies. □

The algorithm implicit in the proof of Theorem 3 requires one to compute the cell cover in advance, and enumerate sequences of cells in order to decide reachability. We next present an algorithm inspired by bounded model checking [7] that implicitly enumerates sequences of cells of increasing length till the upper bound on number of cells is reached, or a safe schedule from the source point to the target point is discovered. The key idea is to guess a sequence of points $x_1, \ldots, x_N$ starting from the source point and ending in the target point such that for every $1 \leq i < N$ the point x_{i+1} is reachable from x_i using rates provided by the multi-mode system. Moreover, we need to check that the line segment connecting x_i and x_{i+1} does not intersect with obstacles, i.e.: $\forall_{0 \leq \lambda \leq 1} (\lambda x_i + (1-\lambda) x_{i+1}) \notin \cup_{j=1}^{k} \mathcal{O}_j$. We write $\text{ObstacleFree}(x_i, x_{i+1})$ for this condition. Algorithm 1 sketches a bounded-step algorithm to decide reachability for multi-mode systems that always terminates for multi-mode systems with sets of closed obstacles defined by linear inequalities thanks to Theorem 3.

Notice that at line 2 of Algorithm 1, we need to check the feasibility of the constraints system, which is of the form $\exists X \forall Y F(X, Y)$ where universal quantifications are implicit in the test for ObstacleFree. If the solver we use to solve the

Algorithm 1. BoundedMotionPlan$(\mathcal{H}, \mathcal{W}, \mathcal{O}, x_s, x_t, B)$

Input: MMS $\mathcal{H} = (M, n, R)$, two points x_s, x_t, workspace $\mathcal{W}$, obstacle set $\mathcal{O}$, and an upper bound B on number of cells in a cell-cover.

Output: NO, if no safe schedule exists and otherwise such a schedule.

$k \leftarrow 0$; **while** $k \leq B$ **do**

Check if the following formula is satisfiable:

$$\exists_{1 \leq i \leq N} x_i \quad \exists_{1 \leq i \leq N, m \in M} t_i^{(m)} \text{ s.t. } (x_s = x_1 \wedge x_t = x_N) \wedge \bigwedge_{\substack{1 \leq i \leq N \\ m \in M}} t_i^{(m)} \geq 0 \wedge$$

$$\bigwedge_{i=2}^{N} \left(x_i = x_{i-1} + \sum_{m \in M} R(m) \cdot t_i^{(m)} \right) \wedge \bigwedge_{i=2}^{N} \textsc{ObstacleFree}(x_{i-1}, x_i)$$

if *not satisfiable* **then** $k \leftarrow k + 1$;

else

Let σ be an empty sequence;

for $i = 1$ *to* $k - 1$ **do**

$\sigma = \sigma :: \textsc{Reach\_Convex}(\mathcal{H}, x_i, x_{i+1}, S)$

return σ;

Algorithm 2. Reach_Convex$(\mathcal{H}, x_s, x_t, S)$

Input: MMS $\mathcal{H} = (M, n, R)$, two points x_s, x_t, convex, open, safety set S

Output: NO if no S-safe schedule from x_s to x_t exists and otherwise such a schedule.

$t_1 = \min_{m \in M} \max \{\tau : x_s + \tau \cdot R(m) \in S\}$;

$t_2 = \min_{m \in M} \max \{\tau : x_t + \tau \cdot R(m) \in S\}$;

$t_{\text{safe}} = \min \{t_1, t_2\}$;

Check whether the following linear program is feasible:

$$x_s + \sum_{m \in M} R(m) \cdot t^{(m)} = x_t \text{ and } \qquad t^{(m)} \geq 0 \text{ for all } m \in M \tag{2}$$

if *no satisfying assignment exists* **then return** NO;

else

Find an assignment $\{t^{(m)}\}_{m \in M}$.

Set $l = \lceil (\sum_{m \in M} t^{(m)}) / t_{\text{safe}} \rceil$.

return the following schedule $\langle (m_i, t_i) \rangle$ where

$$m_k = (k \bmod |M|) + 1 \text{ and } t_k = t^{(m_k)}/l \text{ for } k = 1, 2, \ldots, l|M|.$$

constraints has full support to solve the $\forall$ quantification, we can use that to solve the above constraint. In our experiments, we used the Z3 solver (https://github.com/Z3Prover/z3) to implement the Algorithm 1 and found that the solver was unable to solve in some cases. Fortunately, the universal quantification in our constraints is of very special form and can be easily removed using the Fourier-Motzkin elimination procedure, which results in quadratic constraints that are efficiently solvable by Z3 solver. In Sect. 6 we present the experimental results on some benchmarks to demonstrate scalability.

5 Undecidability

In this section we give a sketch of the proof of the following undecidability result.

Theorem 4. *Given a constant-rate multi-mode system $\mathcal{H}$, convex workspace $\mathcal{W}$, obstacles set $\mathcal{O}$, start state x_s and target state x_t, the reachability problem* $\text{Reach}(\mathcal{H}, S_{\mathcal{W}\setminus\mathcal{O}}, x_s, x_t)$ *is in general undecidable.*

Proof (Sketch). We prove the undecidability of this problem by giving a reduction from the halting problem for two-counter machines that is known to be undecidable [19]. Given a two counter machine $\mathcal{A}$ having instructions $L = \ell_1, \ldots, \ell_{n-1}, \ell_{halt}$, we construct a multi-mode system $\mathcal{H}_\mathcal{A}$ along with non-convex safety $S_{\mathcal{W}\setminus\mathcal{O}}$ characterized using linear constraints. The idea is to simulate the unique run of two-counter machine $\mathcal{A}$ via the unique safe schedule of the MMS $\mathcal{H}_\mathcal{A}$ by going through a sequence of modes such that a pre-specified target point is reachable iff the counter machine halts.

Modes. For every increment/decrement instruction ℓ_i of the counter machine we have two modes $\mathcal{M}_i$ and $\mathcal{M}_{ik}$, where k is the index of the unique instruction ℓ_k to which the control shifts in $\mathcal{A}$ from ℓ_i. For every zero check instruction ℓ_i, we have four modes $\mathcal{M}_i^1, \mathcal{M}_i^2, \mathcal{M}_{ik}$ and $\mathcal{M}_{im}$, where k, m are respectively the indices of the unique instructions ℓ_k, ℓ_m to which the control shifts from ℓ_i depending on whether the counter value is >0 or =0. There are three modes $\mathcal{M}_{halt}, \mathcal{M}_{halt}^{c_1}$ and $\mathcal{M}_{halt}^{c_2}$ corresponding to the halt instruction. We have a special "initial" mode $\mathcal{I}$ which is the first mode to be applied in any safe schedule.

Variables. The MMS $\mathcal{H}_\mathcal{A}$ has two variables $C = \{c_1, c_2\}$ that store the value of two counters. There is a unique variable $S = \{s_0\}$ used to enforce that mode $\mathcal{I}$ as the first mode. For every increment or decrement instruction ℓ_i, there are variables w_{ij}, x_{ij}, where j is the index of the unique instruction ℓ_j to which control shifts from ℓ_i. We define variable $z_{i\#}$ for each zero-check instruction ℓ_i.

Simulation. A simulation of the two counter machine going through instructions $\ell_0, \ell_1, \ell_2, \ldots, \ell_y, \ell_{halt}$ is achieved by going through modes $\mathcal{I}, \mathcal{M}_0, \mathcal{M}_{01}, \mathcal{M}_1$ or $\mathcal{M}_1^1$ or $\mathcal{M}_1^2 \ldots, \mathcal{M}_y, \mathcal{M}_{y\ halt}$ in order, spending exactly one unit of time in each mode. Starting from a point x_s with $s_0 = 1$ and $v = 0$ for all variables v other than s_0, we want to reach a point x_t where $w_{halt} = 1$ and $v = 0$ for all variables v other than w_{halt}. The idea is to start in mode $\mathcal{I}$, and spending one unit of time in $\mathcal{I}$ obtaining $s_0 = 0, w_{01} = 1$ (spending a time other than one violates safety. Growing w_{01} represents that the current instruction is ℓ_0, and the next one is ℓ_1. Next, we shift to mode $\mathcal{M}_0$, spend one unit of time there to obtain

$x_{01} = 1, w_{01} = 0$. This is followed by mode $\mathcal{M}_{01}$, where x_{01} becomes 0, and one of the variables $z_{1\#}, w_{12}$ attain 1, depending on whether ℓ_1 is a zero check instruction or not (again, spending a time other than one in $\mathcal{M}_0, \mathcal{M}_{01}$ violates safety).

In general, while at a mode $\mathcal{M}_{ij}$, the next instruction ℓ_k after ℓ_j is chosen by "growing" the variable w_{jk} if ℓ_j is not a zero-check instruction, or by "growing" the variable $z_{j\#}$ if ℓ_j is a zero-check instruction. In parallel, x_{ij} grows down to 0, so that $x_{ij} + w_{jk} = 1$ or $x_{ij} + z_{j\#} = 1$. The sequence of choosing modes, and enforcing that one unit of time be spent in each mode is necessary to adhere to the safety set.

- In the former case, the control shifts from $\mathcal{M}_{ij}$ to mode $\mathcal{M}_j$ where variable x_{jk} grows at rate 1 while w_{jk} grows at rate -1, so that $x_{jk}+w_{jk} = 1$. Control shifts from $\mathcal{M}_j$ to $\mathcal{M}_{jk}$, where the next instruction ℓ_g after ℓ_k is chosen by growing variable w_{kg} if ℓ_k is not zero-check instruction, or the variable $z_{k\#}$ is grown if ℓ_k is a zero-check instruction.
- In the latter case, one of the modes $\mathcal{M}_j^1, \mathcal{M}_j^2$ is chosen from $\mathcal{M}_j$ where $z_{j\#}$ grows at rate -1. Assume ℓ_j is the instruction "If the counter value is > 0, then goto ℓ_m, else goto ℓ_h". If $\mathcal{M}_j^1$ is chosen, then the variable x_{jm} grows at rate 1 while if $\mathcal{M}_j^2$ is chosen, then the variable x_{jh} grows at rate 1. In this case, we have $z_{j\#} + x_{jm} = 1$ or $z_{j\#} + x_{jh} = 1$. From $\mathcal{M}_j^1$, control shifts to $\mathcal{M}_{jm}$, while from $\mathcal{M}_j^2$, control shifts to $\mathcal{M}_{jh}$.

Continuing in the above fashion, we eventually reach mode $\mathcal{M}_{y\ halt}$ where $x_{y\ halt}$ grows down to 0, while the variable w_{halt} grows to 1, so that $x_{y\ halt} + w_{halt} = 1$.

Starting from x_s—which lies in the hyperplane H_0 given as $s_0 + w_{0j} = 1$ where ℓ_j is the unique instruction following ℓ_0—a safe execution stays in H_0 as long as control stays in the initial mode $\mathcal{I}$. Control then switches to mode $\mathcal{M}_0$, to the hyperplane H_1 given by $w_{0j} + x_{0j} = 1$. Note that $H_0 \cap H_1$ is non-empty and intersect at the point where $w_{0j} = 1$, and all other variables are 0. Spending a unit of time at $\mathcal{M}_0$, control switches to mode $\mathcal{M}_{0j}$, and to the hyperplane H_2 given by $x_{0j} + w_{jk} = 1$ depending on whether ℓ_j is not a zero-check instruction. Again, note that $H_1 \cap H_2$ is non-empty and intersect at the point where $c_1 = 1, x_{0j} = 1$ and all other variables are zero. This continues, and we obtain a safe transition from hyperplane H_i to H_{i+1} as dictated by the simulation of the two counter machine. The sequence of safe hyperplanes lead to the hyperplane H_{last} given by $w_{halt} = 1$ and all other variables 0 iff the two counter machine halts. □

Example 2 (Example of the reduction). Consider an example of a two counter machine with counters c_1, c_2 and the following instruction set.

- $\ell_0 : c_1 := c_1 + 1$; goto ℓ_1
- $\ell_1 : c_1 := c_1 - 1$; goto ℓ_2
- ℓ_2 : if ($c_2 > 0$) then goto ℓ_3; else goto ℓ_0
- ℓ_3 : HALT.

Note that this machine does not halt. We now describe a multi-mode system that simulates this two counter machine. The modes and variables are as follows.

1. Variables $\{c_1, c_2\}$ correspond to the two counters, $\{w_{01}, w_{12}, z_{2\#}\}$ correspond to instructions $\ell_0, \ell_1, \ell_2, \ell_3$ and the switches between instructions, and variable w_3 corresponds to the halt instruction. We also have variables s_0 and $\{x_{ij} \mid 0 \leq i, j \leq 3\}$.
2. Mode $\mathcal{I}$: $R(\mathcal{I})(s_0) = -1$ and $R(\mathcal{I})(w_{01}) = 1$ and other variables have rate 0.
3. Modes $\mathcal{M}_0, \mathcal{M}_1, \mathcal{M}_2^1, \mathcal{M}_2^2, \mathcal{M}_{01}, \mathcal{M}_{12}, \mathcal{M}_{20}$ with rates:
   - $R(\mathcal{M}_0)(w_{01}) = -1, R(\mathcal{M}_0)(x_{01}) = R(\mathcal{M}_0)(c_1) = 1$, and $R(\mathcal{M}_0)(v) = 0$ for all other variables v;
   - $R(\mathcal{M}_1)(w_{12}) = -1, R(\mathcal{M}_1)(x_{12}) = 1, R(\mathcal{M}_1)(c_1) = -1$, and $R(\mathcal{M}_1)(v) = 0$ for all other variables v;
   - $R(\mathcal{M}_2^1)(z_{2\#}) = -1 = R(\mathcal{M}_2^2)(z_{2\#}), R(\mathcal{M}_2^1)(x_{23}) = 1 = R(\mathcal{M}_2^2)(x_{20})$. All other variables have rate 0 in modes $\mathcal{M}_2^1, \mathcal{M}_2^2$;
   - $R(\mathcal{M}_{12})(z_{2\#}) = 1$, and $R(\mathcal{M}_{12})(v) = 0$ for all other variables v;
   - $R(\mathcal{M}_{01})(x_{01}) = -1$, $R(\mathcal{M}_{01})(w_{12}) = 1$, and $R(\mathcal{M}_{01})(v) = 0$ for other v;
   - $R(\mathcal{M}_{20})(x_{20}) = -1$, $R(\mathcal{M}_{20})(w_{01}) = 1$, and $R(\mathcal{M}_{20})(v) = 0$ for other v.
4. Mode $\mathcal{M}_{23}$ with $R(\mathcal{M}_{23})(x_{23}) = -1, R(\mathcal{M}_{23})(w_3) = 1$, $R(\mathcal{M}_{23})(v) = 0$ for other v. Modes $\mathcal{M}_3, \mathcal{M}_3^{c_1}, \mathcal{M}_3^{c_2}$ with $R(\mathcal{M}_3)(w_3) = -1$ and $R(\mathcal{M}_3)(v) = 0$ for all other variables v; $R(\mathcal{M}_3^{c_i})(c_i) = -1, R(\mathcal{M}_3^{c_i})(w_3) = 1$.

The safety set is given by the conjunction of the following seven conditions:

1. $0 \leq w_{01}, w_{12}, x_{ij}, z_{2\#}, s_0 \leq 1$, $0 \leq w_3, c_1, c_2$;
2. at any point, if some x_{ij} is non-negative, then all the other x_{kl} variables are 0, $i \neq k, j \neq l$;
3. at any point, if some w_{ij} is non-negative, then all other w_{kl} are zero, $i \neq k, j \neq l$ and $z_{2\#} = 0$;
4. At any point, if $z_{2\#} > 0$, then all the w_{ij} are 0;
5. At any point, if $s_0 > 0$, then all $x_{ij} = 0$;
6. At any point, if $w_3 > 0$, then variables x_{i3} are 0, and $c_1, c_2 = 0$;
7. At any point, if $x_{i3} > 0$, then $x_{i3} + w_3 = 1$.

The obstacles are hence, the complement of this conjunction. Starting from $s_0 = 1$ and $v = 0$ for $v \neq s_0$, a safe computation must start from $\mathcal{I}$, then visit in order modes $\mathcal{M}_0, \mathcal{M}_{01}, \mathcal{M}_1, \mathcal{M}_{12}, \mathcal{M}_2^1, \mathcal{M}_{20}$, and repeat this sequence spending one unit in each mode. This will not reach $\mathcal{M}_3$ corresponding to the halt instruction.

6 Experimental Results

In this section, we discuss some preliminary results obtained with an implementation of Algorithm 1. In order to show competitiveness of the proposed algorithm, we compare its performance with a popular implementation of the RRT algorithm [18] on a collection of micro-benchmarks (some of these benchmarks are inspired by [21]).

Table 1. Summary of results for the L shaped arena

Dimension	Arena size	OMPLRRT		BoundedMotionPlan	
		Time (s)	Nodes	Time (s)	Witness length
2	100 × 100	0.011	8	0.012	2
2	1000 × 1000	0.076	245	0.012	2
3	100 × 100	0.107	4836	0.183	2
3	1000 × 1000	1.9	1800	0.19	2
4	100 × 100	1.2	612	0.201	2
4	1000 × 1000	94.39	2857	0.206	2
5	100 × 100	3.12	778	2.69	2
5	1000 × 1000	149.4	2079	2.68	2
6	1000 × 1000	105	3822	15.3	2
7	1000 × 1000	319.63	2639	190.3	2

6.1 Experimental Setup

Rapidly-exploring Random Tree (RRT) [18] is a space-filling data structure that is used to search a region by incrementally building a tree. It is constructed by selecting random points in the state space and can provide better coverage of reachable states of a system than mere simulations. There are many versions of RRTs available; we use the *Open Motion Planning Library (OMPL)* implementation of RRT for our experiments. The OMPL library (http://ompl.kavrakilab.org) consists of many state-of-the-art, sampling-based motion planning algorithms. We used the RRT API provided by the OMPL library. The results for RRT were obtained with a goal bias parameter set to 0.05, and obstacles implemented as `StateValidityCheckerFunction()` as mentioned in the documentation [23].

We implemented our algorithm on the top of the Z3 solver [8]. The implementation involves coding formulae in FO-logic over reals and checking for a satisfying assignment. Our algorithm was implemented in Python 2.7. The OMPL implementation was done in C++. The experiments with Algorithm 1 and RRT were performed on a computer running Ubuntu 14.10, with an Intel Core i7-4510 2.00 GHz quadcore CPU, with 8 GB RAM. We compared the two algorithms by executing them on a set of microbenchmarks whose obstacles are hyper-rectangular, though our algorithm can handle general polyhedral obstacles. We considered the following microbenchmarks.

- **L-shaped arena.** This class of microbenchmarks contains examples with hyper-rectangular workspace and certain "L" shaped obstacles as shown in Fig. 1. The initial vertex is the lower left vertex of the square (x_s) and the target is the right upper vertex of the square (x_t). Our algorithm can give the solution to this problem with bound $B = 2$ returning the sequence $\langle x_1, x, x_t \rangle$ as shown in the figure, while the RRT algorithm in this case samples most

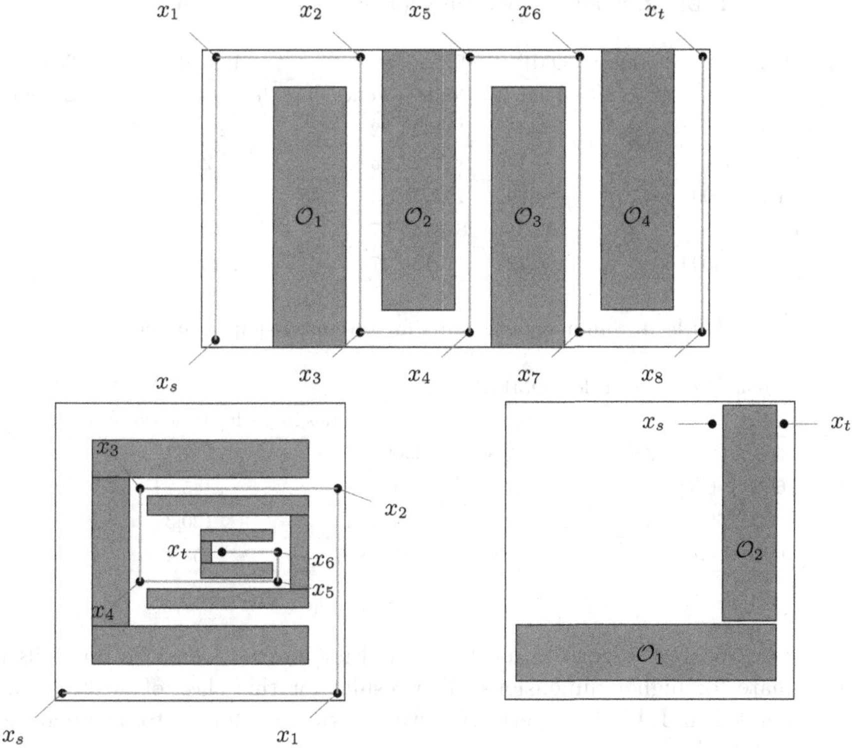

Fig. 2. (a) Snake-shaped arena with four obstacles (left), (b) Maze-shaped arena with three C-shaped patterns (middle) and (c) modified L-shaped arena (right).

of the points which lie on the other side of the obstacles and if the control modes are not in the direction of the line segments x_1x and xx_t, then it grows in arbitrary directions and hits the obstacles a large number of times, leading to a large number of iterations slowing the growth. We experimented with L-shaped examples for dimensions ranging from 2 to 7. In most of the cases, we found that the performance of the BoundedMotionPlan algorithm was better than that of OMPLRRT. Another important point to note is that RRT or other simulation-based algorithms do not perform well as the input size increases, which can be clearly seen from the running times obtained on increasing arena sizes in Table 1. Our algorithm worked better than RRT for higher dimensions ($\geq$3).

- **Snake-shaped arena.** The name comes from the serpentine appearance of the safe sets in these arenas. The motivation to study these microbenchmarks comes from motion planning problems in regular environments. The arena has rectangular obstacles coming from the top and the bottom (as shown in Fig. 2 for two dimensions) alternately. The starting point is the lower left vertex x_s and the target point is x_t. A sample free-path through the arena is also shown

Table 2. Summary of results for the snake-shaped arena

Dim.	Arena size	Obstacles	OMPLRRT			BoundedMotionPlan	
			Time (s)	Nodes	Nodes in path	Time (s)	Witness length
2	350 × 350	3	3.56	13142	72	2.54	4
2	350 × 350	4	4.12	15432	96	4.23	5
2	3500 × 3500	3	4.79	15423	83	2.57	4
3	350 × 350	3	102.3	86314	67	96.43	4
3	3500 × 3500	3	100.22	1013	27	96.42	4

Table 3. Summary of results for the maze-shaped arena

Dim.	Arena size	Obstacles	OMPLRRT			BoundedMotionPlan	
			Time (s)	Nodes	Nodes in path	Time (s)	Bound
2	600 × 600	2	1.8	9500	60	1.3	4
2	6000 × 6000	3	23.5	11256	78	45.23	5
3	600 × 600	2	132.6	90408	71	120.3	5
3	6000 × 6000	3	1002.6	183412	93	953.4	5

in the figure. RRT algorithm performs well for lower dimensions but fails to terminate for higher dimensions. The results for this class of obstacles are summarised in Table 2. Experiments were performed for up to 3 dimensions and 4 obstacles.

- **Maze-shaped arena.** These benchmarks mimic the motion planning situations where the task of the robot is to navigate through a maze. We model a maze using finitely many concentric "C"-shaped obstacles with different orientations as shown in Fig. 2. The task is to navigate from the lower left outer corner to the center point of the square. This kind of arena seems to be particularly challenging for the RRT algorithm and the growth of the tree seems to be quite slow. Also, the performance of our tool degrades as the bound increases due to a increase in the number of constraints, and hence, these examples require more time as compared to the other two microbenchmarks. However, as shown in Table 3, OMPLRRT and `BoundedMotionPlan` perform almost equally well, with the latter being slightly better.
- **Modified L-shaped obstacles.** These set of microbenchmarks contains a hyperrectangular workspace and 2 hyperrectangular obstacles arranged in a "L-shaped" fashion as shown in Fig. 2. The initial vertex lies very close to one of the obstacles. The target vertex is the vertex very close to the start vertex but on the other side of the obstacle. Our algorithm can give the solution to this problem with bound $B = 3$ while RRT algorithm spends time in sampling from the bigger obstacle-free part of the arena. The results are summarised in Table 4.

The micro-benchmarks presented above involved the situations where the target point is reachable from the source point. It is interesting to see the

Table 4. Summary of results for the modified L-shaped obstacles

Dimension	Arena size	OMPLRRT			BoundedMotionPlan	
		Time	Nodes	Nodes in path	Time	Bound
2	100 × 100	0.445	27387	40	0.126	3
2	1000 × 1000	2.57	38612	47	0.132	3
3	100 × 100	115.23	57645	71	92.1	3
3	1000 × 1000	675.62	183412	93	95.23	3
4	100 × 100	287.32	64230	65	283.23	3
4	1000 × 1000	923.45	192453	78	292.53	3
5	100 × 100	523.62	73422	69	534.45	3
5	1000 × 1000	1043	223900	72	533.96	3

Table 5. Summary of results for the unreachable L-shaped obstacles.

Dimension	OMPLRRT		BoundedMotionPlan
	Time (s)	Nodes	Time (s)
2	500 (TO)	5301778	0.0088
3	500 (TO)	7892122	0.032
4	500 (TO)	4325621	0.056
5	500 (TO)	5624609	2.73
6	500 (TO)	4992951	18.34
7	500 (TO)	3765123	213.23

performance of two algorithms in cases when there is no path from the source to target point. For the cases when an upper bound on cell-decomposition can be imposed, our algorithm is capable of producing negative answer. Table 5 summarizes the performance of OMPLRRT and `BoundedMotionPlan` for L-shaped arenas when the target point is not reachable. The timeout for RRT was set to be 500 s, and it did not terminate until the timeout, which is as expected. On the other hand, BOUNDEDMOTIONPLAN performed well, with running times close to those when the target point is reachable.

Discussion. Our implementation of BOUNDEDMOTIONPLAN even though preliminary, compares favorably with a state-of-the-art implementation of RRT. BOUNDEDMOTIONPLAN, in addition, can naturally deal with restrictions on the dynamics of the MMS, that is, with systems such that the positive linear span of the mode vectors is not $\mathbb{R}^n$.

A trend observed in our experiments is that if a large fraction of the arena is covered by obstacles, then the probability of a randomly sampled point lying in the obstacle region is high and this makes RRT ineffective in this situation by wasting a lot of iterations. Another trend is that as the arena size increases, it becomes more difficult for RRT to navigate to the destination points even with higher values of goal bias.

Our algorithm performs better in situations when it terminates early (target reachable from source with shorter witnesses) while the performance of our algorithm degrades as the bound or the dimensions increases since the number of constraints introduced by the Fourier-Motzkin like-procedure implemented in our algorithm grows exponentially with the dimension exhibiting the curse of dimensionality.

7 Conclusion

In this paper we studied the motion planning problem for constant-rate multi-mode system with non-convex safety sets given as a convex set of obstacles. We showed that while the general problem is already undecidable in this simple setting of linearly defined obstacles, decidability can be recovered by making appropriate assumption on the obstacles. Moreover, our algorithm performs satisfactorily when compared to well-known algorithms for motion planning, and can easily be adapted to provide semi-algorithms for motion-planning problems for objects with polyhedral shapes. While the algorithm is complete for classes of safety sets for which a bound on the size of a cell cover can be effectively computed, bounds based on cell decompositions of the safety set may be too large to be of practical use. This situation is akin to that encountered in bounded model checking of finite-state systems, in which bounds based on the radii of the state graph are usually too large. We are therefore motivated to look at extensions of the algorithm that incorporate practical termination checks.

References

1. Alur, R., Courcoubetis, C., Henzinger, T.A., Ho, P.-H.: Hybrid automata: an algorithmic approach to the specification and verification of hybrid systems. In: Grossman, R.L., Nerode, A., Ravn, A.P., Rischel, H. (eds.) HS 1991-1992. LNCS, vol. 736, pp. 209–229. Springer, Heidelberg (1993). doi:10.1007/3-540-57318-6_30
2. Alur, R., Dill, D.: A theory of timed automata. Theoret. Comput. Sci. **126**, 183–235 (1994)
3. Alur, R., Forejt, V., Moarref, S., Trivedi, A.: Safe schedulability of bounded-rate multi-mode systems. In: HSCC, pp. 243–252 (2013)
4. Alur, R., Trivedi, A., Wojtczak, D.: Optimal scheduling for constant-rate multi-mode systems. In: HSCC, pp. 75–84 (2012)
5. Asarin, E., Oded, M., Pnueli, A.: Reachability analysis of dynamical systems having piecewise-constant derivatives. TCS **138**, 35–66 (1995)
6. Branicky, M.S., Borkar, V.S., Mitter, S.K.: A unified framework for hybrid control: model and optimal control theory. Autom. Control **43**(1), 31–45 (1998)
7. Clarke, E., Biere, A., Raimi, R., Zhu, Y.: Bounded model checking using satisfiability solving. Formal Methods Syst. Des. **19**(1), 7–34 (2001)
8. de Moura, L., Bjørner, N.: Z3: an efficient SMT solver. In: Ramakrishnan, C.R., Rehof, J. (eds.) TACAS 2008. LNCS, vol. 4963, pp. 337–340. Springer, Heidelberg (2008). doi:10.1007/978-3-540-78800-3_24
9. Firby, R.J.: Adaptive execution in complex dynamic worlds. Ph.D. thesis, Yale University, New Haven, CT, USA (1989). AAI9010653

10. Frazzoli, E., Dahleh, M.A., Feron, E.: Robust hybrid control for autonomous vehicle motion planning. In: Proceedings of the 39th IEEE Conference on Decision and Control, vol. 1, pp. 821–826. IEEE (2000)
11. Gat, E.: Three-layer architectures. In: Kortenkamp, D., Bonasso, R.P., Murphy, R. (eds.) Artificial Intelligence and Mobile Robots, pp. 195–210. MIT Press, Cambridge (1998)
12. Henzinger, T.A.: The theory of hybrid automata. In: LICS 1996, Washington, DC, USA, p. 278. IEEE Computer Society (1996)
13. Henzinger, T.A., Kopke, P.W.: Discrete-time control for rectangular hybrid automata. TCS **221**(1–2), 369–392 (1999)
14. Henzinger, T.A., Kopke, P.W., Puri, A., Varaiya, P.: What's decidable about hybrid automata? J. Comput. Syst. Sci. **57**, 94–124 (1998)
15. Kato, S., Takeuchi, E., Ishiguro, Y., Ninomiya, Y., Takeda, K., Hamada, T.: An open approach to autonomous vehicles. IEEE Micro **35**(6), 60–68 (2015)
16. Krishna, S.N., Kumar, A., Somenzi, F., Touri, B., Trivedi, A.: The reach-avoid problem for constant-rate multi-mode systems. CoRR, abs/1707.04151 (2017)
17. Latombe, J.: Robot Motion Planning, vol. 124. Springer, Heidelberg (2012)
18. LaValle, S.M.: Planning Algorithms. Cambridge University Press, Cambridge (2006). http://planning.cs.uiuc.edu/
19. Minsky, M.L.: Computation: Finite and Infinite Machines. Prentice-Hall, Inc., Upper Saddle River (1967)
20. O'Kelly, M., Abbas, H., Gao, S., Shiraishi, S., Kato, S., Mangharam, R.: Apex: a tool for autonomous vehicle plan verification and execution. In: Society of Automotive Engineers (SAE) World Congress and Exhibition (2016)
21. Saha, I., Ramaithitima, R., Kumar, V., Pappas, G.J., Seshia, S.A.: Implan: scalable incremental motion planning for multi-robot systems. In: ICCPS 2016, pp. 43:1–43:10 (2016)
22. Schwartz, J.T., Sharir, M.: On the "piano movers" problem. II. general techniques for computing topological properties of real algebraic manifolds. Adv. Appl. Math. **4**(3), 298–351 (1983)
23. Şucan, I.A., Moll, M., Kavraki, L.E.: The open motion planning library. IEEE Robot. Autom. Mag. **19**(4), 72–82 (2012). http://ompl.kavrakilab.org

Author Index

Printed in the United States
By Bookmasters